Josef Raab, Sebastian Thies, Daniela Noll-Opitz (Eds.)

Screening the Americas

Narration of Nation in Documentary Film

Proyectando las Américas

Narración de la nación en el cine documental

INTER-AMERICAN STUDIES
Cultures – Societies – History

ESTUDIOS INTERAMERICANOS
Culturas – Sociedades – Historia

Volume 1

Josef Raab, Sebastian Thies,
Daniela Noll-Opitz (Eds.)

Screening the Americas

Narration of Nation in Documentary Film

Proyectando las Américas

Narración de la nación en el cine documental

wvt Wissenschaftlicher Verlag Trier

Copublished by

Bilingual Press / Editorial Bilingüe

Screening the Americas
Narration of Nation in Documentary Film
Proyectando las Américas
Narración de la nación en el cine documental / Josef Raab, Sebastian Thies, Daniela Noll-Opitz (Eds.). –
(Inter-American Studies | Estudios Interamericanos; 1)
Trier : WVT Wissenschaftlicher Verlag Trier, 2011
    ISBN 978-3-86821-331-7
Tempe, AZ : Bilingual Press / Editorial Bilingüe
    ISBN 978-1-931010-83-2

Cover Image: "ImagiNations" by Sebastian Thies, 2005
Cover Design: Brigitta Disseldorf

Library of Congress Cataloging-in-Publication Data

Screening the Americas : narration of nation in documentary film =
Proyectando las Américas : narración de la nación en el cine documental /
Josef Raab, Sebastian Thies, Daniela Noll-Opitz (eds.).
    p. cm. -- (Inter-American studies = Estudios Interamericanos ; v. 1)
    English and Spanish.
    Includes bibliographical references.
    ISBN 978-1-931010-83-2 (alk. paper) -- ISBN 978-3-86821-331-7 (alk. paper)
    1. Documentary films--United States--History and criticism. 2. Documentary films--Mexico--History and criticism. 3. Documentary films--South America--History and criticism. 4. National characteristics in motion pictures. 5. Nationalism in motion pictures. 6. Motion pictures--Political aspects. 7. Culture in motion pictures. I. Raab, Josef. II. Thies, Sebastian. III. Noll-Opitz, Daniela. IV. Title: Proyectando las Americas.
    PN1995.9.D6S35 2011
    070.1'8--dc23
                   2011035188

© WVT Wissenschaftlicher Verlag Trier, 2011

Publisher:
WVT Wissenschaftlicher Verlag Trier
Postfach 4005, 54230 Trier
Bergstraße 27, 54295 Trier
Tel. 0049 651 41503, Fax 41504
http://www.wvttrier.de
wvt@wvttrier.de

Copublisher:
Bilingual Press / Editorial Bilingüe
Hispanic Research Center
Arizona State University
PO Box 875303
Tempe, AZ 85287-5303
http://www.asu.edu/brp
brp@asu.edu

CONTENTS

II. NARRATING THE NATION FROM ITS MARGINS

III. DISSEMINATIONS: TOWARD A NARRATION OF NATION
  IN POSTMODERN TIMES

IV. DOCUMENTARY FILM AS A MEDIUM OF CULTURAL MEMORY

V. BEYOND THE CANON: REDISCOVERING DOCUMENTARY FILMS AND FILMMAKERS

VI. PERSPECTIVES ON THE PRACTICE OF DOCUMENTARY FILMMAKING

viii

Preface

This volume initiates the interdisciplinary book series "Inter-American Studies | Estudios Interamericanos." The series creates a forum for a critical academic dialogue between North and South on the cultures, societies, and histories of the Americas, promoting an inter-American paradigm that shifts the scholarly focus from methodological nationalism to the wider context of the Western Hemisphere.

More than a century after José Martí wrote about "Our America," as perceived from the South, that the "disdain of the formidable neighbor [i.e., the U.S.A.] who does not know her is our America's greatest danger," this new book series seeks to highlight commonalities and differences in the Americas, to explore transnational and transcultural issues, and to examine the wider contexts of local, regional or national phenomena in the Western Hemisphere. In addition to crossing national and linguistic boundaries, it also aims to transcend the boundaries between academic disciplines and to promote the movement of scholarship past its national confines. In these ways we hope to enliven the emerging field of Inter-American Studies.

This book series is published in Europe by Wissenschaftlicher Verlag Trier and co-published in the Americas by Bilingual Press/Editorial Bilingüe. It is our editorial policy to consider scholarship in both English and Spanish for publication. Manuscripts may be submitted to the series editors or to the publisher. The following volumes, which all appeared in 2011, demonstrate the wide interdisciplinary range of topics covered:

Vol. 1: Raab, Josef, Sebastian Thies, and Daniela Noll-Opitz, eds. *Screening the Americas: Narration of Nation in Documentary Film/Proyectando las Américas: Narración de la nación en el cine documental,*

Vol. 2: Raussert, Wilfried, and Michelle Habell-Pallán, eds. *Cornbread and Cuchifritos: Ethnic Identity Politics, Transnationalization, and Transculturation in American Urban Popular Music,*

Vol. 3: Butler, Martin, Jens Martin Gurr, and Olaf Kaltmeier, eds. *EthniCity: Metropolitan Cultures and Ethnic Identities in the Americas,*

Vol. 4: Gurr, Jens Martin, and Wilfried Raussert, eds. *Cityscapes in the Americas and Beyond: Representations of Urban Complexity in Literature and Film.*

We would like to thank Erwin Otto of Wissenschaftlicher Verlag Trier and Gary Francisco Keller of Bilingual Press/Editorial Bilingüe as well as the members of the series' editorial board for supporting our vision of an innovative, inter-American format of scholarly dialogue.

Josef Raab and Sebastian Thies

Acknowledgments

A number of essays included in this volume originated in the international conference "ImagiNations: Documentaries and the Narration of Nation in the Americas | ImagiNaciones: El cine documental y la narración de la nación en las Americas." We would like to thank the German Research Foundation (Deutsche Forschungsgemeinschaft), the Bielefeld Center for Interdisciplinary Research (Zentrum für interdisziplinäre Forschung), and the Westfälisch-Lippische Universitätsgesellschaft for their generous support of this conference. Seven additional essays were especially commissioned for this volume. The readiness of scholars to contribute to this volume demonstrates how fruitful the approach of the narration of nation is for the study of documentary film. Many thanks for their diligent work and patience are due to the scholars and filmmakers who submitted their work for inclusion in this collection.

For their tireless assistance in reviewing the manuscripts, suggesting revisions, checking sources, editing, proofreading, and layouting we are deeply indebted to Christina Axmacher, Alexandra Berlina, Stefanie Boens, Martin Butler, Luisa Ellermeier, Ines Fricke-Groenewold, Alexander Greiffenstern, Astrid Haas, Birte Horn, Lizbeth Jäger-Alemán, Alexa Kenter, Marietta Saavedra Arellano, Mo Tschache, and David Wood. Finally, we would like to thank the University of Duisburg-Essen for subsidizing the printing of this volume.

Josef Raab, Sebastian Thies, and Daniela Noll-Opitz

Screening the Americas:
Documentaries and the Narration of Nation

SEBASTIAN THIES, DANIELA NOLL-OPITZ, AND JOSEF RAAB

This volume examines—in the context of the Western Hemisphere and with a comparative North/South perspective—the role which documentary film plays in those discourses that Homi K. Bhabha called the "narration of nation." For the "long twentieth century," which spans from the beginning of "moving pictures" to the first decade of the new millennium and has turned out to be exceedingly image-centered, documentary discourses have been central to the construction, transformation, affirmation, and finally to the deconstruction of imagined communities—whether they are local, regional, national, or transnational, political, ideological, ethnic, or gender-specific. The focus of this collection of essays therefore lies on what we would like to call documentary "ImagiNations,"—a concept which points to the friction between, on the one hand, the genre's prime motivation to capture social reality the way it manifests itself to the filmmaker and, on the other, the social imaginaries at work.

A series of aspects underline the importance of this social function of documentary discourse in film, video, television, and recently the Internet. It is often only through the documentary image that occurrences become historical events, which in turn become signifiers of the national or transnational. Documentary images like the pictures of American troops landing in Cuba's *Bahía de Cochinos* in 1961, the Zapruder film of John F. Kennedy's assassination in 1963 (cf. Chanan, *Politics*; Bruzzi), footage by Heynowski and Scheumann of the bombardment of *Palacio de la Moneda* during the 1973 military coup in Chile (cf. Steinmetz/Prase), or the videotaped beating of African American motorist Rodney King by four white police officers in 1991 have entered the collective image memory of a transnational generation of viewers, regardless of ideological orientation or nationality. So did the accidental capture by Gédéon and Jules Naudet of a plane crashing into the World Trade Center (resulting in the documentary *9/11*) or private video footage of the collapsing Twin Towers in 2001. These iconic testimonies of history narrate through the power of images how a reality that the camera does not control is transformed into the epochal (cf. Nichols, *Representing* 38); their fascination is based on the myth of the fall of the legitimate potentate, of the transition from order to chaos, or of the intervention of death in the everyday course of events. Even though these image sequences are only rushes, as opposed to more elaborate forms of documentary discourse, they call up historical plot structures in the viewer (cf. White) that relate to culturally predetermined horizons of expectation with regard to the meaning of history. They also illustrate—more or less explicitly—how documentary film suggests that the social interaction which it represents is embedded in a meaningful social ensemble, i.e., a type of community. Because of the concrete spatialization of social conflicts and political conceits this view of community is always also connected to a notion of territoriality and spatial boundaries. Moreover, filmic discourse defines image types of the local/national and of the other. Establishing what Bourdieu has called social principles of "vision and division," documentary film shapes and visualizes notions of national identity and alterity; whether it is in the service of the hegemonic pedagogy of the national (cf. Bhabha) or whether it subversively represents the margins of society or geographical peripheries, documentary film thus affirms or re-elaborates the boundaries which separate those who participate in society from those who are excluded from it.

All these aspects are called up in documentary film—at times explicitly, at other times subliminally—; frequently they are present only in the background of the social interaction that is being shown. Although we are dealing with rhetorical conventions and cultural constructions that are part of what Frederic Jameson has called the "political unconscious," images of the national, as they are constructed in film, tend to be perceived as depictions of national reality (*Political*). This perception is due to the long-postulated transparency of the documentary medium and to the corresponding truth claim. In this sense, documentary films *represent* imagined communities and simultaneously *create* them in a performative way by promoting political consciousness, a sense of (national) belonging, and cultures of citizenship.

These questions about the narration of nation have long been subordinate, in studies on documentary film, to the prevalent question about the relationship between fact and fiction and thus about the borderlines between the documentary genre and fiction films or experimental art films. Nor did the constructivist theory of nation, which was initiated in the 1980s by Anderson and Hobsbawm (*Nations*; *Invented*) and which took a postcolonial turn with Bhabha (*Nation*) and Chatterjee, consider the specifics of audiovisual and documentary narrations, as it tended to be focused on the foundational fictions of the 19th century. Located at the intersection of film studies and theories of the nation, our volume takes a first step in exploring an area that has not yet received the scholarly attention which it deserves, namely the role of documentary film in the negotiation of national identity.[1] Adopting positions expressed by Homi Bhabha, Chon Noriega, or José David Saldívar, we take *nation* to be a transnational phenomenon that is defined in negotiating processes between self and other, national and international discourses—especially in a field of cultural production which is as internationally intertwined as documentary film.

---

[1] A systematic monograph study on the topic, Sebastian Thies's *The Nation on the Editing Table: Temporality, Mediality, and Imagined Communities in Documentary Filmmaking*, is forthcoming in 2012. A volume that is moving toward exploring the historiography of nationhood by examining national narratives in medial and artistic representations in general is *Narrating the Nation*, edited by Berger/Eriksonas/Mycock.

This transnational dimension of our topic explains the inter-American approach of our volume, which frees documentary film from the methodological nationalism that continues in many current studies of the genre and situates it instead in a broader, hemispheric dialogue. This dialogue is conducted in this book in Spanish and English; we hope to encourage in this way a revision of the language politics prevalent in Inter-American Studies. Dialogue—in Inter-American Studies in general as well as in the study of documentary film in the Western Hemisphere in particular—emanates from the longstanding mutual perceptions of North and South in the area of cultural production. Mutual observation between North and South has brought forth a long series of prominent documentaries such as Drew Associates' *Yanqui, No!* (1960) for Time Life Television, Santiago Álvarez's avant-gardist newsreel *LBJ* (1968) on Lyndon B. Johnson and the assassination of John F. and Robert Kennedy, Michael Rubbo's Canadian NFB production *Waiting for Fidel* (1974) or Oliver Stone's recent *South of the Border* (2009), which explores the mainstream media's misperceptions of the Latin American South. Another case in point is Julianne Burton's influential pioneering study, *The Social Documentary in Latin America*, which examines developments and modes in Latin American documentaries from a U.S. perspective at a time when the genre seemed to have lost (at least temporarily) its avant-garde, political function in North America. As Michael Chanan believes, with documentaries that explore national or communal identity, "[c]onceptually, we are entering the territory—not an accidental metaphor—of what is called cognitive mapping: the construction of mental maps which encode the relative relationships between different locations in the spatial environment" ("Going South" 147). Ideologically marked images of the other and of his/her community and territory reveal the relationship between the documentarian and his/her subject(s) (cf. Martin).

The inter-American component in the construction of a national other, along with phenomena like cultural hybridity, inter-American migration, tendencies of political and economic integration, and questions of cultural and trans/national identity, has triggered countless critical debates in past decades.[2] However, these debates tend to overlook the genre of documentary film, although documentaries, as mentioned above, play a central role in conceptualizing, defining or rejecting national icons and symbols, as they interconnect social imaginaries and documentations of reality.

Our approach to the narration of nation in documentary film is indebted to the pioneers of the genre in the 1920s, when documentaries emerge as a distinct type of

---

[2] Cf., for example, Daniel Mato, "On the Making of Transnational Identities in the Age of Globalization: The US Latina/o-'Latin' American Case;" Earl E. Fitz, "Inter-American Studies as an Emerging Field: The Future of a Discipline;" Caroline F. Levander/Robert S. Levine (eds.), *Hemispheric American Studies*; Sebastian Thies/Josef Raab (eds.), *E Pluribus Unum?: National and Transnational Identities in the Americas/Identidades nacionales y transnacionales en las Américas*; Josef Raab/Martin Butler (eds.), *Hybrid Americas: Contacts, Contrasts, and Confluences in New World Literatures and Cultures*; or Ralph Bauer, "Hemispheric Studies."

film. This is also the time when the postcolonial societies of the Americas start consolidating. Having completed their westward expansion, the U.S.A. assume their hegemony in the American hemisphere through the Spanish-American War and rise to the status of a world power through World War I. Simultaneously, the Latin American nations emancipate themselves from Europe and enter into new, hemispheric dependencies. Canada, finally, gains national independence in 1931. The Scotsman John Grierson, who studied communications at the University of Chicago, was the first to recognize in his filmic, organizational and scholarly oeuvre, the power of documentary film as a medium that can convey to large parts of the population an image of nation and citizenship (cf. Barnouw; Barsam). His 1926 review of Robert Flaherty's South Sea docudrama *Moana* (1926) leads to an initial definition of documentary film. Grierson maintains in his "First Principles of Documentary" that the Hollywood "studio films largely ignore this possibility of opening up the screen on the real world. They photograph acted stories against artificial backgrounds. Documentary would photograph the living scene and the living story" (qtd. in MacDonald/Cousins 97). In retrospect Grierson observes:

> At that time some of us thought the Hollywood film ... was unnecessarily out of touch with the social realities ... We saw the growing complexity of modern affairs; and we thought that if our half-bewildered, half frivolous generation did not master events, it was not unlikely that events would master us. We saw the enormous power of the film medium and felt it had a very special duty to interpret the contemporary scene. (Grierson, qtd. in Deacon 152)

When, starting in 1938, Grierson is instrumental in the establishment of the National Film Board (NFB) of Canada, which is still exemplary for the paradigm of state-funded, non-theatrical documentary production, he describes the role of this non-commercial, didactic genre for Canada thus: "film is a means by which different parts of Canada may be brought alive to each other, international relations taught, and sectionalisms diminished" (qtd. in Druick 41). In this respect, Grierson spesks of a propaganda function of documentary film in Western democracies, which envisages the model of a critical narration of nation that is at the same time affirmative of the system. Grierson's pioneering work on the social function of documentary film coincides with that of the Soviet filmmaker and critic Dziga Vertov, whose position was similarly influential in film history. Under the notion of *kinoglaz* Vertov propagates documentary film as a revolution in terms of the art of filmmaking, focusing initially on the technical potential for innovation that the camera has. At the center of his theory of *kinoglaz* is "the documentary decoding of the visible world and of the world which is invisible for the human eye," which aims at "finding in life itself an answer to a given topic" (Vertov 73, our translation; cf. Hohenberger 11). Hohenberger points out that while Vertov wanted to shape the future complexity of the social through equally complex films, Grierson sought to reduce the complexity of the social to make it fit a film story in order to achieve consensus on an existing reality (cf. 11-12). Both these positions on the social performativity of documentation would later become influential in different areas of documentary film production in the Americas, with Vertov's avant-gardist understanding of the genre influencing especially revolutionary film production in 1960s and 1970s Latin America.

These two decades saw a fundamental change in the production of documentary film, which—emanating from the technological changes in filming and recording technology[3]—establishes the basis for *Direct Cinema* and *cinéma vérité*, two approaches that make it possible to observe the social actors in everyday situations and thus to integrate the quotidian or the subaltern into the narration of the nation. The lighter and less expensive equipment required also lays the basis for a democratization of access to film as a means of the self-determined cultural production of subaltern groups that Julio García Espinosa had described in his manifesto "Un cine imperfecto." These developments had fundamental effects on the ways in which nation was being narrated. In deconstructing social authority, the 1960s also questioned the medial logics of representation used by the preceding generation of documentary filmmakers. For example, voice-over narration is almost liquidated by Direct Cinema as practiced by Robert Drew, Donn A. Pennebaker, Richard Leacock or the Maislies brothers as well as by the experimental newsreels of Cuban director Santiago Álvarez. Beyond the contrary positions of North and South on the cultural, political, and economic imperialism of the U.S.A. and on the "dependency" and "underdevelopment" of the Third World, a radical view of documentary film spreads: it considers documentaries to be a means of "voicing the voiceless," of articulating social heterogeneity and marginalization, as well as—in the extreme case of Third Cinema—a revolutionary weapon against social injustice and inequality.

The focus of this volume is on the transition from this repositioning of documentary film in the 1960s and 1970s, which accompanies the corresponding socio-political changes of those decades throughout the Americas, to yet another shift in the language and aesthetics of documentary film in the 1980s. The debunking of cultural and political utopias of the 1960s and 1970s is accompanied by a disillusionment that involves the postmodern crisis of referentiality and the questioning of the iconicity of the documentary image as well as ways of experiencing the world that are based on social fragmentation and individualization. Furthermore, the experience of migration, exile, and diaspora keeps interrogating the conceptual borders of the nation. These developments impact the narration of nation by deconstructing the imagined community and by stressing the subjectivity of narrative authority. It is especially also the introduction of video technology that leads to new forms of subjective narration in documentaries, a kind of narration whose truth claim—unlike that of films in the 1970s and 1980s— rests not on a methodology and interpretive matrix that orient themselves toward scientific "discourses of sobriety," but on affective intensity, poetic truth, and performativity (Nichols, *Representing*; cf. Bruzzi). The simulacrum of which Baudrillard

---

[3] Because of early camera and sound technology, documentaries from before the times of 1960s *Direct Cinema* necessarily had to perform the subject for the camera, which makes it questionable to apply the fact/fiction distinction (that had been developed later) to them.

has spoken and the hyperreality of an experience of reality that is shaped by mass media are fundamentally changing our relationship to the medium of film (cf. *Simulacra*). Documentaries are starting to test and deconstruct the potential and borders of documentary referentiality; reenactments and formal quotations from fictional genres lead to a blurring of boundaries and to visual synergies between fact and fiction (cf. Haddu/Page). Docudramas, which are based on historical events that they individualize and partly fictionalize, further complicate the fact/fiction distinction, as do biopics. Despite these instances of crisis there has also been something like a deluge of multiplying documentary forms and formats since then. The growing expansion of documentary formats on television, the rise of docu-fictions, as well as the increased presence of documentary films on the big screens of commercial movie theaters in the past two decades (due, to a significant degree, to the success of Michael Moore) mark the beginning of a new phase (cf. Nichols, *Blurred*; Beattie). Video, DVD, Internet television, and P2P exchange are revolutionizing the format, financing, distribution, and reception of documentaries. At the same time the rise of digital media and the availability of Internet platforms like Twitter and YouTube is changing drastically the relationship between producers/consumers of audiovisual media and the technological basis of communication. New types of national and transnational imagined communities are created as a consequence.

In making sense of the complexity of life and in conceiving of nations and communities in documentary film, narration is doubtlessly one of the most effective means the filmmaker can employ. Through voice-over commentary, narrative editing or, in a much more veiled manner, by surreptitiously referring to the narratives of public discourse, plot structures make historical processes understandable and suggest a teleology; they present social interaction implicitly or explicitly as constituting larger imagined communities; and they suggest that the communities of which they conceive are based on specific notions of space and time as well as specific values and ideologies.

As Bill Nichols has pointed out, (especially due to the impact of Direct Cinema) the importance of narration has long been underestimated in film studies.[4] Our volume seeks to correct this oversight by focusing on the numerous ways in which documentaries in and of the Americas tell stories that are offered as commentaries on the identity of nation and/or community, while affirming the political orientation of the filmmaker. These narrations of nation in documentary films of the Americas are explored here in five thematic sections as well as a concluding section in which documentary filmmakers from Argentina, Ecuador, Mexico, and the United States present their individual approaches.

---

[4]   One exception in this regard is Wilma Kiener's study of documentary film, *Die Kunst des Erzählens: Narrativität in dokumentarischen und ethnographischen Filmen.*

1. New Dynamics in the Political Documentary Film

The first section, "New Dynamics in the Political Documentary Film," deals not only with the phenomenon that documentary film as a means of political engagement is enjoying a renaissance but also with the successful return of documentary film to the big screen with filmmakers such as Michael Moore, Patricio Guzmán, and Fernando E. Solanas. Even former U.S. Vice President Al Gore has entered the ranks of filmmakers with *An Inconvenient Truth* (2006). It was especially the polarizing political climate in the U.S.A. under President George W. Bush with its neoconservative backlash that fostered the political positioning of filmmakers as public intellectuals on both sides of the political cleavage lines. Benson and Snee have shown how, following in the footsteps of Michael Moore's *Fahrenheit 9/11*, the most commercially successful documentary film ever, a number of partisan documentaries such as *Fahrenhype 9/11*, *Michael Moore Hates America, Celsius 41.11, George W. Bush: Faith in the White House, Stolen Honor: Wounds That Never Heal, Going Upriver: The Long War of John Kerry* (all of which came out in 2004), determined the political agendas in the presidential elections:

> A fascinating and unexpected development in the 2004 campaign [for U.S. President] was the reemergence of the feature-length documentary film as an outlet for partisan and polemical messages. Documentaries have always held the power to influence public opinion, and historians and critics of documentary have always emphasized its social and political functions, but seldom have documentaries been a major force in a national political election ... it can be argued that they are not "really" documentaries at all—but they do appropriate the form of documentary to lend structure and authenticity to their appeals, even as they draw on other genres and hybrids to create a rhetoric that is a mix of documentary, propaganda, political advertising, and news forms. (2)

Although these new dynamics of political documentaries can be traced back to the agitprop traditions of radical films in the 1960s and 1970s—e.g., Emile de Antonio's U.S. American documentaries of political dissent, Santiago Álvarez's avant-gardist newsreels in Cuba, or the monumental *La hora de los hornos* (1968) by Fernando E. Solanas and Octavio Getino in Argentina—, there are strong indications that this new enthusiasm for political documentaries engenders new semantics of the political, an ambiguous position with regard to the persuasiveness of political language, and a different understanding of the role and narrative authority of a film "author." New dynamics in the political documentary may thus be creating a new narration of nation.

For his exemplary illustration of new dynamics in political documentary film, Wanja von der Goltz selects *Comandante* (2003) by the internationally renowned fiction film director Oliver Stone. In order to explore Stone's documentary techniques, von der Goltz first establishes the characteristics of Stone's docu-fictions (like *Born on the 4th of July* [1989] and *JFK* [1991]), which he then compares to the approach used in *Comandante*. On this basis, von der Goltz demonstrates that while Stone's use of archival footage in *Comandante* differs from that in his docu-fictions, the ideological focus remains primarily on a critique of U.S. society and politics and its narration of nation—as had been the case in his docu-fictions. Drawing a critical portrait of Fidel Castro—which one could have expected from this film—is at best a secondary aim of *Comandante*.

Wiebke Engel chooses Michael Moore's *Fahrenheit 9/11* for her analysis of new dynamics in political documentary film. She illustrates that—far from using a "discourse of sobriety" and an unbiased presentation of facts—Moore employs a highly personalized mode of narration. Through the example of Michael Moore, Engel demonstrates in her essay how author-centered documentaries rely on the strong presence of the filmmaker's I/eye, which turns subjectivity and performativity into constitutive elements of new political documentary film. The innovative dynamics in Michael Moore's *Fahrenheit 9/11* are also the point of departure of Chris Lippard's essay. Lippard analyzes how Steven Greenstreet's *This Divided State* (2005) critically engages with the controversy surrounding Michael Moore's visit to Utah Valley State College (now Utah Valley University). The essay concludes that while Moore questions the narration of national identity in an author-centered approach, Greenstreet's *This Divided State* uses the college—a site of higher education, open debate, and free speech—as the center of his film. On the basis of the rights and values associated with a state institution of higher education, Greenstreet suggests that we need to critically question traditional concepts of national identity.

Hannah Osenberg turns our attention further south—to Chicana filmmaker Lourdes Portillo's *Señorita extraviada* (2001). This documentary investigates the feminicide in Ciudad Juárez, a social phenomenon which has revealed the failure and gendered bias of institutional responses to forms of widespread violence against women in the borderlands between Mexico and the U.S.A. Osenberg demonstrates how Portillo uncovers the socio-cultural structures behind the feminicide by problematizing the dichotomy of public and private. She also focuses on Portillo's distinctive aesthetic, which conveys an acute poetic and ethical awareness of the role of documentary filmmaking vis à vis the traumatic experience of victims of violence and repression at the margins of a failed nation state.

Anne Lakeberg, finally, discusses the semantic transformation of the political in recent Argentinean documentary film through her comparative analysis of *Memoria del saqueo* (2004) by Fernando E. Solanas and *Yo Presidente* (2006) by Mariano Cohn and Gastón Duprat. She contrasts two different generational approaches to conceiving of the people and of the nation's presidents—one still based on the binary oppositions prevalent in 1960s radical filmmaking, the other one emerging from a postmodern deconstruction of both, the people as a collective agent in history and the screen personae of the powerful.

2.   Narrating the Nation from Its Margins

Especially since the 1960s, documentary film, whose creators, according to Louis Menand, "have usually worked in a spirit of advocacy," has increasingly been employed to advocate the rights of marginalized minorities, of people who have suffered injustices or who have been excluded from full social and cultural participation or national citizenship (qtd. in Chanan, *Politics* 23). In fact, the self-determined social function of documentary film has always included a strong interest in depicting the margins of society and in focusing on those areas of the nation that are inhabited by a 'culturally othered' population. With its approach of social critique, documentary film is especially well suited to engage in the narration of nation beyond its homogenizing and power-affirming dimension and to dissect heterogeneity, inequality, and exclusion. In this sense, documentary film has become an instrument that propagates the demands of the oppressed and that gives a voice and platform to the otherwise voiceless. Thus, as Michael Chanan points out, "documentary is a battleground of social and historical truth, and this is one of the main reasons why people make them" (*Politics* 23). Documentaries can offer narrative accounts of society that compete with the versions told by the power elites in order to make a case for a disadvantaged segment of the population. It is often this "spirit of advocacy" that motivates documentarians. Films like Patricio Guzmán's *La batalla de Chile* (1975), Arthur Omar's *Congo* (1972), Diego de la Texera's *El Salvador: el pueblo vencera* (1982), Barbara Kopple's *Harlan County, USA* (1976), Alanis Obomsawin's *Kanehsatake: 270 Years of Resistance* (1993), Nettie Wild's *A Place Called Chiapas* (1998), Eugene Jarecki's *Why We Fight* (2005) or Edward James Olmos's *Walkout* (2006) advocate a cause (as part of a campaign or retrospectively) and offer a platform for minorities. In this way, documentary helps to unsettle distinctions between margin and periphery in society.

Placing the margin(s) in the center (of attention) implies that the documentary film also has to face the issue of representation, as described by Gayatri C. Spivak: by giving a voice to the voiceless, documentaries mediate between social elites and the oppressed masses who do not enjoy the option of a self-determined audiovisuality. In the context of a postmodern reflexivity, this claim to mediation is the nucleus for a controversial debate on the ethics of filmmaking and of modes of mediation, on which Coutinho's *Boca de Lixo* (1993) puts its finger: looking right into the camera, the youngsters in a trash dump of Rio de Janeiro challenge the cameraman, "Que é que vocês ganham com isso? Pra ficar botando esse negócio na nossa cara?" [What do you get out of that? Pointing that thing into our faces?"] (cf. Chanan, *Politics*; "Going South").

This is the background for the essays in our section on "Narrating the Nation from Its Margins," which discuss films that use a variety of ways for positioning diverse marginalized social actors in the center. In Josef Raab's analysis of the docudrama *Salt of the Earth* (Herbert J. Biberman, 1954) the politics of the blacklisted "Hollywood Ten" and the living conditions of mining families are central. The essay demonstrates how this classic docudrama about the 1951-52 strike against the Empire Zinc Mining Company in New Mexico tackles inequalities in terms of ethnicity, gender, class, and political affiliation, as it unites the demands of miners and their wives with those of the blacklisted filmmakers into a plea for "a new way." *Salt of the Earth* is thus discussed here as a case in U.S. film history that insisted on reshaping the U.S. American nation along the demands of the labor, feminist, and civil rights movements of the 1950s and against the repression of McCarthy's House Un-American Activities Committee (HUAC), whose investigations had torpedoed the careers of Biberman and other members of the "Hollywood Ten." Both in terms of its plot and of its history of production and distribution, *Salt of the Earth* narrates the U.S. American nation in a way which suggests that the formerly oppressed can ultimately prevail.

The 1950s are also the starting point for Álvaro Fernández Bravo's essay. His focus is on the Argentinean context, which he explores from a diachronic perspective. The essay concentrates on three documentary films—originating at different moments in Argentina's history—and on the changing role of borders or the periphery in the context of the filmic construction of the nation. Fernández Bravo argues that *Tire dié* (Fernando Birri, 1958) is in the tradition of politically engaged Third Cinema and thus uses a decidedly didactic approach, while *Dársena sur* (Pablo Reyero, 1997) and *La libertad* (Lisandro Alonso, 2001) are part of *Nuevo Cine Argentino*, which is characterized by a far less political film language.

Madalina Stefan and Lorena Ortiz, in their analysis of the Mexican documentary *En el hoyo* (Juan Carlos Rulfo, 2006), also assume an anti-hegemonic narration of the nation from the margins of society. They examine two kinds of discursive strategies. While progress is aestheticized in the film as a topos of modernity, mythical and postmodern strategies like multi-temporal heterogeneity (cf. García Canclini) are used by Rulfo to account for the polyphony of marginalized voices and to delineate the nation as an ambivalent liminal entity.

Gabriela Alemán, for her part, interrogates the filmic construction of the Ecuadorean nation after its return to democracy in the 1980s. She points to the centrality of ethnicity in *Boca de lobo* (Raúl Khalifé, 1982) and *Los hieleros del Chimborazo* (Gustavo Guayasamín, 1980), an aspect that the official discourse had negated for a long time and that these documentary films turn into a constitutive element of the Ecuadorian nation.

Aspects of gender are the focus of Birte Horn's essay, which concentrates on the feminist movement in the United States. Specifically, Horn analyzes the construction of womanhood in U.S. documentary film from the nickelodeons' engagement with the Suffragette Movement of the early twentieth century to Maggie Hadleigh-West's *War Zone* (1998) and thus illustrates the contribution that documentaries can make to the struggle for women's rights. Horn describes some major steps in the development of documentary film as a feminist tool in the United States and she examines how the genre has been used by filmmakers to support, question, and expand notions of womanhood in the United States. Horn's focus lies on films of the second and third waves of feminism, which raised consciousness among women and which combatted sexism and male presumptions.

3. DissemiNations: Toward a Narration of Nation in Postmodern Times

Along with problematizing the truth claim of documentary film, there has been, since the 1980s, a growing tendency toward medial reflexivity, poetic subjectivity, and the performative (cf. Nichols, *Blurred*; Bruzzi; Beattie). These phenomena trigger overwhelming changes in a film genre that is increasingly experimenting with the limits of its epistemological foundations. There is a shift away from the unquestioned narrative authorities of documentary film and of the corresponding authoritarian interpretive matrix of earlier times toward a documentary aesthetic that is characterized much more by ambivalence, aporiae, and poetic forms of reference. The new poetics of documentary form abandon the anti-aesthetic politics of 1960s and '70s documentaries, which had attempted to undermine "bourgeois" aesthetics with approaches like Glauber Rocha's "aesthetics of hunger."[5] In this way, the new documentary aesthetics of the 1980s are connected to the beginnings of the genre, when the poetic—e.g., with the artistic aesthetics of exotic "natural dramas" or city symphonies—was an unquestioned element of documentary film as an art form. The new poetic subjectivity stresses the role of the narrating subject and *auteur* of the film, as illustrated by the success of first-person documentaries and autobiographical videos (cf. Lane; Aufderheide). In this context, *La T.V. y yo* (2002) by Andrés di Tella, with its reflection on the effect of media consumption on membership in national collectives of memory, and *Silverlake Life: The View from Here* (1993) by Peter Friedman and Tom Joslin, with its comments on the social exclusion of AIDS patients and on the preparation for death, constitute two extreme examples of a new kind of intimacy to be found in documentary film.

At the same time, documentary film is rediscovering those traditions of re-enactment and fictionalization which marked the early days of the genre as part of its expressive repertoire but which had been discredited during the decades of Direct Cinema, as more rigid ideas about the scientific truth claims of documentary mimesis were being adopted. These shifts need to be seen in the context of the notion of performativity, which is used in a variety of ways in current research on documentary film and which needs to be briefly addressed in its significance for the narration of nation. From a postmodern perspective, the belief in the accessibility of an authentic reality prior to medialization cannot be upheld. Through the power of the camera,

---

5 Rocha wrote in his manifesto: "We understand the hunger that Europeans and the majority of Brazilians have failed to understand. For the European, it is a strange tropical surrealism. For the Brazilians, it is a national shame. He does not eat, but is ashamed to say so; and yet, he does not know where this hunger comes from. We know—since we made those ugly, sad films, those screaming, desperate films in which reason has not always prevailed—that this hunger will not be assuaged by moderate government reforms and that the cloak of technicolor cannot hide, but rather only aggravates, its tumours. Therefore, only a culture of hunger can qualitatively surpass its own structures by undermining and destroying them. The most noble cultural manifestation of hunger is violence" (13).

documentary film changes the very reality with which the filmmaker is interacting in
his or her documentary practice (cf. Comolli; Renov). The filmmaker's interlocutors
are aware of the practices of medialization; they act as medial subjects and adopt
corresponding roles. Furthermore, documentary film, as a didactic, consciousness-
raising medium, aims at transforming the social reality into which it inscribes itself.
All these aspects imply that reality and its performative transformation in film can no
longer be distinguished. Documentary film reacts by making its own creative process
explicit and thus by destroying the illusion of the medium's transparency by performing a creative process. An example for this approach is Lourdes Portillo's *My
McQueen* (2004), which consists of a discussion between the director and her cameraman on the screen legend Steve McQueen in *Bullit* (Peter Yates, 1968). Cultural
identities and the positioning of film creators are uncovered here as a kind of histrionic
performance. The issue is stressed most memorably in Eduardo Coutinho's *Moscou*
(2009), in which the director has professional actors on stage perform the autobiographical statements of social actors and thus turns the ideal of authentic mimesis in
film into a postmodern aporia.

The significance of performativity is linked to a profound crisis of the referentiality of all systems of signs, with a new conceptualization of semiosis, which transcends the essentialisms in the discourse on cultural identities. With the blurring boundaries between seeming and being, reality and medial virtuality, it suggests a regression to a (neo-)baroque feeling of crisis. What is new about postmodern documentary
film is that the authority of documentary discourse and of the narration of nation is
undercut in the mode of postmodern irony, as described by Linda Hutcheon. An example for this kind of ironic or ludic documentary mode is Ross McElwee's *Sherman's March* (1986), which uses the style of a travelogue to create a documentary film
on the failure of a documentary film project—from the autodiegetic perspective of a
filmmaker whose project of exploring the historical identity of the U.S. American
South suffers from the repeated failure of his flings with the opposite sex.[6] These types
of deconstructing documentary discourse are certainly more frequent in the (alleged)
centers of an increasingly polyfocal cartography of postmodernity. Films like *Ilha das
flores* (1990) by Jorge Furtado, an experimental compilation film on the function of
trash in Western consumer societies, demonstrate, however, that these methods of self-
reflexive irony can also be linked to postcolonial positions.[7]

---

[6] On the paradoxical nature of his endeavors, Ross McElwee commented: "It seems I'm
filming my life in order to have a life to film, like some primitive organism that somehow
nourishes itself by devouring itself, growing as it diminishes" (http://www.imdb.com/title/
tt0091943/).

[7] Especially in the U.S.A., the narration of nation increasingly focuses also on the abnormal,
archaic, and incommensurable, as Maria Luisa Ortega demonstrates in *Espejos rotos*: the
myth of the quotidian is reduced through medialization, for example, to the disturbed dynamics of a family with a pedophile father, juvenile killers of children (Berlinger and
Sinofsky's *Paradise Lost: The Child Murders at Robin Hood Hills*, 1996) or to serial killers (Nick Broomfield's *Aileen Wuornos: The Selling of a Serial Killer*, 1993).

For his exploration of U.S. national identity in the late twentieth century, director Adam Simon uses as his primary material the horror films made by George A. Romero, John Carpenter, Tobe Hooper, Wes Craven and David Cronenberg. As Gabriele Pisarz-Ramírez demonstrates in her essay, Simon's documentary *The American Nightmare* (2003) narrates the nation through the ways in which films like *The Texas Chainsaw Massacre* (1974), *Night of the Living Dead* (1968), *Shivers* (1975), *Halloween* (1978), and *The Last House on the Left* (1972) have unsettled the audience's sense of safety at a time when the nation itself was under attack and in a state of crisis. Pisarz-Ramírez examines the claim made in Simon's documentary that national issues like the Civil Rights Movement, the Cold War, and the Vietnam War led to the creation and popularity of a type of horror film in the late 1960s and in the 1970s that celebrates violence and gore and that plays with audience anxieties as an outlet for the rage that many were feeling against the nation's power elites. In short, Pisarz-Ramírez examines Simon's claim that these horror films transferred the nightmarish social experience onto violent screen fictions.

With Burkhart Pohl the material basis that documentaries use to narrate the nation in postmodern times shifts from horror film and social unrest to music and the city. By analyzing Fernando Pérez's *Suite Habana* (2003), a film indebted to Walter Ruttmann's *Berlin: Die Sinfonie der Großstadt* (1927), Pohl's essay pursues the question of narrating the Cuban nation as an imagined community split between insular revolutionism and diaspora. Pohl concentrates on the ways in which the Cuban director represents with filmic means the relationship of the people portrayed in the film to the Cuban Revolution. He concludes that *Suite Habana* allows for divergent ideological readings of life in Castro's Cuba by representing Cuban reality in a polysemic way, as exemplified through the heterogeneous musical themes and symbols that this documentary uses.

Pohl's focus on uses of a city as metonymic of a national imaginary and on the polysemic approach that documentarians are taking in their engagements with city and nation is continued by Jens Martin Gurr, whose focus lies on Los Angeles and on nonlinear, postmodern narration. Gurr's essay illustrates how the multi-media CD *Bleeding Through: Layers of Los Angeles, 1920-1986* (2003) by film director, novelist, cultural critic and scholar Norman M. Klein transcends the limits of documentary narration: because of the technical options of pursuing different (narrative/documentary) paths that the computer CD format provides, Klein's documentation of Los Angeles from 1920 to 1986 recreates the complexity, multiplicity and dynamics of the city in a way no other medium could. Based on his monograph *The History of Forgetting: Los Angeles and the Erasure of Memory*, Klein's multi-media documentation *Bleeding Through* (which, in addition to the computer CD, also contains a novella) is demonstratively subjective, self-reflexive, intertextual, and revisionist. Engaging in what Gurr calls "interactive multi-medial docu-fiction in hypertext," the work questions our notions of documentary narration of city and nation.

The focus on modes of narration in postmodern times is continued in Sebastian Thies's essay, which examines the narration of nation in Raúl Ruiz's *Cofralandes: Rapsodia chilena* (2004), a first-person documentary and experimental record of the director's return to Chile after having spent several decades in Europe. Ruiz uses a highly poetic, polysemic, intertextual, openly subjective, and self-reflexive style that interweaves fact and fiction and that deconstructs the conventions of ethnographic filmmaking, to which it frequently refers. Thies demonstrates how this work by one of the most renowned *auteurs* of the international avant-garde film scene aspires to a truth claim that is related to a nomadic epistemology and the performative mode in documentary filmmaking. In this narration, as Thies argues, the Chilean nation emerges as a fragmented community that is struggling to deal with the nation's past and to engage in meaningful communication.

4. Documentary Film as a Medium of Cultural Memory

Its privileged relationship to the factual has been considered from the very beginnings of the genre as central for documentary film (cf. Nichols, *Representing* 77-78; Beceyro 86). The power that documentaries have of recreating and preserving the impact of historical events by assembling audiovisual footage from the most diverse sources is illustrated, for example, by *102 Minutes That Changed America* (Nicole Rittenmeyer and Seth Skundrick, 2008), a History Channel compilation of private video images, media reports, fire department and coast guard radio transmissions, phone messages, speeches, interviews with witnesses, and countless other materials on the time that elapsed between the first tower of the World Trade Center being hit on September 11, 2001 and its collapse. But as documentaries abandon, in the postmodern age, the demand for objectivity and factuality, 'softer' concepts of referentiality and of the construction of social knowledge come to the foreground. Among those is the concept of cultural memory, which becomes popular in cultural studies and in the humanities at the same time. This development is reflected in Chilean filmmaker Patricio Guzmán's statement that a nation without documentary films is like a family without a family photo album ("Un país sin cine documental es como una familia sin álbum de fotografías") (cf. Ruffinelli). Memory is understood, in this respect, as a constructed, polyphonic reference to the past which—according to Halbwachs and others—results from social interaction or communication and which has a more subjective and affective dimension than historiographic discourse. Memory opens up for documentary film an access to experiences that are subject to collective repression, traumatization, and forgetting. Therefore documentaries play an important role in coming to terms with a past of violence, dictatorship, ethnocide, and terror.

Collective memory relies on documentaries in two ways: first, the documentary is a medium of remembrance that preserves voices, images, and fragments of other films and media for posterity. Especially postmodern historical compilations like Ken Burns's *The Civil War* (1990) rely on an archeological reconstruction of subjective war experiences and images which boil abstract historical developments down to autobiographical narrations and which thus engage in a certain postmodern historical identification and nostalgia.[8] Second, documentary film in the tradition of Jean Rouch's *cinéma vérité* can play an active part in shaping collective memory in certain social contexts that are threatened by forgetting and official memoricide. For instance, filmmakers of 1960s and 1970s *Tercer Cine* such as Eduardo Coutinho and Patricio Guzmán, whose films had been prevented from completion or censored by the dictatorships in Brazil and Chile, are filming their return to the very people who had been involved in their earlier, uncompleted film projects as social actors and they turn these encounters between present and past into the groundbreaking documentaries *Cabra marcado para morrer* (1985) and *Chile: memoria obstinada* (1997). In this way they make a performative contribution to the memory of the left-wing utopias which characterize the political contexts of the original film projects, while also reflecting on the possibilities and limits of collective memory (cf. Thies, "ImagiNaciones").

The essays collected in section IV of our volume deal with "Documentary Film as a Medium of Cultural Memory" and reflect these two aspects of postmodern memorial culture in documentary film: documentaries as media of remembrance and documentary filmmaking as performative work toward collective memory.

Christof Decker and Itzia Fernández Escareño address the genre of compilation films, which they examine in terms of its formal specifics as well as its narration of nation. After presenting initially the formal and stylistic characteristics of the genre, Decker asks in what ways compilation films can serve as media of cultural memory. His analysis of *Strange Victory* (Leo Hurwitz, 1948), *The Civil War* (Ken Burns, 1990), and *The Atomic Café* (Jayne Loader, Kevin Rafferty, Pierce Rafferty, 1982) focuses on the different ways of remembering war that these works employ. Decker's analysis establishes three categories of how these remembrances of war relate to the narration of the U.S. American nation: unity, division, and disintegration.

Itzia Fernández Escareño, for her part, concentrates on the representation of what is Mexican in the compilation films *La línea paterna* (José Buil and Maryse Sistach, 1995) and *Los rollos perdidos de Pancho Villa* (Gregorio Rocha, 2003) as both films use different registers for constructing a Mexican national identity In *La línea paterna* Buil and Sistach make use of the home movies and ethnographic amateur films of their extended families. Not only are they rewriting the history of their own families in this way, but—emerging from their basis in the private context—they also rewrite regional history. Rocha, instead, works with public images; in *Los rollos perdidos de Pancho Villa* he confronts the imaginaries of the Mexican Revolution while also—in a self-reflexive manner—re-writing the history of film in the U.S. Mexican borderlands.

Another analysis of documentary practices of memory is offered by Daniela Noll-Opitz; she concentrates on an aesthetic of post-memory in Albertina Carri's film *Los rubios* (2003). Noll-Opitz examines Carri's reflexive and performative strategies, as the filmmaker deals with the memory of those Argentineans who have disappeared

---

[8] On postmodern nostalgia in dealing with history, cf. Jameson, *Postmodernism*.

during the country's last military dictatorship. The essay demonstrates how Carri problematizes the use of documentary film as a medium of cultural memory by opposing to those strategies that unambiguously reconstitute and inscribe identities a type of remembrance that asks questions rather than answering them and that doubts the possibility of reconstructing the past in any definitive manner.

5.   Beyond the Canon: Rediscovering Documentary Films and Filmmakers

Compilation documentaries on film history, such as Rocha's above-mentioned *Los rollos perdidos de Pancho Villa* or *Los Angeles Plays Itself* (Thom Andersen, 2003), are currently enjoying much popularity. But also the history of documentary filmmaking itself, which for a long time had been overshadowed in film studies, film theory, and film criticism by a focus on fiction films, is increasingly receiving scholarly attention. In recent approaches to the archeology of documentary discourse, there has been a shift toward the voices of those social groups and filmmakers who had to fight for their medial participation against obstacles put up by patriarchy, ethnic discrimination, and "subdesarrollo" and who were at risk of being forgotten.

It is to this work of revising the canon of documentary film that the essays in section V of our volume are dedicated. Patricia Torres San Martín engages in a revision of Latin American documentary film history by exploring the work of women, which is also the focus of a series of biopics that she initiated and produced: *Opera feminea*. From the perspective of gender studies, Torres San Martín concentrates on the work of the Mexican sisters Adriana and Dolores Elhers as well as Elena Sánchez Valenzuela, which was very influential during the beginnings of documentary filmmaking in Mexico but which has hardly been recognized. The unavailability of original material from those pioneer days of documentary filmmaking illustrates the challenges which this archeological work at the borders of the canon is facing.

While Torres San Martín argues for a revision of the canon of documentary film with regard to gender, Gary Francisco Keller proposes a revision with regard to the subjects of films. His sweeping review of documentaries and fiction films that deal with Mexican Americans, miners, workers' struggles, and the dignity of work starts with the issue of the exploitation of labor in the mines and fields of Hispanic America that began with the Spanish conquest of the Amerindian civilizations. After a historical overview of the conditions of mining in the U.S.A. and Mexico Keller focuses in particular on three films: Herbert J. Biberman's *Salt of the Earth* (1954), Mexican director Marcela Fernández Violante's *Cananea* (1978), which looks back at a 1906 mining revolt that was seminal to the post-revolutionary nationalization of Mexican mines, and Hector Galán's documentary *Los Mineros* (1991). Keller argues that Galán's work is distinctively Chicano in that it depicts Chicano characters while also being financially and artistically controlled by Chicano filmmakers.

Manfred Engelbert, finally, concentrates on the work of the German-born, Chilean director, cameraman, and editor Pedro Chaskel. While Chaskel's films tend to be classified as examples of a seemingly aesthetically unambitious *cine militante*, Engelbert argues through his analysis of *Aquí vivieron* (1964), *Testimonio—hospital psiquiátrico de Iquique* (1968/69), and *Venceremos* (1970) that these works successfully implement a distinct documentary aesthetic, while they also uncover and attack an unjust social order—thus undermining the hegemonic narration of nation.

6. Perspectives on the Practice of Documentary Filmmaking

In our efforts to combine film studies and scholarly practice with filmmaking and creative practice, we had invited several directors of documentary films to present their views on the genre and on their own work. They did so at the conference "ImagiNations: Documentaries and the Narration of Nation in the Americas / ImagiNaciones: El cine documental y la narración de la nación en las Américas," which was held at the Center for Interdisciplinary Research in Bielefeld, Germany. Many of the contributions to this volume originated there. Four documentary filmmakers—from Ecuador, Argentina, Mexico, and the United States—also submitted their ideas in written form for this volume.

Juan Martín Cueva, who lived in Europe for much of the past two decades, presents his documentary *El lugar donde se juntan los polos* (2002) as a narration of the Ecuadorean nation from the decentered perspective of diaspora. According to Cueva, the perceived lack of national belonging and the heterogeneity of Ecuador are responsible for many current Ecuadorean documentaries engaging in a quest for national identity. In this context, Cueva illustrates how his own film highlights indigenous movements and their potential for a new sense of national belonging.

Filmmaker Ernesto Ardito from Argentina situates his documentary *Raymundo* (2002), which he directed in collaboration with Virna Molina, in the narration of the Argentinean nation. The title of this biopic refers to Raymundo Gleyzer, an Argentinean filmmaker who is among the 30,000 people who were abducted and killed during the country's last military dictatorship (1976-83). In his essay Ardito points out that as a work of memorial culture *Raymundo* commemorates Raymundo Gleyzer, while also demonstrating how the militancy of Argentinean cinema of the 1960s and '70s continues in the context of the current social mobilization in Argentina.

Political motivation and the questioning of hegemonic narrations of the nation also characterize the work of Mexican filmmaker Carlos Mendoza, founder of the production company for documentaries, *Canal Seis de Julio*. Contrasting Editorial Clio, a commercial production company and part of Televisa's media empire, with the independent production collective Canal Seis de Julio, Mendoza discusses the opportunities but also the limitations of independent filmmaking, production, and distribution. The price to be paid for artistic freedom in terms of the contents and format of their documentaries and for the critical stance they take toward official narrations of the nation is the uncertainty that comes with precarious channels of distribution and unreliable financing.

The critique of and play with master narratives, finally, is also distinctive for Jesse Lerner's work. Lerner calls up all kinds of documentary traditions and modes, and he self-reflexively undermines any claims to authenticity and 'truth.' In his essay Lerner starts from archaeological methods used at Chichén Itzá to ask: what place, if any, do the Maya have in the modern world, what potential do the living Maya have for entering modernity, and how has Mayan culture been appropriated and misunderstood worldwide? Lerner discusses the avant-gardist, experimental approach he used in his fake documentary *Ruins* (1999), which revolves around the excavation of fragments of Mayan culture; he argues that "the Maya past has proven to be a boundless source of inspiration, ideas and iconography for artists, architects, filmmakers, photographers and other producers of visual culture in Mexico, the United States, Europe and beyond." In speaking of "Maya modernism," Lerner thus questions narratives of Mexican and New World modernity (that privilege metropolitan cultures) and envisages, instead, criss-crossing to-and-fro exchanges throughout the Americas.

The twenty-four essays collected in this volume demonstrate the potential and impact of documentary film in the narration of nation. They take documentary film studies into an area that has been neglected so far, as they explore how various documentary modes and traditions have been used over the past century as discourses on national identity and as vehicles for questioning and revising hegemonic narratives. At the same time, they expand scholarship on narratives of the nation by examining a genre that has not yet received the scholarly attention it deserves in studies of national identity. Finally, this volume—as well as the book series which it initiates—also makes a plea for the discipline of Inter-American Studies, as it suggests interconnections, commonalities, and what Gloria Anzaldúa has called mutual "cross-fertilizations" in the Western Hemisphere, while also promoting the orientation of our academic disciplines past national(ist) confines. In focusing on politics in documentary film (section I), documentaries on and from the margins of the nation (section II), postmodern approaches to narrating the nation (section III), the role of documentaries in cultural memory (section IV), the rediscovery of films and thereby the revision of film history (section V), as well as on the presentation by individual filmmakers of their own documentary approaches and practices (section VI), this volume explores some of the most prominent areas in which documentary film contributes to the narration of nation and it suggests various fields for future research. We made a conscious decision to include essays in both English and Spanish—with essays in Spanish preceded by an abstract in English and vice versa—in order to foster inter-American dialogue and to relativize the dominance of English in Inter-American Studies.

Works Cited

Anderson, Benedict. *Imagined Communities: Reflections on the Origin and Spread of Nationalism.* London: Verso, 1983.

Aufderheide, Pat. "Public Intimacy: The Development of First-Person Documentary." *Afterimage* 25 (1997): 16-18.

Barnouw, Erik. *Documentary: A History of the Non-fiction Film.* New York: Oxford UP, 1993.

Barsam, Richard M. *Nonfiction Film: A Critical History.* Bloomington: Indiana UP, 1992.

Baudrillard, Jean. *Simulacra and Simulation.* Ann Arbor: U of Michigan P, 1994.

Bauer, Ralph. "Hemispheric Studies." *Publications of the Modern Language Association of America (PMLA)* 124.1 (2009): 234-50.

Beattie, Keith. *Documentary Screens: Non-Fiction Film and Television.* Houndmills: Palgrave, 2004.

Beceyro, Raúl. "El documental: La representación de lo político en el documental argentino." *Imágenes de lo real. La representación de lo político en el documental argentino.* Ed. Josefina Sartora and Silvina Rival. Buenos Aires: Libraria, 2007. 85-90.

Benson, Thomas W., and Brian J. Snee, eds. *The Rhetoric of the New Political Documentary.* Carbondale: Southern Illinois UP, 2008.

Berger, Stefan, Linas Eriksonas, and Andrew Mycock, eds. *Narrating the Nation: Representations in History, Media, and the Arts.* New York: Berghahn Books, 2008.

Bhabha, Homi K. *The Location of Culture.* London: Routledge, 1994.

———, ed. *Nation and Narration.* London: Routledge, 1990.

Bruzzi, Stella. *New Documentary: A Critical Introduction.* London: Routledge, 2005.

Burton-Carvajal, Julianne, ed. *The Social Documentary in Latin America.* Pittsburgh: U of Pittsburgh P, 1990.

Chanan, Michael. "Going South: On Documentary as a Form of Cognitive Geography." *Cinema Journal* 50.1 (Fall 2010): 147-54.

———. *The Politics of Documentary.* London: BFI Publishing, 2008.

Chatterjee, Partha. *The Nation and Its Fragments: Colonial and Postcolonial Histories.* Princeton: Princeton UP, 1993.

Comolli, Jean-Louis. "Le détour par le direct." *Cahiers du cinéma* 209 (1969): 48-53.

Curthoys, Ann, and Marilyn Lake, eds. *Connected Worlds: History in Transnational Perspective.* Canberra: ANU E Press, 2005.

Deacon, Desley. "'Films as Foreign Offices': Transnationalism at Paramount in the Twenties and Early Thirties." *Connected Worlds: History in Transnational Perspective.* Ed. Ann Curthoys and Marilyn Lake. Canberra: ANU E Press, 2005. 139-56.

Druick, Zoë. *Projecting Canada: Government Policy and Documentary Film at the National Film Board.* Montreal: McGill-Queen's UP, 2007.

Fitz, Earl E. "Inter-American Studies as an Emerging Field: The Future of a Discipline." *Review of International American Studies (RIAS)* 3.1-2 (Winter/Spring 2008): 32-44.

García Espinosa, Julio. "For an Imperfect Cinema." *New Latin American Cinema. Vol. 1 Theory, Practices, and Transcontinental Articulations.* Ed. Michael T. Martin. Detroit: Wayne State UP, 1997. 71-82.

Haddu, Miriam and Joanna Page, eds. *Visual Synergies in Fiction and Documentary Film from Latin America.* New York: Palgrave Macmillan, 2009.

Hobsbawm, Eric J. *Nations and Nationalism Since 1780: Programme, Myth, Reality.* Cambridge: Cambridge UP, 1990.

————, and Terence O. Ranger, eds. *Invented Traditions.* Cambridge: Cambridge UP, 1992.

Hohenberger, Eva. "Dokumentarfilmtheorie: Ein historischer Überblick über Ansätze und Probleme." *Bilder des Wirklichen: Texte zur Theorie des Dokumentarfilms.* Ed. Hohenberger. Berlin: Vorwerk, 1998. 8-34.

Jameson, Fredric. *The Political Unconscious: Narrative as a Socially Symbolic Act.* New ed. London: Routledge, 2002.

————. *Postmodernism; or, The Cultural Logic of Late Capitalism.* Durham: Duke UP, 1991.

Kiener, Wilma. *Die Kunst des Erzählens: Narrativität in dokumentarischen und ethnographischen Filmen.* Konstanz: UVK, 1999.

Lane, Jim. *The Autobiographical Documentary in America.* Madison: U of Wisconsin P, 2002.

Levander, Caroline F., and Robert S. Levine, eds. *Hemispheric American Studies.* New Brunswick, NJ: Rutgers UP, 2007.

MacDonald, Kevin, and Mark Cousins, eds. *Imagining Reality: The Faber Book of Documentary.* London: Faber and Faber, 1998.

Martin, Michael T., ed. *New Latin American Cinema.* Detroit: Wayne State UP, 2006.

Mato, Daniel. "On the Making of Transnational Identities in the Age of Globalization: The US Latina/o-'Latin' American Case." *Cultural Studies* 12.4 (1998): 598-620.

Menand, Louis. "Nanook and Me: *Fahrenheit 9/11* and the Documentary Tradition." *The New Yorker* 9 August 2004. http://www.newyorker.com/archive/2004/08/09/040809crat_atlarge.

Nichols, Bill. *Blurred Boundaries: Questions of Meaning in Contemporary Culture.* Bloomington: Indiana UP, 1994.

————. *Representing Reality. Issues and Concepts in Documentary.* Bloomington: Indiana UP, 1991.

Noriega, Chon A. *Visible Nations: Latin American Cinema and Video.* Minneapolis: U of Minnesota P, 2000.

Ortega, María Luisa. *Espejos rotos: Aproximaciones al documental norteamericano contemporáneo.* Madrid: Ocho y Medio; Ayuntamiento de Madrid; Área de Gobierno de las Artes, 2007.

Raab, Josef, and Martin Butler, eds. *Hybrid Americas: Contacts, Contrasts, and Confluences in New World Literatures and Cultures*. Münster: LIT Verlag and Tempe: Bilingual P, 2008.

Renov, Michael. "Towards a Poetics of Documentary." *Theorizing Documentary*. Ed. Renov. New York: Routledge, 1993. 12-36.

Rocha, Glauber. "The Aesthetics of Hunger." Trans. Burnes Hollyman and Randal Johnson. https://www.amherst.edu/media/view/38122/original/ROCHA_Aesth_Hunger.pdf.

Ruffinelli, Jorge. "Conversaciones con Patricio Guzmán: No hay lugar para el arte." http://www.patricioguzman.com/index.php?page=entrevista&aid=8.

Thies, Sebastian. "ImagiNaciones perdidas: La narración de la nación en el cine de la diáspora chilena." *Más allá de la nación: medios, espacios comunicativos y nuevas comunidades imaginadas*. Ed. Sabine Hoffmann. Berlin: Tranvía, 2008. 195-216.

Thies, Sebastian, and Josef Raab, eds. *E Pluribus Unum?: National and Transnational Identities in the Americas/Identidades nacionales y transnacionales en las Américas*. Münster: LIT Verlag and Tempe: Bilingual P, 2009.

Saldívar, José David. *Border Matters: Remapping American Cultural Studies*. Berkeley: U of California P, 1997.

Spivak, Gayatri Chakravorty. "Can the Subaltern Speak?" *Marxism and the Interpretation of Culture*. Ed. Cary Nelson and Lawrence Grossberg. Urbana: U of Illinois P, 1988. 271-313.

Steinmetz, Rüdiger, and Tilo Prase. *Dokumentarfilm zwischen Beweis und Pamphlet: Heynowski & Scheumann und Gruppe Katins*. Leipzig: Leipziger Universitätsverlag, 2002.

Vertov, Dziga. *Schriften zum Film*. Ed. Wolfgang Beilenhoff. München: Hanser, 1973.

White, Hayden. *Tropics of Discourse: Essays in Cultural Criticism*. Baltimore: The Johns Hopkins UP, 1986.

Filmography

102 Minutes That Changed America. Dir. Nicole Rittenmeyer and Seth Skundrick. U.S.A., 2008.

9/11. Dir. James Hanlon, Rob Klug, Gédéon Naudet, and Jules Naudet. U.S.A., 2002.

Aileen Wuornos: The Selling of a Serial Killer. Dir. Nick Broomfield. United Kingdom, 1993.

La batalla de Chile. Dir. Patricio Guzmán. Chile, 1978.

Boca de Lixo. Dir. Eduardo Coutinho. Brazil, 1993.

Bullit. Dir. Peter Yates. U.S.A., 1968.

Cabra marcado para morrer. Dir. Eduardo Coutinho. Brazil, 1985.

Celsius 41.11: The Temperature at Which the Brain... Begins to Die. Dir. Kevin Knoblock. U.S.A., 2004.

Chile, la memoria obstinada. Dir. Patricio Guzmán. Canada, France, 1997.

The Civil War. Dir. Ken Burns. U.S.A., 1990.

Congo. Dir. Arthur Omar. Brazil, 1972.

El Salvador: el pueblo vencera. Dir. Diego de la Texera. El Salvador, 1982.

Fahrenheit 9/11. Dir. Michael Moore. U.S.A., 2004.

Fahrenhype 9/11. Dir. Alan Peterson. U.S.A., 2004.

George W. Bush: Faith in the White House. Dir. David W. Balsiger. U.S.A., 2004.

Going Upriver: The Long War of John Kerry. Dir. George Butler. U.S.A., 2004.

Harlan County, USA. Dir. Barbara Kopple, 1976.

La Hora de los hornos. Dir. Octavio Getino and Fernando E. Solanas. Argentina, 1968.

Ilha das flores. Dir. Jorge Furtado. Brazil, 1990.

An Inconvenient Truth. Dir. Davis Guggenheim. U.S.A., 2006.

Kanehsatake: 270 Years of Resistance. Dir. Alanis Obomsawin. Canada, 1993.

LBJ. Dir. Santiago Álvarez. Cuba, 1968.

Los Angeles Plays Itself. Dir. Thom Andersen. U.S.A., 2003.

Michael Moore Hates America. Dir. Michael Wilson, U.S.A., 2004.

Moana. Dir. Robert Flaherty. U.S.A., 1926.

Moscou. Dir. Eduardo Coutinho. Brazil, 2009.

My McQueen. Dir. Lourdes Portillo. U.S.A., 2004.

Paradise Lost: The Child Murders at Robin Hood Hills. Dir. Joe Berlinger and Bruce Sinofsky. U.S.A., 1996.

A Place Called Chiapas. Dir. Nettie Wild. Canada, 1998.

Sherman's March. Dir. Ross McElwee. U.S.A., 1986.

Silverlake Life: The View from Here. Dir. Peter Friedman and Tom Joslin. U.S.A., 1993.

South of the Border. Dir. Oliver Stone. U.S.A., 2009.

Stolen Honor: Wounds That Never Heal. Dir. Carlton Sherwood. U.S.A., 2004.

La T.V. y yo. Dir. Andrés di Tella. Argentina, 2002.

Yanqui, No! Dir. Drew Associates. U.S.A., 1960.

Waiting for Fidel. Dir. Michael Rubbo. Canada, 1974.

Walkout. Dir. Edward James Olmos. U.S.A., 2006.

Why We Fight. Dir. Eugene Jarecki. U.S.A., France, United Kingdom, Canada, Denmark, 2005.

I.

NEW DYNAMICS IN THE POLITICAL
DOCUMENTARY FILM

American History Revisited and Recomposed: Oliver Stone's Docu-fictions

WANJA VON DER GOLTZ

Resumen

La mayoría de las películas de Oliver Stone, por lo general, no se consideran películas documentales ya que muestran características evidentes del género fílmico de ficción conocido como *blockbuster*, incluyendo la presencia de estrellas de cine y el uso de códigos narrativos genéricos. Sin embargo, las así llamadas docu-ficciones de Stone –entre ellas *Born on the 4th of July*, *JFK*, y *Nixon*– narran la identidad nacional de la misma manera como lo hacen muchos documentales: investigan tópicos históricos controvertidos, incluyen material de archivo o representaciones ficticias de imágenes históricas, se basan en una investigación exhaustiva e intentan contribuir con respuestas a la compleja discusión de las relaciones históricas de causa y efecto. Stone desarrolla un estilo periodístico que apoya la imagen de una representación cinematográfica verídica de los hechos históricos. Centra su enfoque en los acontecimientos o épocas claves de la política de los EE.UU. que le permiten analizar los conflictos que se producen entre la población estadounidense y el gobierno que ha elegido. En el contexto del asesinato del presidente Kennedy, la Guerra Fría, la Crisis de los Misiles en Cuba y la Guerra de Vietnam, Stone presenta un gobierno que malinforma y pone en peligro a sus propios ciudadanos, guiado por las ansias de poder y dinero. El documental *Comandante* (2003) sigue esa misma línea: discute la política exterior e interior de los EE.UU., con el trasfondo de la oposición de Cuba y de Fidel Castro a la postura política de los EE.UU. La película, por un lado, parece depender completamente de las estrategias periodísticas de representación; por el otro, no obstante, da la impresión de no estar basada en una investigación minuciosa y de ser evidentemente más tendenciosa que las docu-ficciones de Stone. Por lo tanto, la comparación de las docu-ficciones con películas documentales acentúa la necesidad de enfrentarse críticamente con los métodos narrativos del documental y su contextualización en cuanto a su consideración como portadores de una 'verdad' histórica.

1. Introduction

Throughout his career as a filmmaker, Oliver Stone's involvement with documentary film has been of an ambiguous nature. For about the last 25 years, journalists, scholars, and politicians have continuously been trying to make it known to the public that Oliver Stone's films are everything *but* documentary. His movies have been labeled docu-dramas, docu-fictions, or historical dramas, while names for their director have been swinging back and forth from cinematic historian to fraud. It is only with his more recent films *Comandante* (2003), *Persona non grata* (2003), *Looking for Fidel* (2004), and *South of the Border* (2009) that he has stepped into the realm of 'genuine' documentary filmmaking—provided that a majority of viewers could agree on a definition of the documentary genre. However, many of the issues he tackles in *Comandante*, a film about his three-day interview with then Cuban President Fidel Castro, were already central to his earlier docu-fictions *Born on the 4th of July* (1989), *JFK* (1991), and *Nixon* (1995): the Cold War, the Vietnam War, Cuba's role in global and American politics, and the vague idea that there is something untrue in the way the American political and economic establishment presents itself to its own people and to the rest of the world. Aiming at an understanding of how documentaries help to define a nation's historical narrative, one has to consider that Oliver Stone's docu-fictional movies have—on the one hand—been praised for their role in shaping America's awareness of political processes and institutions, but that they have also been the object of severe criticism in the face of a provocative blending of fact and fiction. If compared to the less obviously fictional materials presented in *Comandante*, however, Stone's docu-fictions might reveal unexpected documentary insights for the larger topics he is concerned with.

It is the aim of this essay to analyze how Stone employs methods of documentary filmmaking in order to tell constructed versions of American history; as a precondition, it is necessary to decide whether or not (some of) Stone's movies are similar enough to what is usually considered the documentary genre to serve as contributions of interest to the present volume. The problem that "[d]ocumentaries adopt no fixed inventory of techniques, address no one set of issues, display no single set of shared characteristics" (Nichols 21) makes it particularly difficult to draw fixed lines between documentary and fiction film. As Michael Renov aptly points out, the "recourse to history demonstrates that the documentary has availed itself of nearly every constructive device known to fiction (of course, the reverse is equally true) and has employed virtually every register of cinematic syntax in the process" (6). Yet, a clear-cut definition might not even be necessary for the present analysis: after all, the main point of interest is not the differences between Stone's films and what is commonly called 'a documentary,' but their similarities: which filmic and narrative tools does Stone borrow from the documentary genre, where does he stay within the conventions of fiction, and to which ends does he combine those two 'languages?'

Two short quotations may serve as a promising point of entry to an assessment of Stone's filmic methods in the light of theoretical discussions of what (potentially) defines documentary film. The first statement is from documentary filmmaker Jill Godmilow, who says that

> [i]f a documentary filmmaker takes up historical materials, it shouldn't be to produce and/or claim to have produced a comprehensive description of the movement of events, but rather to engage the audience ... in a discussion about ideological constructions buried in the representation of history (Godmilow/Shapiro 83).

Talking about his film *JFK*, Oliver Stone expresses a similar attitude: "In hindsight, the film is about more than the murder of a president. It asks the audience to think for itself and begin the process of deconstructing the meaning of its own history" (qtd. in Toplin 15). Both quotations express an approach to historical filmmaking that goes beyond the aspect of accuracy and the so-called 'claim to truth' that the public mind frequently attributes to non-fiction genres. Instead, the statements attest to a quest for a different type of 'truth' that seems to be at the center of both documentary and fiction: "The itinerary of a truth's passage (with 'truth' understood as propositional and provisional) for the documentary is ... qualitatively akin to that of fiction" (Renov 7). This 'truth' does not necessarily evolve from a veridical reconstruction of reality—the notions of 'reality' and 'veridical reconstruction' alone are problematic enough to taint any 'truth' that is supposed to result from their combination—but from the individual approach a (documentary) filmmaker, novelist, scientist, poet chooses to address a given issue. Bill Nichols affirms that "documentary is not a reproduction of reality, it is a *representation* of the world we already occupy. It stands for a particular view of the world" (20; his italics); accordingly, documentary filmmaking becomes a vehicle of subjective expression, of discussion, and of continuous scrutiny. Just like the creators of fictitious texts, creators of documentaries use their chosen mode of expression to tackle topics from a personal point of view; their work takes the shape of a "*creative treatment* of actuality, not a faithful transcription of it" (Nichols 38; his italics).

Still, in their statements about the aims of their filmmaking, both Godmilow and Stone also implicitly stress that their films have a strong connection to actual events of the real world: they "address *the* world in which we live rather than *a* world imagined by the filmmaker" (Nichols XI; his italics). Thus, in addition to being different from the myriads of fiction films that largely deal with imagined worlds, Stone's docu-fictions also stand in opposition to other fiction films that imitate the appearance of a documentary in order to generate interest in a purely imagined object, such as the 'Blair Witch' of *The Blair Witch Project* (1999).[1] Stone does *not* parody the stylistic elements of documentary film in order to lend authenticity to purely fictive contents

---

[1] Bill Nichols reserves the labels "mockumentaries" or "pseudo-documentaries" for this type of film (23), while Alexandra Juhasz and Jesse Lerner use the expression "fake documentaries" (1) in their collection of essays analyzing a wide range of fabricated documentary features. They also acknowledge the legitimacy of the prefixes "mock" and "pseudo" (7).

and/or to analyze the workings of the documentary mode through the lens of the fiction film.[2] Instead, his aims once again seem to resemble those of documentary filmmakers: at the core of his docu-fictions, there is an aspect that originates in the real world and becomes subject to documentary and traditional fictitious approaches to uncovering 'truths.' Stone seems to attest to Bill Nichols' claim that "[f]ilmmakers are often drawn to documentary modes of representation when they want to engage us in questions or issues that pertain directly to the historical world we all share" (xiv)— even if the result comes to be called 'docu-fiction' instead of 'documentary.'

However, if we aim to understand why and where Stone employs those "documentary modes of representation" and why and where he mixes or replaces them with other stylistic devices, it is necessary to develop at least a basic catalogue of features that seem to be essential for documentary film's attempt to combine an explicit relation to the historical world with the individually shaped search for 'truth.' According to Bill Nichols, the most distinctive features of documentary film include

> the use of a Voice-of-God commentary, interviews, location sound recording, cutaways from a given scene to provide images that illustrate or complicate a point made within the scene, and a reliance on social actors, or people in their everyday roles and activities (26).

It cannot surprise that several auditory aspects hold such a prominent position on his list: images in documentary film usually speak less for themselves than the visual components of fiction films (cf. Nichols 30). More than in action-driven or artistically filmed movies, voices—be it a voice-over or an interview that also shows visual images of the speaker—are needed to provide additional information about the shots and scenes that are supposed to 'document' aspects of the topic in question. These shots and scenes are often of a rather fragmented nature and reveal their informative potential only in combination with other narrative structures (such as auditory signals). It is not the editing of visual materials that achieves continuity, but a larger logic or argument that ties together a "wider array of disparate shots and scenes" (Nichols 28), which are linked by their interdependent positions in a historical discourse.

As a consequence, it becomes possible to combine images that seem to have few direct connections—like archival film material and contemporary interviews—to support a superordinate argument and "put a new perspective on past events or events leading up to current issues" (Nichols 33). What these shots and scenes have in common, however, is that they

> have their origin in the historical world we share. On the whole, they were not conceived and produced exclusively for the film. This assumption relies on the capacity of the photographic image, and of sound recording, to replicate what we take to be distinctive qualities of what they have recorded (Nichols 35).

---

[2] The fake music documentary *This Is Spinal Tap* (1984) is probably the most frequently cited example of a fake documentary that succeeds in letting an imagined object appear to be 'of the real world' and that simultaneously foregrounds the narrative and formal characteristics of contemporary documentary features.

One of the basic presumptions about documentary film is that much of its content is supposed to represent actual events authentically in sound and image. In contrast to fiction film, it will indicate those elements that have been fabricated for the film and separate them from the 'historical records.' Social actors instead of actors, re-enacted scenes instead of imagined scenes, found footage instead of created footage all mark a documentary kind of filmmaking and commonly help to distinguish documentaries from fiction films.

In addition, documentary film usually also displays several characteristics that it shares with fiction film, and which contribute largely to the aforementioned difficulty of establishing clear-cut borders between the two genres: "documentary shares the status of all discursive forms with regard to its tropic or figurative character and ... it employs many of the methods and devices of its fictional counterpart" (Renov 3). Documentaries tend to "narrativize the real" (Renov 6) as they attempt to present information that pertains to the historical world in a way that corresponds with their viewers' receptive habits and preferences. In contrast to, for example, a history book, a documentary film about historical events will try to arrange its contents in structures that not only support the line of argumentation, but also appeal to the audience's desire for coherence and emotional dynamic. Therefore, most documentary narratives work along dramatic arcs well-known from fiction and array their plots along, e.g., an investigation, a crisis structure (cf. Renov 2), or a problem solving situation (cf. Nichols 34). Similarly, the characters that are at the center of these plotlines also find themselves in the "ideal or imagined categories" (Renov 2) of hero, genius, villain, victim, etc. Although they are not actors in an imagined story, but social actors in a story that is part of their real lives, they frequently fulfill preselected narrative functions or roles in a carefully balanced dramatic constellation. In order to transform found footage and social actors into working parts of a composed narrative, documentary film employs many of the stylistic commonplaces used in fiction film: poetic language and emotionally intoned narration or music can increase the audience's involvement with distant issues; certain camera angles and techniques can support atmospheres and arguments; close-ups can foster identification with the protagonists; and editing may heavily influence the impact of sequences and determine the way single shots are perceived in the context of the surrounding argument (cf. Renov 2-3). As far as their audiovisual appearance is concerned, documentary films thus are not always easy to separate from their fictive relatives; both types share a certain pool of characteristics that originate in the filmic tradition, in general: "it is not that the documentary *con*sists of the structures of filmic fiction (and is, thus, parasitic of its cinematic 'other') as it is that 'fictive' elements *in*sist in documentary as in all film forms" (Renov 10; his italics).

As a consequence, boundaries between documentary and fiction film are predestined to blur and allegedly immovable definitions are bound to crumble. Forms and function of one genre can be expected to penetrate the other, and vice versa: there is no absolute separation between fiction and documentary. Some documentaries make strong use of practices or conventions ... that we often associate with fiction. Some fiction makes strong use of practices or conventions ... that we often associate with non-fiction or documentary (Nichols XI; cf. also Renov 8).

Just as documentary film relies on stylistic devices tested and refined in fiction film, some fiction films—and here Oliver Stone's movies immediately come to mind—adopt techniques that most viewers associate with non-fiction genres, such as location shooting, hand-held cameras, and found footage. With characteristics shifting between fiction and documentary films, with fake documentaries that imitate non-fiction genres to convey purely fictional messages, and with docu-fictions that combine elements of all types to develop their own approach to historical events and aspects of 'the real world,' there actually remains only one institution which could possibly decide whether a film is a documentary or not: the audience. As Bill Nichols argues, the "sense that a film is a documentary lies in the mind of the beholder as much as it lies in the film's context or structure" (35; cf. also Renov 9, and Juhasz/Lerner 8). The characteristics of any given film combined with the expectations any given viewer develops towards its relation to the historical world will have to serve as the indicators for different labels, from documentary, to fake documentary or docu-fiction, to fiction. Moreover, while some elements of a film may more obviously correspond to claims of authenticity, their attributes do not have to extend to the film as a whole:

> Among the assumptions we bring to documentary ... is that individual shots and sounds, perhaps even scenes and sequences will bear a highly indexical relationship to the events they represent but that the film as a whole will stand back from being a pure document or transcription of these events to make a comment on them or to offer a perspective on them (Nichols 38; cf. Sturken 66).

In sum, the audience will have to decide for themselves whether or not the authentic elements or the general appearance of a film suffice to label it 'documentary;' they will have to negotiate an attitude towards the film that acknowledges its content as well as its form and recognizes the tradition it is a part of or runs against. In case of such complex mixed forms as Oliver Stone's docu-fictions, labels will vary in relation to the individual viewers' experience with documentary film, their involvement with the historical events that are being re-investigated, their attitude towards Stone as a filmmaker and as a person, their expectation towards U.S. American politics and administration, and many other factors. Nevertheless, as the preceding brief introduction to the hybrid characteristics of documentary film should have justified, his films are worth including in an analysis of the narration of nation in documentary film, since they at least communicate a certain awareness of the impact documentary film can have on historical discussions. Furthermore, they promise interesting contributions to the discussion of documentary and fictional narrative traditions with regard to the representation of the historical world. Finally, they might even serve as evidence to Alexandra Juhasz's claim that mixed forms are "received as more than a fiction film plus a documentary; the two systems refer to, critique, and alter each other's reception" (9).

The following section provides a short summary of Oliver Stone's stylistic principles with a focus on those movies that display more obvious similarities to prototypical documentary films—as opposed to his rather 'classic' fiction films, such as *U Turn* (1997) and *Alexander* (2004). A closer look at the representation of the American political and cultural system in the movies *Born on the 4th of July*, *JFK*, and *Nixon* will then reveal some of the most prominent arguments of Stone's social criticism. The predominant tone of those docu-fictions will prepare the ground for a critical analysis of *Comandante* as a film that more explicitly leans towards the documentary genre and less towards conventions usually attributed to fiction, but also as a film that is influenced by Stone's involvement with docu-fictions and conspiracy theories. By juxtaposing *Comandante* to Stone's docu-fictional movies, the concluding observations are intended to develop an understanding of how his films and his exploitation of documentary ingredients contribute to the public awareness and discussion of recent American history.

2. Oliver Stone's Cinematic Style

There are several characteristics that distinguish Oliver Stone's films from the works of most other Hollywood directors. They are dogmatic, iconoclastic, personal, experimental, strongly political, and usually highly controversial. His films do not follow common rules of Hollywood cinema, as they tend to carry strong interpretations and are designed to make the audience feel uncomfortable. Stone says that he has "turned down many far more lucrative 'for-hire' offers" ("Image" 46) to concentrate on movies dealing with his viewpoint on issues of American cultural and political history. Many of his projects reveal deep personal involvement; for example, his experience as a soldier in Vietnam not only motivated the autobiographical war movie *Platoon* (1986), but also triggered Stone's desire to probe further into the social and cultural trauma the U.S. American society suffered from as a result of the Vietnam dilemma. Similarly, his political upbringing and personal attitude towards the political and economic establishment largely determine the way his films deal with historical events: "Stone has taken the images of history and dramatically reenacted, reorchestrated, and retold them through a prism of former 1960s radicalism and late-twentieth-century paranoia" (Sturken 67). In contrast to this personal involvement, however, Stone has—like few other writers or directors—made every endeavor to support his subjective views with a foundation of almost academic research. He has written books and essays[3] to explain the ideas and working processes that created *JFK* and *Nixon*, he

---

[3] Cf., for example, his essays in Robert B. Toplin's collection—such as "Stone on Stone's Image (as presented by Some Historians)," "On Seven Films," and "On *Nixon* and *JFK*"—and his books on *JFK* (1992) and *Nixon* (1995).

has defended his movies at conferences in front of renowned historians, and—what is most crucial to his work as a filmmaker—he has imitated documentary tactics by interweaving his fictional dramas with large amounts of historical archive material or reenactments of historical imagery.

Stone uses historical footage to construct a version of the past that is situated in the present. The combination of realism and imagination makes the audience feel part of repeated historical events that are disguised as first-hand experience. Stone's docudramas involve the viewers in a process of rediscovering, re-interpreting, and maybe even rewriting the records of the past. He fosters a receptive attitude that does not insist on a clear-cut separation of fact and fiction but accepts the blended representation of historical and fictional contents as a valid approach to history:

> Stone reenacts famous documentary photographs, subsuming them into his memory text. In doing so, he enhances the claim of the historical docudrama to represent authentic historical images precisely because the reenactment of historical images has a tendency to replace and subsume those original images (Sturken 74).

That the audience so readily adjusts to this tempering with supposedly fixed categories is largely due to Stone's innovative work with the camera. He explores the possibilities of modern artistic techniques, including various camera angles, quick cutting, morphing, cartoons, flashbacks, black-and-white footage, disturbing sound sequences, and "headache-inducing montage" (Courtwright 190). Amos Vogel expects the viewer to sink into "a kind of psychological numbness" (579), caused by the rapid sequences of visual images and the accompanying soundtrack of hectic drums, gunshots, and overlapping dialogues. In this flow of information, it becomes increasingly difficult to differentiate between found footage, reenactments, and purely fictional segments. In general, Stone's complex, aggressive editing confronts the viewer with a confusing sensory impression that differs considerably from the antiseptic, unemotional receptive experience that usually comes with other forms of history telling in books, essays, and presentations.

While his personal style may distinguish his docu-fictions (and his fictions) from much other popular Hollywood cinema, several of the techniques that dominate his films resemble the repertoire of (other) documentary filmmakers—like Errol Morris or Michael Moore—employing a combination of archive material with new recordings, re-enacted images, narration, etc. As a dramatist, Stone strives for narrative cohesion and condenses the complex facts and assumptions of history into manageable storylines. He makes use of the docudrama genre to combine the characteristics of various other cinematic genres in order to involve the audience as deeply as possible in his version of historical events:

> The docudrama succeeds as a form of popular culture specifically through its exploitation of the dual role of cinema as a representation of the real and a source of fantasy and identification. At the same time, it is a form of cultural reenactment and as such shares in larger cultural processes of memory and healing (Sturken 74).

Social or cultural developments have to be concentrated on a few representative figures. Dialogues, characters, and scenes have to be invented, sometimes in order to represent larger concepts. Historical cause-and-effect relations need to be simplified to fit the narrative structure of a movie plot. Robert A. Rosenstone calls such a condensed historical representation "a generic historical moment, a moment that claims its truth by standing in for many such moments" (26), which means that in a film, the various little facts that are spread out over the field of history are pulled together in a single, cumulative image. Stone's appropriation of documentary styles is part of his strategy to reduce the impact of these changes of facts by making the fictional world he creates as real as possible: he models sceneries and costumes on actual material, he hires military staff to drill the actors for combat scenes, he interviews hundreds of witnesses, and asks experts for advice even on minor details. In his films, he mixes these documentary approaches with elements taken from fictional genres, such as morality tale, initiation story, melodrama, social drama, crime fiction, and many others. Thus, in general, Stone's films combine the contradictions of telling history and imagining history, of what happened and what could have happened.[4] They fulfill the audience's desire to return to the moments of the past, to peep into conference rooms, and to read the minds of people who played a role in a historical development.

3.   The America of *Born on the 4th of July*, *JFK*, and *Nixon*

The three docu-fictions *Born on the 4th of July*, *JFK*, and *Nixon* examine the dark side of American life. They represent history in a form that inquires into the possible and actual deformities of the past. They show failure of leadership, false information policies, moral decline, greed, corruption, weak characters, social pressure, and a ruthless waste of human lives. In doing so, they challenge other versions of public U.S. American history by partly using their very methods—simulation, reenactment, inclusion of found footage, narrativization—to explore alternative angles of historical events.

Born on the 4th of July is an outstanding example of a new tradition of war movies, which emerged after the disaster in Vietnam and shifted the focus from heroism in the face of a foreign enemy towards social and spiritual survival in the battle with an inner enemy—within the individual soldier, within one's own army, in the American government, or even in America's misguided culture in general. Based on the true story of Ron Kovic, a paralyzed Vietnam veteran who turns into a peace activist, the film links an individual fate to "America's discovery of truth through the Vietnam experience" (Davis 136). It opens with the picture book image of an American small town idyll, a community largely built on symbols of love-it-or-leave-it patriotism, political consensus, and individual success in a conformist group. In the

---

[4]   Cf. Marita Sturken's essay, in which she emphasizes the importance of the fantasy of history in contrast to history-telling in Stone's films (65).

course of Kovic's initiation, healthy ambition turns into an ever-growing need to prove oneself in a society that teaches its children "that winning is everything, God hates quitters, communists are banging on our doors, and Uncle Sam needs you" (Roberts/Welky 80). Additionally driven by President Kennedy's appeal to 'do something for your country,' young men try to prove their manhood in a dubious battle. They return as scapegoats for a nation that is not willing to deal with its burden of misguided political and cultural developments.

The main issues of the film openly attack several ideals of American national identity. In Stone's eyes, prior innocence is being destroyed by American arrogance. As U.S. marines slaughter women and children, the director attacks the image of a clean, honest war that had been predominant in fiction and history writing since the victory in World War II. The film shakes America's belief in its "'superior' values and democratic ideals, which have historically helped justify military conflict" (Davis 142) and thus questions the essential social motivation for war and patriotic sacrifice. Even more haunting are those scenes that show the returning soldiers in confrontation with disgusting hospital conditions, hostile war protesters, families who do not know how to handle the remnants of the once so admired sons, and above all, a government that hands out bureaucracy and denial instead of care and sympathy.

Stone cleverly juxtaposes modes of realistic narration with the personal message he wants to convey. As far as realism is concerned, Kovic's status as an eye witness, unsteady TV report-like camera movements, and dialogues that resemble interviews contribute to the feeling of watching a historical representation that comes close to what really might have happened. Like other documentaries, the film creates the impression that the allegedly truthful representational abilities of the camera and the reliability of eye witnesses will increase the degree of 'truthfulness' the film is able to convey. Still, on another level, the film carries an exceedingly subjective message, as it offers Stone and Kovic the opportunity to take cultural revenge on America for having their own patriotic values shattered by a traumatic experience partly forced on them by society. Beyond its objective and subjective qualities, however, *Born on the 4th of July* opened up a chapter of history that had been neglected in public discussion up to that point: the deep fissure in American society resulting from its inability to deal with the consequences of an unwon and unwanted war.

Two years later, the provocative *JFK* approaches history writing from a different perspective: in a controversial and politically explosive way, it attacks an issue that had already been in the center of public discussions and various research projects. Taking up the common disbelief in the explanations for the assassination of president Kennedy, Stone condenses fact, speculation, and fiction into a three-hour summation of his theory of why, how, and by whom Kennedy was murdered (cf. Gunzenhäuser 84). Even more obviously than in *Born on the 4th of July*, the director develops a documentary-style frame for his plot out of archival pieces and a news report-like narrative voice. For example, the film opens with images of Eisenhower warning the population of the rising influence of the military-industrial complex. Combined with excerpts that show Kennedy as a president who is willing to reduce America's involvement in the conflicts of the world, Eisenhower's words are made to appear as a plausible reason for a conspiracy of high-level government staff against the young president. Throughout the movie, Stone mixes more archival footage with reenacted scenes and a largely fictional reproduction of district attorney Jim Garrison's investigation into a possible government conspiracy. He attempts to prove that the American public is being betrayed and kept in ignorance by groups of influential politicians and businessmen. Stone further suggests that the CIA, the military, the mafia, and even vice-president Lyndon B. Johnson might have had the intention of killing Kennedy in order to prolong and escalate the war in Vietnam for financial reasons.

Although the director sacrifices the option of balanced arguments in favor of dramatic impact, although he mixes facts, characters and archival footage,[5] although he gives the audience only a one-dimensional picture of Kennedy's presidency and neglects those pieces of evidence that argue against a conspiracy, *JFK* is the movie that most extensively foregrounds documentary modes of filmmaking. Therefore, it is most likely to replace other historical records in public memory. Stone promoted the film as the version of the story journalists and historians did not dare tell, which caused a public outcry that finally forced the U.S. government to release a multitude of formerly secret documents related to the assassination and the work of the Warren Commission (cf. Vogel 578, and Kurtz 174-75). Thus, in some way *JFK* also undermines the traditional forms of telling history, as it attacks their status as carriers of truth (cf. Sturken 67). By imitating journalistic narrative methods "as something between entertainment and fact" (Stone, qtd. in Goodman 9), Stone manages to provide a picture that is just as truthful or just as false as any other work of historiography, but which—due to its capacity to lend narrative truth to potentially false records—gives the audience the opportunity to feel part of a believable historical experience.

Another four years later, Stone returns to the political atmosphere of the 1950s through the 1970s with his biographical picture *Nixon*. Mainly aiming at a psychological analysis of the controversial president and his social surroundings, the movie only touches upon many of the political issues that were central to the preceding films. Even more than *JFK*, it shifts the focus away from historical accuracy towards insights related to Nixon as a person and as a political leader. Although sometimes sympathetic, it shows Nixon as an ambitious, yet insecure, self-loathing, and strangely paranoid politician torn between the desire for power and an urge to be loved. In examining the individuals and circles around the president the movie leads into a swamp of corruption and political opportunism. Stone presents a multitude of troubling activities at high levels, strange ways of power being wielded beneath the surface of politics. In order to avoid an avalanche of criticism similar to the *JFK* experience, Stone prepared

---

[5] For a more detailed list of alterations in the semi-documentary sequences of *JFK*, cf. Vogel 583. Michael L. Kurtz offers another list of inaccuracies in his essay (169).

the public for his movie and published explanatory texts[6] that were meant to prove the scientific nature of his investigation into Nixon's presidency. The accusations expressed in the film, however, were much too provocative not to cause another uproar among America's politicians and historians: for instance, Stone charges Nixon with prolonging the Vietnam war to secure the support of the right wing for the following election, with playing an important part in several attempts to kill Fidel Castro, and with being indirectly involved in the Kennedy assassination.[7]

At the same time, he wants the viewer to realize that Nixon is not an evil man, but only a marionette used by America's flawed, corrupt, and immoral system. In one of the climactic scenes of the movie, Anthony Hopkins as Nixon sums up the essence of a long career in politics by calling the American political administration a 'beast.' Christopher Wilkinson, Stone's co-writer on the *Nixon* script, defines the term 'beast' as "a metaphor for the darkest organic forces in American cold war politics: the anticommunist crusade, secret intelligence, the defense industry, organized crime, big business, plus the CIA" (qtd. in Toplin 14). Thus, Stone pictures an administration that has finally turned into something non-human, something that works only for power and money and against the people.

4. *Comandante*—Documentary, Docu-fiction, or Fictionalized Documentary?

In contrast to the films discussed in the preceding section, *Comandante* is what most people would call a 'documentary'—and not a 'docudrama' or 'docu-fiction'—without hesitating. It contains the essence of about 30 hours of conversation between Oliver Stone and Fidel Castro, interspersed with archival footage and impressions Stone captured during his stay in Cuba, but no reenactments or explicitly fictional elements. Once again, Stone employs his typical set of visual tools to let off a firework of images, snapshots, and historical bits and pieces that follows Cuba's president on his way from a rebellious student to the leader of one of the last socialist countries in the world. In the context of this essay, the main aim is to examine if and how *Comandante* continues arguments that were already central to Stone's docu-fictions, and in how far the film differs from them with regard to the filmic and narrative elements it employs.

What immediately stands out as one of the film's characteristic features is that—although Stone's unsteady camera movement and quick cuts keep Castro at a certain distance—it is virtually impossible to develop a neutral perspective towards his per-

---

[6] For instance, the appearance of the movie *Nixon* was accompanied by Stone/Hamburg/ Rivele publishing *Nixon: An Oliver Stone Film*, a book that contains the annotated screenplay, interviews, essays, and other documents related to the case.

[7] For a detailed reply to these accusations and a different perspective on the Nixon administration, cf. Stephen E. Ambrose's essay (203-09).

sonal and political history without additional reading. Despite all fragmentation, it is Castro the man instead of Castro the political institution that captures Stone's attention. It is obvious that Stone—while partly losing touch with the bigger issues— tries to show Castro's human side: he seems obsessed with filming his hands and eyes, he tries to make him laugh, he follows him into a cheering crowd. In doing so, he submits to Castro's desire to present himself as a hard-working leader who loves his people and is loved by them in return for the social improvements he has achieved.

While Stone used archive material in his docu-fictions to—for instance—present Kennedy as a saint, make Johnson appear in a dubious light, and analyze Nixon's character, the footage in *Comandante* seems purely demonstrative: Castro talks about the atomic bomb, Stone shows a nuclear explosion; Castro talks about sports, Stone shows an old bicycle; Castro predicts that the capitalist way will lead mankind into extinction, Stone shows clouds hurrying across the sky. While found footage—the *Zapruder* video of the Kennedy assassination, in particular—served as a starting point of a politically explosive investigation in *JFK*, the archival material here contributes to the filmic experience in far less controversial ways: it basically lends the filmed images historical justification. Stone risks joining a trend that Michael Renov detects in many documentary features: "All too frequently … the interest in the visual docu-ment—interview footage intercut with archival material—outpaced the historian's obligation to interrogate rather than simply serve up the visible evidence" (26). In *Comandante*, much of the found footage does not even come close to being eviden-tiary, as it hardly conveys any relevant comments on the dialogues between Castro and Stone. In some scenes, archival material could be meant to add other perspectives to what is happening during the interviews, but these perspectives remain blurred and vague. For example, a close-up of Castro's feet that shows him demonstrating his daily exercise of marching around his office is interlaced with archival shots of someone's feet walking along the furrows of a freshly ploughed field. What is this undefined combination of images supposed to suggest? Is it meant to draw a connection between Castro's youth on his father's sugar plantation and his adult life as a political leader? Does is symbolize his rootedness in Cuba's soil? Is it meant to say that Castro is a simple man at heart, whom history washed into the office of a national leader? Or is it merely decorative padding that matched Stone's rhythmic idea of the sequence and thus made it into the film for aesthetic reasons? The viewer is left without further explanation and cannot do much but focus on the new footage to speak for itself.

A similar lack of controversy arises from the sometimes arbitrary sequence of questions. In a scene of about three minutes length Stone moves quickly from world order to the environment, to drugs, back to world order, to McDonald's. Due to fol-lowing his script or through his editing, he misses the opportunity to obtain any information from Castro that goes beyond standard phrases. Stone admits that during the shooting of *Comandante*, he did not interview Castro "as a journalist. It really was as a director and filmmaker. In my job, I challenge actors. I provoke them" (qtd. in Bardach 1). In fact, when he asks the president about his women, torture, or a secret informer system to control Cuba's population, he almost succeeds in provoking him, but he usually does not contrast Castro's words with other historical sources. As a consequence, information about the incidents referred to is insufficient, since the documentary shots are only used to underscore Castro's words, not to comment on them in a questioning way.

As far as the narration of nation is concerned, *Comandante* can most effectively be viewed from a U.S. American perspective. The film provides only little information about the Cuban people or their leader, but it clearly is a part of Stone's traditional critique of the American system. He manages to present Castro in a way that supports his own attitudes towards the U.S.A. In Castro he finds another person who shares his opinion about a conspiracy around the Kennedy assassination,[8] about the Vietnam War, and about Nixon's psychological deficiencies. Castro criticizes the American people for being uninformed about covert government activities, while the rest of the world knows about CIA and big business involvement in foreign conflicts. Moreover, Stone allows Castro to make the U.S.A. alone responsible for the Cuba Crisis and several other escalations of the Cold War. In contrast, several situations that feature prominently in the film focus on Cuba's positive social achievements and thus indirectly highlight shortcomings of U.S. society: when Castro and Stone walk into a crowd of excited medical students, Stone asks about the tuition fees they have to pay. Studies are free, and among the multicultural group of students there is a girl from New York City who profits from the education available in Cuba. Similarly, when Stone inquires about abortions, Castro informs him that abortion is not only legal, but also medically supervised. By asking apparently innocuous questions, and possibly also through sheer luck, Stone can collect images of situations that, however arbitrary, seem to foreground the social inequities and narrow-minded conservatism he believes to be central to the U.S. American system.

Finally, the way Stone presents Castro himself serves as the essential message about U.S. perspectives of the world. He shows one of America's archenemies as a sympathetic old man who has managed to keep his sphere of power free from U.S. business and corruption. In his film, Stone focuses on Castro's private habits instead of his political principles to bring the public closer to the Cuban president than ever before. The visual language of *Comandante* is designed to eliminate much of the distance between Castro and the viewers; the close-ups of his eyes and hands simulate physical and emotional closeness and block out the larger, inaccessible features of his political office and the controversial role in history that could be expected to permeate the way Castro is perceived in public. In addition, Stone's choice of questions also leans towards an investigation of Castro's private life, and while it might be an honorable achievement for a documentary film to allow the audience to catch a glimpse of a celebrity's more secluded pastime, it still poses a problem for the comprehensibility of

---

[8]   Ironically, in 2006, the documentary film *Rendezvouz mit dem Tod* on German national TV uncovered several pieces of evidence that point towards Castro as a possible initiator of the John F. Kennedy assassination.

the film's political content. Scattered in little pieces over a narrative carpet of private conversation, Stone's ventures into history and current political controversy remain largely incoherent and require extensive background information which the film does not provide.

The archival footage adds a layer of 'evidence' and imitates the 'documentary look' to create the impression that what is being shown has been thoroughly investigated, but it hardly ever contributes information that could help the viewers to develop a more neutral understanding of Castro's and Cuba's image and history. Thus, *Comandante* is less a film about Castro than another step in Stone's attempted deconstruction of the political establishment and public education in the U.S.A. By depicting the communist monster of the American press as a human being, Stone confronts the nation and especially its political and medial institutions with their own form of paranoia and fear of conspiracies. Cuba's and Castro's history are turned into a mirror that is meant to comment on the way the U.S.A. see themselves, their role in world politics, and their relation to their Cuban neighbors.

5. Conclusion: Docu-fictions as a Step towards 'History's Essence'?

Although Stone's docu-fictions have constantly been criticized for blurring the past and for presenting an entirely subjective approach to history, they have had a significant impact on the public discussion of controversial key events in America's recent history. By stressing effect instead of fact they have exerted considerable influence on society, even including the U.S. government. In his docu-fictions, Stone does not try to hide that they contain substantial amounts of fictional ingredients; yet he mixes them with an almost inseparable coating of documentary images and styles in order to convey a more convincing personal version of certain truths about the U.S. American nation. Stone is one of the public's chosen historians; he makes people think about the past and question some of their traditional values. With his films he contributes largely to the process of discovering what Marita Sturken calls "history's essence: the *work* of confronting the past, the *labor* of both confronting what cannot be known and of smoothing it over, the *stuff* of contradiction" (79; her italics).

It is the documentary film *Comandante* in particular that reveals how Stone wants his movies to be perceived. While his docu-fictions still admitted—through their blockbuster form, their usage of celebrity actors, their dramatic staging, etc.—that they mixed fact and fiction, *Comandante* comes in the shape of a documentary and pretends that it is all evidence. Still, it is not Stone's aim to present a well-balanced perspective on a certain topic, but to propagate extreme viewpoints that open up a new discussion about issues subdued or neglected in the American press. It is precisely because of its documentary appearance that the film is even more difficult to situate in relation to current discourses and whichever form of 'truth' it might relate to than Stone's docu-fictions. For audiences outside the U.S.A., *Comandante* must appear strangely biased and lacking controversy; for many American viewers, it could be a counterargument in a one-sided discussion dominated by the mainstream media. Unfortunately, most U.S. TV networks refused to broadcast the film, which ironically adds some new fuel to the fire of Stone's accusations. In the end, we have to believe Oliver Stone that it is not his intention to provide us with the true version of history, but that "it is you, the student of history, who should read for yourself and discover what is true" ("Image" 46). It seems likely that docu-fictions and the controversy that arises from their ingenuous merging of fact and fiction will do more to convince their audience to further investigate the inconsistencies of history than a film that claims to have done most of the investigation itself.

Works Cited

Ambrose, Stephen E. *"Nixon*—Is It History?" *Oliver Stone's U.S.A.: Film, History, and Controversy*. Ed. Robert B. Toplin. Lawrence: UP of Kansas, 2000. 202-12.

Bardach, Ann Louise. "Oliver Stone's Twist—Is the Director's Latest Film Soft on Castro?" *Slate* 14 Apr. 2004. http://slate.msn.com/id/2098860.

Courtwright, David T. "Way Cooler than Manson: *Natural Born Killers.*" *Oliver Stone's U.S.A.: Film, History, and Controversy*. Ed. Robert B. Toplin. Lawrence: UP of Kansas, 2000. 188-201.

Davis, Jack E. "New Left, Revisionist, In-Your-Face History: Oliver Stone's *Born on the Fourth of July* Experience." *Oliver Stone's U.S.A.: Film, History, and Controversy*. Ed. Robert B. Toplin. Lawrence: UP of Kansas, 2000. 135-48.

Godmilow, Jill, and Ann-Louise Shapiro. "How Real Is the Reality in Documentary Film?" *Producing the Past: Making Histories Inside and Outside the Academy*. Ed. Ann-Louise Shapiro. *History and Theory* Theme Issue 36 (1997): 80-101.

Goodman, Walter. "With Fact in Service to Drama." *New York Times* 3 Jan. 1996: C9.

Gunzenhäuser, Randi. "'All Plots Lead Toward Death': Memory, History, and the Assassination of John F. Kennedy." *Amerikastudien/American Studies* 43.1 (1998): 75-91.

Juhasz, Alexandra, and Jesse Lerner. "Introduction: Phony Definitions and Troubling Taxonomies of the Fake Documentary." *F is for Phony: Fake Documentary and Truth's Undoing*. Ed. Alexandra Juhasz and Jesse Lerner. Minneapolis; London: U of Minnesota P, 2006. 1-35.

Kurtz, Michael L. "Oliver Stone, *JFK*, and History." *Oliver Stone's U.S.A.: Film, History, and Controversy*. Ed. Robert B. Toplin. Lawrence: UP of Kansas, 2000. 166-77.

Nichols, Bill. *Introduction to Documentary*. Bloomington; Indianapolis: Indiana UP, 2001.

Renov, Michael. "Introduction: The Truth About Non-Fiction." *Theorizing Documentary*. Ed. Michael Renov. New York; London: Routledge, 1993. 1-11.

Roberts, Randy, and David Welky. "A Sacred Mission: Oliver Stone and Vietnam." *Oliver Stone's U.S.A.: Film, History, and Controversy*. Ed. Robert B. Toplin. Lawrence: UP of Kansas, 2000. 66-90.

Rosenstone, Robert A. "Oliver Stone as Historian." *Oliver Stone's U.S.A.: Film, History, and Controversy*. Ed. Robert B. Toplin. Lawrence: UP of Kansas, 2000. 26-39.

Stone, Oliver. "On *Nixon* and *JFK*." *Oliver Stone's U.S.A.: Film, History, and Controversy*. Ed. Robert B. Toplin. Lawrence: UP of Kansas, 2000. 249-98.

———."On Seven Films." *Oliver Stone's U.S.A.: Film, History, and Controversy*. Ed. Robert B. Toplin. Lawrence: UP of Kansas, 2000. 219-48.

———. "Stone on Stone's Image (As Presented by Some Historians)." *Oliver Stone's U.S.A.: Film, History, and Controversy*. Ed. Robert B. Toplin. Lawrence: UP of Kansas, 2000. 40-65.

———, and Zachary Sklar. *JFK: The Book of the Film*. New York: Applause Books, 1992.

———, Eric Hamburg, and Stephen J. Rivele. *Nixon: An Oliver Stone Film*. New York: Hyperion, 1995.

Sturken, Marita. "Reenactment, Fantasy, and the Paranoia of History: Oliver Stone's Docu-dramas." *Producing the Past: Making Histories Inside and Outside the Academy*. Ed. Ann-Louise Shapiro. *History and Theory* Theme Issue 36 (1997): 64-79.

Toplin, Robert B. "Introduction." *Oliver Stone's U.S.A.: Film, History, and Controversy*. Ed. Robert B. Toplin. Lawrence: UP of Kansas, 2000. 3-25.

Vogel, Amos. "*JFK*: The Question of Propaganda." *The Antioch Review* 50.3 (1992): 578-85.

Filmography

Alexander. Dir. Oliver Stone. Germany, U.S.A., Netherlands, France, UK, Italy, 2004.

The Blair Witch Project. Dir. Daniel Myrick and Eduard Sánchez. U.S.A., 1999.

Born on the 4th of July. Dir. Oliver Stone. U.S.A., 1989.

Comandante. Dir. Oliver Stone. U.S.A., Spain, 2003.

JFK. Dir. Oliver Stone. U.S.A., 1991.

Looking for Fidel. Dir. Oliver Stone. U.S.A., Cuba, 2004.

Nixon. Dir. Oliver Stone. U.S.A., 1995.

Persona non grata. Dir. Oliver Stone. U.S.A., France, Spain, 2003.

Platoon. Dir. Oliver Stone. UK, U.S.A., 1986.

Rendezvous with Death: Why John F. Kennedy Had to Die. Dir. Wilfried Huismann. Germany, 2006.

South of the Border. Dir. Oliver Stone. U.S.A., 2009.

This Is Spinal Tap. Dir. Rob Reiner. U.S.A., 1984.

U Turn. Dir. Oliver Stone. U.S.A., 1997.

Zapruder. Dir. King Horris and Karl Kimbrough. U.S.A., 2000.

Mo(o)re than Anti-Bush Agitprop?!—*Fahrenheit 9/11* and the Question of Post-Nine-Eleven National Identity

Wiebke Engel

Resumen

Michael Moore y su obra fílmica han sido siempre objeto de discusiones muy polémicas. Discusiones que, muy a menudo, se centran en la persona misma de Michael Moore y la cuestión de cómo categorizar su obra dentro del género del documental. No obstante, este ensayo desea analizar el documental *Fahrenheit 9/11* (2004) en términos del cuestionamiento de la identidad nacional estadounidense como consecuencia de las secuelas del 11 de septiembre de 2001. Después de una breve introducción al tema, pretendemos acercarnos sucintamente a Michael Moore como persona controvertida y como director de películas documentales. Esto nos permitirá seguir con un análisis detallado de las estrategias empleadas por Moore en *Fahrenheit 9/11* y de su estructura argumentativa. El enfoque central de nuestro análisis estará puesto en la representación del presidente norteamericano George Bush y en la manera como su gobierno se servía de aspectos esenciales de la identidad nacional para lograr que la máxima cantidad posible de estadounidenses apoyara su guerra contra el terrorismo. Finalmente, este ensayo quiere examinar la forma en que Moore construye su documental como un contra-discurso crítico frente a la generalizada disconformidad en los medios después del 11 de septiembre y durante la "guerra contra el terrorismo."

1. Introduction

According to Benedict Anderson, national identities are culturally constructed and nations are cultural artifacts. In *Imagined Communities* (1983) he argues that a nation "is an imagined political community—and imagined as both inherently limited and sovereign" (6). I agree with Anderson's position that nations are imagined communities created by a society's self-definition. No citizen of a nation—no matter its size—is able to meet all its other members. Nevertheless, there is a feeling of connectedness in every nation. In the United States the sense of national belonging seems to be immensely strong. National pride is very pronounced in comparison to other countries.

98.5% of the population regard themselves as extremely or very proud of being American (cf. Vorländer 294). These feelings of connectedness are supported by symbols, myths and foundational fictions. The continuing use of these myths and guiding images in (popular) culture and public debates keeps them alive and creates a feeling that they are genuine and achievable. Moreover, nations use these discursive constructs to distinguish themselves from other nations and often national symbols and myths turn into unquestioned components of national identity. In the United States concepts like democracy, freedom, Manifest Destiny, or the Frontier have become inherent elements of the country's national identity. However, national identity is not something set in stone. Particularly in times of war or crisis, national identity becomes a contested notion. It turns into a key cipher of emphasizing, questioning, epitomizing and criticizing what it means to be American.

This essay[1] was written against the backdrop of a moment in recent history "when the borderlines between fiction and reality, between imagination and the real, between the message and the medium, between the sacred and the profane, between history and myth … came crashing down on us/U.S." (Vejdovsky 205). September 11, 2001 was a mediated catastrophe—a real-time documentation of the intrusion of terror and death into the lives of millions around the globe. For that reason, images of the two planes hitting the World Trade Center and its resulting collapse burned themselves into our (collective) consciousness. The constant repetition of these images in the media made them increasingly more nightmarish and traumatic.[2] Millions had to witness helplessly the mass murder of more than 3,000 innocent people. Soon, the terrorist strikes came to be interpreted as deliberate attacks on America's national identity and culture. Within hours after the attack a binary constructions of *us/U.S.* versus *them* was dominating the medial and political discourse in the United States (cf. Moritz 195ff.). David Simpson summarizes this binary identity construction as follows:

> *They* are secretive, cowardly, primitive, inflexible: terrorists, followers of Islam. *We* are an open society, honorable, sophisticated, and committed to the global conversation and to respectful dialogue. We stand up in place and identify ourselves; they are anonymous and everywhere. (7, author's emphasis)

This black-and-white differentiation communicates an important message concerning American national identity after Nine-Eleven. It seemed as if the whole American nation was rallying behind President Bush and the war against terrorism. "United We Stand" was the rallying cry communicated by the media, which gave the impression that nobody was challenging the way in which the American government was facing the threat of terrorism.

---

[1] The version printed here is an extension of a chapter taken from my 2007 master's thesis "American Dreams and Nightmares: The Vietnam War and Nine-Eleven in Film and Popular Music."

[2] However, it has also been suggested that this seemingly endless loop of the images may have led to a certain numbing and "trauma fatigue" or even to a trivialization of tragedy.

One who soon came to join the debate about post Nine-Eleven national identity was Michael Moore. After the international bestseller *Dude, Where Is My Country?* (2003), Moore started to work on his political documentary *Fahrenheit 9/11* (2004). The film, which was awarded the Cannes *Palme d'Or* in 2004, takes the events of September 11, 2001 as a starting point for a critical evaluation of the Bush administration, the war in Iraq, and its media coverage. Nevertheless, the central question is: how does a documentary like *Fahrenheit 9/11* engage in discussions on American national identity after the September 11 terrorist attacks? Can it provide its audience with insights "into the use and abuse of power?" This essay will analyze the strategies or narrating, criticizing, and reorienting the nation employed in *Fahrenheit 9/11* and it will scrutinize Michael Moore's view on the complex debate about national identity in the aftermath of September 11, 2001. On the one hand, I will argue that through the manner in which Moore himself edits and comments on his material, *Fahrenheit 9/11* rather follows a distinct agenda employing agitational techniques, subjective viewpoints and a highly emotional tone. On the other hand, I will demonstrate how Moore's documentary nevertheless interrogates concepts of America's national identity such as freedom, democracy, and equal opportunity in order to create an alternative public discourse to challenge the officially disseminated 'truths' concerning the events of September 11, 2001 and the war in Iraq.

2. Michael Moore—Polarizing Persona and Documentary Filmmaker

During the century of its existence, the genre of documentary film in the Americas has undergone numerous changes (cf. the introduction to this volume).[3] The genre's best-known innovator in the past two decades is Michael Moore. I will briefly address some characteristics of his work and demonstrate that documentary films are a popular medium for imagining communities. In a second step, I will shortly categorize *Fahrenheit 9/11* for my purpose of analyzing it as an interrogation of national identity after Nine-Eleven.

Michael Moore, Academy Award-winning director of *Bowling for Columbine* (2002) and author of bestselling books like *Stupid White Men* (2001), is a polarizing figure. People call him either populist or brilliant and some surely consider him to be both. No other American documentary filmmaker has been the subject of such controversial debates as Michael Moore. Alan Rosenthal writes that the most significant purpose of a documentary is "to continue to ask the hard, often disturbing questions so

---

[3] For a detailed introduction to the genre and development of documentary films, cf. Bill Nichols, *Representing Reality: Issues and Concepts in Documentary*; Michael Renov, ed., *Theorizing Documentary*; John Corner, *The Art of Record: A Critical Introduction to Documentary*; and Michael Tobias, ed., *The Search for Reality: The Art of Documentary Film-Making*.

pertinent to our age" (qtd. in Grünefeld 64). This is what Moore's documentaries are known for—whether it is America's culture of violence or the ailing U.S. health care system, Moore does not hesitate to ask troubling and impertinent questions about issues that some people prefer to ignore. Furthermore, his usually rather shabby outward appearance can be seen as a crucial part of his self-dramatization strategy. Instead of signaling distance to the audience and the working-class protagonists of his documentaries, Moore wants to be seen as one of them. He listens to people's problems; he comforts them emotionally and appears as an authentic representative of their interests. In the process, however, Moore stages himself as a modern-day Robin Hood—fighting for the poor, disadvantaged, and exploited American citizens against corrupt economic and political power mongers. Instead of bow and arrow, he uses his camera and biting humor to shoot verbal pins at people he deems responsible for economic, social, and political problems.

Documentary as a film genre started its development in the early 20th century; the then recent invention of motion pictures was used simply to record life and everyday situations. But as Jacobs writes, documentaries soon took over another task: they turned "from random observation to [presenting] selected aspects of reality, vividly acquainting moviegoers with national and international figures and events" (qtd. in Grünefeld 21). Questions concerning national identity, politics or historical events soon turned into popular issues of documentary films. Bill Nichols reminds us that "[t]he term *documentary* must itself be constructed in much the same manner as the world we know and share" (12, author's emphasis) and in a later part of his study he argues that "documentary offers access to a shared historical construct. Instead of *a* world, we are offered access to *the* world" (109, author's emphasis). Consequently, documentary films became a popular medium in times of war and crisis. During the Great Depression, the Second World War, or the Vietnam War era, documentaries were used either to reemphasize or to question American ideals. However, until the late 1980s documentaries rather stayed at the margins of the film industry and were mainly used by various minority groups as a political mouthpiece.[4] In 1989 Michael Moore released his first documentary, entitled *Roger & Me*, which crucially helped to leverage a genre—turning documentaries into a form of political entertainment that appeals to mass audiences. His films crucially contributed to the rising popularity of a genre that had previously often been stigmatized as tiresome or overly instructive.

In the years following *Roger & Me*, documentary films became increasingly successful commercially and attracted constantly growing audiences. Academy Award-winning documentaries like Michael Moore's *Bowling for Columbine* or Davis Guggenheim's *An Inconvenient Truth* (2006) were shown in movie theaters around the globe. In 2006 James McEnteer even heralded a "new golden age" of documentary films (xvi). Despite this proclamation and the ubiquity of the term "documentary film" there is no generally accepted definition of the genre (cf. Grünefeld 15ff.). Moreover,

---

[4]   A case in point is the Latin American social documentary of the 1960s and 70s (cf. Burton-
     Carvajal).

documentaries are not a static genre; they evolve with the taste of the times and the advances of technology. As Bill Nichols writes, "[d]ocumentary as a concept or practice occupies no fixed territory. It mobilizes no finite inventory of techniques, addresses no set number of issues, and adopts no completely known taxonomy of forms, styles, or modes" (12).

Nichols defines four modes of representation: "expository, observational, interactive, and reflexive" (cf. 32 ff.). Moore's documentaries are a mixture of all of these four modes, shifting their emphasis from one of these modes to another. *Expository* documentaries, in Nichols's categorization, make use of montage, images and sounds, and the presented material is commented on by the voice-over of an invisible narrator. While Moore's documentaries do employ montages, images and sounds, the director, instead of mostly documenting and commenting on the events from behind the camera (*observational mode*), appears as a dominant physical and intellectual presence in his own documentaries (cf. Bruzzi 178). Therefore, many parts of Moore's documentaries adopt an *interactive mode*, showing dialogues between Moore and the subjects of his films. Like interactive documentaries in general, Moore's films employ a limited and subjective point of view. This is one of the main points of criticism launched against Moore's works. However, "no documentary can be completely truthful, for there is no such thing as truth while the changing developments in society continue to contradict each other" (Rotha, qtd. in Grünefeld 70). Moore also makes frequent use of satire and parody—trademarks of *reflexive* documentaries. Apart from employing these various modes of representation, Moore's films are known for their intertextuality. The frequent use of popular music, references to American television series or feature films are meant to support Moore's claims and arguments. He employs these crucial elements of identity constructions, but reshapes their meaning and puts them into different contexts. How Moore makes use, in particular, of pop songs and films will be addressed below.

Next to the mixture of various modes of representation, Moore's films predominantly deal with social, economic or political grievances. They are supposed to inform his fellow citizens about these issues, but instead of striking a strictly instructive tone, they are predominantly entertaining in proclaiming their political message; in short, they are *politainment*. Verena Grünefeld points out that Moore's particular way of entertaining the audience gave political statements new mass appeal (cf. 181). According to Jonathan Bignell, a documentary combines both signifiers of observed reality and signifiers of argument (cf. 139). Moore's film observes aspects of America's post-Nine-Eleven reality and gives the appearance that the basic facts he addresses have been meticulously researched.[5] Moore underlines his 'truth claim' by interviewing experts as well as through rare original footage, providing the audience with numerous facts the American news media (had to) withhold from their viewers. His work is not purely factual, though: in order to reach a large mass of people, Moore wraps serious

---

[5]   His website, www.michaelmoore.com, features a chapter listing all the resources Moore had used to support his argumentation in *Fahrenheit 9/11*.

political issues into an entertaining formula. The additional voice-over by Moore, the way of editing the material, fictional sequences, and a strong emotional context point to his political goals. Moore claims to have made *Fahrenheit 9/11* to "see Mr. Bush removed from the White House" (qtd. in Kasindorf). Moore's documentary can be called *agitprop*, since many of his arguments are polemic and present complex socio-political issues in catchy as well as simple formulas and, moreover, have the declared purpose of agitating against George W. Bush and his policies after Nine-Eleven.[6] In his documentaries Moore positions himself as an agitator who provokes certain reactions through his probing and his self-dramatization as a lone, heroic seeker of truth. He also stages himself as an ordinary American, concerned about the well-being and future of his nation. As Stella Bruzzi writes, *"Fahrenheit 9/11 … is an example of agitational cinema: it tried to influence viewers and voters, it sought to disrupt a political regime"* (182). Moore is the one who drives the actions of his films and who questions the truth distributed by political, economic or social leaders. In *Fahrenheit 9/11* the appeal to American ideals like freedom, democracy, and equal opportunities, is juxtaposed with the current reality of the war in Iraq and Bush's politics in order to create a counter-position to the prevalent "united we stand" feeling proclaimed by the mass media and the President. How this is achieved by Moore is an issue to be discussed in the following section.

3. Riding the Emotional Rollercoaster

Fahrenheit 9/11 is characterized by high emotional intensity. Moore incorporates comic and tragic sequences alongside informational ones into the narrative of his documentary. Instead of relying on dry numbers, Moore uses individual stories to substantiate his point of view. He seeks to elicit an emotional response, which is necessary to get people to "see this movie and throw the bastards out of office" (Moore, qtd. in Bruzzi 178).

Fahrenheit 9/11 starts off with George W. Bush's contested victory of the 2000 presidential election and continues in an agitational, subjective and emotionalizing tone. The legitimacy of Bush's presidency is immediately questioned by Moore's voice-over: "Was it all just a dream? Did the last four years not really happen?" Moore positions himself as a commentator in his own documentary and he expresses doubts about Bush as a democratically elected president. To further support his doubts, Moore shows how objections against Bush's election were ignored by the House of Representatives, the Senate and the Supreme Court. These allegations disrupt the image of a well-working system of checks and balances. Moore continues to proclaim his anti-

---

[6] The term "agitprop" has its origins in the Soviet Union of the early 20th century and is coined from the two terms "agitatsiya" (agitation) and "propaganda". Similar to Moore, "The Bolsheviks wished to use art as a weapon in the revolutionary struggle … to stimulate people's understanding of and involvement in such important matters as health, sanitation, literacy or the military situation" (Cuddon 15).

pathy toward Bush by showing his limousine bombarded with eggs on the day of his inauguration. As Verena Grünefeld has written, the rhetoric structure of the establishing shot communicates that democracy was already at risk prior to the terrorist attacks of September 11 (cf. 190). From the establishing shot onwards Moore's documentary communicates that democracy is not only threatened from the outside by terrorists, but from the inside as well. In the eyes of Moore, the greatest danger to a well-working democracy in the United States is President Bush. To further undermine the President's public image Moore employs private snapshots of Bush accompanied by a voice-over asserting that up until then the President had spent 42% of his first term in office on vacation. Here Moore uses what Nichols calls the *reflexive* mode to satirically comment upon the images: "With everything going wrong, he did what any of us would do—he went on vacation." The documentary's prologue closes with what Bruzzi calls "classic Moore cheap shots," which aim at undermining the authority of the Bush administration (180). Seeing Paul Wolfowitz licking his comb or George W. Bush making faces prior to a speech is amusing and challenges the credibility of these political figures. The sad violin music and the way in which Condoleezza Rice, Paul Wolfowitz, and others are exposed appear (to me, at least) to be a prologue to a (national) tragedy. Moreover, politicians are presented as actors preparing for a performance. They hide their faces behind masks; Moore's goal with the narration of nation in *Fahrenheit 9/11* is, to use Bob Dylan's words, to unmask these "masters of war." He stages them as bad actors in a tragic play about the damage done to America's national identity in order to support economic elites, the only group to profit from the war in Iraq and the hysterical fear of terrorism after Nine-Eleven. The prologue focuses on Moore's charges against President Bush, his administration and the media.

To provide proof for its charges, *Fahrenheit 9/11* directly continues with the terrorist attacks of September 11. Moore stylizes the attack on the World Trade Center in a rather artistic manner, focusing on individual recollections. This approach might have several reasons. As mentioned above, September 11 was a mediated catastrophe. The terrorists wanted the world to take part in their perfidious plan, they were well aware that the images of death and destruction would be remembered for a very long time. Such so-called "flashbulb memories," as psychologists and psychiatrists refer to them, are "historic events that are burned into the minds of individuals, communities or whole nations." Furthermore, "these images have "enormous power" and very typically stay "locked into our individual and collective consciousness for better or worse" (Brown/Kulik, qtd. in Moritz 192). Even today, ten years after the terrorist attacks, the images are easily recalled into our (collective) consciousness. Instead of focusing on the all too familiar video footage of the terrorist attacks, in *Fahrenheit 9/11* the screen remains black for almost a minute. Here, Moore makes use of what Nichols calls the *observational* mode and focuses on the power of auditory signs in order to evoke individual memories of the event and its medial representation. Having recreated the attack before the viewer's inner eye, Moore shifts to familiar visuals of the attack's aftermath. We see people crying and others desperately looking for relatives or loved ones. In slow motion and accompanied by violin music, we see others running for their lives as the towers collapse. This sequence illustrates the immense tragedy of Nine-Eleven and invites us to share the loss, grief, and pain of its victims. "As the most significant trauma of modern American history, the events of 9/11 altered everything, and in his response to those events Moore demonstrates the underlying seriousness of his filmic endeavors" (Bruzzi 181). Embedding this sequence into footage of President Bush's (non-)reaction to the attacks, juxtaposed with Moore's reflexive commentary, creates "an unflattering picture of irresolution and even paralysis, one that informs Moore's thesis—of a president in over his head—and pervades the entire film" (Turan). The structure of *Fahrenheit 9/11*'s first 20 minutes prepares the audience for the following argumentation that Moore uses to substantiate his charges against President Bush and his politics.

After this emotional prologue *Fahrenheit 9/11* shifts to a depiction of America in the months following the terrorist attacks. The U.S. Patriot Act, passed six weeks after Nine-Eleven, is a controversial bill which restricts personal freedoms in order to defend national freedom. In this part of the documentary Moore once more steps in front of the camera, making use of the entertaining and polarizing function of his own persona (cf. Grünefeld, 195). While driving around the Capitol in an ice cream truck and reading out the Patriot Act is meant to be deliberately funny, this gimmick does nothing to support Moore's claim that politicians do not read the bills they sign. To further support his charges, Moore uses a comment by a member of Congress who tells him, "we don't read most of the bills" and immediately cuts to an interview with Bush explaining the advantages of a dictatorship. Contrary to the customary celebration of democracy as one of the cornerstones of U.S. national identity, Moore's propagandist cutting and editing presents the nation as moving toward dictatorship, leaving little confidence in a well-functioning democracy (cf. Grünefeld 203).

In the past two decades Michael Moore has gained immense popularity/notoriety, and politicians have come to know him and his strategies well. Against this background, we need to be cautious when, in *Fahrenheit 9/11*, the filmmaker tries to persuade politicians to enlist their children for the military. Most of them evade Moore, and he uses this reaction to his own advantage. As mentioned above, Moore carefully stages himself as one of the people whose aim it is to fight for their rights. In this sequence he wants to demonstrate that these politicians are not willing to send their own children to a war for which they have voted. He stages himself as a substitute victim for "people who actually pay the price for all the posturing out of Washington" (Turan). In order to further accentuate this victim-victimizer dichotomy *Fahrenheit 9/11* continues in an interactive mode. A small-town activist group called "Peace Fresno" and the pensioner Barry Reingold are used as metonymic examples.[7] Their individual experiences are narrated in order to declare the Patriot Act to be a funda-

---

[7] Bignell explains that with metonymic examples "one part of reality is made to stand for a larger real world which it represents" (Bignell 139).

mentally unconstitutional bill. Moore practices what Bignell observes to be the purpose of metonymical examples in documentaries: "In its claim to deliver knowledge and experience of the real world, documentary draws on the myths and ideologies which shape that real world for the viewers of the programme" (139). Moore's metonymical representatives are staged as lawful, patriotic, and peaceful citizens deprived of their constitutional rights of freedom of assembly and speech. This restriction apparently signifies that the fear of another terrorist attack is exploited by the government to intrude into the privacy of innocent people. These individual cases support Moore's controversial thesis of the U.S.A. as a future totalitarian state. He knows that the average American is much more likely to identify with his arguments if they focus on individuals who are deprived of the most cherished rights on which the nation has been founded. In a country which celebrates the freedom of assembly and speech as a crucial part of its national identity, it seems scandalous to disturb the privacy of ordinary, law-abiding citizens for no apparent reason. In this part Moore shifts to a more serious tone, implying that democracy is always at risk and that not only terrorism but the government as well can be a serious threat to it (cf. Grünefeld 203).

Another emotional story he uses to create identification and compassion is the one of a former Bush supporter, Lila Lipscomb. For several years, she encouraged her children and other job-seekers to look at career opportunities in the U.S. military. At first she is depicted as a patriotic, pro-war supporter of Bush. Then her eldest son, who became increasingly frustrated with fighting in an unjustified war, died in the line of duty in Iraq. This event, a Moore shows, abruptly made Ms. Lipscomb change her mind. Once more, her story stands as a metonymical example for a group of parents who have lost their children in one of the wars following the Nine-Eleven terrorist attacks. Instead of relying on the anonymity of casualty figures, Moore provides names and faces. In his former documentaries he "has used 'victims' of the injustices he is exposing as vehicles for bringing the focus back onto himself ... [but] in Lipscomb's case he stays off camera and in the shadows" (Bruzzi, 178). Moore switches his documentary into an observational mode in order to put emphasis on Lipscomb's fate. The sequence of her reading, in tears, the last letter of her son and her nervous breakdown in Washington, D.C., provides *Fahrenheit 9/11*, according to the *New York Times*, with "an eloquence that its most determined critics will find hard to dismiss" (Scott). I can only agree with this statement, since it is beyond doubt that Moore's film draws its energy from such excruciating sequences. I also agree with *USA Today* reviewer Claudia Puig, who writes that Lipscomb "is a willing participant in her own exploitation, choosing to share her pain in service of a broader message: the inhumanity of the war." In an interview with *USA Today*, Lipscomb herself states: "I don't want any more mothers—Americans or Iraqis—to feel this pain" and, moreover, she expresses her hope that Moore's film "will open people's eyes and make them begin to ask questions and start speaking up for themselves" (Strauss). Using the story of a proselytized Bush supporter, Moore tries to make the point that people do change their mind. As a political medium, the film asks U.S. voters to make use of their democratic rights in order to prevent a reelection of George W. Bush. In a way Lipscomb "becomes a more authentic version of Michael Moore, who is always seeking to confront power" (qtd. in Grünefeld, 214). By interrupting her story with footage about American business in Iraq, Moore makes her once more a metonymic example for all U.S. Americans. Instead of supporting the Iraqi people by establishing democracy and freedom, politicians are guided by economic interests, the scene suggests. The individual fates of people like Lipscomb personalize Moore's charges against Bush and his politics. The final sequence of this scene, in which Lipscomb is trying to confront George W. Bush with her pain, is used by Moore to illustrate the distance between the President and the American people. Lipscomb cannot meet him face-to-face since a fence seals off the White House from people like her. This fence becomes a powerful metaphor of division, supporting Moore's claim that the President is not a democratic leader concerned about the well-being of his fellow citizens.

Although this scene from *Fahrenheit 9/11* might be considered overly emotional, it is not fake. The pain of Lipscomb is real and the audience inevitably feels with this woman. Instead of exclusively relying on irony and sarcasm to question Bush's presidency, Moore ably uses individual fates appealing to viewers' emotions in order to convey his position to the audience. He puts into practice what Paul Rotha has stated: "if documentary is going to be significant, we must make films which will move people. ... And if the masses are interested in seeing individuals and following their emotions on the screen, then documentary must embrace individuals" (qtd. in Grünefeld 73). True enough, but if Moore were aiming at an objective narration of nation, he would also need to mention how necessary the fence around the White House is for security reasons.

4.   Music That Emotionalizes even Mo(o)re

Apart from a highly emotional viewer guidance and a polemic narrative structure, Moore makes use of popular music in *Fahrenheit 9/11* to further his goals. In Hollywood blockbusters, music is essential; it also plays a distinct role in documentaries. Music underlining a particular sequence or scene can have a great influence on our perception of the presented visual material. While the images transport certain values in themselves, music can be used to direct the interpretation into a desired direction and to trigger certain emotional responses. Music is centrally important in *Fahrenheit 9/11*; the songs are carefully selected and placed to support the narrative and the director's position. The use of music in voicing social criticism had been successfully used in other documentaries by Moore; e.g. in *Bowling for Columbine*, he uses songs to "add nudges and winks" to his already "sardonic commentary" (Scott). Moore realizes that music is a powerful medium for commenting on national identity. The way music can be connected to personal or national identity is expressed, for example, by Simon Firth, who argues that

The first reason we enjoy popular music is because of its use in answering questions of identity: we use pop songs to create for ourselves a particular sort of self-definition—a particular place in society: the pleasure that pop music produces is a pleasure of iden- tification—with music we like, with performers of that music, with other people who like it. (140)

In *Fahrenheit 9/11* Michael Moore carefully chooses popular songs as background music for striking images, thus creating an auditory viewer guidance on President Bush and his politics. In this manner Moore creates new contexts for crucial depic- tions, a strategy that is entertaining and that allows for socio-political critique.

The documentary's first use of popular music comments on George W. Bush and his attitude toward his political office. The opening sequences of *Fahrenheit 9/11*, which shows the "careless" President golfing, fishing, and cutting wood, is accom- panied by The Go-Goes' "Vacation." It is a song about a person who had escaped the boredom of home by taking a vacation, and now regrets it. Moore adapts the song's original meaning to intimate repeatedly Bush's incompetence and carelessness as U.S. President. He calculates that, instead of serving his fellow citizens, up until September 11, 2001, Bush had spent 42% of his term in office on "vacation."[8] The combination of these images with the "Vacation" song underlines Moore's argument that George W. Bush is "innately lazy and unwilling to face his troubles" (Bruzzi 181); the spectator is expected to be indignant that the President seemingly did not care about the threat of terrorism. The following sequence of the Nine-Eleven terrorist attacks conveys Moore's questionable opinion that they were a direct consequence of Bush's pre- ference of vacations over politics.

Moore continues undermining George W. Bush's trustworthiness with musical support. In a strongly simplified mode, the close business connections between the bin Laden family, the Saudi Royal family, and the Bush family are narrated.[9] Moore believes that the victims' families and the American public in general have a right to know why members of the bin Laden and Saudi Royal family were allowed to leave the USA even though Osama bin Laden planned and financed the attacks, and 15 of the 19 terrorists were Saudi citizens. The complexity of international politics and busi- ness relationships is reduced to a few handy arguments here; to my mind, this is the film's weakest part. Moore deliberately uses simplifications to agitate his audience into the desired direction; to reinforce this agitation, he makes use of two songs. At the beginning of this sequence, Eric Burdon sings "We Gotta Get out of This Place." The song is used to underline Moore's argument that the Bush administration hides the truth about Osama bin Laden. Although the song's lyrics have no apparent connection

---

[8] Cf. Charles Krauthammer, "A Vacation Bush Deserves," *The Washington Post* 10 August 2001.

[9] Close business relations between Saudi Arabia and the Unites States have existed since the 1940s. During the Second World War, President Roosevelt used them to establish the foundations for reliable oil deliveries from Saudi Arabia to the United States (cf. Zinn 413- 414).

to September 11, 2001 and the involvement of the bin Laden family, Moore uses the song's refrain, "we gotta get out of this place/if it's the last thing we ever do," as musical background to a list of names indicating people who were able to leave the U.S.A. after the terrorist attacks. This list shows that several members of the bin Laden family were allowed to leave the country two days after Nine-Eleven without any official questioning. The way Moore continues his montage clearly aims at creating further doubt about Bush's loyalty. The film suggests that the Bush administration does not merely lack interest in finding the instigators of Nine-Eleven, but is actively protecting them. The combination of Burdon's song and the list of names strongly challenges Bush's promise that he would make no distinction between terrorists and those who support them in order to protect the United States from further attacks. The loyalty of other cabinet members like Dick Cheney is also called into question by depicting his involvement in the Halliburton Company as well as its essential role in the war in Iraq. Here the President is "portrayed not just as an untrustworthy politician in his own right but also as a figurehead for a larger, more powerful regime" (Bruzzi 178). Once again this narration shines a light on the U.S.A. as an endangered democracy where the truth is hidden from its citizens and economic profit stands above national security. At the end of this sequence Moore presents us with an uncommented photographic collage of the allegedly close relationship between Bush and bin Laden along with other Saudi leaders; the montage is accompanied by REM's song "Shiny Happy People." Here the irony turns into sarcasm. As if those images alone were not upsetting enough, Moore wants to fuel emotions into a conflagration of sheer anger. By now, "the temperature when freedom burns" appears to have reached a critical point. President Bush, who promised his fellow citizens to do everything possible to "disrupt their [the terrorists'] financial networks [and] to root out and destroy global terrorism"[10] is depicted by Moore as one of the terrorists' closest business partners and friends. Repeatedly, it seems as if economic interests were far more important for Bush's politics than the security of America and its citizens. To further support the thesis that Bush is a threat to America's democratic foundation, the documentary abruptly cuts to a public execution in Saudi Arabia. Moore's voice-over tells the audience that the President's friends are considered notorious violators of human rights by Amnesty International. Despite the tragic contents, the cheerful song and its contrast with the represented scene produce a humorous effect. According to *Los Angeles Times* reviewer Kenneth Turan, "though the situation is so grave we want to cry, Moore is adept at making us smile even when we're not expecting to." As I mentioned earlier, Moore literally invites the viewers to laugh and to cry in compassion for the victims of Bush's incompetence.

Another musical "cheap shot" against Bush follows. Moore shows an uncensored version of Bush's blackened-out military record, combined with "Cocaine" by J.J.

---

[10] Release, Office of the White House Press Secretary, September 20, 2001: "Address to a Joint Session of Congress and the American People" United States Capitol, Washington, D.C., <http://www.whitehouse.gov/news /releases/2001/09/20010920-8.html>.

Cale. First, the song serves as an allusion to Bush's former addiction to alcohol and cocaine. Second, Bush, who frequently calls himself "a war president," has never fought in a war. The Army suspended him from military duty before he was on any battlefield. At first sight, the only purpose of this song-image montage is to reinforce the contradictions between Bush's private and public image. On closer inspection, this song is carefully placed within Moore's argumentative structure since the insinuation of substance abuse is repeatedly picked up in the following part of *Fahrenheit 9/11*.

One of the highlights of *Fahrenheit 9/11*'s soundtrack is Joey Scarbury's song "Greatest American Hero." It is used as a parody on George W. Bush's monomythic[11] post Nine-Eleven rhetoric and appearance. The song accompanies footage with familiar images of Bush landing on an aircraft carrier to declare the mission in Iraq accomplished. Here the President stages himself as the Army man he has never been by displaying what Verena Grünefeld calls a "*Top Gun* appearance" (201). He celebrates himself as America's monomythic hero who has finally prevailed in the struggle of good against evil. By choosing this particular song to accompany the President's self-fashioning Moore stresses again that for him Bush is not a hero, but a brazen liar, declaring a mission accomplished when in Iraq, as seen in the subsequent images, "the roof is on fire." The connotations of the Bloodhound Gang's song "The Roof Is on Fire" changes during the film. U.S. soldiers listen to it during combat; for them, it is "a symbol of the burning Baghdad," as one of them says during an interview. For Moore, presenting the war's atrociousness and chaos, it becomes a symbol of America's failure and arrogance. How can the President declare that the war in Iraq is over, when Americans as well as Iraqis are still dying there? Moore already answered this question several times in the course of *Fahrenheit 9/11*. He uses the image of Bush caring most about his own and his allies' economic gain far more prominently than mainstream American media have done. Instead of being a loyal representative of the United States, Bush appears—in Moore's version of the state of the nation—to care only for large companies and the military industry. The combination of images, music and Moore's voice-over creates the appearance of a president who does not live up to his promises. The portrayal is that of a man not concerned with freedom and democracy in Iraq but merely with the economic advantages of invading countries like Iraq.

The last pop song used in *Fahrenheit 9/11* underlines the image of an apparently baffled George W. Bush. The closing credits are accompanied by Neil Young's "Rockin' in the Free World"—a song from his 1989 album *Freedom*. The song was written, according to Young, in response to the Cold War and the callous social politics of Ronald Reagan and George H.W. Bush. In *Fahrenheit 9/11*, Moore puts

---

[11] In their book *The Myth of the American Superhero*, Robert Jewett and John Shelton Lawrence define the American monomyth as follows: "A community in a harmonious paradise is threatened by evil; normal institutions fail to contend with this threat; a selfless superhero emerges to renounce temptations and carry out the redemptive task; aided by fate, his decisive victory restores the community to its paradisiacal condition; the superhero then recedes into obscurity" (6).

particular emphasis on the line "That's one more kid that'll never go to school / Never get to fall in love, never get to be cool." While this line resounds, a crying Iraqi child and a dead U.S. soldier are shown—images which are disturbing and powerful. The real outcome of the "war on terrorism," Moore implies, is pain and fear as well as many lost lives. Finally, rock music carries the connotation of revolting against the establishment. Therefore, it matches Moore's overall aim—he wants the audience to revolt against the political establishment by voting against a president who violates crucial aspects of America's national identity. Until the very last sequence of the documentary Moore pursues his goal of creating a counter-public to the unquestioning depiction of the war in the network news; music is used to reinforce this aim.

5. President Evil

Since he holds the highest political office in the United States, the president is often seen as the most prominent representative of national identity. As the leader of a nation founded on freedom and equality, he is expected to practice and defend those values—domestically and internationally. But Moore constructs a figure who is far from representing a government "of the people, by the people, for the people." The

president's actions and decisions influence how a country is perceived beyond its national borders. He is usually treated as a person of authority in public and the media. In *Fahrenheit 9/11* things are different: Moore challenges President Bush, disregarding the indefeasibility of his office. Apart from trying to influence the 2004 presidential elections, an additional reason for the filmmaker's disrespectful treatment of Bush appears in the film's prologue, when Moore tries to interview George W. Bush. Instead of answering his questions, Bush tells him: "Behave yourself, will you? Go find real work." Since it is widely recognized that Bush is no great orator, Moore makes use of spontaneous statements that convey the image of a simpleminded and incompetent Bush. *Fahrenheit 9/11* thus focuses on "Bush's perceived stupidity—the inelegancies of speech, stumbles and malapropisms" (Bruzzi 178). The aim of this depiction is to produce a counterstatement to Bush's self-fashioning as a resolute leader in order to question his role as a primary representative of American national identity.

Starting with the movie poster[12], Michael Moore verbally and visually communicates disrespect for Bush and dismisses his authority. Seeing Michael Moore and George W. Bush walking hand in hand makes many viewers smile. According to Moore's homepage, his film "considers the presidency of George W. Bush and where it has led us." This statement corresponds to the message encapsulated in the poster. In it, Moore acts as a visual counterbalance to President Bush. He literally takes him by the hand, exposes his controversial public and private image to us/U.S., and argues for his removal from the White House. Moore does not aim at exposing the controversy surrounding Bush from a bird's eye view, he would rather argue on an interactive level, which is signified by both persons having the same height and standing on the same level. Michael Moore's impish smile communicates that this confrontation will take place whether Bush accepts it or not.

The poster's use of the word "fireworks" also generates a certain sensationalism, which fits the agitational nature of Moore's work. The confrontation of Moore and Bush is marketed as a public event. The exclamation mark at the end of "The fireworks begin June 25th!" makes the announcement more insistent, almost like a command—people have to see this movie. Moore advertises his documentary as a counter-discourse to the prevalent image of Bush and his politics in the mainstream American mass media. The aim of *Fahrenheit 9/11* is to expose what Moore considers the truth about Bush and his politics to the American public. The announcement also creates a link to questions of national identity by alluding to the large public fireworks common in the celebration of Independence Day. Moore, who aims at mobilizing the American public to vote against Bush, would, moreover, like to instill revolutionary sentiments. Similar to the revolutionary slogan "no taxation without representation," *Fahrenheit 9/11* communicates "no reelection without representation." At the same time, the film celebrates the nation, especially its First Amendment. In an interview Moore stated, "I think it would make the founding fathers proud to see the country still survives in their first belief, … that somebody has the ability to express themselves and criticize the top guy" (qtd. in Grünefeld, 219). Like the Declaration of Independence, which features numerous charges against King George III, Moore's documentary features a long list of charges against George W. Bush. People are agitated to start a 'revolution' against the President by making use of their democratic right as voters. Once more American citizens are invited to free themselves from 'tyranny' in order to choose a leader who truthfully represents a free and democratic nation.[13]

Moore portrays the President's inability to lead a country, to run a company, or to be honest to his fellow citizens. First of all, Moore wants the audience to believe that George W. Bush is *the one* to blame for the catastrophe of September 11, 2001.

---

[12] Movie poster source: <www.michaelmoore.com>.

[13] Although Moore wants to remove Bush from office, he does not offer an alternative candidate.

He reduced counter-terrorism funding and ignored the serious threat of terrorism. By intertwining these strongly incendiary accusations, Moore deliberately wants to highlight that Bush is not, as one of his personal advisors, David Frum states, "a good man" with the virtues of "decency, honesty, rectitude, courage, and tenacity" (qtd. in Singer 212). On the contrary, in *Fahrenheit 9/11* George W. Bush is depicted as one of the world's most evil men with dictatorial inclinations. In many sequences concerning the President, Moore employs a subjective point of view and a sarcastic style in order to unsettle the public image of a democratic and resolute ruler. The filmmaker's strong dislike of the President is blatantly stated. According to an article in *USA Today*, "the first President Bush has branded the film a 'vicious personal attack' on his son" (Puig). In fact, many of the President's quotes in *Fahrenheit 9/11* appear rather selective and taken out of context.

> Within the framework of such a clearly targeted, directional film the image created of George W. Bush, though not a fabrication, is entirely subservient to and dictated by Michael Moore's point of view, his perspective reflecting his thwarted desire to assist the removal of Bush from office. (Bruzzi 182)

It therefore often appears hard to distinguish between profound criticism of Bush's politics and Moore's personal dislike of the president, which makes it easy for critics to question the credibility of his documentary. Apart from this all too personal way of scrutinizing the President's authority and trustworthiness, Michael Moore employs another image of Bush which became critically recognized after Nine-Eleven and during the War on Terrorism—the cowboy president. The cowboy embodies many American ideals such as individualism, freedom, toughness and heroism. Fighting evil, negotiating between individuals and the community, the cowboy is seen as an archetypical American hero.

> Since the days of the medieval knights and even well before, horsemen have fascinated mere pedestrians who look up to the mounted riders both literally and figuratively. The man on horseback – symbolizing power, authority, and leadership inspires fear and admiration. The cowboys of the American West, properly the best-known cultural icons of the United States, are heirs to this long heritage of equestrian envy. (Slatta 6)

George W. Bush, a long-time Texas resident and the state's former governor, has often been called a cowboy; apart from his origin, this image is supported by the way he talks and presents himself in public. After Nine-Eleven and especially during the war on terrorism there were "increasing signs that in international affairs the nation is tempted to move with mythic footsteps toward 'cowboy' stances" (Lawrence/Jewett 14). On the one hand, Bush's "Cowboy Diplomacy"[14] helped people to make sense of a sudden war and was supposed to highlight the President's noble character. The simplified binary identity construction of the good United States and the evil enemy was frequently used by Bush in order to gain support for his politics ("Either you're

---

[14] This term is used in a *TIME* Magazine article called "The End of Cowboy Diplomacy" by Romesh Ratnesar, concerning George W. Bush's post-9/11 politics and rhetoric. Cf. <http://www.time.com/time/magazine/article/0,9171,1211578,00.html>.

with us or you're with the terrorists."). Moore questions and satirizes this connotation by showing Bush in a cowboy outfit complemented by Western banjo music. To further ridicule Bush's "Cowboy Diplomacy," Moore makes use of parody. He places Bush's, Cheney's and Rumsfeld's faces onto the bodies of *Bonanza*'s protagonists. Next to the entertaining function, the Western collage signifies that Moore interprets Bush and his administration as a group of cowboys that confuses the complexity of international politics with the fictional Wild West. Bush's war-on-terrorism-slogan, "we smoke them out of their holes," is in fact a line from *Bonanza*. "While the simplicity of myth and the prospect of vengeance offer special comforts in a time of mass murder" (Lawrence/Jewett 16), Moore has a critical viewpoint of the President's cowboy rhetoric. His Bush is more of a Western villain or gunslinger.

> Yet the image of the cowboy has always been a two-sided coin. While some think of him as the tough, virtuous, straight-talking hero of the American West, others prefer to image him as a lawless, wild, shoot-'em up villain that spread mayhem and chaos along the frontier. (Slatta 8)

This depiction creates a strong counterstatement to the predominantly uncritical depiction of the President and his "cowboy politics" in mainstream U.S. media. The President is reenacting frontier justice in a democratic nation, unable to handle the complexities of international affairs in an appropriate manner.

Other ways Moore uses to deconstruct the President's public image are deliberately funny. The "leisure time president" enjoying his ranch appears more concerned with armadillos than with the well-being of his country. Once more, Moore's sarcastic comments and the selective editing create the impression that George W. Bush is not interested in politics at all. Depicting Bush at a desk, at meetings, or at prayer would not have fit the picture Moore wants us to have of him. After September 11, 2001 however, the President appeared to be more actively involved in politics. Moore argues, however, that Bush insidiously exploited the fears of the population for his own purposes. Moore repeatedly paints a black-and-white picture of a complex situation: for him, Bush is a clear-cut imperialist, exploiting the powers of his office in order to invade a "peaceful" country in which a lot of money can be made by the military industry and the oil industry. Carefully placed archival material, like Bush's comment at a White House dinner party, "some call you the elite, I call you my basis," furthers Moore's argument that the President is a lobbyist.

The President's remark that U.S. soldiers "died for a just cause" by "defending freedom" might by now appear as the epitome of hypocrisy. For Moore, these soldiers died a senseless death in an unnecessary war; the noble causes of spreading democracy and freedom in the Middle East are empty shells used to disguise the true intentions for invading Iraq. However, Moore's position misses the complexities of international politics. As mentioned earlier, Moore does not leave any room for ambiguities and he does not present to the viewers of *Fahrenheit 9/11* any socio-political complexities. He aims at an emotional response. Simple formulas like the impossibility for the average American to achieve the American Dream or the power elite's straying from American values are topics with which the audience can easily identify on an emotional level. In this vein, Moore unmasks the mainstream media's staging of the scene of Bush holding a speech in front of a "United We Stand" banner, talking about the war as necessary to save civilization itself to be deeply propagandistic.

As we know, *Fahrenheit 9/11* did not remove George W. Bush from the White House. For a large part, the movie was preaching to the converted—or those about to convert anyway. It is improbable that many of those who supported President Bush decided to watch Moore's film. Even if they did see it, it is an illusion to believe that they left the movie theater as converted Bush haters. I agree with Verena Grünefeld that it would be rather naïve to believe that a/any film can decide America's political future and to accuse Michael Moore of failing to achieve his goal by choosing the wrong strategies (cf. 220). What Moore did achieve is that people went to the movie theaters to see *Fahrenheit 9/11*; until today it is the highest grossing documentary of all times.[15] Moore has created a critical image of the President, questioning his trustworthiness and his defense of American interests and ideals.

6. The Truth Is Out There: *Fahrenheit 9/11* as a Counter-Discourse to the Medial Consent

> Come you masters of war
> You that build all the guns
> You that build the death planes
> You that build the big bombs
> You that hide behind walls
> You that hide behind desks
> I just want you to know
> I can see through your masks
> —Bob Dylan, "Masters of War"

Fahrenheit 9/11 primarily serves as a counter-discourse to the prevalent depiction of President Bush and the war in Iraq in the American news media. In the aftermath of September 11, 2001 and in the wake of the Iraq War, American media were characterized by patriotism on display and a clearly expressed pro-American point of view. Patriotism in this case meant not to scrutinize the war or anything concerned with it. Carter and Barringer write in a *New York Times* article entitled "In Patriotic Time, Dissent Is Muted" that "the surge of national pride that has swept the country after the terrorist attacks on Sept. 11 has sparked the beginnings of a new, more difficult debate over the balance among national security, free speech and patriotism." Television plays a crucial role in the way we perceive reality and imagine our community. In the case of September 11 and its socio-political aftermath, mainstream American news

---

[15] The lifetime grossing of *Fahrenheit 9/11* is $ 119,194,771 and Moore's other documentaries are also featured in the Top 10 of the highest grossing documentaries ever (cf. http://www.boxofficemojo.com/genres/chart/?id=documentary.htm).

media chiefly depicted a community standing united behind the President and his politics. The images of the war in Iraq were often commented on by embedded journalists; the government forbade TV channels to show coffins in the news or other programs. What Moore does in *Fahrenheit 9/11* is to question and criticize this medial consent. His documentary's title alludes to Ray Bradbury's novel *Fahrenheit 451*, a sinister vision of the future United States as a totalitarian nation where books are abandoned, and instead, television controls the public's mind. Moore even adapted the novel's subtitle "the temperature where books burn" into *Fahrenheit 9/11's* tagline: "The temperature when freedom burns." The allusion is provocative, and this is, according to a *New York Times* article, exactly what the *enfant terrible* Moore wants: he aims at presenting "a partisan rallying cry, an angry polemic, a muckraking inquisition into the use and abuse of power" (Scott). Familiar images of the President or news reports are placed in a new context in order to create a critical view of the way the war was presented to the American public. Instead of providing the viewership with an image of a victorious U.S. Army, the film uses footage that highlights the war's atrociousness and chaos as a distinct counter-discourse to the medial consent.

In *Fahrenheit 9/11* Moore draws a parallel to the Vietnam War. The documentary features a clip of a news anchorman interpreting the war in Iraq as "another Vietnam." The idea of seeing the war in Iraq as a second Vietnam appears, on the one hand, quite exaggerated[16], but, on the other hand, shows how present the nightmare of defeat and chaos still is. Many Americans never managed to overcome the "Vietnam Syndrome."[17] Indeed, the Vietnam War has raised many questions concerning national identity and political conformity. As mentioned above, documentaries were a popular medium during the Vietnam War era, producing a counter-discourse to the one-sided depiction of the war by the media and the President. To strengthen his film's emotional appeal, Moore alludes to this recent period of American history that presumably many viewers of his film either remember personally or have heard about. Until today, the Vietnam War remains America's most controversially discussed war, leaving the nation deeply divided.

To further stress parallels, *Fahrenheit 9/11* features a sequence of recruiting new soldiers in the poorer parts of Moore's hometown, Flint, Michigan. Here the film switches into an interactive mode, portraying Moore as an average American who has not forgotten where he comes from: a successful filmmaker, he is still concerned about the wellbeing of people living in his home town. In Flint, with an unemployment rate of 17%, a career in the military often appears to be the only way to escape poverty and unemployment. The military promises education, the basis of the American Dream of upward mobility. Moore interviews a group of African Americans (an ethnic group that is often presented in his movies as oppressed); almost every member of this group has a family member employed by the military. Those images might recall the sit-

---

[16] For a comparison of the Iraq and Vietnam Wars, cf. *Iraq and Vietnam: Differences, Similarities, and Insights* by Jeffery Record and W. Andrew Terrill.

[17] This term was coined in the 1980s by Ronald Reagan.

uation during the Vietnam War, when many African Americans, although not accepted as citizens with equal rights, had to fight in Vietnam. Similar to their situation, the soldiers in Iraq are fighting for dreams that will never come true for most of them. Moore furthermore supports his thesis by showing two Marines recruiting poor people by promising them to fulfill their dreams. In buddy talk manner they tell them that the best way to make money is discipline, and the only way to learn discipline is to join the U.S. Marine Corps. Most of the soldiers serving in Iraq see the military as the only way to education—the basis of opportunities. The next sequence shows images of dead and injured soldiers or civilians as well as images of U.S. soldiers torturing prisoners of war. This part of *Fahrenheit 9/11* combines several messages concerning the war and its real outcome. The war is not like a computer game, although U.S. Army television commercials may present it as being like one. There is no reboot button in order to start over again. In the same way that the Vietnam War was not the imagined Western adventure, the Iraq war has disillusioned many of the interviewed soldiers. The ambivalence of showing the soldiers as victims and victimizers highlights that they increasingly became frustrated living in an alien culture where they are seen as intruders and not liberators. As in the 1970s and 1980s, the veterans are left behind by the government; many of them are suffering from post-traumatic stress disorder or physical disabilities. By using footage not previously seen of dead soldiers/civilians and juxtaposing them with the pro-war depiction of the American news media, Moore challenges the official narration of the war. His documentary makes images of U.S. casualties accessible to a large number of people. The mainstream mass media of a nominally free and democratic country, he suggests, have failed to provide their audiences with the truth about the war in Iraq. Moore implicates them in the strategy of abusing the traumatic events of September 11, 2001 to gain support for a war. America was attacked by terrorists and at the time it would have been considered unpatriotic or un-American to question the accuracy of President Bush's conclusion and his decision to strike back. Moore directly accuses the media of misleading the nation into blind support for an unnecessary war by holding back the truth out of a false sense of patriotism.

The last part of *Fahrenheit 9/11* depicts ordinary Americans as victims of Bush's politics. Primarily poor people or ethnic minorities are presented as the first to defend freedom in times of war. As mentioned above, Moore confronted politicians about enlisting their children in the Army; none of them was willing to do so. This scene questions the status of the United States as a nation in which "all men are created equal." Moore's narration of nation implies that the U.S.A. is not a country with equal opportunities—instead he constructs the image of a few privileged who are exploiting a large mass of people by giving false promises. Interrupting the scene of politicians unwilling to send their own children into war with shots of Bush and Rumsfeld talking about weapons of mass destruction in Iraq makes the President and the Defense Secretary appear untrustworthy. Moore accuses not only politicians, but also the media, which did not fulfill their duty of furnishing the public with accurate information.

While the credits are rolling, we see how the politicians who appear in the prologue take off their microphones and step away from the TV cameras. This image might signify that the politicians—in their public masks—have succeeded in leading the country into a senseless war by exploiting the fears and hopes of Americans, or else that Moore has achieved his aim of unmasking "the masters of war." His documentary has approached the power elites with skepticism and disrespect in order to create a counter-discourse to the prevalent depiction of them in the mainstream media. The people who are supposed to represent America and its values beyond national borders have disguised their real intentions behind medial masks, implies Moore. He reemphasizes this message by accompanying the last sequence with Bush's famous "fool me once, but you can't fool me twice" quotation. The Bush administration has fooled the American nation once, but Moore hopes that Americans will not be fooled another time. Toward this goal has scrutinized official representations, revealing them to be based on private interests.

7. Conclusion

Michael Moore concludes *Fahrenheit 9/11* by quoting from George Orwell's *1984*:

> It is not a matter of whether the war is not real, or if it is, victory is not possible. The war is not meant to be won, it's meant to be continuous. A hierarchical society is only possible on the basis of poverty and ignorance. This new version is the past and no different past can ever have existed.

Orwell's international bestseller creates a memorable image of a totalitarian future based on Nazi Germany and the Soviet Union under Stalin. President Bush's public image of a loyal democratic leader has been turned by Moore into that of a president exploiting his fellow citizens for economic gain. Furthermore, the Orwellian allusion and the film's adapted title create an all too sinister vision of the U.S.A. as a future totalitarian state. Moore uses it to leave the audience with a distinct feeling concerning some crucial aspects of America's national identity. But if the United States, in fact, were such a state, Moore would not be able to make a film like *Fahrenheit 9/11*. People who have the inalienable right of freedom of speech do not tend to think much about this right. *Fahrenheit 9/11* wants to encourage its audience to make use of it and to voice criticism. Freedom of speech is the basis of America's self-description and national identity. Blind trust in political leaders is not patriotic. The government is supposed to be of the people, by the people, for the people and, as mentioned, Moore considers himself a moral citizen concerned about the well-being of his country. He must be aware that he alone cannot change society; nonetheless, *Fahrenheit 9/11* provides many thought-provoking impulses. The audience is invited to think in order to change something about the current situation. With his documentary Michael Moore has shown that "it is possible to intervene in the political and cultural construction of truths which, while not guaranteed, nevertheless matter as narratives by which we live" (Williams, qtd. in Grünefeld 70).

Fahrenheit 9/11, despite its frequently personal point of view and polemics, can be viewed as a quite courageous documentary that asks questions which the majority of American news media did not dare to ask at that time—or as *New York Times* journalist A.O. Scott rightly notes, "The film can be seen as an effort to wrest clarity from shock, anger and dismay, and if parts of it seem rash, overstated or muddled, well, so has the national mood." Instead of relying on an unemotional presentation of facts and figures, Moore's narration of nation wants to entertain, emotionalize and agitate his viewers in order to make them aware of important problems. *Fahrenheit 9/11* is far more than a personal vicious attack on President Bush; it is a documentary revealing many critical insights into questions of national identity, encouraging people to think critically about an imagined community and its slogan, "united we stand".

Works Cited

Anderson, Benedict. "Introduction." *Imagined Communities: Reflections on the Origins and Spread of Nationalism.* Revised Edition. London: Verso, 1983. 1-7.

Bignell, Jonathan. *Media Semiotics: An Introduction.* Second Edition. Manchester: Manchester UP, 2002.

Bruzzi, Stella. "The President and the Image." *New Documentary: A Critical Introduction.* New York: Routledge, 2006. 176-182.

Burton-Carvajal, Julianne, ed. *The Social Documentary in Latin America.* Pittsburgh: U of Pittsburgh P, 1990.

Carter, Bill & Felicity Barringer. "In Patriotic Time, Dissent Is Muted." *New York Times* 28 September 2001. http://www.nytimes.com/2001/09/28/business/media/28TUBE.html?scp=1&sq=In%20patriotic%20times,%dissent%20muted&st=cse.

Corner, John. *The Art of Record: A Critical Introduction to Documentary.* Manchester: Manchester UP, 1996.

Cuddon, J.A. *The Penguin Dictionary of Literary Terms and Literary Theory.* New York: Penguin Group, 1998.

Frith, Simon. "Music and Identity." *Questions of Cultural Identity.* Ed. Stuart Hall and Paul du Gay. London: Sage, 1996. 140.

Grünefeld, Verena. *Dokumentarfilm Populär: Michael Moore und seine Darstellung der amerikanischen Gesellschaft.* Frankfurt: Campus Verlag, 2009.

Jewett, Robert, and John Shelton Lawrence. "The American Monomyth in a New Century." *The Myth of the American Superhero.* Michigan: William B. Eerdmans Publishing Company, 2002. 3-18 .

Kasindorf, Martin & Judy Keen. "*Fahrenheit 9/11*: Will It Change Any Voter's Mind?" *USA Today* 24 June 2004. http://www.usatoday.com/news/politicselections/nation/president/2004-06-24-fahrenheit-cover_x.htm.

McEnteer, James. *Shooting the Truth: The Rise of American Political Documentaries.* Westport: Praeger Publishers, 2006. xvi.

Moritz, Marguerite. "United We Stand: The Constructed Realities of 9/11." *Representing Realities: Essays on American Literature, Art and Culture.* Ed. Beverly Maeder. Swiss Papers in English Language, Volume 16. Tübingen: Gunter Narr Verlag, 2003. 189-201.

Nichols, Bill. *Representing Reality: Issues and Concepts in Documentaries.* Bloomington: Indiana UP, 1991.

Puig, Claudia. "Put Politics Aside: *Fahrenheit 9/11* Will Entertain." *USA Today* 23 June 2004. <http://www.usatoday.com/life/movies/reviews/2004-06-23-fahrenheit_x.htm>.

Record, Jeffrey & W. Andrew Terrill. *Iraq and Vietnam: Differences, Similarities, and Insights.* San Francisco: U of the Pacific P, 2004.

Renov, Michael, ed. *Theorizing Documentary.* New York: Routledge, 1993.

Scott, A.O. "Unruly Scorn Leaves Room for Restraint, but not a lot." *New York Times* 23 June 2004. http://query.nytimes.com/gst/fullpage.html?res=9C0DE5DE1039F930A15755 C0A9629C8B63.

Simpson David. "Introduction: Taking Time." *9/11: The Culture of Commemoration.* Chicago: U of Chicago P, 2006. 1-21.

Singer, Peter. "The Ethics of George W. Bush." *The President of Good and Evil: Questioning the Ethics of George W. Bush.* New York: Plume/Penguin Group, 2004.

Slatta, Richard W. "Cowboy Life & Legend." *Cowboy—The Illustrated History.* Ed. J.E. Sigler. New York: Sterling, 2006. 6-8.

Strauss, Gary. "9/11 Documents a Mother's Grief." *USA Today* 28 June 2004. http://www.usatoday.com/life/movies/news/2004-06-28-fahrenheit-lipscomb_x.htm.

Tobias, Michael, ed. *The Search for Reality: The Art of Documentary Film-Making.* Ann Arbor: Braun-Brumfield, 1998.

Turan, Kenneth. "*Fahrenheit 9/11*: Michael Moore's Partisan yet Provocative Film Commands Attention." *Los Angeles Times* 23 June 2004. http://www.calendarlive.com/movies/reviews/cl-et-turan23jun23,2,2756103.story?coll=cl-movies-top-right.

Vejdovsky, Boris. "Nine-Eleven-Two-Thousand-And-One: The Morning After and the Melancholy Streets of Manhattan." *Representing Realities: Essays on American Literature, Art and Culture.* Ed. Beverly Maeder. Swiss Papers in English Language, Volume 16. Tübingen: Gunter Narr Verlag, 2003.

Vorländer, Hans. "Reaktionen auf den 11. September 2001." *Länderbericht USA.* Ed. Lösche, Peter & Hans Dietrich von Löffelholz. Bonn: Bundeszentrale für Politische Bildung, 2004. 294.

Zinn, Howard. "A People's War?" *A People's History of the United States: 1492-Present.* Twentieth Anniversary Edition. New York: HarperCollins Publishers, 1999. 407-42.

Filmography

An Inconvenient Truth. Dir. Davis Guggenheim. U.S.A., 2006.

Bowling for Columbine. Dir. Michael Moore. Canada, U.S.A., Germany, 2002.

Fahrenheit 9/11. Dir. Michael Moore. U.S.A., 2004.

Roger & Me. Dir. Michael Moore. U.S.A., 1989.

M and M's for Everyone: Michael Moore, Steven Greenstreet, and Identity in Utah Valley

CHRIS LIPPARD

Resumen

La primera parte de este ensayo se ocupa del exitoso documental *Fahrenheit 9/11* (2004) dirigido por Michael Moore. Nuestro análisis se realiza en el contexto de las actuales tendencias de las películas documentales estadounidenses y del estado de ánimo post-11 de Septiembre. Siguiendo esta línea, en la primera parte, investigamos la forma en que el film cuestiona la noción de una identidad estadounidense y proponemos lugares que sustentan y, además, otros que socavan un significado más progresista y productivo de los EE.UU. Finalmente, llegamos a la conclusión de que el trabajo de Moore pone de relieve su propia identidad como cineasta. La segunda parte de este trabajo se centra en la manera como *This Divided State* (2005) de Steven Greenstreet presenta la controversia suscitada por la visita de Moore al centro conservador de Orem, en Utah. Aunque el título de la película de Greenstreet se refiere, evidentemente, más a Utah, la película, sin lugar a dudas, se sirve de este estado para dar cuenta de las luchas por la identidad a nivel nacional. Así nos muestra de qué manera los individuos utilizan diversos artefactos y símbolos de la identidad estadounidense para construir su propia relación con el estado y la nación. Recurriendo a estrategias diferentes de las de la película de Moore, *This Divided State* desafía a su audiencia a cuestionar los conceptos tradicionales sobre la identidad.

While it is true that the term 'America'—in its guise as 'the United States'—is commonly and inevitably a contested term, there are times at which the stakes are higher than at others. The events of September 11, 2001 have certainly provoked such a period. Contestation of the image of America, of how the nation can be re-imagined, has been fierce. This is true certainly of sites, whether literal or intellectual/imagined, that are very directly tied to the events of that day, but also to those which might seem more remote. Thus, the control of what kind of ideas and images of America may be available at the memorial-site of the erstwhile Twin Towers has provoked one organization (the Drawing Center) to pull out of its planned home, and another (the International Freedom Center)—having already severely circumscribed its proposed activ-

ities in the face of opposition to anything which might be perceived as in any way critical of U.S. policy—to be evicted.[1] Meanwhile, in the school history textbook market,
debate was joined about the appropriateness or otherwise of including in descriptions
of 9/11 material on the ways in which American policy might have influenced the attack. Is there room for debate and analysis, or is any such thing now deemed anti-
American?[2] The re-emergent anti-intellectual trend in the defining of the American nation can be discerned too in areas less directly related to 9/11: in the desire to recall
moments in American history as so intimately a part of the meaning of the country as
to be immune from critical analysis. In a September 2005 issue of *The Nation*, under
the by-line, "Patriotic Bore," Daniel Lazare, reviewing several new books on the
founding of the American nation, concludes that "[l]iberal historians have succumbed
to the country's celebratory mood, praising an American Revolution that never was"
(31). His argument is that while they might cite somewhat different evidence for their
claims, liberal historians are as prone as their more conservative peers to write history
that privileges the celebration of America as a great country, and consequently ignores
the complexity, the messiness of history: for example the fact that the indigenous population—not to mention the slaves—commonly supported the British as a defense
against land-hungry, and sometimes blood-thirsty, settlers. Of course this celebration
of nation is part-and-parcel of any country's self-definition, an element in the cultural
and political negotiation of what a nation stands for. Filmmaker Michael Moore has
been a part of this debate for some time and had previously re-envisaged the U.S. as
The Big One: a name more reflective, he argues in his 1997 film of that title, of the
role and disposition of the country in the world than is the bland description, 'United
States.'

My purpose in this essay is to discuss how notions of identity—and also, inevitably, notions of the nation—were brought up by Michael Moore's visit to Utah Valley
State College just before the 2004 Presidential election as portrayed—or reimagined—
in Steven Greenstreet's film, *This Divided State* (2005).[3] But first a few words about
the state of American documentary with regard to its depiction of nation. The success
of documentaries at the U.S. box office in 2004 pleased film critics and many also
noted the especial prominence of political documentaries.[4] The chief exhibit here is
Michael Moore's *Fahrenheit 9/11* (2004), which took in more money at the U.S. box-
office than any previous documentary. Moore's film is evidently a rallying-cry to

---

[1] Cf. Dunlap for details of these events, and Mandell for an insightful analysis of their
    implications.

[2] The clearest attempt to provide such an analysis of American policy in relation to 9/11 is
    Foner's *Give Me Liberty!* Cf. both "Teaching 9/11" articles by Wiener for further discus-
    sion of the issues at stake.

[3] Utah Valley State College became Utah Valley University in July 2008.

[4] Cf. Arthur and other articles from the same special edition of *Cineaste*, "Political Docu-
    mentary in America Today," which includes the comments of eleven academics and media
    specialists on this phenomenon.

those in the U.S. (and to a less clear extent those outside) for whom the Bush administration's agenda is anathema, and one of its key rhetorical tropes, as so often in
American political discourse, is to argue that this government is indeed un-American—that it has betrayed American values and positioned the country as standing for
something which it has not and indeed does not—since the policies pursued are self-
serving and destructive of the country's political traditions and long-term interests.
These latter interests are to be distinguished from those of a wealthy corporate elite for
whose benefit the war abroad is engaged and civil liberties at home abrogated. For me,
joining the line around the block and watching the film on opening night in Salt Lake
City, as for others throughout the country unenamored of the George W. Bush administration, this was much less a documenting experience than an act of solidarity and
comfort: an attempt to be, at least briefly, in the majority, joining with others to
register opposition to Washington. Most of us were glad that Moore's film was there
to rally around even if some of us disagreed with some of his politics, or, at least,
several of his rhetorical strategies.

Various reasons have been suggested for the relative prominence of the documentary in U.S. cinemas in recent years. Certainly the status of the form has risen,
leading to increased advertising budgets and improved distribution from companies
such as New Yorker and Sony Picture Classics. From 1996 to 2002, an average of fif-
teen documentaries per year opened on U.S. screens, but by 2004 that figure had
reached fifty, with non-studio distributors taking the lead. *Fahrenheit 9/11* opened in
an impressive 868 theaters with huge takings of $25,115 per theater average.[5] In ad-
dition both critics' and readers' polls in film magazines over the last couple of years
have started to feature more documentaries.[6] It is harder, of course, to say why this is
happening, how long the trend will last, and finally, how many of these films are, in a
broad or narrow sense, part of a political debate that seeks to define America and its
values. New technologies have helped, while to some extent the phenomenon may be
tied to the rise of reality television and the demise of real news—embedded reporters
and a lack of political analysis. The notion that the country was divided by the debacle
of the 2000 election and subsequent events, thus promoting the appearance of oppo-
sitional social activist agendas on the screen is certainly tenable—thus much of the
best of American documentary since September 11 has been rhetorically opposed to

---

[5] A convenient place to access box-office analysis is at <http://www.hollywood.com>. More
specifically, cf. Bowen's comments on *Fahrenheit 9/11*. Paul Arthur also analyzes these
figures.

[6] Jonathan Rosenbaum, probably the most academically respected of U.S. newspaper critics,
comments that 2004 "was such a strong year for documentaries, in overall quality and public reception, that I easily could come up with a top ten list devoted exclusively to them."
However, only *March of the Penguins*, apparently a non-political documentary, though
claimed on the right as an argument for 'family values,' appears in the 2005 *Film Comment*
readers' poll.

Bush's assertion that "either you are with us or you are with the terrorists" (Bush).[7] Rather than emphasizing an axis of evil—expanded after the event from Wahhabi-influenced Islamic fundamentalism, to include a diverse group of (selected) secular Arab dictators, shi'i theocracy and unreconstituted communists, with the whiff of re-newed social agendas in Latin America not so far off—post-9/11 documentaries, while often acknowledging the al-Qaeda threat, foreground division at home: corporations bilking their employees out of pension-funds (Enron, World Com, the airlines), and government lying and distorting to justify its ambition (weapons of mass destruction, Saddam's supposed links with al-Qaeda, the fabricated Niger uranium deal and Valerie Plame).[8]

These films, like most documentaries, use a wide range of techniques and a va-riety of different materials in order to build their cases/tell their stories—ominous background music, witty animations and slow motion are prominent but the most im-mediately striking thing about many of them is their dependence on the personality of the filmmaker or narrator to entertain and sustain momentum. Moore's films, like those of Judith Hefland and 2004 Sundance winner, *The Corporation* fit this model. It often leads to the depiction of a personal questing or testing as in, say, *Supersize Me*, in which Morgan Spurlock shows that, somewhat unsurprisingly perhaps, eating at McDonald's all the time is really bad for you.

For me the most effective political documents remain films such as Lourdes Portillo's examination of the disappearances and murders of female employees of Juarez *maquiladoras* in *Señorita Extraviada* (2001), a film which works for many crit-ical audiences partly because, while the revelation of ineptitudes and cover-ups is telling and unequivocal, not all pieces of the puzzle are there to be explained. Additionally, the exploitative actions of the multi-nationally owned plants, though remaining in the background, still tower over the film, locating the critique of one problem within the larger one of corporate deregulation and the combination of trade laws and poverty to disempower large numbers of people. Perhaps the most exciting political film I have seen from the U.S. from the early 2000s is Travis Wilkerson's *An Injury to One* (2001), a film balanced delicately between documentary and experi-mental poles, as it reveals the brutal silencing of union organizers and the abuse of Butte, Montana by the Anaconda copper mining company over many years. Labor songs in which the words appear on screen and music is played but no voices heard, potently illustrate the struggle of the miners, and the recordings of lengths, depths,

---

[7] President Bush's address to the Joint session of Congress and the American People on September 20, 2001 was widely reported in newspapers across the world. Cf. Bumiller for the *New York Times* report.

[8] Relevant films here include Robert Greenwald's series *Unprecedented: The 2000 Presi-dential Election, Uncovered: The Whole Truth about the Iraq War, Unconstitutional: The War on Our Civil Liberties*, and *Outfoxed: Rupert Murdoch's War on Journalism*, as well as *The Corporation, Enron: The Smartest Guys in the Room, Why We Fight*, and *The Fog of War*.

costs and quantities, plus diary excerpts from Dashiell Hammett in his Pinkerton days, advance the narrative in a formally-engaging and consciousness-building manner. Portillo and Wilkerson remain firmly absent from their films. This is not to say, of course, that their attitude to their material or ideological positions are hidden or de-nied—far from it—but their individual personalities are unimportant to the text. The first-person political documentaries of Moore and Hefland, following in the tradition of the somewhat less political work of Werner Herzog and Ross McElwee, depend partly, as I have suggested, on the persona of the filmmaker: vibrant, outgoing, de-termined. While Hefland's work has been narrowly focused, single-issue advocacy, Moore, especially since *Fahrenheit 9/11*, has become a lightning-rod for political dis-sent—and the reimagining of an America in which this matters. He is unmistakable: dressed down in jeans and a baseball cap, unshaven, overweight, seemingly without pretense, his roots in and allegiance to the working-class fundamental to his visual rhetoric. His fearless, unembarrassable pursuit of CEOs and members of Congress is thus enhanced by a choice of clothing that contrasts so sharply with theirs. Perhaps this is why the opening salvos of *Fahrenheit 9/11* that show the Bush team being wiped, smoothed and powdered in preparation for the cameras both works and yet proves dis-concerting. Of course politicians are dolled-up for the camera. When Paul Wolfowitz, in mock-impatience with his handlers, licks his comb, then pulls it through his hair, the audience gasps in horror or feels superior. But we must wonder: one, why this action is so different from all the other means of behind-the-scenes grooming?—and, two, while we should care a lot about much that Wolfowitz instigates, who gives a damn about his personal hygiene? It's a cheap-shot, without political relevance: humor at the expense of substance.[9]

I feel rather the same way about one of the film's best-known jibes, the image of Bush, having been told of the attack on the Twin Towers while reading *My Pet Goat* with a class of young school-children, continuing to sit there for (up to) seven min-utes.[10] Although celebrated as a damning comment on the President's incompetence by several reviewers, including B. Ruby Rich in *Sight and Sound*,[11] one wonders just what he could or should have done at that moment. Now, Moore's film, of course, makes many much more effective critiques of government policy, as when, for exam-ple, he follows military recruiters trying to snare poor, mostly non-white youth at a downscale shopping mall or, more explicitly, as he targets the business-connections between the 'House of Bush' and the 'House of Saud.' Here Moore inserts a series of shots of Bush senior and junior, Cheney, Rumsfeld, Powell, Rice *et cetera* squeezing the hands of and metaphorically raising a glass to the Saudi royal rulers. The montage

---

[9] Ella Taylor makes a similar point in her thoughtful *LA Weekly* review, "Burning Bush."

[10] The actual length of time was probably somewhat less. It is measured as approximately five minutes in Alan Peterson's right-wing critique of Moore's film, *Fahrenhype 9/11*.

[11] For example, Mark Cousins, also in *Sight and Sound*, Roger Ebert in the *Chicago Sun-Times*, Peter Bradshaw in *The Guardian*, Kenneth Turan in the *Los Angeles Times*, Ella Taylor in the *LA Weekly*, and Damon Wise in *Empire* online.

is accompanied by REM's "Smiling, Happy People" and concludes, abruptly, with footage of a public beheading in Jeddah—it takes two swings of the sword. At one point, watching over the permanent U.S. guard outside the Saudi embassy in DC, Moore is approached by the police, and, in his usual manner, attempts to engage an officer in conversation: "Are they giving you any trouble, the Saudis?" he inquires. "No comment," replies the cop. To which, Moore, "I'll take that as a 'Yes.'" It's a wonderful comic moment in part because it flies in the face of impartial analysis: Moore knows what he is doing in going for this laugh, and he cuts the grounds out from underneath possible critique—we all know that objectivity is impossible, subjectivity inevitable. As Errol Morris points out: "Movies are movies [they are neither true nor false]" (qtd. in Arthur 20). Still, if you are picking at power's secrets and lies, the relation to truth seems to matter—after all, the fate of nations is at stake.

Images of race have been especially important and contentious in defining many American nations and there are moments at which racial and national stereotyping in *Fahrenheit 9/11* seem close to smugness—despite the desire to speak truth to power. Moore strays into somewhat racist imagery in his 'kow-towing to the Saudis' montage: the danger of fueling anti-Arab sentiment in the U.S. ignored.[12] Derogatory, stereotypical images of other nations are deployed again, later in the film, in Moore's pastiche of Bush's 'coalition of the willing': Palau and Costa Rica are proclaimed first—intoned in a portentously drawn-out manner, accompanied by images of garlanded dancers and a horse and cart respectively, mocking their military potential. Next up is Iceland (Vikings), Romania (vampires), Morocco (musicians, snakes, monkeys), and the Netherlands (pot-smoking kids). In between, as Moore emphasizes how few troops this group brings to the operation, he inserts additional images of underdevelopment—most starkly a high angle of an (apparently African) woman working at a grinding stone beside a mud hut. This rhetoric of insignificance plays into another national stereotype and also a key issue to have surfaced since 9/11: U.S. ignorance of the rest of the world. How much does it matter that so many Americans know so little about other countries and people? To certain officials in the government and the FBI, not a lot—carrying forward a policy or investigation is what counts, not understanding why people might feel and act as they do.[13] We must assume that Moore would not agree, but his film's visual rhetoric suggests otherwise, arguing against an informed foreign policy and greater cultural sensitivity. In American political documentary, one fine place to look at this issue is in Petra Eperlein and Michael Tucker's *Gunner Palace* (also 2004), where we see American troops making fun of the efforts of Iraqis to speak English, and one parading around with basketball-netting on his head in impersonation of an archetypal imam. Another place, more encouragingly perhaps, is Jahane Noujaim's *Control Room*

---

[12] For an analysis of how U.S. perceptions of Saudi Arabia have changed since 9/11, cf. Gresh.

[13] John Simmons's Associated Press report quotes Executive Assistant Director Gary Bald as saying "You need leadership. You don't need subject matter expertise." Cf. also David Johnson's report on the possible consequences of this thinking.

(2004) on al-Jazeera, in which U.S. marine, Lieutenant Josh Rushing, increasingly thoughtfully, does value the qualities of understanding and information, and struggles to fit them into his mission as PR man for the invasion of Iraq.[14]

I will return to some of the above issues as I discuss *This Divided State*—the state in question is Utah, but the term 'state' is deliberately ambiguous here. On the one hand, Utah is an exception—less divided, for example, than any other state in the union in its support for Bush over Kerry in 2004. Greenstreet's film, however, shows that, in fact, Utah is exemplary of issues at debate throughout the *nation*-state. Even in what one character in the film refers to as the most conservative city (Orem) in the most conservative county (Utah county) in the most conservative state (Utah) in the nation, there is a strong divide. This is not simply a party political debate or one for or against Bush and the war in Iraq; it is also one about the role of a college of higher education—an institution, indeed, planning to introduce graduate programs and hoping to become a full-fledged university. Should such a facility reflect the dominant values of the community in which it sits? Or is the overriding imperative that of intellectual inquiry and the free exchange of ideas? There is little question, I think, of director Greenstreet's stance on whether Michael Moore should have been allowed to speak at the college—he should have been—or that Greenstreet is more sympathetic to Moore's message than to that of slick conservative Fox television talk-show host, Sean Hannity, who ended up speaking at Utah Valley State the week before Moore. Still, his film generally avoids the pitfalls of *Fahrenheit 9/11* as it plunges into the divide.

The main players are as follows. All-American students Jim Bassi and Joe Vogel, President and vice-President of the Student Union, have invited Moore: the pair make a photogenic team of ex-missionaries for the Mormon church, one tall and the other short, clean-cut and well-spoken. There are several interviews with Bassi; in the most featured he wears sports shorts and a sweat-shirt as he toys with the basketball that sits on his lap. In the opposite corner is Kay Anderson, a member of the community who emphasizes that Orem is, as indeed it proclaims on the sign as you enter the town—and the film—"Family city, U.S.A." Greenstreet follows this image with those of a crossing-guard, fireworks, the flag, mountains, billboards advertising missionary accessories, and the Freedom car-wash, and Mormons walking through leafy fall streets to church. We see Bush/Cheney signs, dominant in a county where registered Republicans outnumber Democrats by twelve to one. But Greenstreet also slips in a shot of the closed Geneva Steel plant, a reminder that the ills of American industry have affected Utah County too. Such family-values must be preserved, Anderson believes, by protecting Orem from outside influences so that it may remain a sanctum of clean-living and responsibility in a world plunged into drug-abuse and disrespect. He offers to write the school a check for a considerable sum if it agrees to cancel Moore's

---

[14] Rushing's openness led, once *Control Room* was released, to his being ordered not to give further interviews. He was transferred to the Marine Corps Motion Picture and Television office in Los Angeles and left the Marines in October 2004. In September 2005, he accepted an offer to become a journalist for the English language al-Jazeera International.

invitation. We also see a lot from faculty—apparently united in their support of Moore's right to speak, and students: more divided.[15] Greenstreet, raised as a Mormon and a student at the LDS-sponsored Brigham Young University at the time he began work on the film, does not appear on camera himself.

The furore surrounding Moore's visit is in fact several times presented as a great thing in itself—an apathetic student body is suddenly energized and engaged. We see one open discussion forum in which a Togolese student—named for Ephraim, one of the Mormon prophets—temporarily silences the anti-Moore students as he asks them to learn, from restrictions abroad, the value of the freedom of speech for which America should stand. UVSC President and faculty are more concerned with the institution of the College than with the nation in their defense of free speech and civil debate.[16] If Moore's appearance meant their victory in the former case, they were somewhat less successful in providing a forum for the latter. To balance Moore's visit—as student President Bassi insisted had always been a part of the plan—the UVSC Student Union duly invited Sean Hannity to speak on campus the week before. Both Hannity and Moore gave the performances of showmen, scoring points and 'rallying the troops,' as the media attention to the event had perhaps made inevitable. Together they made a mockery of UVSC's desire to stage civilized, intellectual debate. Moore's appearance prominently featured the repetition of chants with the support of guest, Roseanne Barr. Greenstreet does not show her, and arguably lets Moore off somewhat lightly, though he does show the ejection—with Moore's apparent approval—of Nader supporters, angry at his embracing of pro- Iraq war Kerry and the Democrats. Greenstreet in fact devotes slightly more time, around twelve minutes, to Hannity's rhetorically-skilled but excruciating performance. After quizzing a 'self-confessed' liberal student in the audience, Hannity responds to questions from the floor. We see two UVSC professors ask critical questions over a barrage of jeers. The second of these is a young, long-haired Philosophy professor, whom Hannity first pretends to think a student, then, with a withering look, acknowledges as a teacher, before further classifying him, to the audience's delight, as an "angry liberal." At the

---

[15] We do not hear from any non-college affiliated residents of Orem, whatever their political orientation, who support Moore's appearance at UVSC. By making Anderson, plus briefly his wife and some attendees at Hannity's talk, the representative of the town, Greenstreet does somewhat simplify—and, arguably parody—a community that is certainly conservative but not entirely without dissenting voices.

[16] At a public debate in advance of Moore's visit, we see College President, William Sederburg opine that: "As these issues emerge, civility needs to be the key word that we respond to. We need to have civil discourse, we need to learn how to deal with uncomfortable issues. ... and we need to respect a variety of points-of-view which might not necessarily agree with us at all times." Philosophy professor, Pierre Lamarche makes the link to the educational institution more specifically: "Colleges and universities are supposed to be free markets of ideas. It is what they are. That implies that all perspectives, all points-of-view are welcomed and encouraged, including and especially those with which we may disagree strongly. That's what a college is."

same time, the questioner must overcome the mockery of those seated around him, as he asks Hannity to justify "the move to a neo-conservative foreign policy that assumes that democracy can be imposed from the top down." The professor is brave to beard the lion in his den, but Hannity, holding all the cards—the stage, the microphone, the audience, his experience in the limelight—rather than avoiding the question altogether, uses it to make his own point: "What you Liberals do not understand is that 9/11 changed everything." Thus for the right's media commentators, 9/11 is a reason not for changing their own outlook on the world but for depicting alternate views as unacceptable, incomprehensible, irresponsible, or ignorant—in the literal sense of the word. Unlike Ephraim, the Togolese student, the young professor is unable, even temporarily, to silence the hecklers, and, indeed, the complaints continued to roll in after Moore had come and gone. We see Bassi, now in suit-and-tie, checking his messages a couple of days after the event. Sitting in his office, under a painting of George Washington praying beside his horse at Valley Forge in the Revolutionary War, Jim is surrounded by a close-up wedding photograph, another image of himself and Vice President Joe, with their wives, and a few Western Americana tchotchkes. He is engagingly wry in his reactions to the angry messages to which he dutifully listens. His first under-his-breath comment, in response to an irate caller's personal axis-of-evil consisting of Moore, Hitler and Castro—will Jim now invite the other two?—is a mock-response to the Hitler option: "Can't. He's dead." If Moore's and Hannity's supporters find comfort in the presence of their heroes and the like-minded, Jim's consolation is his wife. "I have a wonderful wife," he quietly intones. In fact, Jim's reprieve from Utah County politics, set up by the sense of nation suggested by his office furnishings, involves a couple of American icons: M and M's and blissful marriage. The former are symbolic of the comfort offered by the latter in a shared project with his wife: every October 20th will now be M and M day in memory of Moore's visit, a second anniversary created with his partner. What this brief scene does, I would argue, is construct a distinct series of markers of identity, both personal and national that Bassi can use to counter the intolerance directed at him from the surrounding community.

Films like those I have been discussing form just one strand in the response of popular culture to the U.S. government's attempts to reimagine America. "Air America" attempted to dent the Right's control of radio talk show airwaves, while John Stewart and Stephen Colbert, on cable channel Comedy Central, apparently provide much of the nation's youth with its political information—from a viewpoint distinctly unfriendly to Hannity's vision of America.[17] Bumper stickers pick up on the debate over the officially unified, unofficially fiercely divided state: "One Nation under Surveillance," and the relationship between America and others: "We're making enemies faster than we can kill them." Amongst popular singers, several proved less enamored of President Bush than *Fahrenheit 9/11*-featured Britney Spears. (Surely Bush can't reciprocate her approval of his performance!) Bruce Springsteen has played the game before, and seen

---

[17] Air America ceased broadcasting and filed for bankruptcy at the beginning of 2010, after almost six years on air. Stewart and Colbert, on the other hand, are going strong.

his "Born in the USA" co-opted for patriotic purpose quite different from his original design; inveterate Bush critic Steve Earle, the Dixie Chicks and Iris de Ment who followed up her searingly satiric "Wasteland of the Free" with "I Want My Country Back" all sang out against Bush by arguing that his America was inauthentic, not theirs and not the true America. Perhaps they have created new anthems for future dissent. In the meantime, however, the archetypal song which fights for an America imagined as something fiercely different from that constructed by the wrathful whims of the plutocrats remains "This Land Is Our Land," with which, accompanied by appropriate iconic images of American-ness, Greenstreet chooses to conclude his film.

Woody Guthrie's song is explicitly a reimagining of the nation as *ours*—it has a history in both American documentary and political lampoon—I am thinking here, in the first case, of its coming on the radio, in the Maysles brothers' direct cinema classic, *Salesman*, as the protagonist, the Rabbit, drives around the bizarre mock-Arab city of Opa-Locka, Florida, with its minareted city hall and street names out of *Ali Baba*. The effect is heavily ironic as the Rabbit, unable to find the street he wants, drives in circles, muttering the exotic names to himself. The title of Guthrie's song with its possessive pronoun means that its referent can be easily re-interpreted, and this was the strategy adopted by web-animators, Jib-Jab in their version of "This Land" prior to the 2004 Presidential election: Bush and Kerry alternatively claim that they will win America. "This land will surely vote for me," each is made to sing, until, at the end of the song, they join forces, united in opposition to a native American who sings, "This land *was* my land." Since copyright on the song has apparently expired, one might say it does "belong to you and me."[18] In *This Divided State* it accompanies a mosaic of specifically American images which suggest, perhaps, who *we* are in this instance: the civil rights, labor and women's movements, immigrants and the statue of Liberty, soldiers in and returning from the war against fascism, Paul Robeson, Martin Luther King, and Woody Guthrie himself, plus baseball and the glorious western landscape epitomized by Yosemite's El Capitan, and American suburbia. There are several images redolent of Frank Capra's films about the ordinary man, though we also see images with somewhat different class connotations: the Charleston and a pirouetting dancer, plus the corporate image of a McDonald's clown, and the firing range. The vision of America thus created is quite complex. The total effect, I think, is to form an

---

[18] Ludlow Music, who had the copyright on Guthrie's song, argued that Jib-Jab's video infringed that copyright, while Jib-Jab claimed the copyright had lapsed. For details of the contested copyright, see the Electronic Frontier Foundation's website at http://www.eff.org/cases/jibjab-media-inc-v-ludlow-music-inc.

Bruce Springsteen has since sung the song at the inauguration of President Obama in 2010, evidently in the belief that the new administration would, indeed, redefine the United States in a way more friendly to his and Guthrie's (quite different) political beliefs. It was also performed outside the Wisconsin State Capitol building in Madison in February 2011 in protest against Governor Scott Walker's desire to strip public sector workers of their collective bargaining rights. See http://www.woodyguthrie.org/news.htm for more on the history of the song.

alternative idea of what American identity might mean—an opportunity for individual and collective rights which offers dignity to its people, yet remains open to the outside world while also indicating contrary currents and showing that this is a divided nation-state, as the red and blue illustrates. Lars von Trier created a somewhat similar, though more coherent and more pessimistic, collage of images of famous photographs of the poor as the conclusion of *Dogville*, part of his own ongoing critique of what it is to be American—or perhaps of how we all are. But I will finish with a different touchstone from the world of the narrative feature film. Released at the end of 2005 was George Clooney's *Good Night and Good Luck* about Edward R. Murrow, seemingly very much a plea for a critical media, one that will hold the powerful to account and foster dissent. Evidently the same kind of question regarding a college's independence of its community, might be asked about America's major media-outlets, existing as they do within the 'communities' of big business—Disney, GE Viacom, Clear Channel and the News Corporation.

Works Cited

Arthur, Paul. "Extreme Makeover: The Changing Face of Documentary." *Cineaste* 30.3 (Summer 2005): 18-23.

Bowen, Kit. "*Fahrenheit 9/11* Burns up Competition." Hollywood.com. 27 June 2004. http://www.hollywood.com/news/id/2401410.

Bradshaw, Peter. "Film of the Week: *Fahrenheit 9/11*." *The Guardian* 9 July 2004, Friday Review: 14.

Bumiller, Elisabeth. "Bush Pledges Attack on Afghanistan unless It Surrenders bin Laden now; He Creates Cabinet Post for Security." *New York Times* 21 September 2001: A1.

Bush, George W. "President's Address to a Joint Session of Congress and the American People." United States Capitol Washington D.C. 20 September 2001. http://www.whitehouse.gov/news/releases/2001/09/20010920-8.html.

Cousins, Mark. "Fahrenheit 9/11." *Sight and Sound* 14.9 (September 2004): 60.

Dunlap, David. "Governor Bans Freedom Center at Ground Zero." *New York Times* 29 September 2005: A1.

Ebert, Roger. "*Fahrenheit* Holds Bush's Feet to Fire; Moore's Documentary Gives the President Rope to Hang Himself." *Chicago Sun-Times* 24 June 2004: 47.

Electronic Frontier Foundation. http://www.eff.org/cases/jibjab-media-inc-v-ludlow-music-inc.

Foner, Eric. *Give Me Liberty! An American History*. New York: Norton, 2004.

Gresh, Alain. "Saudi Arabia, a Kingdom Divided." *The Nation* 22 May 2006: 18-22.

Johnson, David. "FBI Counter Terror Officials Lack Experience, Lawyer Says." *New York Times* 20 June 2005: A13.

Lazare, Daniel. "Patriotic Bore." *The Nation* 12 September 2005: 31.

Mandell, Jonathan. "9/11 and 'Inappropriate Art.'" *Gotham Gazette* September 2005: 8-9.

"Political Documentary in America Today." Special issue. *Cineaste* 30.3 (Summer 2005): 29-36.

Rich, B. Ruby. "Mission Improbable." *Sight and Sound* 14.7 (July 2004): 14-16.

Rosenbaum, Jonathan. "Besides *Sideways*." *Chicago Reader* 5 January 2005: 7.

Solomon, John. "Terrorism Expertise not Priority at FBI." Associated Press report 19 June 2005. http://www.usatoday.com/news/washington/2005-06-19-fbi-terrorexpertise_x.html.

Taylor, Ella. "Burning Bush." *LA Weekly* 24 June 2004. http://www.laweekly.com/2004-06-24/film-tv/burning-bush/.

Turan, Kenneth. "No Holds Bared." *Los Angeles Times* 23 June 2004: E1, 6-7.

Wiener, Jon. "Teaching 9/11." *The Nation* 26 September 2005: 25.

———. "Teaching 9/11: What the Textbooks Say." *History News Network* 19 September 2005. http://hnn.us/articles/15810.html.

Wise, Damon. "Fahrenheit 9/11." *Empire* 9 July 2004. http://www.empireonline.com/incine mas/reviewcomplete.asp?FID=10087.

Woody Guthrie—Official Website. http://www.woodyguthrie.org/news.htm.

Filmography

An Injury to One. Dir. Travis Wilkerson. U.S.A., 2002.

Control Room. Dir. Jehane Noujaim. U.S.A., 2004.

Enron: The Smartest Guys in the Room. Dir. Alex Gibney. U.S.A., 2005.

Dogville. Dir. Lars von Trier. Denmark, Sweden, Norway, Finland, UK, France, Germany, Netherlands, 2003.

Fahrenheit 9/11. Dir. Michael Moore. U.S.A., 2004.

Fahrenhype 9/11: Unravelling the Truth about Fahrenheit 9/11 *and Michael Moore*. Dir. Alan Peterson. U.S.A., 2004.

Fog of War. Dir. Errol Morris. U.S.A., 2003.

Good Night and Good Luck. Dir. George Clooney. U.S.A., France, UK, Japan, 2005.

Gunner Palace. Dir. Petra Eperlein and Michael Tucker. U.S.A., 2004.

March of the Penguins. Dir. Luc Jacquet. France, 2005.

Señorita Extraviada. Dir. Loudes Portillo. Mexico, U.S.A., 2001.

Supersize Me. Dir. Morgan Spurlock. U.S.A., 2004.

The Big One. Dir. Michael Moore. U.S.A., UK, 1997.

The Corporation. Dir. Mark Achbar and Jennifer Abbot. Canada, 2003.

This Divided State. Dir. Steven Greenstreet. U.S.A., 2005.

Outfoxed: Rupert Murdoch's War on Journalism. Dir. Robert Greenwald. U.S.A., 2004.

Unconstitutional: The War on Our Civil Liberties. Dir. Robert Greenwald. U.S.A., 2004.

Uncovered: The Whole Truth about the Iraq War. Dir. Robert Greenwald. U.S.A., 2003.

Unprecedented: The 2000 Presidential Election. Dir. Robert Greenwald. U.S.A., 2002.

Why We Fight. Dir. Eugene Jarecki. U.S.A., France, UK, Canada, Denmark, 2005.

Exterminio de la mujer. Representaciones del poder y la estetización de la femineidad en *Señorita extraviada* de Lourdes Portillo

HANNAH F. OSENBERG

Abstract

With *Señorita extraviada* (2001), Lourdes Portillo's homage to the women of Ciudad Juárez, the filmmaker focuses on binary oppositions in terms of gender roles and on structures of repression passed down socially and historically in Mexico, which degrade women, making them a culturally encoded, devalued and objectified component of a patriarchal discourse of power. Through a very particular aesthetic style, the polarity between genders is staged in the film and informs all levels of the filmic discourse. Based on the dichotomy between the public and the private, *Señorita extraviada* explores the underlying socio-cultural structures of the feminicides from the ideologically motivated subject-position of the director. It highlights the role of the woman as an exploited symbolic element and stresses the crucial significance of her body as territory and medium.

The symbolism employed in the film also serves to modify and reduce the potentially sensationalist quality of the images of violence and pain. It marks an ethical approach to the film's topic which takes the form of poetic imagery, emotive experience and reflection, all linked by a particular rhythm of montage. From the vantage point of feminist theory, the manner in which Portillo stages femininity can be read as both performance and critique. On the one hand, her focus on feminine attributes and characteristics condemns the established discourse of power which turns women into passive victims of violence and institutionalized misogyny; on the other, it also highlights femininity as an expression of courage and power.

1. Introducción

Con *Señorita extraviada* (2001) –el homenaje de Lourdes Portillo a las mujeres de Ciudad Juárez–, la cineasta se centra en las oposiciones binarias respecto a los roles de género y en las estructuras de represión que, transmitidos social e históricamente en

México, degradan a la mujer y la convierten en un componente del discurso patriarcal de poder, un componente que ha sido codificado, devaluado y objetivado culturalmente. En todos los niveles de la película, se organiza y se acentúa conscientemente la polaridad entre los géneros utilizando, de manera individual, la estetización como recurso estilístico de la narración fílmica. Sobre la base de la dicotomía entre el discurso público y el discurso privado, el film investiga las estructuras socioculturales que subyacen en el feminicidio desde la postura, ideológicamente motivada, de la directora. Este enfoque resalta el rol de la mujer como elemento simbólico explotado y destaca la importancia crucial de su cuerpo como medio y territorio.

Asimismo, el simbolismo empleado en la película modifica y atenúa el efecto del carácter potencialmente sensacionalista de las imágenes de violencia y sufrimiento. De la misma manera, el simbolismo manifiesta un aproximamiento ético al tema del filme a través de las imágenes poéticas, la experiencia emocional y la reflexión, que se acoplan por medio de un montaje rítmico. Al discutir el acercamiento de Portillo al tema, sobre la base de la teoría feminista, constatamos que la manera en que presenta la feminidad puede ser interpretada igualmente como manifestación y crítica. Su enfoque, orientado a los atributos y características de la mujer, condena, por un lado, el discurso establecido del poder que convierte a las mujeres en víctimas pasivas de la violencia y de la misogonia institucionalizada. Por el otro, también realza la feminidad como una expresión de valentía y poder.

2. Feminicidio y 'desorden' cultural

'Fictional' narratives have become both the site where victims are mourned and the means by which justice can be restored. Cultural producers have filled the vacuum left by state officials who continue either to shun their responsibility or to conceal the guilty. (Volk/Schlotterbeck 54)

En relación con los asesinatos de mujeres cometidos en los últimos años en la frontera mexicano-estadounidense de México, la directora Lourdes Portillo es una de aquellas productoras culturales que –según la cita de Volk y Schlotterbeck–, llenan la laguna de información que dejan las instituciones estatales. Portillo, quien actualmente reside en San Francisco, EE.UU., nació en el Estado de Chihuahua, en el que se encuentra Ciudad Juárez, núcleo urbano donde se cometen los asesinatos que dieron comienzo a *Señorita extraviada* (2001). Es una de las primeras documentalistas[1] que se ha ocupado, desde una perspectiva feminista, de la serie de asesinatos de mujeres que, desde principios de los años noventa, son perpetrados en esta ciudad industrializada, ubicada en medio del desierto entre el 'primer' y el 'tercer' mundo. *Señorita extraviada* es un documental en el que se cuestionan el trasfondo y los modos de representación de este

---

[1] El primer contacto entre ella y los parientes de las víctimas, por un lado, y representantes estatales, por el otro, se efectuó en 1998.

feminicidio.[2] Enfoca la dimensión de complicidad de la sociedad que posibilita la creación de un espacio de impunibilidad en el cual la desprotección de la mujer la convierte en un componente simbólico de la victimización. En este sentido, Segato afirma:

> La tesis feminista fundamental de que los crímenes sexuales no son obra de desviados individuales, enfermos mentales o anomalías sociales, sino expresiones de una estructura simbólica profunda que organiza nuestros actos y nuestras fantasías y les confiere inteligibilidad. En otras palabras: el agresor y la colectividad comparten el imaginario de género, hablan el mismo lenguaje, pueden entenderse. (Segato 6)

La representación de la mujer como víctima de sus condiciones socio-culturales hace que ésta puede ser analizada como portadora de una serie de codificaciones histórico-culturales, que se vinculan al hecho de ser objeto de estrategias de derrocamiento sistemático en las que la violencia ejercida en su cuerpo simboliza el 'desorden' cultural dentro de una red de complejos ritos de apropiación. Heaven expresa:

> La disciplina social y política de las mujeres está efectuada a través de su sexualidad, y con el uso de la violencia sexual como arma de la represión política. Esta violencia está dirigida no sólo a los cuerpos atacados, sino a través de ellos al cuerpo político, de modo que ambas, persona y sociedad, quedan tan desintegradas que se paralizan. (Heaven; cit. en Mora 120)

Para contrarrestar el pretexto del simple móvil sexual, es preciso establecer nuevas perspectivas de análisis que consideren aspectos tales como las relaciones de poder – marcadas por una extrema desigualdad–, el territorio y el género. Al referirse a los asesinatos de Juárez, Sergio de la Mora utiliza el término "guerra," una guerra sin armas convencionales, "una guerra en contra de las mujeres mexicanas jóvenes, pobres y morenas" (118). O, más explícitamente, en contra de aquellas mujeres que emigran de Centroamérica –solas, en la mayoría de los casos– para encontrar trabajo en una de las numerosas maquilas a lo largo de la frontera, o con la esperanza de poder cruzar la frontera hacia los EE.UU.

> Allí se muestra la relación directa que existe entre capital y muerte, entre acumulación y concentración desreguladas y el sacrificio de mujeres pobres, morenas, mestizas, devoradas por la hendija donde se articulan economía monetaria y economía simbólica, control de recursos y poder de muerte. (Segato 3)

Los discursos actuales explicitan que abordar el significado territorial del espacio fronterizo desde la teoría sigue siendo de gran importancia. Con todo, lo que se ha convertido en una necesidad mucho más perentoria es explorar el constructo metafórico derivado de él. Consiguientemente, el discurso fronterizo es interpretado como uno que enfatiza las interacciones y transformaciones étnicas, identitarias y de género, y, como tal, es transferible a cualquiera situación fronteriza binaria (cultural, política). No obs-

---

[2] Según Segato: "Si en el genocidio la construcción retórica del odio al otro conduce a la acción de su eliminación, en el feminicidio la misoginia por detrás del acto es un sentimiento más próximo al de los cazadores por su trofeo: se parece al desprecio por su vida o a la convicción de que el único valor de esa vida radica en su disponibilidad para la apropiación" (13).

tante, en el contexto del feminicidio de Ciudad Juárez, esta interpretación sólo puede ser admitida de manera bastante restringida, puesto que la presencia de las estructuras hegemónicas centralistas, el desarrollo del poder estatal y el regreso a una consciencia nacional y territorial que se enlaza a estas estructuras, apenas pueden ser ocultados en la realidad de la frontera entre México y los EE.UU.

3. El cuerpo como territorio

> Ciudad Juárez, estado de Chihuahua, frontera Norte de México con El Paso, Texas, es un lugar emblemático del sufrimiento de las mujeres. Allí, más que en cualquier otro lugar, se vuelve real el lema 'cuerpo de mujer: peligro de muerte.' (Segato 3)

La forma de violencia que se ejerce contra las mujeres está directamente relacionada con su femineidad y no hay ninguna otra explicación que parezca ser más evidente. Las mujeres son violadas, torturadas y mutiladas. A menudo, tienen los órganos sexuales cercenados o desfigurados y algunas presentan cuchilladas en la espalda. También hay ocasiones en que les cortan el cabello y las atan con los cordones de sus propios zapatos. El asesino se apropia de la víctima en dos niveles: uno que afecta directamente a la mujer, la castiga, la humilla. Pretende disciplinar, dominar y, comete, por lo tanto, un crimen de carácter moralista. Pero, también hay otra interpretación apoyada en la idea de que el significante 'cuerpo femenino' es usado como medio, como portavoz de un sistema de comunicación entre el autor y un destinatario. Este último representa una instancia suplementaria –más allá de la víctima–, a quien van dirigidas partes del discurso del sujeto-autor. Este destinatario metafórico tiene un papel muy complejo, de importancia decisiva, incluso antes de cometerse el crimen. El acto violento como tal forma parte de la comunicación, o sea su resultado contiene un mensaje implícito.[3]

La teoría de la dimensión discursiva de los asesinatos y del cuerpo como medio cambia la interpretación del feminicidio. Las estructuras misóginas indican la falta de importancia individual de la víctima al ejecutar el asesinato de una mujer genérica. Por tanto, cabría formular la hipótesis de que, tal vez, se trate más de la comunicación entre los sujetos-autores y los destinatarios ausentes que del exterminio de la víctima, la cual, por medio de su cuerpo, adoptaría, en este caso, la función de ser material disponible.

Michel Foucault constata en su debate sobre la ocupación política del cuerpo humano y su función marcada por las relaciones del poder que: "It is largely as a force of production that the body is invested with relations of power and domination. [T]he body becomes a useful force only if it is both a productive body and a subjected body" (25-26). El acto de subyugación puede manifestarse a través del uso de la violencia, pero ésta puede ser evitada a través de una apropiación sutil del cuerpo y de sus fuerzas, en la medida en que pasa a ser parte de la creación estratégica de las redes de la

---

[3] Para profundizar este aspecto, cf. el sistema de comunicación de la violencia según Segato (8; 12).

llamada microfísica del poder (Foucault 26), que genera el despliegue de un sistema de control. La importancia del cuerpo de la mujer como uno de los elementos esenciales de su situación en el mundo fue destacada ya a mediados del siglo XX por Simone de Beauvoir (41). Judith Butler retoma esta idea fundamental describiendo el cuerpo femenino como una constante central de la identidad social de la mujer y haciendo hincapié en el hecho de que: "The body is not a self-identical or merely factic materiality; it is a materiality that bears meaning, if nothing else, and the manner of this bearing is fundamentally dramatic" (272). Todas estas razones hacen necesario considerar el significado del cuerpo en los asesinatos ritualizados, aunque no sólo como el objeto primario del abuso sexual, sino más bien en una función espacial que abarque todos los aspectos anteriormente mencionados. El cuerpo encarna un territorio que se representa a sí mismo como tal y, al mismo tiempo, funciona como un área que puede ser utilizada por las otras categorías relevantes del feminicidio.

El dominio sobre este espacio-cuerpo posibilita la manifestación de aspectos como las circunstancias territoriales, el reparto jerárquico de poderes y las estructuras de género. De esta manera, se instituye un ejemplo en el cual el abuso del cuerpo femenino es representante simbólico de la disposición y del control. No se trata de un cuerpo individual, sino de un concepto, reducido a su apariencia y a lo que queda de significado inmanente. El cuerpo reproduce en este momento la situación socio-histórica de la subordinación de la mujer y resulta ser una mera codificación cultural materializada.[4] El cuerpo físico se contrapone a un cuerpo simbólico e, instrumentalmente, es 'sacrificado' por éste. El cuerpo simbólico adquiere relieve y se pone de manifiesto mediante la ejecución escenificada del cuerpo físico.

Rita Laura Segato desarrolló una hipótesis acerca de las estructuras de fondo del feminicidio de Ciudad Juárez, según la cual se pueden deducir "características del régimen patriarcal en un orden mafioso" (9) dentro de un "segundo Estado" o "Estado paralelo" (16). Este "Estado paralelo" se sirve de la mujeres y de sus cuerpos para "una exhibición de capacidad de dominio" (10), representando un orden social impune e inoficial. El concepto de "dominio absolutista sobre un territorio" (13) sería aquí, por un lado, el estímulo, la prueba alegable en cualquier momento, para poder cometer, de manera impune, los delitos de la más brutal dimensión. Por otro lado, presenta la posibilidad de acceder a una red donde el poder estatal es ínfimo, tanto a nivel humano como a nivel material (cf. 13). En esta aproximación, la conexión entre factores económicos, políticos y socioculturales es inmanente e interdependiente. De este modo, los asesinatos repetitivos de un sólo tipo de víctima se convierten en un medio de expre-

---

[4] Como tampoco resulta razonable enfocar el cuerpo dejando de lado las descripciones que le asignan su trascendencia, éste no debe ser considerado como destinatario marcado pasivamente de códigos culturales y contextos predeterminados. Para no privarlo de su existencia y función independientes, cabría argumentar con Butler que "the gendered body acts its part in a culturally restricted corporal space and enacts interpretations within the confines of already existing directives" (277).

sión de la imposición violenta y ritualizada de una estructura de poder corporativa, consolidada frente a cualquier intento exterior de destruirla. Esto y, además, la impunidad continua alimentan un ciclo constante que se reproduce con cada asesinato. Según Segato:

> Uso y abuso del cuerpo del otro sin que éste participe con intención o voluntad compatibles, la violación se dirige al aniquilamiento de la voluntad de la víctima, cuya reducción es justamente significada por la pérdida del control ... sobre su espacio-cuerpo. (6)

Segato se refiere así a un canibalismo –aquí denominado apropiación– representado por el acto de consumir al otro (a la mujer), terminando con su completa destrucción física. Este canibalismo constituye un acto "mediante el cual el otro perece como voluntad autónoma y su oportunidad de existir solamente persiste si es apropiada e incluida en el cuerpo de quien lo ha devorado. El resto de su existencia persiste sólo como parte del proyecto del dominador" (7). Por consiguiente, el "consumidor" no sólo adquiere el poder sobre el cuerpo y la voluntad, es decir, territorio y rol sexual, sino también sobre la vida y la muerte. No se trata solamente de la apropiación que el hombre realiza de la mujer, sino, a la vez, del completo derrocamiento de la mujer. En este sentido, Segato postula:

> En un régimen de soberanía, algunos están destinados a la muerte para que, en su cuerpo, el poder soberano grabe su marca; en este sentido, la muerte de estos elegidos para representar el drama de la dominación, es una muerte expresiva, no una muerte utilitaria. (7)

Se puede concluir que es un concepto del cuerpo femenino estructurado en varios niveles: símbolo politizado, medio de comunicación, territorio codificado y portador simbólico de un lenguaje masculino de violencia. Y aunque la relación entre todos los asesinatos cometidos desde 1993 nunca pueda comprobarse y, tal vez, tampoco exista, están vinculados por la dimensión de extrema violencia y por el ostensible sistema represivo que demuestran y que multiplica la calidad del terror. Esta violencia implica un mensaje, tiene una función comunicativa que se manifiesta, a manera de ejemplo, en las víctimas. Deja sus huellas en ellas sin que los agresores sean necesariamente conscientes de ello y se dirige a los destinatarios que han de interpretarlo.

El nexo entre los mencionados aspectos de poder e impotencia en las relaciones de género, el derrocamiento doloso y la violenta subordinación de la mujer, además el dominio sobre su espacio-cuerpo como portador de un significado simbólico, manifiesta también el enfoque de *Señorita extraviada*. La película permite adentrarse en esta perspectiva a través de una representación fílmica cuya estética y estructura narrativa indican un cambio respecto a las formas de representación dentro del género documental.

4. La estetización de la realidad

Documentaries are a negotiation between filmmaker and reality and, at heart, a performance. (Bruzzi 154)

En la historia reciente del cine documental el uso cada vez más libre de las posibilidades artísticas e interpretativas y el cuestionamiento de las limitaciones normativas se
ven confrontadas con el deseo de inmediatez y pureza en la imagen documental y con
el afán profundamente arraigado de una representación 'auténtica' de la realidad. Uno
de los problemas fundamentales se encuentra en los interrogantes de cómo es la realidad y cuál es la posición que el documental toma frente a ésta. Asimismo, en la cuestión de si el documental negocia abiertamente lo que pretende reflejar y de qué forma
lo efectúa. Tradicionalmente, la relación realidad-ficción en el cine documental ha sido
analizada a partir del convencimiento de una diferenciación normativa entre los dos
términos. Eva Hohenberger asegura que en cada film, junto a la impresión de realidad,
subyace una ficción; la ficción de experimentar como realmente presente, lo que debe
de estar siempre ausente: personas, paisajes, la realidad prefílmica (50). El espectador,[5]
por consiguiente, no reconoce el documento y el material usado dentro de la narración,
sino que tiende a percibir, en primer lugar, la ficción de la realidad fílmica, es decir,
"la realidad de los significantes es rechazada en favor de la instancia imaginaria de la
diégesis, la cual es considerada como lo único real de la película" (51). El término
diégesis se equipara con la ficción y se contrapone a lo real. De este modo, Hohenberger niega al discurso documental la posibilidad de transportar autenticidad. En cambio,
describe la construcción de la realidad como elemento ficcional y, por tanto, como parte de las formas de representación que ella rechaza *a priori* para el documental.[6]

La realidad fílmica tiene su origen en la materialidad de la que deriva, a la que
hace referencia y por la cual es determinada. Su carácter y sus límites están definidos y
su capacidad de retratar y reproducir la realidad está limitada por la cámara. El arte de
la representación fílmica está en analizar el mundo extra-diegético para modificarlo y
estructurarlo según una percepción subjetiva. La profundidad de las imágenes no se
debe a la reproducción realista del mundo visible, sino a su contenido interpretativo, a
la manifestación estética de pensamientos y sensaciones subjetivas y a la posibilidad

---

[5]   Sin querer ignorar en absoluto la importancia de la incorporación al lenguaje del enfoque
      de género, deseamos especificar que 'espectador' se refiere al 'receptor' y este término se-
      rá usado aquí como denominador neutral de sexo, que incluye tanto a la destinataria como
      al destinatario. Esta decisión se debe a la carencia en el español de alternativas lingüísticas
      que en este contexto de análisis cinematográfico no resultan semánticamente satisfactorias.

[6]   En su argumentación de 1988, Hohenberger se encuentra en una fase intermedia, en una
      problemática de transformación inherente al cambio. Y aunque, por un lado, su indagación
      crítica de los conceptos normativos que considera contradictorios, demuestra el fuerte de-
      seo de un cambio del paradigma y de la renovación de las estructuras canónicas de repre-
      sentación e interpretación; por el otro, su posición, prácticamente, rechaza la renovación de
      estos conceptos y presenta afinidad con las mismas ideas normativas que critica.

de expresar las experiencias humanas en imágenes y, además, de colocarlas, crearlas y
enlazarlas.

En 1935, Walter Benjamin –entre otros–, criticaba, en su ensayo "La obra de arte
en la época de su reproductibilidad técnica," que la estetización convertiría todo en
objetos de consumo placentero y que esto conduciría, en contraposición, a la politización del arte, operando así en oposición a la minimización y la transfiguración de la vida política y de la miseria (cf. Trebeß 39). Este acercamiento crítico a la realidad puede ser interpretado, en la actualidad, de manera constructiva con una argumentación en
favor de las posibilidades creativas. La estetización del arte puede sensibilizar y crear
accesos más amplios, puede sustituir la inmovilidad por la vivacidad y favorecer la conexión entre la obra de arte y la vida real.

> Subjective camera movement, impressionistic montage, dramatic lightning, and compel-
> ling music: such elements fit comfortably within a realist style but, in documentary,
> they are traditionally subordinated to a documentary logic, which is governed, in turn,
> by the protocols of the discourses of sobriety. (Nichols 100)

Nichols expresa que el uso de recursos estilísticos asociativos y poéticos, que van a la
par de una representación supuestamente auténtica, puede causar, de hecho, un efecto
de distanciamiento. La idea inicial de un discurso de sobriedad forma parte de una posición sumamente normativa ante cualquier tipo de características que tradicionalmente se asociaba más con el cine experimental o de ficción. Más allá de los límites nor-
mativos, también existe una orientación hacia una complejidad y autorreflexión pro-
fundizada y, con ello, hacia un enlace de los aspectos expresivos, poéticos y retóricos.
Aunque el uso de formas de representación performativas presente un contraste entre
los recursos creativos y referenciales y pueda distraernos de los aspectos formales y
del contexto político de un film, hay que admitir que posibilitan otras formas de proceder –ya no restringidas al discurso ficcional–, capaces de ampliar, reanimar y profundizar la discusión en torno al documental.

Stella Bruzzi trasciende la categoría de performatividad introducida por Nichols
y sostiene que el documental performativo aprovecha el elemento de la performance
para enfatizar, en el marco de un contexto no-ficcional, la imposibilidad de representaciones auténticas en este género cinematográfico (cf. 153). Si bien el documental puede referirse a una realidad no-fílmica, es sólo mediante la interacción entre ella y su
correspondiente forma fílmica, la diégesis, que esta realidad cobra trascendencia. Según este concepto, la 'verdad' del documental performativo nace de la transformación
de los hechos reales en elementos performativos y es, por lo tanto, de carácter construido.

La performatividad rompe supuestamente con las normas y las tradiciones del
documental, aunque éstas, prácticamente, no consideran el aspecto de la producción y
el montaje de una película como elementos tradicionalmente performativos, escenifi-
cados. Bruzzi intercede por la 'de-mascarada' de parámetros imposibles de cumplir en
torno al significado de las condiciones de producción y sugiere:

The use of performance tactics could be viewed as a means of suggesting that perhaps documentaries should admit the defeat of their utopian aim and elect instead to present an alternative "honesty" that does not seek to mask their inherent instability but rather to acknowledge that performance—the enactment of the documentary specifically for the cameras—will always be the heart of the non-fiction film. (155)

La afectividad inmanente a las expresiones estéticas y la reflexión acerca de la posición del sujeto en la obra de arte, que resultan de un acercamiento performativo, enlazan este debate teórico con el documental de Lourdes Portillo. La escenificación poética, emotiva y mística del feminicidio suscita empatía y desea que el espectador pueda interiorizarse en la situación.[7] Destaca el hecho de que en la película no haya, por ejemplo, una exposición de cuerpos femeninos desfigurados. Imágenes de tal índole son sustituidas por un simbolismo casi mágico, partiendo de un enfoque estético y de una estructura narrativa sumamente expresiva que enfatizan el nivel del contenido.

Mediante la representación estetizada de la diégesis respecto a la ilustración de la ausencia de las mujeres y de la muerte, la directora nos conduce mucho más cerca de una realidad no-fílmica[8] de lo que hubiera podido lograr el intento de reflejar la realidad de manera supuestamente objetiva. La conceptualización estética de esta película permite, además, el acceso a una confrontación dicotómica entre la historicidad y la conciencia estilística expresiva, entre la escenificación y el carácter testimonial de las imágenes. Se desarrolla una oscilación entre los enfoques, de manera análoga al discurso víctima-autor. Y es que mientras un elemento exige la concentración en sí mismo, el otro se refiere justamente a lo que representa. Es decir, las técnicas poéticas comprenden una acentuación de sus propias características expresivas, de la misma manera que se atienen a la pretensión referencial de historicidad. Mediante ellas Portillo construye dicotomías como, por ejemplo, la de 'justicia' e 'injusticia' o –como pareja opuesta– emoción y razón, caracterizando el discurso personal versus el discurso oficial. Por consiguiente, el carácter referencial del documental se manifiesta en un hilo narrativo, mientras que, paralelo a éste, surge otro hilo en forma de una posición escenificada del sujeto, que obviamente hace alusión a un contexto de referencia ideológicamente marcado.[9]

Para prevenir una posible carencia de referencialidad, la directora recurre, en varias ocasiones, a material televisivo y de archivo, fotos y grabaciones directas de las declaraciones de las instituciones estatales. Además, establece acotamientos claros entre los dos niveles de representación: las secuencias son separadas por transiciones ne-

---

[7] Según Nichols, el carácter performativo de un documental tiene como meta la reacción moral del espectador. Ya su propia forma (fílmica) ejemplifica el acceso ético elegido, de manera que el espectador se enfrente a los hechos (cf. 99). Más que esperar una actividad política o crítica ideológica, este acceso procura, en cierto sentido, provocar al espectador o sugerirle el cuestionamiento de su moral.

[8] Para el tema de las relaciones entre las distintas realidades del documental, cf. Hohenberger 29.

[9] Cf. p. ej. la representación a través de enfoques internos y de cámara subjetiva, pág. 89.

gras que disminuyen el contraste entre la percepción sensorial y la racional, entre el discurso del sujeto-autor y la víctima, entre la representación subjetiva y los 'testimonios históricos.' El documental concede así al espectador un momento de reflexión para comprender lo que ha visto, antes de entregarle la siguiente información. Estas pausas facilitan, sobre todo, el experimentar y tomar conciencia sensorialmente, para, posteriormente, también poder enfrentarse al tema de manera racional.

Con el ritmo de las imágenes, su distribución y la estrategia narrativa, la película no intenta trastornar al espectador con las exposiciones de terror, sufrimiento, dolor y violencia en contra de las mujeres, tampoco pretende romantizar a la víctima o apelar a la morbosidad. Mediante una técnica muy sui generis establece, por un lado, un estrecho vínculo entre el film y el espectador y, por el otro, restablece la dignidad humana en la representación de víctimas y las familias afectadas. Así trabaja en contra del silencio y del olvido y ofrece un espacio a las familias en el que pueden articular su pena de manera clara y digna. *Señorita extraviada* propone, en la plasticidad de su discurso, establecer una relación con el espanto que no aterre al espectador o lo lleve a rechazarlo.

5. Lo político se vuelve personal

Señorita extraviada comienza con la introducción al tema realizada por la directora quien se sirve de una narración en *voice-over*, que acompaña a la cámara en su acercamiento físico y mental al lugar de los sucesos. Este tono personal es característico de la película en su totalidad y se muestra no sólo por el uso de la propia voz de Portillo (y su función de instancia narrativa), el papel de periodista que asume o su breve aparición delante de la cámara. Su presencia como individuo en los sucesos se observa, también, en la concepción del nivel gráfico, donde adopta una posición subjetiva ante un asunto público y convierte así lo político en asunto personal.

Gran parte de la película se dedica a presentar cómo se organizan las familias y los voluntarios para reivindicar públicamente sus exigencias de justicia. La directora enfatiza la absoluta falta de protección en que se encuentran las mujeres de Ciudad Juárez frente a las instituciones locales y estatales. Como afirma González:

> Portillo has found a way to represent both the 'invisibility' of the murdered women and the over-visible brutal images of death doled out by mainstream journalism. While the cultural proclivity has been to narrate the young women's deaths with suggestions of their own complicity—the archetypal tale of the lost girl in the big city —the institutional and economic factors producing such high levels of violence are left unexamined. (235)

A pesar de la evidente acusación en contra del manejo de las instituciones estatales y las políticas de representación, el discurso político en *Señorita extraviada* a veces parece relativizado por medio de la estetización y del acercamiento subjetivo al tema. Sin embargo, es precisamente este sentido altamente metafórico de las imágenes que conlleva un sutil mensaje político. Este discurso no se basa en las imágenes de las mujeres desfiguradas o en los significados que pueden derivarse de ellas. Al contrario, Portillo explora la manera en la cual los representantes gubernamentales enfrentan la serie de homicidios, los enredos y las explicaciones poco convincentes, así como la falta de referencia al derrocamiento simbólico que amenaza al sexo femenino. La búsqueda de las posibles interpretaciones acerca de lo que acontece en Ciudad Juárez lleva a la directora a preocuparse de los hechos de fondo en el entorno de las victimas y a denunciar la pasividad institucional. Mediante su trabajo crea conciencia sobre los sucesos, deseando favorecer así la creación de movimientos de apoyo.

Para *Señorita extraviada* Portillo utiliza "narrativas con lente exotizante orientalista, apropiado para la mentalidad colonialista usada por los reporteros de los medios de Estados Unidos cuando cubren tópicos sociales o políticos en el tercer mundo" (Mora 128). Aquellas tomas estetizadas cuestionan las convenciones del cine documental y manifiestan un acercamiento al ámbito de lo imaginario. Al entrelazar estas formas expresivas con un acercamiento periodístico a los hechos, la película evidencia las fricciones entre las dos modalidades. La directora retoca la imagen de la realidad en favor de una intención que trasciende el sensacionalismo de la prensa, la que hace un despligue de cuerpos femeninos torturados y formula profusas hipótesis. Portillo configura la realidad según su propia percepción de los acontecimientos, aunque sin manipular o polarizar de manera excesiva.

La película evoca a menudo la mirada de los afectados mediante el uso de la cámara subjetiva, por lo que el espectador percibe el mundo desde su punto de vista.[10] Al favorecer la identificación del espectador con los afectados, la película lo involucra personalmente y le sugiere una perspectiva determinada acerca de los hechos. En cambio, no da crédito a las declaraciones y explicaciones oficiales entregadas por las autoridades estatales y, en consecuencia, no les concede relevancia en la argumentación de su film. Participa en el conflicto tomando parte por las víctimas, hecho que se manifiesta en reiteradas ocasiones, mediante el carácter afectivo y empático de las tomas. De esta manera, también, a nivel emotivo, sensibiliza al espectador para que reflexione sobre el contenido.

> Once the film was finished it received international attention because for the first time the girls were humanized. Up to that moment they had been just statistics or 'poor brown woman,' not human beings who deserved action and justice on their behalf. (Portillo, "Filming" 230)

La directora crea un lazo rítmico de tristeza y poesía, usa a menudo la cámara lenta, emplea música de fondo y utiliza una gran cantidad de tomas de carácter simbólico y religioso. "La connotación que yo quería darle a esa película con la música y con la manera de cortar y con las flores y todo, es un réquiem" afirma Portillo ("Filmmaker's"). Por medio de este réquiem, la muerte se convierte en un *leitmotiv* que aparece de una forma muy independiente y omnipresente. Su repetición continua integra al espectador, quiere reducir su distancia hacia los sucesos, dirigir su atención

---

[10] Cf. los planos punto de vista de los familiares como, por ejemplo, en el caso de Eva Arce.

hacia un aspecto determinado y, asimismo, lo guia como un hilo rojo por la narración. Portillo usa esta música cargada de afectos, especialmente, en las representaciones estetizadas de las mujeres de Ciudad Juárez y en las escenas que describen la actuación de los familiares de las víctimas. Con esto, no sólo las mujeres asesinadas, sino también sus familiares se asocian con lo sagrado del réquiem, poniendo de manifiesto la solidaridad e implicación personal de la directora. Actitud que tiene su expresión particularmente en las escenas carentes de voz, en las que se muestran a mujeres atravesando la ciudad y pintando cruces como símbolo de su lucha y resistencia o, también, a través de las fotografías y los volantes que aparecen en la pantalla. En estas tomas, la gran cantidad de símbolos explicitan el concepto de ausencia mejor que cualquier forma de verbalización.

Sin embargo, Lourdes Portillo no se empeña en dramatizar momentos o secuencias aisladas, sino que apela a la activación de todo el nivel emotivo del espectador mediante la individualización de algunas víctimas y la presentación, profundamente humana, de sus familiares. Sin considerar su función informativa y de esclarecimiento, este documental puede considerarse ante todo un homenaje a las mujeres de Ciudad Juárez. Es el desafío de la película, además de intentar conseguir que se haga justicia a estas mujeres, que se las reconozca y presente como mujeres.

La directora parte de la noción del documental como construcción performativa de la realidad, la que puede ser escenificada en el cine sin echar mano de la representación mimética. La concepción de sus imágenes tampoco pretende compensar o minimizar. Más bien persigue producir una profunda consciencia de la dimensión de su significado a través del enlazamiento de la experiencia emotiva y la reflexión de lo experimentado.

6. Narraciones de lo no decible

According to the filmmaker, *Señorita extraviada* deals with the "two different languages" of Mexican society, "the said and the unsaid." Portillo's interest was to tell the story based on a culturally specific way of telling stories, one that stresses the eloquence of the unsaid. (González 236)

Los momentos de lo no decible son los que provocan una respuesta intensamente emotiva. La cámara presta una atención particular a las reacciones profundamente humanas, a los gestos, las miradas y los momentos silenciosos. Con frecuencia, se detiene en estas imágenes, como si quisiera hablar a través de ellas. Al contrastar la escenificación del silencio con las escenas donde hay presencia de la voz narradora, se manifiesta una elaboración muy particular y poética del silencio. Algunas tomas dan la impresión de querer clavarse en la memoria del espectador: la risa infantil e indiferente de una niña, cuyo rostro, después de ser entrevistada acerca de los asesinatos, revela, lentamente, una expresión grave y angustiada que parece reflejar la sucesión de pensamientos inquietantes que atraviesan por su mente; las miradas absortas de los padres, marcadas de dolor y tristeza, cuando, una y otra vez, han de relatar la historia de la muerte de su hija recordando todos los sucesos en detalle; las incontables fotografías, los volantes, los recortes de periódico, insertados por la directora entre las imágenes de las entrevistas y las últimas conclusiones, documentos frente a los cuales, el espectador permanece, por algunos momentos, solo.

> There is an intricate play between the respectful and empathic portrayals of the surviving women … and the memorial still images … Portillo conveys the propagation of these easily reproducible images of death and the connection each contains for the living. (González 237)

Se trata, ante todo, de la visualización de algo, a menudo, desatendido dentro del discurso oficial, es decir, de concederles humanidad a las mujeres asesinadas, incluso más allá de su muerte. Estas son presentadas como seres con una vida auténtica, real. De esta manera a nivel de la representación fílmica, se les permite recuperar su personalidad, sin que sean reducidas al número de un expediente, o al motivo de una foto traumatizante, o, a ser responsables de su propio destino como lo sugiere el discurso oficial.

En la película la ausencia de sonido como medio de expresión estética representa aquello para lo cual no existen palabras adecuadas. Asimismo, se manifiesta el silencio en su función social, como parte de la sociedad y del discurso oficial respecto al feminicidio. Este silencio yace en el centro de una presentación aciaga y lúgubre de los motivos y trasfondos de los asesinatos, casi como si resultase de algún acuerdo secreto. A este contexto remite *Señorita extraviada* al asumir el motivo de las palabras que faltan y de las imágenes que hablan por sí solas.

El silencio alborota la sociedad, alimenta desconfianza, transmite la incompetencia de las instituciones, niega la importancia de los acontecimientos e impide que cesen los crímenes. El silencio corresponde también a la actitud que la parte oficial impone a las familias y activistas, a los críticos y testigos, y, del mismo modo, a la eliminación de informaciones, testimonios y pruebas de parte de las instituciones.

En oposición al silenciamiento oficial, el lenguaje fílmico de *Señorita extraviada* conlleva una función muy clara: a través de él, los familiares de las víctimas se articulan y pueden experimentar la reflexión sobre su doloroso trauma como el comienzo de un proceso curativo. En este marco, romper con el silencio constituye parte de la lucha contra la represión y el olvido. En consecuencia, las declaraciones de las personas afectadas "revelan que hablar sobre violencia, crimen, e injusticia social puede funcionar como las armas imprescindibles para otorgarse poder" (Mora 132).

7. El simbolismo de la femineidad

Señorita extraviada sustituye la representación directa de la muerte y la violencia por el uso de estrategias y objetos simbólicos, que subrayan la omnipresencia de ambos factores sin su representación física. Asimismo, el simbolismo enfatiza la conciencia de pérdida y ausencia. De esta manera, la película vuelve a dar vida a las mujeres muertas para así explicitar su existencia anterior.

Las imágenes de tacones blancos expuestos en el escaparate de cristal de una zapatería, los rostros femeninos maquillados, los cabellos largos de mujer movidos por el viento, las flores en el desierto, un vestido artísticamente drapeado, retratado a cámara lenta –de aspecto casi espectral–, los zapatos de mujer tirados en el desierto y los rostros angelicales estilizados, todas estas imágenes influyen en la mirada del espectador. Evocan en el espectador aquellas características típicamente femeninas que son otorgadas a la mujer por la mirada masculina: un cuerpo sin alma, un objeto fetiche dentro del discurso de género tradicional. Pero la película no representa a la mujer como víctima –un papel que inevitablemente encarna debido a su asesinato–, sino la presenta como un ser humano enérgico y convencido, que demanda justicia y reclama sus derechos. Algunos aspectos del interés de Portillo por el contexto feminista se manifiestan en la perspectiva de la mujer en su función socio-histórica[11] y la suposición de un concepto de asesinato misógino-patriarcal. Su acto de escenificar la femineidad parece ser igualmente una crítica y una manifestación.

La película pretende ver a la mujer como mujer, con toda la femineidad que le pertenece y postula que así es como también los hombres la ven y la califican para, finalmente, degradarla a la condición de víctima. Por lo tanto, la femineidad en *Señorita extraviada* significa a la par, naturaleza y estatus, fuerza y peligro de ser sometida a estructuras establecidas en contra de la mujer. Pero también implica emoción y sensibilidad, para cuya expresión la directora utiliza conceptos connotados tradicionalmente con lo femenino.

Los símbolos omnipresentes de la femineidad se presentan como alusiones que pueden aparecer en la función de sustitutos y que, sin embargo, en su mera forma visual no logran expresar de manera unívoca en qué medida se sirven de contextos no-fílmicos. Una multiplicidad de motivos indica, repetidamente, la ausencia de las mujeres asesinadas de Ciudad Juárez, por ejemplo, a través de ropa sin dueño y de objetos pertenecientes a las víctimas, que ahora funcionan como sustitutos. Tales objetos, directamente vinculados a las víctimas, tienen un gran valor simbólico, en varios momentos, incluso, llegan a tener un caracter de fetiche.[12] Con el uso de las características simbólicas pertenecientes a los órdenes hegemónicos de género, éstos pueden "reconfirmar, interrumpir, y trastornar la manera en que las identidades sociales y los papeles están inscritos en el cuerpo" (Mora 129). Y es que las imágenes de la película no persiguen presentar a la mujer como un ser frágil y vulnerable, sujeto a la merced del va-

---

[11] Cf. también la identidad inestable descrita por Judith Butler, la cual postula que la identidad no es origen, sino manifestación de una temporalidad concebida como socio-histórica. Butler describe la performatividad e inestabilidad de la identidad de género con las siguientes palabras: "Significantly, if gender is instituted through acts which are internally discontinuous, then the *appearance of substance* is precisely that, a constructed identity, a performative accomplishment which the mundane social audience, including the actors themselves, come to believe and to perform in the mode of belief" (271).

[12] "Un fetiche es siempre un significante de la ausencia, una especie de 'objeto suplente'" (Hohenberger 54, traducción de la autora).

rón, indefensa ante la mirada frívola, sensacionalista del espectador. Al contrario, estas imágenes se unen a la pretensión de sensibilizar y agudizar la mirada consciente y, a menudo, crítica ante el significado de los atributos femeninos. En cierto modo, sentencian el discurso sobre la mujer como víctima pasiva de la violencia institucionalizada y la misoginia. Además hacen hincapié en el compromiso de las mujeres de Ciudad Juárez, en su firme propósito de cambiar la situación y luchar contra la injusticia. Como conclusión afirma Mora que "Portillo recodifica los cuerpos de las mujeres y la ornamentación femenina con una aureola de energía que destaca la organización y fuerza femeninas" (Mora 130).

Nos encontramos, entonces, ante una femineidad enfatizada por una autora que, por un lado, parece escandalizarse de los reproches misóginos de la conducta supuestamente 'provocativa' de las mujeres. Por el otro, sugiere que precisamente aquellos atributos de la femineidad también se convierten en el motivo de la perdición de las mujeres: los tacones que les impiden cualquier movilidad, el maquillaje y la ropa que las hacen parecer disponibles; a fin de cuentas, su apariencia física las clasifica y las desindividualiza.

Lourdes Portillo muestra una consciencia clara de que las estructuras de poder patriarcal y de la criminalidad política convierten a la mujer en víctima. Justamente para subrayar esta perspectiva usa los atributos de la femeneidad como recursos estilísticos feminizados hasta conseguir que la mujer simbolice cierta pureza e inocencia dentro del laberinto de las maquinaciones de un poder carente de escrúpulos. Y aunque la mujer constituya el foco de atención y esté siempre presente, ella misma sólo aparece al margen y, la mayoría de las veces, de manera simbólica. Prudentemente Portillo mueve su ruego personal al centro del discurso fílmico: la mujer como mujer y su hado predeterminado. Ella es motivo en doble sentido; es objeto y motivo de acción al mismo tiempo.

El acto de 'hacer visible' es otro leitmotiv de este documental; hacer visible la presencia de lo existente y también de lo invisible: las desaparecidas. Los primeros planos recurrentes de los ojos de las afectadas sirven de contrapeso tanto a la ya mencionada puesta en escena del simbolismo femenino que desindividualiza y crea uniformidad, como también a la referencia continua a la mujer y a la identidad social que se le atribuye. Según el análisis de Mikhail Bakhtin respecto a la concepción del cuerpo grotesco en la obra de Francois Rabelais, los ojos contrastan con el cuerpo y son considerados como la expresión de lo individual, de la vida interior del ser humano (358). Desde esta perspectiva, estos planos son elementos gráficos que muestran el empeño de Portillo de no presentar a la mujer con un simple perfil de víctima y privarla, en consecuencia, de cualquier significado individual. El foco de atención se dirige a una mujer concreta y a lo que su mirada refleja. De este modo, la autora permite al espectador, a lo largo de la narración, una doble perspectiva: la mirada de una mujer de Ciudad Juárez hacia afuera, hacia lo que la rodea, el intento de ver con sus ojos. Por otro lado, a la vez, es la perspectiva de la mirada de esta mujer enfocada desde fuera, el primer plano de un ojo, perteneciente a una cara determinada que se destaca entre la gente.

Este régimen binómico de la mirada representa el contraste continuo entre los dos polos opuestos a través del cual en todos los niveles de esta película se interpreta la dualidad de las estructuras sociales al igual que la binariedad de género. Los recursos estilísticos utilizados crean y destacan –por medio del colorido, del enfoque, del sonido, del montaje y de la estructura narrativa– una oposición simbólica tanto al discurso hegemónico como a la estructura sistemática de represión. Pero de la misma manera como la película opone las mujeres asesinadas a los supuestos sujetos-autores, la vida a la muerte, lo masculino a lo femenino, también la directora escenifica la tristeza y la pérdida frente al coraje y la esperanza, y persigue, de este modo, la meta de evitar que la visualización del dolor sea la parte esencial de su película. A pesar de realzar así la injusticia y el sufrimiento que viven las mujeres de Ciudad Juárez, ante todo, quiere promover en el espectador el deseo de ayudar y de participar activamente en la reclamación de cambios estructurales y para denunciar las estrategias políticas de desempoderamiento.

Para lograrlo, la perspectiva de Portillo siempre se mantiene fija en los distintos papeles de la mujer, estableciendo así una imagen integral de un sujeto que en el hegemónico régimen de representación se reduce a tan sólo un objeto. El documental une a la mujer, como objeto, víctima y mero símbolo instrumentalizado de un constructo histórico-social, con la mujer enérgica y valiente, comprometida con la lucha contra su opresión. Es esta última mujer, la que forma parte de la imagen de esperanza y resistencia con la que las mujeres de Ciudad Juárez se dirigen unitariamente a la cámara –y con ella al público–, toma con la cual termina *Señorita extraviada*.[13]

Bibliografía

Bakhtin, Mikhail. *Rabelais and His World*. Bloomington: Indiana UP, 1984.

Beauvoir, Simone de. *The Second Sex*. New York: Vintage Press, 1973.

Bruzzi, Stella. *New Documentary. A Critical Introduction*. London: Routledge, 2000.

Butler, Judith. "Performative Acts and Gender Constitution. An Essay in Phenomenology and Feminist Theory." *Performing Feminisms. Feminist Critical Theory and Theatre*. Ed. Sue-Ellen Case. Baltimore: The Johns Hopkins UP, 1990. 270-82.

Foucault, Michel. *Discipline and Punish. The Birth of the Prison*. New York: Vintage Books, 1977.

González, Rita. "The Said and the Unsaid. Lourdes Portillo Tracks Down Ghosts in *Señorita extraviada*." *Atzlán. A Journal of Chicano Studies* 28.2 (2003): 235-40.

Hohenberger, Eva. *Die Wirklichkeit des Films. Dokumentarfilm, ethnographischer Film, Jean Rouch*. Hildesheim: Georg Olms Verlag, 1988.

---

[13] Quiero dar las gracias a Marietta Saavedra, Daniela Noll-Opitz y Sebastian Thies por el apoyo, la crítica constructiva y por haber hecho posible esta publicación.

Mora, Sergio de la. "Asesinato, mujeres y justicia en *Señorita extraviada* de Lourdes Portillo". *Cinémas d'Amérique Latine* 12 (2004): 116-32.

Nichols, Bill. *Blurred Boundaries. Questions of Meaning in Contemporary Culture.* Bloomington: Indiana UP, 1994.

Portillo, Lourdes. "Filming *Señorita extraviada.*" *Aztlán. A Journal of Chicano Studies* 28.2 (2003): 229-34.

————. "Filmmaker's Workshop by Lourdes Portillo. Presentation and Discussion." Fourth Bielefeld InterAmerican Studies Symposium: *Of Fatherlands and Motherlands: Gender and Nation in the Americas.* ZIF, Bielefeld. 30 de nov. 2006.

Segato, Rita Laura. "Territorio, soberanía y crímenes de segundo Estado. La escritura en el cuerpo de las mujeres asesinadas en Ciudad Juárez." *Serie Antropología* 362 (2004): 6-9.

Trebeß, Achim, ed. *Metzler Lexikon Ästhetik.* Stuttgart: J.B. Metzler, 2006.

Volk, Steven S. y Marian E. Schlotterbeck. "Gender, Order, and Femicide. Reading the Popular Culture of Murder in Ciudad Juárez." *Aztlán. A Journal of Chicano Studies* 32.1 (2007): 53-58.

Filmografía

Señorita extraviada. Dir. Lourdes Portillo. México, EE.UU., 2001.

Transformaciones de lo político en el documental argentino. Representaciones de pueblo y poder en *Memoria del saqueo* (2004) y *Yo Presidente* (2006)[1]

ANNE LAKEBERG

Abstract

The economic and political crisis in Argentina in 2001, which culminated in the so-called *cazerolazo*, had a fundamental impact on cultural and social life. It set off a growing politicization of the masses, which led to a profound reconceptualization of the nation-state. This period of crisis and post-crisis provides the context for the analysis of two documentary films—*Memoria del saqueo* (2004), directed by Fernando E. Solanas, and *Yo Presidente* (2006), directed by Mariano Cohn and Gastón Duprat. The representation of social reality in the two films is informed by the political discourses that were current in Argentinean society at the time. However, there is a stark contrast with regard to the ways in which the two documentaries address politics and social transformations. This essay argues that the documentary aesthetic is fundamental for an understanding of how the modern world is conceptualized, particularly with regard to the nation-state, the mise-en-scène of its politics, and the popular resistance to hegemony. It demonstrates that the strategies of representing the political in documentary filmmaking are changing and that the reexamination (or deconstruction) of basic categories such as the political body or social space is profoundly transforming the political.

1. Introducción

En diciembre de 2001 Argentina atrae la atención del mundo. Los bancos congelan las cuentas bancarias privadas, la gente sale a la calle y logra la renuncia del presidente De la Rúa, provocando con ello una sucesión caótica de presidentes. Las circunstancias económicas que trajeron consigo la desaparición de una gran parte de la clase media –y con ella la base más relevante que sostiene a la comunidad imaginada de la nación–,

---

[1] Agradezco a Sebastian Thies, Marietta Saavedra Arellano y a Daniela Noll-Opitz por sus valiosos comentarios.

tienen profundas consecuencias en la vida política, social y cultural.[2] Motivan la politización, sobre todo, de aquéllos que sufren directamente la crisis económica. Uno de los efectos de esta crisis se aprecia en el renacimiento del pueblo como una categoría referencial dentro del imaginario social.

La época de crisis y poscrisis nos sirve de contexto para el análisis de los documentales argentinos *Memoria del saqueo* (2004) y *Yo Presidente* (2006). Los imaginarios y los debates sociales de esa época influyen en la manera como se construye la diégesis[3] de estas películas. En ellas la idea de un estado-nación basada en una comunidad imaginada será reemplazada, por lo menos, parcialmente, por el concepto foucaultiano de un estado que es solamente una abstracción mitizada que fracasa en sus esfuerzos de sostener su supuesta unidad.[4]

Por lo tanto, surge la cuestión de cómo se narra esa "abstracción mitizada" en las representaciones culturales. Homi Bhabha relaciona la función social de la nación con sus narraciones y, de este modo, pone el lenguaje en el centro del interés: "It is the project of *Nation and Narration* to explore the Janus-faced ambivalence of language itself in the construction of the Janus-faced discourse of the nation" (3). Guiados por esta premisa nos proponemos analizar, en ambos documentales, el lenguaje fílmico como elemento fundamental de la construcción de la nación. Así, examinaremos la pluralización de perspectivas para mostrar la forma como se está transformando actualmente el concepto de lo político ganando nociones y perdiendo estructuras. Ya no se restringe tan sólo a la esfera pública, sino abarca también lo privado, incluyendo la intimidad del hogar. Lo político no se considera ya necesariamente un producto del pueblo, de la nación, de los políticos o de las hegemonías nacionales. Mas bien hay un cambio en la percepción de lo social centrado en una nueva sensibilidad del carácter construido de las prácticas sociales. En este sentido, un cine político puede ser también el que aspira a cambiar las formas de ver y entender lo social.

En consecuencia, usamos, el concepto de lo político en un sentido amplio. Por un lado, siguiendo a Foucault (*Discipline* 27), nos apoyamos en su concepto de la "microfísica de poder" que describe las relaciones de poder como "innumerable points of confrontation, focuses of instability, each of which has its own risks of conflict, of struggles, and of an at least temporary inversion of power relations" (27). Por otro lado, tomamos en cuenta aquellos conceptos tradicionales que entienden lo político como una plena identificación con el concepto de la nación.

---

[2] Cf. Arfuch para un análisis de la crisis.

[3] La diégesis se define como "la historia comprendida como pseudo-mundo, como universo fictico cuyos elementos se ordenan para formar una globalidad. Su significado es más amplio que el de la historia a la que acaba de englobar: es todo lo que la historia evoca y provoca en el espectador" (Aumont 114).

[4] "But the state, doubtless no more today than in the past, does not have this unity, individuality, and rigorous functionality, nor, I would go so far as to say, this importance. After all, maybe the state is only a composite reality and a mythicized abstraction whose importance is much less than we think" (*Security* 109).

El lente a través del que miramos las narraciones de la nación son los documentales citados, los cuales emplean lenguajes propios para construir y reconstruir el momento histórico en cuestión. Cada lenguaje se caracteriza por una estética específica que es compartida con las otras obras fílmicas. Constatamos así que *Yo Presidente* (2006) participa por su estética en el nuevo cine argentino, siendo altamente significativo que los directores del film, Mariano Cohn y Gastón Duprat, se hayan conocido por su trabajo para la televisión –realizan a finales de 1990, el programa *televisión abierta*–, porque las experiencias ganadas allí marcan, también, el lenguaje utilizado en los filmes. Su primer largometraje experimental *Enciclopedia* (2000) muestra "la sucesión de personajes intercalados por imágenes puras, casi abstractas" (Noriega 10-11) y tematiza la extrañeza que puede resultar de la actuación de seres mostrados sin maquillaje. *Yo Presidente*, por su parte, cuenta la sucesión de los presidentes alrededor de la crisis en un tono "que está en las antípodas del documental político" (Gorodischer s.p.).

En contraste, *Memoria del saqueo* se caracteriza por un legado estético surgido, entre los años sesenta y setenta, en el contexto del cine militante y que, en la actualidad, ha visto su reformulación en una nueva ola de cine militante. La continuidad de este legado se encuentra en su director, Fernando E. Solanas, figura prominente del cine argentino desde los años sesenta y setenta. Es uno de los fundadores del Grupo Cine Liberación,[5] movimiento que da a conocer su ideología en el manifiesto "Hacia un tercer cine" publicado en conjunto por Solanas y Octavio Getino (cf. Solanas/Getino 55-91). Dirige, también con Getino, *La hora de los hornos* (1968), el primer documental de este grupo que, concebido como un acto vanguardista revolucionario (cf. Solanas/Getino 6), recibió de inmediato la atención de la crítica ganando varios premios internacionales. *Memoria del saqueo*, por su parte, se puede considerar como una continuación de las ideas del primer film de Solanas, quien en su página web afirma: "A treinta y cinco años de *La hora de los hornos*, he querido retomar la historia desde las palabras y gestos de sus protagonistas." Esta película es parte de un ciclo de documentales de Solanas que comprende *La dignidad de los nadies* (2005), *Argentina latente* (2007), *La próxima estación* (2008) y *Tierra sublevada* (2009). Con la última película Solanas completa el "fresco sobre la Argentina contemporánea" (Solanas). La figura de Solanas y su obra siguen siendo una referencia para los documentalistas de hoy en día, aunque de forma desigual y polarizada. Para la generación de documentalistas militantes contemporáneos la obra de Solanas es una fuerza integradora, mientras que para el nuevo cine argentino sirve más bien para posicionarse frente a Solanas por medio del contraste.

---

5 "Ellos negaban la artesanía y la actitud artística al decir: 'Nosotros trabajamos antes que nada como luchadores políticos.' Por consiguiente, trataron de transformar a sus espectadores y los modos de recepción tradicionales poniendo debajo de la pantalla una pancarta que decía: 'Cada espectador o es un cobarde o un traidor. Frantz Fanon'" (Schumann 25, traducción de la autora).

A pesar de un cierto antagonismo, los dos documentales comparten también rasgos comunes, tanto con respecto a sus contenidos como en cuanto al lenguaje fílmico o estilo. Coinciden en la idea de que el documental no es simplemente una fiel representación de la realidad, sino un lenguaje propio que se basa en los elementos característicos del cine, tales como el montaje, la estructura narrativa y el sonido. Ambos muestran una gran libertad en lo que se refiere a la puesta en escena de lo "real." Tanto *Yo Presidente* como *Memoria del saqueo* manipulan a los sujetos sociales representados de acuerdo a su argumentación política. No obstante, en nuestro análisis nos centraremos, sobre todo, en las diferencias.

Las dos películas enseñan que la crisis ha provocado la aparición y re-aparición de lenguajes distintos en el campo del cine documental. Una comparación de ambos lenguajes fílmicos ayudará a situar cada obra dentro de un contexto más amplio y permitirá hacer visible las ideas de lo político que yacen en el trasfondo. La importancia de lo específico de los lenguajes reside en la idea de que, a través de las narraciones, se construyen identidades y representaciones del mundo social.

El análisis enfoca la representación del pueblo, por una parte, y la representación de los políticos, por la otra. Para ello se hace hincapié en la puesta en escena de los cuerpos, tomando en cuenta que el escenario político los transforma en símbolos del poder (cf. Diehl 43). Para entender tal transformación se concibe el cuerpo físico como resultado de las prácticas sociales y mediáticas. Siguiendo a Judith Butler, el cuerpo y la identidad correspondiente son producto de adscripciones sociales. No existe un cuerpo natural que sirva como evidencia para la identidad del sujeto. En un nivel analítico, la creación de identidades por medio del cuerpo se relaciona con el concepto de la nación. La existencia de un cuerpo originario tanto como la comunidad imaginada se deconstruyen y desembocan en la valorización de cuerpos débiles con múltiples identidades y un estado definido como "composite reality" (Foucault, *Security*).

Después de una descripción de los dos movimientos estéticos a los que pertenecen las dos películas, el análisis seguirá una estructura comparativa contrastando separadamente las diversas categorías de lo político que aparecen en ellas.

2. Transformaciones de lo político: una comparación entre el cine militante y el nuevo cine argentino

Como se ha indicado con anterioridad, la crisis argentina de 2001 llevó a cuestionar lo que, generalmente, se denominaba como lo político. La desconfianza hacia los políticos, el sistema político y el sistema económico como resultado de la inestabilidad de los gobiernos de esa época afectó también la producción cinematográfica. En el cine se buscaban caminos viables para la representación que tomaran en cuenta los cambios en la percepción de lo social y que reflexionaran sobre los hechos que afectaban el país.

Aquellos cineastas que retoman las pautas del cine militante de los años sesenta y setenta, abogan por una estética e ideología que concibe al director como actor social y político, el que usa el medio audiovisual para posicionarse políticamente. El cine militante se caracteriza, desde el momento de su surgimiento,[6] por una relación estrecha con la política partidaria, ya que muchos grupos de cineastas formaban, en ese tiempo, parte del brazo político de un partido apoyando la lucha política con su herramienta, la cámara. Así, el Cine Liberación realizó, después de *La hora de los hornos*, dos documentales en favor del Peronismo –*La Revolución Justicialista* (1971) y *Actualización Política y Doctrinaria* (1971) (cf. Solanas/Getino 61)–, los que se articulan en torno a entrevistas a Juan Domingo Perón, quien en ese momento estaba exiliado en España. En estas películas, el compromiso político es lo que sirve de motor para el trabajo cinematográfico. En una declaración del grupo Cine Liberación, Solanas y Getino describen esta relación de la siguiente manera: "Nuestro compromiso como hombres de cine y como individuos de un país dependiente, no es ni con la cultura universal, ni con el arte, ni con el hombre en abstracto; es, ante todo, con la liberación" (Solanas/ Getino 9). El cine se convertía así en un instrumento para "la liberación de las masas argentinas." La dimensión política del cine residía en la movilización de las masas y la incitación a una acción liberadora, la que implicaba un desafío a las estructuras de distribución encontrando su expresión en la realización de proyecciones, a veces clandestinas, en barrios marginales, y dirigidas a una audiencia de trabajadores, estudiantes e intelectuales. La relación entre el cine y la política se refleja en los documentales por medio de una estrecha relación entre forma y contenido, es decir, entre estética e ideología. Para Ana Amado la relación del cine y la política en aquella época puede describirse como "un vínculo absoluto, condensado en la tensión entre forma y contenido –la dupla que replicaba en el cine la de estética e ideología" (Amado 158).

La crisis de 2001 como una fisura en la realidad social que divide la historia en un antes y un después, provocó la re-politización de gran parte de la sociedad y, con ello, un resurgimiento del cine militante.[7] Éste vuelve a ganar fuerza y se transforma en el compañero por excelencia de las movilizaciones masivas cuya expresión máxima son los cacerolazos de diciembre de 2001.[8] En ese tiempo surge el mito del cineasta como un hombre solitario que sale a la calle a documentar la realidad que le rodea, una

---

[6] El panorama político de aquel tiempo está marcado por la dictadura de la junta militar liderada por Juan Carlos Onganía, después del golpe de estado de 1966. La dictadura militar y la inestable situación política provocaron la radicalización de las organizaciones populares (cf. Tcach).

[7] "En ese sentido, los grupos de cine militante existen sólo en tanto y en cuanto la crisis no sólo se hace presente, sino que muestra el rostro más feroz de las políticas neoliberales. Y de esta manera se constituyen como experiencias estéticas desde la crisis, y 'gracias' a ella. La mayoría de estos grupos surgieron luego de los sucesos de diciembre del 2001 y son impensables sin ella: puede pensarse que son 'hijos' de la crisis" (Puente s.p.).

[8] *Cacerolazo* se llaman las manifestaciones en las que los manifestantes traen ollas y sartenes de las casas y las usan como tambores. Las manifestaciones del 19 y 20 de diciembre de 2001 fueron los cacerolazos más grandes de la historia y provocaron la renuncia del presidente Fernando de la Rúa. En nuestro contexto se usa este término, específicamente, para referirnos a la protesta de aquellos días.

realidad explosiva y prometedora en cuanto a la reaparición de la fuerza popular.[9] Se forman nuevos grupos cineastas, o ganan fuerza otros que se habían constituido antes, respectivamente el M*ovimiento documentalista* que se forma antes de la crisis, DOCA, una asociación de cineastas documentales que operan bajo el lema "una idea en la cabeza y una cámara en la mano," *Cine Ojo* –vinculado orgánicamente al Partido Obrero (PO)– y *Contraimagen* –promovido por militantes y simpatizantes independientes del Partido Trabajador Socialista (PTS)–, por nombrar algunos. La crisis dio impulso a nuevos debates políticos y llevó a que muchos de estos cineastas retomaran la ideología de grupos como el Cine Liberación o el Cine de Base de Raymundo Gleyzer. Así lo señalan los directores de *Raymundo* (2002) y *Corazón de Fábrica* (2008) Ernesto Ardito y Virna Molina, cofundadores de DOCA, en una entrevista realizada por la autora:[10]

> El cine tenía un objetivo concreto que era servir a esa lucha, o servir a esa huelga o esclarecer y llevar claridad o otro punto de vista distinto a la comunidad en general, para seguir abriendo el debate, para discutir. El objetivo principal era hacer crecer la conciencia política de la gente y rescatar el interés en un montón de cosas, que no existían y creo que es en este sentido … nos sentimos, como que sí, que hay que continuar ese camino, hay que continuar esa lucha sobre todo hoy. Porque hoy estamos peor que en los sesenta, setenta. Hoy hay mucho menos debate, mucho menos conciencia, mucho menos conciencia política … (Lakeberg s.p.)

La cita muestra que se sigue pensando el documental como un estímulo para suscitar debates políticos, que –como señalan Ardito y Molina–, en la actualidad no encuentran cabida en el espacio público. De este modo, el documental quiere incentivar un proceso de concientización de la sociedad. Los directores del cine militante –hoy en día al igual que antes– se consideran voceros que pueden alcanzar a un público mayoritario y, de tal manera, difundir las ideas y críticas que no son divulgadas en los medios masivos estatales, ni tampoco en los privados. Aunque las discusiones en los circuitos del cine militante siguen vitales, se pone en cuestión la obra de los cineastas de los sesenta y setenta y se buscan nuevas expresiones estéticas de lo político. Pero, de todos modos la premisa fundamental no se ha perdido: el cine militante sigue inscrito en la tradición del documental como arma política.

Fernando Solanas representa el legado vivo del cine militante no solamente por su obra, sino también por sus actividades políticas. Fundó, entre otros, el movimiento político, social y cultural "Proyecto Sur" por el cual participó como candidato a la presidencia de la república en las elecciones realizadas en 2007. Un tema central del movimiento es la lucha en contra de la deuda externa, tema enfocado también en *Memoria del saqueo*. Su postura militante se manifiesta también en su recién estrenado docu-

---

[9] Un trabajo que retoma esa idea del cineasta solitario que sale a la calle a documentar es: *El compañero que lleva la cámara. Cine militante argentino* (cf. Puente/Russo). Para más detalles acerca de la ideología del DOCA cf. la página web del movimiento.

[10] Los directores Ernesto Ardito y Virna Molina, entrevistados en Buenos Aires en junio del 2007, actualmente ya no son miembros del DOCA.

mental *Tierra sublevada* (2009) que forma parte del fresco sobre el país iniciado con *Memoria del saqueo*. Al igual que el nuevo cine militante, la obra reciente de Solanas es una reacción significativa a la crisis al reinterpretar la realidad social con un lenguaje fílmico que se inscribe en la militancia en razón de sus premisas políticas, su estética y su simbología.

Opuesto a estas tendencias del cine militante, hay otro movimiento de cine en la Argentina actual que, irónicamente, se conoce con el mismo nombre que en los años setenta había sido usado para el cine de Solanas y Getino, el "nuevo cine argentino." Esta denominación se aplica hoy, especialmente, al cine de ficción, pero proponemos ampliarla también para el documental ya que muchas películas se destacan por cruzar o cuestionar el deslinde entre documental y ficción. Por ende, lo que estas obras tienen en común no es necesariamente el formato. Aunque en el nuevo cine argentino se incluye un grupo muy heterogéneo de cineastas, éstos comparten rasgos comunes relativos al lenguaje cinematográfico y a la postura frente a la vida contemporánea social y política.[11] De la misma manera que las nuevas generaciones de cineastas militantes, también ellos son "hijos de la crisis," ya que la peculiaridad de su estética se corresponde con la atmósfera social resultante de ésta y sus películas se ubican, en su gran mayoría, en el presente. La crisis –que deja estallar un pasado inestable y dibuja un futuro inseguro–, intensifica la necesidad de reubicarse en la contemporaneidad, rechazando las proyecciones hacia el futuro y la nostalgia del pasado. Según Wolf: "A la pregunta de qué es hoy la Argentina y qué podemos decir de ella, los nuevos cineastas responden con historias y sistemas de representación que están fijados en la pura contemporaneidad" (33). El rechazo de la militancia del pasado provoca una búsqueda de nuevos significados de lo político. El imprevisible mundo contemporáneo pide su reformulación:

> El cuestionamiento a la repartición de tareas entre los que son y los que no son políticos apareció a lo largo de la modernidad de varios modos, y la mítica consigna que como una bandera en llamas atravesó el año 2002 argentino, "que se vayan todos," pone de relieve una vez más esta creencia firmemente asentada. Los acontecimientos de diciembre de 2001 mostraron lo diluido y lo corroído de la trama tejida con la tela de la sociedad, pero también evidenciaron las nuevas formas que lo político va adquiriendo en el imprevisible mundo contemporáneo. (Mundo 66)

Del reconocimiento de que la sociedad es débil y la política traicionera, surge la posibilidad de cuestionar lo que se ha dado por sentado. Esta búsqueda de sentido desatada por la crisis será el leitmotiv del nuevo cine argentino. Esta forma de hacer cine se ocupa de deconstruir cualquiera ideología o utopía que proponen imaginar un futuro.

---

[11] "Más que una generación, que se ve obligada a reconocer a sus padres, el grupo es una tendencia estética que se produjo desde mediados de los noventa. El nuevo cine argentino se caracteriza por su heterogeneidad, por su falta de un programa que agrupe a los cineastas en una generación. Sin embargo, si hay algo que une al movimiento es su espíritu voluntarioso de transformación y su manera de establecer un diálogo con el país, el cine anterior y entre ellos mismos" (Varas/Dash 193-94).

Lo contemporáneo es la inspiración con la que cuentan los cineastas. Y si se narra la historia nacional, como en *Yo Presidente*, la narración destruye y reinterpreta las visiones anteriores, reemplazándolas por un análisis que se niega a incorporar soluciones políticas.

La crítica y los estudios de cine se han preocupado de investigar las dimensiones políticas que, según ellos, sí residen en las obras del nuevo cine argentino. El ensayista argentino Daniel Mundo argumenta en su ensayo "Apuestas políticas del nuevo cine argentino" en favor de un cine contemporáneo que hable desde un lugar ideológicamente indefinido, pero al mismo tiempo se pregunta:

> ¿Cómo es eso que una película que narra un fragmento de la vida cotidiana, que no se quiere manifestar ni se respalda en una consigna ideológica, que se ubica en la antípoda de lo que corrientemente se entiende por cine político o comprometido, que renuncia a la mirada omniabarcadora y se contenta con captar una de las inumerables capas de la realidad, termine siendo una obra política? (67)

Una posible respuesta a esta pregunta, –que es afín a nuestra interpretación–, nos la da Gonzalo Aguilar, quien de esta manera abre el debate acerca de una reformulación de lo político.

> El hecho de que al hablar de la política en las películas del nuevo cine argentino se desemboque en su negación (como prepolítica o despolitización) nos lleva a preguntarnos si no se trata de redefinir su estatuto. Ya no como algo que se encuentra desplazado (lo inédito sería entonces siempre prepolítica) o suprimido (la diferencia, entonces, sólo puede ser despolitización), sino como una categoría que adquiere nuevas potencias y cualidades en un medio cuya función se ha transformado. (136)

Estas nuevas "potencias" y "cualidades" se pueden relacionar con aquello que en los estudios culturales, Néstor García Canclini llama "poderes oblicuos." En su obra *Culturas híbridas* (1998), pone en tela de juicio la bipolaridad de la estructura social y constata que "los cruces entre lo culto y lo popular relativizan la oposición entre hegemónicos y subalternos, concebida como si se tratara de conjuntos totalmente distintos y siempre enfrentados" (323). Lo oblicuo en este sentido es lo que se niega a ser expresado por relaciones verticales, la concepción del mundo social a través de una estructura bipolar que, como resultado, parece reducir las relaciones de poder, dejando de lado lo transversal y lo sinuoso.

En el caso del cine militante –y, por lo tanto, también en *Memoria del saqueo*– la bipolaridad entre pueblo y políticos o, en otras palabras, entre subalternos y hegemonía, es un elemento fundamental y sirve de base narrativa; por el contrario, el nuevo cine argentino, da cuenta de una "sociología de rejas," como titula García Canclini la idea de una sociología que se preocupa de las interdependencias, las mezclas extrañas y contradictorias (cf. 322).

La representación de los poderes oblicuos se manifiesta no solamente en el contenido de las películas de este movimiento. Existe un afán entre los directores del nuevo cine argentino por reflexionar sobre su propio lenguaje cinematográfico y la forma fílmica en general. Las ideas resultantes desembocan en una postura crítica frente al cine como medio de comunicación y a su valor testimonial. En consecuencia, tienden a buscar un lenguaje propio capaz de visualizar la incomodidad con aquellos sistemas representativos que los directores consideran anacrónicos.[12]

Con respecto a la noción de lo político, las transformaciones que se registran en el lenguaje cinematográfico –no solamente en el del nuevo cine argentino, sino también en el cine militante–[13] no tienen que ver sólo con la crisis nacional argentina. Antes bien responden a transformaciones globales. La política nacional pierde peso, ya que la nación se enfrenta a sobrepoderes inter-, supra- y transnacionales, ya sean económicos o políticos. Queda de manifiesto la creciente fuerza de las organizaciones transnacionales no gubernamentales y de las constelaciones regionales (UE, Mercosur). De este modo surgen discusiones sobre lo que Luhmann llama la sociedad mundial (*Weltgesellschaft*), las constelaciones posnacionales, la pregunta sobre la gobernamentalidad de un mundo que –al menos, parcialmente– enfrenta problemas y riesgos similares. La nación en crisis implica también la crisis de la categoría pueblo y de cómo hablar de lo político hoy en día. El pueblo, como concepto, no puede quedar en pie si su gemelo conceptual, la nación, padece una profunda transformación semántica.

En los imaginarios contemporáneos aparece un concepto que se opone al entendimiento tradicional de lo popular y que se denomina la *masa posmoderna*. Según Sloterdijk:

> Es una masa carente de potencial alguno, una suma de microanarquismos y soledades que apenas recuerda ya la época en la que ella –excitada y conducida hacia sí misma a través de sus portavoces y secretarios generales– debía y quería hacer historia en virtud de su condición de colectivo preñado de expresividad. (18)

Siguiendo a Sloterdijk, referirse al pueblo como tal se vuelve difícil. Si la idea del pueblo se ha diluido en el mundo posmoderno y globalizado, se replantea la pregunta de ¿a quién dirigirse con el cine y cómo hacerlo? Mientras el cine militante afirma la necesidad de un "pueblo," (re)construyéndolo como referencia para las luchas políticas y su visión de lo político, el nuevo cine argentino constata que el pueblo se ha vuelto un mito. En la esfera privada es en donde el NCA encuentra su visión de un mundo que se caracteriza por el cuestionamiento de valores y conceptos que han sido fundamentales pero que, según ellos, hoy en día están desapareciendo.

---

[12] El documental *Los rubios* (2005) de Albertina Carri es un ejemplo muy interesante de tal tendencia (cf. también el artículo de Daniela Noll-Opitz en este mismo volumen).

[13] Aunque defiendan el cine como arma que sirve para la lucha social, los directores entrevistados del nuevo cine militante constatan que el trabajo en el marco de un partido les parece imposible. Posición que es también el resultado de la poca confianza que actualmente existe en el sistema político y sus partidos.

3. "Un día explota ardorosa la pasión, la muchedumbre se hace pueblo": la representación del pueblo en *Memoria del saqueo*

Las imágenes del cacerolazo en *Memoria del saqueo* son centrales para la representación fílmica del pueblo. Muestran un pueblo unido en la acción contra la política oficial. Las imágenes se caracterizan por la masa de cuerpos en movimiento, sonidos salvajes y confusos y una cámara que, a causa de toda esta agitación, no sabe adónde dirigirse. Tal registro de los hechos es una estrategia que pone el centro de interés en los sucesos filmados y da énfasis al papel del director como observador participante.

La filmación consigue que el pueblo incorpore el rencor transformado, la unión de intereses diversos, la solidaridad. Así se da al colectivo la posibilidad de oponerse al sistema. Como resume Díaz del Moral:

> La población es la masa, el banco de peces, el montón gregario, indiferente a lo social, sumiso a todos los poderes, inactivo ante el mal, resignado con su dolor. Pero, aún en ese estado habitual de dispersión, subyace en el espíritu de la multitud el sentimiento profundo de su unidad originaria; el agravio y la injusticia van acumulando rencores y elevando el tono en su vida afectiva, y un día, ante el choque sentimental que actúa de fulminante, explota ardorosa la pasión, la muchedumbre se hace pueblo, el rebaño se transforma en ser colectivo. (43-44)

En el documental de Fernando Solanas tenemos ante nuestros ojos justamente el momento de la transformación: el pueblo y la necesidad de organizarse son el fundamento de la argumentación. Es un pueblo en el que "descansan la resistencia y una conciencia inalienable" (Aguilar 146). En este sentido es un concepto de "masa" opuesto al de Sloterdijk quien entiende por ello un número de individuos que carece de una expresión colectiva.

La diégesis de *Memoria del saqueo* está marcada por el contraste esquemático entre la subalternidad y el poder que resalta desde la secuencia titular. Las imágenes de pobreza victimizan a las personas subalternas por medio de la perspectiva de la cámara en contrapicado que los aplasta contra el suelo mostrándolos despojados de poder y articulación. Estas imágenes de la subalternidad se contraponen a los espacios de poder que se muestran desde un ángulo picado, representándolos, de esta manera, como omnipotentes e inalcanzables. La situación que se dibuja así es desesperanzadora. La sucesión de imágenes ensambladas en un montaje expresivo provoca efectos de ruptura en el espectador e intensifica la impresión de una profunda fisura entre la sociedad y la clase política.

Frente a estas imágenes, el pueblo como protagonista colectivo se construye cinematográficamente por medio de las imágenes del cacerolazo, las que aparecen inmediatamente después de la secuencia titular y se repiten al finalizar la película. De esta manera, la estructura temporal circular[14] del documental se basa en las tomas de las

---

[14] "El tiempo circular está determinado por una sucesión de acontecimientos ordenados de tal modo que el punto de llegada de la serie resulte ser idéntico al de origen" (Casetti/Di Chio 152).

manifestaciones como punto de partida y punto de llegada, lo que confiere a estas protestas un especial énfasis como momento clave en la historia del "saqueo." Con respecto al tratamiento estético de las imágenes en cuestión, se destaca la falta del comentario en off. Es muy significativa la ausencia de la *voice of god* cuando la película representa el pueblo. En contraste, en las escenas en las que se muestra la esfera hegemónica, el comentario en off asume un papel protagónico, dado que provee e interpreta las imagenes e informaciones que apoyan la argumentación.[15] En el caso de la multitud del cacerolazo, el documentalista opta por la fuerza de las imágenes en vez de guiarnos con sus palabras. El espectador ve cuerpos en movimiento que enfrentan a la policía y escucha un sonido sincrónico abrumador. El impacto de las imágenes y la falta del comentario animan a identificarse plenamente con lo visual: se crea la impresión de que nada existe entre el espectador y el pueblo.

Si en la secuencia titular de la película se construye un contraste irreconciliable en términos espaciales por medio de la perspectiva de la cámara –monumentales espacios de poder versus espacios minimizados de pobreza–, aquí es el pueblo quien llega a reconquistar los espacios de poder convirtiéndolos de nuevo en "propiedad popular." En la secuencia de cierre, la cámara entra en la Casa Rosada –Sede del Poder Ejecutivo de Argentina– y recorre los pasillos sin representantes del gobierno, en tanto que este vacío se va llenando con el ruido de los tambores de los manifestantes. En esta escena, la superposición de un sonido extradiegético crea un asincronismo entre la imagen y el sonido que se transforma en metáfora.[16] La invasión de los agresivos ruidos callejeros en el espacio solemne de la casa de gobierno destruye su inaccesibilidad, su aura de poder y devuelve,por un instante, el poder al pueblo. Esta metáfora es también adecuada para ver el papel que asume el mismo director en este proceso, puesto que la cámara –que representa en esta escena su punto de vista– encarna también la toma de conciencia del pueblo. En consecuencia, es él mismo quien guía al pueblo hacia la "reconquista" de los espacios de poder.

4. Lo que es está lejos: la representación del pueblo en *Yo Presidente*

Mientras que en *Memoria del saqueo* el pueblo se narra en base a una visión épica, *Yo Presidente* evita crear esta impresión. El pueblo se muestra como una muchedumbre, la cual celebra a sus presidentes con una histeria frenética y, paradójicamente, después

---

[15] Según Nichols el comentario en off tiene la siguiente función: "El comentario ofrece una orientación didáctica hacia la argumentación. El comentario guía nuestra comprensión de la visión moral y política que ofrece el texto documental. A diferencia de la perspectiva, desvía nuestra atención del mundo representado dirigiéndola hacia el discurso del texto, hacia las representaciones de una lógica documental" (174).

[16] Según Marcel Martín: "La metáfora consiste en hacer un paralelo entre un contenido visual y un elemento sonoro, en que el segundo está destinado a señalar el significado del primero mediante el valor gráfico y simbólico que posee en cierto modo" (128).

lucha contra la injusticia de estos gobiernos contra el pueblo. De este modo, la película cuestiona al pueblo como actor colectivo, cuya imagen se caracteriza por sentimientos de distancia y de ambigüedad.

Mientras que la cámara activa[17] de Fernando Solanas recorre la calle cediéndole la palabra a sus paisanos y observando la dura lucha contra la represión del estado, en *Yo Presidente* no se convive con el pueblo en los lugares públicos, sino que se explora el espacio privado del poder, relegando al pueblo, aparentemente, a un papel secundario.

En *Yo Presidente*, para referirse al pueblo, se usan imágenes televisivas que son introducidas una y otra vez para hacer un resumen de los sucesos históricos claves de cada presidencia. Estas imágenes, denominadas por Schejtman como "imágenes-hits de archivo" (12), evocan frecuentemente la estética de los sueños según el lenguaje convencional del cine de ficción: hay un elaborado trabajo sobre sus colores y los perfiles se desdibujan. Resalta, sobre todo, el blanco de los planos. Los contrastes transforman las imágenes en blanco y negro y hacen que éstas se vean borrosas. En algunos casos, se introduce artificialmente otro color, como por ejemplo, cuando se ven las imágenes de un atentado y la sangre de un herido estalla en un rojo brillante. En otro caso, se emplea la cámara lenta y lo representado adquiere un significado adicional que lo aleja de su valor testimonial. Acerca de la cámara lenta Walter Benjamin constata: "So, too, slow motion not only presents familiar qualities of movement but reveals in them entirely unknown ones which, far from looking like retarded rapid movements, give the effect of singularly gliding, floating, supernatural motions" (18). De esta manera la cámara lenta no sólo revela movimientos que, de otra manera, no hubiéramos percibido, sino que trasciende la supuesta realidad y pierde su relación inmediata con ella implícita en la mímesis documental. Por medio de los efectos descritos se pone énfasis en la polisemia de lo visual y se sugieren diversas lecturas posibles. Esto implica que al espectador se le dificulta la identificación con el pueblo. Así, a pesar de que las imágenes sean parecidas, el público no se involucra emocionalmente como en el caso de *Memoria del saqueo*.

Y si no es ya la estética peculiar de las imágenes, es la palabra la que establece una distancia entre el espectador y el pueblo. Mientras el espectador sigue las imágenes estéticamente defamiliarizadas, oye la voz de un ex-presidente que da su versión de los hechos o habla de alguna cosa que banaliza lo visto: se habla de pasatiempos, de la nariz prominente de De la Rúa, etc. Imágenes –como la gente manifestándose, la agresión de los policías, los cuerpos en agitación–, que en el documental de Solanas tienen tanta fuerza e inmediatez, en *Yo Presidente* pierden su impacto por lo que Nichols

---

[17] El movimiento propio de la cámara tiene implicaciones. Casetti y di Chio formulan: "El movimiento de cámara, gracias a su cohesión y a su concentración espacial y temporal, induce a un mayor sentido de inmediatez y de la verdad, da siempre idea de una presencia real" (94).

llama la reflexividad estilística.[18] Ésta provoca que las imágenes se perciban como a través de un velo. Parecen ser un sueño o fragmentos de una película de acción, cualquier cosa, menos un testimonio de la realidad histórica.

En cuanto al contenido fílmico, el pueblo pierde importancia no sólo por la peculiar puesta en escena, sino porque los directores del documental representan la cúspide del poder desde sus refugios privados. Si en *Memoria del saqueo*, tanto la diferenciación espacial entre lo hegemónico y lo subalterno como su transgresión, son premisas sobre las que se construye la diégesis, en *Yo Presidente* se juega con las implicaciones sociales de esta división espacial y se invierte su simbología. Apoyándonos en la teoría espacial elaborada por la socióloga alemana Renate Ruhne explicaremos brevemente cuáles son las implicaciones de esta inversión. Según ella la diferenciación de los espacios es, sobre todo, una construcción social que se reproduce por medio de estructuras que han sido internalizadas por los individuos:

> De esta manera la separación y diferenciación espacial (y material) de la esfera pública y el espacio privado se han cargado de un significado social. Así, los espacios públicos y los espacios privados no se produjeron únicamente a través de una separación y diferenciación del sustrato espacial, sino que se relacionaron con estructuras muy específicas de interacción y actuación, reglamentos normativos y también con una simbología distinta cuya respectiva orientación se deja describir fundamentalmente con las palabras claves de "lucha" por un lado, y "paz casera" por el otro. (Ruhne 89, traducción de la autora)

La división entre lo privado y lo público se convierte, entonces, en una red de instrucciones para la actuación social. El espacio privado se entiende como espacio individual, íntimo, que no debe ser penetrado por los demás. En cambio, el espacio público es aquél donde se realiza la acción social, la "lucha." *Yo Presidente* trabaja con la división espacial en tanto que trastorna esta semántica: el espacio público se vacía de su explosividad y la intimidad del espacio privado se convierte en escenario para deconstruir la narración hegemónica sobre los protagonistas de la política argentina. Al no respetar las estructuras de la actuación social, normalmente invisibles y dadas por hecho, el documental abre el espacio para reflexionar sobre ellas y, así, sobre una de las bases fundamentales de la sociedad moderna.

Al contrario de *Memoria del saqueo*, el pueblo no constituye un sujeto revolucionario en *Yo Presidente*. La multitud se presenta aquí –afín al pensamiento de Sloterdijk–, como una masa carente de potencial alguno. Esto se consigue por medio de varias estrategias narrativas: la distancia que los directores crean entre el carácter testimonial y la puesta en escena peculiar de las imágenes, la inversión del significado del espacio público y, finalmente, la negación de adoptar la postura popular.

Esta negación parece ser parte de un implícito diálogo crítico con el cine militante que desemboca en una propuesta estética propia del nuevo cine argentino frente a la

---

[18] Segun Nichols la reflexividad estilistica describe estrategias que "quebrantan convenciones aceptadas. ... Se introducen fisuras, inversiones y giros inesperados que dirigen nuestra atención hacia el trabajo del estilo" (108).

realidad social. Propuesta que se caracteriza por el rechazo de los directores a ejercer su autoridad narrativa de manera tan explícita como lo hace Solanas. Mientras éste establece el sentido por medio de la modalidad expositiva,[19] Cohen y Duprat aparentan dar más libertad al espectador. Su posición política no se encuentra tanto a nivel de contenido, sino, primero, en el deseo de deconstruir y subvertir las narraciones hegemónicas o dogmáticas, ya sea de los discursos oficiales televisivos o de los discursos esquemáticos de la militancia de izquierdas como en *Memoria del saqueo*. De esta manera, *Yo Presidente* se inscribe en la estética del nuevo cine argentino en el que domina la incomodidad con la categoría pueblo que, sobre todo, sirve como "una manera de encuadrar" (Rancière 95). El pueblo figura como lo *otro*, a lo que no se tiene acceso:

> En el pueblo como *otredad*, en cambio, predomina la opacidad entre las relaciones, la inaccesibilidad a esa cultura ajena, y la sospecha, no siempre explícita, de que en los artefactos populistas no se muestra la cultura popular, sino la imagen idealizada que se tiene de la misma. La paradoja de este gesto es que debe negar la cultura popular a la vez que se hace un acercamiento a ella: se la representa como vacío, ausencia u opacidad, pero *algo* se representa. (152)

La opacidad de la representación del pueblo en *Yo Presidente*, visualizada por medio de los efectos antes descritos, evita la directa identificación de parte del espectador. Al mismo tiempo, la relación con los representantes de la hegemonía política también se caracteriza por la misma imposibilidad de identificación. Surge, entonces, la pregunta sobre la necesidad de contrastar entre ambas representaciones. ¿Es tal vez necesario construir al pueblo en contraste con sus líderes para que su fuerza se desate en las imágenes? En este documental, las figuras de los líderes políticos, –como veremos después–, son deconstruidas, ridiculizadas, son objeto de una burla abierta. ¿Es tal vez por eso que el pueblo tampoco puede quedarse en su pedestal?

5. La fiesta de los traidores: la representación de los presidentes en *Memoria del saqueo*

En la película de Solanas, las estrategias de representación con la que se describe la cúspide del poder se distinguen claramente de la manera como se construye el pueblo. Un elemento fundamental, utilizado por Solanas, es la peculiar puesta en escena de los cuerpos de los ex-presidentes, la que difiere diametralmente de la película de Cohn y Duprat. Nos serviremos del concepto de cuerpo político de Paula Diehl para esaminar este aspecto. Diehl explica que el cuerpo tiene un papel de importancia primordial en el mundo político ya que no sólo representa la política, sino, de igual manera, la produce de manera performativa. El cuerpo político tiene que legitimar y representar el po-

---

[19] La modalidad expositiva se define según Nichols como un texto que "se dirige al espectador directamente, con intertítulos o voces que exponen una argumentación acerca del mundo histórico. Los textos expositivos toman forma en torno a un comentario … en el cual las imágenes sirven como ilustración o contrapunto … y hacen hincapié en la impresión de objetividad y juicio bien establecido" (68).

der y, al mismo tiempo, coexiste en una difícil y contradictoria relación con el cuerpo físico. Afirma Diehl que: "el cuerpo político/simbólico está vinculado estrechamente con el mundo de la representación y por eso no puede morir. El cuerpo físico, en cambio, es material y mortal, pero al mismo tiempo es portador de la representación política" (43, traducción de la autora). Celikates y Rothöhler aclaran con respecto a la performatividad del cuerpo político:

> En el cuerpo del político se unen pragmática y estética –es decir, producción y representación de la política–, en una instancia estéticamente definible, a la cual se pueden atribuir procesos políticos y la cual, en caso de duda, se puede hacer responsable de esos procesos. (62, traducción de la autora)

A este binomio cuerpo político-cuerpo físico, se añade el cuerpo mediático como un tercer concepto propuesto por Diehl, un cuerpo que no es ni político ni privado y forma parte de la construcción de la figura mediática del político (59). La aplicación de este concepto es particularmente fructífera en el análisis de la representación de los políticos en este documental, dado que el ex-presidente Carlos Menem fue un excelente ejemplo de la forma como jugó con los medios de comunicación, una relación caracterizada por la mutua dependencia. Menem se puso y fue puesto en escena por medio de clichés, fantasías de riqueza y potencia sexual que más parecían las características de protagonistas de telenovelas. Menem se construyó y fue construido según una "lógica de consumo y entretenimiento" (Diehl 58). Solanas, al usar material de archivo recurre a esta construcción mediática del ex-presidente, al mismo tiempo que lo recontextualiza históricamente para integrarlo en su línea de argumentación. Esta representación de Menem critica la imposibilidad de la existencia de un campo político que sea autónomo de la lógica de consumo. La evidencia de este proceso de comodificación es el cuerpo de Menem que representa la traición política del neoliberalismo al pueblo por medio de una imagen que es consumible, o para decirlo con Rothöhler y Celikates, que reúne estética y pragmática bajo una lógica de consumo y entretenimiento.

En el documental, este argumento se evidencia en las imágenes fílmicas de Menem que muestran al ex-presidente jugando al golf, bailando tango y junto a los *Rolling Stones*. Algunas de estas imágenes han sido tratadas con filtros, colores etc, en la post-producción. Llegan a funcionar como códigos visuales que solamente se aplican a la representación de los "enemigos" del pueblo, es decir, los medios de comunicación, los presidentes, los jueces, etc. A manera de ejemplo, nos serviremos de una secuencia en la que se intercalan –en un montaje asociativo y extremadamente rápido– imágenes de talkshows, de fiestas y de símbolos de riqueza haciendo uso de la estética de videoclip.[20] Carlos Menem aparece una y otra vez en medio de este flujo de imágenes. Muchas de estas tomas se destacan por sus colores fuertes, connotadores de lo

---

[20] La estilización de las imágenes evidencia lo que comparten ambos documentales: conceptos de narración documental que no se basan en la idea de una fiel representación. Se puede definir con el concepto de reflexividad estilística (cf. Nichols 108) y que en este contexto funciona para construir un contrapunto a través del contraste logrado mediante el tratamiento de las imágenes.

irreal del mundo televisivo que hacen alusión a una hiperrealidad, una realidad fetichizada creada por los medios. Realidad que está en fuerte contraste con la realidad social descrita por Solanas.[21]

La secuencia está enmarcada por imágenes de la decadencia –fábricas en desuso, locales cerrados y gente durmiendo en la calle–, en las que dominan los colores grisáceos. En este mundo gris estallan los colores que introducen la secuencia en cuestión. Cuando ésta termina, vuelven las imágenes de la decadencia nacional, se ve la calle de una villa miseria anegada por el agua. La secuencia descrita ejemplifica cómo en *Memoria del saqueo* se establecen los signos de diferenciación a través del tratamiento creativo de la imagen documental que, en su artificialidad, puede ser reconocida por el espectador como parte de un efecto brechtiano de defamiliarizacion que impacta en su percepción del mundo representado.

6. Lo que circula alrededor: la representación de los presidentes en *Yo Presidente*

En *Yo Presidente* la representación de los presidentes se realiza, aparentemente, de manera más directa ya que las imágenes son tomadas de entrevistas realizadas originalmente para esta película y no, como en el caso de *Memoria del saqueo*, tomas de archivo. Sin embargo, el sentido se construye más bien de manera indirecta por medio de los objetos que circulan en torno a los políticos y por medio del montaje y la filmación. Así, los cuerpos de los políticos forman parte de una densa red de atributos contradictorios y ambiguos.

La peculiaridad de la representación fílmica de los protagonistas reside en su inclusión en la realidad profílmica (cf. Hohenberger 30)[22], y por tanto, en el proceso de la filmación. No se eliminan las indicaciones de los realizadores ni los lapsos de tiempo muerto. Al contrario, el foco de atención se centra en las indicaciones, los momentos de descanso, de preparación del escenario, y del proceso de la producción. Esa estrategia pone a los supuestos protagonistas más bien en los márgenes de la narración.

---

[21] El concepto de hiperrealidad describe, según Baudrillard, el siguiente fenómeno: "The end of the spectacle brings with it the collapse of reality into hyperrealism, the meticulous reduplication of the real, preferably through another reproductive medium such as advertising or photography. Through the reproduction from one medium into another the real becomes volatile, it becomes the allegory of death, but it also draws strength from its own destruction, becoming the real for its own sake, a fetishism of the lost object which is no longer the object of its representation, but the ecstasy of denegation and its own real extermination: the hyperreal" (72).

[22] "Se refiere a la realidad que está presente en el momento de la filmación. Se la puede reconstruir a base de la película misma o, si existen, a base de documentos sobre el proceso de la filmación. De la relación que tiene la realidad profílmica con la realidad no-fílmica (y la realidad profílmica en el caso del documental ha sido antes realidad no-fílmica) se puede concluir qué fragmento de la realidad escogió el director" (Hohenberger 30, traducción de la autora).

Durante las entrevistas, los protagonistas se muestran con extrema nitidez usando primeros y primerísimos planos. La composición del encuadre pone la cara del entrevistado no en el centro, sino a un costado cortando la mitad de la cara. La asimetría y el hecho de que se descentralice la figura del protagonista socavan la importancia que parece concederle el enfoque. El uso de primeros y primerísimos planos es propio del cine de ficción, donde se emplean especialmente cuando se quieren mostrar las emociones más profundas de un personaje provocando el efecto de no haber "baranda entre el espectáculo y el espectador," penetrando en la vida en vez de sencillamente observarla. De tal manera permite "todas las intimidades," según Martín (44-45).

La búsqueda del personaje sin maquillaje, del "Yo" de los representantes políticos, de la autenticidad de sus actuaciones tiene lugar por medio de estrategias fílmicas que no dejan escapar ningún gesto no intencional: éstas incluyen también el trabajo con el sonido que ocupa un papel central en la creación de sentido. El sonido traiciona lo dicho por los presidentes, asociando sus opiniones con arbitrariedad. Cuando, por ejemplo, los ex-presidentes aparecen hablando de sus pasatiempos, su alimentación, etc., se sobrepone el sonido de otra respuesta a la misma pregunta confluyendo así, varias respuestas de ellos a la misma pregunta. Por consiguiente, lo expresado carece de inmediatez y aparece como parte de una puesta en escena que sigue las instrucciones de los directores. Son ellos quienes insisten en la repetición criticando una y otra vez la velocidad de las afirmaciones monológicas, la claridad de la pronunciación etc. El efecto conseguido al sobreponer las distintas versiones es la arbitrariedad que implica el contenido de las respuestas y pone de manifiesto la artificialidad del escenario que ha sido creado y elegido por los directores. Estas estrategias narrativas quitan, por un lado, el aura de autoridad a los políticos y, por el otro, matizan de arbitrariedad lo que se dice y lo que se mira.

El cuerpo y la voz de los protagonistas pierden su importancia, las manifestaciones del cuerpo privado junto a la pérdida de control sobre el cuerpo político producen un conflicto en la representación de estos dos cuerpos. Esto se debe, especialmente, a las huellas visibles de la vejez, lo que conlleva la percepción de la materialidad corporal. Con la representación de los cuerpos envejecidos, los directores crean una puesta en escena contraria a la que ha sido institucionalizada por los canales televisivos. Este "modo institucionalizado de informar" –como lo llama Gustavo Jalife– se convierte en una narrativa hegemónica. Este modo, finalmente, no es "neutro, ni independiente de las relaciones que los medios periodísticos entretejen a diario con el poder" y se basa en "el encadenamiento de las palabras e imágenes estandarizadas que precipitan un sentido pre-fabricado" en vez de abrir un espacio de reflexión. Según el autor, *Yo Presidente* revela la farsa de la representación política: "farsa es el nombre del juego cuyas reglas Duprat y Cohn develan con singular maestría."

El presidente Menem, que en *Memoria del saqueo* y, por lo tanto, según el "modo institucionalizado de informar" se mostraba como un mujeriego deportivo, sale en *Yo Presidente* con una mosca sobre la nariz. La mirada iritada del ex-presidente y la siguiente exterminación de los insectos realizada por sus guardaespaldas con *Raid* y un matamoscas eléctrico –objeto que recuerda el uso de la picana como instrumento de tortura durante la dictadura–, producen, por el contrario, una representación fuera de control. La rigidez con la que se pretende salvar la representatividad de su imagen se relaciona con la necesidad de que el cuerpo exponga "en la política visualmente lo que representa" para que se "legitime la actuación política y se reconozca la autoridad de los políticos" (Diehl 42-43).

En el documental de Cohn y Duprat, los ex-presidentes no se representan con la dignidad que correspondería al cargo político que habían detentado. Sus cuerpos son cuerpos débiles. Y se sienten continuamente amenazados por peligros anónimos. Los guardaespaldas que circulan en torno a los cuerpos dan énfasis a la necesidad y el deseo de protección que tienen estos personajes. Todo lo que se mueve a su alrededor sirve para caracterizarlos. El control sobre su propia imagen mediatizada se les ha escapado. Gustavo Noriega de la revista *El Amante* afirma: "Los inquietantes entornos; los utensilios que circulan como armas, teléfonos, insecticidas, trofeos, fotos, retratos. La película arma y desarma a los presidentes como si fueran muñecos" (11).

La película los presenta como títeres que se dejan poner en escena por los realizadores. Son estos momentos los que sirven de "foco de inestabilidad" y en los que ellos subvierten las relaciones de poder dando cuenta de la "microfísica de poder" (Foucault, *Discipline* 27). Durante toda la película los directores indican a los presidentes qué hacer y cómo performar frente a la cámara. Juegan con gestos y elementos representativos que, siendo dictados, revelan el simulacro del poder. Como resultado, su posible lectura no desemboca en la legitimación de los poderosos sino, al contrario, en la deconstrucción de la performatividad del poder.

Se pueden dar varios ejemplos de este procedimiento: uno es el plano que muestra a Alfonsín haciendo su gesto de campana. Se muestra al político ya viejo, en su casa bien arreglada usando un encuadre bien trabajado, simétrico, donde el cuerpo sólo parece ser parte del decorado. En otro momento, cuando De la Rúa sigue la indicación de los directores y levanta el teléfono, no le es posible evitar una sonrisa artificial, forzada, que destruye toda solemnidad y pone en evidencia lo construido del gesto. De la misma manera, Menem dice las consignas de su campaña con voz cansada, monótona y desprovista de la energía de antes. Los débiles cuerpos de los tres políticos ya no pueden funcionar como legitimación del poder político.

Al contrario del lenguaje que se usa en los discursos políticos televisivos, el lenguaje cinematográfico de *Yo Presidente* dista mucho de respetar los parámetros del "modo institucionalizado de informar." Desmantela ante los ojos del espectador el funcionamiento de la representación de los cuerpos políticos. Tematiza lo corporal que existe al margen de la representación mediática y que, por la intimidad del trato, de pronto sale a la superficie. Se cuestionan los parámetros sobre cuya base se construye el mundo en los medios, la intocabilidad de las autoridades, la separación del espacio en público y privado, la distancia entre lo humano y lo político. Por consiguiente, el político figura como algo ajeno, lejano, extraño, preocupante que, al mismo tiempo, no podría ser más cercano, más humano, menos mitificado.

El lenguaje cinematográfico en *Yo Presidente* se caracteriza por conflictos constantes entre el contenido de la imagen, el sonido y el tratamiento de ambos. El picado que se usa de manera constante al principio de *Memoria del saqueo* para dar énfasis al poder hegemónico, se usa sólo una vez en las entrevistas de *Yo Presidente*: De la Rúa es filmado con ironía cuando, en picado, se le muestra hablando de su enfermedad y explicando el funcionamiento de un "stent." Los contrastes que se establecen en *Memoria del saqueo* entre los diferentes cuerpos –el cuerpo vulnerable, marcado por la pobreza y el cuerpo representativo que, como si fuera de hierro, parece ser invulnerable–, se reproducen en *Yo Presidente* en la imagen de un solo cuerpo. Esta estrategia narrativa aporta a la creación una sensación de ambigüedad, resultado de una profunda subversión del lenguaje cinematográfico y las adscripciones sociales que forman parte de las prácticas sociales y de las políticas de representación.

7. Conclusión

Los dos documentales comparten rasgos comunes y presentan, además, características que los diferencian. Común a ambos es que las técnicas usadas evidencian que la idea de que el documental es una representación fiel de la realidad social, ha sido reemplazada por un tratamiento creativo de la imagen documental. Las imágenes estilizadas que hacen alusión a una reflexividad estilística dan cuenta de este fenómeno. Ambos documentales, además, se enfrentan a una realidad contemporánea, altamente influenciada por lo medios masivos y las formas de representación que éstos han establecidos de manera dominante. En *Memoria del saqueo* lo vemos en el tratamiento que se le da al cuerpo mediático del Presidente Menem, y en *Yo Presidente*, se reflexiona durante toda la película sobre el fenómeno denominado por Gustavo Jalive como "modo institucionalizado de informar." Ambas películas también comparten –al igual que los movimientos cinematográficos en los que se inscriben– una cierta reflexión posmoderna sobre la realidad social. Asimismo, se puede constatar que los dos movimientos en que se inscriben los documentales, presuponen mutuamente la existencia de su contraparte: tanto el nuevo cine argentino como el cine militante actual se constituyen por un proceso de mutua diferenciación.

Sin embargo, más allá de las similitudes se perfilan dos visiones distintas de lo político. El cine militante sustenta un concepto de lo político que está estrechamente ligado con el estado-nación, la toma del poder por el pueblo y la participación de éste en los procesos políticos. De ahí surge que para los cineastas militantes el pueblo *sea* la nación. Y esta nación tiene la función de englobar bajo su fuerza coercitiva a la "suma de microanarquismos" de la multitud, porque de esta manera se posibilita la reorientación hacia una comunidad imaginada nacional. Finalmente es la nación, y su potencial de identificación, la que hará realidad la liberación de un país, que de la dependencia colonial pasó a depender de una clase política. Según la posición militante, esta última no ha conseguido garantizar a la mayor parte de la población una existencia digna y, más que nada, ha provocado una crisis económica, social y política que desembocó en

2001 en la desaparición de la clase media del país. El documental *Memoria del saqueo* es representativo de un cine concebido como arma política, con una argumentación coherente y, por ultimo tendenciosa. Su objetivo es crear un espectador ilustrado, que, por el conocimiento adquirido a través del documental, sea capaz de participar en el escenario político que le rodea. En resumen, el documental tiende a la construcción mediática del renacimiento de un pueblo útopico.

Para los cineastas del nuevo cine argentino, el conjuro de un pueblo unido parece extemporáneo y el estado-nación, un concepto que ha fallado y que poco tiene que ver con la realidad de la gente como para ser una oferta de identificación. *Yo Presidente* da cuenta de una sociología de rejas que rechaza un lenguaje esquemático. Su visión de lo político reside en la capacidad de reflexión sobre el medio audiovisual, por un lado, y, por el otro, sobre los fundamentos de la sociedad moderna y con ello, la política. Y, por último, informa sobre la relación entre los modos de representación y el objeto representado. La satírica representación de los ex presidentes desemboca en la exploración de prácticas sociales que (de)construyen cuerpos simbólicos, pueblos utópicos y el estado-nación como unidad funcional y estética.

Bibliografía

Aguilar, Gonzalo. *Otros mundos. Un ensayo sobre el nuevo cine argentino.* Buenos Aires: Santiago Acros Editores, 2006.

Amado, Ana. "Las políticas del cine político." *Pensamiento de los confines* 18 (julio 2006): 157-58.

Arfuch, Leonor. "Kultur, Kunst und Politik in der argentinischen Postkrise." *kultuRRevolution. Zeitschrift für angewandte Diskurstheorie* 51 (2006): 48-56.

Aumont, Jacques. *Estética del cine.* Barcelona: Paidós, 1985.

Baudrillard, Jean. *Symbolic Exchange and Death.* Thousand Oaks/London/New Dehli: Sage Publications, 1993.

Benjamin, Walter. "The Work of Art in the Age of Mechanical Reproduction." *Media and Cultural Studies. Keyworks.* Ed. Meenakshi Gigi Durham y Douglas Kellner. Oxford: Blackwell Publishing, 2008. 18-40.

Bhabha, Homi K. "Introduction. Narrating the Nation." *Nation and Narration.* Ed. Homi K. Bhabha. London: Routledge, 1990. 1-7.

Butler, Judith. *Gender Trouble. Feminism and the Subversion of Identity.* New York: Routledge, 1990.

Casetti, Francesco y Federico Di Chio. *Cómo analizar un film.* Barcelona: Paidós, 1991.

Celikates, Robin y Simon Rothöhler. "Die Körper der Stellvertreter. Politische Repräsentation zwischen Identität, Simulation und Institution. *Mr. Smith Goes to Washington, The Parallax View, The West Wing.*" *Inszenierungen der Politik. Der Körper als Medium.* Ed. Paula Diehl y Gertrud Koch. München: Wilhelm Fink Verlag, 2007. 57-75.

Díaz de Moral, Juan. *Historia de las agitaciones campesinas andaluzas. Córdoba: antecedentes para una reforma agraria.* Madrid: Alianza Editorial, 1969.

Diehl, Paula. "Körper, Soap Operas und Politik. Die Körperinszenierung von Fernando Collor de Mello und Silvio Berlusconi." *Macht – Performativität, Performanz und Politiktheater seit 1990.* Ed. Birgit Haas. Würzburg: Königshausen und Neumann, 2005. 41-59.

Doca. Documentalistas argentinos. 23 de marzo 2011. http://www.docacine.com.ar/.

Foucault, Michel. *Discipline and Punish.* Middlesex: Penguin Books, 1991.

———. *Security, Territory, Population. Lectures at the Collège de France 1977-1978.* Houndmills: Palgrave Macmillan, 2007.

García Canclini, Néstor. *Culturas híbridas. Estrategias para entrar y salir de la modernidad.* México: Grijalbo, 1989.

Gorodischer, Julián. "Menem se la pasó hablando de Charly García." *Página 12* 17 de septiembre de 2006. http://www.pagina12.com.ar/imprimir/diario/suplementos/espectaculos/2-3822-2006-09-17.html.

Hohenberger, Eva. *Die Wirklichkeit des Films. Dokumentarfilm, ethnographischer Film, Jean Rouch.* Hildesheim: Georg Olms Verlag, 1988.

Jalife, Gustavo. "'La venganza fue terrible. *Yo presidente,* manual de uso del político argentino." *Rayando los confines* (2006). http://www.rayandolosconfines.com.ar/critica_yopresi.html.

Lakeberg, Anne. "Entrevista a Raymundo Ardito y Virna Molina." Buenos Aires, junio 2007. Sin publicar.

Lie, Sulgi. "Der Ruhm des Beliebigen. Zur politischen Filmästhetik von Jacques Rancière." *Inszenierungen der Politik. Der Körper als Medium.* Ed. Paula Diehl y Gertrud Koch. München: Wilhelm Fink Verlag, 2007. 193-210.

Luhmann, Niklas. *La sociedad de la sociedad.* Barcelona: Herder, 2007.

Martín, Marcel. *El lenguaje del cine.* Barcelona: Gedisa, 2005.

Mundo, Daniel. *Pasatiempos. Lecturas políticas de la contemporaneidad argentina.* Buenos Aires: Santiago Acros Editores, 2006.

Nichols, Bill. *La representación de la realidad. Cuestiones y conceptos sobre la realidad.* Barcelona: Paidós, 1991.

Noriega, Gustavo. "Que de lejos parecen moscas." *El Amante* 137 (2006): 10-11.

Puente, Maximiliano de la. "Estética y política en el cine militante argentino actual." *Cuestión* 14 (otoño 2007). http://perio.unlp.edu.ar/question/numeros_anteriores/numero_anterior 14/nivel2/articulos/ensayos/delapuente_1_ensayos_14otono07.htm.

——— y Pablo Russo. *El compañero que lleva la cámara. Cine militante argentino.* Buenos Aires: El autor, 2007.

Rancière, Jacques. *Breves viajes al país del pueblo.* Buenos Aires: Nueva Visión, 1991.

Ruhne, Renate. *Raum, Macht, Geschlecht. Zur Soziologie des Wirkungsgefüges am Beispiel von Unsicherheiten im öffentlichen Raum.* Opladen: Leske+Budrich, 2003.

Schejtman, Natalí. "Chiquitos." *El Amante* 137 (2006): 12.

Schumann, Peter. *Handbuch des lateinamerikanischen Films*. Frankfurt a.M.: Vervuert, 1982.

Sloterdijk, Peter. *El desprecio de las masas. Ensayo sobre las luchas culturales de la sociedad moderna*. Barcelona: Paidós, 2002.

Solanas, Fernando E. *"Memoria del saqueo* (2004)." 8 de marzo 2011. http://www.pino solanas.com/memoria.htm.

───── y Octavio Getino. *Cine, cultura y descolonización*. Buenos Aires: Siglo XXI Editores, 1973.

Tcach, César. "Golpes, proscripciones y partidos políticos." *Nueva historia argentina. Violencia, proscripción y autoritarismo (1955-1976)*. Ed. Daniel James. Buenos Aires: Editorial Sudamericana, 2003. 49-54.

Varas, Patricia y Robert Dash. "(Re)imaginando la nación argentina: Lucrecia Martel y *La ciénaga*." *El cine argentino de hoy. Entre el arte y la política*. Ed. Viviana Rangil. Buenos Aires: Editorial Biblos, 2007.

Wolf, Sergio. "Las estéticas del nuevo cine argentino. El mapa es el territorio." *El nuevo cine argentino. Temas, autores y estilos de una renovación*. Ed. Horacio Bernardes, Diego Lerer y Sergio Wolf. Buenos Aires: Fipresci/Tatanka, 2002. 29-39.

Filmografía

Argentina latente. Dir. Fernando Solanas. Argentina, Francia y España, 2007.

Enciclopedia. Dir. Mariano Cohn, Adrián de Rosa y Gastón Duprat. Argentina, 2000.

La dignidad de los nadies. Dir. Fernando Solanas. Argentina, Brazil y Suiza, 2005.

La hora de los hornos. Dir. Fernando Solanas y Octavio Getino. Argentina, 1968.

Memoria del saqueo. Dir. Fernando Solanas. Argentina, Francia y Suiza, 2004.

Yo Presidente. Dir. Mariano Cohn y Gastón Duprat. Argentina, 2006.

II.

NARRATING THE NATION
FROM ITS MARGINS

Negotiating Equality: *Salt of the Earth* and the Narration of Nation

JOSEF RAAB

> Experience hath shewn, that even under the
> best forms [of government] those entrusted
> with power have, in time, and by slow
> operations, perverted it into tyranny.
> —Thomas Jefferson

Resumen

En el marco de la narración de la nación, este artículo examina el drama documental del director Herbert J. Biberman *La Sal de la Tierra* [*Salt of the Earth*, 1954] enfocándolo desde dos perspectivas diferentes: una en cuanto a su contenido y otra respecto a la producción y distribución del film. En relación con su contenido, *La Sal de la Tierra* se basa en un hecho histórico: la huelga de los mineros mexicanos americanos en Nuevo México, entre 1950 y 1952. En el contexto de la polémica acerca de la identidad nacional de los EE.UU., el film se posiciona claramente a favor de los huelguistas, quienes también tuvieron la posibilidad de participar en la creación del guión. La clase de comunidad que la película propaga –como modelo de identidad nacional para los EE.UU.–, se caracteriza por las múltiples transgresiones de las líneas fronterizas, que tienen por consecuencia una revisión, sobre todo, de las fronteras étnicas y de género, ya que toda la comunidad de los huelguistas persigue la misma meta, es decir, mejores condiciones de vida para los mineros y sus familias. La historia de la producción y distribución de *La Sal de la Tierra* documenta asimismo la nación estadounidense: Biberman y otros cineastas, a quienes como resultado de las investigaciones del Comité McCarthy no les fue permitido trabajar en los estudios de Hollywood a causa de sus tendencias potencialmente comunistas, lograron, a pesar de muchas dificultades, eludir la censura de la clase dirigente. El hecho de que *La Sal de la Tierra* se haya convertido entretanto en un clásico de la historia del cine preservado por la biblioteca nacional (Library of Congress), puede ser estimado como una esperanza del triunfo final de las fuerzas democráticas estadounidenses.

1. Introduction

In 1809 Thomas Jefferson told the citizens of Wilmington that "the best principles of our republic secure to all its citizens a perfect equality of rights" (16: 336). By the early 1950s—before the 1954 Supreme Court ruling in the case Brown v. Board of Education of Topeka and the 1964 Civil Rights Act—this "perfect equality of rights" had still not become a legal reality, and McCarthyism had deeply undermined these "best principles of our republic." Thomas Jefferson seems to have been well aware that the equal opportunity to secure "life, liberty, and the pursuit of happiness" that he had envisaged for the young republic was not a given in the United States—neither in his own time nor a century and a half later. In 1824 he complained of "too many parasites living on the labor of the industrious" (letter to William Ludlow, September 6, 1824). While the nation had been founded on the ideal of equality, slavery remained in place and women's suffrage did not exist. As Howard Zinn points out, passage of the Bill of Rights, which went into effect in 1791, was aimed at safeguarding equality, as the Amendments "seemed to make the new government a guardian of people's liberties: to speak, to publish, to worship, to petition, to assemble, to be tried fairly, to be secure at home against official intrusion." However, as Zinn continues, "[w]hat was not made clear ... was the shakiness of anyone's liberty when entrusted to a government of the rich and powerful" (99). Time and again the national democratic principle of equality was threatened by special interests in politics and economy. In the middle of the twentieth century one of the major instruments of control used by an all too powerful government was the House Un-American Activities Committee (HUAC), established in 1938, given permanent status in 1945, and operating until 1975. Its task was to investigate potential disloyalty and subversive activities by private citizens, public employees, and by organizations suspected of communist or fascist leanings. Among its early victims was a group of ten screenwriters and film directors known as the "Hollywood Ten," who were cited for contempt of Congress on November 25, 1947 for refusing to testify to HUAC.[1] Studio executives fired those members of the Hollywood Ten who were working for them and they barred them from future employment in the film industry. In addition, the Hollywood Ten were each sentenced to one year in prison.[2]

---

[1] A short documentary entitled *The Hollywood Ten* was made by the Southern California Chapter of the National Council of the Arts, Sciences & Professions in 1950. The names of those involved in making the film are not given—for fear of HUAC reprisals. This documentary is contained on the DVD edition of *Salt of the Earth*. It declares that from among the initial group of directors and writers who refused to testify to HUAC "all ten are now in federal prison, serving one-year sentences" and that the country will have to choose between the Bill of Rights and the Thomas Committee of HUAC.

[2] Howard Zinn points out that even after the Senate had censored Senator Joseph McCarthy in December 1954 for "conduct ... unbecoming a Member of the United States Senate," the witch hunt against the alleged threats of Communism continued: "Congress was putting

Among the Hollywood Ten was film director Herbert J. Biberman. While Elia Kazan went along with the reactionary climate of the times, cooperated with HUAC by "naming names," and directed *On the Waterfront* (1954) as an indictment of labor unions and leftist politics and as a defense of those who decide to "name names," Biberman stuck to his political convictions and to his belief that the First Amendment guaranteed his right to refuse testimony. He was released from prison after serving six months of his one-year sentence. Blacklisted in Hollywood, he decided to pursue film-making outside the studio system and co-founded the Independent Productions Corporation (IPC) with film producer Paul Jarrico, who had also been blacklisted. IPC, in cooperation with the International Union of Mine, Mill and Smelter Workers, made *Salt of the Earth*, a fictionalized version of a strike by mostly Mexican American zinc miners in New Mexico, in which the union's women's auxiliary took over the picketing once a court order had forbidden picketing by the miners. Biberman's *Salt of the Earth* came out the same year as Kazan's *On the Waterfront*, although most cinema owners in the United States, for fear of reprisals, decided not to show Biberman's film.

Biberman combats the ideological narration of the U.S. American nation by 1950s McCarthyism and by films in its service (like *On the Waterfront*) with his own ideological narration of an imagined community that demands equality across ethnic and gender divides and that demonstrates the dignity of labor as well as celebrating the victory of the common people over the oppressive interests of big business. As Homi K. Bhabha has observed, the question of which community ultimately defines the nation can never be settled, since answers to it are highly dependent on ideologies and (self-)identifications. Therefore, for Bhabha, "the nation, as a form of cultural *elaboration* ..., is an agency of *ambivalent* narration" ("Introduction" 3, emphasis in the original). In other words: both *Salt of the Earth* and *On the Waterfront* narrate the U.S. American nation of the early 1950s and neither can give the definitive version of national identity. While Kazan consented to the practices of HUAC, Biberman dissented, maintaining that his dissent was in the interest of the nation and its founding principles.[3]

That the founding principle of equality continues to be a major challenge for the United States in the 21st century is illustrated, for example, by Samuel P. Huntington's problematic *Who Are We?: The Challenges to America's National Identity*. While Huntington criticizes affirmative action programs as leading to reverse discrimination and as being thus inherently unequal, he also speaks of the "challenges ... from other-national, subnational, and transnational identities"—cultural identities that he deems far from equal to what he calls "America's core Anglo-Protestant culture," which he

---

through a whole series of anti-Communist bills. ... The liberals in the government were themselves acting to exclude, persecute, fire, and even imprison Communists" (431).

[3]   Howard Zinn remarked in an interview that, in his mind, "dissent is the highest form of patriotism. In fact, if patriotism means being true to the principles for which your country is supposed to stand, then certainly the right to dissent is one of those principles. And if we're exercising that right to dissent, it's a patriotic act" (Bosco 1).

seeks to defend (5, 17). Casting a suspicious eye toward cultural difference, Huntington narrates the U.S. American nation as being imperiled by those who do not fit his
view of "America's core Anglo-Protestant culture." For him, anyone and anything
outside this "core" constitutes the margin that is trying to alter the nation. As Homi
Bhabha states, "[e]ach time the question of cultural difference emerges as a challenge
to relativistic notions of the diversity of culture, it reveals the margins of modernity"
("Introduction" 6). Specters of a nation under siege are called up and under the guise
of patriotism or nationalism the "core" of the nation becomes more equal than its
"margins." As Timothy Brennan remarks, "nationalism is an ideology that, even in its
earliest forms in the nineteenth century, implied unequal development" (59). Especially in times of crisis, the nation is reinterpreted and narrated from the perspective of
those in power, who have the ends and means to propagate their vision. Siri Hustvedt
notes in this context: "national histories ... blur and hide and distort the movements of
people and events in order to preserve an idea" (170).

In the 1950s HUAC and McCarthy narrated a nation threatened by Communists,
labor unions, and progressive artists. Movements demanding equal rights for ethnic
minorities and women were likewise perceived as a threat. The major Hollywood studios supported the othering of the margins of the nation. Gary Keller has demonstrated
the racist implications of the 1934 Hollywood Production Code, which celebrated
Anglo-American-ness and "Americana such as home, motherhood, community, puri-
tanical love, and the work ethic," while creating a "them" as the antagonists that "reject and seek to destroy the proper set of American (Anglo) values. ... 'Them' not only
includes blacks, Hispanics, and Indians, but usually any ethnic group when it is depicted ethnically" (26).[4] Sixty years later, in 1994, a publication by the National Council of *La Raza* still complains that "Latinos are more likely than other groups to receive portrayal in the media that reinforces crude and demeaning cultural stereotypes.
Positive media portrayals of Latinos are ... uncommon" (21).

---

[4] Building on Keller's research, Charles Ramírez Berg, in *Latino Images in Film*, has established "six basic stereotypes [of Latinas/os in U.S. film]: el bandido, the harlot, the male
buffoon, the female clown, the Latin lover, and the dark lady" (66, cf. ch. 3). In contrast to
the standard Hollywood fare, Berg calls Biberman's *Salt of the Earth* "progressive" in
view of it being the only 1930s through 1960s "social problem film" in the United States
that has a female protagonist, who, in addition, is not Anglo (120). Berg remarks that
Salt—along with very few other films to come out of the studio system, namely *The Lawless*, *Giant*, and *The Ring*—is among the very few exceptions that "treated Chicanos
humanely and contributed meaningfully to the discourse on American prejudice" (126).
  Berg's list of stereotypical portrayals of Latinas/os in film and television is expanded
and updated by David Maciel and Susan Racho. They include the perpetual *bandolero*, the
péon, the drug dealer and drug user, the urban gang member, the prostitute, and the maid as
additional prominent depictions. Moreover, they point out that even in "mainstream films"
set in areas that are heavily populated by Chicanas/os "Chicanas/os are [generally] invisible" (94-95).

In the 1950s most Latina/o characters were played by white actors and usually the depiction poked fun at the presumed shortcomings of the Latina/o. So director Herbert J. Biberman, producer Paul Jarrico, screenwriter Michael Wilson, and actor Will Geer set out to go against the grain of the Hollywood studios that had blacklisted them. Rather than indulging in stereotypes of "spicks" and "reds," and denouncing the margins of the nation, they embarked on a film project dedicated to humanizing and celebrating the story of a successful strike by mostly Mexican American miners aided by their wives, who took over the picketing once the men were legally barred from using this maneuver. While the filmmakers wanted to document the margin's demands for equality, they did not choose the format of a documentary film but rather that of a docudrama (or "photoplay," as the opening credits call *Salt of the Earth*). The format of the docudrama allowed them to use voice-over commentary and invented scenes, while still trying to narrate the actual, historical events faithfully.

Documentary film of course also makes use of invention and commentary frequently. These devices characterized the genre before the days of "Direct Cinema," when illustrating the message proved more important than accuracy of details. Eric Barnouw has pointed out that the rise of advocacy in documentaries during the 1930s and 1940s "also involved matters of form. ... The typical film of advocacy was shot like a silent film, with 'voice-over' narration added. ... Some narrators were characterized but most were abstract voices ... resonant with authority and backed by impressive music" (161).[5] If we take what Jeffrey Youdelman calls "captur[ing] the essence of the situations and personalities" to be the guiding principle of documentation in film, then *Salt of the Earth* comes close to being a documentary, although we read in its opening credits that "[t]he characters in this photoplay are fictitious." True, some names have been changed—for example Bayard, NM becomes "Zinctown, NM" and the Empire Zinc Mining Company becomes the "Delaware Mining Company." Some events have been highlighted and others omitted. Conversations are staged. However, *Salt of the Earth* is remarkable for its use of actual locations of the historical events as well as for having many of the protagonists in the labor dispute play themselves. Moreover, *Salt* refrains from stereotyping Latinas/os and uses a Mexican actress (Rosaura Revueltas) as the protagonist and for the voice-over. The film relies on neorealist style to defend its cause of equality and to narrate the nation from its margins. In 1992, in recognition of the artistic and historical achievement of *Salt of the Earth*, the Library of Congress chose this film for inclusion in the United States National Film Registry.

---

[5] Concerning the advocacy of documentary film, which he sees exemplified in the work of Michael Moore, Louis Menand writes: "It's not surprising that documentary-makers have usually worked in a spirit of advocacy. They are people sufficiently committed to a point of view to go to the trouble of obtaining expensive equipment, carting it into the field, shooting miles of film under often unpleasant or dangerous conditions, and spending months or years splicing the results into a coherent movie" (1).

In analyzing the documentation of the mining strike undertaken in this against-all-odds docudrama, I will argue that *Salt of the Earth* unifies the political goals of the miners, their wives, and the blacklisted filmmakers in its advocacy of equality. The kind of equality which the film proposes crosses gender, ethnicity, and class lines—ten years before U.S. lawmakers dared give a legal basis to a more comprehensive equality in the Civil Rights Act of 1964. However, the demand for equal access to Hollywood facilities and finances, to production labs and movie theaters went unfulfilled for many of the blacklisted filmmakers until the 1970s. Thus the plot of the film as well as the history of the film's production and reception narrate the U.S. American nation in the 1950s and thereafter. In retrospect, current narration usually casts *Salt* as a triumph. As the DVD cover boasts, this is "[t]he only American blacklisted film." As such, *Salt of the Earth* challenges narrow definitions of U.S. national identity and argues for a reconsideration of the nation's founding principle of equality. To illustrate this film's unique significance, I will first discuss its genre (docudrama) and historical backgrounds. I will then move on to examining the multiple border crossings that are staged in *Salt of the Earth* as an argument for far-reaching equality. Last, I will discuss the blacklisting of the film itself and its eventual endurance as a national narrative.

2. The Truth Claim of Documentary and Docudrama

What is a documentary and does such a thing as fictionalized documentation exist? If documentary film can make a truth claim[6] for itself, does this mean that the fictionalized documentation of a docudrama is necessarily less "true"? Michael Renov believes that "all discursive forms—documentary included—are, if not fictional, at least *fictive*, this by virtue of their tropic character (their recourse to tropes or rhetorical figures)" (7). Capturing events, characters, and scenes in film frames automatically implies selection, arrangement, foregrounding, and interpretation. The film document cannot mirror an external reality but it can guide readers in contemplating and interpreting this external reality. As Bill Nichols states, "[i]n documentaries we find stories or arguments, evocations or descriptions that let us see the world anew" (Nichols, *Introduction* 3). Ideally, documentary expands our previous familiarity with the film's subject, the cinematic experience guiding our position toward the presented subject. The degree of difference between documentary and docudrama, however, remains a matter of case-by-case debate. So does the question about the limits of the documentary genre. I agree therefore with Nichols's view that "our own idea of whether a film is or is not a documentary is highly susceptible to suggestion. ... We believe what we see and what is represented about what we see at our own risk" (*Introduction* xii). What distinguishes "the documentary tradition," writes Nichols, is its "impression of authenticity" (*Introduction* xiii). This impression is created through audiovisual means

---

[6]   For more on the truth claim of documentary film, cf. the introduction to this volume.

and additional textual information, but those same techniques can also be used by other genres.

Nichols argues that "there are two kinds of [documentary] film: (1) documentaries of wish-fulfillment [which he calls 'fictions'] and (2) documentaries of social representation [which we typically call 'non-fiction']" (*Introduction* 1). The latter, writes Nichols,

> give tangible representation to aspects of the world we already inhabit and share. They make the stuff of social reality visible and audible in a distinctive way, according to the acts of selection and arrangement carried out by a filmmaker. They give a sense of what we understand reality itself to have been, of what it is now, or of what it may become. These films also convey truths if we decide they do. ... Documentaries of social representation offer us new views of our common world to explore and understand" (*Introduction* 1-2).

Agreeing with Nicholls and Renov, Keith Beattie writes that the "documentarian draws on past and present actuality—the world of social and historical experience—to construct an account of lives and events." Using the conventions of the documentary genre, the filmmaker implies that her/his "documentary depiction of the socio-historical world is factual and truthful." This implication offers the basis for the truth claim of documentary film, which defines the genre, in Beattie's words, "as a work or text which implicitly claims to truthfully represent the world, whether it is to accurately represent events or issues or to assert that the subjects of the work are 'real people'" (10). But this claim overlooks the impact of the presence of a camera (and usually also of a film crew), which transforms the events and actions that are meant to be documented. Moreover, each documentarian can capture an external reality only through his or her own lens—through the lens of his or her own interests, talents, and past experiences.[7]

Louis Menand reminds us that the name "*documentaire*" originally described "movies of ordinary life, exotic places, and current events. The word suggests observational neutrality, a documentation, an unretouched record of what's real; and if that was the promise it was betrayed almost from the start" (1). The captured "reality" is inevitably changed in the act of capturing it; and the captured footage is then usually edited to highlight a certain aspect or interpretation. Moreover—largely because of technical and logistic limitations—the documentary genre, from its beginnings, relied on reconstructions and reenactments. As Jeffrey Youdelman has pointed out, in the 1920s through the 1950s,

---

[7] Documentary film is not, as a rule, free from a subjective evaluation of the issues it addresses. On the contrary, Nichols has spoken of the "interpretive arena [into which] most independent documentarists have stepped" and "which might in other arguments be called editorializing, persuasion, orientation, ideology, propaganda. ... Interpretation builds on facts, however. Its forms and its canons of validation depend upon referentiality, an evidentiary base, and documentary logic" (*Representing* 189-90).

the author's recourse to invention sometimes took the form of reenactment. Initially rooted in technological limitations, reenactment also rested on principle. It didn't occur to the old documentarists that such activities on their part were "manipulative." In fact, reenactment often proceeded with great care ... [Filmmakers] learned about their subjects and created episodes meant to capture the essence of the situations and personalities. Reenactment usually involved the difficult task of directing non-professional actors, but the belief in the legitimacy of reenactment also extended to fictionalizing and using trained professional actors. (401)

Much of this characterization of the work of the so-called "old documentarists" also applies to *Salt of the Earth*, the fictionalized and personalized reenactment of events surrounding the fifteen-month strike of mining workers in Bayard, New Mexico from October 1950 through January 1952.

A pioneer among the group to whom Youdelman refers as "old documentarists" was Robert Flaherty. As numerous film historians have noted, he arranged and staged many of the scenes in his classic *Nanook of the North* (1922); performed scenes were repeated and re-shot when they did not meet with the director's approval. In his attempt to document the life of the Inuit, Flaherty individualized his depiction, a strategy that is credited with having contributed to the film's success (cf. Menand 2).[8]

Politically, especially through the work of the Workers' Film and Photo League in the 1920s and 1930s and New Deal productions of social awareness, documentary film tended to be situated toward the left. Ian Aitken writes that while the left-leaning tendencies of the beginnings of documentary film in the 1930s cannot be generalized, there exists a common social democratic political stance in the early phase of documentary filmmaking: "The ideological discourse of the documentary film movement during the 1930s can be positioned to the left of dominant conservatism, to the right of Marxist and socialist opinion, and within a constellation of centrist ideologies associated with currents of social democratic reform" (Aitken 31). In general, U.S. documentaries in the 1930s and 1940s—from Ralph Steiner and Willard Van Dyke's *The City* (1939) to Frank Capra's *Why We Fight* series (1942-44)—have been characterized as working in a propagandist tradition.

During the 1950s, however, the decade when *Salt of the Earth* was made, documentary filmmaking in the United States was dominated by *direct cinema* and by the view of the documentary as "a plotless, commentary-less, vérité-style record of life as it is—the notion of the documentarian as a fly on the wall" (Menand 2). The master of this inside-look documentary is Frederick Wiseman.[9] He, however, spoke of his own films as "reality fictions," claiming that "[a]ll the material is manipulated so that the final film is totally fictional in form although it is based on real events" (qtd. in

---

[8] For Bill Nichols's discussion of the close relationship between Robert Flaherty's *Louisiana Story* and fiction film (particularly Orson Welles's *Touch of Evil*), cf. *Representing* 182-84.

[9] Wiseman's *Titicut Follies* (1967) presents a record of life at the Massachusetts Correctional Institution at Bridgewater. The film documents the activities of inmates deemed criminally insane and of the institution in which they were held to the point that the Massachusetts Supreme Judicial Court ordered the picture to be withdrawn from circulation.

Menand 2). In this same vein, the opening credits of *Salt of the Earth* announce that "[t]he characters depicted in this photoplay are fictional," while also specifying that "[o]ur scene is New Mexico," where most parts of the film were actually shot (using the very location where the actual strike had taken place).

It will have become clear by now that the border between documentary film and fiction film cannot be clearly drawn. With docudrama as a blend between documentary and fiction, the distinctions get even murkier.[10] Bill Nichols wrote concerning the use of realism in documentary and fiction film that "[i]n fiction, realism serves to make a plausible world seem real; in documentary, realism serves to make an argument about the historical world persuasive" (*Representing* 165). The docudrama *Salt of the Earth* certainly does both.[11] Nichols further perceives in the documentary genre a "tendency ... to bridge evidence and argument, the concretely historical and the conceptual generalization" (*Representing* 177). This is also the approach of *Salt of the Earth*, which takes the concrete historical event of a successful miners' strike as the basis for general statements on equality, women's rights, and the dignity of labor. In this manner, *Salt* combines historiography with political commentary—another common feature of documentary film (cf. Nichols, *Representing* 177).

Moreover, documentaries tend to combine performance with 'authentic' material, fiction with fact.[12] Whether this strategy impedes their truth claim is debatable. Keith Beattie sums up the discussion as follows: "Depending on which interpreters are read, the meeting of fact and fiction results in either the subversion of documentary claims to authenticity and veracity, or, innovative and productive approaches to documentary representation" (146). Both interpretations have also been used to assess the 'truth' of docudrama.

---

[10] Filmmaker Leslie Woodhead calls docudrama a "crossbreed from the techniques of fiction and the factual claims of journalism and documentary" and he deems it the genre's "fundamental requirement to re-create as accurately as possible using the techniques, forms, and values of imaginative drama" (478).

[11] *Salt of the Earth* also shares some features with what Bill Nichols has categorized as the performative documentary. Nichols writes: "Performative documentary clearly embodies a paradox: it generates a distinct tension between performance and document, between the personal and the typical, the embodied and disembodied, between, in short, history and science. One draws attention to itself, the other to what it represents. One is poetic and evocative, the other evidential and referential in emphasis. Performative documentary does not hide its signifieds in the guise of a referent it effortlessly pulls from its hat. These films stress their own tone and expressive qualities while also retaining a referential claim to the historical. They address the challenge of giving meaning to historical events through the evocations they provide for them" (*Blurred* 97-98).

[12] Stella Bruzzi has therefore cautioned against the truth/reality claim of documentaries. She views especially documentary films of the 21st century as displaying a "renewed ... interest in the more overt forms of performativity: reconstruction, acknowledgement of an interplay with the camera, image manipulation, performance. Documentary now widely acknowledges and formally engages with its own constructedness, its own performative agenda" (252).

For Ian McBride docudrama is a "reenactment of events" and thus "the true, true story" (487). McBride further observes that the motivation of docudrama makers is that of potential intervention: they aim "at delivering the audience a picture of the unglimpsed ... with all the hallmarks of authority and credibility" because they believe in "a potential for energising change if only by informing the audience well about something others would prefer they remain in ignorance of" (488, 489).[13] Docudrama, writes British filmmaker Leslie Woodhead, wants "simply to tell to a mass audience a real and relevant story involving real people" (478). It does so, as John Caughie has remarked, by relying "on dramatic codes and conventions for the basis of a fictional narrative that makes reference to factual or possible situations, people and events." But on the other hand, Caughie continues, docudrama also "draws heavily on ... a 'documentary look', a style which creates the impression of facticity within a fiction by replicating the visual language of documentary film through techniques such as shaky camera shots and a reliance on natural lighting" (Beattie 148; cf. Caughie 27).

Apart from its closeness to a documentary like the later *Harlan County, USA* (1976) by Barbara Kopple, *Salt of the Earth* also bears numerous similarities with fiction film. In terms of subject matter as well as concerning the debate between fact and fiction, we are reminded foremost of Sergei Eisenstein's *Strike* (1925). Like Biberman's *Salt*, Eisenstein's *Strike* eschews simple classification as either fiction or documentation.[14] However, this resistance to categorization does not diminish the 'truth' of the depictions and issues or the truth claim of the films.

---

[13] Derek Paget agrees. Among the five characteristics he has named for docudrama, Paget mentions the genre's potential goals of aiming "to re-tell events from national or international histories, either reviewing or celebrating these events" and "to portray issues of concern to national or international communities in order to provoke discussion about them" (61). Docudrama thus participates in the narration of nation.

[14] Nichols writes about Eisenstein's early masterpiece: "Here is a political, and documentary style of filmmaking that blurs all our received notions of where the bounds of social representation lie" (*Blurred* 107-08). Nichols goes on to point out that, in his view, the conventional approach of contrasting Dziga Vertov, the documentarist, to Sergei Eisenstein, the fiction filmmaker, does not really hold: "I prefer to treat fiction and nonfiction as a blurred or fuzzy boundary and to examine ways and means of addressing the real historiographically, as with Eisenstein, or in the present, ethnographically, as with Vertov. In these terms, Eisenstein is a neither/nor figure: neither fiction as we have known it nor documentary as it has come to be defined locate his work effectively. Powerful as fiction, *Strike* is also the most impressive achievement in documentary representation since *Who Killed Vincent Chin?*" (109).

For a more critical view of Eisenstein, cf. Joanne Hershfield's "Paradise Regained: Sergei Eisenstein's *Que viva México!* as Ethnography," in which Hershfield speaks of Eisenstein's documentation of an "imaginary," rather than a "real" Mexico.

3. The Story Behind *Salt of the Earth*

Bill Nichols reminds us that "contesting the nation-state" has long been a common practice in documentary film (*Introduction* 148ff). In the United States, the Workers' Film and Photo Leagues of the 1920s and 1930s

> produced information about strikes and other topical issues from the perspective of the working class. ... They adopted a participatory mode of filmmaking, consistently identifying and collaborating with their worker-subjects, thus avoiding the risk of portraying them as powerless victims. This was a cinema of empowerment that sought to contribute to the radical social movements of the 1930s and to build community from a grassroots, oppositional level rather than from a top-down, governmentally orchestrated one. (*Introduction* 148-49)

Filmmakers working in the tradition of these Leagues, writes Nichols, "proposed a sense of community based on actions, and changes, that governments seemed unprepared to accept, or make. Their films took up positions that opposed the policies of governments and industries" (*Introduction* 148).

Herbert J. Biberman, who also "opposed the policies of governments and industries"—both in his films and in his life—belongs to this tradition. Although he works in docudrama and fiction film, his movies are neither escapist entertainment nor 'nice stories' but political statements. In his book *Salt of the Earth: The Story of a Film* Biberman recounts a conversation about his film project that he had with an investor in 1951:

> "... These stories you're talking about. They sound pretty radical to me. Why don't you make a nice mystery story?"
> "The country has a surfeit of them now. The only thing radical about our stories is that they're about real people." (Biberman 33)

Wanting to make a film about 'real people' and to offer an alternative to the standard fare of the big Hollywood studios that had blacklisted him, Biberman was drawn to news reports about a strike in New Mexico in which the picketing was done not by the striking miners but by their wives. Having been denied his citizen rights (of free speech and of remaining silent), having served a politically motivated prison sentence, and having suffered unjust exclusion from his workplace (the Hollywood studios), Biberman naturally felt drawn to trade unions.

James J. Lorence[15] notes that Mexican-American mining workers of the Southwest were among the most committed members of the Mine-Mill union because of the union's commitment to civil rights and to promoting racial equality in the workplace. Allegations of the Communist infiltration of unions mattered little to these Mexican-American unionists; what did matter to them were the improvements that the union had brought to African American workers and the solidarity between Anglos and Mexican Americans that characterized the union. The Mine-Mill union charged that

---

[15] For my account of the film's backgrounds I rely primarily on James J. Lorence's superb and thorough study of the suppression of *Salt of the Earth*.

Empire Zinc wanted to maintain discriminatory wage levels between Anglo and Mexican-American workers in order to promote tensions in the labor force and thereby to keep the workers disunited. As Lorence summarizes: "from the union perspective, the basic issue was the demand for economic equality. However, pensions and benefits also became important issues as negotiations unfolded. Contrary to the film's argument, mine safety and underground conditions were not major points of dispute" (25-26).

At the Empire Zinc Mining Company in Bayard, NM wage negotiations between the union and the company had started in July 1950. Since no progress was being made at the negotiating table, a strike began in October 1950. After many violent attempts to put an end to the strike and after support for the strikers had come in from many sources, including a miners' union in Mexico, the company finally agreed to negotiate in January 1952, which ended a strike that had cost the union 113,360 dollars in fines as well as over 1,100 person-days in jail. In its long history and ultimate success, the strike had united two separate movements of the time, namely the Anglo progressive labor movement and the Chicano Left that was constituting itself at that time.

The leaders of this combined effort, Clinton Jencks and his wife Virginia, play themselves (although with changed names) in *Salt of the Earth*. Jencks had been sent by the union's International as an organizer; he lived in the Bayard mining community, and he was regarded as a Communist agitator by the company. In a 1996 interview Jencks "remained firm in his conviction that a new level in human equality was achieved as a result of the strike and that the women 'expressed a new sense of unity, especially after the mass jailing, which brought them together'" (Lorence 40). But his wife felt disappointed with the union's continuing practice of relegating women to a subordinate position. James Lorence recapitulates:

> Virginia Jencks's sour reaction to Mine-Mill's disappointingly conventional perspective on women's union activities suggests that the strike had failed to alter long-standing assumptions concerning gender relations. But when Michael Wilson, a gifted playwright, crafted the screenplay that was to become *Salt of the Earth*, a more inspirational outcome became possible. Through his skillful creation of a composite character in Esperanza and a blend of fiction and reality in his story, Wilson moved to redeem the strike's vision through an upbeat interpretation of the events described. The reality both within Local 890 and the International was much more complex, as later experience would confirm. (41)

Although filming did not begin until after the end of the Bayard strike, *Salt of the Earth* reinforced the success of the strikers and put the demand for equality on a broader basis than issues of work and pay.

Herbert J. Biberman found in the strike the material for a narration of the nation and an opportunity for propagating the U.S.A.'s principle of equality. He recalls the genesis of the film's plot:

> Paul Jarrico had gone away on a few weeks vacation with his family. He had heard of an extraordinary strike in progress in New Mexico. The strike had been called against

> New Jersey Zinc in Bayard, New Mexico, by Local 890 of the Mine, Mill and Smelter Workers Union. This old and militant union had been expelled from the C.I.O. for alleged Communist influence. The local union membership was largely Mexican-American. Several months before, when the strikers were faced with a Taft-Hartley injunction prohibiting the miners from picketing, the women of the local union's Ladies Auxiliary had taken over the picket line from their miner-husbands and were holding it with dramatic bravery and resourcefulness. The Jarricos drove there. (37)

Having been imprisoned for refusing to answer HUAC's question about his past or present membership in the Communist Party and having been expelled from the Hollywood studios himself, Biberman must have been attracted to what he calls an "old and militant union [that] had been expelled from the C.I.O. for alleged Communist influence." Biberman and Jarrico asked screenwriter Michael Wilson—also blacklisted—to write the script for a film on the strike.

Wilson was reluctant. Concerned about authenticity, he told Biberman and Jarrico:

> Fellows, we have to give up trying to write stories about real people from our point of view. ... If I do this story, I want to do a story from the point of view of the people of Local 890. And if I do this story, they are going to be the censors of it and the real producers of it ... in point of view of its content. If you think something's great and they think it's lousy, the're going to win. And vice versa. (Biberman 38)

So Wilson went to Bayard, NM late in 1951 to get a first-hand impression, to speak with strikers and listen to their concerns. He was interested in their views on the strike and on their future. Then he went to work on the script.

Wilson returned to Bayard in the spring of 1952 with his draft for *Salt of the Earth*

> to hold an open meeting at the union hall, at which time union members offered vigorous criticism of the draft treatment. While generally supportive of the draft, miners and their families called for a number of revisions. ... [S]ome scenes seemed unreal and were removed or altered; stereotypical portrayals of Mexicans as sexually promiscuous or prone to chronic alcoholism disappeared. Yet the essential integrity of Wilson's treatment, including his decision to focus on women's issues through the interaction between Esperanza and Ramón, remained intact. Biberman summarized the projected outcome as a film that would be 'neither a story of the strike nor a story of male chauvinism,' but rather an account of women's 'emergence' and their 'decisive contribution' to 'victory in [the] struggle for the group—the class.' (Lorence 58-59)

In *The Suppression of "Salt of the Earth": How Hollywood, Big Labor, and Politicians Blacklisted a Movie in Cold War America*, James J. Lorence estimates that most union members in Bayard were involved in the process of planning the film; all in all, over four hundred people seem to have read the script before production began (cf. Lorence 73).

With the supreme goal in mind that the film should be "true to life from start to finish," a production committee was set up for *Salt of the Earth* that consisted of film professionals, miners, and members of the Women's Auxiliary—continuing the tradition of the Workers' Film and Photo Leagues of the 1920s and 1930s of "community participation." As Lorence reports:

> To coordinate the activities of IPC and Local 890, a production committee was established, composed of film company personnel and union members, including four IPC representatives and eight union and auxiliary members. This democratic procedure ensured full community participation in the production process; the committee "took up everything," including both matters of details and "artistic decision." The committee had "policy-making" duties and was responsible for "seeing that [the] picture ran true to life from start to finish." ... the union spirit was contagious, and it produced a strong sense of group ownership. (73)

That the Hollywood professionals shared the management of the film with Local 890 gave *Salt of the Earth* unanimous endorsement by those whose cause it portrayed.

In terms of form and cast, Biberman also went against the conventions of classical Hollywood cinema of the 1930s and 1940s, where, as Linda Williams points out, "realism meant highly polished performances by known actors who could imitate real people in the simulated, meticulous reconstructions of the real world created on the studio sound stage. These reconstructions were carried out according to the conventional rules of story-telling, lighting, *mise-en-scène*, and editing" (62). Biberman, however, cast the relatively unknown Mexican actress Rosaura Revueltas in the female lead (rather than using an Anglo actress for a non-Anglo role—as Hollywood convention had it—and rather than using a well-known star); he cast a non-actor, union leader involved in the strike (Juan Chacón) in the male lead.[16] Apparently "Biberman balked at the idea of Anglos in the lead roles" (Lorence 69). Along with Chacón, many more members of miners' families appear in the film. As A. Manuel Meléndez[17] recounts,

> Thirteen of the nineteen members of the nonprofessional cast were local Mexican American residents and union members. An unnamed and unknown number of members of Local 890 appear in the film as extras. The dignity of their participation on film suggests that finally the image of Chicanos—in this case, of Nuevomexicanos—had plied its way through the layers of distortion to form a more fully rounded view of men and women creating their own history and acting with their own agency and determination. (123-24)

Concerning location, Biberman also wanted for *Salt of the Earth* to be authentic. Rather than using a studio, he shot most of the film on location in the New Mexico desert, using primarily natural light (cf. Williams 62).[18]

In terms of the composition of the film crew, *Salt of the Earth* likewise went against the rules of Hollywood. By the end of 1952, as James Lorence reports, "Jarrico

---

[16] Chacón was the newly elected president of Local 890.

[17] It is unfortunate that Meléndez keeps getting the names of the film's creators wrong, speaking of "Henry" (rather than Herbert J.) Biberman and Paul and Sylvia "Jerrico" (rather than Jarrico).

[18] While he was barred from the major studios, Biberman could have used lots in the Los Angeles area for the film—as did Orson Welles, who shot most of *Touch of Evil* (1958; set in South Texas) in and around Venice, CA.

and Biberman had assembled a team that included several blacklistees, as well as three African-Americans, whose employment broke with Hollywood's standing Jim Crow hiring practices" (68-69).

As to the representational style of *Salt of the Earth*, Linda Williams concludes that Biberman's "break with Hollywood's conventional realism was ... in the name of a greater realism" and resulted in "an authenticity of social context" that one expects from documentary film but not necessarily from drama (62).[19] *Salt of the Earth* documents a cause and the efforts of the people involved in it. It is not a newsreel depiction, though, but a staged and partly fictional reenactment in the service of the cause it portrays. As Lorence remarks, "the people of Local 890 had been desperate for equality and saw the film as a way to get their story to a wider public" (197). This spirit of advocacy and the modes of depiction selected because of it do not make the film or the cause any less real or true.

The advantage of the kind of "fictional realism" that *Salt of the Earth* uses is that the audience feels close to the events and characters on screen. As Bill Nichols has noted: "Fictional realism has most often been celebrated for its self-effacing quality. It allows unimpeded access to the world of the representation" (*Representing* 180). Biberman and his crew of professionals entered the world on which "the world of the representation" is based, they included many elements of this represented world (locations, characters, issues) in their film and they were thus able to decrease the distance between *Salt*'s audience and its "world of representation."

To Biberman this world and its cause—at bottom the cause of equality—are thoroughly American. *Salt of the Earth* is thus a narration of the nation. To stress this point, the opening credits, alluding to the national anthem of the United States, announce: "Our scene is New Mexico, Land of the free Americans who inspired this film, home of the brave Americans who played most of its roles." The language stresses the (widely unrecognized) citizenship of Mexican Americans.

The issues of national/community significance are personalized (using the strategy that Flaherty used in *Nanook of the North*) and they are dramatized, boiled down to what screenwriter Michael Wilson has termed "a love story." After spending a number of weeks with Local 890 in Bayard, NM late in 1951, Wilson summarized his take on the script he was to write as follows:

---

[19] Williams believes that "[i]n many ways the contrivance of a voice-over, the unusual mix of professional and non-professional actors and the obvious low-budget look of the whole production, make the film appear even more manipulated, less a seamless imitation of reality. Biberman's theme called for a form that could emphasize the social and historical embeddedness of his characters even if this meant sacrificing in some of them a range of emotional expression that a cast of entirely professional actors could give it. He thus borrowed qualities from the documentary film—a form which concentrates on social conditions to the relative exclusion of drama—in order to give his film an authenticity of social context that Hollywood films about minority groups had never before achieved" (62).

"Well, the core—it's something—something like this: A love story. A Mexican-American miner and his wife. In love. And divided—by everything outside themselves. He, consumed by hatred of the discrimination that surrounds his people and his family. Can't think of anything else. She, feeling ignored—overburdened—despairs of life itself. Their situation becomes intolerable. The men strike. And they hold fast. The company—finds a legal maneuver, and prepares to break the strike. The men are lost. Desperate women, suddenly appear out of nowhere—so far as their husbands are concerned—and offer to take over the battle—they become important. The struggle for equality moves to a new level, which includes the old. Because the men can't overcome company discrimination against them unless they overcome their own against their women. A people will either unify itself for the real struggle—or fail in it. That's it! The theme: The indivisibility of equality. The story: A husband's struggle to accept as his equal the wife he loves. A wife's insistence that love include respect. The resolution: The women lead the men to victory on all fronts because in social struggle *they* call on and embrace every living soul in their community—the men included." (Biberman 39)

As Wilson assesses the situation of the strikers and plans his script, equality is the central issue—on the level of gender, ethnicity, and class. With this discussion of a national issue as it affects the lives of a Mexican American couple and their community, Wilson individualized the conflict and showed its impact on "real people." He was in good company.

4.   Equality and Multiple Border Crossings

In 1952, the year that Wilson completed his script for *Salt of the Earth*, John Grierson wrote of the "overriding humanist factor" that he perceived in the Red Clydesdale movement, an association of socialist and communist groups in Great Britain.[20] To Grierson, this "overriding humanist factor" assumes "more and more validity as the harder forces of political organisation have taken control of the thoughts we had and the sympathies we urged." Working against such political control, Grierson sees his own documentary depictions of "the working man on the screen and all that" as approaches he owed to his "masters," among them Keir Hardie (qtd. in Aitken 32).[21] Documentations of workers and common people as well as of their causes—often from a socialist perspective—were an international phenomenon in the 1950s.

---

[20] Grierson had been dismissed in 1945 from his post as Commissioner of the National Film Board of Canada, charged with alleged Communist sympathies, and had returned to Scotland, where he was to start hosting a television program in 1957 that showed parts of outstanding documentaries.

[21] Hardie was a leading figure in labor politics; Ian Aitken describes his political stance thus: "His socialism was based on moral premises derived from the Bible, and he believed socialism to be the 'embodiment of Christianity in the industrial sphere'" (Aitken 32).

In Latin America, the 1950s mark the beginning of what Julianne Burton terms the "social documentary."[22] She points out that during the 1950s and 1960s documentary filmmaking in Latin America has an unavoidably political agenda:

> In Latin America ... the urge to self-expression was almost invariably circumscribed by inescapable social, economic, and political realities. This explains why, even when not explicitly political in origin or orientation, this surge of experimental and documentary activity would soon acquire a political dimension. (18-19)

A masterpiece of the genre, *La Hora de los hornos* (1968) by Octavio Getino and Fernando E. Solanas, was to influence a whole generation of filmmakers.

While the "social documentary" was on the rise in Latin America, in the U.S.A., documentaries accompanied the historical developments of the civil rights movement. A notable film in this context is *Crisis: Behind a Presidential Commitment* (1963) by Robert Drew and Drew Associates, which documents the attempts of Alabama governor George Wallace to prevent two African American students from enrolling at the University of Alabama. Documentary attention to Mexican Americans did not come until later. But by the late 1960s, short documentaries motivated by political activism started to proliferate as part of the Chicano Movement's demands for the recognition of Mexican Americans and for an end to discrimination. Notable examples include *Huelga* [*Strike*, 1966], made by the United Farm Workers Association and narrated by César Chávez, about the Delano grape strike in California from 1965 to 1970. Documentary representations of the Chicana/o cultural heritage—combined with demands for Chicana/o recognition and rights—include Luis Valdez's *I Am Joaquin* (1969), Jesús Treviño's *Yo soy chicano* (1972), and Sylvia Morales's *Chicana* (1979). Maciel and Racho estimate that "[b]y 1990 more than 100 documentaries [by and about Mexican Americans] (including television documentaries) had been completed and exhibited" (99).

Herbert J. Biberman preceded Chicana/o filmmakers in changing the image of Mexican Americans on screen. He saw his enterprise of making *Salt of the Earth* as a patriotic act and thus as one of his contributions to the narration of nation and to the negotiation of U.S. national identity. In his book on the making and distribution of the film he wrote,

> The American, the human struggle for dignity and the "right to push everything up with us," must not be labeled and thereby discarded. ... Of all things, patriotism may not be weighed, cannot be weighed in scales of public polls. The poll of polls remains the individual conscience. It is the seed of America as a great society. (313)

Biberman also expresses his gratitude to the businessmen who supported his freedom of speech, investing an initial 35,000 dollars in the film project, and who—despite the

---

[22] Burton calls *Tire dié* (1958-60) "the founding social documentary of the New Latin American Cinema Movement" (18). On *Tire dié*, cf. Álvaro Fernández Bravo's essay in this collection.

political difficulties and the uncertain outcome of the enterprise—"would not refuse to gamble on a democratic America" (36).

His concern for a "democratic America" drew Biberman to the issues of gender inequality, racial discrimination, and economic exploitation that are at the heart of *Salt of the Earth*. James Lorence recounts that

> One Local 890 unionist flatly asserted the conviction of most Hispanos that "the issue of the Empire Zinc strike was equality." The problem of racial discrimination and unequal wages transcended the influence of imported union organizers like Clint Jencks. "The issues were there, and would have been there even if El Palomino [Jencks] had never been born." (44)

The national issues of race and gender discrimination coalesced in the Bayard strike with the issue of economic oppression. They could all be subsumed under the national principle of equality that was being widely disregarded. Having suffered from this disregard at the hands of HUAC and the Hollywood studio executives, Biberman, Jarrico, and Wilson felt compelled to tell a story of a successful struggle for an equality that extended to gender, race, economic opportunity, and political representation. When Wilson came back to Hollywood from his first stay in Bayard in 1951, he told Biberman, "There are battles for equality taking place there on so many levels I can hardly unskein them yet myself" (Biberman 39). Likewise, Jarrico spoke of his desire to depict the "dignity of woman, labor and a racial minority" (qtd. in Lorence 58). As the filmmakers realized and as the film itself illustrates, these various domains of equality are all interrelated.

In their desire to promote equality, the filmmakers created a docudrama that combines historical fact with political vision and commentary, a film that presents an idealized imagined community by altering, embellishing, or romanticizing the strike's progression and outcome.

The main issue which *Salt* embellishes is the role of women in the strike. The film makes Esperanza Quintero, the wife of the strike leader Ramón Quintero, the protagonist: the voice-over[23] that comments on the events and fills in some of the backgrounds is hers, and the first and last scenes of the film show close-ups of her face (Illustrations 1 and 2).

---

[23] Stella Bruzzi has observed that a major distinction between the use of voice-over in documentary as opposed to fiction film is that "whereas in a fiction film the voice-off is traditionally that of a character in the narrative, in a documentary the voice-over is more usually that of a disembodied and omniscient narrator," which makes documentary voice-over come across as "inevitably and inherently didactic" (47). While, according to Bruzzi, "the narrational voice" of documentary is "distortive and superimposed onto it," Biberman manages to use Esperanza's voice-over to fill in background information and to foreground the women's perspective and their contribution to the strike's success. Bruzzi further points out that only in the 1970s and 1980s did documentarists realize that "a woman's voice embodied protest because women had traditionally been sidelined by history and documentary alike" (65).

Illustration 1: First close-up frontal shot of Esperanza

Illustration 2: Final close-up frontal shot of Esperanza

In the initial close-up, Esperanza's face has a clothing line across it, which suggests that she has been struck out. The pain of daily chores and pregnancy, the disregard of a husband who forgets her name's day and who does not agree with her suggestion of making sanitation in the miners' shacks one of the strike demands show in her face, which is set off against their shack and the desert landscape. By the end of the film, however, Esperanza's face (Illustration 2) is beaming with hope (as her telling name implies); her eyes are no longer downcast but looking up expectantly. There are still many hardships ahead, but the experience of a community sticking together to prevent her family's eviction and of a husband praising her and agreeing with her that, as they rise, they will pull everyone up with them has given her confidence. Equality in her family, in the mining camp and in her husband's workplace is now within reach.

As the film opens, we see Esperanza from the back, chopping wood. The scene is gloomy: the screenplay points out that at Esperanza's first appearance "we sense her weariness in toil by the set of her shoulders" and the guitar music is "grave, nostalgic" (Biberman 315). While the music was changed in the editing process from guitar music to a dramatic, foreboding tune, there is nonetheless a sense of toil and dispossession. Visually, this atmosphere is conveyed, for example, through what the screenplay describes as follows: "Close Short: A sign attached to a fence. It reads: PROPERTY OF DELAWARE ZINC, INC. Vista Shot: The zinc mine in the distance" (Biberman 316). Acoustically, the sense of toil and dispossession is created through Esperanza's voice-over:[24]

> How shall I begin my story that has no beginning? My name is Esperanza, Esperanza Quintero. I am a miner's wife. This is our home. The house is not ours. But the flowers ... the flowers are ours. This is my village. When I was a child, it was called San Marcos. The Anglos changed the name to Zinc Town. Zinc Town, New Mexico, U.S.A.

---

[24] The text of the voice-over, as it is reproduced here, is based on the film script that appears as an appendix to Biberman's book *Salt of the Earth: The Story of a Film*. In the actual, edited film, however, the sequence of some of the sentences of Esperanza's opening monologue was changed.

Our roots go deep in this place, deeper than the pines, deeper than the mine shaft[s].
In these arroyos my great grandfather raised cattle before the Anglos ever came. The
land where the mine stands—that was owned by my husband's own grandfather. Now it
belongs to the company. Eighteen years my husband has given to that mine. Living half
his life with dynamite and darkness.

Who can say where it began, my story? I do not know. But this day I remember as
the beginning of an end. (Biberman 315-17)

The following ninety minutes stage this "end" of "the old ways" of inequality in the
family, in the camp, and in the workplace. We are reminded right from the film's
beginning of loss: two generations earlier the land we are seeing still belonged to the
Mexican American families, but then "the Anglos" came and changed everything, says
Esperanza's voice-over—including a name change away from a patron saint to "Zinc
Town," a settlement with the sole purpose of mining zinc for the company's profit. By
the end of the film, though, Esperanza's voice-over announces: "I knew we had won
something they could never take away, something that I could leave to my children,
and they, the salt of the earth, would inherit it."

The expression "salt of the earth" takes up the religious connotations of the name
"San Marcos" and of the baptismal scene halfway through the film. The well-known
line from Jesus's Sermon on the Mount addresses poor working people (like the
miners), mainly fishermen; it is the poor laborers, who are for Jesus "the salt of the
earth," i.e., what is basic and good and necessary. Yet Jesus cautions: "but if the salt
have lost his savor, wherewith shall it be salted? It is thenceforth good for nothing, but
to be cast out, and to be trodden underfoot of men" (Mk. 9.50; Lk. 14.34, 35). The
words of Jesus describe the situation of both the miners involved in the Bayard, NM
strike and deprived of their equal rights as well as the independent, blacklisted
filmmakers who struggled to make the film, and who were deprived of their livelihood
and careers. The strikers and their families were as powerless and, indeed, down-
trodden as the filmmakers. In the end, both groups prevailed against all odds in their
projects. Neither group, it turned out, had "lost [its] savor."

Significantly, Jesus's remarks on "the salt of the earth" are followed by "Ye are
the light of the world. A city that is set on a hill cannot be hid" (Joh. 8.12; 9.5). Of
course this wording brings to mind John Winthrop's reference to the Puritan Americans of the 1620s and 1630s being like "a city upon a hill." It may also be seen as an
implication of the model character of the miners' community portrayed in the film.
The community prevails because its members stick together.

This implied reference to foundational terminology contributes to making *Salt of
the Earth* a quintessentially American tale, a national narrative—revolving around the
issue of equality. At the union meeting that makes the walkout official, a miner (Charley Vidal) is speaking in Spanish as several women enter the meeting hall: "tenemos
varias quejas, hermanos, y muchas demandas, pero todo esto se puede traer a un punto
básico: la igualdad." This is when the women take their seats, signifying that they, too,
need to be included in the strikers' demands for equality. While Charley Vidal calls for
"la unidad de todos los hombres trabajadores," the film also calls for unity and

equality across the gender divide. Consuelo, the speaker of the women at the union meeting, makes the point that: "if the issue is equality, like you say it is, then maybe we ought to have equality in plumbing, too." The women demand running hot water in the company-owned miners' homes, which, we are told, is already standard in other (i.e., Anglo) mining camps. Earlier on, when Esperanza tells Ramón that better sanitation has to be one of the workers' demands, Ramón answers her that what is most important is "the safety of the men" and that therefore "first we gotta get equality on the job, then we'll work on those other things." Ramón's reaction foreshadows that of the union meeting, which "tables" the issue. Thus, at the outset, there are various efforts toward equality going on side by side. Ramón's reaction to racial discrimination is that "we [Mexican Americans] want equality with Anglo miners: same pay, same conditions." Esperanza's reaction to racial discrimination is a demand for equal sanitation. Fittingly, the most prominent sign carried by the picketers—seen most often on the screen—reads, "WE WANT EQUALITY."

The binary opposition of Mexican-American and Anglo-American is addressed in a variety of respects, indicating that it permeates the narrated nation and its culture. Homi Bhabha has spoken of "the western nation as an obscure and ubiquitous form of living the *locality* of culture." He goes on to explain: "This locality is more hybrid in the articulation of cultural differences and identifications—gender, race or class—than can be represented in any hierarchical or binary structuring of social antagonism" ("DissemiNation" 292). While *Salt of the Earth* does rely on binary oppositions and "social antagonism," it combines multiple binaries and shows through their interconnectedness the manifold nature of social conflict and grievances.

Crossing the ethnic borderline on issues of work, safety, pay, and housing is only part of the story. Ethnic equality is intertwined with gender equality, as we will see in the interaction between Esperanza and Ramón later on. It is also intertwined with class equality. When Mr. Alexander, the plant manager, drives up to the picket line with a Mr. Hartwell from the company's "eastern office," two representatives of the upper/ managing classes enter the picture, signified also by their ties and their luxurious car. Alexander tells Hartwell about the picketers: "Well, they're like children in many ways. Sometimes you have to humor them, sometimes you have to spank them. And sometimes you have to take their food away." As Ramón approaches them, the following exchange takes place:

> *Mr. Alexander*: I know your work record. You were in line for foreman when this trouble started, do you know that? Yessir, you had a real future with this company. But you let those reds stir you up, and now they'll sell you down the river. Why don't you wake up, Ray? That's your name, isn't it? Ray?
> *Ramón*: My name is Quintero, Mr. Quintero.

In this way Ramón refuses to be treated like a child or like a slave (sold "down the river") and asserts his right to class equality by demanding to be addressed as "Mr. Quintero" rather than being subsumed in a misnamed mass.

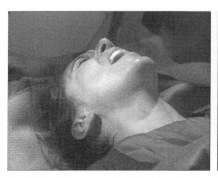 

Illustration 3: Esperanza in labor in a shack   Illustration 4: Ramón being beaten by two
at the picket line   of the sheriff's men

But resistance to inequality takes its toll. This suffering is conveyed most impressively in parallel, alternating shots of Esperanza in labor and Ramón being beaten by two of the sheriff's men (Illustrations 3 and 4). As the film keeps cutting back and forth between the two scenes, both characters scream each other's name in pain. Esperanza has to give birth without the assistance of a doctor or midwife, since she is at the picket line when labor begins; the company doctor will not come out to the picket line and she has no money to go to a hospital. At the same time, Ramón is helpless: picked up after stopping a scab, he is handcuffed in a sheriff's car out in the desert, where the sheriff's men keep punching him in the stomach.

The brutality of the system is further illustrated in the film's prison scene: women and children on the picket line have been arrested and are crammed into a prison cell—without food or bathrooms. Esperanza and her baby are among the detained. Taking over a *film noir* technique, *Salt of the Earth* repeatedly shows the shadow of the prison bars on the bodies of the Mexican American inmates.

Illustration 5 demonstrates the inhumanity of the ruling system of inequality. In the film's spirit of advocacy, the faces of the two boys are marked by the shadows of the iron bars. With the boy on the right, the shadow appears as a cross on his face; with the boy on the left, the wide open eye and the open mouth convey incomprehension and vulnerability.

The nation that is narrated by *Salt of the Earth* is not one of equality or harmonious plurality. Bhabha writes that "[w]e may begin by questioning that progressive metaphor of modern social cohesion—*the many as one*—shared by organic theories of the holism of culture and community, and by theorists who treat gender, class, or race as radically 'expressive' social totalities" ("DissemiNation" 294). This is what *Salt of the Earth* does from the very beginning, e.g. by setting up "the Anglos" in Esperanza's initial voice-over monologue as the other who has taken over land and resources. So there cannot be a national community of "the many as one" because of the inequality of power, possession, and means. By the end of the film, however, when the mining company is ready to negotiate, a national version of "the many as one" seems more within reach. The path toward this possibility of a more equal nation is paved through the mining community, which serves as a model for a future national community. In this idealized mining community borderlines are crossed, as the original, separate demands are combined into the overreaching demand for equality on all levels—as women and men, Mexican Americans and Anglo Americans, old and young join forces in pursuing the same goal.

Illustration 5: Children are detained along with their mothers

The joint efforts of the diverse members of the mining community can stop the wheels of the system of inequality. At first, the power of the mining corporation is symbolized by turning wheels that keep generating profits—regardless of the risk to the workers. But the film demonstrates the power of the community to stop the capitalist machinery. When the miners decide to go on strike after one of them (an Anglo) has been injured badly in an accident under ground, Ramón signals to stop the conveyer belts. Biberman uses the close-up of a wheel standing still (Illustration 6) to demonstrate the shift in power and to signal that communal effort may defeat corporate oppression. Once the corporation calls in the sheriff's department to move the picketing women, the women's power to halt the enforcement machinery is symbolized by them pushing against a sheriff's car, which makes the car's tire turn without moving forward (Illustration 7). We get two shots of this rotating tire—in between them we see the

women pushing against the car, after the second shot of the rotating tire we see the
women pulling out the spark plug cables of the car's engine. The viewer guidance and
the spirit of advocacy are strong in this scene: Esperanza's voice-over makes us side
with her; she is carrying her baby, while the law enforcement agents, wearing gas
masks, are carrying rifles from which they shoot tear gas. The four men—sheriff's
badges on their chests and Stetsons cocked on their heads—are depicted in a low-angle
shot, which makes them appear as a menacing, male, Wild West force used by an
unjust alliance of corporate and judicial power to fend off women and children.
Dramatic music sets off the callous authorities against the life-affirming women, who
had only a few moments earlier been singing and dancing on the picket line.

Illustration 6: The miners stop the conveyor   Illustration 7: The women picketers stop the
belt and go on strike.   sheriff's car.

We witness the power of community solidarity—the united underdogs who can resist
the cold forces of inequality. Their singing of "Solidarity Forever" (to the tune of
"Glory, Glory, Hallelujah") underlines the strategy that makes them strong (fore-
shadowing Lech Wałęsa's Solidarność movement in Gdańsk in the 1970s and 1980s)
and is at the same time a call for viewer solidarity. So were the depictions in earlier
scenes of support letters and relief shipments coming in from all over the country and
of women from other mining camps joining the picketers. Solidarity in the idealized
group leads to helplessness in the opposing camp, as illustrated when the sheriff's men
beg those in the prison cell to stop shouting, and a close-up pans to a boy behind bars
sticking out his tongue at the law enforcers.

     In this utopian national narrative we see equality on the rise in terms of race and
especially in terms of gender. Old models of behavior and old centers of authority are
challenged through the crossing of borderlines. An example: After a court order has
forbidden the miners to continue their picketing, a union meeting is turned into a community meeting so that the women can also have a say. Men and women then vote that
the women, the so-called "ladies auxiliary," should continue the picketing, which is
supported by some of the male centers of familial authority but not by all, also not by
the strike leader Ramón. Even when Esperanza joins the picketing women, he is re-

luctant to take care of their three children while she is on the picket line. But eventually Ramón comes around to accepting and even appreciating the women's solidarity. Reading in a magazine that the company president likes to go hunting, Ramón and some other miners also go hunting, subconsciously aligning themselves with the old centers of authority. The company and the sheriff's department try to use this opportunity to evict Ramón's family from their company-owned home in order to "scare some sense into" his neighbors. But once again the solidarity of the idealized community wins the confrontation with the callous bearers of authority: children throw stones at the assistant sheriffs who are trying to empty out the shack and women carry the Quinteros's belongings right back into their home. Ramón rushes back from his hunting expedition. When the sheriff tells him to "make them [the women defying his men] behave," Ramón replies: "You know how it is, Sheriff. I can't do nothing. They won't listen to a man no more." Then more miners arrive in solidarity to stop the eviction.

Romanticizing the situation, the film shows Ramón holding his baby and telling the community in his concluding monologue: "Thanks, sisters and brothers. Esperanza, thank you for your dignity. You were right: together we can push everything up with us as we go." This idealized vision, although straying from rote documentation, offers interpretive guidance (cf. Nichols) to audiences; it also marks this docudrama as a new, not yet established narrative of an egalitarian national community.[25] The "humanist factor," of which John Grierson had written in 1952, while *Salt of the Earth* was being filmed, is fully recognized here. Agreeing with Grierson, screenwriter Michael Wilson believes that a writer has to "struggle tenaciously to preserve human values in all his work," and producer Paul Jarrico insists that films can change the views of audiences[26]: "if you could change [the viewers'] attitude toward women,

---

[25] As Ellen Baker has argued, the ending of the film is more conclusive and optimistic than the historical developments in Grant County's mining community: "The movie shows a fundamental transformation taking place in the relations of husbands to wives, a transformation made possible by a change of gender consciousness and by he success of the strike. The transformation is clear and unambiguous; the old way is distinguished from the new, and the new way is chosen. It is a transformation that will be sustained and enjoyed by the coming generations. The film's portrayal of transformation, though, was itself an effort to settle and make permanent in a cultural artifact that which was far more volatile in real life. For the conflicts taking place in Grant County were not fully resolved—for individuals or families, or in terms of gender relations more broadly. ... [W]hile positive and powerful, the change of consciousness proved inadequate for sustaining activism in the ladies' auxiliary. In fact, Auxiliary 209 disbanded only a few years after *Salt of the Earth* was made" (245, 247).

[26] This persuasive power of film did not go unnoticed by business and industry. As Eric Barnouw recounts, there was widespread use of the film medium by corporations in the United States during the 1950s as an instrument of influencing public opinion: "During the first decade after World War II, production of industry-sponsored films—mostly short—rose in the United States to some 4000 films per year. Some were for intra-company use as

workers, Blacks, and minorities in general—*and you could*—then that was an important contribution. Sure [the powers that be] wouldn't let us make a really revolutionary
picture, but if we were good writers and skillful at our craft we could subtly affect the
content" toward progressive ends (qtd. in Baker 200).

In order to alter the ways audiences think about these issues, *Salt of the Earth*
presents Ramón as a character who substantially changes his own views—especially
on gender equality. Ramón's epiphany is prepared in the film by two scenes. In the
first one, while his wife is in jail, he and a male neighbor hang up laundry outdoors,
complaining how long is takes to heat water to do the wash. The neighbor tells him
that they also need to work toward "sex equality," explaining that "lo que es bueno
para el hombre es bueno para la mujer." The other scene occurs when Esperanza
comes home from jail: she asks Ramón, who at that time still disapproves of her
involvement with the picketers, whether he has to keep her down in order to feel
worthy himself the same way the Anglo miners had kept him down to feel worthy
themselves: "Why are you afraid to have me at your side? You still think you can have
dignity only if I have none?"[27] This rhetorical question is of course directed at viewers,
appealing to their sense of equality. Esperanza's plea "I don't want anything lower
than I am. I'm low enough already. I want to rise. And push everything up with me as
I go," is echoed in Ramón's final monologue ("together we can push everything up
with us as we go") to signify that he has now understood that the perpetuation of hierarchies and inequality will not ultimately lead to a better society.

Apart from gender, ethnicity is the main area for which the film advocates solidarity. The models in this regard are the Anglo union organizer Barnes and his wife.
They and other Anglos live with the Mexican-American mining families and do not
look down on Mexican Americans. On the contrary, when the foreman asks Barnes to
tell the miners to go back to work, he replies: "They don't work for me; I work for
them." Later on, while Barnes is at Ramón's house, Ramón questions Barnes's membership in the community on the basis of ethnic and cultural heritage, as Barnes does
not recognize that the portrait in the Quintero house is of Benito Juárez. Serving as a
model of intercultural awareness, Barnes admits that he has "a lot to learn" about
Mexican Americans. His wife links the issues of ethnicity and gender, pointing out
that "wives don't count in the Anglo locals either." In this manner, she, too, propagates
the film's demand that solidarity and equality cannot be limited in any arena.

In this vein, as mentioned above, the creators of *Salt of the Earth* also crossed
borders of authorial control in making their film, realizing that the crossing of borders
and the plea for solidarity and equality in the film's plot needed to be echoed in power
sharing when it came to the making of the film. Therefore the miners depicted in *Salt
of the Earth* had a significant say in how their lives and the issues of their strike were

---

training films, or as records of research. Many others went into theaters, schools, clubs,
churches, to influence the climate of ideas" (219).

[27] During their argument, when Ramón is ready to strike her but doesn't, Esperanza tells him
that "that would have been the old way."

to be represented. As A. Manuel Meléndez writes, basing his views on James J. Lorence's study,

> The project deliberately sought to get at true history, economy, and culture. The method called for the filmmakers to establish sustained and close working collaborations with the people whose story they wished to bring to film. The filmmakers' willingness to give up authorial control in favor of 'getting the story right' is unprecedented in the history of U.S. film. (118)

This seems true enough: it is hard to imagine Robert Flaherty allowing Allakariallak (who plays Nanook) and his family to have a say in how the Inuit were to be portrayed in *Nanook of the North*.

Under the major headings of equality and activism, different groups and individuals had their own particular hopes for *Salt of the Earth*, as Ellen Baker explains. For the women in the mining camp the film was "a way to rekindle women's activism, which dwindled after the strike ended in January 1952;" for "the union participants" it presented a way "to get their story out;" for Juan Chacón "*Salt of the Earth* 'help[ed] to expose the lie' that Mexicans were 'naturally inferior,' a lie told by the mining companies to prevent Anglo-Mexican unity;" and for the film professionals the project presented an opportunity to do creative, socially meaningful work despite the blacklist (220-22). As Baker concludes,

> For all of these participants, the essence of making the movie was making connections to others, just as Biberman had described. *Salt of the Earth* brought workers and artists together and had the potential to connect both groups to American audiences more broadly. It was this challenge to the isolation imposed by the blacklist and by anticommunism more broadly that most threatened the mining industry and the film industry. And it was the potential to bring people together that, ironically, allowed both the mining industry and the film industry to unite in order to stifle *Salt of the Earth*. (222)

5. Despite McCarthyism: Production, Distribution, Reception

Producer Paul Jarrico was struck by the parallels between the situations of the New Mexico miners and the blacklistees in Hollywood. As James Lorence relates:

> As a committed feminist, Sylvia Jarrico embraced the story with enthusiasm, but no more so than her husband, Paul, who was deeply impressed with the parallels between the Empire/Mine-Mill story and the blacklisted artists' own political and economic predicament. Whereas Mine-Mill had been expelled from the CIO for alleged Communist influence, the blacklistees had been 'kicked out of Hollywood' ... for the same reason. Convinced that this was the material IPC [the Independent Productions Corporation set up by Biberman and Jarrico] had been looking for, he told Biberman and Scott that "this is a story that's got everything. It's got labor's rights, women's rights, minority rights, all in a dynamic package." (58)

The other IPC members concurred and decided to commit "what Jarrico called a 'crime to fit the punishment' already meted out to the victims of the blacklist" (Lorence 58).

The completion of the film was by far not the end of IPC's troubles. In 1953 and 1954, the United States were not ready for *Salt of the Earth* and its demand for universal equality. Given the ideological climate of the 1950s, it is hardly surprising that the film encountered serious resistance from its inception. Even before the cameras began to roll in Bayard, the *Hollywood Reporter* proclaimed that a "commie" film was being shot in New Mexico under "direct orders from the Kremlin." California Republican congressman Donald Jackson, an active HUAC member, was soon denouncing *Salt of the Earth* from the floor of the House of Representatives, charging that the film was being made "under Communist auspices" as part of an attempt to undermine the U.S. war effort in Korea. In a speech on February 24, 1953 Jackson promised to do all he could "to prevent the showing of this Communist-made film in the theaters of America" (Lorence 79ff). Laboratories refused to process the film once it had been shot, thus delaying postproduction work for months. The visa of Mexican actress Rosaura Revueltas was revoked, and she was not allowed back into the United States to promote the film.

Once postproduction was completed and the film was ready to be shown, movie theaters would sometimes announce *Salt of the Earth* and sell tickets for it but would then never show the film. The reason for the general boycott was that *Salt of the Earth* was the inaugural film project of the IPC, formed in 1951 by film professionals who were convinced they could circumvent the industry's blacklist by working outside the studio system. Theater owners did not want to risk being boycotted themselves by the big studios in the future as a reprisal for collaborating with IPC. There were some screenings of *Salt of the Earth* in New York City and San Francisco, generally to enthusiastic crowds and warm reviews. Lorence summarizes:

> contemporary critical reaction was mixed, but in most cases *Salt* received positive, often outstanding reviews. Many commentators, while endorsing the film's gripping social realism, added disparaging remarks concerning stilted portrayals of management and alleged propaganda content. (195)

There were also successful screenings in Toronto (promoted by Canadian unionists in their Labor Day Parade) and Mexico City. Apparently, Diego Rivera's reaction to the film was: "¡stupendo!" (Lorence 152).

But in the United States, *Salt of the Earth* invariably met with widespread boycotts throughout the country. In his book, Biberman recalls the situation in 1955:

> Even when we knew that our resistance had been rendered pitifully weak, we persisted, to prevent the total obliteration of resistance. What gave us hope in this formative, present moment of change was what seemed to be the recognition by the nation of the fact of injury to *itself*. (214)

According to Biberman, the nation itself was coming to realize that its principles (especially those of free speech and equality) were under attack and that the narration of nation orchestrated by Joseph McCarthy, Donald Jackson, and others was false.

Not surprisingly, in the United States the film was especially espoused by Mexican Americans and by labor unions: "Juan Chacón always viewed *Salt* as the expression of the Mexican-American spirit, as well as an effective organizational tool," writes Lorence (197). Through the success of the strike and through the involvement of Mexican Americans in making the film, this ethnic group felt "elevated" and experienced a sense of "pride" and ownership. In 1955 a group of Los Angeles Chicano unionists proposed a campaign to open the movie theaters of the Southwest to showing *Salt*. While this campaign did not materialize, the initiative revealed to Biberman "*Salt*'s power as an instrument of self-identified value to Mexican-Americans seeking to achieve 'cohesion as a minority' and 'increased strength'" (Lorence 198).

Because of the massive resistance and obstacles with which the film met in the United States, IPC launched a campaign for its international distribution. In 1954 the film garnered much critical acclaim in Eastern Europe. It won the awards for "best picture" and "best actress" at the 1954 Czech International Film Festival. In France, *Salt of the Earth* won the 1955 International Grand Prize from the Académie du Cinema de Paris. But later, when IPC's distribution division "closed a deal with the Chinese government, the United States government nullified the sale. ... Finally, in 1959 the United States Information Agency blacklisted *Salt* for foreign distribution, which meant that IPC was unable to convert blocked foreign currency into dollars by exhibiting the picture overseas" (Lorence 153). Donald Jackson continued his diatribes against the film, charging that it was "'carrying distortion, inaccuracy, and American-made Red propaganda to millions of human beings,' who were likely to accept the picture's images as 'a true expression of American life'" (qtd. in Lorence 154). Half a century later, however, James J. Lorence judges the Communist content of and influence on *Salt of the Earth* to be largely fictitious.[28] But when the film first came out, the political climate of the 1950s led to reviewers, governmental officials, and Hollywood magnates detecting in the film the Communist ideology against which HUAC had been warning them.

In 1964, ten years after making *Salt of the Earth*, Herbert J. Biberman wrote that "McCarthy had been jettisoned, but McCarthyism persisted in the basic assumptions under which we lived. One was free to attack our mores, institutions, personages without limit or fear, so long as one also despaired and offered no alternatives" (223).[29] But with its utopian vision of interlaced multiple border crossings toward greater equality *Salt of the Earth* had offered alternatives. Biberman believed that this was the reason

---

[28] Lorence writes: "In reality, despite the film's persuasive power, its impact owed little to direct Communist Party influence. The Communist intellectual leadership in Hollywood had been largely frustrated in its attempt to significantly alter the film. If propaganda was to be found in *Salt*, it resided in the strong argument the film makes against unrestrained capitalism, which was hardly the exclusive property of the CP" (197).

[29] Lorence has found that "because the specter of the Communist menace lingered long after the Senate's action, the lives of both the *Salt* activists and Mine-Mill leaders were to be influenced for years by the project. For some, the persecution persisted long after the film controversy had disappeared from public consciousness" (171).

why the government, the film industry, and the distribution channels had suppressed the film in the United States.

Despite our sympathies for Biberman and his film we need to bear in mind that the counter-narrative of the nation that *Salt of the Earth* offers in resistance to HUAC and the national inequalities of the 1950s is by no means authoritative either. Homi Bhabha therefore asks "whether the *emergence* of a national perspective—of an élite or subaltern nature—within a culture of social contestation, can ever articulate its 'representative' authority in that fullness of narrative time, and that visual synchrony of the sign" ("DissemiNation" 295).

Despite Biberman's and IPC's tireless efforts *Salt of the Earth* went almost unseen in the U.S.A. until the late 1960s. But then it became an important document for raising consciousness in terms of class, ethnicity, and gender equality.[30] For example, the film was screened in 1968 at one of the early organizational meetings of the United Mexican American Student Association (UMAS) (cf. Meléndez 122). It was rediscovered and embraced by America's New Left to become a staple of labor rallies, campus film clubs, and art houses. Moreover, it became a rallying tool for the burgeoning women's movement in the 1970s. As Victor Navasky estimates, *Salt of the Earth* "anticipated both the feminist and independent film-producing movements by more than a decade (not to mention its premature concern for the Chicanos)" (qtd. in Lorence 200-01). It stood as a testimony to free speech and as a sign of resistance and hope for the blacklistees in Hollywood, it "represented an alternative consciousness of the artist's social responsibility," and it survived as an "'extraordinary assault on HUAC.'" In short, the appearance of a provocatively independent film production offered hope to the outcasts of Cold War America" (Lorence 201).

Ultimately, as Gary Francisco Keller writes in his contribution to this volume, *Salt of the Earth* assumed a timeless quality: "As the women find their voice, the film's affirmation of perseverance, justice, as well as gender and racial equality appears almost as radical and rousing today as it did in the dark days of McCarthyism" (377). Assessing the legacy of the film, Keller states that while "[t]he makers of *Salt of the Earth* struggled to find theater owners willing to show their incendiary movie, ... it has become a classic cult film, at least on college campuses. To paraphrase William Faulkner's Nobel Prize speech, *Salt* 'not only endures, but prevails'" (374). James J. Lorence agrees that this

> film, little seen in its own time, has become a symbol of an alternate vision of America in the 1950s, a view that emphasizes conflict and confrontation. The *Salt* story challenges the consensus view of race relations, gender roles, and class harmony and signifies a historical counter-trend, which existed side by side with a "culture of conformity."

---

[30] While, according to Louis Menand, *Fahrenheit 9/11* illustrates that Michel Moore is "a populist ideologue who boils everything down to a single article of belief: the rich screw the poor" (3), the "article of belief" is much more complex and multi-faceted with Herbert J. Biberman, who portrays the interrelatedness of different kinds of inequality.

... For all the vicissitudes of its troubled history, *Salt of the Earth* remains a fragile celluloid monument to that culture of resistance. (202-03)[31]

The vision of resistance and equality, of the triumph of the underdog, that Biberman put on the screen in *Salt of the Earth* may also be credited with having given rise to the documentary engagement with labor disputes, e.g. in Barbara Kopple's *Harlan County, USA* (1976) or Michael Moore's *Roger & Me* (1989). Especially with Kopple, there is a distinct similarity to Biberman in terms of outlook and approach.[32]

Like the film itself, its reception is also a national narrative and a comment on American national identity. Both illustrate the ideological struggles and the hierarchies that characterized the U.S. in the 1950s and that have not yet ended today. (The "Patriot Act" may serve as a case in point.) *Salt*'s utopian, democratic, inter-American vision of equality, nonetheless, stands firm as a plea for changes to the dystopian realities.

6. Conclusion

Salt of the Earth presents a narration of the nation from its margins and a patriotic plea for equality in the nation. As a docudrama set in rural New Mexico, it resists the bias for the metropolis and for a metropolitan perspective on its subjects of which Michael Chanan has complained with regard to documentaries. Chanan notes that the *nuevo cine latinoamericano*, which started in the 1960s, brought about a change. Its creators "discover[ed] that the exotic isn't other and somewhere else but on their own doorstep, and not at all exotic but full of teeming humanity, impoverished and deprived." Chanan believes that what distinguishes the films of the *nuevo cine latinoamericano* is that "they escape the distorted imagery of the dominant cinema's imaginary, simply by rendering visible the previously unseen, overlooked, and excluded" ("Going" 149). In

---

[31] Lorence sums up *Salt*'s intervention in the negotiation of national identity and in the struggle to preserve the nation's principles as follows: "For Chicanos, Hollywood leftists, mainstream liberals, and principled conservatives, the *Salt* controversy was significant as a call to conscience and a test for civil liberties. The battle for the film was, in the words of Simon Lazarus, an 'honorable chapter' in recent American history. With the passage of time, Herbert Biberman, Paul Jarrico, and Michael Wilson reemerged as exemplars of the dissenting tradition. Their politics aside, the *Salt* group stood almost alone against thought control and censorship in a period of grave constitutional danger; and they emerged as people of courage who insisted that the Bill of Rights be honored, despite the pressures exerted by the forces of political conformity. As Biberman declared in 1970, the moral of the story was a warning to the oppressors: 'Be careful whom you blacklist—he may be extolled as a hero in the next, if not his own generation'" (202).

[32] James McEnteer characterizes her as follows: "Barbara Kopple has enlarged the scope of documentary discourse by reporting on social upheavals and cultural trends in ways that clearly delineate the relationship of individual trajectories/lives/narratives to a larger political and economic context. Kopple uses personal stories to undermine the feel-good economic fables that corporate culture deploys to mask oppressive behaviors" (xviii).

this sense, *Salt of the Earth* can be said to have preceded the *nuevo cine latinoamericano* through its unprecedented representation of Mexican Americans.[33]

The film engages in what John Grierson has defined as the task of documentaries: "the creative treatment of reality" (qtd. in McEnteer xv). In this creative treatment the underdogs gain power and dignity, coming a step closer to equality. Thus *Salt of the Earth* positions itself against the tendency that Homi Bhabha identified as "the attempt by nationalist discourses persistently to produce the idea of the nation as a continuous narrative of national progress, the narcissism of self-generation, the primeval present of the *Volk*" ("Introduction" 1). Expanding on the position of Benedict Anderson, Bhabha speaks of the nation as "a system of cultural signification" that is filled with ambivalence and that relies on "the representation of social *life* rather than the discipline of social *polity*" ("Introduction" 1-2). This is the path that *Salt of the Earth* follows. Its narration of the nation focuses on the common people, women, workers, ethnic minorities; in other words, on the liminality of national culture.[34]

Salt of the Earth enacts on screen the position expressed by Thomas Jefferson in his First Inaugural Address of 1801, namely that "the minority possess their equal rights, which equal law must protect, and [which] to violate would be oppression." Jefferson would likely have admired the Bayard mining strike and the film based on it, since he wrote to James Madison in 1787: "I hold it, that a little rebellion, now and then, is a good thing, and as necessary in the political world as storms in the physical" (6: 65). That *Salt of the Earth*, which launched such a "little rebellion," was chosen in 1992 by the Library of Congress as one of 25 films to be added to the National Film Registry that year can be seen as a sign of hope for the ultimate victory of the nation's founding principles.

Biberman stands in the tradition of Thomas Jefferson, believing that the principles of the nation (foremost: equality) need to be defended, and that at times rebellion is the only appropriate defense of U.S. national identity and of a de-centered, alternative narration of the nation. At the end of his book on the background of *Salt of the Earth* he writes,

---

[33] *Salt of the Earth* also precedes (by more than half a century) the Declaration of Guayaquil, which was passed in 2009 at a meeting of over one hundred Latin American and Caribbean documentarists in Ecuador and which states as two of the four goals it posits for documentary film that in order to reflect the America that they would like to be seen, the genre needs to "grant a vital space to all who work for transformation within our pluriculturalism" and to "give meaning to the struggles taking place against key hegemonic imaginaries which manipulate and negate the essential qualities of our realities." By pursuing these goals, the manifesto affirms, the documentary in the Western Hemisphere can be "a form of building identities, of historical memory, and … a helper in building active communities at every level" ("Going" 153-54).

[34] Bhabha believes that "it is from the liminality of the national culture that the figure of the people emerges in the narrative ambivalence of disjunctive times and meanings" ("DissemiNation" 304).

In 1947 I offered a statement to the Un-American Activities Committee which they would not permit me to read and would not read themselves. Its last lines seem as appropriate to end my part of this book as they seemed to me to be then:
"In this hearing I will not merely rely upon the Constitution—I will fight for it and defend it against all possible intimidation. Here, as well, I am a free man—accustomed to slow, hard, patient, and passionate defense of what I believe to be American." (314)

Works Cited

Aitken, Ian. *The Documentary Film Movement: An Anthology.* Edinburgh: Edinburgh UP, 1998.

Baker, Ellen R. *On Strike and on Film: Mexican American Families and Blacklisted Filmmakers in Cold War America.* Chapel Hill: U of North Carolina P, 2007.

Barnouw, Eric. *Documentary: A History of the Non-Fiction Film.* Second rev. ed. New York & Oxford: Oxford UP, 1993.

Basco, Sharon. "In Pursuit of Equality, Life, Liberty, and Happiness: An Interview with Historian Howard Zinn." TomPaine.com. July 3, 2002. http://www.tompaine.com/Archive/scontent/5908.html.

Beattie, Keith. *Documentary Screens: Non-Fiction Film and Television.* Houndmills: Palgrave, 2004.

Berg, Charles Ramírez. *Latino Images in Film: Stereotypes, Subversion, Resistance.* Austin: U of Texas P, 2002.

Bhabha, Homi K. "Introduction: Narrating the Nation." *Nation and Narration.* Ed. Bhabha. London: Routledge, 1990. 1-7.

———. "DissemiNation: Time, Narrative, and the Margins of the Modern Nation." *Nation and Narration.* Ed. Bhabha. London: Routledge, 1990. 291-322.

Biberman, Herbert. *Salt of the Earth: The Story of a Film.* Boston: Beacon P, 1965.

Brennan, Timothy. "The National Longing for Form." *Nation and Narration.* Ed. Homi K. Bhabha. 44-70.

Bruzzi, Stella. *New Documentary: A Critical Introduction.* Second ed. Abingdon & New York: Routledge, 2006.

Burton, Julianne. "Toward a History of Social Documentary in Latin America." *The Social Documentary in Latin America.* Ed. Burton. Pittsburgh: U of Pittsburgh P, 1990. 3-30.

Caughie, John. "Progressive Television and Documentary Drama." *Screen* 21.3 (1980): 9-35.

Chanan, Michael. "Going South: On Documentary as a Form of Cognitive Geography." *Cinema Journal* 50.1 (Fall 2010): 147-54.

———. *The Politics of Documentary.* London: BFI Publishing, 2008.

Hershfield, Joanne. "Paradise Regained: Sergei Eisenstein's *Que viva México!* as Ethnography." *Documenting the Documentary: Close Readings of Documentary Film and Video.* Ed. Barry Keith Grand and Jeannette Sloniowski. Detroit: Wayne State UP, 1998. 55-69.

Huntington, Samuel P. *Who Are We?: The Challenges to America's National Identity.* New York: Simon & Schuster, 2004.

Hustvedt, Siri. *The Summer Without Men: A Novel*. New York: Picador, 2011.

Jefferson, Thomas. *The Writings of Thomas Jefferson*. Ed. Andrew A. Lipscomb, Albert Ellery Bergh, and Richard Holland Johnston. Washington: Thomas Jefferson Memorial Association, 1907.

Keller, Gary D. "The Image of the Chicano in Mexican, United States, and Chicano Cinema: An Overview." *Chicano Cinema: Research, Reviews & Resources*. Ed. Keller. Tempe, AZ: Bilingual Review/Press, 1985. 13-58.

Keller, Gary Francisco. "Mining and the Dignity and Indignities of Work: From *Salt of the Earth* to Hector Galán's *Los Mineros*." *Screening the Americas: Narration of Nation in Documentary Film / Proyectando las Américas: La narración de la nación en el cine documental*. Ed. Josef Raab, Sebastian Thies, and Daniela Noll-Opitz. Trier: Wissenschaftlicher Verlag Trier / Tempe, AZ: Bilingual P, 2011. 369-386.

Lorence, James J. *The Suppression of* Salt of the Earth: *How Hollywood, Big Labor, and Politicians Blacklisted a Movie in Cold War America*. Albuquerque: U of New Mexico P, 1999.

Maciel, David R., and Susan Racho. "'*Yo soy chicano*': The Turbulent and Heroic Life of Chicanas/os in Cinema and Television." *Chicano Renaissance: Contemporary Cultural Trends*. Ed. David R. Maciel, Isidro D. Ortiz, and María Herrera-Sobek. Tucson: U of Arizona P, 2000. 93-130.

McBride, Ian. "Where Are We Going, and How and Why?" *New Challenges for Documentary*. Ed. Alan Rosenthal and John Corner. Second ed. Manchester: Manchester UP, 2005. 484-92.

McEnteer, James. *Shooting the Truth: The Rise of American Political Documentaries*. Westport, CT & London: Praeger, 2006.

Meléndez, A. Gabriel. "Who Are the 'Salt of the Earth'?" *Expressing New Mexico: Nuevomexicano Creativity, Ritual, and Memory*. Ed. Phillip B. Gonzales. Tucson: U of Arizona P, 2007. 115-38.

Menand, Louis. "Nanook and Me: *Fahrenheit 9/11* and the Documentary Tradition." *The New Yorker* 9 August 2004. http://www.newyorker.com/archive/2004/08/09/040809crat_atlarge.

National Council of *La Raza*. "Out of the Picture: Hispanics in the Media." 1994. *Latin Looks: Images of Latinas and Latinos in the U.S. Media*. Ed. Clara E. Rodríguez. Boulder, CO: Westview P, 1997. 21-35.

Nichols, Bill. *Blurred Boundaries: Questions of Meaning in Contemporary Culture*. Bloomington & Indianapolis: Indiana UP, 1994.

———. *Introduction to Documentary*. Bloomington & Indianapolis: Indiana UP, 2001.

———. *Representing Reality: Issues and Concepts in Documentary*. Bloomington and Indianapolis: Indiana UP, 1991.

Paget, Derek. *No Other Way to Tell It: Dramadoc/Docudrama on Television*. Manchester: Manchester UP, 1998.

Renov, Michael, ed. *Theorizing Documentary*. New York & London: Routledge, 1993.

Williams, Linda. "Type and Stereotype: Chicano Images in Film." *Chicano Cinema: Research, Reviews & Resources*. Ed. Gary D. Keller. Tempe, AZ: Bilingual Review/Press, 1985. 59-63.

Woodhead, Leslie. "Dramatised Documentary." *New Challenges for Documentary*. Ed. Alan Rosenthal and John Corner. Second ed. Manchester: Manchester UP, 2005. 475-84.

Youdelman, Jeffrey. "Narration, Invention, and History." *New Challenges for Documentary*. Ed. Alan Rosenthal and John Corner. Second ed. Manchester: Manchester UP, 2005. 397-408.

Zinn, Howard. *A People's History of the United States*. 1999. New York: Harper Perennial, 2010.

Filmography

Chicana. Dir. Sylvia Morales. U.S.A., 1979.

The City. Dir. Ralph Steiner and Willard Van Dyke. U.S.A., 1939.

Crisis: Behind a Presidential Commitment. Dir. Drew Associates. U.S.A., 1963.

Fahrenheit 9/11. Dir. Michael Moore. U.S.A., 2004.

Giant. Dir. George Stevens. U.S.A., 1956.

Harlan County, USA. Dir. Barbara Kopple. U.S.A., 1976.

The Hollywood Ten. Dir. Southern California Chapter, National Council of the Arts, Sciences & Professions. U.S.A., 1950.

La Hora de los hornos. Dir. Octavio Getino and Fernando E. Solanas. Argentina, 1968.

Huelga. Dir. United Farm Workers Association. U.S.A., 1966.

I Am Joaquin. Dir. Luis Valdez. Mexico, U.S.A., 1969.

The Lawless. Dir. Joseph Losey. U.S.A., 1950.

Louisiana Story. Dir. Robert J. Flaherty. U.S.A., 1948.

Nanook of the North. Dir. Robert J. Flaherty. U.S.A., France, Canada, 1922.

On the Waterfront. Dir. Elia Kazan. U.S.A., 1954.

Que viva México! Dir. Sergei M. Eisenstein. Soviet Union, U.S.A., Mexico, [filmed in 1930-32]. Completed by Grigori Aleksandrov. Soviet Union, 1979.

The Ring. Dir. Kurt Neumann. U.S.A., 1952.

Roger & Me. Dir. Michael Moore. U.S.A., 1989.

Salt of the Earth. Dir. Herbert J. Biberman. U.S.A., 1954.

Strike. Dir. Sergei M. Eisenstein. Soviet Union, 1925.

Tire dié. Dir. Fernando Birri. Argentina, 1958.

Titicut Follies. Dir. Frederick Wiseman. U.S.A., 1967.

Touch of Evil. Dir. Orson Welles. U.S.A., 1958.

Why We Fight. Dir. Frank Capra. U.S.A., 1942-44.

Yo soy chicano. Dir. Jesús Treviño. Mexico, U.S.A., 1972.

MargiNaciones: usos del margen en la narración de la nación

ÁLVARO FERNÁNDEZ BRAVO

> Pienso que la condición sine qua non para que
> haya imagen es la alteridad.
> —Serge Daney
>
> Una imagen es siempre la imagen del otro.
> —Jean-Louis Comolli

Abstract

This essay focuses on three Argentinean documentaries comparing the changing role of the margin in the filmic construction of the nation. *Tire dié* (1958), directed by Fernando Birri, can be considered as a direct precursor of Third Cinema political engagement and as such uses a didactic approach by giving a voice to the voiceless. *Dársena sur* (1997), directed by Pablo Reyero, and *La libertad* (2001), directed by Lisandro Alonso, however, both come out of the so-called *Nuevo Cine Argentino* and are marked by a much less explicit political stance.

In *Tire dié* the margin is indispensable for Birri's image of the Argentinean nation, constructed as a bipolar world of a poor rural society (living at the margins) that is in stark contrast to a wealthy one (living in the urban center). The opposite is true for *Dársena sur* and *La libertad*: although in both films margins are explored in the portrayal of members of lower social classes, the margin no longer separates two distinct worlds. Instead, the division between center and margin dissolves and everything turns out to be marginal. The margin thus loses its implication of exclusion, which it still had in *Tire dié*. While the emancipatory discourse of *Tire dié* seeks to overcome the margins, *Dársena sur* and *La libertad* present a nation that is entirely marked by the margin and question this situation—without giving easy solutions or answers.

1. Alteración de las imágenes

Mi trabajo se propone reconstruir una genealogía discontinua del documental en la Argentina a partir de un problema específico: la exploración de la cultura nacional como el reconocimiento de sus márgenes. Mi atención nace de una investigación más amplia que realicé sobre la formación de los patrimonios culturales en América Latina y, en lo que sigue, me interesa examinar la posición de los márgenes como insumo determinante de la identidad colectiva.

Uno de los descubrimientos que hice en esa investigación –centrada en colecciones, exhibiciones y museos–, es que los márgenes han sido una cantera abundante donde imaginar, abastecer y problematizar la idea de nación. La definición del contenido de la cultura nacional ha encontrado en los márgenes una fuente inagotable de recursos simbólicos. En el caso del cine argentino, también los márgenes han despertado la atención de los directores, en particular en el género documental y sus variantes híbridas contemporáneas. Existe una tradición documental que intentaré releer y comparar con dos filmes recientes que, en mi opinión, pueden ser analizados en diálogo con la tradición documentalista iniciada por Fernando Birri con *Tire dié* en 1958. Las películas sobre las que voy a hablar marcan un cambio en la politización estética que estalló en los años sesenta. Me concentraré, por lo tanto, en *Tire dié*, en tanto filme precursor de un cine realista y social, pero donde la politización del Tercer Cine es todavía incipiente. Las películas contemporáneas con las que quiero comparar este documental – *Dársena sur* (1997) de Pablo Reyero y *La libertad* (2001) de Lisandro Alonso–, son filmes donde es posible reconocer rasgos de un nuevo lugar de la política en el arte. Tanto *Tire dié* como *Dársena sur* y *La libertad* marcan un antes y un después de la relación entre el cine y la política de los años sesenta.[1]

Creo que la convocatoria de esta publicación resulta oportuna, ya que en el cine argentino reciente ha cobrado importancia una marca realista donde algunos componentes característicos del documental se derraman sobre la producción cinematográfica ficcional y no ficcional.[2] Asimismo, como ha señalado David Oubiña: "La estética dominante con la que suele identificarse a los nuevos filmes argentinos se caracteriza por un rescate del universo sumergido de los marginales" (29). Abundan películas que toman como objeto la marginación social y lo hacen apelando a procedimientos característicos del documental. Entre los ejemplos más significativos del cine de ficción podemos mencionar *Pizza, birra, faso* (1997) de Adrián Caetano y Bruno Stagnaro, *Mundo grúa* (1999) de Pablo Trapero, *Bolivia* (2001) de Adrián Caetano y *La ciénaga* (2001) de Lucrecia Martel. En algunos casos, lo marginal ingresa por el repertorio temático – el mundo marginal urbano en *Pizza, birra, faso*, la desindustrialización en *Mundo grúa*–, en otros, por la convocatoria de actores no profesionales –*Bolivia, La ciénaga*–; hay otros casos en que la inclusión de prácticas propias del documental –como la entrevista en *Los rubios* (2003) de Albertina Carri–, señalan una marca realista común a todos estos filmes.

---

[1]   Sobre Birri, cf. Burton y Bernini. Pablo Reyero reconoce a Birri como una influencia. Silvina Díaz, en un artículo reciente, explora este mismo problema sobre un corpus de filmes argentinos de los sesenta y los noventa (cf. también Beceyro, *Cine y política* 12).

[2]   Sobre documentales recientes cf. Aguilar "Los precarious," "Renuncia;" Beceyro et al., "Estética," "Cine documental: la objetividad," "Cine documental: la primera;" y Dieleke/ Fernández Bravo.

La presencia del registro realista permite hablar de un regreso del documental y la incorporación de algunos de sus procedimientos en el cine de ficción, con la consiguiente disolución de las fronteras entre los géneros (cf. Dieleke/Fernández Bravo). La reemergencia del género documental –tanto en documentales propiamente dichos, como *Bonanza* (2001) de Ulises Rosell o *Dársena sur*, o en filmes más híbridos, fuertemente permeados por los procedimientos característicos del documental como *Balnearios* (2002) de Mariano Llinás o *La libertad*–, permite plantear algunas preguntas acerca de su estatus e intentar adelantar algunas hipótesis acerca de la reemergencia del documental en el cine argentino contemporáneo. ¿Cómo se articula el documental en los filmes actuales y cuál es la relación con su modo de representación característico? ¿Por qué "regresan" los realismos al cine y a la literatura y qué marcas específicas tiene este regreso?[3] ¿Qué cambia en los documentales actuales respecto de sus antecesores de los años sesenta y qué signos caracterizan esta transición? ¿Por qué lo marginal resulta atractivo para los jóvenes cineastas y qué lugar ocupa lo marginal en la representación de la nación? ¿Es posible establecer una relación entre el regreso del documental y la debilidad argumental de algunas películas actuales?

En primer lugar, quisiera recuperar algunos elementos del documental de Birri que me parecen fundadores de esta tradición.[4] Como se sabe, *Tire dié* fue producto de un trabajo colectivo en el que intervinieron muchas personas y una institución, el Instituto de Cine de la Universidad Nacional del Litoral, en la ciudad de Santa Fe, Argentina. La Escuela Documental de Santa Fe ya plantea una voluntad pedagógica de mostrar un mundo invisible, externo y fronterizo con el mundo urbano y moderno, y reúne otros rasgos propios de un cine no tradicional, opuesto al canon cinematográfico.[5] La

---

[3] Vale señalar que también en la literatura existe un conjunto de obras realistas interesadas por lo marginal; la más sobresaliente es la novela *Cosa de negros*, de Washington Cucurto, también en la poesía o en autores ya más establecidos como Rodolfo Enrique Fogwill, analizados por Ludmer. Hal Foster plantea hipótesis en esta misma línea en *The Return of the Real*.

[4] Aunque el así llamado Nuevo Cine Argentino proclama su voluntad de ruptura con el cine que lo precedió, Mariano Llinás, director de *Balnearios*, reconoce las escenas iniciales de *Tire dié* como un emblema del cine documental que él prefiere y cita en su propia película estadísticas absurdas que evocan las estadísticas de *Tire dié* al comienzo de la película. Aunque la relación entre Birri y los cineastas jóvenes no es muy visible, el reconocimiento de Llinás y su propia cita indican la persistencia de *Tire dié* como referente local del género (cf. Llinás). Pablo Reyero menciona a *Los inundados* de Birri como uno de los filmes significativos en la tradición cinematográfica argentina e incluye a Birri entre los directores que más admira (cf. Toibero).

[5] También el Nuevo Cine Argentino emerge de las escuelas de cine, en particular durante la década de los noventa con la Fundación Universidad del Cine (FUC), dirigida por Manuel Antín. *La ciénaga*, *Bonanza*, *Mundo grúa* y otras películas fueron filmadas con apoyo o en el ámbito de las escuelas de cine. Mariano Llinás reconoce su deuda con la FUC en la entrevista citada de 2002, donde sintetiza una historia del Nuevo Cine Argentino desde su perspectiva como realizador. Como *Tire dié*, todas estas películas son producidas con bajo

exhibición de la película en escenarios no comerciales –donde incluso fueron invitados los protagonistas pobres de la película–, indica una práctica típica de ese momento histórico que expresa su distancia del cine comercial, es una producción alejada del "modo industrial" con el interés pedagógico de lograr la concientización de la audiencia.

La película está articulada en torno a un conjunto de oposiciones binarias, propias del momento en el que fue filmada y en las que me gustaría detenerme. La más obvia está en el título, *Tire dié* [*Throw me a dime*], que reproduce el habla popular y se refiere a "tire diez (centavos)," como un pedido de limosna formulado por los niños pobres junto al tren. El filme presenta un margen donde se encuentran los sectores populares subrepresentados en las estadísticas oficiales con las que comienza la película. De este modo, el tren que conecta el barrio popular con la ciudad[6] plantea un eje de oposición que, según veremos, está ausente en los documentales contemporáneos con los que me interesa comparar la película de Birri. Así, los ciudadanos –las mujeres que van a la peluquería, los pasajeros que leen el diario en el tren–, son habitantes de una sociedad que todavía se imaginaba a sí misma como próspera y moderna, y parecen también indiferentes a la pobreza. Estos sujetos urbanos son acusados por su desinterés por el mundo marginal y, simultáneamente, son representados en el film como un componente de esa sociedad. A la vez, uno puede imaginárselos como una audiencia imaginaria a la que la película intenta educar e interpelar. La voz del locutor evoca la figura del informativo, pero es llevada al absurdo por los datos que entrega: el típico programa de noticias –una subespecie del documental– es denunciado como portador de una información incompleta e inexacta. El comienzo tiene una marca fuertemente irónica en el que las estadísticas se muestran insuficientes para dar cuenta de lo real y, en este sentido, la misma capacidad informativa de los datos resulta cuestionada. La ciudad rica y los suburbios pobres se relacionan antagónicamente en el documental cuyo título, sin embargo, realza la importancia de lo marginal como signo distintivo.

La segunda mitad del cortometraje se enfoca en las historias de vida de los pobladores que son las marcas más perdurables del documental, representadas bajo la óptica del cine de observación. La pobreza de los márgenes es aquello que define a la comunidad y, en la medida en que ese suplemento se derrama sobre toda la imagen nacional, opera también como una sinécdoque. Aunque es sólo una parte, es la parte más visible de la identidad colectiva. De esta manera, si bien el margen es materia de denuncia, también provee de imágenes útiles para componer una idea de nación. Los pobladores, por su parte, aunque lamentan su pobreza, parecen arraigados en su espacio, reivindican su "progreso" y no manifiestan deseos de abandonarlo. El caso más evidente es el testimonio de Doña Lola, que cuenta las peripecias de su vida en ese pobre arrabal. ¿Cómo entender el lugar central de los márgenes? El espacio identificado en el documental es lo contrario de los espacios globales, se trata de un sitio capaz de promover la pertenencia, (fortaleciendo la identidad colectiva), y posee rasgos nítidos, no

---

presupuesto, en escenarios naturales y apelando en muchos casos a actores no profesionales.

[6]   Sobre la oposición Buenos Aires-interior cf. Gorelik.

presentes en otros espacios. Por esa razón, la cámara se interesa en el margen: por su capacidad de capturar allí rasgos idiosincrásicos, genuinos, una diferencia capaz de definir la subjetividad.

Si bien *Tire dié*, en contraste con *La hora de los hornos* (1968) –el documental de Fernando Pino Solanas filmado pocos años después–, apela muy escasamente al montaje y parece una película más próxima al "observational mode of representation," como lo define Nichols (cf. Bernini 157), la oposición entre la estadística oficial –índice de la prosperidad de una sociedad moderna, con instituciones estatales, educación y servicios, etc.– en contraste con el mundo desvalido de la periferia de Santa Fe –sin escuelas, ni servicios, ni trabajo–, son una declaración explícita de la politización incipiente que caracterizaba en esos años a la cultura argentina y latinoamericana. No hay una relación pacífica entre las dos partes de la película: el comienzo marca una diferencia significativa con el retrato de la pobreza de la segunda parte. La relación entre el margen y su contraparte, la ciudad rica, es fundamental porque una cara completa a la otra, aunque "lo real" quede asociado con la pobreza –la prosperidad es falsa, engañosa y por lo tanto los datos que la sustentan pierden legitimidad, al ser severamente cuestionados por la "encuesta social"–. También en el nivel formal es un megamontaje, donde unas imágenes se contraponen a las otras: ciudad y periferia, lujo superfluo y miseria. El filme se postula como un engranaje en el movimiento de la integración marginal de los individuos y, en ese sentido, sí es un film político: lo marginal es político y la política se hace en los márgenes. Como observa Bhabha:

> Una vez establecida la liminaridad del espacio-nación, y una vez que su diferencia significante es desplazada del "afuera" fronterizo a su finitud de "adentro," la amenaza de la diferencia cultural ya no es más un problema del "otro pueblo." Se vuelve una cuestión de otredad del pueblo-como-uno. El sujeto nacional se escinde en la perspectiva etnográfica de la contemporaneidad de la cultura y provee tanto una posición teórica como una autoridad narrativa para las voces marginales o el discurso minoritario. (Bhabha 187)

El margen se encuentra así en el interior de la subjetividad colectiva, dividiéndola y politizando esa división.

Una parte del problema que el documental intenta responder es la "medición de la desposesión." No sólo la desposesión material, la pobreza, sino también la desposesión de imágenes, la falta de información confiable (datos, representaciones, estadísticas sobre la pobreza). Sin embargo, paradójicamente, el cuestionamiento del informativo y del contenido de su información –denunciada como superflua– afecta a la propia objetividad del film. No podemos negar la función pedagógica al añadir a la estadística oficial, como suplemento, la "encuesta social" que exhibe, como en un libro didáctico, las condiciones de vida de los marginados. El margen altera el significado de la identidad colectiva y le otorga un nuevo contenido donde los márgenes resultan indispensables.

De este modo, el margen adquiere un valor necesario, y aunque quiera ser abolido, como parece proclamar el film, no resulta posible ni conveniente hacerlo; el margen es funcional porque opera como una cantera de imágenes que alimentan un inventario ("encuesta") a partir del cual se construye una imagen nacional, aunque –insisto– no todos los componentes de ese inventario tienen el mismo valor. El margen entrega un contenido distintivo que es proyectado sobre la nación y la invade; es útil, funcional e imprescindible para definirla.[7]

2. Recursos humanos

Quisiera continuar con un tema próximo a mi propio objeto de investigación, la Formación del Patrimonio Cultural en colecciones y museos. Una de mis hipótesis en el estudio de la formación del patrimonio cultural está vinculada a la idea de un patrimonio vacío, despoblado de objetos auténticos, el que durante el auge de los museos en América Latina, se dirigió a los márgenes para abastecerse de materia con la que dotar de contenido a la identidad colectiva. La cultura popular, lo indígena, las tradiciones, el folclore y la literatura oral serán las fuentes para llenar el depósito vacío de la subjetividad colectiva con componentes genuinos. Aunque la barbarie era enemiga de la civilización, se volvió, en este ámbito, materia esencial y así fue manipulada y clasificada en el orden museal para construir una imagen de la nación. ¿Cómo vincular el documental con el museo? Creo que un lazo aparece en su voluntad de representar la identidad colectiva apelando a fragmentos[8] y al collage en el que se superponen imágenes contradictorias: los ranchos y los edificios, los niños pobres y las mujeres ricas que van a la peluquería, el ferrocarril y el hambre.

Me interesa en particular la relación entre el documental, la cultura y la nación. La exploración del arrabal urbano en *Tire dié*, como un suplemento que "completa" una imagen de la nación que, por otra parte, está formada por estadísticas, establece un dualismo constitutivo y "congela" el margen, asignándole un valor adicional que modifica el conjunto "nación." La estadística habla de una sociedad moderna, dotada de instituciones civiles, leyes, derechos, ciudadanía, etc., pero el documental indica que esas estadísticas dejan algo afuera, un resto que excede y complementa esa misma imagen. "Al llegar a las orillas de esta ciudad organizada la estadística se hace incierta" –proclama el locutor–, poco antes de ingresar en el mundo del *Tire dié*, en una de las escenas preliminares al ingreso en la comunidad retratada en la película. De este modo, los residuos y los márgenes de la modernización capitalista parecen un material

---

[7] Quiero destacar un rasgo importante de la película: su aspiración a dar cuenta de una condición nacional. Si bien habla de Santa Fe y sus suburbios, sitúa a la región en "el feraz litoral argentino" e incluye referencias a Buenos Aires y Rosario; los trenes junto a los cuales mendigan los chicos, vienen o se dirigen a las ciudades más ricas y el contraste alude a ellas. En síntesis, el film se detiene en una problemática general que sin duda habla de la nación y aspira a interpelar a su público en esos términos: el interior, como el margen miserable, completa el sentido de la nación, lo altera, pero sirve también para darle sentido.

[8] Hans Ulrich Gumbrecht en *The Powers of Philology: Dynamics of Textual Scholarship* habla del fragmento como un bien manipulable y útil en la formación de totalidades simbólicas. El fragmento vale más por su versatilidad que por su contenido.

necesario y central para componer la imagen de la nación. Este procedimiento comprende tres elementos.

En primer lugar, las imágenes de la ciudad que evocan un referente moderno y rico, observado en una toma aérea y acompañado de la información estadística, en parte parodiada; en segundo lugar, hay otro componente que consiste en los márgenes interiores y desconocidos de la nación: los ranchos y sus habitantes. Y entre estos dos mundos antagónicos está el tercer elemento, el propio documentalista, y su acción de vincular entre sí esas dos dimensiones antagónicas y opuestas que son "unidas" y complementadas en el trabajo con la imagen. La película muestra así el mundo marginal y lo muestra a la nación como una imagen oculta de sí misma; al mostrarlo se produce la identificación de la parte con el todo, la sinécdoque de la representación característica de la operación-museo, el cine como un "musée du réel," para emplear una expresión de Jean-Luc Godard. Como en el museo, lo marginal tiene un valor adicional funcional a la audiencia, a la que se busca interesar en el margen e, igual que en el museo, las imágenes resultan fetichizadas, cosificadas, dotadas de atributos en los que el yo y el otro quedan entrelazados.

Tire dié indica una acción, la de interrogar la subjetividad en un sector fronterizo, situado en los márgenes de la ciudad y explorarlo. El hecho de que las estadísticas no lo consideren crea una oportunidad a la intervención cinematográfica: montar un archivo paralelo, más realista, capaz de entregar un componente ausente en la imagen de la nación. ¿Cómo dar contenidos a la cultura nacional? ¿De qué dotarla? *Tire dié* sugiere que hay que proporcionar a la nación algo que está en sus bordes, y que, a la vez, es materia interior, inferior, ubicada en la base y en lo infantil. Infancia y margen forman el zócalo inferior de la nacionalidad: las tomas en picada, donde los chicos están en una posición inferior y forman un margen ínfimo que nutre al centro, lo explica y justifica.

Curiosamente, aunque lo marginal es rechazado y denunciado por la retórica de la película ("hay muchos, demasiados ranchos"), existe una dependencia y un interés insoslayable por ese componente para construir la representación de la nación: la nación se hace con los márgenes; la pobreza y la marginación son la materia útil para formar la subjetividad. ¿Por qué lo son? Una posible razón es porque el subalterno –según lo ha señalado Gayatri Spivak en un ensayo fundamental y John Beverley para América Latina no habla por sí mismo, ni posee la capacidad de representarse a sí mismo, "es hablado por otro." Quien ejecuta esta acción de re-presentación es el cineasta, al que me gustaría pensar en relación con la estadística oficial. Los cineastas completan la información estadística con imágenes y entrevistas donde hablan los subalternos y, de ese modo, terminan por sumar un elemento ausente. Sin márgenes no hay nación, la nación se forma en los márgenes. En algún sentido, el documental precisa de aquello que está excluido, porque su discurso se alimenta de lo marginal: si lo marginal desapareciera, si los ranchos fueran reemplazados por edificios –como reclaman algunos de los pobladores que trabajaron en la construcción de edificios, pero viven en casas precarias–, el documental social debería cambiar de tema. La identidad subalterna es relacional, no ontológica, como lo indica John Beverley (cf. 30). El margen opera ante la nación como un insumo relacional que permite la intervención del intelectual –del cineasta en este caso– para negociar y traficar imágenes. En el margen es donde el documentalista consigue autolegitimarse.

Pero el margen aquí no se encuentra en los bordes externos de la nación, sino en su interior. Explorar la exclusión es navegar hacia adentro. La lengua hablada en los márgenes, no obstante, plantea el problema de la representación. Aunque el film toma el habla popular para el título, hubo dificultades técnicas que impidieron grabar las voces de los entrevistados. Así, fue necesario convocar a actores profesionales –María Rosa Gallo y Francisco Petrone– y sus voces fueron superpuestas a las de los auténticos protagonistas. Los actores no sólo asumen en el filme la voz del subalterno, sino que, en algunos casos, corrigen las imperfecciones y errores del habla popular. Como ha señalado Emilio Bernini, es posible interpretar esta operación dando privilegio a la información social, al "contenido" que la película buscaba transmitir (cf. 160).

Sin embargo, creo que habría que entender esta operación como algo más que una lealtad con la misión de denuncia. Al superponer la voz de los actores, se hace explícita la imposibilidad de que hablen los subalternos por sí mismos, pero también evidencia que hablan por otro, que no son ellos mismos. El contraste entre la imagen y el sonido –el tono, la pronunciación, el énfasis sobre todo de María Rosa Gallo– pone de manifiesto este procedimiento. Como las voces originales no quedan completamente ocultas tras las voces de los actores, es posible reconocer el mismo acto de re-presentación como una intervención; la usurpación de la voz subalterna por la voz de los actores hace explícito el procedimiento documental. Aunque el título del cortometraje recupera el habla popular, esa misma habla está oculta, corregida y "traducida." Es decir, la exhibición de los materiales, el modo de producción, la intervención de las voces de los actores, manifiestan la mediación: casi no escuchamos las voces de los subalternos, y si las escucháramos, quizás no las entenderíamos. Sólo la intervención del documental nos permite acceder a ese mundo remoto o, más bien, a la mediación articulada en el film que es, por eso mismo, nada más que eso: una mediación y no la realidad.

3.   "Can the Subaltern Speak?"

Quisiera continuar con las otras dos películas que quiero analizar en esta tradición discontinua del documental. Si en *Tire dié* podemos reconocer la evidencia del "hacerse cargo" de la voz del otro, "to speak for" en términos de Gayatri Spivak, en *Dársena sur* y *La libertad* ese recurso está cuestionado. Ambos filmes recuperan el mandato formulado por Birri y se lanzan a explorar los márgenes de la nación, la periferia urbana en un caso, el mundo rural en el otro: la identidad en la diferencia; pero la representación recorre otros caminos y está despojada de la pretensión didáctica de *Tire dié*. El ventrilocuismo del Otro desaparece e indirectamente resulta cuestionado.

Dársena sur está planteado como un filme bastante tradicional en términos formales. Sus materiales son característicos del documental: entrevistas, testimonios, escenarios interiores y exteriores reales, composición de un lugar y sus habitantes. En contraste con *Tire dié*, no se dirige a un público nacional al que busca educar, sino parece hablar más bien a un espectador internacional, aunque se alimente de ciertas formas típicas del cine local. Los relatos de vida característicos del documental evocan el "observational mode of representation" y pueden ser considerados como "magnificaciones" de los que presentaba Birri.

El esquema binario planteado en *Tire dié*, articulado en la oposición ciudad-margen y en la relación estadística oficial-suplemento marginal se ha modificado. El esquema binario supone la mediación cinematográfica para exhibir aquello que la estadística oficial no muestra. Pero en estos otros dos filmes –según intentaré demostrarlo– uno de los bordes ha desaparecido: el margen es todo. El margen ha perdido su condición de "afuera," como aparecía en *Tire dié*. Ahora se trata de un territorio insular, donde la división entre interior y exterior se ha disuelto (cf. Ludmer). La ciudad es bien una parte del paisaje posindustrial o, bien son las prácticas culturales urbanas las que han invadido los márgenes. Al desaparecer uno de los bordes del esquema aparecen algunos interrogantes: ¿cuál es el lugar del mediador documental en *Dársena sur* y *La libertad?*, ¿es posible que la alteración de la mediación atenúe el componente político? Lo político aparece en la cultura, con frecuencia, como dispositivo pedagógico y, en estos filmes, la voluntad pedagógica nacional se ha transformado.[9] Lisandro Alonso lo declara: "Yo no quiero contar una historia, lo único que me interesa es observar" (85).

En esta nueva configuración el eje comparativo se ha modificado radicalmente. Lo marginal sigue convocando la atención de la cámara en la representación de la identidad colectiva, aunque no del mismo modo. La comparación enfatizada en la cita de Solanas –el montaje que intercala la escena de los chicos corriendo junto al tren, la imagen en contrapicada de un rascacielos en Buenos Aires–, está ausente en *Dársena sur*.

La película de Pablo Reyero –estrenada en 1997– cuenta la experiencia de una comunidad marcada por la pobreza y la marginación, localizada a muy poca distancia de Buenos Aires, a sólo 5 km de la Casa de Gobierno. Los protagonistas viven en la costa del Río de la Plata, cerca del Polo Petroquímico de Dock Sud, sitio en el que funciona una planta procesadora de coque, que luego de ser prohibida en Holanda, fue desmantelada y, luego, rearmada en ese lugar. Esta localidad, a pesar de su cercanía de la ciudad, tiene un modo de vida semirural: sus habitantes tienen gallinas, crían cerdos y emplean caballos y botes para desplazarse; viven sumergidos en la precariedad y rodeados de basura. Las historias de vida que se narran –a diferencia de las microhistorias de la pobreza presentadas en *Tire dié*–, son biografías bastante completas. De "El Negro," el primer personaje entrevistado, se cuenta su origen, nacimiento, cómo fue criado y se le pregunta por su destino y situación. Igual que doña Lola en *Tire dié*, el Negro dice que no quiere irse de donde vive. Se aferra a su lugar y se identifica con él. Nuevamente el subalterno habla a través de la mediación documental, pero aquí el elemento comparativo aparece debilitado y con su disolución desaparece la posibilidad de

---

[9] Creo que en *Dársena sur* sí la hay; no hay un juicio, ni culpables, ni un planteamiento político nítido, pero sí hay intención de mostrar lo abyecto.

resolver la contraposición en un relato emancipador. La nación como unidad y eventual eliminación de la diferencia ha desaparecido; tampoco se vislumbran posibilidades (ni deseos) de salir. Si *Tire dié* realzaba la oposición, incluso cuando se enfoca exclusivamente en el mundo marginal (el tren con sus pasajeros burgueses, el trabajo de los pobres y su relación con el mundo urbano), en *Dársena sur* la comparación está ausente. El plano secuencia que abre la película muestra, en una toma circular, las refinerías de petróleo y los edificios próximos al barrio que parecen rodearlo, como si se tratara de una isla rural y contaminada, incrustada en un océano urbano e industrial. No hay un recorrido que ubique a los personajes en un extremo, porque no hay extremos.

El margen es aquí la cultura del descarte, la basura, las ruinas del capitalismo que se amontonan, alimentan y también enferman a quienes viven allí. La exploración interior, entonces, se monta sobre el mandato de Birri, internándose en un espacio muy próximo a la ciudad y, sin embargo, desconocido. También aquí el film responde a un imperativo moral, el de mostrar las imágenes de un mundo ignorado y llamar la atención sobre las condiciones de vida de sus habitantes. Éstos, sin embargo, aunque ceden a la autocompasión instigada por el entrevistador, no manifiestan deseos de cambiar su modo de vida. Más bien se aferran a él, porque el margen los define. Todos los espacios recorridos son lo opuesto de los no-lugares de Marc Augé: están definidos y marcados, incluso por su miseria, como espacios propios.[10] Así, el Negro rechaza los edificios de departamentos (los compara con cárceles) y vindica la libertad de su vida junto a los residuos petroquímicos a los que define como "naturaleza," aunque sabe que "la tierra está llena de basura." Los chanchos, como en *Tire dié*, viven junto a las personas, se alimentan de la basura próxima a sus casas. Los pobladores no quieren abandonarlos porque es lo único que tienen. En rigor, es difícil reconocer una clara nostalgia o el deseo de un mundo urbano, moderno, limpio, que parece aún más distante para los habitantes del Dock Sud que para los protagonistas de *Tire dié*. El padre del Negro se lamenta de que sus hijos no conozcan el zoológico, acaso porque él mismo tuvo un pasado cercano a la ciudad; los protagonistas jóvenes de los noventa, por el contrario, no añoran un mundo que desconocen y que sólo les despierta indiferencia.

Aunque la historia de Liliana –el segundo personaje de la película– es terrible, también ella reivindica la solidaridad recibida de sus vecinos en Dock Sud. Su identidad como mujer tiene un espesor propio: la violencia sexual, la opresión y el engaño explican su historia a partir de su condición femenina. Hay allí un incipiente discurso político –quienes la ayudan son sobre todo, otras mujeres–, pero que no llega a expresarse en una reivindicación colectiva. Su relato queda sumido en el universo de lo personal y restringido al ámbito de la isla urbana. Por último, la historia de "El Ruso" aparece teñida por la imagen de su padre alcohólico. El Ruso es explícito: abandonó los sueños, no aspira a tener auto o una piscina, emblemas de la cultura urbana moderna y burguesa, no sueña con salir del margen.

---

[10] Esta observación es de Gonzalo Aguilar, en el nuevo cine "escasean los lugares globales (los 'no-lugares' de Marc Augé), a la vez que se acentúan las localidades que muestran el carácter periférico de esa cultura" ("Los precarios" 16).

En los tres casos, se trata de jóvenes y el documental se (y les) pregunta por un futuro que no promete cambios. En contraste con *Tire dié* y sus personajes víctimas de un sistema social que los condena a la miseria, nada indica que estas historias vayan más lejos que la condición de sus propios protagonistas. Al haber desaparecido el contrapunto burgués –los edificios opuestos a los ranchos, los pasajeros que leían el diario en el tren del filme de Birri e ignoraban a los chicos pobres que corrían junto al ferrocarril– tenemos un mundo que es únicamente margen, volcado sobre sí mismo, sin voluntad de transformarse. En este territorio "inmune a las mutaciones históricas" (Ludmer 106), la idea de la cohesión nacional, de un escenario en el que el margen y el centro se unan y se neutralicen mutuamente –el puente ferroviario de *Tire dié*, que actuaba como barrera entre dos mundos asimétricos, pero que podía convertirse en lo contrario–, ha desaparecido y con él, el relato emancipatorio que depositaba esperanzas en la unión de los opuestos. En *Tire dié*, los "demasiados ranchos" hablaban de un tren para salir de la miseria que nunca llevaba a los chicos, de pobladores que merecían un acceso digno a la sociedad civil. ¿Se trata, en el caso de *Dársena sur*, de una imagen de la nación? Mucho menos que en Birri. El documental no aspira a extender los relatos de vida hacia la nación ni tampoco a dar una imagen totalizadora. La película de Reyero fue producida con apoyo de tres fundaciones, dos de ellas internacionales –la Rockefeller y la McArthur–, la Fundación Antorchas de Buenos Aires y el Instituto Goethe. Su recorrido y audiencia son transnacionales[11] –el film recibió escasa atención en la Argentina–, pero sobre todo la película no aspira a instruir al público argentino acerca de su país. *Tire dié* era exhibida en funciones públicas multitudinarias con el propósito de "educar" y difundir una realidad desconocida, en cambio *Dársena sur*, producida por Lita Stantic –la productora más exitosa del Nuevo Cine Argentino, responsable de *Mundo grúa*, *La ciénaga*, y *Bolivia*, entre otras– señala una inserción del documental en el circuito internacional. El margen empieza a funcionar como un exitoso objeto de marketing y puede ser usado como marca nacional para ingresar en el mercado global de imágenes donde existe una audiencia permeable a este tipo de relatos. La contaminación, la pobreza y la marginación encuentran su público internacional. Tradicionalmente esas imágenes no eran asociadas con la Argentina, pero los nuevos documentales parecen reconocer en ellas valores útiles: la originalidad, la autenticidad, e incluso la fealdad del margen tienen un mercado.

---

[11] La internacionalización del cine significó un reconocimiento veloz para estas películas, a través del circuito de los festivales internacionales (*La libertad* y el último documental de Reyero, *La cruz del sur* (2003) fueron premiados en Cannes). A diferencia de *Tire dié*, y de los filmes vinculados a instituciones educativas, *Dársena sur* fue producido por Lita Stantic. La película no parece aspirar a presentar una descripción global de la sociedad (o de la nación). Sólo se trata de observar. No obstante, ya en *Tire dié* hay un interés por las historias de vida de la pobreza y el margen, que en los filmes más recientes se ensancha y abandona la mirada "elevada:" como en los documentales de Robert Flaherty, *La libertad* filma "desde abajo," con la colaboración del sujeto filmado –Misael Saavedra– casi un coproductor de la película.

En todos estos filmes –como decía al comienzo– el lugar de la política ha cambiado. Aunque la película *Dársena sur* habla del proceso de precarización laboral y de marginación, característico del gobierno de Carlos Menem, tiempo en que fue filmada, no hay ninguna referencia en ella a ese momento histórico. Como en *Tire dié*, el testimonio habla por sí mismo y, de este modo, hay una resistencia explícita a las definiciones ideológicas. Asistimos así a una representación distanciada, donde lo político se encuentra en algunos rincones –el género es uno de ellos, los jóvenes como un colectivo marginado es otro–, pero parece deliberadamente alejado de explicaciones abarcadoras o sueños de cambio.

Una razón posible es precisamente la renuncia de los personajes a conectarse con el afuera. Dentro del margen disminuye la posibilidad de la reivindicación y la política se vuelve un asunto interno y de menor importancia. El margen se ha internalizado y se ha expandido, lo cubre todo, pero su presencia ominosa también recluye, aísla, fragmenta. *Dársena sur*, con su agenda local e introspectiva rehuye una política "nacional" y pedagógica.

4. Un espejo vacío

En *La libertad*, a diferencia de los otros dos documentales, casi no hay oralidad. El protagonista apenas intercambia algunas palabras casuales en dos oportunidades, pero durante la mayor parte del filme, asistimos a su existencia cotidiana de hachero solitario, casi un eremita, aislado en el escenario rural de la Provincia de La Pampa, dedicado a su actividad rutinaria y silenciosa.

El camino recorrido en *La libertad* –en mi opinión–, extiende algunas de las líneas de Birri y del cine realista, pero también las cuestiona. Por un lado, se trata de un film independiente, producido con un escaso presupuesto y al margen del circuito comercial. Lisandro Alonso dirigió la película a los veinticinco años con un presupuesto de treinta mil dólares. La circulación de la película es la más internacional de las tres, ya que fue seleccionada, primero, para el Festival de Buenos Aires y, casi inmediatamente después, para el de Cannes: de esta forma, obtuvo en los festivales su primer reconocimiento (antes de los festivales, no había sido exhibida públicamente). Del mismo modo que en los otros dos filmes, no hay actores profesionales ni escenografía. La película se rueda en escenarios naturales, en una zona rural de la Provincia de La Pampa y cuenta la historia de un hachero, Misael Saavedra, que vive solo en el campo, tala árboles que luego vende, come, duerme, caza, cocina y tiene escaso contacto con el mundo social. Los espectadores asistimos a una sucesión de imágenes que completan un día de la vida del personaje. En un grado más agudo que en *Dársena sur*, la cámara observa sin intervenir, a menudo bajo el formato de cámara excéntrica[12] (el protagonista sale del cuadro y nos quedamos viendo un paisaje sin seres humanos).

---

[12] Raúl Beceyro et al. definen la cámara excéntrica como uno de los rasgos que definen un "estilo documental" ("Cine documental: la objetividad" 17).

La virtual ausencia de lengua hablada crea un efecto de distancia, que está en contradicción con la proximidad de la cámara durante todo el film. ¿Cómo enunciar la condición de su personaje sin habla? ¿Se trata de un documental etnográfico? ¿Qué se propuso Alonso al filmar un día de la vida del hachero Misael Saavedra? Como señala Gonzalo Aguilar, el film se aparta de la modalidad piadosa característica de la mirada sobre lo marginal en el cine argentino y eligió el camino de celebrar la retirada del mundo del consumo, con el que, sin embargo, el protagonista negocia cuando vende su producción de troncos, que son comprados como "postes" (cf. "Renuncia" 17). En efecto, una de las escenas "ficcionales" muestra al protagonista negociando la venta de esos postes con un acopiador local de madera.[13]

Aunque, desde el ángulo del interés por el personaje, *La libertad* se acerca a *Tire dié* y a *Dársena sur* —un personaje rural, pobre, alejado de la ciudad y sus "beneficios"–, la composición del protagonista se distancia radicalmente de las otras dos películas. Frente a la pobreza sórdida, a la basura y a la precariedad que rodean a los protagonistas de los otros dos filmes, el personaje de Lisandro Alonso tiene dignidad; aunque vive en condiciones de escasez y privación, no pide nuestra compasión, ni tampoco demanda una salida (en esto se acerca a los personajes de *Dársena sur*). En realidad, la salida ya se ha producido y se manifiesta en su elección de alejarse del mundo urbano en búsqueda de la libertad representada en la naturaleza. Si en *Tire dié* el tren que los chicos no toman nunca, representa su marginación de la abundancia del mundo urbano, en *La libertad*, la emancipación va en dirección opuesta. Se encuentra lejos del consumo, de las instituciones y de la sociedad civil de las cuales el hachero parece haberse distanciado por propia voluntad. Misael Saavedra no tiene nostalgia por el mundo urbano, pero convive con él: escucha la radio, usa una gorra de béisbol, compra una bebida gaseosa, llama por teléfono, e incluso maneja un auto. Sus hábitos son modernos y urbanos. Lo que ocurre es que la relación entre el mundo rural y el mundo urbano se ha alterado. Misael no está lejos de la civilización, aunque esté deliberadamente ausente de la ciudad. No la necesita, porque la cultura de la ciudad llega hasta él y él sabe cómo usarla. No hay perspectiva de salida, ni de progreso, el tiempo vital es como el tiempo narrativo del film: circular, cíclico, testimonio de un asceta que goza de su existencia solipsista e insular. No se trata aquí de la isla urbana, pero tampoco podríamos decir que es un escenario plenamente rural: las fronteras entre ambos mundos se han derretido y con ellas, el interés por el otro lado del margen.

La debilidad de la narración argumental ha sido señalada como un rasgo del cine argentino contemporáneo y también se aprecia en esta película.[14] ¿Cómo entender la

---

[13] Alonso declara en una entrevista haber introducido una alteración en la rutina de Misael: "La única diferencia en su trabajo cotidiano es que no vende la madera sino que trabaja por un sueldo" (Aguilar, "Renuncia" 15).

[14] Beceyro et al. afirman que "… *Pizza, birra, faso* primero y *Mundo grúa* después se caracterizan por dos rasgos. Uno temático, de pertenencia social de sus personajes, para decirlo rápidamente, los personajes son pobres. Y una cuestión formal: ausencia de vertebración narrativa" ("Estética" 34).

indiferencia por la fábula? En *La libertad* se manifiesta en el distanciamiento extremo de la cámara respecto de su personaje. Aunque la cámara acompaña al personaje en su actividad cotidiana desde cerca y somos testigos de un conjunto muy minucioso de acciones –vemos al hachero trabajando, defecando, comiendo, durmiendo la siesta–, nunca sabemos cuáles son las condiciones de posibilidad de su existencia: ni su origen, ni las razones de su elección laboral, ni las condiciones históricas, sociales, económicas de la situación en que se encuentra, trabajando aislado en el monte y con un contacto mínimo con otros seres humanos. ¿Tuvo otras opciones que ésta? ¿Dónde está su familia? ¿Quiénes son sus relaciones? ¿Cuál es su pasado, su historia, el relato que articula su posición en el mundo? En contraste con los dos filmes anteriores, la entrevista está ausente y Saavedra habla sólo con su cuerpo. Como señala el director:

> No ... me interesaba informar como en un noticiero cuánto ganaba un hachero o cuántos árboles corta por día. Quería observar atentamente y poner al espectador en esa situación, que se pregunte qué tiene que ver lo que está viendo con su propia libertad ... La única manera que encuentro es no dar información, no poner diálogos, dejarlo solo al personaje. ... Es un espejo, pero vacío. (Alonso 87)

Una vez más, el documental se imagina en oposición al informativo: sin embargo, aunque muestra lo real, se resiste a proclamar la transparencia de la imagen como lo hacía Birri. Pero, sobre todo, cuestiona la posición del informante[15] que Birri y, hasta cierto punto Reyero, aún conservaban. No hay un itinerario pautado para el espectador, sino, más bien, un conjunto de preguntas y un enigma.

Cabría preguntarse si la historia de Misael Saavedra es una historia sobre el margen. Del mismo modo que en *Dársena sur*, la modificación de la estructura binaria centro-margen, hace que el margen también aquí pierda sentido y por eso es que la posición de la cámara abandona toda voluntad de explicación. No sabemos nada acerca de las condiciones que impulsaron a Misael Saavedra a su vida de eremita posmoderno, pero sí sabemos que negocia con el mundo exterior –vende su producción y discute su precio, habla por teléfono con su familia, practica un módico consumo de subsistencia–, para preservar su libertad y profundizar su fuga hacia adentro. No es que Misael no salga de su isla rural: sale sólo para volver a entrar; paga un tributo que le permite preservar su autonomía.

Es posible pensar que la ausencia de pedagogía, explicación o enseñanza es como una contestación al cine social y un alejamiento deliberado del uso del margen para hablar de la nación. Igual que los relatos de vida de *Dársena sur*, la historia de Misael rehúsa insertarse en un conjunto más amplio, no alude a una totalidad mayor que lo comprenda ni sirve para pensar en otra cosa que no sea en esas imágenes, suficientemente enigmáticas en sí mismas y desprovistas de un metadiscurso que nos guíe para entender la peripecia del protagonista. La ausencia de fábula nos priva también de una moral o un argumento.

---

[15] Sobre el informante en el arte etnográfico, cf. Foster.

La política está en otra parte, en posiciones de sujeto y acciones privadas de oposición y contraste frente a las cuales el espectador queda desconcertado. Nada de lo que los personajes hacen queda inserto en una estructura dramática. Si en *Tire dié* las palabras del subalterno debían ser traducidas por actores profesionales para llegar más claramente a la audiencia, en *Dársena sur* y *La libertad* ese programa ya no funciona. *La libertad* simplemente descarta esa alternativa y subraya algo que ya estaba presente en el cine de Birri: el documental como punto de partida para pensar (y no como un puerto seguro donde completar una imagen social, apaciguando la mala conciencia pequeño burguesa). La película de Alonso, aún más que la de Reyero, plantea un conjunto de preguntas con el menor número posible de pautas para responderlas, y se aleja del rezo repetitivo y monótono –"hay muchos, demasiados ranchos"– capaz de clausurar la imaginación. Aunque el documental se alimente de los márgenes hiperreales, el sitio de la mirada no significa negar la potencia para incentivar las preguntas despertadas por lo imaginario, ni para petrificarlo: el subalterno no puede hablar pero sí puede mostrarnos sus preguntas. Somos nosotros quienes debemos hacernos cargo de ellas y emplearlas para intentar entender la nación en sus márgenes.

Bibliografía

Aguilar, Gonzalo. "Los precarios órdenes del azar." *Milpalabras* 1 (2001): 14-24.

———. *Otros mundos. Un ensayo sobre el nuevo cine argentino.* Buenos Aires: Santiago Arcos, 2006.

———. "Renuncia y libertad. Sobre una película de Lisandro Alonso." *Milpalabras* 2 (2001): 12-20.

Alonso, Lisandro. "El misterio del leñador solitario (entrevista con Lisandro Alonso)." *El amante* 111 (junio 2001): 84-90.

Beceyro, Raúl. *Cine y política.* Caracas: Ediciones de la Dirección General de Cultura de la Gobernación del Distrito Federal, 1976.

——— et al. "Cine documental: la objetividad en cuestión." *Punto de vista* 81 (abril 2005): 15-23.

——— et al. "Cine documental: la primera persona." *Punto de vista* 82 (agosto 2005): 27-36.

——— et al. "Estética del cine, nuevos realismos, representación (debate sobre el nuevo cine argentino)." *Punto de vista* 67 (agosto 2000): 31-38.

Bernini, Emilio. "Politics and the Documentary Film in Argentina during the 60s." *Journal of Latin American Cultural Studies* 13.2 (August 2004): 155-70.

Beverley, John. *Subalternity and Representation. Arguments in Cultural Theory.* Durham: Duke UP, 1999.

Bhabha, Homi. *El lugar de la cultura.* Traducción de César Aira. Buenos Aires: Manantial, 2002.

Burton, Julianne. *Cinema and Social Change in Latin America.* Austin: U of Texas P, 1986.

Comolli, Jean Louis. *Voir et pouvoir.* Paris: Verdier, 2004.

Cucurto, Washington. *Cosa de negros*. Buenos Aires: Interzona, 2003.

Daney, Serge. *Cine, arte del presente*. Buenos Aires: Santiago Arcos, 2004.

Díaz, Silvina. "La construcción de la marginalidad en el cine argentino." *La civilización y la barbarie en el cine argentino*. Ed. Ana Laura Lusnich. Buenos Aires: Biblos, 2005. 111-22.

Dieleke, Edgardo y Álvaro Fernández Bravo. "Documentales argentinos y brasileños. Un mapa en fragmentos." *Grumo* 6.1 (2007): 9-16.

Foster, Hal. *The Return of the Real. Art and Theory at the End of the Century*. Cambridge: The Massachussets Institute of Technology P, 1999.

Gorelik, Adrián. "Buenos Aires y el país. Figuraciones de una fractura." *La Argentina en el siglo XX*. Ed. Carlos Altamirano. Buenos Aires: Ariel, 2001. 45-58.

Gumbrecht, Hans Ulrich. *The Powers of Philology. Dynamics of Textual Scholarship*. Chicago: U of Illinois P, 2003.

Llinás, Mariano. "Reportaje a Mariano Llinás." *El Amante* 124 (agosto 2002): 87-92.

Ludmer, Josefina. "Territorios del presente. En la isla urbana." *Pensamiento de los confines* 15 (diciembre 2004): 88-96.

Nichols, Bill. *Representing Reality. Issues and Concepts in Documentary*. Bloomington: Indiana UP, 1991.

Oubiña, David. "El espectáculo y sus márgenes. Sobre Adrián Caetano y el nuevo cine argentino." *Punto de vista* 76 (2003): 24-30.

Spivak, Gayatri. "Can the Subaltern Speak?" *Marxism and the Interpretation of Culture*. Ed. Cary Nelson and Lawrence Grossberg. Chicago: U of Illionis P, 1988. 271-313.

Toibero, Emilio. "Breve diálogo con Pablo Reyero." *Enfocarte. Arte y comunicación en red* 23 (2004). http:// www.enfocarte.com/4.23/cine2.html.

Filmografía

Balnearios. Dir. Mario Llinás. Argentina, 2002.

Bolivia. Dir. Adrián Caetano. Argentina, Países Bajos, 2001.

Bonanza. Dir. Ulises Rosell. Argentina, 2001.

Dársena sur. Dir. Pablo Reyero. Argentina, 1997.

La ciénaga. Dir. Lucrecia Martel. Argentina, Francia, España, 2001.

La cruz del sur. Dir. Pablo Reyero. Argentina, Francia, 2003.

La hora de los hornos. Dir. Fernando Pino Solanas. Argentina, 1968.

La libertad. Dir. Lisandro Alonso. Argentina, 2001.

Los rubios. Dir. Albertina Carri. Argentina, 2003.

Mundo grúa. Dir. Pablo Trapero. Argentina, 1999.

Pizza, birra, faso. Dir. Adrián Caetano y Bruno Stagnaro. Argentina, 1997.

Tire dié. Dir. Fernando Birri. Argentina, 1958.

El regreso de los Runas[1]: una aproximación al documental ecuatoriano de los años ochenta

GABRIELA ALEMÁN

Abstract

This essay explores the way documentary film served to re-/construct cinematographically the idea of an Ecuadorian nation state after the return of democracy in the 1980s. By looking at the strategies used in *Boca de lobo* (1982), directed by Raúl Khalifé, and *Los hieleros del Chimborazo* (1980), directed by Gustavo Guayasamín, we can observe the first steps taken by audiovisual media to separate themselves from the ethnic analysis of the social sciences and the social realist interpretations of literature.

Quisiera enmarcar el acercamiento al documental ecuatoriano de los años ochenta en el contexto de una cita del General Guillermo Rodríguez Lara, Presidente de la República y líder de la "revolución nacionalista" que gobernó el Ecuador de 1972 a 1976. El contexto de la cita es la presencia del general en la Región Amazónica, donde se había reunido con un grupo de dignatarios locales para discutir sobre el desarrollo del área. En el diálogo Rodríguez Lara declaró que el gobierno se ocuparía de transformar la infraestructura de la zona, construyendo carreteras, escuelas e implementando una agricultura "mejorada" que incentivaría la exportación de productos locales. Los líderes le preguntaron de qué manera se reconciliarían los derechos de sus comunidades –ya amenazadas por la colonización de las tierras amazónicas promovida por el poder central– con las mayores exportaciones dirigidas a las ciudades y al exterior. Rodríguez Lara no respondió directamente, sino invocó a sus ancestros y subrayó que él siempre había creído que todos los ecuatorianos eran en parte indígenas, todos compartiendo la misma sangre del Inca Atahualpa y que, aunque reconocía desconocer el origen de esa sangre entre sus antepasados, estaba seguro que también corría por sus venas. Rodríguez Lara aseguró: "Ya no hay más problema indígena, todos nos volvemos blancos cuando aceptamos los objetivos de la cultura nacional." Este discurso nacionalista llamaba a un "blanqueamiento" y homogeneización del país donde se pretendía canjear la etnicidad por una membresía en el Estado nación "donde los objeti-

---

[1] "Runa" significa ser humano en el idioma quechua o quichua.

vos culturales, sociales y hasta las características físicas de la clase dominante serían
tomados por los miembros de esa otra clase para generar cambios y movimientos culturales, sociales y biológicos" (Stutzman 47).

En términos culturales la ideología estatal impulsaba la eliminación de toda diferencia y sus programas de "cultura para todos," en realidad, terminaron impulsando
una cultura para nadie. El discurso estatal recurría a eufemismos para desidentificar a
los actores sociales –los indígenas–, a quienes pasó a llamar campesinos. A partir de
las leyes dictadas en esa época –como la Ley Nacional de Cultura de marzo de 1973–
se buscaba: "Exaltar el sentimiento nacional y afirmar la conciencia de los valores particulares de la patria ecuatoriana" (Art. 1).

Al blanquear, o proclamar una nación únicamente mestiza, se pretendía convertir
el Ecuador en una nación sin marcas étnicas, donde todos los ciudadanos colaborarían
al progreso nacional. Éste era el discurso del estado ecuatoriano, pero la realidad se
volvió contra él: los años setenta en Ecuador estuvieron fuertemente condicionados
por las movilizaciones campesinas que luchaban por sus tierras, reivindicaciones que
estaban en contra de los programas de desarrollo y progreso promovidos desde el gobierno. Como señala Sánchez-Parga:

> Lo más importante de esta movilización campesina será la (re)emergencia de nuevos (u
> olvidados) actores sociales, cuya presencia no sólo cuestionará el proyecto de nación
> sino que pone también en evidencia los serios y profundos obstáculos con los que en
> realidad se enfrentan los planes desarrollistas del Estado; al nivel cultural señala una tal
> "diferencia" al interior del país, que a partir del reconocimiento de lo étnico será necesa-
> rio repensar la misma cultura con otros parámetros teóricos y políticos. (55)

Si he dado una larga vuelta para volver al principio es porque lo que ocurrió, en
términos culturales, en los años ochenta en Ecuador, está muy ligado a los plantea-
mientos y negaciones de la década anterior. El retorno a la democracia en 1979 constituye el replanteamiento de lo que es la cultura nacional, pues es en la década de los
ochenta en que se comenzará a hablar de culturas en plural:

> El proceso democrático que se instaura en el Ecuador conlleva a una paulatina desiden-
> tificación entre Estado y sociedad, la que repercute en una relativa "desnacionalización"
> de la cultura y de las identidades colectivas. (Sánchez-Parga 130)

El cambio se señala en el discurso inaugural del presidente Jaime Roldós (1979–
1981) en el Congreso, que, en parte, fue pronunciado en quichua; este cambio de postura se acentuó cuando el sucesor de Roldós, Osvaldo Hurtado (1981–1984), se presentó en el Congreso con la leyenda de la banda presidencial escrita en shuar. Luego
de una década de gobiernos militares, el efecto no era solamente simbólico, ya que el
discurso del gobierno, enfrentado al imperativo de la integración nacional, mostraba
haber aceptado el dilema estatal de reconocer "la particularidad étnica" (Sánchez-
Parga 109); tampoco hay que perder de vista que el cambio democrático se dio con la
participación en las urnas de las grandes masas indígenas, que, por primera vez, tenían
la oportunidad de entrar en la arena de la participación y responsabilidad ciudadana
(Sánchez-Parga 77).

Lo indígena "blanqueado" vuelve al debate nacional, en muchos sentidos, como "el regreso de lo reprimido," después del intento del aparato estatal de hacerlo desaparecer durante décadas; aunque no es el lugar para profundizar el tema, cabe señalar que es un largo proceso en término culturales, desde la creación de la Casa de la Cultura (en singular) en la década de los cuarenta. Toda la ciencia social de los años setenta y los ochenta coincidía en señalar que la desaparición de lo étnico era simplemente una cuestión de tiempo; como lo indica Galo Ramón, no había una posición clara en las ciencias sociales –ni en la literatura, si el realismo social sirve de ejemplo de la misma tendencia– capaz de imaginar la supervivencia de las distintas etnias en el futuro. La aculturación, palabra que hoy en día requiere de desempolvo, pero que entonces resultaba ineludible, era considerada como el destino final de toda nuestra diversidad cultural y lingüística. El problema de los cineastas documentalistas era, entonces, en parte, ¿cómo hacer otra cosa que archivar una cultura en vías de desaparición?

En el terreno de lo audiovisual la década de los ochenta marcó una línea divisoria en términos de posibilidades de producción: el Banco Central del Ecuador (BCE) –fundado en la década de los veinte– se "reconvirtió" en un instituto también emisor de cultura que auspiciaba desde el Centro de Difusión Cultural una "política de democratización y popularización de la cultura, apoyando la producción artística" (Sánchez-Parga 101). Además, el incipiente movimiento de cineastas, centrado sobre todo en Quito –la capital, situada en la región andina–, había logrado dar una vuelta de tuerca a un reglamento que permitía la exoneración de impuestos a tres organismos: la Unión Nacional de Periodistas (UNP), la Casa de la Cultura Ecuatoriana (CCE) y la Sinfónica Nacional. Esto significó que, durante tres años, dos de estos organismos –la UNP y la CCE– se convirtieron en productores y así se consiguió mantener un rodaje sostenido de cortometrajes nacionales que, entre 1980 y 1983, eran exhibidos en los cines comerciales precediendo a los largometrajes programados. A su vez, el BCE financió la producción de una serie de documentales relacionados con su afán "democratizador" de la cultura. Queda para otro trabajo mirar cuánto de la producción de esos años abordó el tema de las culturas nacionales, la manera como lo hizo y qué significó en términos reales el afán democratizador del Banco Central. Lo que pretendo en esta primera aproximación al documental ecuatoriano de los años ochenta es mirar, a través de dos documentales: *Boca de lobo* (1982) de Raúl Khalifé y *Los hieleros del Chimborazo* (1980) de Gustavo Guayasamín, de qué manera lo indígena se mueve del margen al centro del discurso cinematográfico y así se reconfigura, desde ese espacio fílmico, el espacio de la nación ecuatoriana en la pantalla. No he tomado estas películas al azar, ambas tuvieron, en su momento, reconocimiento internacional –*Boca de lobo* en el Festival de Oberhausen (Alemania) y *Los hieleros del Chimborazo* en el Festival de La Habana (Cuba)– y son de los pocos documentales de esos años que continúan "vivos" –en términos de su circulación– a través de su exhibición para las nuevas generaciones en la Sala Audiovisual del Banco Central; a la vez, son representativas de las dos fórmulas de producción más importantes de esa década. *Boca de lobo* fue "producida" por la CCE mientras la producción de *Los hieleros del Chimborazo* fue financiada por el BCE. La clave de estas dos cintas se encuentra en su intento de representar lo irrepresentable y al intentar hacerlo, asumen una testimonialidad mortuoria anclada en el trauma. En las cintas se produce una tensión que emerge entre textos preparados como elegías para personas ausentes, que, incómodamente, se empeñan en irrumpir en una representación que no tiene paciencia con ellas, y los contenidos que se sublevan contra ese destino. Los documentalistas subvierten así su propia labor archivista de lo indígena al sugerir que los mismos indígenas se rebelan en contra de su obsolescencia y en contra de la desaparición temprana de ciertas prácticas culturales.

1. *Boca de lobo*

El regreso de lo étnico al discurso nacional se presenta como un discurso traumático. Cathy Caruth postula que: "El trauma no sólo funciona como un testamento del pasado, sino que registra la fuerza de una experiencia a la cual no se tiene pleno acceso" (151, mi traducción).[2] Si aceptamos esta tesis, entonces, la marca étnica, blanqueada en la historia, no podrá formularse en términos narrativos tradicionales, dado que no existe una "memoria narrativa" o para nuestro caso, una memoria fílmica del momento anterior. La habilidad de recordar o contar el pasado está invariablemente ligada a la imposibilidad de tener acceso a él desde el presente y sólo podrá aparecer a modo de *flashbacks* "que no están integrados plenamente a la conciencia colectiva" (Caruth 152). ¿Cómo se narra entonces lo que supuestamente no está? Éste parece ser el punto de partida de *Boca de lobo*. El documental sobre el pueblo de Simiatug de la Provincia de Bolívar, en la Sierra ecuatoriana, está basado en una investigación de la antropóloga Susana Andrade:

> Susana tenía toda la información antropológica, pero al final en el documental no hay nada de eso, quiero decir, no es un documental antropológico. Pensó ser eso: un documental etnográfico, de las relaciones interétnicas, en este pueblo mercado, las relaciones de dominación donde sin embargo existe toda una rebeldía subyacente de la población indígena ... (Alemán, "Entrevista a Raúl Khalifé")

Se podría argumentar que lo que imposibilita la narración antropológica es reconocer la imposibilidad de contar una historia comprensible sobre Simiatug. Una narración donde la voz del entrevistado, un comerciante mestizo, podría ser la fuente que aporta información, datos, conocimiento; voz que en las primeras escenas de *Boca de lobo* nos comunica:

> Hay mucha diferencia entre el campesino, el indio, el cholo, el mestizo. En nuestro país hay esa diferencia y, cómo le digo, el indio es la ignorancia, el indio no entiende, el indio se encierra en algo y es como un animal. Es mal llevado, de a buenas, con consideraciones, no entiende ...

---

[2] "Trauma does not simply serve as record of the past but precisely registers the force of an experience that is not yet fully owned."

La opción del director es, sin embargo, abrir la obra a una polifonía donde las "voces" están siendo continuamente minadas por las imágenes, posibilitando, de este modo, "el regreso de lo reprimido" a través de los intersticios del choque entre lo audible y lo visible. La estructura del documental está planteada como la imposibilidad de la comprensión absoluta de lo que nos cuenta y en el que el espacio de lo sonoro invade constantemente la imagen.

Boca de lobo cuenta la historia de un pueblo a punto de desaparecer, un pueblo abandonado por la población mestiza y que está siendo ocupado por los indígenas, con gran pesar de los pocos habitantes "blancos" que aún quedan en Simiatug.

Al comienzo del documental vemos una toma panorámica de los Andes, seguida por un plano general de una ladera por donde suben dos campesinos montados en sus mulas e, inmediatamente después, un camión trepando por el camino que lleva al pueblo. Escuchamos desde un comienzo un viento de páramo ensordecedor que barre el paisaje andino –viento que luego funcionará, junto a la neblina como *leitmotiv* del documental– y una voz femenina descorporalizada que explica que "boca de lobo" es la traducción de Simiatug al castellano, enseguida viene el texto del comerciante mestizo que ya hemos mencionado. En los veinte minutos de duración sólo aparecerán cuatro momentos de sonido sincrónico que coincidirán con las entrevistas a tres mujeres mestizas y a un dirigente campesino; el resto del documental está montado sin ninguna sincronía. Es importante notar que el uso de sonidos no sincrónicos para crear un contrapunto audiovisual ha sido teorizado desde los años veinte y posibilitó movimientos de ruptura en los experimentos vanguardistas de los años sesenta, donde el sonido intentaba desmentir permanentemente lo que el espectador esperaba de la imagen (Russo 238). Me gustaría detenerme en el último segmento del documental, donde esta experimentación –con implicaciones en la manera de relatar "lo traumático"– está presente. Si el documental se va armando, a través de las "voces"[3] del pueblo como un juego de oposiciones binarias: blanco-natural, ciudad-campo, desarrollo-estancamiento, vida-muerte, entonces –como ya dijimos–, los discursos chocan con las imágenes. Cerca del final vemos a una mujer indígena caminando por las calles del pueblo abandonado y escuchamos la voz de otra mujer, una mestiza, que canta y luego reza, dejando entrar la dimensión y el peso de lo religioso al documento fílmico. Según Chávez,

> Para el mestizo la adaptación religiosa no representó ningún problema, nacido dentro del catolicismo, ha seguido su desarrollo dentro de él. El catolicismo monoteístico corresponde a la nacionalidad ecuatoriana; la gente, la nación, es muy católica en la esencia de su infraestructura. (cit. en Stutzman 66)

La oposición blanco-natural, cruzada por lo religioso, se vuelve "verbo" cuando prosigue el documental. Seguimos escuchando la voz de la mujer mestiza mientras vemos a un grupo de indígenas, que cargan un ataúd, llegando a la entrada de un cementerio, el cielo poblado de cruces:

---

[3] Es interesante notar el desplazamiento de la imagen a la voz, no sólo en términos del documental, sino en lo que se podría llamar el momento multicultural ligado al fenómeno de la posmodernidad.

A mi manera de pensar creo que los que van a vivir eternamente son los naturales ...
Las cuatro familias blancas que estamos, nos vamos a morir ... esto va a quedar como
principió, va a quedar solamente a manos de los naturales ...

El "como principió" de la cita se refiere al trauma de lo "étnico" como principio de la
nación que aquí queda planteado a través de la bruma –de la historia y el páramo– y
del viento que lo barre todo.

2. *Los hieleros del Chimborazo*

Si en *Boca de lobo* la voz humana tiene un peso importante, peso anclado además en la
historia, en *Los hieleros del Chimborazo* las imágenes toman la delantera para volver a
la narración ahistórica y desprovista de voces. Por esta razón quisiera seguir indagando
sobre la naturaleza de lo traumático:

> La historia que cuenta un *flashback* ... es una historia que literalmente *no tiene lugar*, ni
> en el pasado, donde no fue experimentada plenamente, ni en el presente, en que la
> precisión de sus imágenes y su recreación no son entendidas plenamente. (Caruth 153)

Las únicas dos instancias en que nos situamos en un espacio y tiempo concretos,
son cerca de la mitad del documental: cuando el espacio diegético del documental se
sitúa en un mercado y, al final, cuando aparece un texto escrito sobre una pantalla
negra, con toda la carga de autoridad que posee la palabra escrita, para contarnos la
verdad de los hieleros. El resto de la película, de 25 minutos, transcurre en la atempo-
ralidad del páramo andino donde nada parece haber cambiado en siglos. Volvemos así
al momento en que nos deja el final de *Boca de lobo*: en el principio de los tiempos,
donde el hombre, la mujer y el niño "naturales" se enfrentan a la naturaleza inmiseri-
corde. Quizá la estrategia de los realizadores sea un intento de repoblar el espacio de lo
ecuatoriano con la marca de la diferencia, de lo étnico, mientras reconocen la imposibilidad de articular un discurso que narre esa historia. Lo que queda en la pantalla, lo
que el espectador ve, es el quiebre que caracterizaba a la sociedad ecuatoriana de los
años ochenta. La imagen fílmica del no-lugar visibiliza el trauma pero también *inventa*
una memoria nacional. Dice Susan Hayward:

> Las naciones son el producto de la territorialización de la memoria. La memoria aquí
> suplanta una memoria colectiva, una cultura compartida, las memorias compartidas de
> un pasado colectivo. (90)

El texto que leemos en la pantalla al final de la película nos informa que:

> En tiempos de la Colonia, los hieleros del Chimborazo bajaban con 150 mulas a las
> poblaciones costeñas de Babahoyo, Pueblo Viejo y Vinces. Los hieleros participaron en
> las luchas de la Independencia. Emboscaron al ejército español y guiaron por sus cha-
> quiñanes a las tropas patriotas que obtuvieron su primera victoria en las cercanías de
> Guaranda el 9 de noviembre de 1820. Han transcurrido desde entonces:
> 160 años
> 195 gobiernos.

El presupuesto nacional se ha incrementado de menos de 400.000 pesos en la presidencia de Flores a más de 47 mil millones de sucres para 1980. Sin embargo, para ellos, la
historia se quedó en la Colonia ...

En ese intento de construir un pasado y de re-territorializar la memoria *Los hieleros
del Chimborazo* se sitúan en el momento anterior a la nación mestiza, pero haciéndolo
a su vez, en una operación paradójica, en el mismo momento del quiebre de la ilusión
de esa nación mestiza.

3. A modo de conclusión

Boca de lobo inserta su narración directamente en la imposibilidad de reconciliar una
cultura nacional con la marca de la diferencia de lo étnico, las voces descorporalizadas
de su narración circulando por las calles desiertas del pueblo de Simiatug así lo confirman:

> Tiempo de antes nosotros nos llevábamos bonito con la gente indígena, ahora están
> portándose mal, dicen que nosotros somos igualitos a ellos; que ellos son la misma cosa
> que nosotros. Claro que uno les dice que ellos son indios y que nosotros somos blancos
> pero ellos dicen que somos todos iguales.

Los hieleros, por su parte, cuestiona –como lo hacen las organizaciones indígenas
de la época– a la sociedad que "en términos económicos transforma [a los indígenas]
en campesinos pauperizados, asediados por el comerciante, por el prestamista" (Ministerio de Bienestar Social 86). En la única secuencia hablada de la película, vemos a
un hielero –el individuo marcado por la época histórica– insultando, reclamando para
que los comerciantes del mercado compren su hielo y no el de la fábrica: esa imagen
del hombre pauperizado y borracho es la que confronta el texto final, con toda su carga
traumática.

Es así como ambos documentales intentan narrar la nación ecuatoriana desde el
espacio negado de lo étnico para reformular una memoria narrativa distinta del discurso oficial de la décadas precedentes, aunque también existe una contradicción, que
sería la tensión del documentalista ante su papel de embalsamador y su rol como constructor y agente cultural. Todo esto prepara el camino para el surgimiento de algo así
como un gótico andino; o sea, un entramado en donde lo reprimido se cuela en el discurso en forma de presencias sobrenaturales y sus equivalentes fílmicos (sonorización
y las voces en *off*). No es una coincidencia, entonces, que en *Los hieleros de Chimborazo* y en *Boca de lobo*, la presencia del frío cale tan fuerte en la composición: el
frío sería algo así como la materialización atmosférica del proceso de individuación
social que la modernidad produce.

Finalmente se podría hablar de un "anti-sublime." Si, como señala Burke, lo sublime es la representación de lo imposible o de su sugerencia por medio de la representación, los indígenas de ambos documentales representarían esta suerte de concre-
ción gótico-sublime que se insinúa continuamente, pero que no puede mostrarse de
lleno. Algo así como una "pedroparamización" del mundo rural: desolado, fantasmáti-

co, pero incapaz de totalizar la realidad predeterminada de antemano por las ciencias sociales y el propio discurso del realismo social. Sería aquí donde el cine empieza a buscar su propia voz, fuera del regazo confortante de la literatura realista y lejos del grito de batalla de las ciencias sociales.

Bibliografía

Alemán, Gabriela. "Entrevista a Raúl Khalifé." Realizada en mayo 2004. No publicada.

Burke, Edmund. *A Philosophical Enquiry into the Origin of Our Ideas of the Sublime and Beautiful*. London: Oxford UP, 1958.

Caruth, Cathy. "Introduction." *Trauma, Explorations in Memory*. Ed. Cathy Caruth. Baltimore: Johns Hopkins UP, 1995. 151-157.

Fundación Ecuatoriana de Estudios Sociales. *Cultura, estado y sociedad*. Quito: 1991.

Hayward, Susan. "Framing National Cinemas." *Cinema & Nation*. Ed. Mette Hjort and Scott Mackenzie. New York: Routledge, 2000. 63-74.

Hjort, Mette, and Scott Mackenzie, eds. *Cinema & Nation*. New York: Routledge, 2000.

Ministerio de Bienestar Social. *Política estatal y población indígena*. Quito: Abya-Yala, 1984.

Ramón, Galo. *El regreso de los Runas*. Quito: COMUNIDEC, 1993.

Russo, Eduardo. *Diccionario del cine*. Buenos Aires: Paidós, 2003.

Sánchez-Parga, José. *Actores y discursos culturales, Ecuador: 1972–88*. Quito: Centro Andino de Acción Popular, 1988.

Silva, Erika. "El terrigenismo: opción y militancia en la cultura ecuatoriana." *Teoría de la Cultura Nacional*. Ed. Fernando Tianajero. Quito: BCE-CEN, 1986.

Stutzman, Ronald. "El Mestizaje: An All-Inclusive Ideology of Exclusión." *Cultural Transformations and Ethnicity in Modern Ecuador*. Ed. Norman E. Whitten. Urbana: U of Illinois P, 1981. 45-94.

Trujillo, Jorge, ed. *Indianistas, inidianófilos, indigenistas, entre el enigma y la fascinación: una antología de textos sobre el "problema" indígena*. Quito: ILDIS/Abya-Yala, 1992.

Filmografía

Boca de lobo. Dir. Raúl Khalifé. Ecuador,1982.

Los hieleros del Chimborazo. Dir. Gustavo Guayasamín. Ecuador, 1980.

Voces subversivas y mito en la narración de la nación. *En el hoyo* (2006) de Juan Carlos Rulfo

MADALINA STEFAN Y LORENA ORTIZ

Abstract

This essay focuses on the narration of the nation (cf. Bhabha, *Nation*) in the documentary film *En el hoyo* [*In the Pit*] (2006) by Juan Carlos Rulfo. The film narrates the process of constructing the *Periférico* in Mexico City from the point of view of the workers and thus adopts an alternative, subversive perspective on the Mexican nation.

Part of the subversive power of Juan Carlos Rulfo's narration of the nation resides in the use of the documentary film form, whose relation to reality has been a polemical topic in academic debates. The subversive perspective in this counter-narrative is complemented by a distinct use of temporality that interweaves the linear time of progress in the context of a "deficient" Latin American modernity with the circular time of myth, thus showing the ambivalence of the nation in the discursive interstices. In the documentary, this temporal dissociation is accompanied by a polyphonic and hybrid portrait of the capital of a male-connoted Mexican nation. The double character of this portrayal reveals the film's intention to reconceptualize the Mexican nation as a liminal figure.

1. Introducción

El documental *En el hoyo* (2006), premiado en el festival de Sundance (Utah, EE.UU.) del mismo año, puede entenderse en el contexto de la narración de la nación como un ejemplo de una poderosa contra-narrativa (cf. Bhabha, "DissemiNation" 302), es decir, un discurso anti-hegemónico que narra la nación desde la perspectiva de los intersticios y los márgenes sociales. El director Juan Carlos Rulfo –mexicano, hijo del reconocido escritor jalisciense Juan Rulfo–, reivindica una comunidad imaginada (cf. Anderson) nacional y mexicana, distanciándose de los conceptos tradicionales del Estado Nación concebidos desde la cúspide del poder. La película documenta, desde la perspectiva de los trabajadores, la construcción del segundo piso del Periférico, uno de los proyectos viales más ambiciosos de la historia de la Ciudad de México, construido en

el periodo en que Andrés Manuel López Obrador era Jefe de Gobierno del Distrito
Federal (2000-2005). En el documental, el contexto urbano se constituye en el microcosmos de la nación mexicana y, en su realización, se advierten dos estrategias discursivas distintas. Por un lado, se trata de la estetización del progreso como tópico de la
modernización nacional; por el otro lado, la película refuerza las fricciones y rupturas
discursivas de la narración de la nación al deconstruir los conceptos hegemónicos sirviéndose de estructuras narrativas míticas y estrategias posmodernas, como la heterogeneidad multitemporal (cf. García Canclini, *Culturas*). De esta manera, Juan Carlos
Rulfo abre paso a la polifonía de las voces marginadas y a la hibridez para reconcep-
tualizar la nación como una figura ambivalente y liminal.

Para abordar el tema del discurso de la nación, este artículo recurre al concepto
de la comunidad imaginada, de Benedict Anderson cuyas ideas acerca del papel fundamental de la imprenta para la construcción de la nación han sido discutidas extensa-
mente en el contexto de los estudios mediáticos y, también, son productivas en el ámbito del género documental. La relación entre el documental y la identidad nacional se
ve profundamente afectada por la crisis de la referencialidad, o sea, el cuestionamiento
epistemológico de la posibilidad de una representación fiel de la realidad histórica. Si,
anteriormente, se le atribuían al documental las características de objetividad y autenticidad, en la actualidad se extiende la idea de que éste no constituye una fuente objetiva
de información. Incluso, los documentalistas han sido acusados de echar mano de la
ficcionalización y de la manipulación subjetiva.[1] Esta crisis también ha puesto en tela
de juicio el lugar de la enunciación y ha contribuido así a un cambio paradigmático a
nivel de los regímenes de representación (cf. Hall), surgiendo, de esta manera, nuevos
estilos y, también, modalidades reflexivas, performativas (cf. Nichols, *Representing*) y
deconstructivistas en la representación documental de la historia.

Frente al reto de una representación documental fidedigna, *En el hoyo* opta por
capturar la realidad mexicana desde una perspectiva parcial y marginal. Se muestra la
distopía de la gran ciudad desde la perspectiva del conflicto de clases, de la corrupción
y de la pobreza, sin dejar de lado el lugar subversivo de la enunciación de los obreros y
la dignidad de su vida, a pesar de las pésimas condiciones de trabajo en que se mue-
ven. El documental –de ochenta minutos de duración– es el resultado de tres años de
filmación en los que el director Juan Carlos Rulfo –al igual que sus personajes–, estuvo presente día a día en la construcción del segundo piso del Periférico de la Ciudad de
México y, de este modo, pudo captar el transcurrir de la vida de los obreros, tanto en
su jornada laboral como en sus momentos de ocio.

El presente artículo quiere analizar la manera como este documental hace uso de
los mencionados cambios paradigmáticos; asimismo enfoca el modo como el cineasta
se apropia de las estrategias subversivas narrando la nación mexicana desde abajo,
rompiendo así el modelo tradicional y hegemónico de la narración de la nación.

---

[1] "The documentarist makes endless choices. He selects topics, peoples, vistas, angles, lenses,
juxtapositions, sounds, words. Each selection is an expression of his point of view, whether
he is aware of it or not, whether he acknowledges it or not" (Barnouw 313).

2. La ciudad latinoamericana, sus modernidades complejas y sus temporalidades disyuntivas

La película documental aborda la vida laboral en la megaurbe mexicana en el marco de una compleja reflexión sobre la (post-) modernidad, por eso es imprescindible, en un primer paso, situar la interpretación de la película en el contexto teórico latinoamericano de los estudios urbanos. Como el mismo cineasta aclaró en una entrevista, el reto al que se enfrentaba su documental era encontrar los medios para lograr el retrato de la ciudad, reinventando y adecuando los códigos estéticos: "Cómo entrarle a esta ciudad, cómo ver la Ciudad de México sin caer en clichés; siento que no está tratada y está muy maltratada audiovisualmente" (Corzo). Esta cita subraya la actitud consciente del director frente a la representación estereotipada y, –al enfatizar la entrada como posicionamiento estratégico del cineasta frente a la realidad representada–, recuerda la metáfora de Néstor García Canclini en su libro *Culturas híbridas*, cuando describe los distintos tipos de acercamiento a la ciudad de las diversas ciencias sociales:

> Pero ¿cómo hablar de la ciudad moderna, que a veces está dejando de ser moderna y de ser ciudad? ... El antropólogo llega a la ciudad a pie, el sociólogo en auto y por la autopista principal, el comunicólogo en avión. Cada uno registra lo que puede, construye una visión distinta y, por lo tanto, parcial. (37)

Si la metáfora de García Canclini envuelve la idea de que la ciudad representa la modernidad, por analogía, los diversos acercamientos a la ciudad pueden ser entendidos como entradas en la modernidad. En el contexto del documental, la metáfora de García Canclini puede aplicarse al regimen de miradas como expresión de las múltiples estrategias en el tránsito interminable entre las entradas a la modernidad y las Salidas de ella.

En la representación del contexto urbano, el director se enfrenta al problema que García Canclini abordó al rechazar el tópico de la modernización "deficiente" latinoamericana (cf. *Culturas* 65) preguntándose "¿por qué nuestros países cumplen mal y tarde con el modelo metropolitano de la modernización?" (68). Según García Canclini, este problema surge porque se mide el grado de modernidad a través de "imágenes optimizadas de cómo sucedió este proceso en los países centrales" (68). Para indicar que el modernismo se dio de una manera gradual hasta en el mismo "centro" –Europa– (71), diferencia entre los conceptos de "modernización," el cual se refiere al ámbito de los procesos económicos, y de "modernismo" que se aplica a la esfera cultural. En comparación con Europa, expresa que en América Latina también "hubo rupturas provocadas por el desarrollo y la urbanización que, si bien ocurrieron después, fueron más aceleradas" (72). Esta diferenciación permite entender que el modernismo latinoamericano se da conjuntamente con una "modernización deficiente" (65).

Esta constatación conlleva también en sí la imposibilidad de considerar sólo un tiempo como medida universal, frente al cual se sitúa el concepto predominante de la heterogeneidad multitemporal, que se sirve de la idea de la simultaneidad de lo no simultáneo. Como explica Sieber refiriéndose a las obras de Lechner, Martín Barbero y

Piscitelli respectivamente, el concepto del "atraso" se convierte en "discontinuidad si-
multánea," en la "modernidad no contemporánea," en el asincronismo –tanto temporal
como espacial– entre el centro y la periferia (121). La aparente contradicción de la coexistencia de las temporalidades es inteligible en el marco del concepto de la heterogeneidad multitemporal de la cultura moderna la cual "es consecuencia de una historia en
la que la modernización operó pocas veces mediante la sustitución de lo tradicional y
lo antiguo" (García Canclini, *Culturas* 72). La heterogeneidad multitemporal está estrechamente interrelacionada con la modernidad y, por lo tanto, con el Estado Nación,
ya que este último es la consecuencia del orden impuesto por la modernidad y lleva
consigo la idea de que cada objeto y cada sujeto tienen un lugar natural (cf. Bauman).

En este marco teórico, es necesario tener presente la afirmación de García Canclini de que, en la realidad globalizada, los determinismos científicos no son adecua-
dos para describir lo existente. Argumenta que estos supuestos determinismos, que se
muestran coherentes y cohesionados, interiormente son demasiado complejos y están
atravesados por muchas aristas como para imponerse "objetivamente." Incluso estas
mismas metodologías pueden ser descritas como narraciones, como conjuntos de relatos que surgen desde experiencias y vivencias dadas, desde percepciones particulares
de la realidad.

Las metáforas y narraciones son productoras de conocimiento en la medida en
que intentan captar lo que se vuelve fugitivo en el desorden global, aquello que no se
deja delimitar por las fronteras, sino que las atraviesa. Las metáforas tienden a figurar,
a hacer visible, lo que se mueve, se combina o se mezcla. Las narraciones buscan tra-
zar un orden en la profusión de los viajes y las comunicaciones, en la diversidad de
"otros" (cf. García Canclini, *La globalización* 57-58).

3. Ambivalencia y mito en la narración de la nación

En correspondencia con las ideas de Zygmunt Bauman, el teórico postcolonial Homi
K. Bhabha explica que en los discursos hegemónicos sobre la nación –englobados en
lo que denominó "pedagogía de la nación"–, la élite impone la noción de una unidad
social homogénea expresada en el concepto de una nación monolítica al que se une la
idea de que el surgimiento del Estado Nación siempre tiene lugar en el "signo de la
modernidad" (cf. "Introduction" 1). Como también lo hace García Canclini con su
concepto de la heterogeneidad multitemporal, Bhabha destaca la coexistencia de temporalidades disyuntivas que producen una profunda ambivalencia del concepto de la
nación moderna. Esta disyunción temporal –existente a pesar de las tendencias características homogenizadoras del discurso de la nación–, se manifiesta a nivel de los modos de narración:

> What I want to emphasize in that large and liminal image of the nation with which I be-
> gan is a particular ambivalence that haunts the idea of the nation, the language of those
> who write of it and the lives of those who live it. It is an ambivalence that emerges from
> a growing awareness that, despite the certainty with which historians speak of the

'origins' of nation as a sign of the 'modernity' of society, the cultural temporality of the nation inscribes a much more transitional social reality. (Bhabha, "Introduction" 1)

De estas afirmaciones puede abstraerse que la ambivalencia surge como consecuencia de la heterogeneidad nacional y de la polifonía. Al mismo tiempo, sugiere la idea de que cualquier comunidad imaginada es de carácter narrativo, lo que significa que su recepción admite una variedad de interpretaciones. De acuerdo a la aproximación de Jan Assmann, la construcción identitaria siempre coincide con un proceso narrativo (cf. 52) que recurre a un autorretrato colectivo de carácter imaginado (cf. 18); de este modo, la narratividad y sus múltiples interpretaciones adquieren una importancia trascendente. En un sentido más amplio, las narraciones también pueden ser escenificaciones y prácticas culturales que se entienden dentro de lo que Assmann denomina mito. La importancia del mito en la narración de la nación, se aprecia en la afirmación de que el mito "construye mundos imaginarios, evocados más que descritos, a través de arquetipos o figuras del inconsciente y de creaciones tipológicas que son las irrupciones dramáticas del alma en una sociedad determinada" (Mardones 186). Assmann acentúa el hecho de que el carácter imaginario del mito ha permitido la suposición de una cercanía ideológica entre el mito y la religión posibilitando, en consecuencia, una oposición dicotómica entre mito y logos. Sin embargo, Rössner pone énfasis en la imposibilidad de equiparar lo mítico y lo irracional e indica que se trata más de una alternativa, que de una cosmovisión irracional, es decir, de otro tipo de ratio (cf. 27). Asimismo Gilbert Durand se refiere al posible carácter racional del mito al afirmar que el mito es

> un sistema dinámico de símbolos, de arquetipos y de esquemas, sistema dinámico que, bajo el impulso de un esquema, tiende a componerse en relato. El mito es ya un esbozo de racionalización, puesto que utiliza el hilo del discurso. ... Lo que importa en el mito no es exclusivamente el hilo del relato, sino también el sentido simbólico de los términos ... y el análisis de los isotopismos simbólicos y arquetípicos que es el único que puede darnos la clave semántica del mito. (56, 339, 343)

Hans Poser contribuye a invalidar la dicotomía entre logos y mito advirtiendo que los residuos del pensamiento mítico surgen justamente en el marco menos esperado, es decir, en modelos racionalistas que son develados como utopías creadas a base de figuras míticas (cf. Rössner 24).

Del mismo modo, Bhabha reconoce que "nations, like narratives, lose their origins in the myths of time and only fully realize their horizons in the mind's eye" ("Introduction" 1). Por consiguiente, en su concepto de la narración de la nación, pone el acento en el carácter construido de la comunidad imaginada señalando que ambas, nación y narración, están conectadas mediante el mito del tiempo. La pérdida de los orígenes de la nación en el mito, significa que la narración de ella requiere de la narración de sus orígenes, los que van más allá de su existencia como tal. El mito adquiere, de este modo, una función afirmativa en la narración de la nación y constituye un elemento subversivo que mina el discurso de la modernidad y de la nación hegemónica.

Estas dos cosmovisiones diversas implican la coexistencia de temporalidades disyuntivas por el hecho de que, mientras el progreso y la modernidad se basan en la idea del tiempo lineal, la cosmovisión popular y mítica, acude a un tiempo ritual y circular. En consecuencia, el análisis de la narración de la nación puede ser realizado considerando las temporalidades disyuntivas (cf. Bhabha, *Location* 204). En este contexto, Bhabha pone de manifiesto que la ambivalencia y la disyunción temporal son causadas por los componentes divergentes del discurso de la narración de la nación y el carácter heterogéneo de la comunidad imaginada. El pueblo representa un elemento fundamental para definir la performatividad de la nación en oposición a los discursos de élite que –como ya se ha dicho– Bhabha denomina pedagogía de la nación:

> The people are neither the beginning nor the end of the national narrative; they represent the *cutting edge* [acentuación en el original] between the totalizing powers of the social and the forces that signify the more specific address to contentious, unequal interests and identities within the population ... This is because the subject of cultural discourse–the agency of a people–is a split in the discursive ambivalence that emerges between the pedagogical and the performative. ("DissemiNation" 297, 299)

La polifonía y, sobre todo, las voces marginadas, –las cuales se atribuyen en gran parte a la polifonía–, muestran la ambivalencia de la narración de la nación (cf. Bhabha, "DissemiNation" 301). Por eso, es necesario realizar una reconceptualización de esa nación (cf. 299) que surge en los intersticios discursivos. Aquella disociación temporal de carácter liminal, que se expresa en las representaciones de la nación (cf. 295), se manifiesta a distintos niveles en el documental analizado. Uno de los niveles va estrechamente ligado a la problemática de la representación verosímil del mundo histórico y concierne directamente a las temporalidades disyuntivas, ya que éstas pueden ser pensadas como uno de los ejes cruciales que originan la imposibilidad de comparación entre el mundo histórico y la realidad fílmica presentada en el documental.

4. *En el hoyo*

En el hoyo se muestra la historia de ocho obreros mexicanos que convergen en el mismo espacio urbano y con el mismo objetivo: la construcción de una de las obras viales más ambiciosas de la historia de México. Aquel espacio urbano, la Ciudad de México, se concibe como un microcosmos de la nación mexicana, la cual se narra haciendo referencia a la lógica de la modernización. Por lo tanto, el segundo piso del Periférico da lugar a ser interpretado como un significante metafórico de la modernidad y del progreso de la nación, un símbolo del avance de la comunidad imaginada. La metáfora del segundo piso se refiere a una perspectiva o a un discurso que coexiste como perspectiva alternativa sobrepuesta a la primera. Se trata de un motivo en la narración audiovisual que, tanto literal como metafóricamente, produce un desdoblamiento a nivel espacial, temporal y semántico.

El motivo del desdoblamiento significa, en el campo de la espacialidad, la convergencia de la periferia y el centro en un mismo escenario, representando los conflictos sociales que implican el encuentro entre la subalternidad y las clases hegemóni-cas. El desdoblamiento, en el campo temporal corresponde a las reflexiones acerca de la heterogeneidad multitemporal, que conjuga las temporalidades disyuntivas de la modernidad con la temporalidad cíclica y atávica de los mitos populares. En el campo semántico, el desdoblamiento produce un efecto subversivo al descentralizar el discur-so nacional monológico y hegemónico mediante la introducción de la perspectiva mar-ginada.

Por lo tanto, la figura del segundo piso, con su polisemia, constituye un complejo símbolo colectivo (cf. Link 9) y posibilita la representación de la nación utilizando el microcosmos de la ciudad. Esta dimensión nacional del espacio urbano puede apreciar-se por el uso recurrente de símbolos nacionales como, por ejemplo, la bandera mexica-na. Para recrear lo nacional desde lo popular, la película utiliza, además, entre otras, referencias a la comida típica, a la ensalada de nopales, a las tortillas y –a nivel auditi-vo–, a la música de banda. Elementos que forman parte de muchas otras alusiones para recordar al espectador la ubicación geográfica y esbozan, al mismo tiempo, un espacio de construcción identitaria que define el territorio nacional mexicano en el marco de las geografías imaginarias.

4.1. Hibridez, polifonía y masculinidad: la capital de la nación

El documental pretende capturar el ambiente de esa geografía imaginaria y de aquello que caracteriza a sus habitantes. Al respecto, Juan Carlos Rulfo afirma que "lo que in-tento determinar es de quién es esta ciudad, de los que la hacen o los que viven en ella, quiénes hacen que se mueva y le dan vida" (Macarúa Sánchez). En este contexto llama la atención la interrelación que establece entre los ciudadanos y la ciudad, debido a que –en congruencia con la teoría de Bhabha–, atribuye a la performatividad de los ha-bitantes, la creación de la ciudad en movimiento. Ciudad que es, a su vez, una ciudad en proceso de hibridación, aunque "es muy difícil mostrar la mexicanidad que se vive en la capital porque es tan polifacética y hace que todo tipo de cosas confluyan, existan y sucedan en un mismo espacio" (Macarúa Sánchez).

El propósito del director de retratar este espacio en proceso, lleva en sí la necesi-dad de dar voz a la población híbrida, la que, en concordancia, está marcada por la migración y la diversidad cultural y social. Rulfo expresa que "de repente me di cuenta de que estaba con unos diez o quince trabajadores originarios de varias partes de la re-pública que llegaron a este lugar buscando chamba" ("Juan Carlos capta la vida"). La presentación de las perspectivas de los trabajadores pone énfasis en un momento dis-cursivo crucial, ya que la gran variedad de gente que habita o migra a la ciudad regis-tra una multiplicidad de voces y perspectivas desde la cual emerge lo que Juan Carlos Rulfo denomina la "mexicanidad" (Macarúa Sánchez). Se produce, de esta manera, una imagen de la mexicanidad que, bajo el enfoque de la teoría de género, se caracteri-za por estar estrechamente vinculada a la masculinidad. La baja presencia de mujeres en el filme, los diálogos, los comentarios y el lenguaje entre los obreros, lo sitúa en un

ambiente machista y misógino. En consecuencia, el retrato de la ciudad que el documentalista presenta, al hacerla "hablar por sí misma," o más bien, a través de sus porta-
voces –los habitantes que la animan–, reproduce en su seno la exclusión y marginación
de lo femenino.

Se dice que las ciudades son de quienes las habitan. Toriz afirma:

> Será necesario observar el detalle, los fragmentos, el incidente: para habitar la ciudad es
> preciso escribirla. Necesario será también recordar que las fuerzas históricas del presen-
> te se diluyen y desembocan en el sujeto que las dice: la ciudad sólo acontece en el cuer-
> po que la registra, en las palabras que la nombran: la ciudad es el lenguaje.

El registro de lengua coloquial caracteriza el habla de los obreros al conversar de lo
público y de lo privado, pasando de lo uno a lo otro y viceversa. Muestran parte de lo
que acontece en sus vidas, sus planes, sus fracasos, sus creencias religiosas y políticas,
su afición al fútbol, a las mujeres y hasta sus preferencias culinarias. Dan a conocer
una radiografía de la ciudad, de "su ciudad," utilizando un vocabulario florido, lleno
de doble sentido, salpicado de injurias y silbidos. De esta forma se muestra que la ciudad también tiene la voz de quienes la habitan, la trabajan, la caminan, la sufren y la
viven. La Ciudad de México, con más de quince millones de habitantes, no es la excepción, moviéndose en el variado contraste entre la hipermodernidad y la miseria. De
ahí que, en un mismo espacio, se dé la ineludible convivencia entre pobres y ricos.

Amalia Signorelli en su artículo "Clases dominantes y clases subalternas, el control del ecosistema urbano," opina que el espacio urbano agudiza los antagonismos de
intereses provocados por una participación diferenciada y desigual en los procesos de
producción y reproducción de la vida social. Por esta razón, la ciudad no puede ser ex-
perimentada de la misma manera por todos sus habitantes:

> En cada época histórica, si la ciudad representa una oportunidad, lo es más para unos
> que para otros. Para unos será el espacio de ejercicio del poder y la dominación, mien-
> tras que para otros representa el instrumento de la opresión, la marginación y la explota-
> ción. (Signorelli 331)

Ésta es la imagen que trasmite *En el hoyo* al revelar una capital mexicana dividida por la diferencia de clases sociales: el obrero que trabaja a marcha forzada en el le-
vantamiento de un puente que atravesará toda la ciudad y el automovilista que hará uso
del mismo cuando esté listo:

> Es el drama humano, parte de la ciudad más grande del mundo; la parte triste es que po-
> cas veces hay comunicación entre obreros y automovilistas; ellos trabajan para los otros
> cuando, es curioso, los obreros nunca se subirán al segundo piso porque ni viven por
> ahí, ni tienen auto. (Gamaliel)

4.2. Desde abajo

Documentar la construcción del segundo piso del Periférico en el marco de la narración del progreso nacional comprende un enfoque de la parte subalterna y dependiente

del pueblo, o sea, los trabajadores. Los personajes hablan desde abajo, no sólo en sentido figurado, también, literalmente, se encuentran "en el hoyo." Rulfo da comienzo a su documental en las profundidades del hoyo en que se construyeron los cimientos de la obra vial y, al mismo tiempo, se inicia la comunicación del director con los obreros. Desde abajo, empieza a ganar su confianza, consiguiendo confesiones, chistes, canciones y momentos memorables.

La película tiene ocho personajes, algunos de ellos conocidos por sus apodos, como el "Chabelo" –a quien sus más allegados llaman "Chaparro"–, quien vive la vida con optimismo, o el "Grande," quien, en más de una ocasión, quiere demostrar su hombría al hablar de las mujeres que ha tenido. También aparecen el "Guapo," el "Chómpiras" y Vicencio, el "Voyeur" –quien se autodenomina "el cabo de los guerreros"–, además de dos trabajadores nocturnos, a saber, Agustín, un taxista que se mueve por las calles de una Ciudad de México iluminada por los tres millones de automovilistas que circulan por sus pistas, y Natividad, una mujer encargada de cerrar la calle donde están las obras. Mujer que se mostrará como la "más espiritual" y aferrada a las leyendas urbanas.

El director se aleja del melodrama y presenta a los personajes sin idealizarlos. De la misma manera en que introduce al obrero que camina por una varilla arriesgando su vida, lo hace también con el que duerme siesta o juega a las cartas después de comer. Sin embargo, desde el punto de vista de su estatus social, todos comparten una perspectiva marginal, ya que, en la jerarquía social, ocupan un lugar inferior al de los integrantes de la clase media que son los que utilizarán el segundo piso. El director retrata la realidad desde esa perspectiva subalterna y, al mismo tiempo, deja constancia de un momento de la memoria histórica de la ciudad y sus habitantes. Los obreros son dignificados por el trabajo y en su marginación mediante la forma en que Rulfo realiza la representación fílmica de esa realidad.

Pierre Bourdieu, en su artículo "La identidad como representación," dice que el actor urbano está expuesto desde el lugar social que ocupa en la estructura de múltiples y variados discursos sobre la realidad, discursos que logra introyectar en la forma de esquemas de percepción, valoración y acción (cf. Reguillo Cruz 29-30). Se puede deducir, entonces, que la lectura y la perspectiva que los obreros tienen de la Ciudad de México, no es la misma que la que tienen los automovilistas.

En este contexto se destaca el Voyeur. Su nombre es bastante sugestivo en relación con el régimen de la mirada que adopta el documental. Se trata de un trabajador que, desde la altura de una parte de la construcción, observa el tráfico y a los automovilistas, quienes disponen de mayor movilidad, así como de la posibilidad de mirar trabajar a los obreros. La subalternidad del Voyeur está caracterizada por su movilidad reducida; no obstante, su posición en la altura, le permite mirar también las piernas de las mujeres que pasan por la construcción, transgrediendo su intimidad, sin que ellas puedan advertirlo. Es así que, a pesar de tener menos movilidad, logra invertir las relaciones de poder, un poder que ahora yace en su mirada. Por consiguiente, la escenificación del *gazing* implica tanto la inversión de la mirada como de las jerarquías sociales. No es gratuito que esta alteración del régimen de la mirada coincida –a manera de una referencia al nivel metanarrativo–, con la mirada de la misma cámara que documenta estas escenas. Rulfo afirma que

> el conocimiento de los obreros del día a día es más profundo que el de uno. Si tú no tienes chamba mañana te deprimes; en cambio como ellos no tienen nada seguro, lo que les interesa son cosas más inmediatas: qué va a pasar con su mujer o a dónde van a ir el fin de semana. Con este trabajo, me he dado cuenta de que, en general, la gente del pueblo tiene una especie de permeabilidad frente a los acontecimientos y eso mismo es quizá lo que los hace resistir. Sus angustias no son las mismas que las de nosotros. Sus intereses van en otra dirección. Ellos no son los que van a usar el segundo piso, porque desde donde viven ni de chiste van a venir a pasear hasta acá. (Espinosa de los Monteros)

En consecuencia, se puede concluir que el documental parte desde la perspectiva de los obreros, de la gente marginalizada, lo que, efectivamente, significa la narración de la nación desde abajo. Se trata de un lugar de enunciación que altera el régimen de representación (cf. Hall). El lugar de enunciación y la mirada del documentalista adquieren un carácter subversivo con respecto a la narración de la nación, ya que podemos ubicar el discurso en la gente misma, hecho que trae consigo la ambivalencia de la nación indicada por Bhabha.

4.3. ¿Personajes con voz?

Juan Carlos Rulfo consigue la subversión de la narración de la nación dando voz a aquéllos que no la tienen, a los marginados. Dado que se vale del recurso de las entrevistas, es importante ocuparse de la manera como se realizan y se presentan. En el documental predominan las entrevistas interactivas junto al "pseudodiálogo" o el "pseudomonólogo." Nichols constata:

> The visible presence of the social actor as evidentiary witness and the visible absence of the filmmaker (the filmmaker's presence as absence) gives this form of the interview the appearance of a 'pseudo monologue' … Frequently the filmmaker is neither seen or heard, allowing witnesses to speak for themselves. (*Representing* 54)

En este tipo de entrevista, la instancia narrativa polifónica –constituida por las voces marginadas–, sustituye a la voz de un narrador omnisciente, tanto en su apariencia de *voice-over* como en la de sonido grabado en directo. La aparente ausencia del cineasta y de su voz, como instancia narrativa perceptible e intradiegética en la película, parece entregar el control y abrir paso a las enunciaciones de los actores sociales. Por otra parte, al omitir la mediación realizador-sujeto-espectador, el pseudomonólogo crea la impresión de que el documental se dirige de manera directa al espectador e, incluso, hace posible no respetar la convención de evitar la mirada directa a la cámara (cf. Nichols, *Representing* 54). Esta impresión de una mediación inobstaculizada es acentuada a través del papel de testigos que desempeñan los actores sociales como representantes de una perspectiva alternativa al discurso hegemónico: "We are encouraged to believe that these voices carry less the authority of historical judgment than that of personal testimony" (Nichols, "The Voice" 23).

Además, la narración polifónica del documental puede ser interpretada como una estrategia discursiva, ya que las entrevistas deben ser entendidas como discursos jerárquicos (cf. Nichols, *Representing* 50). El pseudomonólogo y el pseudodiálogo, como ya lo indican sus denominaciones, sólo fingen un monólogo o, respectivamente, un diálogo, es decir, un espacio libre de jerarquías:

> The interview format prohibits full reciprocity or equity between the participants. The interviewer's skill is his or her ability to appear at the service of the interviewee whose speech actually he or she controls, somewhat in the manner of a ventriloquist. (52)

En ambos casos, las preguntas y los comentarios que dejarían entrever la posición del director y, por lo tanto, las jerarquías, no llegan al espectador. Se trata, en todo caso, sólo de la ilusión de una mediación inobstaculizada, conseguida en un proceso de montaje que elimina las jerarquías.

Existen, sin embargo, escenas que evidencian este orden jerárquico subyacente en las que este orden se altera. En la primera escena, el Chaparro, a quien, al parecer, le han hecho una pregunta acerca de sus preocupaciones, hace un comentario breve sobre el trabajo y la comida antes de repetir la pregunta enfrentándose a la cámara. Su pregunta no será contestada ya que la película sigue, mediante un corte, con el hilo temático de la comida (*En el hoyo* 14.12). La segunda escena implica una pregunta más concreta. Después de que el Chaparro opina que "ningún presidente es bueno, aquí, aquí en el mundo" se dirige hacia la derecha donde parece haber alguien y continúa diciendo "todos tenemos que chingarle, ¿no?" Al darse cuenta de que no recibirá respuesta cambia de postura y se dirige directamente a la cámara expresando "¿no lo ve así?" (*En el hoyo* 47.27). Tampoco recibirá respuesta a esta pregunta. Las dos escenas significan una alteración del orden jerárquico debido a que los papeles han sido invertidos, porque no es el director quien hace las preguntas. En consecuencia, el hecho de que el Chaparro no obtenga respuesta, pone en tela de juicio la presencia de una mediación inobstaculizada.

Se puede concluir que el documental no supera del todo las jerarquías discursivas y que, al fin y al cabo, las voces que escucha el espectador siempre son filtradas por la percepción y el énfasis del cineasta. Aunque no puede olvidarse de que se trata de una problemática inherente a la práctica de la película documental, Rulfo logra reforzar la impresión de autenticidad de su filme mediante el enfoque en las personas como instancias narrativas. Este proceder transmite la idea de que el discurso hegemónico ha sido reemplazado por el testimonio íntimo de los actores sociales. Por esta causa, podría decirse que el director asume una posición ambivalente y reflexiva frente a la modalidad de representación documental, dado que no excluye estas escenas.

4.4. Transgresiones y espacio

La identidad social de los sujetos, en este caso, de los personajes, está dada y establecida por los espacios, los escenarios y los lugares sociales que el sujeto hace suyos en la
medida que le proporcionan una idea de quién es, quién ha sido y cuáles son sus posibilidades objetivas. Rossana Reguillo Cruz, en su libro *En la calle otra vez*, señala:

> El referente situacional se constituiría en el lazo entre el espacio y la representación que
> se hace el sujeto para sí mismo y para los demás sobre su identidad: estructuras de plau-
> sibilidad como determinantes del ajuste entre la situación y las posibilidades objetivas
> del sujeto. Es decir, el lugar social como determinante de los itinerarios cotidianos en
> los que se establecen las relaciones con la ciudad. (33)

El lugar de origen de muchos de los trabajadores del segundo piso del Periférico
es el campo y así surge un interesante contraste entre éste y la ciudad, cuando el director decide llevar la cámara hasta las viviendas de algunos de sus personajes. Martín
Barbero, en su ensayo sobre medios y culturas del espacio latinoamericano, afirma que
el mundo popular se inserta en la dinámica urbana mediante las transformaciones de la
vida laboral, de la identificación de las ofertas culturales con los medios masivos y,
también, del progreso con los servicios públicos.

El director juega con los espacios de la ciudad y el campo, el primero como el lugar de trabajo del obrero y el segundo, como su terruño. El documental baila al ritmo
de lo urbano y lo rural. Para lograr este equilibrio, Rulfo recurre a la entrevista que entra como voz en *off*, sólo después vemos al personaje. Ésta es una técnica muy utilizada para entretejer y pasar de un plano a otro sin que el espectador sienta la brusquedad
del cambio de espacios, como sería pasar de la ciudad al campo. Rulfo manifiesta que
"esta gente trae el ritmo del campo a la ciudad, pero también el lenguaje. Estaba ansio-
so por captar esas cosas personales e íntimas en sus propias palabras" (Alsedo).

El director sale del lugar de trabajo con algunos de los personajes. Los acompaña
a sus hogares, se involucra en su espacio vital y logra un cierto grado de intimidad con
ellos. En estas escenas –a diferencia de los planos utilizados en la zona de construcción del puente–, Rulfo se desprende del tripié y deja atrás los *travellings*, los paneos y
se sale de la formalidad técnica. Utiliza la cámara en mano para adentrarse de una manera más íntima y libre en el mundo rural de los personajes. Así se descubre una perspectiva diferente sobre la vida del obrero, como en el caso del Chómpiras, que orgullo-
so le muestra su casa nueva recorriendo la cocina, el baño, el cuarto de visitas y hasta
el dormitorio de su hija, a quien vemos en un retrato colgado en la pared.

García Canclini señala que la modernidad no es sólo un espacio al que se entra o
se sale, es más bien, una situación de tránsito interminable entre las ciudades y el campo, entre las metrópolis y los países subdesarrollados:

> El análisis cultural de la modernidad requiere poner juntos los modos de entrar y salir de
> ella. Pero dicho así es equívoco, porque sugiere que la modernidad sería un periodo his-
> tórico o un tipo de prácticas con el que uno podría vincularse eligiendo estar o no estar.
> A menudo se plantea en estos términos, y toda la discusión se reduce a lo que debe ha-
> cerse para entrar o salir. El artesano que debería convertirse en obrero, el migrante que

quiere mejorar yendo a la ciudad o a un país desarrollado, el intelectual o el artista que se incorpora al avance tecnológico. Son situaciones de pasaje que sugieren un cambio de estado. (*Culturas* 333)

Éste es el caso de muchos de los obreros, como, por ejemplo, el Guapo, que emigra a la capital con la certeza de que su situación económica será mejor. Y lo dice claramente, cuando está en el campo, en la casa de su madre: "Allá hay más dinero que aquí. Aquí trabajas el día y te lo pagan a cincuenta pesos" (*En el hoyo* 52.56).

Pero también está aquél que, cansado de la modernidad, anhela volver al campo, como sucede con otro de los personajes, Vicencio, quien, en su contexto rural, se ve feliz, montado a caballo, llevando sombrero y botas. García Canclini asegura que

algo semejante ocurre con los que quieren salir. Huir de las megalópolis y regresar a la naturaleza, buscar en un patrimonio histórico sacralizado la *di-solución* [acentuación en el original] de los conflictos modernos, liberar al conocimiento o al arte de la compulsión del progreso. (*Culturas* 333)

El espacio urbano tiene una gran potencialidad, precisamente por albergar en un mismo lugar diferentes temporalidades que están cargadas de significados. Mas en el caso de los obreros, el espacio rural también es el espacio de su vida cotidiana; el campo es, también, un espacio delimitado y colmado de contenidos. El constante cambio entre el espacio urbano y el rural indica la realidad cíclica de los trabajadores que entran y salen de la ciudad, situación que afianza las transgresiones entre las temporalidades.

4.5. *Transgresiones y temporalidades*

El documental refleja la complejidad de la urbanidad mexicana no sólo en relación con la diversidad social y lingüística, sino, también, hace hincapié en los procesos de la hibridación cultural. Este tema se trata, principalmente, mediante la referencia a una leyenda mexicana urbana que remite a las creencias populares y los mitos. En ella se puede apreciar el modo como coinciden las temporalidades disyuntivas deconstruyendo la idea de la homogeneidad nacional. La leyenda cuenta que el diablo iba pidiendo almas como ofrendas para que las construcciones se mantuvieran en pie y no se cayeran. Ya al comienzo del filme se hace referencia a ella, cuando una voz femenina en *off* afirma que "todas las obras grandes necesitan almas para que amarren, como si le echaras abono. Aquí han pasado muchas cosas, cosas que son inexplicables y las cuentas y no te creen. Quieres contar cosas para que te crean y no te creen" (*En el hoyo* 03.50). La creencia popular acentúa las fricciones causadas por las temporalidades, las cuales se retoman audiovisualmente en una escena posterior. Esta segunda puesta en escena de la leyenda se inicia con Natividad –la guardia de noche–, y se sirve de un ambiente mágico[2] que, en primer lugar, es creado a nivel visual. Como son sólo los focos de los camiones que traspasan la niebla causada por las trabajadoras que barren

---

[2] Lo mágico es, según Rössner, un posible sinónimo válido para lo mítico (cf. 29).

unos vidrios rotos, las personas grabadas a contraluz se vuelven siluetas, abstracciones de sí mismas. La tensión se refuerza mediante la banda sonora, en la cual se escucha el ruido de los vidrios junto a una melodía que crece y decrece en volumen y que da la impresión de un misterioso vértigo disonante. Estos elementos crean un fuerte contraste con las otras escenas del filme que, en su mayoría, han sido filmadas de día y carecen de este carácter misterioso y mágico, o *unheimlich*, en el sentido freudiano. Sobre todo, es importante que la temporalidad misma de estas escenas fantasmagóricas diverja fuertemente del resto de la película. Durante la narración mítica, el espectador tiene la impresión de ver las imágenes a cámara lenta, mientras, en oposición, la escena posterior muestra la construcción del segundo piso a cámara rápida, de tal manera que los trabajadores parecen hormigas. La cámara rápida concuerda con la temporalidad del progreso y de la modernidad y su discrepancia con la temporalidad mítica introduce dos temporalidades distintas que representan igualmente dos cosmovisiones dispares. La transgresión de las temporalidades y de las cosmovisiones se ve favorecida por la intercalación de una imagen de la Vírgen de Guadalupe, que forma parte de las escenificaciones a cámara lenta (*En el hoyo* 22.16). Aparentemente la fe religiosa, simbolizada por la figura santa, marca una oposición a lo racional. No obstante, debido a que se muestra la coexistencia de la cosmovisión arcaica –que de por sí ya es sincretista– y la cosmovisión moderna, la dicotomía entre mito y logos se deconstruye. La complementariedad de las dos cosmovisiones se pone de relieve a través de una toma en la cual aparece una cruz cuya figura es casi idéntica a la forma de los pilares inacabados del segundo piso que se ven en el trasfondo (*En el hoyo* 24.35).

En este contexto, Natividad encarna la actualización del arquetipo del guardián del umbral, quien vigila la entrada en lo desconocido y, aunque los arquetipos significan la actualización de las representaciones simbólicas en el inconsciente, éstas se ven afectadas por las alteraciones de los estilos narrativos en el transcurso del relato fílmico. Por consiguiente, estas representaciones pueden disentir constantemente del sentido tradicional sin que los arquetipos sean alterados. Debido a que no se trata de motivos, sino de la estructura arquetípica de la diégesis "se puede demostrar la supervivencia literaria de los grandes temas y de los personajes mitológicos" (Eliade 162). El arquetipo del guardián del umbral –que forma parte de los mitemas de la separación y de la partida– se introduce al iniciarse el documental, a nivel audiovisual, en la primera secuencia de la película que muestra la toma de un hoyo –una excavación abismal– desde el que habla una persona. La puesta en escena de la subalternidad presenta, al mismo tiempo, los mitemas de la llamada y del descenso. "El destino ha llamado al héroe, y ha transferido su centro de gravedad espiritual del seno de su sociedad a una zona desconocida" asegura Campbell (60). La visualización del descenso cautiva por su estética ya que el hoyo aparece desde la oscuridad y vuelve a desaparecer en ella. El juego de luz y tinieblas produce la impresión de que el cineasta ilumina y vuelve visible lo desconocido que está en la oscuridad porque se trata del descenso para rescatar las voces marginadas que representan lo desconocido, las enunciaciones desde los márgenes de la nación, como el director mismo afirmó en una entrevista: "Me interesa mucho la gente que aparentemente es invisible" (González).

Si se considera la afirmación del cineasta, cuando al referirse a la realización del filme manifiesta que el proyecto "ha tenido una estrella especial ... porque cada vez que se necesitaba algo, llegaba. No ha sido fácil, pero todo se dio de forma mágica" (Olivares 2), también, por lo menos, a nivel paratextual, está presente el mitema de la ayuda sobrenatural que facilita el camino. Por lo demás, se aprecia que el director no se reduce al discurso fílmico, sino que incluye la práctica de la filmación en la estructura mítica. En este contexto, los mitemas de la iniciación, de las pruebas y de las victorias representan la idea lacaniana del estado del espejo, es decir, de la dificultad de encontrarse a sí mismo en el "otro." El mitema del obstáculo coincide con las palabras de Bhabha: "And by exploring this Third Space, we may elude the politics of polarity and emerge as the others of ourselves" (*Location* 38).

El hecho de que la película recurra a estas estructuras míticas puede relacionarse con la pretensión de construir fílmicamente una comunidad imaginada donde las voces de los obreros constituyen –de la misma manera que el discurso hegemonial– la narración de la nación. Es decir, se trata de dos facetas del mismo discurso o como diría Juan Carlos Rulfo:

> *El hoyo* [acentuación en el original] es una idea coloquial de que estamos en el hoyo. El segundo piso puede estar en el hoyo. Pero al final todos lo estamos, es decir, todo lo que sucede allí es reflejo inmediato de todos nosotros, no sólo de los obreros. Quiero que tú como espectador llegues a la conclusión de que tú, estés donde estés, eres parte del hoyo. ("Juan Carlos capta la vida")

Para complementar la estructura mítica, el regreso del mundo sobrenatural, el retorno al mundo, se da en la práctica de la documentación fílmica. El documental lleva las voces rescatadas de esta otredad al mundo moderno, lo que podría interpretarse en el marco del mitema de la posesión de los dos mundos, como se verá más en adelante.

En consecuencia, el hecho de que la película recurra a la leyenda del diablo indica una transgresión en las temporalidades. La cosmovisión mítica corresponde a un tiempo ritual y circular mientras que la cosmovisión de la modernidad se basa en la temporalidad lineal del progreso, del pensamiento racional de la Ilustración y de la secularización. Las temporalidades disyuntivas constituyen la ambivalencia, la ruptura narrativa con el discurso nacional y se refieren tanto al concepto de la heterogeneidad multitemporal como al énfasis puesto en la heterogeneidad, la polifonía y la hibridez de la nación.

Siguiendo a Bhabha, el desdoblamiento de las temporalidades narrativas en el documental puede atribuirse a que la narración de la nación pierde su origen en el mito, vale decir, en su equivalente de la temporalidad opuesta al progreso. En consecuencia, el documental pone el acento en que la narración de la nación no puede excluir el tiempo mítico, por lo cual tampoco puede mantenerse en pie el concepto de la oposición entre el tiempo mítico irracional y el tiempo lineal del pensamiento racional de la Ilustración:

Sí, sé que suena a lo más banal. Pero detrás está México que nos estorba, que tachas de populista y que no tiene nada que ver con el progreso. Con este documental estamos tratando de hacer algo que vaya más allá de la cuestión partidista, más allá de la temporalidad, intento que hable la Ciudad de México en un contexto más amplio de tiempo. ("Juan Carlos capta la vida")

En este contexto, el discurso de Natividad –mencionada anteriormente–, constituye una metarreferencia a la compleja relación entre el mundo histórico y la realidad fílmica del documental: Querer contar las cosas para que la gente las crea es el difícil oficio del documentalista. Las fricciones causadas por las dos cosmovisiones distintas pueden ser registradas en las fricciones que se dan entre la realidad híbrida del mundo histórico que intenta capturar el documentalista y la realidad fílmica que ve el espectador. Rulfo afirma en una entrevista que "al hacer un documental estás en la realidad completa" (Espinosa de los Monteros). Al contestar la pregunta acerca de la diferencia entre el director de cine documental y el de ficción, Rulfo describe el peculiar nexo entre la realidad fílmica y el mundo histórico que observa en el documentalista:

El de ficción tiene una parte muy interior, de trabajo en casa, pensando en sus historias. El documentalista es un pata de perro. Sales a la calle y te encuentras el material. Muchas veces no tienes claro lo que tienes que hacer y la realidad te dice por dónde. El de ficción tiene que tener toda la mesa puesta para poder filmar, mientras que el de documental tiene que tener mucho valor para empezar y mucha paciencia para terminar. (González)

Si la realidad marca los procesos de hibridación y la coexistencia de cosmovisiones y temporalidades disyuntivas, entonces surge la necesidad de desarrollar estrategias para posibilitar la representación de las ambivalencias de la narración de la nación. La solución de esta problemática coincide con el mitema que faltaba para complementar la estructura mítica del documental: el mitema de la posesión de los dos mundos. El descubrimiento del héroe en el mitema del retorno es que los distintos mundos son dos lados de la misma realidad. El uso de la documentación de la realidad contemporánea que enfoca a la gente misma y el nivel de compromiso personal del receptor muestra que el director recurre a una estrategia narrativa mitopoética que lo inscribe en el turno performativo al que se refieren Nichols y Bruzzi:

Y esto significa también un cambio en el camino general de trabajo. Siempre he trabajado con la vida de mi abuelo, de mi padre y la vida familiar. Los recuerdos, la tradición y la memoria de México. … Esta vez es mi cuento. Me toca hablar de mi contexto. Son las anécdotas de mi tiempo. ("Juan Carlos capta la vida")

Las palabras de Juan Carlos Rulfo indican que la elección de documentar el presente compromete al espectador –quien comparte el mismo presente– a formarse una opinión acerca del grado de verosimilitud de la representación. "Se trata de cine que se finca en la convicción de que la propia audiencia con sus mismos e impresionados ojos realizará sus propias conclusiones" asegura Koehler.

5. Conclusión

El documental *En el hoyo* puede ser entendido como un intento de lograr un retrato subversivo de la capital de la nación mexicana, un retrato que plasma la vida, la pobreza, las esperanzas y la realidad de los obreros, quienes narran la nación desde una perspectiva peculiar y ambivalente, desde abajo. El discurso nacional del progreso y de la modernidad se aborda utilizando el espacio urbano considerado como el microcosmos nacional.

El efecto subversivo en la narración de la nación se alcanza mediante la polifonía, la diversidad de los lugares de enunciación y de las temporalidades disyuntivas en las que se reproducen las múltiples rupturas discursivas. Por lo tanto, Juan Carlos Rulfo crea un espacio en el cual la nación es concebida como una figura liminal poniendo énfasis en la heterogeneidad de la población y en la ambivalencia discursiva de la narración de la nación.

La ambivalencia del lugar de enunciación se manifiesta en el peculiar enfoque de una multitud de voces marginadas que narran la nación desde la experiencia vivencial de los pueblos rurales de la periferia, o desde abajo, desde los abismos u "hoyos" urbanos. Dicho con las palabras de Bhabha: "The margins of the nation displace the centre; the peoples of the periphery return to rewrite the history and fiction of the metropolis" ("Introduction" 6). Con este enfoque centrado en la gente marginada, el cineasta toma una posición estratégica que le permite crear una narración polifónica y subversiva que otorga un mayor grado de verosimilitud a la representación documental mediante el carácter testimonial de las enunciaciones.

Las distintas temporalidades ponen de manifiesto la disyunción del discurso hegemonial de la nación introduciendo el mito y el tiempo circular. Así la disociación de las temporalidades en las representaciones de la nación constituyen el efecto de diseminación de la nación, descrito por Bhabha. Esta puesta en escena del desdoblamiento de las temporalidades no es solamente una referencia al concepto de la heterogeneidad multitemporal, sino también es la inscripción en un momento discursivo paradójico de la narración de la nación, ya que propone una nación que pierde su origen en el mito.

La última imagen del documental, es precisamente la de un *travelling* aéreo de ocho minutos, al sobrevolar el segundo piso del Periférico ya terminado y lo que falta por terminar. "The history is told from the eye of the aeroplane which becomes that 'ornament' that holds the public and the private in suspense" afirma Bhabha ("Introduction" 6) y su afirmación coincide con estas últimas imágenes que imposibilitan ver, tanto el final de la obra, como decidir si se trata de una salida o de una entrada en la ciudad moderna. Recordando la metáfora de García Canclini, este final abierto es consecuente y concuerda con el tránsito interminable de entrar y salir de la modernidad. Finalmente es importante que no se trate de una obra cerrada, porque así significa la abstracción del proceso abierto y del cambio permanente de la ciudad. En este sentido, el documental adopta las características del proceso de la renegociación identitaria de la nación y del proceso de hibridación de la nación desde una perspectiva marginalizada: "La obra se propone como una estructura abierta que reproduce la ambigüedad de nuestro mismo ser-en-el-mundo; por lo menos tal como nos lo describen la ciencia, la filosofía, la psicología, la sociología" (Eco 322).

El documental es también el registro de un momento histórico de la Ciudad de México, la construcción del puente más grande y extenso hasta este momento, donde junto a él, los albañiles son las voces de la identidad de un México en busca de una modernidad utópica, de un país en construcción, en crecimiento, inacabado como el segundo piso del Periférico. Hecho que queda retenido y salvaguardado en la memoria colectiva, tal como lo explica Nichols en el primer párrafo del prefacio de su libro *Representing Reality*:

> Utilizing the capacities of sound recording and cinematography to reproduce the physical appearance of things, documentary film contributes to the formation of *popular memory* [la acentuación es nuestra]. It proposes perspectives on and interpretations of historic issues, processes, and events. (ix)

Este poder discursivo de que dispone la película documental, según Eitzen (cf. 414), puede ser reconocido en este filme ya que contribuye a la formación de la memoria del México contemporáneo haciendo evidentes las rupturas discursivas en el discurso de la nación. Al ser el retrato de la capital de la nación mexicana, ya su nombre –"*En el hoyo*"– advierte que se trata de una contra-narrativa, de una película que mina los discursos tradicionales.

Bibliografía

Alsedo, Quico. "Juan Carlos Rulfo y el México invisible." *El Mundo*, 14 de Mayo de 2007. http://www.elmundo.es/2007/05/14/cultura/2122785.html.

Anderson, Benedict. *Imagined Communities. Reflections on the Origin and Spread of Nationalism*. London: Verso, 1985.

Assmann, Jan. *Das kulturelle Gedächtnis*. München: Beck, 2000.

Barnouw, Erik. *Documentary. A History of the Non-Fiction Film*. Oxford: Oxford UP, 1983.

Bauman, Zygmunt. *Postmodernity and Its Discontents*. Cambridge: Polity P, 1997.

Bhabha, Homi K. "DissemiNation. Time, Narrative, and the Margins of the Modern Nation." *Nation and Narration*. Ed. Homi K. Bhabha. London: Routledge, 1990. 291-322.

———. "Introduction. Narrating the Nation." *Nation and Narration*. Ed. Homi K. Bhabha. London: Routledge, 1990. 1-7.

———, ed. *Nation and Narration*. London: Routledge, 1990.

———. *The Location of Culture*. London: Routledge, 1994.

Bourdieu, Pierre. "La identidad como representación." *La teoría y el análisis de la cultura*. Ed. Gilberto Giménez. Guadalajara: Universidad de Guadalajara, SEP, Comecso, 1987. 473-81.

Calcagno, Luciana. "Mientras tanto." *El Ángel Exterminador. Revista Digital de Cine* 1.2 (nov-dic 2006). http://www.elangelexterminador.com.ar/articulosnro.3/enelhoyo.html.

Campbell, Joseph. *El héroe de las mil caras. Psicoanálisis del mito.* México, D.F.: FCE, 1959.

Corzo, Hugo. "Realiza documental sobre segundo piso." *Reforma*, 15 de agosto de 2004. Página oficial de *En el hoyo.* http://www.enelhoyo.com.mx.

Durand, Gilbert. *Las estructuras antropológicas de lo imaginario.* Madrid: Taurus, 1981.

Eco, Umberto. *Sobre literatura.* Barcelona: RqueR, 2002.

Eitzen, Dirk. "Against the Ivory Tower. An Apologia for 'Popular' Historical Documentaries." *New Challenges for Documentary.* Ed. Allan Rosenthal and John Corner. Manchester: Manchester UP, 2005. 409-18.

Eliade, Mircea. *Aspectos del mito.* Barcelona: Paidós, 2000.

Espinosa de los Monteros, Silvina. "Fílmica hacía el Periférico." *La Revista.* Página oficial de *En el hoyo.* http://www.enelhoyo.com.mx.

Gamaliel, Luna. "Filma Juan Carlos Rulfo desde el segundo piso." *El Universal*, 21 de Agosto de 2004. http://www2.eluniversal.com.mx/pls/impreso/noticia.html?id_nota=240786&tabla=notas.

García Canclini, Néstor. *Culturas híbridas. Estrategias para entrar y salir de la modernidad.* México: Grijalbo, 1989.

———. *La globalización imaginada.* Buenos Aires: Paidós, 2005.

González, Mario. "El documentalista es un pata de perro." *La Opinión*, Torreón, Coahuila. Página oficial de *En el hoyo.* http://www.enelhoyo.com.mx.

Hall, Stuart. *Representation. Cultural Representations and Signifying Practices.* London: Sage, 2001.

"Juan Carlos capta la vida en un inmenso agujero en el D.F." *Rolling Stone.* Página oficial de *En el hoyo.* http://www.enelhoyo.com.mx.

"Juan Carlos Rulfo lleva la realidad de la clase obrera a la gran pantalla con *En el hoyo.*" *Gara*, 10 de mayo de 2007. http://www.gara.net/paperezkoa/20070510/17336/es/Juan/Carlos/Rulfo/lleva/realidad/¬clase/obrera/gran/pantalla/En/hoyo.

Jung, Gustav. *El hombre y sus símbolos.* Barcelona: Luis de Caralt, 1977.

Koehler, Robert. "*En el hoyo.*" *Variety.* Página oficial de *En el hoyo.* http://www.enelhoyo.com.mx.

Levi-Strauss, Claude. *Mito y significado.* Madrid: Alianza, 1987.

Link, Jürgen, Jochen Hörisch y Hans G. Pott. *Elementare Literatur und generative Diskursanalyse.* München: Fink, 1983.

Macarúa Sánchez, Sara. "Segundo piso del periférico En el hoyo." *Monitor.* Página oficial de *En el hoyo.* http://www.enelhoyo.com.mx.

Mardones, José María. *El retorno del mito.* Madrid: Síntesis, 2000.

Martín Barbero, Jesús. "Medios y culturas en el espacio latinoamericano." *Pensar Iberoamérica* 5 (enero-abril 2004). http://www.oei.es/pensariberoamerica/ric05a01.htm.

Nichols, Bill. *Representing Reality. Issues and Concepts in Documentary*. Bloomington: Indiana UP, 1991.

———. "The Voice of Documentary." *New Challenges for Documentary*. Ed. Allan Rosenthal and John Corner. Manchester: Manchester UP, 2005. 17-33.

Olivares, Juan José. "*En el hoyo*, película con un puente como personaje principal, dice Rulfo." *La Jornada*. Página oficial de *En el hoyo*. http://www.enelhoyo.com.mx.

Reguillo Cruz, Rossana. *En la calle otra vez. Las bandas: identidad urbana y usos de la comunicación*. Guadalajara: Iteso, 1995.

Rössner, Michael. *Auf der Suche nach dem verlorenen Paradies*. Bodenheim: Athenäum, 1988.

Sieber, Cornelia. *Die Gegenwart im Plural. Postmoderne, postkoloniale Strategien in neueren Lateinamerikadiskursen*. Frankfurt a.M.: Vervuert, 2005.

Signorelli, Amalia. "Clases dominantes y clases subalternas, el control del ecosistema urbano." *La teoría y el análisis de la cultura*. Ed. Gilberto Giménez. Guadalajara: Universidad de Guadalajara, SEP, Comecso, 1987. 329-43.

Toriz, Rafael. "Las ciudades, el lenguaje y la voz que las habita." *Antroposmoderno* (octubre 2007). www.antroposmoderno.com/antro-version-imprimir.php?id_articulo=1100.

Filmografía

En el hoyo. Dir. Juan Carlos Rulfo. México, 2006.

The Role of Documentaries in Redefining American Womanhood: From the Suffragette Movement to *War Zone* (1998)

BIRTE HORN

Resumen

En las últimas décadas, películas documentales han servido para atraer la atención de la audiencia hacia ciertos temas de índole social y cultural. Enfocando la temática de la nación y de la femineidad, podemos constatar que directoras y directores de películas feministas han recurrido cada vez más al género fílmico documental para negociar y redefinir el concepto de la femineidad en las diferentes etapas del movimiento feminista norteamericano. Este ensayo se propone dilucidar cómo películas documentales, en las últimas cinco décadas, han servido para afirmar y cuestionar el concepto de la femineidad en los EE.UU.

1. Introduction

Popular documentary films have been part of movie theater programs for quite some time now: Michael Moore, with his highly polemic films *Roger and Me* (1989), *Bowling for Columbine* (2002), *Fahrenheit 9/11* (2004)[1], or *Sicko* (2007); Morgan Spurlock, with an overdose of McDonald's in *Supersize Me* (2004); or environmental films such as Alastair Fothergill and Mark Linfield's *Earth* (2007). These big *docu-tainment* films illustrate some of the new paths that the documentary genre has recently taken. Even though there is not one particular form which documentary film necessarily uses (cf. Nichols, *Reality* 12), most documentary filmmakers have considerably smaller budgets available for their endeavors than creators of fiction films, and perhaps also less desire for special-effects entertainment. Their primary goal is documentation for the sake of making statements. To make a statement, to bring arguments before the viewer, and to negotiate a particular topic of social and/or cultural relevance is a common aim of the majority of documentaries. One such topic has been gender and

---

[1] For a critical examination of the film *Fahrenheit 9/11* see Stella Bruzzi's *New Documentary*, p. 176-182 as well as Wiebke Engel's essay in this collection.

the performance of gender. Over the past 40 to 50 years we can observe that documentary films, especially those by women filmmakers in the U.S., have made strong statements about the place and status of women in American society, correlating with larger social changes concerning sexuality and gender.

In this essay I am therefore going to look at how documentary films have been utilized to negotiate and redefine the term "womanhood" and its meaning in the United States. My main focus lies on the work of women filmmakers since the 1970s, as part of the feminist movement in the U.S. I am going to illustrate how documentaries have represented particular developments within the American feminist movement. The documentary films which will be mentioned should be regarded as an exemplary selection from a wide range of materials. After defining the term "womanhood" as it is used in this text, I will shortly discuss the unique qualities of documentary film before addressing some of the documentaries that were produced in the service of feminist movement in the Unites States. Focusing on a more recent example of a documentary narration of nation through a critical look at gender, I will study the film *War Zone* (1998) by Maggie Hadleigh-West in greater detail.

2. Womanhood

The term "womanhood" is rather abstract. Different communities at different times may understand this expression in any number of ways. As this essay is concerned mainly with women in the United States, with a particular focus on the film *War Zone*, which was produced towards the end of the 1990s, I will try to establish briefly how the concept of "womanhood" was discussed in the U.S. from the late 1980s to the early 2000s.

Womanhood has been defined as "an achieved status, and its criteria vary for different social groups" (Imamura 292). Some societies may see womanhood achieved only when a woman is caring for a husband and children, others value economic success and self-reliance (cf. Imamura 292). In 1995 anthropologist Gail Landsman stated that "no model of womanhood has dominance in American culture at present" (33). Landsman explains that in society and media motherhood and work life are presented as an insurmountable dichotomy. Apparently being a mother and committing to a workplace outside the home is a challenging concept which "evokes intense anxiety over the work ethic, family values, and notions of proper womanhood" (Brush 721). Arguments differ from those who support formal equality for men and women to those who insist on biological differences inexorably effecting socially diverging roles:

> Given the differences between men and women in reproductive biology and in socialization, gender-neutral laws inevitably lead to greater hardships for women. These policy positions are grounded in what have been viewed as competing ideological positions, often termed natural rights versus natural roles, or equality versus difference (Landsman 34).

Interestingly enough, both positions were supported by voices within the feminist movement at the time (34).

In the 1990s a number of studies about the relation between bodies, culture and subjectivity were published, many of them by feminist sociologists (cf. Dellinger/Williams, Lorber/Martin, McCaughey). All these works discuss how women "embody" gender, i.e. create meaning of their bodies and personalities through gender performance. Dellinger and Williams illustrated that women may bond over make-up and that make-up has the ability to make them feel both empowered and constrained. McCaughey observes how some women have learned to challenge concepts of the "weaker sex" in self-defense classes which make them "feel more assertive and confident in their everyday lives" (Schrock/Reid/Boyd 318). One significant aspect of gender embodiment is formed by women's expectations of how they are seen and appraised by men. A 2002 study by Gagnd and McCaughey shows that women who underwent cosmetic surgery "view themselves through the male gaze and feel more confident and liberated as their bodies become more palatable to the patriarchal imagination (qtd. in Schrock/Reid/Boyd 318) In conclusion, we can only affirm that womanhood, as much as gender, is a dynamic term and depends on performance and subjective assessment. However, the wide range of views and angles makes the idea of womanhood a topic which lends itself to close scrutiny—also in documentary films.

3. Documentary Films

Much like the definition of "womanhood" is a dynamic and shifting process, the genre of documentary film evades clear and easy categorization. As Bill Nichols succinctly puts it:

> Documentary as a concept or practice occupies no fixed territory. It mobilizes no finite inventory of techniques, addresses no set number of issues, and adopts no completely known taxonomy of forms, styles, or modes. The term documentary must itself be constructed in much the same manner as the world we know and share. Documentary film practice is the site of contestation and change. (*Reality* 12)

Even though documentary film may take any form or shape, and we should be aware that "elements of style, structure, and expositional strategy draw upon pre-existent constructs, or schemas, to establish meaning and effects for audiences" (Renov 3), the average viewer may still perceive a documentary film as "closer to the truth" than a fiction film. At the very least, viewers often "expect that what occurred in front of the camera has undergone little or no modification in order to be recorded on film and magnetic tape" (Nichols, *Reality* 27). Other scholars expect the audience to be more aware of the problematic "truth claim" or of the alleged "factual representation" of documentary film and knowledgeable about filmic productions and thus approach the genre in a more critical manner:

> The spectator is not in need of signposts and inverted commas to understand that a documentary is a negotiation between reality on the one hand and image, interpretation

and bias on the other. Documentary is predicated upon a dialectical relationship between aspiration and potential, that the text itself reveals the tensions between the documentary pursuit of the most authentic mode of factual representation and the impossibility of this aim. (Bruzzi 6-7)

In the early 1990s Bill Nichols identified four distinct modes of documentary film: expository, observational, interactive, and reflexive (cf. Nichols, *Reality* 33 ff.) Since then he has added the performative mode and the poetic mode to his roster (cf. Nichols, *Introduction* 99 ff.) These modes, according to Nichols, stand out as "the dominant organizational patterns around which most texts are structured" (*Reality* 32). At the same time Nichols uses his documentary modes to present a certain chronological development inherent in the documentary tradition. In the poetic mode the filmmaker represents the topic of his/her film in a very subjective manner. Exemplary for this method are filmmakers of the Soviet montage theory (cf. Eisenstein/Leda 38 ff.) during the 1910s and 1920s. The expository mode of documentary usually shows images which are explained, and, in most cases, evaluated, by an off-screen narrator. Here, the voice provides an argument and the images support this view (cf. Nichols, *Reality* 34). In the late 1950s, Nichols suggests, filmmakers began to focus more on the "social actors" in a film. The filmmaker enters the picture (sometimes quite literally) and may serve as a "mentor, participant, prosecutor, or provocateur in relation to the social actors recruited to the film" (Nichols, *Reality* 44). At times we can even find films that are very specifically about the interaction with the social actors and the historical world. The result is that "the text leads less to an argument about the world than to a statement about the interactions themselves and what they disclose about filmmaker and social actors alike" (Nichols, *Reality* 45). In the context of the film *War Zone*, which is going to be discussed in greater detail below, this interactive mode of documentary film, is of particular significance.

Reflecting on his/her own work, the filmmaker may use meta-commentary, i.e. speaking to the audience about "the process of representation itself" (Nichols, *Reality* 56) when immersed in the reflexive mode. Seeing this mode of creating documentary films as yet a further development in social and cultural issues, we can determine certain aspects similar to literary post-modernism: the self-reflexivity of the author and the questioning of the medium (Nichols, *Reality* 60). The last mode Nichols has introduced so far is the performative mode. Again, steeped in post-modern aesthetics, this mode breaks with conventional methods:

> In short, the performative documentary breaks from traditions of empirical evidence, accepted conventions of representing "reality" and classical narratives structuring the elaboration of the filmic text. The performative documentary eschews empiricism, realism, and narrative. Instead it favours an aesthetico-temporal structure of associated but fragmentary filmic events. These events are clustered around the subjectively perceived citizenship, and both collective and individual memory. Through its expressive qualities, the performative documentary rejects any preoccupation with ontology as empirical thinking imagines it. It re-frames the profilmic event as phenomena subjectively perceived, weaving fragments of representation into an aesthetic response of knowledge and rhetorical truth (Craig).

Nichols's modes of documentary have met with some criticism. Bruzzi notes that "his categories are often—and increasingly—defined negatively, that is in terms of what they do *not* as opposed to *do* represent" (3). Renov sees documentary not necessarily as an opposition to fictional films but argues that "documentary shares the status of all discursive forms with regard to its topic or figurative character and that it employs many of the methods and devices of its fictional counterpart" (3). I agree that Nichols's taxonomy seems at times too limiting and at others arbitrary. Nevertheless, the illustration of elements which are unique to particular styles and times can be helpful in the analysis of a documentary film. Thus I will come back to some of Nichols's observations in the following chapter about womanhood, feminism and documentaries.

4. Feminism and Documentary Films

Feminism has swept the world—and especially the United States—in a series of waves.[2] The first wave was represented by the suffragette movement of the late 19th and the early 20th century, fighting for women's civil and legal rights with a strong focus on the right to vote, which was eventually granted on a national basis in 1920 (cf. Wheeler). The suffragettes battled for political emancipation while still caring for their home and family. Documentary films of that time are hard to find, especially as the concept of "documentary," as we understand it today, did not exist. Some British and a few American newsreel documents of the suffragette movement have survived from the times of the nickelodeon, which are nowadays of historical and cultural importance, concerning the earliest feminist movement in the United Stats. Though the nickelodeon materials consist mainly of fiction films aimed at entertaining their audience, these documents still yield information on social and cultural issues such as sexual politics, power struggles, and the shift of social values as seen by the movie makers.

Historian and writer Kay Sloane has retrieved a number of films from the early 1910s dealing with suffragettes and their movement. Her 35-minute documentary *Suffragettes in the Silent Cinema* introduces different points of view on the social and media context of the early suffragette movement in the United States. Among the films Sloane examines is the 1913 U.S. production *What 80 Million Women Want*. Filmed in New York, the movie follows one of the leaders of the British suffragette movement, Emmeline Pankhurst, on a lecture tour of America in October 1913, making a strong point for the vote for women (cf. Crawford 221). Even though the suffrage movement

---

[2] For a more detailed overview of the development of feminism, see Jennifer Mather Saul's book *Feminism* or the collection of critical essays on feminism and literary theory, *Feminism: Critical Concepts in Literary and Cultural Studies* by Mary Evans. A critical reappraisal of most recent developments in feminism can be found in Natasha Campo's *From Superwomen to Domestic Goddesses: The Rise and Fall of Feminism*.

was taken up as a subject primarily in fiction film, the struggle was nevertheless a public one and it was using film in its early days as a tool to reach a wide audience.

5. The Second Wave

In the 1960s, a time of turmoil and civil rights battles all across the United States, the feminist movement entered what has been called the second wave. Like their suffragist predecessors, women once again started to question gender roles and traditional value systems on which they had been brought up. Encouraged by an atmosphere of change, many women felt the need to liberate themselves from stereotypes; they demanded independence from men in general. Whereas before and even during the 1960s, issues considered to be women's issues, such as birth control or abortion, were mainly discussed by men[3], towards the middle of the decade more women began to demand agency in their own lives. Womanhood was no longer to be a term which referred primarily to the family sphere and little outside of it, but it included work life, social engagement, and gender equality. On a much broader basis than the suffragettes, women from the late 1950s to the early 1980s were concerned with issues such as economic gender equality and the rights of female minorities, i.e. African-American, Asian or Latina women.[4] Political action was the central instrument tied to radical plans of changing the nation to create a better life for women. Largely united by a strong sense of community, feminists of the second wave often pursued their goals with an aggressive purpose that frightened conservatives. Women spoke up and were noticed. They

> questioned nearly everything, transformed much of American culture, expanded the idea of democracy by insisting that equality had to include the realities of its women citizens and catapulted women's issues onto a global stage. Their greatest accomplishment was to change the terms of debate, so that women mattered. (Rosen 3)

In tune with the radical mood of the 1960s and 1970s, feminist documentary films of that time were often highly political. Tracing back their roots to anti-war organizations, women filmmakers began to make "self-consciously feminist films, and other women began to learn filmmaking specifically to contribute to the movement" (Lesage 222). The format of many of these films was relatively straightforward. Influenced by *cinéma vérité*, i.e. with as little manipulation by the filmmaker as pos-

---

[3] Public television echoes some of the issues which were publicly debated at the time. CBS's *Birth Control and the Law* (1962), and *Abortion and the Law* (1965) deal with the topic at hand in an extremely conservative manner. Male reporters focus on the moral, social, legal, and psychological aspects of birth control and abortion. In both productions clergymen, lawyers, and physicians (all male) are interviewed, who, not surprisingly, oppose birth control and abortion. Women, who have to cope with problems of birth control, abortion or childrearing are hardly to be seen anywhere in these television debates.

[4] A closer examination of feminist struggles by diverse ethnic groups at that time appears in Benita Roth's book *Separate Roads to Feminism: Black, Chicana, and White Feminist Movements in America's Second Wave*.

sible, documentaries were often set up as interviews with women or as observations of their interactions with regard to a particular topic. *Growing Up Female* (1971) by Julia Reichert and Jim Klein, for example, looks at the socialization of American women. Six girls and women between the ages of four and thirty-five, of various ethnic and class backgrounds, talk about what and who influences their self-perception as women in the United States. One focus for women documentary filmmakers was the collective struggle towards emancipation and equality. Films such as *The Woman's Film* (1971) by the women of San Francisco Newsreel, or Margaret Lazarus and Renner Wunderlich's *Taking Our Bodies Back: The Women's Health Care Movement* display female agency aimed at raising the consciousness of the, presumably primarily female, audience and at offering a safe platform for discourse. In *The Woman's Film* women talk about their preconceptions of marriage and the reality of their married lives, about childrearing as well as employment inside and outside the home, and about their husbands' expectations concerning their roles as wives. *Taking Our Bodies Back* observes women acknowledging and demanding their rights concerning healthcare. The film addresses a wide range of issues, such as self-help, birth at home, abortion, breast cancer research, gynecological examinations, the attitudes of pharmaceutical companies, hysterectomy, and healthcare for women of color. Violence against women becomes a topic for women filmmakers as well. JoAnn Elam's film *Rape* (1975) brings together—in an environment that is entirely void of standard patriarchal discourse—women who had experienced sexual violence. Elam's film is also highly interesting in terms of form:

> Coming out of an experimental film tradition, Elam uses both Brechtian intertitles and a symbolic iconography intercut with a video transfer of a conversation she taped with rape victims one night in one of the women's apartment. The women's conversation forms the sound track of the film, and Elam both heightens and comments wittily on their points by repeating some of their lines in the intertitles. The film is an angry one that elaborates a whole new filmy style adequate to treating the subject of rape with neither titillation nor pathos. The women filmed are impassioned and intellectual. They are discussing their experiences with the group's support and within the security of domestic space; most of them are political activists in organizations against rape, and all saw the making of this film as an explicitly public act. (Lesage 235)

Considering Nichols's modes of documentary film it is rather obvious that, depending on the individual background of the filmmaker, the techniques and modes within a documentary film may vary widely within one and the same period of time.

Reactions to the sometimes rather aggressive stance of women filmmakers and their outcry for equality also came in the form of documentary films. In 1978 ABC aired a program called *Men Under Siege: Life with the Modern Woman* in its *Close-Up* series. Here men talk about how the changing roles of women in the United States affect them in various areas of life, such as work, sexual relations, marriage and family life. The show reflects on how new, and, often enough, uncomfortable, duties and responsibilities have produced both anxiety and transformations in the life of American men. Both the documentaries by women filmmakers, as well as responses such as

Men Under Siege reveal the challenging process of social and cultural change in the United States during the 1960s and 1970s and thus participate in the narration of nation. However, women and ethnic minorities were not the only groups clamoring for recognition and better treatment. Entwined with the feminist movement of the 1970s, lesbian women demanded a public place and acceptance in the new social structures of the nation. As documentary film was one of the tools for feminist and lesbian filmmakers to gain acknowledgement, I would like to offer a short excursion into lesbian documentaries during the feminist second wave in the United States.

6. Feminists, Lesbians, and the Queer Movement

Second-wave feminists were the first to openly recognize and include lesbian women within the movement. However, the relationship between lesbians and heterosexually oriented feminist groups was not always easy and free from stereotypes, as "feminists sometimes feared that lesbian-feminists would stigmatize the whole women's movement as being made up of 'nothing but a bunch of man-hating dykes'" (Faderman, *Odd Girls* 209).[5] Even within the lesbian community a diversity of groups made for difficult progress:

> Lesbian-feminists were especially critical of what they saw as the superficiality of the 'liberal' feminist and gay demands for social change. They attempted to educate the older groups. For example, they exhorted feminists to become lesbians and lesbians were told they must become feminists in order to aid the battle against male supremacy (Faderman 209-10).

Not surprisingly, a number of lesbian feminists felt betrayed and rejected by straight women and vice versa. As lesbian and gay documentary films began to appear[6] in the early 1970s, the visibility of these groups increased in the public discourse. Though the first documentaries from this movement are very much male-oriented, women filmmakers have since then contributed numerous works to this field. Today the Queer Community, or perhaps better the numerous glbt[7] communities, consider documentary films as an important instrument to

> resurrect historical memory and to permit the marginalized to bear witness as well as to build an image base that reflects our diversity and counters the distorted and misleading representations. Documentary film is an indispensable media [sic!] for the glbtq community to re-evaluate and reposition ourselves in different contexts (Bartone).

[5] These trends are also observed in the development of gay and lesbian communities in Los Angeles in: Faderman and Timmons, *Gay L.A: A History of Sexual Outlaws, Power Politics, and Lipstick Lesbians*.

[6] See for example Ken Robinson's *Some of Our Best Friends* (1971), followed by Arthur Bressan's *Gay U.S.A.* (1977) and Peter Adair's *Word Is Out* (1977). For an introduction to glbtq documentaries, see Bartone; Holmlund/Fuchs.

[7] *Glbt*, or sometimes *lgbt*, is the commonly used abbreviation for gay, lesbian, bisexual, transgender, and queer.

Queer documentary films have increased in number, especially since the 1990s, confronting society with a variety of topics. Some examples are Greta Schiller and Robert Rosenberg's *Before Stonewall: The Making of a Gay and Lesbian Community* (1984), Debra Chasnoff's *It's Elementary: Talking About Gay Issues in School* (1996), and Meema Spadola's *Our House: A Very Real Documentary about Kids of Gay and Lesbian Families* (1999). These films have helped not only to increase visibility of queerness in the United States but also to challenge existing definitions of sexuality and gender performance in American society. Once more expanding the definition of womanhood, lesbian women, their families, social lives and self-determination must also be subsumed under this term. The growth of lgbt communities and their public acknowledgement are representative of a more general trend in American society, and American feminism in particular: a growing diversity within social and cultural discourses.

7. The Third Wave

With the radicalism of the 1970s abating, the mid-1980s saw the advent of the so-called third wave of feminism. First used by feminist groups concentrating on multiracial aspects of feminism (cf. Drake 99), it quickly developed into a term encompassing young women from a wide range of backgrounds with an equally wide range of ideas and aims.

American feminism had reached a point where an emphasis on diversity had taken the place of the strong sense of a communal effort that had driven feminists only a decade before. As much as American society was in a process of diversification, so was the feminist movement. Documentary films of that period reflect these shifts very well. The range of topics women and feminist filmmakers dealt with expanded exponentially. Some films dealt with the struggles of defining womanhood in the modern world such as *She's Nobody's Baby: American Women in the 20th Century* (1981), while others presented the struggle between motherhood and work-life in the professional and corporate world of men, e.g. *Windows on Women* (1985), or showed the problems of single mothers, e.g. *And Baby Makes Two* (1983).

Yet another development in terms of gender performance occurred with regard to the female body. Women showing physical strength began to appear in film and television, for example the character of Ripley in the *Alien* (1979ff.) movies. For the first time a female action hero "demonstrated that women did not have to look as though they stepped directly from a beauty parlor when they battled foes" (Innes 3). The documentary film *Pumping Iron II: The Women* discussed a variety of perceptions of the female body. Whereas *Pumping Iron* (1977) had celebrated the physique of male bodybuilders, most prominent among them the young Arnold Schwarzenegger, *Pumping Iron II: The Women* follows four women as they prepare for the 1983 Caesar's Palace World Cup Championship. The film concentrates on the tight regimen the women put on themselves in order to achieve their vision of a perfect female body. Even though bodybuilding was not as popular as baseball or football, the film

Pumping Iron II: The Women does hint at the world of sports recognizing a change in agency, as women extend the definitions of what it means to be "feminine."

Feminists of the third wave have often been criticized by those of the second wave for being supposedly extremely self-centered, only interested in individual gain and failing to consider what, or who, came before them, who else may be concerned in the present, or what long-term goals should be pursued (cf. Drake 98). At a 2002 conference at Barnard College in New York, feminists of both generations came together to discuss women's rights since the 1960s. Veteran feminist Letty Cottin Pogrebin said about the work of her generation: "We were action-oriented in a public context. We had to challenge laws, change patterns, alter behavior" (qtd. in Friedlin). Other participants focused on more positive developments achieved by the feminist movement: "We changed society. Without *Fear of Flying* there would be no *Sex in the City*. My daughter wouldn't feel empowered" (qtd. in Friedlin). Nevertheless, second wave feminists have passed a severe verdict on the women profiting from their work; as Erica Jong put it: "We have produced a generation of uppity women who feel entitled" (qtd. in Friedlin).

Women of the third wave grew up during a time when feminism had already become an integral part of society. They grew up with a "sense of entitlement feminism made possible" (Drake 99). Though gender equality has not been reached entirely even today, the theoretical and legal background has largely been established. For third-wave feminists, laws against sexual harassment or rape, the possibility of legal abortion in every state, or the theoretical entitlement to pursue any job they want have always been part of their lives. As Findlen writes in the introduction to *Listen Up: Voices from the Next Feminist Generation*:

> We are the first generation for whom feminism has been entwined in the fabric of our lives. … Maybe not as unified as the generation that preceded us. Maybe we're just not as categorizable. … So what may appear to be a splintering of this generation comes from an honest assessment of our differences as each of us defines her place and role in feminism. We are determined, as Sonja D. Curry-Johnson writes, "to bring our whole selves to the table." (xii-xiv)

While one could argue that second-wave feminism was a particularly radical force and that it is fairly easy to put a finger on who the participants were and what their aims were, it is extremely difficult to do the same for third-wave feminism. Perhaps the best way to define third-wave feminism is to emphasize the variety of issues and participants as a unifying factor:

> Even as different strains of feminism and activism sometimes directly contradict each other, they are all part of our Third Wave lives, our thinking, and our praxes: we are products of all the contradictory definitions of and differences within feminism, beasts of such a hybrid kind that perhaps we need a different name altogether. (Heywood/Drake 3)

The world in which the third wave moves is certainly different from the one the second wave fought in. Therefore we need to analyze issues such as gender performance, the female body, sexuality and sexual orientation, single mothers, work life, etc. in a context of contemporary society and politics. The diversity of third wave feminism is echoed in the topics chosen by the filmmakers of the 1990s and early 2000s, as they narrate the U.S. American nation with a focus on gender.

Self-esteem, sexuality, and normative beauty are some of the most widely discussed topics. *Girls Like Us* (1997) explores experiences of teenage sexuality and pregnancy, and *Growing Up With the Self Image of American Girls* (1998) addresses self-awareness and lifestyles, as well as observing what others expect of girls in that age group. *Beautopia* (1998) exemplifies the questioning of ideals of beauty in the world of supermodels such as Elle MacPherson and Claudia Schiffer. However, beauty and identity formation does not only concern white middle- and upper-class women. In *Lockin' Up* (1997), the Jamaican-born filmmaker T. Nicole Atkinson looks at beauty from a particular ethnic background. In a similar vein, *Nappy* (1997) portrays African Americans talking about why they have chosen to stop straightening their hair and go 'natural.'

A significant number of films deal with ethnic minorities and their economic exploitation in a society still dominated by white Americans. *Maid in America* (2005), for example, addresses the vast number of Latina immigrants working as housekeepers and nannies in Los Angeles, and *Behind the Labels* (2001) portrays Chinese and Filipina women who pay high fees to work in garment factories on the Pacific island of Saipan, the only U.S. territory exempt from U.S. labor and immigration laws.

The growing discussion of gender, gender performance, sexuality, and sexual orientation is represented in numerous documentary productions. In *Cancer in Two Voices* (1994), audiences may glimpse into the lives of two lesbian women, one of whom is diagnosed with fatal breast cancer. *In My Father's Church* (2004) addresses the conflict of gay marriage and Christian faith. Here, a young lesbian woman is set on getting married to her partner in the town's United Methodist church of which her father is the pastor. The film presents the women's struggle for acceptance by the church and its community as well as the troubled relationship of religion and homosexuality in a very frank and sympathetic fashion. A further example of this group of films is the sensitive portrayal of a female-to-male gender identity transition over a period of 15 months in *Sir: Just a Normal Guy* (2003).

As we have seen, the relationship of documentary film and feminism has gone through a number of significant changes over the past decades. Women's documentaries of the 1970s confronted a variety of areas radically challenging male domination, both in public and in private life. Nevertheless, the value attributed to documentaries addressing these issues was often minimal (cf. Erhart, esp. pages 10-13). During the 1980s and 1990s the work of women filmmakers dealing with gender issues in documentaries changed substantially and became less obscure. No longer was the collective struggle, the leftist-activist fight for equal rights, a priority. Now issues such as individual feminism, race, and gender became the center of attention. The numerous forms of relationships among women and alternative forms of women's agency were and are topics for the work of women filmmakers. The term "womanhood" has never been as ambiguous and as varied as in the past 20 years, and it is likely to become even more polysemous as feminism itself stretches to encompass ever wider definitions of what it means to be a woman.

The documentary films mentioned above use voice-over narration, interviews, and uncommented observational footage. If we tried to adopt Nichols's modes of documentary film to these productions, we would have to acknowledge that most films include technical and aesthetic features of different modes, be it poetical, expository or interactive. We should consider these modes to be a variety of possible styles of documentary films; however, a chronological development should not be assumed.

Consequently, both in terms of issues addressed, and technique, it is almost impossible to categorize a documentary film as belonging to the second or third wave movement, and perhaps we should try to overcome the tendency to classify a film as belonging to the one or the other. Jennifer Drake suggested a different approach to feminism and feminist issues:

> I'm also uncomfortable using concepts like "the Second and Third Waves" or "feminist generations" as the only way to organize current feminist debates. Conversations that invoke these terms do point to real generational differences, but the "wave" metaphor also emphasizes continuities within feminist thought and action and acknowledges differences within feminist movements. Rather than thinking of feminist generations or waves only in terms of an age-based mother/daughter, teacher/student divide—more binary thinking—it seems productive to consider how these terms suggest feminist movements understood as changing, informed by particular locations, and specific struggles. (Drake 98)

One example of understanding feminist issues as a concern connected to particular times, places, or topics is Maggie Hadleigh-West's 1998 documentary film *War Zone*.

8. Maggie Hadleigh-West's *War Zone* (1998)

Maggie Hadleigh-West's *War Zone* is not the first film to deal with the sexual harassment of women on public streets. As early as 1977, experimental filmmaker Sheila Paige produced the short documentary *A Film on Street Harassment*. Paige's film is "a multi-phase investigation: how women feel about verbal harassment by men" (The Filmmakers' Cooperative).[8] Thus, *War Zone* is an example of the continuity of issues within the feminist movement, further supporting the notion that a strict categorization of the American feminist movement along generational lines is neither possible nor very useful. Hadleigh-West, for example, deals with a topic which concerns American womanhood as a whole, i.e. a communal struggle, reminiscent of the subject matter of

---

[8] Unfortunately, I was not able to obtain that film in order to make a more detailed comparison between Hadleigh-West's and Paige's documentaries, however, I think it is still interesting to note that the issue of verbal harassment of women is as much a topic in 1998 as it was a decade earlier.

second-wave feminists. She also displays some aggression in her approach to the topic, even though this feeling stems less from a political, but more from a personal attitude. Furthermore, this aggressiveness could as well be read as a sign for a typical third-wave feminist, used to the discourse and praxis of equal rights for any gender. But, no matter which generation of feminists, if any, the filmmaker might belong to, the most important aspect of her documentary is its influence upon the discourse of renegotiating images of American womanhood in the context of national identity.

The 'war zone' into which Hadleigh-West ventures, along with her audience, consists of the sidewalks of several major cities in the United States. The combatants are, on the one hand, Hadleigh-West herself, and, on the other, men who engage in sexually infused comments, wolf-whistling or simply staring. According to Hadleigh-West's website, *War Zone* is about "sex, power and what happens when men—either knowingly or unknowingly—threaten a woman's right to walk undisturbed on the streets" (YoMaggie).

By going out on the street, capturing and commenting on her experiences, Maggie Hadleigh-West speaks out against a certain type of behavior in her own culture that she finds offensive. In most Western societies it is quite common for men to 'check out' a woman in the streets, make comments and innuendos, whereas the woman, in most cases, whether flattered or not, is supposed to ignore these remarks. Hadleigh-West calls this social practice "street abuse" (cf. Oppenheimer 1). Even though one might argue that there is a difference between a man "only" looking at a woman's physique or actually commenting on it, be it in a complimentary or in a ridiculing fashion, the filmmaker herself sees little difference: "Men who look at my ass or breasts, make comments or make kissing noises cause me to feel creepy and self-conscious. It's still sexual" (Oppenheimer 3). Hadleigh-West's aim is to empower women in general, beginning with herself: "This film is my way of taking back the streets, letting men know that it is not okay to treat me like a piece of meat, or to treat any other woman that way" (Hadleigh-West, qtd. in FilmForum). Recommendable as that aim may be, we need to be aware of the fact that Hadleigh-West's film is highly subjective and that she is not representative of the whole of American womanhood. Having said that, however, it is very much her attitude, her point of view and her head-on approach that make Hadleigh-West's film so powerful and so attractive for a wide audience.

The way she set up her film is simple and straightforward. She armed herself with a handheld Super-8 camera and a microphone[9] and walked down various sidewalks in New York City, San Francisco, Chicago, and New Orleans, dressed in a light, black summer dress, and black leggings, ready to confront any man making suggestive remarks or caught staring. Sleeveless, the dress featured a substantial cleavage as well as large areas of bare skin on Hadleigh-West's back. We can assume that the filmmaker chose this dress to make sure she was attracting attention to provide her with ample material in terms of looks and comments.

---

[9] For more detail on the technical equipment as well as on the set-up on the streets, cf. Jean Oppenheimer at http://www.theasc.com/protect/jan99/hassle/pg1.htm.

Two other cinematographers accompanied Hadleigh-West: Eileen Schreiber, who usually stayed a few feet behind her, and Todd Lieber, who kept a camera on Hadleigh-West from across the street. Both cameras would be ready to zoom in on any action as it happened. It was important for the filmmaker to have at least one other female camera operator with her, because "street abuse is so subtle. It's the kind of thing men aren't particularly familiar with, so I wanted another woman's perspective. She would be able to see it more readily than a man" (Oppenheimer 4).

The reactions of the men who saw themselves confronted by Hadleigh-West varied. While many felt embarrassed and several tried to run away (with the filmmaker enthusiastically chasing after them), some became violent, pursued Hadleigh-West and/or physically assaulted her. Others tried to grab the microphone or knock the microphone and/or the camera away. One man actually smashed the camera into the filmmaker's head, while another hit her with his fist. While violence should not be excused, we have to consider that Hadleigh-West readily invaded people's private space, followed men around to extort comments and obviously enjoyed her provocative role in the film.

However, the film is not simply a 76-minute accumulation of men being confronted on the streets. Hadleigh-West positions street interviews, stationary interviews with women from all over the country, voice-over narration, POV shots filmed by herself, and footage of the two other cameras, next to each other, throughout the film, thereby giving *War Zone* a very distinct individual voice. If we were to apply Nichols's terms of documentary modes, we would most probably situate Hadleigh-West's film in the interactive category. As the whole film is very much about the confrontation between Hadleigh-West and the men on the streets, *War Zone* is a good example of the interactive mode. However, the film includes voice-over narration and other techniques which, according to Nichols, would belong to other modes.

Combining observation and active participation, the filmmaker takes the audience with her onto the streets, inviting the viewer to experience the day-to-day sexism she encounters 'first hand.' Through narration and interviews Hadleigh-West's film is politically reflexive and calls social conventions into question. While women have often been given the part of the 'victim' in documentaries, Hadleigh-West consciously claims agency in her film. Though she has been criticized for the aggressiveness with which she confronts the men in the streets, almost to the point of bullying them, in doing so she successfully turns the table on the macho behavior that is generally taken for granted and that she seeks to challenge. At the same time she presents an image of a strong woman taking charge, turning away from the idea of women as the 'suffering' or 'weaker' sex. Personally and actively putting herself in the midst of addressing social issues, Hadleigh-West discloses her agenda:

> This is a film that I believe will speak to women in a very personal way. But it is also a film for men—men who understand that just because they know they can get away with street abuse, doesn't mean they have the right to do it. It's a film that will awaken men to the experience of women. A film that can ultimately participate in the liberation of men. Liberating them from antiquated ideas of masculinity and bring them into the

millennium with a more genuine and individual definition of manhood. (Hadleigh-West, qtd. in FilmForum)

Whether or not Hadleigh-West has been or will be successful in enlightening men about the experiences of women on public streets is debatable. Another problem is that the filmmaker can hardly be considered representative of the majority of women in the United States. Nor will most women approach the streets in such a provocative manner. Nevertheless, by vigorously confronting a particular form of discrimination against women in contemporary society, Hadleigh-West offers her audience the opportunity to rethink notions of the roles and acceptable behavior of women and men concerning this particular issue of American womanhood and Western culture. How successful and valuable *War Zone* is considered to be by the U.S. government becomes clear when we see that since 2002 Hadleigh-West's film was used as an educational tool of the Department of Defense to introduce all branches of the military to issues of sexism, sexual harassment and sexual assault (cf. YoMaggie).

9. Conclusion

Beginning with the earliest moving images of the suffragette movement and developing into widely varying artistic representation of issues of social and/or cultural relevance for women, documentary film has been an important medium to illustrate the diversity and advances of political and personal definitions of womanhood in the U.S. over the past 100 years. The understanding of womanhood has expanded from the image of a woman as wife and mother, to the acknowledgement of her freedom of choice regarding motherhood, work-life, sexual orientation, etc. Women in the United States have changed the public notion of what it means to be a woman. Documentary films have accompanied the feminists' struggle throughout the decades, challenging traditional gender roles and propagating freedom and self-determination for all women. They have engaged in the narration of nation from a distinctly gendered point of view. Public debates—from the right to vote to street harassment to changing one's gender—are dealt with in documentary film, both documenting the issues and influencing public opinion. The film *War Zone* is a good example of a documentary through which a woman filmmaker wishes not only to demonstrate behavior which she deems to be discriminatory but also to change male attitudes.

Works Cited

Bartone, Richard C. "Documentary Film." *glbtq: An Encyclopedia of Gay, Lesbian, Bisexual, Transgender, and Queer Culture.* Ed. Claude J. Summers. Chicago, 2002. http://www.glbtq.com/art/documentary_film.html.

Baumgardner, Jennifer, and Amy Richards. *Manifesta: Young Women, Feminism, and the Future.* New York: Farrar, Straus, Giroux, 2000.

Brush, Lisa D. "Worthy Widows, Welfare Cheats: Proper Womanhood in Expert Needs Talk about Single Mothers in the United States, 1900 to 1988." *Gender and Society* 11 (Dec. 1997): 720-46.

Bruzzi, Stella. *New Documentary: A Critical Introduction*. Second ed. London: Routledge, 2006.

Campo, Natasha. *From Superwomen to Domestic Goddesses: The Rise and Fall of Feminism*. Bern: Peter Lang Publishing, 2009.

Craig, Robert Carl. "Phil Hoffman—Passing Through/Torn Formations and the Performative Documentary." http://www.horschamp.qc.ca/new_offscreen/phil_hoffman.html.

Crawford, Elizabeth. *The Women's Suffrage Movement: A Reference Guide, 1866-1928*. 1999. London: Routledge, 2001.

Dellinger, Kirsten, and Christine L. Williams. "Makeup at Work: Negotiating Appearance Rules in the Workplace." *Gender & Society* 11 (Dec. 1997):151-77.

Drake, Jennifer. "Review Essay: Third Wave Feminism." *Feminist Studies* 23.1 (1997): 97-108.

Eisenstein, Sergei, and Jay Leda. *Film Form: Essays in Film Theory*. New York: Harcourt, Brace, 1959.

Erhart, Julia. "Performing Memory: Compensation and Redress in Contemporary Feminist First-Person Documentary." *Screening the Past*. http://www.latrobe.edu.au/screeningthe past/firstrelease/fr1201/jefr13a.htm.

Evans, Mary, ed. *Feminism: Critical Concepts in Literary and Cultural Studies*. London: Routledge, 2001.

Faderman, Lillian. *Odd Girls and Twilight Lovers*. New York: Penguin Books, 1991.

———, and Stuart Timmons. *Gay L.A.: A History of Sexual Outlaws, Power Politics, and Lipstick Lesbians*. New York: Basic Books, 2006.

Film Forum. http://www.filmforum.org/archivedfilms/warzone.html.

Filmmakers' Cooperative, The. http://www.film-makerscoop.com/-

Findlen, Barbara. *Listen Up: Voices from the Next Feminist Generation*. Seattle: Seattle P, 1995.

Friedlin, Jennifer. "Second and Third Wave Feminists Clash Over the Future." *Women's eNews* 26 May 2002. http://www.womensenews.org/article.cfm/dyn/aid/920/context/cover.

Heywood, Leslie, and Jennifer Drake, eds. *Third Wave Agenda: Being Feminist, Doing Feminism*. Minneapolis: U of Minnesota P, 1997.

Holmlund, Chris, and Cynthia Fuchs, eds. *Between the Sheets, in the Streets: Queer, Lesbian, Gay Documentary*. Minneapolis: U of Minnesota P, 1997.

Imamura, Anne E. "The Loss That Has No Name: Social Womanhood of Foreign Wives." *Gender and Society* 2 (Special Issue, Sept. 1988): 291-307.

Inness, Sherrie A. *Action Chicks: New Images of Tough Women in Popular Culture*. New York: Palgrave Macmillan, 2004.

Landsman, Gail. "Negotiating Work and Womanhood." *American Anthropologist*. New Series 97 (Mar. 1995): 33-40.

Lesage, Julia. "The Political Aesthetics of the Feminist Documentary Film." *Issues in Feminist Film Criticism*. Ed. Patricia Erens. Bloomington: Indiana UP, 1990. 222-237.

Lorber, Judith, and Patricia Yancey Martin. "The Socially Constructed Body: Insights from Feminist Theory." *Illuminating Social Life*. Ed. Peter Kivisto. Thousand Oaks, CA: Pine Forge Press, 1998. 183-206.

McCaughey, Martha. "The Fighting Spirit: Women's Self-defense Training and the Discourse of Sexed Embodiment." *Gender & Society* 12 (Mar. 1998): 277-300.

Media Resource Center, University of California, Berkeley. "Documentary Classics." http://www.lib.berkeley.edu/MRC/documentaryclassics.html.

Mulvey, Laura. "Visual Pleasure and Narrative Cinema." *Visual and Other Pleasure*. Ed. Laura Mulvey. Bloomington: Indiana UP, 1989. 14-28.

Nichols, Bill. *Introduction to Documentary*. Bloomington and Indianapolis: Indiana UP, 2001.

———. *Representing Reality*. Bloomington: Indiana UP, 2002.

Oppenheimer, Jean. "In *War Zone*: Filmmaker Maggie Hadleigh-West Hits Manhattan's Sidewalks to Confront Men About Their Abusive Treatment of Female Pedestrians." American Society of Cinematographers, January 1999. http://www.theasc.com/protect/jan99/hassle/pg1.htm.

Renov, Michael, ed. *Theorizing Documentary*. New York: Routledge, 1993.

Rosen, Ruth. *The World Split Open: How the Modern Women's Movement Changed America*. New York: Viking P, 2001.

Roth, Benita. *Separate Roads to Feminism: Black, Chicana, and White Feminist Movements in America's Second Wave*. Cambridge: Cambridge UP, 2004.

Ryan, Mary P. *Womanhood in America: From Colonial Times to the Present*. New York: New York Viewpoints, 1975.

Saul, Jennifer Mather. *Feminism: Issues and Arguments*. Oxford: Oxford UP, 2003.

Schrock, Douglas, Lori Raid, and Emily M. Boyd. "Transsexuals' Embodiment of Womanhood." *Gender and Society* 19 (Jun. 2005): 317-35.

Wheeler, Marjorie Spruill, ed. *One Woman, One Vote: Rediscovering the Woman Suffrage Movement*. Troutdale, OR: New Sage Press, 1995.

YoMaggie. http://www.yomaggie.com/films.html.

Filmography

A Film on Street Harassment. Dir. Sheila Paige. U.S.A., 1977.

Abortion and the Law. Dir. David Lowe. U.S.A., 1965.

Alien. Dir. Ridley Scott. U.S.A., UK, 1979.

And Baby Makes Two. Dir. Judy Katz and Oren Rudavsky. U.S.A., 1983.

Beautopia. Dir. Katharina Otto-Bernstein. U.S.A., 1998.

Before Stonewall: The Making of a Gay and Lesbian Community. Dir. Greta Schiller and Robert Rosenberg. U.S.A., 1984.

Behind the Labels. Dir. Tia Lessin. U.S.A., 2001.

Birth Control and the Law. CBS. U.S.A., 1962.

Bowling for Columbine. Dir. Michael Moore. U.S.A., 2002.

Cancer in Two Voices. Dir. Lucy Massie Phenix. U.S.A., 1994.

Earth. Dir. Alastair Fothergill and Mark Linfield. U.S.A., UK, Germany, 2007.

Fahrenheit 9/11. Dir. Michael Moore. U.S.A., 2004.

Gay U.S.A. Dir. Arthur J. Bressan, Jr. U.S.A., 1978.

Girls Like Us. Dir. Tina Di Feliciantonio and Jane Wagner. U.S.A., 1997.

Growing Up Female. Dir. Jim Klein and Julia Reichert. U.S.A., 1971.

Growing Up With the Self Image of American Girls. Dir. Christina Bellantoni and Elizabeth Pickett. U.S.A., 1998.

In My Father's Church. Dir. Charissa King. U.S.A., 2004.

It's Elementary: Talking About Gay Issues in School. Dir. Debra Chasnoff and Helen Cohen. U.S.A., 1996.

Lockin' Up. Dir. T. Nicole Atkinson. U.S.A., 1997.

Maid in America. Dir. Anayansi Prado. U.S.A., 2005.

Men Under Siege: Life with the Modern Woman. ABC. U.S.A., 1978.

Nappy. Dir. Lydia Ann Douglas. U.S.A., 1997.

Our House: A Very Real Documentary about Kids of Gay and Lesbian Families. Dir. Meema Spadola. U.S.A., 1999.

Pumping Iron II: The Women. Dir. George Butler and Charles Gaines. U.S.A., 1985.

Rape. Dir. Joann Elam. U.S.A., 1975

Roger and Me. Dir. Michael Moore. U.S.A., 1989.

Sicko. Dir. Michael Moore. U.S.A., 2007.

She's Nobody's Baby: American Women in the 20th Century. Prod. HBO and Ms Magazine, 1981.

Sir: Just a Normal Guy. Dir. Melanie LaRosa. U.S.A., 2002.

Some of Our Best Friends. Dir. Ken Robinson. U.S.A., 1971.

Suffragettes in the Silent Cinema. Dir. Kay Sloane. U.S.A., 2003.

Supersize Me. Dir. Morgan Spurlock. U.S.A., 2004.

Taking Our Bodies Back: The Women's Health Movement. Dir. Margaret Lazarus and Renner Wunderlich. U.S.A., 1974.

War Zone. Dir. Maggie Hadleigh-West. U.S.A., 1998.

What 80 Million Women Want. Dir. Will Louis. U.S.A., 1913

Windows On Women. Prod. Suzanne Singer. U.S.A., 1985.

Woman's Film, The. Dir. Louise Alaimo, Judy Smith and Ellen Sorren. U.S.A., 1971

Word Is Out: Stories of Some of Our Lives. Dir. Peter Adair et.al. U.S.A., 1977.

III.

DissemiNations:
Toward a Narration of Nation
in Postmodern Times

Documenting Horror: *The American Nightmare* and the Narration of Nation

GABRIELE PISARZ-RAMÍREZ

Resumen

Este artículo se ocupa con el filme documental sobre películas de horror de Adam Simon que tiene por título *The American Nightmare*. La tesis central del filme es que las películas de horror de los finales de los años sesenta y de los comienzos de los años setenta fueron influidas por los acontecimientos sociales y políticos de la época y su medio de documentación tanto en la temática, como en lo estético. Los sucesos como la guerra de Vietnam, los asesinatos políticos de Martin Luther King, John F. Kennedy y Robert Kennedy, el Watergate, así como los movimientos de mujeres y de derechos civiles llevaron a un clima de inseguridad o, bien, incertidumbre en relación a los valores sociales y nacionales. Simon muestra que directores de cine como George A. Romero, Wes Craven, David Cronenberg y otros reaccionaron ante este clima de miedo presentando a la sociedad americana en sus filmes como monstruosa. El ensayo investiga la construcción de nación en el filme documental de Simon y su estrategia fílmica de mezclar el hecho y la ficción, la representación de traumas sociales y la presentación de películas de horror como jeremiadas sobre el estado de la sociedad americana en los años sesenta y setenta.

In *Horror as Pleasure*, Yvonne Leffler describes as one of the general aesthetic conditions of "pleasurable" horror the audience's assumption that the horror that is created is entirely fictional. The feeling that the fictional characters "cannot step outside the fictional world or do anything in our extrafictional reality," is, according to Leffler, a precondition of the entertainment value of horror (260-61). The line between the real world and the stories told in horror movies, Leffler contends, is always clear.

Adam Simon's documentary *The American Nightmare* suggests just the opposite. It covers the breakthrough films of five horror genre masters—George A. Romero, John Carpenter, Tobe Hooper, Wes Craven and David Cronenberg. With films such as *The Texas Chainsaw Massacre, Night of the Living Dead, Shivers, Halloween,* and *The Last House on the Left,* these directors produced a set of movies that distinguished themselves from earlier productions through their shocking violence and their lack of a reassuring ending. In his documentary Simon tests his general hypothesis that the horror films produced by these directors in the late 1960s and 1970s were a direct outcome of the American reality of that period—a time of social turmoil, war, and national crisis. Simon strives to give an explanation for the popularity of these movies in this period, which critics have called the Golden Age of American independent horror films, or briefly, The Gory Age.

Against the still quite common judgment that horror movies are trivial films which cater to the desire for gory scenes in an unenlightened audience, Simon presents the horror films by Hooper, Craven, Romero, Carpenter, and Cronenberg as an expression of the rage, anxiety and unease that accompanied what many people experienced as a time of social unrest. Linking these films to the psychological shock brought about by events such as the Vietnam War, the assassinations of John F. Kennedy, Robert Kennedy, and Martin Luther King, as well as to the Civil Rights and the Women's Movement, he makes the argument that horror films are a violent and enraged response both to the growing distrust of the American establishment and to the anxieties brought about by the radical changes in American society—in short, that the American nightmare acted out in the horror movies represented what to many was a nightmarish condition of society itself.

The American Nightmare was financed and first screened by the Independent Film Channel in 2000. It has had an international distribution and was shown at the German Berlinale in 2001. Described by director Adam Simon as a film essay, it is a compilation film which draws mostly on interviews with film directors and critics as well as on historical film and newsreel footage. In an interview with *Filmmaker* in 2000, Simon explains how he grew up in a family of politically active parents who exposed him to the reality of political rallies and police monitoring:

> My older brothers and my mother and father were very active politically in the period of this film [*Night of the Living Dead*]. They were always taking me to demonstrations, and I was horrified by them; I thought, this is chaos! I didn't know who to be more afraid of, the line of blue-helmeted cops holding their batons or these crazed demonstrators. The first time I saw a movie like *Night of the Living Dead*, which dropped you in the middle of this kind of situation, I saw these two things as being connected. ("Exquisite Corpses" 84)

The striking opening of the documentary presents a montage of archival newsreel material from the 1960s and 1970s and film clips from horror movies of the times. Simon uses the archival footage oft the Vietnam War and of events such as the Kent State University riots, and juxtaposes it with brief clips from *The Texas Chainsaw Massacre*, *Night of the Living Dead*, *The Crazies*, and other horror films. Very quickly the newsreel footage and the horror movie footage seem to blend into an indistinguishable stream of violent and disturbing images. An intended and distressing effect of this montage is the impression that the newsreel images of mutilated corpses in Vietnam and of firing national guards are actually more shocking than the gory scenes of the horror films.

This deliberate and visible collapse of fact and fiction in Simon's documentary reveals him as a postmodern documentarian who engages with a newer, more contingent, relative truth, a truth of meaning-making processes. As Linda Williams has pointed out, postmodern documentaries, rather than being defined as essences of truth, can be seen as "a set of strategies designed to choose from among an horizon of relative and contingent truths" (14). Both fiction and documentary must be seen as foregrounding the subjective construction of experience. While there is no objective observation of truth, there is always an interested participation in its construction (16). Already in 1983, in his seminal essay "The Voice of Documentary," John Nichols observed an increasing hybridization of documentary and fictional discourses, a process that leads to increasingly blurred genre conventions of both discourses. In this process, documentary discourses give up their claim to objectivity, while fictional discourses import conventions of the documentary (cf. Nichols). By linking horror movies to the social experience of the 1960s and 1970s, Simon thus not only formulates a relative truth, he also points to the constructedness of documentary truth at large.

As postmodern media culture is undermining the category of objectivity, contemporary documentaries seek new ways to authenticate their version of reality. In order to do so, Simon uses various strategies of authentication. *The American Nightmare* combines various visual and auditory materials: apart from extensive interviews with the directors, Simon also lets film critics such as Carol Clover, Adam Lowenstein and Tom Gunning speak in order to support his thesis, and he uses montage. All three instances: the critics, the directors, and Simon's montage of horror film and newsreel material, transmit the same "truth," which becomes more plausible through this strategy: that the horror movies of the 1960s and 1970s are both a representation of and a direct response to the social chaos of this time.

The late 1960s and the 1970s were characterized by decisive social, political and economic developments such as the struggle for civil rights, the protests against the Vietnam War, the alienation of substantial sections of the young middle class from the American Dream, as well as by a seemingly permanent recession, uncontrollable inflation and rising unemployment, which altogether created a sense of loss and anxiety with many Americans. The omnipresence of the war in the nation's media in the 1960s and early 1970s, as well as the ubiquity of images of police violence against political activists, rebellious students, and civil rights campaigners led to a massive loss of trust in the political leadership and to a deep crisis of American identity. Marilyn Young compares Vietnam to an "acid bath in which received myths dissolved" and that "presented a serious threat to the nation's very sense of self" (201). Especially for those whose sense of identity primarily depended on idealized representations of the nation, the country's leaders, and a clear-cut idea of one's proper role in relation to others in the patriarchal family, the defeat in Vietnam, the resignation of a president, and the youth, sexual, and feminist revolutions were particularly disenchanting developments significantly contributing to a general lack of self-esteem (cf. Ryan/Kellner 171). While most Americans in the 1950s did not doubt the essential goodness and su-

periority of their society, and while the validity of the American establishment was only seldom questioned, the subsequent period brought about a growing uneasiness concerning an establishment that, as events such as Watergate or Vietnam showed, had
turned out to be untrustworthy.

According to Michael Ryan and Douglas Kellner, there were various cinematic
responses to the pervasive social changes of the period in the American movie industry
(cf. 169ff). First, there was an impulse to reconstruct stabilizing representations of self
and world in order to counterbalance anxiety and fear through a dramatization of romance and the family as sources of nurturing and trust. A second compensatory strategy focused on the reassertion of male heroism and of national military power in films
such as in *Missing in Action, Rambo* or *Star Wars*. A third version of coming to terms
with the tensions and fears related to political leadership, feminism, and social crisis
was played out in paranoid projections of social monstrosity. The horror films Simon
addresses in his documentary are of this latter kind. As he contends, they became a vehicle for social critique and for provocative statements against American conservatism
that were too radical for Hollywood cinema.

As early as 1975, in a seminal essay, "The American Nightmare: Horror in the
70s," Robin Wood had pointed to the significance of late 1960s and early 1970s horror
movies in the context of the American nation's identity crisis in this period, drawing
on Freud's theory of repression and the "return of the repressed"(64). While Simon
acknowledges this earlier study in the title of his documentary, he is particularly interested in the specific representational parallels between newsreel images and horror
images. In the interviews he conducted with the directors, he explores the relationship
between social trauma and the concrete practices of representation in the horror films.
Extensive interview sequences foreground the directors' personal motivations for
making horror movies and highlight the link between their experiences and specific
cinematic decisions. What emerges from the interviews is a sense of distress as well as
a great deal of rage. As the directors recall how they experienced the era, all of them
recollect feelings of incredulity, helplessness, fear, and frustration, as well as a general
sentiment of being at the mercy of a system that was no longer considered trustworthy.
While Wes Craven remembers that "everybody knew somebody who had been
wounded in Vietnam," and that he was struck by the assassinations of Robert Kennedy
and Martin Luther King as well as by the Watergate affair as mysteries which undermined his faith in the establishment, George Romero recalls feeling scared by what he
describes as the "blue-collar kind of monster," mentally dead people that he frames
into the apt metaphor of "dead people walking around." Tobe Hooper tells about
primal fears from his childhood related to corpses and torture which were brought to
life when he saw the news coverage of Vietnam. All of the directors in the interviews
convey a sense of the fragility of the nation's life and they all look back on feelings of
rage and confusion.

Simon's documentary suggests that the horror films these directors produced dramatize this fragility as well as the rage and destructive potential they sensed in the

American society of that period. *The American Nightmare* shows how the directors encoded the movies in ways that correlated with the collective traumata and media experience of violence that surrounded them. While older horror classics such as *Franken-
stein, Dracula* or *King Kong* were set in foreign locales or at least presented the threat
as entering the country from abroad, concluding with the domestic order safely restored, films such as *Night of the Living Dead* and *The Texas Chainsaw Massacre*
were set in the American heartland (Pennsylvania) and Southwest (Texas) and ended
on the disquieting note that the evil lingers in our midst.

The plots of the movies dramatize monstrous brutality and sadism emanating
from members of American society. This becomes particularly evident in the construction of the core unit of national identity, the family, in these films. Throughout the documentary Simon focuses on scenes in the movies in which the home and the family
become sites of violence. *The Texas Chainsaw Massacre* presents a family of slaugh-
terhouse workers who all have been put out of work by mechanization and who have
taken to cannibalism. In *Night of the Living Dead*, a child is shown eating her father
and killing her mother with a hoe. In *The Last House on the Left*, the middle class parents of a girl murdered by a youth gang become bestial killers themselves. All of
these films do suggest the crisis not only of family values but of community at large.
The families presented carry pathological features in many cases: *Night of the Living
Dead* presents a patriarchal father more concerned about preserving his authority than
about protecting his wife and child from the zombies, and *The Texas Chainsaw Massacre* shows a three-generation family of men who do not only practice brutish violence against their victims but are violent in their interpersonal relations as well. Apart
from the fact that these films are characterized by extreme violence, in many of the
movies the line between mad killers and 'normal people' is blurred, suggesting that
monsters are no longer creations of mad scientists or bloodsucking vampires, but are
bred by society itself.

The American Nightmare proposes that the scenarios of violence in the movies
and the fears evoked by them also correlate, on an iconographic level, with the shocking images of violence that reached American TV viewers through the media coverage
of the war in Vietnam. Documentary images of Vietnam scandalized American viewers as they confronted audiences—for the first time—with uncensored images of the
war, and because they sharply contradicted the vision of a fast, clean and successful
war that had been promoted by the American government. One example of the power
and potency of these images is the famous photograph of naked Vietnamese children
running down a road following a Napalm attack that Nick Ut shot for Associated Press
(1972), an image that was repeatedly and effectively employed by anti-war protesters.
Simon uses this image to contextualize scenes from Wes Craven's *The Last House on
the Left*. Craven himself recalls in the interview that the images of Vietnam as well as
of the police violence during the Kent State riots confirmed his impression that "there
was nothing to be trusted in the establishment" and that "the war had come home in
very strange ways." In several scenes Simon uses the outline of an old-fashioned

1970s TV screen to frame both the movie and newsreel images, suggesting parallels between them.

Some of the films, as Simon makes clear, transgress the boundaries between documentary and fictional discourses in referring directly to newsreel images about the war abroad and about police squads fighting social activists at home. In *Night of the Living Dead* the black sole survivor of the zombies' attack on a farmhouse, the African American Ben, is killed by a posse of redneck sheriffs who in their search for zombies fire at all moving targets. This scene bears a striking parallel to Southern lynching parties and to images of search-and-destroy units in Vietnam, who in their hunt for enemies indiscriminately killed civilians and children. The image of dogs used by the sheriffs to find their targets bears similarities to newsreel images showing police forces who set their dogs on non-violent protesters. As Adam Lowenthal, one of the critics interviewed by Simon, observes: "You can not not think of lynchings. You cannot not think of freedom marches in the South. You cannot not think about the Civil Rights struggle when watching these images."

Images of dogs hunting down protesters were a televised 'reality' with which viewers were familiar, and it was these images that, as director John Landis points out, were "real horror images." Simon also highlights iconographic parallels between the horror footage in the final scenes of *Night of the Living Dead* and documentary footage about Vietnam. The scene shows how Ben's dead body is treated like a piece of dead flesh when the sheriffs carry him with hooks without touching him physically, throwing him on a pile of corpses and dousing him with gasoline. Simon juxtaposes the stills of this scene with documentary footage of the My Lai massacre, images that show piles of slain civilians who were murdered by American firing squads. The 'reality effect' of this movie was heightened by the fact that it was shot in black and white, just like the newsreel images of that period. One scene in Wes Craven's *The Last House on the Left* depicts the execution of one of the two girls tortured by the teenagers who kidnapped them. Craven traces the camera work and angle in this scene directly to a report he had watched on the news that documented the execution of a Vietnamese prisoner. The iconic picture by photojournalist Eddie Adams (who won the Pulitzer Prize for it) depicts an unarmed man who is brutally shot by South Vietnam's national police chief Nguyen Ngoc Loan during the 1968 Tet offensive. Craven admits that "that methodical execution style was translated directly to the shooting of Mary at the lake."

Make-up artist Tom Savini, who is also interviewed by Simon, recalls how his Vietnam experience enabled and encouraged him to break with the romantic tradition of presenting violence. Traditionally, scenes that depicted violent deaths were dominated by the use of slow-motion and quick-cut editing, thus avoiding an overly realistic depiction of the killing. Savini, who was drafted to fight as a soldier in Vietnam after he had finished photography school, relates that the images he saw in Vietnam encouraged him, in his later work, to present violence the way it was: ugly and real. Remembering that he was extremely scared and that he, like everybody around him, tried to deal with his fear by "turn[ing] off my emotions," he describes how he tried to view the dead bodies he saw through his camera in terms of special effects. He shot pictures of corpses and used them to study and practice special effects that were later used in films such as *Dawn of the Dead.*

Simon's documentary suggests that while the newsreel clips appear as a visible expression of the disorder in society, the horror films work as a cultural manifestation of the invisible effects of this disorder. They present horrific visions of national life antithetical to the American Dream. In that respect they stand in the tradition of the Jeremiad, that Puritan rhetorical device which laments the state of society and the discrepancy between its promises and its reality. According to Sacvan Bercovitch, secularized forms of the Jeremiad have considerably shaped public discourse in America, which is still seen by many as the Promised Land. As Bercovitch explains, the essence of the Jeremiad is its unshakeable optimism that things can be set right. But where is the optimism in the horror movies? One might suggest that the violence with which patriarchal family structures are destroyed, with which an old order and the value system of the 1950s are rejected in these movies, also makes room for new visions. As some of the directors admit, there was a tremendous energy behind the changes going on in society; it was a process that felt, as Romero puts it, like "there was a new society devouring the old one." It is particularly one movie, David Cronenberg's *Shivers*, which explores one of these visions in all its ambivalence in his imagination of a society infected with the virus of eroticism. While the virus itself is presented as quite disgusting and ferocious, leading people to behave not like rational beings but like animals, the optimistic ending of this movie shows the protagonist giving up his resistance against the amorous attacks of a crowd of naked women, suggesting that change might be as beautiful as it is terrifying.

A general problem of compilation films, as Hilmar Hoffmann has pointed out, is the issue of making a very heterogeneous set of material fit an intended purpose. As interviews and archival film material have a force of their own, it presents a challenge to the documentarian to stage them in a coherent way in order to suggest a particular 'version' of reality. Simon's project of staging the horror film directors as mouthpieces of a troubled society is not invariably successful. While Wes Craven and George Romero both give thoughtful and reflected evaluations of the contexts of their movies, this is not always the case with the observations of the other filmmakers. While some of their statements appear rather shallow, others raise ethical questions which are never addressed in the documentary. When Tobe Hooper talks about his dislike for family gatherings in relation to his representation of family in *The Texas Chainsaw Massacre*, or when make-up artist Tom Savini describes his experience of seeing corpses in Vietnam as a good visual preparation for the realistic imitation of such scenes in horror movies, these statements leave the viewer in doubt about the social and political responsibilities of those who make them. The most illuminating remark concerning such statements is a self-ironical observation by John Landis, director of *American Werewolf* and *Blues Brothers*, who explains that viewers who saw Hitchcock movies felt themselves in the hands of a master who precisely calculated what turned out to be a comfortably scary feeling, while in these movies, as he claims, the viewer felt that he was not in the hands of a master but in the hands of a maniac. In some cases, as with director John Carpenter, it is apparent that the critics' statements make much more sense in explaining his films than Carpenter's own observations. At times Simon's intention of presenting the directors as social critics who, through filmmaking, wanted to deal with the trauma of increasing violence in the media seems forced, if only since it neglects the economy of filmmaking, in which young and unknown directors constantly attempt to draw attention to themselves not by social criticism but by the most spectacular film possible.

The documentary does not have a voiceover, intentionally avoiding explanations of what viewers see because, as Simon has stated in an interview, he wanted to put his audience "more into the kind of position that they're in when watching a narrative film—both willing and happy to interact with the film and figure it out for themselves" ("Exquisite Corpses" 108). If we take the documentarian, as Stanford film critic and director Jan Kravitz has recently done,[1] as a "ventriloquist" whose voice, if not heard in the documentary itself, is translated through his selection of images, the question arises which 'voice' can be heard through Simon's editing decisions. To give an answer to this question, I would argue that his selection of scenes from horror movies suggests that the voice heard in his documentary is as much that of a social critic as that of a horror fan. *The American Nightmare* lays out markers of an intended reception for at least two groups of viewers. On the one hand, Simon constructs the horror film as an expression of a troubled society, removing its makers from their dubious position as creators of shock and gore into the position of chroniclers of society's ills. His documentary thus addresses itself to a critical audience that approaches horror films with a certain distance and to whom Simon appeals through the informed opinion of critics such as Clover, Gunning, or Lowenstein. On the other hand, he also speaks to an audience of horror lovers, who are attracted by the abundance of horror footage in the film.

The composition of the audience can be—if very incompletely—guessed from the reviews that the documentary has received. Reviewers obviously employed different discursive filters in reading the film: while reviewers who do not engage in horror fandom appreciate the documentary for its explanation of horror material and for its claim of seriousness with respect to this popular genre, reviewers who disclose themselves as fans value the film for its extensive inclusion of interview material with the directors as well as for its nostalgic qualities in recreating these early movies for them, while they often discard the critics' opinions as negligible.[2] *The American Nightmare*

---

[1] Jan Kravitz, "The Documentary Filmmaker as Ventriloquist." Kravitz took issue with Bill Nichols's statement, in "The Voice of Documentary," that in the 1980s, a period which he calls the stage of "reflexivity" in documentary filmmaking, many directors had "lost their voice" (cf. Nichols 18).

[2] Especially German fan reviews celebrate the documentary exactly for its uncensored presentation of horror material.

displays a certain sensationalism in privileging the bloodiest scenes, the most grue-
some episodes from the movies. The documentary includes many scenes that have
been censored in the versions of these films available in most European countries—if
they are available at all. This decision may result from Simon's desire to appeal to horror film audiences who appreciate these films for their shock effects and who often de-
plore their restricted availability.[3]

The American Nightmare is an illuminating documentary that identifies and portrays a popular horror subgenre which blossomed during the cultural upheaval of the
late 1960s, which thrived on the public distrust and disillusionment of the 1970s, and
which continues flourishing to the present day. Many of the horror movies from the
1960s/1970s have experienced recent remakes or sequels that are quite successful, Romero's recently launched *Land of the Dead* (2004) being only one example. But the
past few years have also seen the emergence of a new cycle of extremely violent horror films that shock their viewers by what critic David Edelstein has called "torture
porn"—i.e. by the hyperreal, explicit and in its nature pornographic representation of
torture.

Like the horror films of the 1960s/1970s, the new movies attract not only hard-
core horror fans but huge audiences. The film *Hostel* (2005) returned 20 million dollars on the opening weekend. The extremely brutal movie *Wolf Creek* (2005) was
equally successful, and both *Saw* (2004) and *Hostel* have seen sequels since their re-
leases. *Hostel* particularly stands out since it takes the merging of fictional and documentary discourses yet a step further than the horror films of the 1960s and 1970s. The
film's plot dramatizes the journey of two young American tourists in Europe who are
lured into the Slovak city of Bratislava where they have been promised inexpensive
sex and entertainment. As it turns out, the prostitutes whom they meet are traders who
sell the two youngsters to an establishment catering to rich businessmen who draw
pleasure from torturing people to death.

The images in this film draw their 'authenticity' from a seemingly objective,
quasi-documentary representation of torturing and killing procedures. As drills gouge
into kneecaps, and eyes are cut out of their sockets, *Hostel* invites viewers to share the
sadistic voyeurism of the victimizers, transgressing not only genre conventions between documentary and fiction but ethical borders as well. Unlike the horror movies of
the 1960s and 1970s, *Hostel* does not encourage sympathy with the victims, who are
presented as replaceable objects rather than complex human beings throughout the
film.

The film's extreme violence does not only respond to the changing tolerance
threshold of audiences used to watching fictionalized violence in the media on a regu-

---

[3] Simon's own horror films have so far been little acknowledged. In 1990 he made *Brain
Dead*, a psychological horror-thriller based on a story by Charles Beaumont; *Carnosaurs*
followed in 1993, a low-budget dinosaur horror film that was a box office success but did
not, as Simon admits, lead to many subsequent directorial opportunities (cf. "Simon Says"
327).

lar basis, it obviously also reacts to the lifting of taboos from discussing torture as a viable strategy in public discourses.[4] While alluding directly, in one scene, to images of the Abu Ghraib case when one of the torture victims is shown with his head covered in a black hood, the film's voyeurism more generally comments on a media landscape where pictures documenting violence invite curiosity rather than compassion. The fact that the Abu Ghraib pictures, with their spectacle of torture showing perpetrators posing, gloating, over their helpless captives, were distributed via the world wide web to millions of people thus indeed illustrates what Susan Sontag has called a "culture of shamelessness"(29).

While the changed media landscape may explain the extreme violence and callousness of *Hostel*, it cannot account for this and other new films' enormous box-office returns. Without intending to construct a similar relationship between these horror movies and their societal context as Simon does with their 1960s/1970s predecessors, it is not too far-fetched to suggest that the success of these new films can to a certain degree be explained with the societal paranoia following 9/11 and the internal "war on terrorism" that affected many Americans' concept of self and nation. *Hostel*'s director Eli Roth explains what he regards as the reasons for the success of his film:

> America is terrified because they have no idea when any of this is going to end. George Bush has everyone terrified because of all these terror alerts—terror alert orange—every holiday there is a terror alert and every time you travel it's a nightmare. All that terror that you feel, all that anxiety. It gets stored up and you have to let it out. ... You need an outlet to be afraid and experience fear, where it's okay to be screaming. It's an incredible release, which people need desperately right now and that's why they are flocking to these horror films.

Although Roth can hardly be regarded as a social critic, he may be correct in assuming that the contemporary American horror films function as a sounding board for the structures of feeling of a post-9/11 America that—like the America of the late 1960s and the 1970s—was marked by the loss of self-assurance, by fear and insecurity. *Hostel* dramatizes emotions of helplessness, loss of control and impotence, thus reactivating real fears of a nation that, in the years after 9/11, saw itself surrounded by terrorists and forces of evil, that was traumatized by the September 11 attacks, by abductions and executions of Americans in Iraq, and by the situation of a never-ending war in that country. The horror films of the 1960s/1970s responded to the crumbling of a dearly held national image in all its shocking implications. In a time of menacing terrorism, but also of imperial strategies in fighting it in the Bush era, horror films again appeared to have succeeded in producing potent nightmare images that comment on the terror of a nation and project it onto the screens of movie theaters.

---

[4]   An extensive debate was stirred up, for example, by American lawyer and Harvard professor Alan Dershowitz' argument in favor of a legal basis for torture after 9/11 (cf. Dershowitz).

Works Cited

Bercovitch, Sacvan. *The American Jeremiad.* Madison: U of Wisconsin P, 1978.

Dershowitz, Alan. *Why Terrorism Works: Understanding the Threat, Responding to the Challenge.* New Haven and London: Yale UP, 2002.

Edelstein, David. "Now Playing at Your Local Multiplex: Torture Porn. Why Has America Gone Nuts for Blood, Guts, and Sadism?" *New York Magazine* Jan. 28, 2006. <http://nymag.com/movies/features/15622/>.

Hoffmann, Hilmar. *"Und die Fahne führt uns in die Ewigkeit": Propaganda im NS-Film.* Frankfurt a.M.: Fischer Taschenbuch Verlag, 1988.

Kravitz, Jan. "The Documentary Filmmaker as Ventriloquist." Roundtable with Jan Kravitz. Stanford University. Jan. 23, 2009.

Leffler, Yvonne. *Horror as Pleasure: The Aesthetics of Horror Fiction.* Stockholm: Almqvist & Wiksell International, 2000.

Nichols, Bill. "The Voice of Documentary." *Film Quarterly* 36.3 (1983): 17-30.

Roth, Eli. Interview with Lorna Allen on *Hostel. Close-up Film.* <http://www.close-upfilm.com/features/Interviews/eli_roth.html>.

Ryan, Michael, and Douglas Kellner. *Camera Politica: The Politics and Ideology of Contemporary Hollywood Film.* Bloomington, Ind.: Indiana UP, 1988.

Simon, Adam. "Exquisite Corpses: Interview with Adam Simon, Filmmaker." Scooter McCrae. *The Magazine of Independent Film* 8.4 (2000): 82-87, 108-09.

———. "(Adam) Simon Says...: *Paradoxa* Interview with the Director of *The American Nightmare.*" Steven Jay Schneider. *Paradoxa* 17 (2002): 323-33.

Sontag, Susan. "Regarding the Torture of Others." *New York Times* May 23, 2004, 24ff.

Williams, Linda. "Mirrors without Memories: Truth, History, and the New Documentary." *Film Quarterly* 46.3 (1993): 9-21.

Wood, Robin. "*The American Nightmare*: Horror in the 70s." *Hollywood from Vietnam to Reagan.* 1979. New York: Columbia UP, 1986. 63-84.

Young, Marilyn. "Dangerous History: Vietnam and the 'Good War.'" *History Wars: The Enola Gay and Other Battles for the American Past.* Ed. Edward T. Linenthal and Tom Engelhardt. New York: Metropolitan Books, 1996. 199-209.

Filmography

The American Nightmare. Dir. Adam Simon. U.S.A., 2003.

American Werewolf. Dir. John Landis. United Kingdom, U.S.A., 1981.

Blues Brothers. Dir. John Landis. U.S.A., 1980.

Brain Dead. Dir. Adam Simon. U.S.A. , 1990.

Carnosaurus. Dir. Adam Simon and Darren Moloney. U.S.A., 1993.

The Crazies. Dir. George A. Romero. U.S.A., 1973.

Dawn of the Dead. Dir. Zack Snyder. U.S.A., Canada, Japan, France, 2004.

Halloween. Dir. John Carpenter. U.S.A., 1978.

Hostel. Dir. Eli Roth. U.S.A., 2005.

Land of the Dead. Dir. George A. Romero. Canada, France, U.S.A., 2005.

The Last House on the Left. Dir. Wes Craven. U.S.A., 1972.

Missing in Action. Dir. Joseph Zito. U.S.A., 1984.

Night of the Living Dead. Dir. George A. Romero. U.S.A., 1968.

Rambo. Dir. Ted Kotcheff. U.S.A., 1982.

Saw. Dir. James Wan. U.S.A., Australia, 2004.

Shivers. Dir. David Cronenberg. Canada, 1975.

Star Wars. Dir. George Lucas. U.S.A., 1977.

The Texas Chainsaw Massacre. Dir. Tobe Hooper. U.S.A., 1974.

Wolf Creek. Dir. Greg Mclean. Australia, 2005.

La polifonía de la ciudad: *Suite Habana* (2003) de Fernando Pérez

BURKHARD POHL

Abstract

This essay discusses Fernando Pérez's documentary *Suite Habana* (2003), which earned considerable acclaim not only at the Cuban festival in Havana but also at film festivals in San Sebastián and Cartagena. Examining features such as montage, narration, sound, and the representation of the city and its inhabitants, the essay asks in how far *Suite Habana* transgresses the dichotomy of documentary v. fiction film.

Suite Habana is first presented as belonging to the genre of the city symphony film—one of the most prominent historical referents is Walter Ruttmann's *Berlin: Die Sinfonie der Großstadt* (1927). Then a detailed analysis demonstrates that montage and sound are central to creating a filmic suite. However, *Suite Habana* avoids folkloric musical stereotypes and creates instead what the essay calls a "rhythmic musical collage." Finally, addressing the question whether *Suite Habana* should be considered a politically engaged film, the essay analyzes how the attitude of Havana's inhabitants toward the Revolution is depicted here. It concludes that there is no simple answer to be given since *Suite Habana* represents Cuban reality in a polysemic way, relying on heterogeneous musical themes and symbols. This strategy allows for different ideological readings of everyday life in Castro's Cuba.

En los años noventa, muchas imágenes fílmicas sobre La Habana provenían del extranjero. Como apunta Raúl Rubio, a finales de la década se pudo observar un aluvión de "Cuban-themed cinema ... that globalized the situation in Cuba" (s.p.). En este sentido, para el público europeo fue crucial la eclosión del proyecto *Buena Vista Social Club* llevado a cabo por Ry Cooder y Wim Wenders. Independientemente de la alta calidad musical del CD y del documental correspondiente, ambos ayudaron a cimentar un imaginario que identifica a Cuba con la música del son y el bolero, por un lado, y con las calles del casco antiguo de La Habana, incluidos el Malecón y los viejos coches estadounidenses, por el otro. Formaron un imaginario de la cultura popular cubana basado en determinados estereotipos culturales exotistas y, además, explotado también por la creciente industria del turismo.

El éxito de *Buena Vista Social Club* (Wim Wenders, 1999) condujo a la filmación de numerosas películas –ficcionales y documentales– sobre la música y la realidad cubanas, generalmente de menor difusión: largometrajes como *Cuba feliz: Road movie musical* (Karim Dridi, 2000), *Paraíso* (Alina Teodorescu, 2003), *Habana Blues* (Benito Zambrano, 2005), *Habana, Havana* (Alberto Arvelo, 2004), o el documental *Havanna, mi amor* (Uli Gaulke, 2000). Fernando Trueba rodó una trilogía de documentales musicales que incluye *Blanco y negro* (2003) –título programático sobre un concierto en conjunto del cubano Bebo Valdés y el cantor Diego "Cigala"–, *Calle 54* (2000) y *El milagro de Candeal* (2004). Sobre todo España, en vísperas del centenario de la fecha 1898 en que España perdió Cuba, su última colonia americana, se destacó con películas que evocaban el pasado colonial y se preocupaban de la actual relación transatlántica entre turismo y migración, a menudo, desde una "perspectiva extranjerizante" (Santaolalla 182). *Cuarteto de La Habana* (1999) de Fernando Colomo y *Cosas que dejé en La Habana* (1997) de Manuel Gutierrez Aragón pertenecen a este grupo, de la misma manera que otras más comprometidas como *Flores de otro mundo* (Icíar Bollaín, 1999) y *Agua con sal* (Pedro Pérez Rosado, 2005). Una mirada distinta brinda el documental *Balseros* (2002) de los catalanes Carlos Bosch y Josep M. Domenech, con co-guión de David Trueba, que presenta un acceso "interactivo" al destino de sus protagonistas desde la perspectiva del reportaje televisivo.

En los años noventa, la producción cinematográfica del Instituto Cubano de Arte e Industria Cinematográficos (ICAIC) cayó en gran medida a causa de la escasez de medios. Sin embargo, apoyadas por coproductores internacionales, se dio el éxito internacional de las películas de Tomás Gutiérrez Alea, *Fresa y chocolate* (co-director Juan Carlos Tabío, 1993) –"el primer éxito mundial del cine cubano" (Schumann 131)– y *Guantanamera* (1995), y la difusión de *Alicia en el pueblo de maravillas* (Daniel Díaz Torres, 1991), prohibida en Cuba. El mismo Díaz Torres colaboró con productores y actores alemanes para rodar la comedia policíaca *Kleines Tropicana* (1997) y, *Hacerse el sueco* (2000). En el nuevo milenio, el ICAIC, apoyado también por la coproducción internacional, ha estabilizado la cuota de producciones a un modesto nivel de seis largometrajes y diez cortometrajes en 2003.[1]

El cine de Fernando Pérez ocupa un lugar propio en este panorama. Nacido en 1944, Pérez colaboró con Gutiérrez Alea en los años sesenta, para emprender después una larga carrera como director y guionista. Desde los años setenta, ha rodado alrededor de quince documentales y ha colaborado en producciones para el célebre Noticiero Latinoamericano del ICAIC. En 1988, estrenó su primer largometraje de ficción, *Clandestinos*, sobre un grupo opositor al régimen de Batista, seguido por *Hello Hemingway* (1990), también ambientado en la época prerrevolucionaria. Con *Madagascar* (1994), se adentró en el presente del período post-1989. *La vida es silbar* (1998), la única película cubana producida en aquel año (cf. Schumann 134), fue galardonada con el pre-

---

[1] Otro problema lo constituye la situación precaria de las salas de cine y la baja en la difusión de cine extranjero; situación lamentada por el propio Ministerio de Cultura Cubano (cf. *Producción cinematográfica*).

mio Goya español –si bien obtuvo escasa proyección (33.000 espectadores)–, y en varios festivales internacionales (La Habana, Sundance, Viña del Mar, Rotterdam, Oslo), lo que confirmó el reconocimiento nacional e internacional de Pérez, quien es conocido por su discurso crítico y poético sobre la realidad cubana. Con *Suite Habana*, estrenada en 2003, Fernando Pérez volvió al cine documental después de dieciocho años. Como *La vida es silbar*, *Suite Habana* se filmó en coproducción entre el ICAIC y la empresa española Wandafilms, especializada en el cine latinoamericano. De este modo, la película es también un ejemplo ilustrador de la estrategia de supervivencia del ICAIC, que tiende a la coproducción como modelo predominante. *Suite Habana* suscitó, en Cuba, el mayor interés de la crítica y del público después de *Fresa y chocolate*. A nivel internacional fue nominada a la Concha de Oro de San Sebastián y galardonada con el Signis Award de este festival, al mismo tiempo recibió el premio a la mejor película tanto en el Festival de La Habana como en el de Cartagena de Indias. En Europa, se convirtió en obra de referencia gracias a la buena acogida en San Sebastián. La recaudación española fue modesta –con unos 209.567 € logrados entre 43.126 espectadores–, pero considerablemente alta tratándose de una producción promocionada como "documental" (cf. *Cine*).[2] Poco después siguió una edición europea en DVD.

1. Entre el documental y la ficción

Suite Habana se organiza alrededor de los quehaceres diarios de sus protagonistas. Hay pocas tomas panorámicas con imágenes emblemáticas del paisaje urbano, como la estatua del Cristo de La Habana, el faro, las columnas, y el Malecón. La escenografía típica pertenece más a los ciclistas que a los coches de los años prerrevolucionarios. La vida exterior es una realidad urbana, que recuerda los contenidos de documentales observacionales, mostrando la decrepitud, pero también la actividad del centro habanero. La Habana de Fernando Pérez se identifica aquí con las herramientas y lugares de trabajo, con los interiores de las viviendas y los diversos escenarios de congregación pública; en conjunto, un espacio que no cumple con el imaginario internacionalmente estereotipado.

Un factor de su favorable recepción entre la crítica y el público parece ser su carácter híbrido. En los paratextos de la película, se tropieza con una sorprendente variedad de clasificaciones –que a su vez condiciona una determinada lectura– desde "documental sociológico" (Torreiro) o "docudrama" (*Cine*) hasta "poema" (Trigon film), o, incluso, "película de ficción" (carátula DVD). El *Diario del Festival de San Sebastián* afirma que "no es un documental, ni es una ficción" dándole, por lo tanto, una

---

[2] Las 25 películas españolas con mayor recaudación se situaron por encima de los 168.000 espectadores. Entre los documentales, *Buena Vista Social Club* atrajo a 114.381 espectadores, *Calle 54* tuvo 67.921, y *El milagro de Candeal* 55.431, mientras que *Balseros*, con temática cubana, sólo se cifra con una audiencia de 16.666 espectadores. A modo de comparación: rodada por un director de culto y tratando un tema polémico nacional, *La pelota vasca* (Julio Medem, 2003) tuvo más de 377.000 espectadores (cf. *Cine*).

identidad binaria (3). Por otra parte, el portal Cubacine del ICAIC, califica a *Suite Habana* de documental.

¿En qué consiste, por tanto, el "efecto documental" (Hohenberger 29) atribuido a la película? Roger Odin define la lectura "documentarizante" ("documentarisante") como la interacción entre los distintos niveles externos e internos de la película; en concreto, distingue entre cuatro "modos de producción:" por el receptor (sus hipótesis) y la institución (codificación paratextual), por el genérico y el "sistema estilístico" del filme (275). En *Suite Habana*, la falta de genéricos más allá del título y la productora, se acercaría a esta convención documentarista según Odin. A nivel de estilo, el uso de (pocos) insertos explicativos, el enfoque en la vida privada de los personajes no-profesionales, la cámara digital y la transmisión directa del ruido callejero, son elementos que determinan desde el principio una lectura "documentarizante."

Entre los cinco modos del documental que define Bill Nichols, *Suite Habana* no se adapta a una sola categoría. No hay intervención auditiva de una voz autorial, casi tampoco, diálogo intradiegético, se sigue "la modalidad de observación" (Nichols, *Representing* 32-44) para la representación directa de la cotidianidad cubana. Por otro lado, *Suite Habana* se aparta, desde el principio, de la presunta neutralidad y objetividad de un cine directo, mediante el uso de un montaje trabajado, de la banda sonora independiente, del silencio forzado, artificial de los protagonistas, y con el "efecto cámara" (Maqua 208) de una cuidada puesta en escena. Como retrato de la capital –mediado por el montaje rítmico de imagen y sonido–, *Suite Habana* se inscribe en la tradición de las *city symphonies* establecida por Walter Ruttmann en 1927, que cuestiona las fronteras entre el documental y la ficción. A nivel de la narración, la estrategia hermenéutica y elíptica en la presentación de las vidas individuales se acerca a los esquemas diegéticos de la ficción. El *making of* revela que algunas escenas inventan una realidad profílmica inexistente, como la lluvia artificial en las imágenes finales de la guardia nocturna, o la preparación del mercado donde Amanda compra maní; una construcción de la realidad, que el propio Pérez parece admitir al hablar de la "manipulación de sentimientos" (Elizalde s.p.). En vez de pretender la representación directa del reportaje, se busca dar una "impression of reality" (Rosen 87). Según diferentes propuestas acerca de la teoría del documental, se podría hablar bien de un documental "mezclado" (Burton 5) y "poético" (Izod/Kilborn 426-33), o bien, "artístico" (Carroll 49) o de la modalidad "performativa" (Nichols, *Blurred* 92-106), más preocupado de la expresión estética que de otros modos dirigidos a la información y a la didáctica. La transgresión entre el documental y la ficción hace de *Suite Habana* una heredera de las estrategias del Nuevo Cine Latinoamericano cuyas producciones, según Julianne Burton, guardan "close ties to the documentary mode" (21).

En las próximas páginas, seguiré más de cerca estas transgresiones a través de las estrategias fílmicas del montaje, la narración y el sonido. Después, se discutirá la representación de la ciudad y la sociedad, que recibe especial importancia bajo un enfoque documentarizante y político. Más que *oponer* personajes y paisajes, la imagen de

La Habana *expone* las relaciones entre el individuo y la sociedad a una interpretación abierta.

2. Montaje y narración, el ritmo sinfónico

Filmada en cinco semanas entre abril y mayo de 2002, la película trata de un día cualquiera en La Habana, de sol y lluvia, de trabajo y ocio. Empezando con las imágenes del amanecer y terminando en la noche, se muestran las actividades privadas y profesionales de quince habitantes de la ciudad, identificados con nombre y edad. Doce de ellos se convierten en "personajes," al reaparecer entre los créditos finales con nombre completo y un resumen de su situación personal y sus sueños.

La composición cuenta con una estructura circular, que empieza y termina con la guardia nocturna frente al monumento a John Lennon, en montaje alterno con tomas del faro que ilumina la Habana nocturna. Si el faro se interpreta como una metáfora poco favorable del régimen –lectura posible, pero no la única–, la continua referencia al insigne inglés permite diferentes connotaciones. Anuncia, desde el comienzo, el papel de la música en la película y, sobre todo, introduce, a través del cantante de "Imagine," la isotopía del sueño utópico, al mismo tiempo que reivindica una inscripción transnacional y transcultural de la sociedad cubana –con Los Beatles como referencia clave de la generación de Pérez–, y que invoca el prestigio del artista comprometido que se propone hacer un cine "político" (cf. abajo). Todavía más que el Che, cuya imagen se ve en diversos sitios, Lennon es el héroe emblemático de la película y es integrado como un personaje más.[3]

El montaje alternante de diferentes vidas privadas crea la ilusión de una simultaneidad de imágenes –que fueron filmadas durante varias semanas–, desde una cámara omnipresente. Un elemento ficcional es su estructuración en diferentes (sub-)secuencias cronológicas y acronológicas, determinadas por efectos sonoros y otros tipos de interpunción fílmica: planos autónomos, ruidos y temas musicales emblemáticos, cambios de ritmo y de duración de planos, o una imagen concluyente, como el apagado de un ventilador o el cierre de una puerta. Aunque el principio del montaje alternante impide una continuidad estricta de acciones y personajes, se organizan unidades semánticas, bien sea a nivel narrativo y cronológico –la lluvia, el almuerzo, la tarde–, o bien, mediante un tema musical común, y/o la yuxtaposición y asociación iconográfica (el avión – las palomas; las palomas – el color blanco).

El final consta de dos epílogos: el primero constituido por imágenes ya conocidas de las olas rompiendo en el Malecón al sonido y ritmo de "Quiéreme mucho," cantada por Omara Portuondo. El segundo son los créditos finales, con la presentación gráfico-verbal de los personajes que aclara alguna u otra pregunta del espectador.

---

[3] La importancia de Lennon como personaje paradigmático es resaltada por la utilización de una cita suya como epígrafe de *La vida es silbar*.

En la tripartita tipología del documental "sinfónico" de la era muda, esbozada en
su tiempo por Grierson (110), la película de Pérez se adaptaría más al modo "poético"
(frente a lo "musical" y lo "dramático"). El modelo genérico de *city symphony* connota
una totalidad dentro de un orden limitado; el objeto (la ciudad) es el resultado de una
suma de actividades separadas (cf. 110). Por ejemplo, la sinfonía de Ruttmann parte de
una estructura de 24 horas, separadas en "actos," donde se mezclan el registro dramático y el sinfónico. Aunque la película de Pérez comparte esta estructura temporal básica, el modelo de suite alude a la sucesión de varias piezas cortas con variaciones sobre
el mismo tema –la vida en La Habana–, pero empleando diferentes ritmos y *tempi*.[4] La
variación se logra por la insistencia en ciertos motivos (las manos, las naves) y personajes, y por la repetición de determinadas estrategias formales (paneo, *zoom* horizontal), que se vuelven a combinar a lo largo de la película.

El título *Suite Habana* incluye también un juego de palabras para un público internacional. En la transmisión fonética del título, algunos pensarán en "Sweet Havanna" como "Dulce Habana." Una connotación legítima de declaración de amor a la ciudad, corroborada por el epílogo de la canción "Quiéreme mucho." Por otra parte, la or-
tografía señala precisamente su distinción de eslóganes ingleses demasiado tópicos.[5]

El montaje intrasecuencial así como la transición entre secuencias, confirman la
connotación paratextual de suite. La suite como sucesión de variaciones es un leitmotiv paratextual y estructural. En vez de ofrecer un mero collage asociativo de imágenes, la película pone en relación sonido e imágenes. Se emplea un ritmo variado, entre
pausado, con tomas largas, y montajes rápidos que aceleran la acción. Momentos de
meditación y descanso se combinan con secuencias de corte acelerado y sonido eleva-
do.

A nivel de secuencia, el montaje convergente sigue una estrategia proléptica, basada en el juego de distancias. Raras veces, se recurre al panorámico como *establishing shot*. Se empieza con un primer o un primerísimo plano, como la bombilla del
faro o las manos de la estatua de Lennon, para sólo después abrir la vista hacia un plano general integrador.

Por ejemplo, los preparativos de la función travesti empiezan ya con las primeras
imágenes después del genérico: Unos primeros planos enfocan los zapatos de mujer
que cuelgan de la mano de Iván, de treinta años, quien trabaja en la lavandería de un
hotel. Los zapatos se llevan al zapatero y reaparecen como objeto sólo cerca del final
de la película, traicionando las expectativas del público –que puede suponer que los
zapatos pertenecen a la hermana–, cuando es Iván quien los lleva en su actuación nocturna.

---

[4]   Una lejana referencia intertextual podría ser la *Suite Cubana*, que el músico de jazz Bebo
      Valdés compuso entre 1992 y 1997.

[5]   Como anécdota, cabe citar el ejemplo del diario alemán, *Hamburger Abendblatt*, que anun-
      cia una presentación de la película efectivamente bajo la falsa ortografía inglesa (14 de
      agosto 2005).

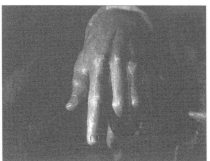

Primera toma: primer plano del faro   Segunda toma: plano detalle de la estatua de
                                             John Lennon

Especial atención recibe el manejo del *match-cut*, que cumple con funciones narrativas y temáticas y que suele incluirse en una serie de primeros y primerísimos primeros planos. Un magnífico ejemplo es el corte a manera de *shot/reverse-shot* entre dos personajes (Waldo, Natividad) que están mirando la misma transmisión televisiva. No sólo se unen dos espacios privados, sino se comenta la relación entre Revolución y ciudadano (cf. abajo). Otro recurso narrativo son los movimientos de cámara, sobre todo, paneos horizontales y verticales. Según Comolli, el paneo "organiza la toma como acción" e introduce un elemento ficcional-diegético en el documental (259). Por ejemplo, en la primera escena de la casa de Norma y Waldo, después de que Norma ha salido, la cámara hace un inexplicado paneo izquierdo hacia la puerta del dormitorio, esperando que ésta se abra y que salga Waldo (3.33-3.48).

La repetitividad de ciertas imágenes puede evocar así un ritmo de crescendo y desenlace. En la mencionada suite (11.56-14.12), interviene dos veces la voz de una mujer que grita el nombre de un chico. En esta instancia, el grito repetido pertenece al conjunto de ruidos que constituyen una "Suite Habana" propia. Sólo al repetirse un grito parecido por tercera vez en una secuencia posterior (42.25), la imagen se integra en uno de los hilos narrativos: es el grito de una vecina que avisa al joven Francisquito de la llegada de su padre.

Con la colaboración activa del espectador, se consigue un efecto dramatúrgico y ficcional que se extiende por toda la película. La narración elíptica y fragmentada de las vidas personales construyen breves episodios de una intriga. Elementos iconográficos y con alto valor simbólico invitan a crear hipótesis sobre el porvenir de los personajes y el desenlace de cada relato. La combinación de imágenes fragmentarias con escueta información textual y auditiva convierte a las personas en personajes.

Convertida en película "muda" a nivel de diálogo, *Suite Habana* explora la fuerza connotativa y emocional del montaje que caracterizó a los primeros documentales "sinfónicos" de los años veinte. Más allá de la función narrativa, el montaje asociativo y contrastivo es prolífico en significados. Estética y temáticamente, se recurre a una semántica de oposiciones entre luz y sombra, día y noche, sol y lluvia. En este contexto, hay que mencionar los diversos textos verbales –grafiti, letreros– que aparecen en el paisaje urbano. Si estos textos contribuyen, en parte, a la interpunción narrativa como títulos de subsecuencia ("Revolución," "El Rincón de la Paciencia," "Miami"), también funcionan como planos autónomos que añaden una interpretación extradiegética, no exenta de ironía. En la secuencia que trata de la partida de José Luis a Miami, introducida por el letrero "Cuba," el magnífico montaje paralelo entre imagen, sonido y letras asocia una simple pregunta escolar con el contexto político de la identidad nacional: un largo plano secuencia de palomas volando hacia el mar (33.45-34.30) prepara la interacción entre la isla y la diáspora. La pregunta en *off* de José Carlos, durante una función de payaso, con los colores de la bandera cubana, acompaña en montaje alternante a las tomas del aeropuerto del que está saliendo su hermano. Dentro del diálogo de la fiesta infantil, se monta la imagen de un avión de la línea aérea "Continental" que lleva impresa la bandera estadounidense, que comparte los mismos colores –rojo, blanco y azul– con la bandera cubana. Este montaje con los dos personajes –la niña con la bandera cubana en el balcón de su casa, y el emigrante en el avión norteamericano– muestran que Cuba está en ambos lados; Cuba y los EE.UU. están más próximos los unos a los otros de lo que piensan.

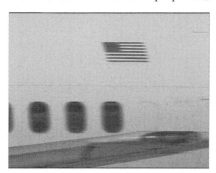

Dos veces ...   rojo, blanco y azul

Al tratar temas humanos existenciales, *Suite Habana*, desde una semántica binaria de claroscuros (cf. Padrón), recurre a estrategias de subjetividad que estimulan una honda reacción emocional. En el encuentro paulatino de varios de los personajes, se evoca un tono de solidaridad doméstica y de convivencia privada, entre padres e hijos, entre vecinos y familiares, entre hermano y hermana. Las historias individuales de los protagonistas dejan las huellas de la muerte, de las penurias financieras, y los sueños incumplidos. En la subsecuencia de la despedida y la pérdida, se unen la partida en avión de Jorge Luis con la visita de Francisco a la tumba de su esposa. Significativamente, la imagen inmediatamente anterior al epílogo enfoca, en primerísimo primer plano, la lluvia en los ojos de John Lennon, connotando lágrimas.

    El intercambio de la focalización externa del documental con planos de focalización interna, prepara la identificación del espectador con los protagonistas y crea "scenes of empathy" (Plantinga). Primerísimos primeros planos acercan los personajes al espectador y exhiben sus sentimientos, como las lágrimas de la madre en la despedida de su hijo, o la puesta en escena de antiguas fotos de familia que recuerdan momentos de felicidad pasada rellenando lo ausente en las historias de los personajes mudos. El *over-the-shoulder-shot* de la anciana frente al televisor o del médico frente al espejo hacen compartir su percepción visual y un momento íntimo de reflexión. La focalización interna se simula, incluso, en relación con ciertos objetos, como el ventilador enfrente de la cama de Jorge Luis.

3. El sonido de la metrópolis

De mayor importancia para la intensidad emocional y semántica de la recepción, el sonido ocupa un lugar primordial al yuxtaponer diferentes registros y estrategias de sonorización. El *sound editing* entre varios niveles y modalidades de sonido rompe la ilusión de inmediatez objetiva y añade claves de interpretación.

En la representación de los protagonistas –es decir, dejando el diálogo *off-trac–*, es precisamente la ausencia del sonido original, el silencio de las voces, lo que convierte y hasta mitifica la actividad mostrada. Por otra parte, se aprovechan como sonido diegético los ruidos callejeros y caseros. El sonido figura en función de un montaje asociativo, complementario a la imagen, para lograr un conjunto casi musical. Sirva como ejemplo la subsecuencia "Suite Habana" compuesta por imágenes de la ciudad bulliciosa: una voz radiofónica anuncia la "suite habana, interpretada por," a lo que sigue el ruido de las máquinas de construcción y el estrépito urbano de gritos y coches, unido al ritmo de tambores[6] (11.56-14.12). La equilibrada duración de planos imita un rítmico collage musical.

En el sonido musical, una banda sonora extradiegética se superpone ocasionalmente al sonido diegético, produciendo un efecto de elaboración poética. Esta banda original extradiegética de piano y *synthesizer* que se caracteriza por ser minimalista y meditativa ha sido compuesta por Edesio Alejandro responsable también de la música de *La vida es silbar*. No coincide con los estereotipos folklóricos de las habituales representaciones de la música cubana. Los restantes temas musicales abarcan una variedad de estilos y tradiciones musicales de raíz cubana. Hay canciones sincrónicas, emitidas en directo, o desde la radio, o la televisión, que contrastan o complementan las connotaciones de la imagen fílmica. El cambio de un tema musical a otro acentúa el corte narrativo. Por ejemplo, la canción "La tarde" de Sindo Garay acompaña una secuencia yuxtapuesta de asociaciones sobre el atardecer y el crepúsculo, que terminan en el letrero rojo "Revolución" (54.21-55.55). Del mismo modo, el tema "Mariposas" de Silvio Rodríguez, sobre una memoria nostálgica, dialoga con las imágenes de varios

---

[6] Los tambores recuerdan de lejos su empleo en una de las secuencias finales de *La vida es silbar* como índice de identidad cubana.

protagonistas mayores, para terminar con una lograda puesta en escena de Amanda en el primer plano, y de una foto de matrimonio, en blanco y negro, puesta en la pared. La música crece en protagonismo en los veinticinco minutos en que la cámara sigue a los personajes durante la vida nocturna. En la secuencia clave, "un momento memorable del cine cubano" –según el director Daniel Díaz Torres–, cinco ambientes y temas musicales relacionan a los personajes entre sí e interpretan sus sueños individuales (60.10-68.50). Primero, el extracto de "El lago de los cisnes" con el baile del supuesto albañil Ernesto, después el "Amén" cantado a coro en una iglesia, seguido de una pieza en saxofón tocada por Heriberto, que se halla entre los feligreses; el ambiente animado del salón Beny Moré y de un estadio de béisbol, y finalmente la performance de Iván como *drag queen* sobre el tema "Ya no hace falta" de Bamboleo, cuya letra sobre la separación de una mujer de su pareja ("déjame vivir en paz") contribuye a la pregunta sobre la relación entre el hombre y el sistema en la Revolución (cf. abajo).

En esta secuencia, el montaje traiciona una vez más las expectativas del público, preparado para escuchar los sonidos del concierto de salsa. En un momento contrapuntístico y unificador a la vez, el himno religioso permanece *on-track* y sustituye como *sound-bridge* el sonido sincrónico tanto en el salón de baile como en el estadio. La música religiosa es una fuerza integradora que refuerza la sublimación del habanero y de sus actividades. Música y arte logran agrupar a la gente y representan la verdadera esencia de sus sueños; esa información, que se dará en los créditos finales, se anticipa en el montaje de las actuaciones de Iván, Ernesto, Heriberto y Julio, filmadas en planos americanos y medios. Al añadir los temas de Nueva Trova (Silvio Rodríguez), rumba (Omara Portuondo) y bolero (Sindo Garay), la banda sonora constituye una propia suite como conjunto de estilos y tradiciones híbridas que componen el panorama musical cubano.

En este montaje polifónico de piezas musicales más o menos solemnes y de ambientes festivos, vuelve a evocarse una comunidad espiritual y emocional que había estado ausente durante las imágenes del día, convirtiendo el canto en un himno a la Revolución. Además, la película realiza un homenaje a la cultura popular en un sentido más amplio, que incluye diversos tipos de espiritualidad, con un insólito predominio de la religión cristiana, representada además por el Cristo de La Habana. De esto modo, *Suite Habana* celebra la diferencia.

3.1. Excurso: intertextos fílmicos

El documental de Fernando Pérez pretende dar una imagen poética de La Habana a través de sus habitantes y de un uso especial del montaje y sonido. *Suite Habana* se inscribe así en la tradición de las *city symphonies* que aparece, en Europa, en el cine mudo de los años veinte del siglo pasado, pero que cuenta con varios predecesores también en América Latina. Aunque Pérez declara la influencia del filme paradigmático de Walter Ruttmann, *Berlin. Die Sinfonie der Großstadt* (1927), podrían citarse también antológicos documentales latinoamericanos como el franco-brasileño *Rien que les heures* (Alberto Cavalcanti, 1926) y el cubano *PM* (Sabá Cabrera Infante/Orlando Ji-ménez Leal, 1960), documental recién recuperado para el público internacional por Ju-lian Schnabel en los genéricos de *Before Night Falls* (2000).[7] Entre las producciones extranjeras basta con recordar la trilogía *Koyaanisquatsi/Powaqquatsi/Naqoyquatsi* (1982-2002) de Godfrey Reggio, en la cual la banda sonora de Philipp Glass encubre el sonido sintópico, y los documentales de Basilio Martín Patino *Canciones para des-pués de una guerra* (1971) y *Madrid* (1987), en los cuales la música se convierte en protagonista.

La obvia interrelación con Ruttmann se insinúa, al menos, con dos recursos: pri-mero, se hace una película "muda," por el silencio de los personajes y el uso de una banda sonora adicional; segundo, se insertan textos explicativos que funcionan de cier-ta manera como el inserto del cine mudo. A diferencia de Ruttmann y del modelo de *city symphony*, Pérez no renuncia a los personajes para hacer del paisaje urbano su úni-co protagonista, sino que afirma la subjetividad de los destinos individuales. Ruttmann hizo el elogio casi futurista de la capital bulliciosa e industrializada; Pérez muestra también lugares públicos como el aeropuerto, como hospitales y colegios, pero se con-centra en la experiencia individual.

Por una parte, *Suite Habana* está inscrita en el documentalismo internacional[8]; por otra, recuerda al apogeo del documental cubano en los primeros años de la Revolu-ción, con un inmenso número de filmes: Santiago Álvarez (*Now*, 1965), Octavio Cor-tázar (*Por primera vez*, 1967) o Tomás Gutiérrez Alea (*Memorias del subdesarrollo*, 1968), entre otros. El propio Pérez empezó rodando documentales, por ejemplo con Santiago Álvarez, incluido un cortometraje sobre la cantante Omara Portuondo (*Oma-ra*, 1983), la cual volvió a la escena en *Buena Vista Social Club* y cuya voz aparece en el epílogo de *Suite Habana*.

A nivel intratextual, *Suite Habana* retoma el tono y varios motivos de sus ante-riores películas, preocupadas con los destinos individuales, pero representativos de al-gún modo, de los habitantes de la capital. También en *Madagascar* y *La vida es silbar* lo poético y la música habían desempeñado un papel estratégico. En *Suite Habana*, se recurre a estrategias del cine de ficción, técnicas de montaje, de suspenso, incluso de lo cómico.

En suma, *Suite Habana* se ubica entre una tradición tanto nacional como transna-cional. Pérez reivindica un puesto como "auteur" e inscribe su declaración de amor a la capital en una tradición internacional experimental. En las entrevistas sobre la pelí-cula, el director subraya, precisamente, ese experimentalismo. En este sentido, cuando

---

[7]   Bajo una definición muy amplia, Julianne Burton cita como "city symphonies," además de *Che, Buenos Aires* (Fernando Birri, 1966), algunas producciones ficcionales que desarro-llan historias urbanas y episódicas mediante una estética documentalista, como *Rio, qua-renta graus* (1955) de Nelson Pereira dos Santos, *Chuquiago* (1977) de Antonio Eguino o *Valparaíso, mi amor* (1969) de Aldo Francia (cf. 21).

[8]   Pérez habla también de las "actuaciones" de esquimales en los documentales de Flaherty (cf. García Hernández s.p.).

en Cuba el documental no tiene muchos adeptos por haberse perdido el contexto inmediato del cine revolucionario, *Suite Habana* significa una reflexión sobre la viabilidad del documental cubano a más de cuarenta años de la Revolución.[9]

4. El ciudadano y la Revolución

Más que otros lugares en el mundo, cualquier representación fílmica de La Habana, ficcional o documental, se enfrenta a una lectura "documentarizante" (cf. Odin). Por tanto, como demuestra la recepción de *Suite Habana*, difícilmente se puede escapar de una valoración políticamente interesada. En una de las muchas entrevistas al respecto, Fernando Pérez admitió una calidad "política" de su obra en un sentido universal, es decir, mediante el distanciamiento de cualquier discurso propagandístico: "lo que no quisimos fue hacer un discurso político desde la política misma, sino desde la vida" (García Hernández s.p.). Afirma, además, que la película da un "reflejo de la vida en La Habana, sin juzgarla" (Elizalde s.p.). Declaraciones que no impidieron interpretaciones controvertidas por parte de la prensa internacional, considerándola tanto procastrista –por ejemplo, por parte de la exiliada Zoé Valdés– como por crítica al régimen, una lectura que predominó en la prensa española y en Miami.[10]

De hecho, a pesar del afán estético y "poético," *Suite Habana* da varias claves para interpretaciones sociológicas ambiguas. Pese al interés en representar la diversidad social cubana, no abarca todos los sectores sociales. Aunque la estrechez económica se trasluce en las fachadas deshechas y en los interiores modestos, la película no busca la denuncia de la situación económica. Sus protagonistas, en su mayoría, están integrados en la sociedad mediante algún trabajo, por precario que sea: de construcción, en ferrocarriles, en una fábrica, en una lavandería, como zapatero, médico y ex-profesores; los lugares de trabajo también abarcan los logros de la Revolución como la sanidad, la fábrica de productos "hechos en Cuba" y la escuela, que sabe integrar a un chico con síndrome de Down. Por su profesión (por ejemplo, profesor de marxismo) o alguna imagen del Che en la pared, a veces exhiben un compromiso con la Revolución o con el Estado. La iluminación de las habitaciones en tonos de rojo, amarillos y dorados, y los primeros planos de las manos y las herramientas, no sólo estetizan el trabajo, sino también la precariedad cotidiana.

Por su edad, los protagonistas representan un panorama transgeneracional entre los 10 y los 97 años. La diversidad étnica se refleja relativamente; la mayoría son blancos, mientras que la población afroamericana sólo está presente con los hermanos Ra-

---

[9] De hecho, igual que en otras cinematografías nacionales, en el nuevo milenio ha aumentado la producción de cortometrajes documentales en Cuba (cf. *Producción cinematográfica*).

[10] En las tapas de diferentes copias piratas DVD vendidas desde EE.UU. por Internet, la película se promociona como subversiva al régimen: "Documental que muestra la dureza de vivir en Cuba ... Muestra el lado que no le gusta a la gente;" "Cuba quiere verla. El Gobierno la censuró. *Suite Habana* está prohibida."

quel e Iván, y en los ambientes del salón Beny Moré. Bajo la perspectiva de género, domina la figura del trabajador masculino, mientras que las mujeres pertenecen a la tercera edad, con excepción de la obrera fabril, Raquel (43 años). En consecuencia, la película escenifica una división laboral entre hombres trabajadores y mujeres como madres y en función maternal (Caridad, Norma, Inés, Natividad) e, incluso, como objeto sexual, en una secuencia humorística dominada por la mirada masculina (17.00-17.36).[11] Por otra parte, el discurso de género se cuestiona en el transformismo de varios personajes masculinos, que se maquillan y actúan como bailarín, *drag queen* y payaso. La identidad se convierte en diversas actuaciones, subrayada por la oposición entre día y noche. Otras transformaciones nocturnas descubren al zapatero Julio como el "elegante" del salón de baile y a la abuela Norma como pintora. Por tanto, si bien se esboza un panorama quizá incompleto de la población, sí se exponen diferentes identidades y opciones individuales entre las que destaca la vocación por el arte (baile, actuación, pintura, música). Los sueños hablan de paz familiar y de una carrera como artista –y no de Cuba o de alguna utopía política. La película termina con el plano de Amanda, de 79 años, económicamente la más necesitada de todas, y la única persona sin sueños.

En *Suite Habana*, Fernando Pérez emplea un "enfoque microhistórico" (García Borrero 91) que investiga la realidad cubana a través de historias y perspectivas individuales. Una estrategia contraria al juicio histórico de Grierson sobre la forma sinfónica como representación de un objeto colectivo, masivo (cf. 110). La Revolución forma el contexto y no entra en el discurso verbal transmitido. La narración y la puesta en escena minimizan la presencia explícita del contexto político, por lo que destacan las contadas referencias icónicas, en las que sí se hace presente. La realidad cubana es aludida en diferentes imágenes y mediante diferentes elementos fílmicos. Las tomas de letreros públicos insertan las palabras "Cuba" y "Revolución" en el paisaje urbano. Se menciona la diáspora (Jorge Luis), y se incluye un guiño de la censura, como la breve exhibición de un libro del escritor exiliado Jesús Díaz (José Carlos). El plano del letrero "Revolución" (55.45-55.55), dentro de una secuencia temática sobre el motivo del crepúsculo (cf. arriba), podría ser una irónica connotación política, pero también, anticipar, a nivel diegético, la transformación en la vida de los protagonistas que adoptan otra identidad durante la noche.

Mediante la puesta en escena, el ser humano, en ocasiones, se relaciona explícitamente con la Revolución. Los héroes oficiales y consagrados se yuxtaponen a los héroes cotidianos: la anciana Natividad que mira a Silvio Rodríguez en la televisión, los guardias sentados frente a la estatua de Lennon. En una elegante yuxtaposición, construida sobre la profundidad de campo, se reúnen en un plano dos generaciones de la Revolución: el joven Ernesto Díaz con un retrato del Che que está pegado en la pared de su casa. Una imagen que se repite dos veces seguidas, en alternancia, una vez más,

---

[11] La secuencia combina tomas de traseros de paseantes femeninas y de hombres mirones con una olla a presión. No se menciona, sin embargo, la prostitución, que sí se tematizó en *La vida es silbar*.

con la estatua de Lennon, integrada como ícono en la vida cotidiana. En la composición de estos planos, la película parece preguntar por la supervivencia de la Revolución y de sus héroes en los hijos y nietos. Una posible lectura indica la continuidad –el joven ayudando a reconstruir la casa– y, a la vez, un desplazamiento hacia otros terrenos, como la lucha por la igualdad cultural y sexual; o bien, la búsqueda de la felicidad individual como base de la felicidad colectiva. Alcanzan una función metonímica por el montaje paralelo de acciones y encuadres similares: por ejemplo, el de los obreros Iván, Heriberto y Francisco en bicicleta, una imagen clave que recuerda el comienzo de *Madagascar*. Los protagonistas llevan vidas "ejemplares" que se alejan de una pauta pre-establecida. El paralelismo del montaje convierte sus destinos en variaciones sobre un mismo tema: la condición del hombre en la Revolución. En este sentido, los protagonistas de *Suite Habana* serían representantes de *otro* "hombre nuevo."

El crepúsculo y la revolución   Dos Ernestos

Mención aparte merecen, en este contexto, las imágenes televisivas, que contrastan al individuo con la "realidad" política como un mundo aparte. Primero, las manifestaciones masivas, cuyas imágenes son intercaladas en distintos momentos (14.30; 54.21), referidas a diferentes horas. Dos personajes, el marido de Norma y la anciana Natividad, de 97 años, están mirando la tele aparentemente todo el día, y siempre la misma imagen. La repetición de la misma imagen de una multitud vociferante con banderas cubanas, transmite un comentario paródico acerca del rutinario entusiasmo de la fiesta revolucionaria. Entre las tomas de la multitud frenética, se percibe muy brevemente, filmado en primer plano lateral, una persona (¿Fidel?) en el podio. La escena comprueba, por una parte, la integración de la Revolución en la vida cotidiana, con la anciana como muda compañera, cuya mirada se enfoca mediante un *zoom* hacia un primer plano lateral. Por otra, el espectáculo colectivo expuesto en el televisor choca con la soledad y pasividad de la espectadora. La Revolución mediada por la televisión está distante del individuo, en esta lectura, *Suite Habana* no se encuentra tan lejos de *La vida es silbar*. Una segunda emisión televisiva se refiere al cantautor Silvio Rodríguez, coetáneo de Pérez, cantando "Mariposas" (57.33-60.10). Como uno de los registros musicales preferidos por la Televisión Nacional –según Eßer y Frölicher– la canción de la Nueva Trova figura como representante cultural de la Revolución Cubana. La canción de Silvio Rodríguez forma parte del registro poético de la película, mediante el *zoom*, que combina su letra, que habla sobre el recuerdo, con una foto que está en la pared, mostrando una Amanda mucho más joven. Sin embargo, al mismo tiempo de rendir homenaje al cantautor –como otro "héroe" público al lado de Lennon–, la secuencia de "Mariposas" también recuerda la existencia de un arte oficial, frente a otro que se descubre en los clubes nocturnos.

La pregunta implícita versa sobre la condición del ser humano bajo la Revolución. A través de la sublimación del trabajo y del ocio humano, se presentan héroes cotidianos. Cuando insiste en los sueños de los personajes, crea suspenso y muestra la diversidad en la narración de las vidas personales, es así como la película subraya que el hombre debe ser libre para desarrollar su individualidad. Por otra parte, necesita de la solidaridad y la comunidad –sólo así, podríamos deducir–, puede funcionar una Revolución. De este modo, *Suite Habana*, sirviéndose del género documental, renueva ideas expuestas en algunos de los largometrajes anteriores de Fernando Pérez.

5. Conclusión

En su esbozo de una poética del documental, Michael Renov habla de cuatro funciones que puede cumplir una producción documental: registrar, persuadir, analizar y expresar (cf. "Toward"). Sin duda, la película de Fernando Pérez se dedica, sobre todo, a la cuarta función, con su preocupación por la estética del filme, pero no excluye por completo a las otras. *Suite Habana* cumple con la característica de los largometrajes anteriores de Pérez, que Raúl Rubio considera un "response-oriented cinema" bajo un doble enfoque "perfecto" e "imperfecto;" es decir, un cine que emplea los códigos del cine transnacional, sin renegar de la estrategia didáctica del cine cubano de los sesenta. Fernando Pérez combina el melodrama y un lenguaje emotivo con la reflexión social. En palabras de Beat Borter, se trata de un cine destinado a "moving to thought" (141). Mientras sus dos primeros largometrajes reflejaban y explicaban la Revolución desde su historia y prehistoria, los siguientes empezaron a ahondar en el presente y la reflexión sobre sus contradicciones. Creo que este doble enfoque didáctico-emotivo también se halla en *Suite Habana*, aunque las técnicas de subjetividad conllevan una identificación afectiva muy intensa. Ahora bien, no se ofrece una interpretación explícita ni única de la realidad habanera, muy por el contrario: al permitir tanto una lectura disidente como afirmativa, *Suite Habana* aglutina a diferentes públicos europeos, norte- y sudamericanos, como el logrado ejemplo de una película transnacional.

En *Madagascar* y *La vida es silbar*, Pérez desarrolla historias individuales que expresan una especie de "exilio interior" (Rubio s.p.) relacionándose con motivos como la migración y la orfandad. *La vida es silbar* utiliza el silbo –la negación del habla– como símbolo de la libertad de expresión y de insumisión, e incluye la sátira del discurso burocrático, cuando palabras como "doble moral" y "oportunismo," escucha-das de la boca de un ciudadano insumiso, causan desmayo entre los transeúntes. En *La vida es silbar*, se parte de la soledad de la ciudad y de sus habitantes, soledad remediada sólo en parte durante el transcurso de la narración. La madre del mulato Elpidio, "Cuba," es una madre ausente.

En *Suite Habana*, los personajes han dejado de hablar por completo. Están solos por momentos, pero asimismo están acogidos por la solidaridad familiar. Son personas que han vivido la Revolución, cuyos hijos formarán la futura Cuba. Expuesta al juicio del espectador, la imagen de la capital cubana se abre hacia una interpretación polisémica, una imagen polifónica de temas musicales y símbolos heterogéneos. *Suite Habana* organiza un universo propio, que resulta, en forma y contenido, dialéctico y conciliador a la vez. La Habana, representada por sus habitantes, es una ciudad entre la derrota y la reconstrucción. La "contaminación" del documental con elementos ficcionales –narración, cámara y montaje, "actuación" de los protagonistas reales, puesta en escena de situaciones "reales"–, permite a la película ofrecer una interpretación performativa de la realidad que, precisamente, por ello logra presentar lados "invisibles" de la capital.[12]

Pero más allá de una estrecha y exclusiva lectura política, La Habana según Pérez es un paisaje cultural y una utopía soñada. No en vano el comienzo y el cierre se centran en la figura de John Lennon, un héroe pacífico de la cultura mundial, la cual constituye el público de *Suite Habana*. Fiel a la letra de la canción más famosa de Lennon, "Imagine," la composición de Fernando Pérez invita precisamente a la recepción constructiva de la imaginación.

Bibliografía

Borter, Beat. "Moving to Thought. The Inspired Reflective Cinema of Fernando Pérez." *Framing Latin American Cinema*. Ed. Ann Marie Stock. Minneapolis: U of Minnesota P, 1997. 141-61.

Burton, Julianne. "Toward a History of Social Documentary in Latin America." *The Social Documentary in Latin America*. Ed. Julianne Burton. Pittsburgh: U of Pittsburgh P, 1990. 3-30.

Cabello, Gabriel. "Construyendo tiempo. Los ensayos cinematográficos de José Luis Guerín." *Ciberletras. Revista de crítica literaria y de cultura* 12 (2004). http://www.lehman.edu/ ciberletras/v12/cabello.htm.

Carroll, Noël. "Dokumentarfilm und postmoderner Skeptizismus." 1996. Trad. Jutta Doberstein. *Bilder des Wirklichen. Texte zur Theorie des Dokumentarfilms*. Ed. Eva Hohenberger. Berlin: Vorwerk 8, 2000. 35-68.

Cine y audiovisuales. Base de datos de películas calificadas. Ministerio de Cultura del gobierno de España. http://www.mcu.es/bbddpeliculas/cargarFiltro.do?layout=bbddpelicu las&cache=init&language=es.

---

[12] Una parecida estrategia entre narrativa y documental persiguen los "ensayos cinematográficos" del español José Luis Guerin (cf. Cabello).

Comolli, Jean-Louis. "Der Umweg über das *direct*." 1969. Trad. Stefan Barmann, Eva Ho-henberger. *Bilder des Wirklichen. Texte zur Theorie des Dokumentarfilms*. Ed. Eva Ho-henberger. Berlin: Vorwerk 8, 2000. 242-65.

Cubacine. El portal del audiovisual cubano. ICAIC. 22 de febrero de 2010. http://www. cubacine.cu.

Diario del Festival de San Sebastián. 18 de septiembre de 2003. http://www.sansebastian festival.com/admin_img/diarios/archivos/diario_55.pdf.

Díaz Torres, Daniel. "Redención de la melancolía. (Sobre *Suite Habana*, una película de Fer-nando Pérez)." *La Jiribilla* 121 (agosto 2003). http://www.lajiribilla.cu/2003/n121_08/ 121_02.html.

Elizalde, Rosa Miriam. "Fernando Pérez, director de cine. 'Suite Habana' no admite interpre-taciones políticas." *Rebelión* 1 de octubre de 2003. http://www.rebelion.org/hemeroteca /cultura/031001sh.htm.

Eßer, Thorsten y Patrik Frölicher. "Von der Schlitztrommel zum Synthesizer. 500 Jahre Mu-sik auf Kuba." *Kuba heute*. Ed. Ottmar Ette y Martin Franzbach. Frankfurt a.M.: Ver-vuert, 2001. 683-731.

García, Rocío. "Cuba ha sido y es todavía un sueño posible." *El País digital* 19 de septiembre de 2003. http://www.elpais.com/diario.

García Borrero, Juan Antonio. "Las iniciales de la ciudad. La libertad expresiva en el cine de Fernando Pérez." *Cinémas d'Amérique Latine* 12 (2004): 75-91.

García Hernández, Arturo. "*Suite Habana* propone un discurso político desde la vida." Artí-culo de opinión. *La Ventana, Portal informativo de la Casa de las Américas* 19 de sep-tiembre de 2003. http://laventana.casa.cult.cu/modules.php?name=News&file=article& sid=1464.

Grierson, John. "Grundsätze des Dokumentarfilms." 1933. Trad. Wilhelm Flöttmann. *Bilder des Wirklichen. Texte zur Theorie des Dokumentarfilms*. Ed. Eva Hohenberger. Berlin: Vorwerk 8, 2000. 100-13.

Hamburger Abendblatt. 14 de agosto de 2005.

Hamdorf, Wolfgang M. "*Suite Havanna*." *Filmdienst* 23 (11 de noviembre de 2004): 48.

Harguindey, Ángel S. "Un demoledor documental cubano." *El País digital* 19 de septiembre de 2003. http://www.elpais.com/diario.

Hohenberger, Eva. "Dokumentarfilmtheorie." *Bilder des Wirklichen. Texte zur Theorie des Dokumentarfilms*. Ed. Eva Hohenberger. Berlin: Vorwerk 8, 2000. 8-34.

Izod, John y Richard Kilborn. "The Documentary Film." *The Oxford Guide to Film Studies*. Ed. John Hill y Pamela Church Gibson. Oxford: Oxford UP, 1998. 426-33.

Krebs, Geri. "Lenin und Lennon in Havanna." *Der Freitag* 26 de diciembre de 2003. http:// www.freitag.de/2004/02/04021801.php.

López, Ana. "Revolutions and Dreams. The Cuban Documentary Today." *Studies in Latin American Popular Culture* 11 (1992): 45-57.

Manso Sendán, Geovannys. "Los universos visuales de Fernando Pérez." *Miradas. Revista del audiovisual* (s.a.).http://www.miradas.eictv.co.cu/index.php.

Maqua, Javier. "El estado de la ficción. ¿Nuevas ficciones audiovisuales?" *Historia general del cine*. T. XII: El cine en la era audiovisual. Ed. Manuel Palacio y Santos Zunzunegui. Madrid: Cátedra, 1995. 199-219.

Nichols, Bill. *Blurred Boundaries. Questions of Meaning in Contemporary Culture*. Bloomington/Indianapolis: Indiana UP, 1994.

———. *Representing Reality. Issues and Concepts in Documentary*. Bloomington: Indiana UP, 1991.

Odin, Roger. "Film documentaire, lecture documentarisante." *Cinémas et réalités*. Ed. Jean-Charles Lyant y Roger Odin. Saint Étienne: Université de Saint Étienne, 1984. 263-78.

Padrón, Frank. "Una Habana que llora (y que sueña...)." *La Jiribilla* 121 (agosto 2003). http://www.lajiribilla.cu/2003/n121_08/121_06.html.

Plantinga, Carl. "The Scene of Empathy and the Human Face on Film." *Passionate Views. Film, Cognition, and Emotion*. Ed. Carl Plantinga y Greg M. Smith. Baltimore/London: Johns Hopkins UP, 1999. 239-55.

Producción cinematográfica. Ministerio de Cultura de la República de Cuba. 22 de febrero de 2010. http://www.min.cult.cu/loader.php?sec=estadisticas&cont=prodcinematografica.

Renov, Michael. *The Subject in Documentary*. Minneapolis: U of Minnesota P, 2004.

———. "Toward a Poetics of Documentary." *Theorizing Documentary*. Ed. Michael Renov. London: Routledge, 1993. 12-36.

Rodríguez Marchante, E. "*Suite Habana*: La tristeza cubana desvelada en los rostros de la mera gente." *ABC.es* 19 de septiembre de 2003. http://www.abc.es.

Rosen, Philip. "Document and Documentary." *Theorizing Documentary*. Ed. Michael Renov. London: Routledge, 1993. 58-89.

Rubio, Raúl. "Political Aesthetics in Contemporary Cuban Filmmaking. Fernando Pérez's *Madagascar* and *La vida es silbar*." *Ciberletras* 13 (julio 2005). http://www.lehman.cuny.edu/ciberletras/v13/rubio.htm.

Santaolalla, Isabel. *Los 'otros.' Etnicidad y 'raza' en el cine español contemporáneo*. Zaragoza: Prensas Universitarias, 2005.

Schulte, Anna. "'Ich bin süchtig nach dieser Stadt.' Der Dokumentarfilm *Suite Habana*. Ein authentisches Portrait über den Alltag in der kubanischen Hauptstadt." *Lateinamerika Nachrichten* 366 (2004). http://www.lateinamerikanachrichten.de/?/artikel/368.html.

Schumann, Peter B. "El cine cubano en el contexto de la política cultural." *Todas las islas la isla. Nuevas y novísimas tendencias en la literatura y cultura de Cuba*. Ed. Janett Reinstädtler y Dieter Ingenschay. Madrid/Frankfurt a.M.: Iberoamericana/Vervuert, 2000. 123-35.

Seguin, Jean-Claude. "El documental español del tercer milenio. Las formas de la trans-gresión." *Miradas glocales. Cine español en el cambio del milenio*. Ed. Burkhard Pohl y Jörg Türschmann. Frankfurt a.M.: Vervuert, 2007. 55-69.

Theis, Peter. "Soy Havana. (Film Review: *Suite Habana*)." *Offoffoff Film*. (1 de mayo de 2004). http://www.offoffoff.com/film/2004/suitehabana.php.

Torreiro, M. "Retratos en claroscuro." *El País digital* 3 de octubre de 2003. http://www.elpais.com/diario.

Filmografía

Agua con sal. Dir. Pedro Pérez Rosado. Puerto Rico, España, 2005.

Alicia en el pueblo de maravillas. Dir. Daniel Díaz Torres. Cuba, 1991.

Balseros. Dir. Carlos Bosch y Josep M. Domenech. España, 2002.

Before Night Falls. Dir. Julian Schnabel. Estados Unidos, 2000.

Berlin. Die Sinfonie der Großstadt. Dir. Walter Ruttmann. Alemania, 1927.

Blanco y negro. Dir. Fernando Trueba. España, 2003.

Buena Vista Social Club. Dir. Wim Wenders. Alemania, Estados Unidos, Gran Bretaña, Francia, Cuba, 1999.

Calle 54. Dir. Fernando Trueba. España, Francia, Italia, México, Bélgica, 2000.

Canciones para después de una guerra. Dir. Basilio Martín Patino. España, 1971.

Che, Buenos Aires. Dir. Fernando Birri. Argentina, 1966.

Chuquiago. Dir. Antonio Eguino. Bolivia, 1977.

Clandestinos. Dir. Fernando Pérez. Cuba, 1988.

Cosas que dejé en La Habana. Dir. Manuel Gutierrez Aragón. España, 1997.

Cuarteto de La Habana. Dir. Fernando Colomo. España, 1999.

Cuba feliz: Road movie musical. Dir. Karim Dridi. Francia, Cuba, 2000.

El milagro de Candeal. Dir. Fernando Trueba. España, 2004.

Flores de otro mundo. Dir. Icíar Bollaín. España, 1999.

Fresa y chocolate. Dir. Tomás Gutiérrez Alea y Juan Carlos Tabío. Cuba, España, México, Estados Unidos, 1993.

Guantanamera. Dir. Tomás Gutiérrez Alea. Cuba, España, Alemania, 1995.

Habana Blues. Dir. Benito Zambrano. España, 2005.

Habana, Havana. Dir. Alberto Arvelo. Venezuela, 2004.

Hacerse el sueco. Dir. Daniel Díaz Torres. Cuba, España, Alemania, 2000.

Havanna, mi amor. Dir. Uli Gaulke. Alemania, 2000.

Hello Hemingway. Dir. Fernando Pérez. Cuba, 1990.

Kleines Tropicana. Dir. Daniel Díaz Torres. Cuba, España, Alemania, 1997.

Koyaanisquatsi. Dir. Godfrey Reggio. Estados Unidos, 1982.

La pelota vasca. Dir. Julio Medem. España, 2003.

La vida es silbar. Dir. Fernando Pérez. España, Cuba, 1998.

Madagascar. Dir. Fernando Pérez. Cuba, 1994.

Madrid. Dir. Basilio Martín Patino. España, 1987.

Memorias del subdesarrollo. Dir. Tomás Gutiérrez Alea. Cuba, 1968.

Naqoyquatsi. Dir. Godfrey Reggio. Estados Unidos, 2002.

Now. Dir. Santiago Álvarez. Cuba, 1965.

Omara. Dir. Santiago Álvarez y Fernando Pérez. Cuba, 1983.

Paraíso. Dir. Alina Teodorescu. Alemania, 2003.

PM. Dir. Sabá Cabrera Infante y Orlando Jiménez Leal. Cuba, 1960.

Por primera vez. Dir. Octavio Cortázar. Cuba, 1967.

Powaqquatsi. Dir. Godfrey Reggio. Estados Unidos, 1988.

Rien que les heures. Dir. Alberto Cavalcanti. Francia, Brasil, 1926.

Suite Habana. Dir. Fernando Pérez. Cuba, España, 2003.

The Politics of Representation in Hypertext Docu-fiction: Multi-ethnic Los Angeles as an Emblem of 'America' in Norman M. Klein's *Bleeding Through: Layers of Los Angeles, 1920-1986*

JENS MARTIN GURR

Resumen

Este ensayo se ocupa de *Bleeding Through* (2003), una obra que combina una novela breve de 37 páginas con un documental interactivo multimedia (DVD-ROM) que sucede en la ciudad de Los Angeles en el siglo veinte (1920-1986). Pretendemos demostrar que la presentación de la ciudad puede ser considerada una representación, con gran frecuencia, subversiva, de las complejidades de Los Angeles en la actualidad como símbolo emblemático de los EE.UU. La obra hace uso pleno de las posibilidades que ofrece un medio digital para representar la complejidad, la multiplicidad y las dinámicas de la urbe. En un primer paso, estableceremos el contexto para el análisis centrado en las ideas básicas de Norman Klein en su monografía *The History of Forgetting: Los Angeles and the Erasure of Memory* (1997) en la que *Bleeding Through* se basa en gran medida. Demostraremos que la reflexividad de la obra de Klein –altamente sofisticada– y su intento de crear una textualidad no lineal pone de relieve los problemas que surgen al querer representar la complejidad de la ciudad en una forma lineal 'tradicional' y remite al hipertexto de *Bleeding Through*. En un segundo paso, enfocaremos las implicaciones estéticas y políticas del formato. Sirviéndose de las estrategias y estéticas de documentales del hipertexto *Bleeding Through* radicaliza las tendencias hacia la reflexividad, la subjetividad y el artificio –supuestamente opuestas a la objetividad del realismo–, muy presentes en los documentales de las últimas décadas. En conclusión, este ensayo muestra cómo la obra a través de su enfoque subversivo de las estrategias hegemónicas de la planificación urbana y de la segregación étnica subvierte la visión convencional de la hegemonía de un Los Angeles multi-étnico –a veces de manera implícita, aunque a menudo explícitamente– y, a la vez, de los EE.UU. en su totalidad.

Consider this: the computer is fundamentally an aesthetics of assets. ... Thus, if ever there were an aporetic model of story, it is the digital. However, we must never trust any use of aporia that suggests it is a problem to be solved. That is like saying that unreliable narrators are a problem, rather than the heart of the modern novel. ... Perhaps we have lost the sense of what gives story presence: Absence. ... I came up with a model that captures the immersive power of a Balzac novel or a stream-of-consciousness journey through a city (Musil, Joyce, Proust, even Melville—the ship as city—and Virginia Woolf). The structure works like this: ... Each tier [of the DVD] comments on a specific medium that tries to make the city intelligible as it erases, collectively forgets, survives from day to day. The history of forgetting is a distraction from the basic reality of urban life in Los Angeles, its quotidian power of survival (Klein, "Bleeding Through" 42).

1. Introduction

How does one represent, synchronically as well as diachronically, the complexity of Los Angeles, city of Hollywood myths and inner-city decay, of ceaseless self-invention and bulldozed urban renewal, of multi-ethnic pluralism and ethnic ghettos, a city where both the promises and problems of 'America' have crystallized to the present day? For while the discourses of urban utopia and urban crisis with all their contradictory ideological implications are as old as the concept of 'city' itself (cf. Mumford, Gassenmeier, and Teske), Los Angeles has always been imagined in particularly polarized ways:

> According to your point of view, Los Angeles is either exhilarating or nihilistic, sun-drenched or smog-enshrouded, a multicultural haven or a segregated ethnic concentration camp—Atlantis or high capitalism—and orchestrating these polarized alternatives is an urban identity thriving precisely on their interchangeability (Murphet 8).[1]

Los Angeles, of course, has long been a center of attention for urbanists as well as for scholars of urban planning and of cultural representations of the city. It has been the subject of innumerable studies, the locale for countless novels, documentary films and particularly of countless feature films.[2] However, one of the most impressive renderings of the complexities of 20th-century Los Angeles, and surely one of the most ambitious attempts to do justice to these complexities by presenting a wealth of material in a highly self-conscious form of hypertext, is Norman M. Klein's multi-media docu-fiction *Bleeding Through: Layers of Los Angeles, 1920-1986*.[3]

---

[1] This passage is also cited in Bénézet 56.

[2] From among the innumerable studies, cf. for instance Davis, Fulton, Klein, *Forgetting,* Murphet, Scott & Soja, Soja, *Thirdspace,* "Exopolis" and "Los Angeles," Ofner & Siefert.

[3] Largely written by Klein and programmed by Rosemary Comella and Andreas Kratky, it was co-produced by The Labyrinth Project at the Annenberg Center for Communication at the University of Southern California and the ZKM—Zentrum für Kunst und Medien—Karlsruhe.

Bleeding Through, which combines a 37-page novella with a multimedia documentary DVD[4] on twentieth-century Los Angeles, is based on the fictitious story of "Molly," who moved to L.A. in 1920 when she was 22 and whose life and times the narrator of the novella attempts to chronicle.[5] The question whether or not she killed her second husband (or had him killed) at some point in 1959 serves as a narrative hook to launch the reader and user of the DVD on a quest through layers of 20th-century Los Angeles. Thus, as the cover blurb appropriately notes, *Bleeding Through* is "a loosely constructed documentary underlying a flexible literary journey, it is an urban bricolage held together by the outline of a novel spanning sixty-six years."[6]

In this essay, I will argue that *Bleeding Through* makes full use of the opportunities afforded by the digital medium to represent the complexity, multiplicity and dynamics of the city in a way no other medium could. I will first establish the contexts for an analysis of Klein's multi-media documentary by outlining the key findings of Klein's 1997 monograph *The History of Forgetting: Los Angeles and the Erasure of Memory*, on which *Bleeding Through* is based to a considerable extent. *The History of Forgetting*, however, also provides the context for *Bleeding Through* in another sense: the flaunted self-reflexivity of Klein's distinctly non-academic and often highly literary work and its attempts at creating a non-linear textuality also highlight the problems of representing the complexity of the city in any 'traditional' linear form, in print or in a documentary film. These problems of representation demonstrably lead to the non-linear format of multi-media hypertext in *Bleeding Through*. By outlining the relationship between the novella and the documentary and by highlighting some of the features and design principles of the interactive DVD, I will then show how *Bleeding Through* re-presents the complexity of 20th-century Los Angeles by taking us on a revisionist tour of its history since the 1920s and by pointing out the extent to which fictitious urban imaginaries—the innumerable *films noirs*, detective films and thrillers set in L.A.—have shaped perceptions of the city and even the city itself. The essay goes on more explicitly to point out the aesthetic and political implications of the multimedia format, of what one might call 'interactive multi-medial docu-fiction in hypertext.' Deploying the narrative and aesthetic strategies of hypertext documentaries, *Bleeding Through* demonstrably heightens and radicalizes the tendencies towards self-reflexivity, subjectivity and flaunted artifice as opposed to allegedly objective realism—apparent in documentaries in recent decades. In conclusion, I will show how the work's subversive view of hegemonic strategies of urban planning and ethnic segrega-

---

[4] References to the novella, where this source is not clear, will be abbreviated BT, references to the DVD will be given by tier and chapter.

[5] For the connections between Molly's story and the material on the cultural history of L.A., cf. the additional texts in the *Bleeding Through* booklet by Klein's collaborators on the project, Shaw 52, Kinder 54f., Comella 59 and Kratky 60.

[6] Klein's collaborator, Rosemary Comella, calls it "a sort of stream-of-consciousness interactive bricolage-documentary overlaying a fictionalized story based on a real person" (59).

tion undercuts conventional representations of multi-ethnic L.A. and—sometimes by implication, but often explicitly—of the Unites States as a whole.

2. Establishing Contexts: The Problems of Representing Urban Complexity in Klein's *History of Forgetting*

Klein's 1997 monograph *The History of Forgetting: Los Angeles and the Erasure of Memory* is itself highly unusual in its mix of genres: Parts I and IV are scholarly studies of 20th-century urban planning in L.A. and of the impact of filmic representations on the urban imaginary of the city, Part II is the imaginative recreation of the perspective on the city of a Vietnamese immigrant in a novella of some 65 pages (151-215), while Part III is a collection of creatively essayistic "docufables" (217).[7] Klein names as one of his key themes "the uneven decay of an Anglo identity in Los Angeles, how the instability of white hegemonic culture leads to bizarre over-reactions in urban planning, in policing, and how these are mystified in mass culture" (17).

Referring to what is surely the most drastic urban redevelopment project in 20th-century Los Angeles, Klein states that "Bunker Hill [became] the emblem of urban blight in Los Angeles, the primary target for redevelopment downtown from the late twenties on" (52). The Bunker Hill Renewal Project, begun in the 1950s and not scheduled to end before 2015, brought the virtually total razing of a neighborhood, the flattening of the hill and the construction of the high-rise buildings now popularly regarded as constituting "Downtown L.A." Similarly, Klein comments on the razing of the "old Chinatown, old Mexican Sonora ... the old Victorian slum district, and other *barrios* west of downtown, [which] were leveled, virtually without a trace" (97). Commenting on an eerie commonality of all these 20th-century urban renewal projects in L.A., Klein writes:

> Except for Chinatown, every neighborhood erased by urban planning in and around downtown was Mexican, or was perceived that way (generally, they were mixed, often no more than 30% Mexican). ... While East L.A. may *today* seem the singular capital of Mexican-American life in the city, the mental map was different in the forties. The heartland of Mexican-American Los Angeles was identified as sprawling west, directly

---

[7]   In his "Outline" in the Introduction, Klein sets out his plan for the book as follows: "In the chapters that follow (Part I), I will examine the map of what is left out in downtown Los Angeles, how urban myths (social imaginaries) have been used as public policy. In the second part, I present a docu-novel, (or novella) based on Vietnamese immigrants who live in areas affected by these policies. In the third part, I present docufables from other residents in these communities, particularly about how their memories are affected by public traumas: drive-by shootings, racist neglect, policies toward immigrants, the Uprising of 1992, and so on. And in the final parts, I examine how literature and other media use techniques of the 'unreliable narrator,' and how the corporate uses of 'unreliable' memory are transforming the cultures of Los Angeles" (17).

past downtown, from north to south. Bunker Hill was identified as "Mexican" by 1940, like Sonoratown just north of it ... and particularly Chavez Ravine (132-33).[8]

In *History of Forgetting* as well as in a number of essays, Klein further shows how the urban imaginary of Los Angeles has been shaped by images of the city in film, from *noir* to *Blade Runner* and beyond, creating "places that never existed but are remembered anyway" ("Absences" 452), even arguing that the ideology of noir and neo-noir films, these "delusional journeys into panic and conservative white flight," also help "sell gated communities and 'friendly' surveillance systems" ("Staging Murders" 89).

More immediately, *Bleeding Through*—though the details do not all fit—is clearly based on one of the short docufables in part III of the book: in a mere three pages, "The Unreliable Narrator"[9] tells the story of 93-year-old Molly Frankel, who moved to the city in the 1920s, ran a shop for decades and rented out most of her spacious Victorian house in Angelino Heights to a large Mexican family. Towards the end of the text, the experimental and tentative nature of these musings is pointed out by self-reflexively sketching a genealogy in a number of references both to the tradition of the unreliable narrator and to accounts of the constructedness of historiography and memory since the eighteenth century: "the Münchhausens and Uncle Tobys ... German and Central European fiction after 1880 ... the absent presence that in Michelet's words are 'obscure and dubious witnesses' (1847) ... the broad crisis of representation in cinema" (233).

A similar concern with forms of representation is apparent in the chapter entitled "The Most Photographed and Least Remembered City in the World" in *History of Forgetting*. Klein here comments on previous fictional films and documentaries seeking to record the history of ethnic Los Angeles, such as Kent MacKenzie's *The Exiles* (1961) or Duane Kubo's *Raise the Banner* (1980) and the way in which even these well-intentioned films evade the issue of the razing of ethnic neighborhoods: "The twin beasts that erased much of downtown—racist neglect and ruthless planning—leave only a faint echo in cinema, because generally one will distract the other, or because cinema, by its very apparatus, resembles the tourist imaginary" (249). Klein here speaks of the

> utter instability of cinema as a formal record, and the fact that audiences enjoy this paramnesiac sensation, as memory dissolves. ... The layering of erasures is essential to moving the narrative along, to its simultaneity, its unreal solidity, its anarchic orderliness (253).

Anticipating the self-conscious concern with narrative form in *Bleeding Through*, Klein notes in *History of Forgetting* that when he began to write about the 20th-century transformations of Los Angeles, "I noticed that my scholarship was beginning to resemble fiction" and speaks of the "crossed identity" fostered by this type of writing,

---

[8]   Klein also refers to the "policy of shutting out downtown to non-whites ...since the 1920s" (132).

[9]   "Unreliable Narrators" is also the title of a chapter in the novella (26-34).

"[making] the scholar both reader and character within the same text" (6-7). Even more directly linking the arrangement of a wealth of materials to the writing of fiction, he comments: "In many ways the materials I have assembled look like research gathered by a novelist before the novel is written, before the writer turns the contradictions into a character-driven story" (7). In a highly revealing footnote, he further comments on his concern with form:

> I am trying, with as much modesty as possible, to identify a form of literature that is not simply 'hybridized,' or 'de-narratized,' and certainly not deconstructed—not a blend of others but a structure in itself, a structure that is evolving ... By structure, I mean *how to generate alternatives within the text itself, within the style itself* (*Forgetting* 20, note 10, italics in the original).[10]

In *History of Forgetting*, Klein even points forward to *Bleeding Through* by employing—if only half-seriously—the techniques of hypertext. In a short section entitled "Brief Interruption" in the "Introduction," in a reference to theories of memory and forgetting, he states: "The only solution for this introduction is a kind of hypertext (click to page 301). For the reader also interested in memory theory ... I have included an Appendix ... Read it now or read it later, whenever is suits you" (14).[11] *The History of Forgetting* in its frequently scrupulous and highly self-conscious concern with narrative form thus clearly anticipates *Bleeding Through*.[12]

3. *Bleeding Through*: Multimedia Docu-fiction on the Erasure of Multi-ethnic Los Angeles

While *History of Forgetting* addresses more directly the perversions of city planning driven by greed and racism, *Bleeding Though* tackles them more obliquely if more experientially. It does so by juxtaposing two formats: the "traditional" narrative of

---

[10] Cf. *History of Forgetting*: "There are clear signs that both critical theory and cultural studies have generated what amounts to a new category of literature (as yet unnamed). What names there are sound a bit early in the cycle right now, clearly not what this (genre?) might be called ten years from now: docu-novels, 'mockumentaries,' false autobiographies, public autobiography; 'faction'; phonebooks or chatlines as variations of personal essay; public autobiography; 'witnessing' ...; historiographic metafiction. I would rather not add more labels. Instead, I'll stick to the term 'history.' That is problematic and fictive enough already" (7).

[11] Elsewhere in the Introduction, he refers to the effect of his strategies of representation in the book as those of "digital simulations," "special effects, a morphing programme in slo-mo, when the simulation is naked, when the tiger is obviously three frames away from turning human" (BT 16). This morphing of one image into the next is precisely one of the most impressive features of *Bleeding Through*.

[12] On the other hand, establishing a connection between the contextual material for Molly's story on the DVD and *The History of Forgetting*, the narrator of the novella comments on "numerous characters in the background [of Molly's story] who may show up, but certainly will appear in future volumes of *The History of Forgetting*" (BT 29; cf. 32).

Klein's novella on the one hand and a multimedia DVD on the other hand. The documentary is thus held together by the underlying story of Molly and her life in L.A. between 1920 and 1986.

Klein's constantly self-reflexive 37-page novella "Bleeding Through" has a highly self-conscious first-person narrator who tells the story of Molly and—just as centrally—his attempts to reconstruct it:

> I couldn't trust any of her stories. Not that her facts were wrong. Or that she didn't make an effort. [But] she'd fog out dozens of key facts. Whenever I noticed, she would blow me off, smiling, and say, "So I lose a few years." ... But there were seven memories in the years from 1920 to 1986 that were luminously detailed. (10)[13]

It is these seven memories of key stages of Molly's life around which the novella and the DVD are structured, and which serve to explore 66 years of developments in the city.

Set largely within the three-mile radius near downtown L.A. in which Molly spent most of her life, the documentary deals with neighborhoods such as Boyle Heights, Bunker Hill, Chavez Ravine, Chinatown and Echo Park, the disappearance of which was chronicled in *History of Forgetting*. As the narrator explains here, this area was the site of the most drastic urban renewal projects in the country continuing over decades: "Hundreds of buildings gone: that could just as easily have been caused by carpet bombing, or a volcano erupting in the central business district" (BT 12). The same area around downtown, however, is also the center of a filmic universe: "Inside those three miles, under the skyline dropped by mistake into downtown ten years ago [in the 1980s] more people have been murdered in classic Hollywood crime films than anywhere else on earth" (BT 12).[14]

The documentary database includes hundreds of images, maps, newspaper clippings, drawings and sketches, historical film clips and (for copyright reasons[15]) film

---

[13] The "preface" on the DVD, displayed above a vintage photograph of downtown L.A. with City Hall still by far the tallest building, similarly makes clear the central principle of this "cinematic novel archive" (Klein, "Absences" 453) and already highlights its major concerns: "An elderly woman living near downtown has lost the ability to distinguish day from night. Rumors suggest that decades ago, she had her second husband murdered. When asked, she indicates, quite cheerfully, that she has decided to forget all that: 'I lose a few years.' Three miles around where she is standing, more people have been 'murdered' in famous crime films than anywhere else in the world. Imaginary murders clog the roof gutters. They hide beneath coats of paint. But in fact, the neighborhoods have seen something quite different than movie murders; a constant adjustment to Latinos, Japanese, Filipinos, Jews, Evangelicals, Chinese. What's more, in the sixties, hundreds of buildings were bulldozed. And yet, pockets remain almost unchanged since 1940."

[14] The novella refers to "290 murder films ... shot no more than five minutes from Molly's house" (31). The narrator later states that "Since the Seventies, murders have been relocated a few blocks west, because gunfire looks more ironic underneath the L.A. skyline at night, seen best from the hills in Temple-Beaudry" (BT 37).

[15] For this, cf. Comella's short essay on the "making of" *Bleeding Through*; especially p. 58.

snippets recognizably re-enacting key scenes of famous L.A. films merely by repeating the camera movements in basically empty streets in the original locations, but
without actors.[16] Furthermore, there are numerous interviews with long-term residents,
sometimes elaborate captions, as well as narrative commentary by Norman Klein.[17]
Klein's video commentary frequently gives clues as to the story behind the disappearance of Molly's husband Walt, which adds a playful dimension of detective game to
the navigation experience, because, such is the underlying fiction, the point of navigating *Bleeding Through* in the first place is to act as a detective on the hunt for such
clues. However, as the narrator of the novella comments, "The journey through the
evidence is more exciting than the crime itself. We want to see everything that is
erased to make the story legible" (BT 37).

The first "Tier" of the documentary, "The Phantom of a Novel: Seven Moments," structured around the seven key moments of Molly's life in L.A. between
1920 and 1986, is dominated by historical photographs of people and places in the
neighborhoods surrounding Bunker Hill. Thumbnails of these photographs are arranged in random sequence and can be selected by the user; alternatively, the user can
go through the photo archive by enlarging each photo to almost the size of the screen
and then continuing either with the photograph on the left or on the right. Making full
use of the technical possibilities, the sequence of photographs is not fixed but rather
randomly selected from the archive. Additionally, with each phase of Molly's life,
there is a short narrative comment by Norman Klein in a window in the corner—a
commentary that can be opened and closed by the user. The narrator of the novella describes this first tier as "a visual, interactive radio program ... a kind of modern novel
on a screen with hundreds of photos and Norman as narrator. You might say they are
also a docu-fictional movie" (BT 43).

Tier 2, "The Writer's Back Story," which the narrator of the novella describes as
"more like a contextualization," is largely made up of newspaper clippings and establishes the context of other people and places more loosely connected to Molly's story.
It collects newspaper clippings covering events and developments occurring during

---

[16] The re-shot sequences of films such as *Falling Down*, *Heat*, *Training Day*, *Chinatown*, *The
Last Boy Scout*, *T-Men*, *The Omega Man*, *D.O.A.*, *To Live and Die in L.A.* are frequently
iconic scenes with the downtown towers looming in the background. In addition, this section also features maps of L.A. pointing out key locations used in these films.

[17] The narrator of the novella (whom one is likely to have identified as "Norman Klein") refers to his materials as follows: "I have about a thousand photographs and newspaper articles, over two hundred relevant movies on file, and over twenty interviews, along with
hours of interviews with Norman Klein; and hundreds of pages of text" (BT 27; cf. 33, 38,
42, 43). The narrator also comments on the way the documentary is to be perceived: "I
turned toward my research on Molly's life, as if I could edit her sensations into a story that
was symphonic in some way, or contrapuntal. ... I could gather data for Molly's story, and
embed it like bots under the skin: newspaper clippings, historical photographs, and patches
of interviews. Then I could assemble my assets into a vast database, for a search engine
that could be selected according to the senses" (BT 11).

Molly's life, with references to the prohibition and illegal distilleries, the ban on inter-racial marriages in the state of California in a 1932 newspaper clipping, the controver-sial reception of a 1941 anti-Semitic speech by Charles Lindbergh, the deportation of Japanese Americans during World War II, illicit gambling, the McCarthy era with its Red Scare and the building of air-raid shelters—frequently interspersed with innumer-able sensationalist clippings reporting murders in Los Angeles. Additionally, explana-tory captions beneath newspaper clippings and photographs contextualize develop-ments, with comments, for instance, on the ambivalent views of Chinatown in the 1920s as both "an exotic place in the popular imagination" and a place "considered as an eyesore, as more brown and black races converged at the Plaza" (DVD 2:1).

Tier 3, "Excavation: Digging behind the story and its locale," is described in the novella as "the aporia of media itself" (BT 43). In five sections, it offers a wealth of further material, here arranged thematically rather than chronologically. There is a sec-tion entitled "People Molly Never Met But Would Make Good Characters in Her Story," featuring randomly arranged interviews with twelve residents (including Nor-man Klein) of these neighborhoods, who comment on their experiences within the so-cial and ethnic developments in 20th-century L.A., the Zoot Suit Riots, fear of violent police officers, ethnic festivities, Anti-Communist witch-hunts during the McCarthy era, the 1947 murders of Elizabeth Short—the "Black Dahlia"—and of Bugsy Siegel, or the treatment of Japanese Americans during WW II. Largely consisting of film and video sequences, it is a "vast 'ironic index' of what Molly left out, forgot, couldn't see. It samples from the back-story that gets lost when the movie or novel is made legible" (BT 43). It is also described as

> a meta-text (not a deconstruction). It is the structure of what cannot be found, what Molly decided to forget, what Molly never noticed, what passed before her but was lost to us. It is proof that no novel or film (documentary or fiction) can capture the fullness of how a city forgets, except by its erasures. (BT 38f.)

Thus, neither the novella nor the DVD are to be regarded as a higher-level com-mentary one on the other; they are mutually complementary: just as the DVD can be seen as a vast exploration of the themes outlined in the novella, the narrative frequent-ly comments on the contents of the DVD: "Next day, I went into a newspaper morgue, looking for articles on Walt's disappearance. Instead, I found fifty ways to kill a man between 1959 and 1961 (along with five suicides). I've scanned all the articles into a database for you" (BT 24). In the novella, the fictional story of Walt's disappearance is constantly related to current developments chronicled on the DVD, tying the wealth of documentary material back to the underlying quest narrative: "Among police photos, I find what should be Walt's body. … Then I discover that on the same day, the down-town editor cancelled photos about racist crimes, particularly the railroading of blacks and Latinos" (BT 25).

With Molly as its protagonist, *Bleeding Through* shifts attention from hegemonic white males and draws attention to the role of minorities in L.A.'s complex history: Molly, "a twenty-something girl from a Jewish home in the Midwest" (DVD 1:1; cf.

BT 13), is herself a newcomer and an outsider when she arrives in the city in 1920. As Bénézet points out, "Through Molly, Klein articulates a gendered and minority-oriented revision of the city's history" (69).

From the very beginning, both the novella and the DVD characterize Molly's neighborhood as a multi-ethnic one.[18] Much of the material centers on transformations in 20th-century multi-ethnic L.A., whether in references to "Brooklyn Avenue with its famous mix of Jews and Mexicans, Japanese and other 'swart' young men" (BT 15; cf. 40), to "restrictions against the black community on Central Avenue, especially when by 1924 membership of the Klan reached its highest number ever" (BT 30), to the tearing down of Chinatown for Union Station (built in 1939), to the history of mixed Japanese and Mexican neighborhoods, with a Japanese American family man running a Mexican grocery store (DVD 3:1), the 1943 Zoot Suit Riots, the Watts rebellion, or the turning of Little Tokyo into "Bronzeville" during World War II, when African Americans and Mexicans moved into the area while the Japanese Americans were held in deportation camps away from the West Coast (BT 22).

The changes in 20th-century Los Angeles are rendered in a fascinating if oblique way in the frequent pairings of an old photograph and a recent one taken from exactly the same angle; some of these are made to blend into one another in impressive overlay montage.[19] Thus, there is a pair of photos taken on the corner of Spring and Main Street in the 1920s and today, in which a shop sign "D.W. Wong Co. Chinese Herbs" disappears and a billboard advertising Green River Bourbon morphs into a billboard advertising a $ 7,000,000 lottery draw in Spanish (DVD 1:2), in another of these morphs, juxtaposing 1941 Main Street with a contemporary image, "Fond's Pants Shop" on 655 Main Street (with "Ben's Barber Shop" and "Adams Radios & Appliances" next to it) turns into "Dongyang Machine Co." (DVD 1:3). A further morph overlays a 1943 image of City Hall as clearly the tallest building among a few small shops in small two-story buildings with a modern image of City Hall surrounded by anonymous corporate glass-and-steel blocks; yet another pair of photographs morphs the area around the South Hill Street funicular "Angels Flight," with buildings around six floors in height, into the present-day high-rise towers of downtown.

Indeed, the drastic changes imposed by radical urban development projects in areas such as Bunker Hill may well be seen as the central theme of the documentary DVD. The section "Collective Dissolve: Bunker Hill," in film sequences from Kent McKenzie's 1956 documentary *Bunker Hill* and *The Exiles* (1961), maps as well as photographs from the 1890s to the 1960s attempts to recreate Bunker Hill before the massive demolition program that cleared the area for what is now regarded as "downtown" L.A. A long sequence from McKenzie's *Bunker Hill* refers to the Community Redevelopment Agency's major plan to relocate 8,000 residents of the neighborhood,

---

[18] In his insert narrative accompanying the DVD preface, Klein refers to a family of "Latinos renting downstairs" in Molly's house.

[19] For the use of such techniques in city films, particularly in Pat O'Neill's L.A. film *Water and Power* (1989), cf. MacDonald 232-34.

to demolish all buildings and to sell the land and have modern office and apartment complexes built (DVD 1:6). This chapter of the DVD also displays images from 1959 and 1960 showing the large-scale demolition of Bunker Hill. A sequence from Gene Petersen's 1949 film "*... And Ten Thousand More*" [housing units] also refers to the problem of "slums" in L.A. and the need for urban development. This sequence is captioned "The myths of urban blight."[20] Similarly, the photograph of a model "Redevelopment Study for Bunker Hill, March 22, 1960" is captioned "Cooking statistics to justify tearing down Bunker Hill" (DVD 1:6). Indeed, statistics on the housing situation and living conditions in Bunker Hill appear systematically to have been distorted in order to win public support for the demolition of this predominantly Mexican neighborhood. In the caption underneath a sequence from McKenzie's *The Exiles*, the fact that "this was a brown and black identified downtown center" is explicitly identified as "one of the reasons it was torn down" (DVD 3:3).

In the interview section, residents comment on racial segregation in L.A. Japanese American Bill Shishima recounts his experience of having to leave Los Angeles in May 1942 as an 11-year-old to be interned away from the coast with his family; retired African American fire-man Arnett Hartsfield reports coming to Los Angeles in 1929, "when we couldn't even cross Washington Boulevard on Central Avenue [because of segregation]" (DVD 3:1). Finally, Esther Raucher recalls her experience of first coming to downtown as a white child and of staring at African Americans: "As a child ... I don't think I'd seen a black person ... That's how segregated the city was that you would never see a black person" (DVD 3:1).[21] Tying such developments to the underlying story of Molly, a clip from Jeremy Lezin's 1975 documentary *A Sense of Community* with references to illegal immigrants working in L.A. is captioned "With each year, Molly felt the massive immigration from Latin America change the rules in her world" (DVD 1:7).

All in all, in keeping with *The History of Forgetting*, *Bleeding Through* thus shows how 20th-century Los Angeles, in the process of becoming increasingly multiethnic demographically, continued to erase the visible traces of this diversity in favor of a de-ethnicized all-American look and feel modeled on the needs of a largely white elite and enforced by representing non-white L.A. along the lines of the paranoid and implicitly racist aesthetic of innumerable *noir* murder films. It remains to be shown that the attempt at an open, non-hierarchical and anti-hegemonic representation of these complexities is closely tied to the non-linear and de-centered form of the multimedia hypertext documentary.

---

[20] On the discourse of crisis and the frequently disastrous consequences of large-scale restructuring plans in L.A., cf. Soja, "Los Angeles, 1965-1992").

[21] In *History of Forgetting*, Klein refers to the "policy of shutting out downtown to nonwhites ... since the 1920s" (132).

4. Implications of the Form: Hypertext Docu-fiction as Radicalized Historiographic Metafiction and Political Commentary

The experience of navigating *Bleeding Through* is a fundamentally contradictory one: on the one hand, by making sophisticated use of the technological possibilities of the multimedia database, the fast-paced, multi-dimensional, overpowering, non-hierarchical, multi-faceted documentary recreates the urban experience of 20th or even 21st-century L.A.; on the other hand, there is a nostalgic quality to the experience, which partly arises from the use of vintage photographs, film clips and newspaper clippings which appear to work against the grain of the high-tech mode of presentation—in keeping with Klein's views expressed in the *The History of Forgetting* on the constant self-reinvention of the city and the concomitant memoricide of previous layers of its history. While these aesthetic and experiential implications of the form are worth noting, its implicit politics are a momentous, though elegantly inobtrusive, complement to the more explicit political commentary also packaged into *Bleeding Through*.

Repeated references to the editorial decisions that went into the compilation of the material, the frequently self-reflexive narrator of the novella as well as the meta-narrative[22] titles of the DVD's three "tiers"—1: "The Phantom of a Novel: Seven Moments," 2: "The Writer's Back Story," 3: "Excavation: Digging behind the Story and Its Locale"—already point to the fact that this documentary database fiction self-reflexively foregrounds its own narrative constructedness. This is continued throughout the DVD. In between the interviews with eleven other residents of the central L.A. neighborhoods, Klein in interview clips comments on his thoughts on Molly, on the writing of the novella, on his own first coming to Los Angeles.

> When we began these interviews ... we were continually locating details that were half remembered, badly remembered or often forgotten and lost and couldn't possibly be known to her. ... And it seems that we became almost more interested in locating what she couldn't find, what she had to forget, what she couldn't locate. ... It's such a great pleasure to not be constrained simply by the legibility of the story. ... The complexity becomes such a great pleasure. It's such a pleasure noticing what she wouldn't have noticed. ... So in a way the absences become much more present in these interviews than anything else (DVD 3:1).

Postmodern literary and filmic explorations of the city, it is true, have already dissolved distinctions between genres, between fiction and discursive exploration; they have self-reflexively highlighted the ambiguous role of the writer or film-maker as both observer and participant in urban interactions; they have highlighted the dissolution of traditional views of the city and have frequently attempted to make the city itself legible as a text; they have set out formally to represent the multiplicity, polyphony and fragmentation of the city through multiple, polyphonic and fragmented textuality (for some of these tendencies, cf. Teske). Similarly, in keeping with the views on

---

[22] For the concept of metanarrative as distinct from metafiction, cf. Fludernik and Nünning.

the narrativity and constructedness of historiography in the work of Hayden White, Michel de Certeau and others, many recent documentaries, constantly foreground artifice, subjectivity etc.[23] Furthermore, precisely the fact that the documentary needs to be manipulated by the individual viewer for anything to be visible at all further reminds us of the mediality and the constructedness of what we are witnessing. The medium thus constantly draws attention to itself—in contrast to much traditional documentary film-making which relies on the reality effect of suggesting that what we see is somehow evident and can hardly be questioned; hence the paradox inherent in much documentary film-making that is meant to be anti-hegemonic, subversive etc. but through its very narrative form frequently cannot help being suggestive and (since the viewer is essentially passive[24]), imposes a view of the world. *Bleeding Through*, however, in contrast to even the most advanced filmic documentaries, which still inescapably rely on the linearity of film, makes full use of the digital medium to disrupt linearity.

Thus, while documentaries, which are originally meant for collective viewing, induce forms of collective medial experience, the effect of *Bleeding Through* specifically relies on a highly individual experience. The constant need to "do" something in the process of navigating *Bleeding Through*—all clips are very short, hardly anything happens without being triggered by the user, who is essentially assigned the role of a detective in search of the story and ist contexts—thus not only foregrounds the mediality, narrativity and construction of the material, it also activates the viewer. In keeping with the promise of the medium,[25] the non-linear presentation of the material thus precludes closure, stimulates the discovery of knowledge rather than imposing it and thus fosters learning without being explicitly didactic.

The aesthetic and political implications of the form can fruitfully be accounted for with reference to the concept of rhizomatic structures. As proposed by Deleuze and Guattari (7-13), rhizomes are characterized by the principles of "connectivity," "heterogeneity," "multiplicity," "asignifying rupture," "cartography" and "decalcoma-

---

[23] For a discussion of these tendencies, cf. Aitken, Hohenberger, Nichols.

[24] I am aware of course that the tradition especially of British cultural studies has long pointed out the viewer's active role in the constitution of meaning of TV, film and other forms of popular culture; for a discussion of the productive role of the viewer, cf. especially Winter. Nonetheless, the constant need for active manipulation and the flaunted non-linear and hypertextual nature of the program in contrast to the reception of even the most experimental, fragmentary, "postmodern"—but ultimately still "fixed and invariable" documentary film is bound to have consequences for the constitution of meaning.

[25] In a laudatory review of *Bleeding Through*, Helfand comments on the "digital revolution's promise of new literary forms" and the "brief blossom and fade [of the] experiments in online interactive fiction"] and—speaking of the "many unfulfilled dreams" of the genre, regards *Bleeding Though* as living up to the promises of the form's technological possibilities (n.p.). For analyses of the technological and literary implications of the digital form and their repercussions in literary studies from the early 1990s classics to more recent accounts, cf. Aarseth, Bolter, Burnett, Ensslin, Gaggi, Hayles, Landow, McGann, Sloane.

nia."[26] If, as Burnett has argued, "[h]ypertext is rhizomorphic in all its characteristics" (28)—and Klein's work makes full use of the medium—*Bleeding Through* may be characterized as fully rhizomatic, with all the non-totalizing and anti-hegemonic implications Deleuze and Guattari famously ascribe to rhizomatic discourses. Thus, the multimedial, multivocal, multi-perspectival, interactive, non-sequential and highly self-reflexive experience of navigating *Bleeding Through* brings out "traits that are usually obscured by the enforced linearity of paper printing" (Burnett 3) and, like hypertext generally, serves to undercut, liquefy and question established and hegemonic representations with their frequently unquestioned dichotomies and *"hierarchies violentes"* (sensu Derrida).

As Marsha Kinder argues in her short essay in the booklet of *Bleeding Through*, "database narratives [are] interactive structures that resist narrative closure and expose the dual processes of selection and combination lying at the root of all stories" (54).[27] *Bleeding Through* is narrative 'enough' so as to create interest and curiosity, but it flaunts its constructedness and constantly requires the user to select from a wealth of narrative items and, by means of a succession of such choices, consciously to perform himself the acts of selection and combination usually hidden behind the surface of conventional narrative. Database fictions, in foregrounding the arbitrariness of such choices and enabling users to choose differently next time (but never exactly to retrace their steps), are potentially subversive purely in their form in that they expose as a construction and fabulation what narrative traditionally represents as a given. By making each journey through the material necessarily a different one—and by thus presenting what is merely material for a story as subject to change and human intervention—these narratives also contribute to the activation and mobilization of the user in ways that even the most advanced self-reflexive fiction—which is still subject to the unchangeable linearity of print—cannot achieve (cf. Kinder 54).

True to the "democratic form" of hypertext digital media, *Bleeding Through*, not least by means of its very form, thus serves to deconstruct hegemonic constructions of history by constantly drawing attention to the medial, discursive, constructed nature of such conceptions. As a user, one is never allowed to forget that this is a revisionist,

---

[26] For a discussion of the rhizomatic nature of hypertext along the lines of these characteristics, cf. Burnett.

[27] Bénézet's allegedly original coinage of the term "database narrative" and her claim to harmonize what were previously regarded as the incompatible formats of narrative and of database (56-57) are hardly as original as she asserts—she here merely follows Marsha Kinder's essay "Bleeding Through: Database Fictions," which already attempts a synthesis based on her reading of *Bleeding Through: Layers of Los Angeles, 1920-1986* (cf. 54). Curiously, much of what Bénézet presents as the results of "[her] analysis" (63) is explicitly stated in Klein's text or the accompanying essays or is blatantly obvious anyway: "There are many reasons that may have led Klein and his team to privilege a recombinant poetics. My analysis suggests that the presentation of an openly multifaceted, critical, and self-reflexive creation was one important motivation" (63).

anti-hegemonic, at times polemical re-construction of a repressed, alternative Los Angeles.

5. Representing Los Angeles, Representing 'America'

What makes *Bleeding Through* even more directly political is that it self-reflexively draws attention to the political implications of its narrative procedures and even explicitly links its own constructedness to a history of political fabrications from the Cold War to the George W. Bush administration. In this vein, the narrator of the novella self-consciously comments on his narrative procedures:

> I need a different model for the unreliable narrator as well as for the fragrant noir world, vital though these have been for modern literature, detective stories, cinema suspense; and for lies the State Department delivered on broadcast news during the Cold War. (This is 1986 remember. You the reader may have more grisly forms of unreliable news to deal with) (BT 28).[28]

A similarly self-reflexive passage on the DVD draws attention to the fact that part of the material originally collected for the documentary was destroyed in a computer crash; however, more than merely suggesting the haphazard, selective and necessarily incomplete nature of even the most scrupulously undertaken reconstruction project, this passage again closely associates the contingencies influencing the production of *Bleeding Through* with contemporary political events:

> On November 1 [2002], an electric surge boiled two hard drives for 'Bleeding Through.' Perhaps the Day of the Dead came by phone, reminding us that all media looks better as a sketch. We lost four programs. ...
>
> November 9: The drives still smell like burnt upholstery. ... On TV, we watch George W. Bush take charge of our future. The Pentagon was working on a Stinkpot called Stench Soup, so foul smelling that it could stop a crowd. ... They are trying to decide if it would make a good "non-lethal" weapon.
>
> The last paragraph [on Bush and the Pentagon's stink bomb] is completely accurate. The rest is what works for you.
>
> March 23, 2003: A last gasp for the project. The troops are less than 100 miles from Baghdad (Tier 3, "The Lost Section").[29]

The novella, too, ties events in L.A. back to the grand national questions, turning what seems a novella and documentary on L.A. into a *pars pro toto* representation of 20th-century America. For instance, the problems of violence and murder in L.A. are tied to the "longstanding American distrust of urban democracy" (25):

---

[28] This passage also shows how the documentary relies on explicitly or implicitly situating not only the story level (1920-1986) but also the time of production and initial reception (2002/2003) in their political and cultural contexts far beyond ethnic life in Los Angeles.

[29] The text is here presented in written form reminiscent of a typed diary entry.

Many Americans believe, as they did in Jefferson's day, that equality can survive only in a small town. By contrast, fascism flourishes in crowds. ... I prefer to make Walt's murder a critique of urban capitalism; but then crime becomes a defense of the suburbs (25).

In his essay "Absences, Scripted Spaces and the Urban Imaginary: Unlikely Models for the City in the Twenty-First Century," written while he was also working on *Bleeding Through*, Klein describes the results of drastic urban renewal projects. After a long section on some of L.A.'s contemporary problems, he explicitly relates contemporary L.A. to the problems of the U.S. and the world at large:

> In short, the global civilization has begun to settle in. We see its monuments more clearly, its glitter, its brutality. ... This is a world that has more than lost its way. It is the best and the worst of all possible worlds, dominated by scripted spaces and social imaginaries inside a level of surveillance, top-heavy economic fragility and media feudalism .... And yet its possibilities are extraordinary. (451)

Even more explicitly, this 2002 essay links genre-specific urban imaginaries of Los Angeles, ruthless urban planning and reactionary and paranoid U.S. politics in general (especially of the Bush era). Interestingly, it then comments on this conjunction of urban imaginaries of L.A. and grand national themes as being central to *Bleeding Through*, thus suggesting that it should be seen as far more than a multimedia documentary on the changing face of Los Angeles. This passage needs to be quoted at some length:

> During the noir film era, from about 1944 to 1958, the horizontal imaginary city [of Los Angeles] evolves into a complex grammar. ... This noir grammar has become the standard way for broadcast media to dis-report the news, to generate a highly conservative, fundamentally reactionary vision of the world that finally covered up key information about the presidential election of 2000, the Enron scandal, the War on Terrorism, the anthrax attacks, Homeland Rule. ... Of course, noir reportage has always been a mode of distraction. [But now], that distraction has become national presidential policy, and CNN, Fox, CNBC policy as well ... So 2002 shows us a noir scenography as our national vision. We have extended this noir staging into national obsession with surveillance as well. ... I am currently trying to engage these issues inside a cinematic novel /archive entitled *Bleeding Through: Layers of Los Angeles, 1920-1986* ("Absences" 452-53).

Engaging with various forms of appropriating the city—from the most direct version proceeding by means of bulldozers to fictionalized and medialized forms in filmic urban imaginaries—, *Bleeding Through* as itself an appropriation of the city is a unique form of cultural expression in an urban context, in which it takes up a diagnostic as well as catalytic function, seeking to raise awareness and potentially to influence policy-making and urban planning. By celebrating the ethnic and cultural diversity of Los Angeles in the face of ruthless urban redevelopment based on racism and greed, and by explicitly linking this anti-hegemonic view of the city to the grand national themes of the years after 9/11, the war on terror and the beginning disaster in Iraq, the multimedia documentary thus also contributes to national discourses and once more makes Los Angeles in all its multiplicity and ambivalence an emblem of 'America.'

Works Cited

Aarseth, Espen J. *Cybertext: Perspectives on Ergodic Literature.* Baltimore, MD and London: Johns Hopkins UP, 1997.

Aitken, Ian, ed. *Encyclopedia of the Documentary Film.* New York: Routledge, 2005.

Bénézet, Delphine. "Recombinant Poetics, Urban *Flânerie*, and Experimentation in the Database Narrative: *Bleeding Through: Layers of Los Angeles, 1920-1986.*" *Convergence: The International Journal of Research into New Media Technologies* 15.1 (2009): 55-74.

Bolter, Jay David. *Writing Space: Computers, Hypertext, and the Remediation of Print.* Mahwah, NJ: Lawrence Erlbaum Associates, 2001.

Burnett, Kathleen. "Toward a Theory of Hypertextual Design." *Postmodern Culture* [online journal] 3.2 (January 1993). http://muse.jhu.edu/login?uri=/journals/postmodern_culture/v003/3.2burnett.html.

Comella, Rosemary. "Simultaneous Distraction: The Making of *Bleeding Through Layers of Los Angeles, 1920-1986.*" Norman M. Klein et al. *Bleeding Through.* Book included in Norman M. Klein et al., *Bleeding Through: Layers of Los Angeles, 1920-1986* [DVD and Book]. Karlsruhe: ZKM digital arts edition, 2003. 56-59.

Davis, Mike. *City of Quartz: Excavating the Future in Los Angeles.* New ed. Brooklyn, NY: Verso Books, 2006.

Deleuze, Gilles, and Félix Guattari. "Introduction: Rhizome." *A Thousand Plateaus: Capitalism and Schizophrenia.* Trans. Brian Massumi. London and New York: Continuum, 2004. 3-28.

Ensslin, Astrid. *Canonising Hypertext: Explorations and Constructions.* London: Continuum, 2007.

Fludernik, Monika. "Metanarrative and Metafictional Commentary." *Poetica* 35 (2003): 1-39.

Fulton, William. *The Reluctant Metropolis: The Politics of Urban Growth in Los Angeles.* Baltimore: Johns Hopkins UP, 2001.

Gaggi, Silvio. *From Text to Hypertext: Decentering the Subject in Fiction, Film, the Visual Arts, and Electronic Media.* Philadelphia: U of Pennsylvania P, 1997.

Gassenmeier, Michael. *Londondichtung als Politik: Texte und Kontexte der City Poetry von der Restauration bis zum Ende der Walpole-Ära.* Tübingen: Niemeyer, 1989.

Hayles, N. Katherine. *Electronic Literature: New Horizons for the Literary.* Notre Dame, Ind.: U of Notre Dame P, 2008.

Helfand, Glen. "Read Only Memory: A New Interactive DVD Mines Provocative Layers of Storytelling." *San Francisco Chronicle.* http://www.sfgate.com/cgi-bin/article.cgi?f=/g/a/2003/09/18/blthrough.DTL.

Hohenberger, Eva, ed. *Bilder des Wirklichen: Texte zur Theorie des Dokumentarfilms.* Berlin: Vorwerk 8, 2006.

Kinder, Marsha. "Bleeding Through: Database Fiction." Klein et al. *Bleeding Through.* Book included in Norman M. Klein et al., *Bleeding Through: Layers of Los Angeles, 1920-1986* [DVD and Book], with additional texts by Rosemary Comella, Marsha Kinder, Andreas Kratky, Jeffrey Shaw. Karlsruhe: ZKM digital arts edition, 2003. 53-55.

Klein, Norman M. "Absences, Scripted Spaces and the Urban Imaginary: Unlikely Models for the City in the Twenty-First Century." *Die Stadt als Event: Zur Konstruktion urbaner Erlebnisräume.* Ed. Regina Bittner. Frankfurt/Main: Campus Verlag, 2001. 450-54.

———, et al. *Bleeding Through: Layers of Los Angeles, 1920-1986* [DVD and Book]. Karlsruhe: ZKM digital arts edition, 2003.

———. "Bleeding Through." Klein et al. *Bleeding Through.* Book included in Norman M. Klein et al., *Bleeding Through: Layers of Los Angeles, 1920-1986* [DVD and Book], with additional texts by Rosemary Comella, Marsha Kinder, Andreas Kratky, Jeffrey Shaw. Karlsruhe: ZKM digital arts edition, 2003. 7-44.

———. *The History of Forgetting: Los Angeles and the Erasure of Memory.* 1997. New York: Verso, 2008.

———. "Staging Murders: The Social Imaginary, Film, and the City." *Wide Angle* 20.3 (1998): 85-96.

Kratky, Andreas. "How to Navigate Forgetting." *Bleeding Through.* Norman M. Klein et al. *Bleeding Through.* Book included in Norman M. Klein et al., *Bleeding Through: Layers of Los Angeles, 1920-1986* [DVD and Book]. Karlsruhe: ZKM digital arts edition, 2003. 60-61.

Landow, George P. *Hypertext 3.0: Critical Theory and New Media in an Era of Globalization: Critical Theory and New Media in a Global Era.* Baltimore, MD: Johns Hopkins UP, 2006.

MacDonald, Scott. "Ten+ (Alternative) Films about American Cities." *The ISLE Reader: Ecocriticism, 1993-2003.* Ed. Michael P. Branch and Scott Slovic. Athens, GA: U of Georgia P, 2003. 217-39.

McGann, Jerome. *Radiant Textuality: Literature After the World Wide Web.* New York: Palgrave Macmillan, 2001.

Mumford, Lewis. *The City in History: Its Origins, Its Transformations, and Its Prospects.* London: Secker & Warburg, 1961.

Murphet, Julian. *Literature and Race in Los Angeles.* Cambridge and New York: Cambridge UP, 2001.

Nichols, Bill. *Representing Reality: Issues and Concepts in Documentary.* Bloomington: Indiana UP, 1991.

Nünning, Ansgar. "On Metanarrative: Towards a Definition, a Typology, and an Outline of the Functions of Metanarrative Commentary." *The Dynamics of Narrative Form: Studies in Anglo-American Narratology.* Ed. John Pier. Narratologia, vol. 4. Berlin, New York: de Gruyter 2005. 11-58.

Ofner, Astrid, and Claudia Siefen, eds. *Los Angeles: Eine Stadt im Film/A City on Film: Eine Retrospektive der Viennale und des Österreichischen Filmmuseums, 5. Oktober bis 5. November 2008.* Marburg: Schüren, 2008.

Scott, Allen J., and Edward. W. Soja, eds. *The City, Los Angeles and Urban Theory at the End of the Twentieth Century.* Berkeley: U of California P, 1997.

Shaw, Jeffrey. "The Back Story: Reformulating Narrative Practice." *Bleeding Through.* Book included in Norman M. Klein et al., *Bleeding Through: Layers of Los Angeles, 1920-*

1986 [DVD and Book], with additional texts by Rosemary Comella, Marsha Kinder, Andreas Kratky, Jeffrey Shaw. Karlsruhe: ZKM digital arts edition, 2003. 52.

Sloane, Sarah. *Digital Fictions: Storytelling in a Material World.* Stamford, CT: Ablex Publishing, 2000.

Soja, Edward W. *Thirdspace: Journeys to Los Angeles and Other Real-And-Imagined Places.* Oxford: Blackwell, 1996.

———. "Los Angeles, 1965-1992: From Crisis-Generated Restructuring to Restructuring-Generated Crisis." *The City: Los Angeles and Urban Theory at the End of the Twentieth Century.* Ed. Edward. W. Soja and Allen J. Scott. Berkeley: U of California P, 1996. 426-62.

———. "Exopolis: The Restructuring of Urban Form." Soja. *Postmetropolis: Critical Studies of Cities and Regions.* Oxford: Blackwell, 2000, 233-63.

Teske, Doris. *Die Vertextung der Megalopolis: London im Spiel postmoderner Texte.* Trier: WVT, 1999.

Winter, Rainer. *Der produktive Zuschauer: Medienaneignung als kultureller und ästhetischer Prozess.* München: Quintessenz, 1995.

Filmography

A Sense of Community. Dir. Jeremy Lezin. U.S.A., 1975.

... And Ten Thousand More. Dir. Gene Peterson. U.S.A., 1949.

Blade Runner. Dir. Ridley Scott. U.S.A., Hong Kong, 1982.

Bleeding Through: Layers of Los Angeles, 1920-1986. Dir. Norman M. Klein. U.S.A., 2003.

Bunker Hill. Dir. Kent MacKenzie. U.S.A., 1956.

Chinatown. Dir. Roman Polanski. U.S.A., 1974.

D.O.A. Dir. Rudolph Maté. U.S.A., 1950.

The Exiles. Dir. Kent MacKenzie. U.S.A., 1961.

Falling Down. Dir. Joel Schumacher. U.S.A., UK, France, 1993.

Heat. Dir. Michael Mann. U.S.A., 1995.

The Last Boy Scout. Dir. Tony Scott. U.S.A., 1991.

The Omega Man. Dir. Boris Sagal. U.S.A., 1971.

Raise the Banner. Dir. Duane Kubo. U.S.A., 1980.

T-Men. Dir. Anthony Mann. U.S.A., 1947.

To Live and Die in L.A. Dir. William Friedkin. U.S.A., 1985.

Training Day. Dir. Antoine Fuqua. U.S.A., Australia, 2001.

Water and Power. Dir. Pat O'Neill. U.S.A., 1989.

Nomadic Narration and Deterritorialized Nationscape in *Cofralandes: Rapsodia chilena* (2004) by Raúl Ruiz

SEBASTIAN THIES

Resumen

En Cofralandes. Rapsodia chilena (2004), el cineasta chileno Raúl Ruiz, autor de una vasta obra de cine de vanguardia y de ficción, narra un viaje de retorno a su país de origen después de una larga ausencia en la diáspora europea. Estudia la comunidad imaginada de su patria, poblada de personajes grotescos y alegóricos que performan idiosincrasias chilenas y evocan un imaginario cultural lleno de reminiscencias folclóricas, mitos y contradicciones. Redescubre un país que está todavía marcado por la fragmentación social, la incomunicación y la lucha para superar el pasado conflictivo de la dictadura militar. El documental, narrado en primera persona, es una mezcla entre un video-diario de viaje, cargado de emotividad y poesía, y un filme-ensayo que explora, de manera reflexiva, los límites del mismo género documental. Ruiz, en su simbolismo surrealista, opta por una estética radicalmente amimética y polisémica que se inscribe en la modalidad performativa del documental.

El presente artículo examina la forma en la cual se concibe la nación a base de la narración de su espacio. Los escenarios locales, los suburbios, el paisaje, los espacios monumentales, los no-lugares posmodernos, todos se recrean desde una perspectiva marcada por la diáspora y la deterritorialización. Lo que surge es una particular forma de narración nómada, que proporciona a la nación un *global sense of place*, una percepción global de la localidad como propuesta por Doreen Massey. Deconstruye cualquier forma de esencialización y cosificación de la nación, cuyo espacio se concibe entre fragmentado y fluido, pero siempre penetrado por las fuerzas de la globalización. Al mismo tiempo, cuestiona las formas etnográficas convencionales del discurso documental desde la perspectiva de una epistemología nómada, irreverente e iconoclasta, así como la conciben Deleuze y Guattari.

1. Introduction

This essay examines the (de)construction of nationhood in Raúl Ruiz's *Cofralandes: Rapsodia chilena* (2002)[1] by focusing on how the film narrates and visualizes the spatial formations of the nationscape. *Cofralandes* reconfigures a series of those spatial formations related to the construction of the nation's imagined community—the middle class suburbs, the Andean landscape, Santiago's monumental cityscape, and the nation's non-places[2]—from a perspective deeply marked by the experience of diaspora.[3] They are rendered in a particular nomadic narration which evokes what Massey has called a *global sense of place*.[4] Territorial space is conceived, thus, in ways which display, simultaneously, the effects of social fragmentation and the liquefying impact of transnationalization on the perception of space. These narrative strategies are complemented by a metanarrative discourse which undermines the strategies of conventional ethnographic narration of space by applying a form of nomadic epistemology to documentary discourse.

Cofralandes is a first-person documentary and experimental filmic travelogue of a journey to the filmmaker's homeland Chile after decades of living in Europe.[5] Instead of the conventional documentary realism, the film's *auteur* opts for an audiovisual language which is highly polysemic, self-reflexive and poetic. Challenging the boundaries between fact and fiction and deconstructing the genre conventions of ethnographic filmmaking, *Cofralandes* received Chile's Altazor price for the best documentary in 2004. As part of a collage-like style, the film makes constant use of conventions of documentary discourse: expert interviews, testimonies, archival material as well as the portrait shots and landscape photography typical of ethnographic filmmaking, but its particular approach to documentary filmmaking is profoundly subjective and rejects simple forms of realistic mimesis. In one of the iconoclastic statements characteristic for Ruiz's artistic standing as one of the most renowned

---

[1] *Cofralandes* is composed by four separate parts called *Rapsodia chilena*, *Evocaciones y valses*, *Rostros y rincones*, and *Museos y clubes en la región antártica*. Co-financed by the Chilean *Secretaría de Educación Pública*, the film is part of the Cineteca virtual de Chile and is accesible via http:\\www.arcoiristv.com. Thus, *Cofralandes* stands for innovative forms of documentary film in the Network Age.

[2] See below for an explanation of Marc Augé's concept of "non-place."

[3] Ruiz uses a similar approach to the narration of nation in the TV series *La recta provincia* (2007), a fiction mini series which treats a series of topics related to the construction of the homeland from a diasporic perspective (cf. Vázquez Rocca).

[4] Appadurai refers to a similar notion with his concept of the "production of locality" (cf. 178-200).

[5] It shares the return narrative from exile or diaspora with a series of Chilean documentaries by some of the most prominent exiled Chilean filmmakers and intellectuals: *Acta General de Chile* (1985) directed by Miguel Littín, *Chile: Memoria obstinada* (1996) by Patricio Guzmán, *La cueca sola* (2003) by Marilou Mallet and *Calle Santa Fé* (2007) by Carmen Castillo. Cf. also Thies, "ImagiNaciones."

directors/auteurs of the international Avant-garde film scene, the filmmaker claims that the documentary truth in *Cofralandes* is based on a particular quality of subjective experience: "Mi película es documental, porque está hecha sobre cosas vistas o vividas. Todas las cosas que están ahí las he visto o imaginado, lo que en este caso es lo mismo" (Medel).[6] The film aspires to a truth claim related to the performative mode in documentary filmmaking as described by Nichols (cf. 93ff.) and Bruzzi (cf. 185ff.), according to whom documentary truth is created by the performative intervention of the filmmaker and the film's subjects in the pro-filmic reality which the film is to record. The Chilean nation is documented by Ruiz in this experimental film as being peopled by a host of grotesque characters and allegoric figures exhibiting national idiosyncrasies and conjuring up childhood memories, national myths and folklore. Their performances evoke an imagined community imbued with a sense of social fragmentation, lack of communication, and the struggle to overcome the nation's conflictive past.

The latter aspect is created by a particular form of nomadic narration which derives from a certain diasporic or exilic subject position. When the nation is being narrated from the experience of exile or diaspora, one inevitably finds the traces of deterritorialization, social fragmentation, and alienation inscribed in the filmmaker's positioning vis-à-vis his or her lost homeland, as Hamid Naficy posits in his influential study *Accented Cinema* on exilic and diasporic filmmaking. One can conceive this diasporic construction of nationhood as being informed by a dialectic relation between two superimposed narrations: one being autobiographic, marked by discontinuity and contingence, the other being ethnographic and showing the characteristics of "national pedagogy" (Bhabha, *Location* 221)—i.e., a longing for belonging, continuity and cultural homogeneity. The result is a highly ambivalent subject position which is conscious of its precariousness and constructed character. The shifting positions between, on the one hand, fetishizing and, on the other, rejecting the lost homeland—turn the diasporic subject into a voice in disaccord with national pedagogy and the epistemological matrix of national ethnography the latter is conventionally based on. It is a voice from the margins of the nation or, to be more exact, from the interstices between various national discourses, being as such profoundly revealing as to the crises and processes of transnationalization the modern nation has undergone in recent decades.

The subtitle of *Cofralandes'* first part calls the documentary a *Chilean Rhapsody*. The polyvalent term "rhapsody" connects the montage with a late romantic genre of musical composition of particularly loose formal structure on the one hand, and, on the other, with a narrative tradition which originated in Greek antiquity and is characterized by a particular relation to orality, performativity, and nomadism. According to Pindar, the Greek *rhapsodos*, or "singer of stitched verse," was a travelling artist who sang epic poetry, improvising and threading together the episodes of the hero's journey, myths, legends and jokes without following a pre-established structure (cf. Bahn/

---

6 "My film is a documentary, because it is made of things seen or lived. Every single thing in it has been seen or imagined by me, which, for our concerns, means just the same thing". (All translations in this essay are by myself).

Bahn). In the same sense, *Cofralandes* is informed by a particularly loose structure, which is an expression of the narrator's nomadism both in terms of spatiality and the topoi displayed. The film thus aspires to transpose some aspects of this classic foundational fiction to contemporary Chilean film. In the second part of *Cofralandes*, there is an explicit reference to the South American rural cultural memory of the *paya* or *payada*, which is suggested in a veiled manner to be part of the legacy of the ancient oral art, the rhapsody, come alive in today's Chile.[7]

The word "rhapsody" is thus a reference to a nomadic concept associated with, firstly, the eminently national oral tradition of old, the paya, secondly, with Ruiz's diasporic and cosmopolitan subject position as an auteur filmmaker, and, thirdly, with a particular approach to documentary (auto)ethnographic narration. The "stitched verse" of the rhapsody is a highly appropriate image for an Avant-garde montage which threads together surreal and concrete audiovisual poems, visual puns, grotesque performances of Chilean everyday culture, impressions from the Chilean landscape and encyclopedic information, all enmeshed by the narrative frame of the filmmaker's seemingly erratic geographical meanderings. In accord with the overall ludic and self-reflexive style, which is omnipresent in Ruiz's vast filmic oeuvre, the role of the filmmaker/rhapsode and his nomadic narration in *Cofralandes* is informed by two conflicting *structures of feeling*[8] produced by deterritorialization: on the one hand, there is a fragmented sense of belonging, related to the trauma of displacement and a diffuse sentiment of loss, grief and nostalgia, as described by Naficy (cf. 25ff.). On the other, there is an irony, playfulness and detachment present in this return narrative, which differs markedly from earlier examples in Chilean accented cinema, as it appeals to a much more cosmopolitan, self-reflexive and performative approach to the homeland. There is, thus, in Ruiz's filmmaking a liberating dimension to the experience of deterritorialization. It lies somewhere between the pathos of Said's radical postcolonial critic who conceives of himself as exiled from all places[9] and the almost

---

[7] Rediscovering the rhapsody through the paya constitutes a highly effective postcolonial appropriation of the cultural heritage that the so-called Old World claims for itself. This goes unnoticed by the filmmaker's French journeyman companion in the second part of *Cofralandes*, Bernard Pautrat, who is simply bewildered by the endlessly repetitious recitations of the payadores. The ritual temporality of the payadores' performance evokes an anachronistic, suspended mobility, contrasting to the restless cosmopolitan form of deterritorialization associated with the European travelers.

[8] Applied to the accented cinema by Hamid Naficy, the term "structure of feeling," as coined by Raymond Williams, describes a "set of undeniable personal and social experiences ... 'that is still in process, often indeed not yet recognized as social but taken to be private, idiosyncratic, and even isolating, but which in analysis (though rarely otherwise) has its emergent, connecting, and dominant characteristics'" (qtd. in Naficy 26), giving rise to social, cultural and institutional formations.

[9] Referring to Ernst Auerbach, Said quotes Hugo's Didascalian meditations to describe this radical posture of the critic: "The man who finds his homeland sweet is still a tender beginner; he to whom every soil is as his native one is already strong; but he is perfect to whom the entire world is as a foreign land" (7).

libidinal transgressive joy of identity-loss and role playing described by Augé in his conception of the non-places of "supermodernity" (103).

Although the film addresses political issues and painful experiences of fragmentation and isolation, the narrator's position is always marked by a playful unreliability. The first person documentarian is taken in by the "mentira con chispa," the Chilean art of lying with tongue in cheek, as one protagonist states in the first part of the film. Suspending thus the documentary claim for mimetic representation of social reality, *Cofralandes* tells the truth by lying, i.e., by making explicit its ludic approach to the narration of nation. The film's narration of nation produces an effect of authenticity in as far as it questions self-reflexively the possibility of documentary discourse of rendering reality in a truthful manner. It thus aspires to a poetic truth claim much more related to the epos of antiquity than that of conventional documentary film.

2.   The Documentarian as "National Geographer"

One of the fundamental discursive strategies of the narration of nation in film is the visualization of space—that is, the cognitive mapping of national territory. Conventionally, this territory is conceived of as a homogeneous and cohesive entity enclosed by fixed boundaries and imbued with a certain essentialized national character. In documentary filmmaking, however, this cohesiveness and homogeneity of the spatial extensions of the nation cannot be considered as simply given, housed in a container, and accessible to mimetic representation. Instead, territoriality has to be constructed by means of a narration which structures the imagined world (or "diegesis")[10] so as to produce an excess of meaning to "real," profilmic space.[11] As the frame constructs the spatial dimensions of the documentary image on the grounds of both limiting and focusing the perception of space[12], the ethnographic documentary needs to expand the diegesis beyond the image by making use of certain rhetoric tropes of spatialization in order to evoke territoriality. This spatial rhetoric is highly conventionalized and deeply rooted in our political unconscious (cf. Jameson), particularly with regard to common-sense assumptions about territorial integrity and the naturalized spatial belonging of the nation people. This is how film is able to imbue the topography of "real," profilmic space with a topological dimension that associates space with semantics of community and identity.

Although any attempt to list the highly diverse tropes of spatialization in documentary film will necessarily be incomplete, we will sketch a number of examples in order to contrast them, in a second step, to the Ruizian approach of constructing a

---

[10] Diegesis is the story understood as a pseudo-world, as the fictional universe whose elements fit together to form a global unity (cf. Aumont 89ff).

[11] The category of *profilmic reality* has been introduced by Souriau as referring to the reality photographed by film. For a description of the different levels of reality according to Souriau, cf. Buckland 47.

[12] Synchronic soundscapes, on the contrary, tend to suggest spatial integrity (cf. Chanan 115ff).

"global sense of place" (Massey). Panorama shots of landscapes with monuments and landmarks, for example, usually signify immutability and the spatial particularity of the nation; in this sense, they extend the space conceptually beyond the frame by means of a synecdoche. Traveling shots on roads or rails, instead, bridge the interstitial spaces in between different scenarios and signify spatial connectivity; they suggest, at the same time, that space is narrated from the subjective point of view of a "national geographer," who takes on an important role in translating geographic space into national territory. A systematic conceptualization of the nation as a spatial entity may be evoked by using a topological opposition between scenarios configured as center vs. periphery, urban life vs. nature, or rich vs. poor. By representing space in a polarized fashion and by omitting the interstitial spaces, the documentary discourse may suggest the all-embracing reach of an allegorical narration of nation within the framework of a logic of closure. Net topologies, on the contrary, allude to the function of communication connecting distinct and distant spaces and produce an image of community which transcends the local and face-to-face interaction.[13] On a much more abstract level, representations of space in a Lefebvrian sense (cf. 38)—including cartographies, signboards, architectural language etc.—may also signify the spatial integrity of national territory from the perspective of planners, urbanists and social engineers.

National territory, however, remains an abstract entity if it is not related to a social practice and a sense of place. It is locality—and not the abstractly configured territory—which is peopled by typical characters in their corresponding milieus. Locality bears an inscription of everyday practice and its ruses described by De Certeau. It is also the spatial order of locality in which the course of experienced history becomes materially manifest by leaving its traces, ruins and relics (cf. Augé 54-55). Pierre Nora's *lieux de mémoire*—both the intimate and the public ones—are imbued with this sense of locality, showing how community changes over time while still guaranteeing the relation between habitat and its inhabitants to be relatively stable. Locality in national pedagogy is thus traditionally related to the subjective experience of community and has a highly affective appeal to its members or "inhabitants." The documentarian as "national geographer" has to find a narrative strategy which extends this affective appeal of locality as well as the particularism of a place and its social milieus in order to construct the cognitive cartography of a nation's territory.

3. Visualizing a Global Sense of Place: Nomadic Narration of the Nationscape in *Cofralandes*

We have described these techniques of visualizing the territorial extension of a nation and embedding the nationscape in local settings in some detail because *Cofralandes* sets out to deconstruct such conventional forms of the spatial narration of nation. The film creates a particular nomadic perspective on the nationscape. It does so by combin-

---

[13] With regard to a description of polar and net topologies, cf. Frahm 269ff. and 293ff.

ing a highly poetic *affective cartography* of the nation and a *mise en abyme*[14] of trad-itional techniques of ethnography and landscaping. In addition, it explores those interstitial "non-places" which transcend the reach of national territoriality and are thus usually omitted as a setting in its own right in the documentary narration of na-tion. All these topoi of spatial narration are bound together in something like a film essay reflecting on the limits of traditional national pedagogy.

The first part of *Cofralandes* undermines the system of coordinates of national geography by using a narrative frame which, right from the outset, thoroughly blurs the boundaries between fact and fiction in documentary discourse. Undoubtedly, ethnographic discourse allows for a certain measure of subjectivity in the narration of space, as is constitutive, for example, for the travelogue genre, and it may even refer to spaces belonging to wholly different spatial orders when such reference is episte-mologically framed in terms of encountering the Other.[15] In *Cofralandes*, however, Ruiz opts for a much more radical approach to constructing the cultural location of ethnographic discourse. Instead of using the journey through diegetic space as an initiation for an internal journey of self-discovery, the film's narrator mostly refrains from "real" movement through the diegetic world and, instead, imagines or remembers the topographical displacement, or else dreams of it in a floating movement through the nationscape.

An earthquake at night takes on the metaphorical function of destabilizing the narrator's system of coordinates and leaves him in a wake dream, pondering childhood me mories and enmeshing them with impressions of his current journey to Chile, his diasporic "home" in France as well as a recent voyage to Asia. This narrative frame introduces a stream of consciousness technique, which turns out to be extremely provocative and iconoclastic. The film simply does not distinguish between "real" and "imaginary" objects or spaces, as the above-mentioned Ruizian quote on the indif-ference of things seen or imagined suggests (cf. Ruiz in Medel, page 275 above). It allows for an erratic spatial and temporal movement between these objects in ways which do not guarantee territorial cohesiveness. Instead, the film addresses the dis-continuities and fragmentation of space and time as well as the multiple associative superimpositions in which spaces are experienced from a diasporic or locally disem-bedded perspective.[16]

One of the principal narrative techniques stressing the narrator's dreamlike state of contemplative, melancholic rapture is his voice. It is charged with affectivity and

---

[14] Narratology conceives the *mise en abyme* as a technique of embedding a reproduction of the image (or narration) within the image (or narration) and producing thus a mirroring effect, which conveys the constructedness, fictionality and self-reflexivity of the narration.

[15] This can be exemplified by the treatment of ritual space in the classic example of visual anthropology, *Les maîtres fous* (1954) by Jean Rouch.

[16] Giddens introduces the concept of the disembedding factors of modernity, positing that modernity fosters "relations between 'absent' others, locationally distant from any given situation of face-to-face interaction" (18).

poetic sensibility and, simultaneously, it is indicative of a picaresque lack of reliability, which makes it extremely difficult to distinguish truth from lies. While in conventional ethnographic narration in documentary film we either find the neutral, disembodied focalization of the voice-of-god narrator or a narrator's point of view immersed in the concrete circumstances of the diegetic world, *Cofralandes* presents an aporetic locus of enunciation charged with both affective nearness and painful distance. Thus, the way in which the film constructs narrative subjectivity is an open challenge to those strategies of authentification of ethnographic discourse which show truth either to be a form of disembodied epistemic knowledge or else embodied in the privileged position of the eye witness. The first-person narrator in *Cofralandes*, instead, is never shown as an on-screen persona but his diegetic presence is being made palpable in a continuous and fleeting process of associating and disassociating it with the point of view of the camera.[17] With constant oscillations between embodiment and disembodiment, presence and absence, the film deconstructs the narrative subject of documentary discourse which remains suspended somewhere between testimony, an actor's performance, and a mere discourse effect.

At the same time, the fleeting and unsure presence of the narrator in the diegetic world informs the ways in which space is constructed in the film. The liminality of the narrative subject that has no clear contours and commits constant transgressions corresponds to a lack of closure or containment in the logical organization of space. Thus, at the beginning of the film, the dreamy autodiegetic narrator recalls an intimate *lieu de mémoire*, the forlorn country home in Limache. He evokes the childhood memory of the "cuentos de la vieja Paulina" and peoples this place at the periphery of the postmodern nation, in a rash of surreal fantasies, with masses of allegoric characters—personae clad as *pasqueros* (Santa Clauses) and butlers blend the innocence of childhood imagery with a clearly menacing performance, as they evoke and satirize the Chilean history of violence and militarism under the Pinochet dictatorship. Blind men are shown hitting their sticks against shields and cardboards carried by demonstrators who demand their expulsion. The hermetic symbolism in this sequence transcends facile interpretation, evoking a trauma which is both personal and collective. It sets the coordinates for the impressions and vignettes the film rhapsodically threads together.

The following sequence is introduced by one of the many incidents in which the narrator seems overly preoccupied with defining the space and the calendar time of his cultural location: Santiago de Chile, a Sunday at 10 o'clock in the morning, a week after his arrival in Chile. His fruitless intentions to stabilize the present locality evoke an order of place and time which is principally determined by being in flux, being only an instance of a life-long journey. A paused pan of Santiago's skyline, which is ac-

---

[17] Street scenes, for example, are mostly shot through the lens of a subjective hand camera, with interlocutors addressing the camera directly, eliciting some kind of response; the scene in a Parisian Chinese restaurant which includes a staged dialogue between Ruiz and his travel companion Bernard Pautrat, on the contrary, disassociates the camera perspective and the narrator's point of view.

companied by Violeta Parra's song about the utopic Cofralandes, where "everything happens" and people do not suffer from hunger because "the houses are made of bread and the towers of cheese," is juxtaposed in swift, associative moves by the places the narrator has travelled before coming to Chile on this occasion: from France, his diasporic homeland, to Tokyo, and from Tokyo to a past journey to Chiloe. The juxtaposition of these spaces is metaphoric in the sense in which Bhabha associates the term with the diasporic constitution of the modern nation:[18] The juxtaposition of the different spatial orders signifies on both spaces. It evokes a sense of movement and uprooting and breaks up the territorial order of the nationscape. In order to bring the different spatial orders together in a diasporic apperception of the world, the film uses visual motifs as a *tertium comparationis*—the carps in the aquarium of a Parisian Chinese restaurant dissolve into carps in a Japanese pond, the merry-go-round of an amusement park in Tokyo reminds the narrator of a trip to a forgotten amusement park in Chiloe. These motifs make it possible for the narrator to affectively relate the different spaces to each other by (re)discovering a familiar motif in a space that seems distant and different; simultaneously, they also signify the diasporic condition of the narrator—the fish in the pond and the wheel of fortune symbolize his transitory existence and the experience of being caught in a continuous and inescapable state of flux.

Once the cosmopolitan identity of the narrator has been established through these narrative techniques, the filmmaker is shown to explore the locality of urban life in Santiago. Although the apperception of locality corresponds to the pronouncedly idiosyncratic point of view of the diasporic narrator, the following incidents and encounters with Chilean reality indicate that the deterritorialized sense of place functions as common ground shared by the diasporic subject and the imagined community of his homeland. The latter is shown to be caught in processes of social fragmentation, the long-term consequences of the 1970s and 1980s military dictatorship and the disembedding factors of neoliberal globalization and world wide connectivity.

The first spatial dimension of the nationscape explored by the narrator is the neighborhood of his home in Santiago. His wanderings unveil a suburban cityscape: an unlikely setting for a narration of nation as it is hardly distinguishable from similar places in any other cultural context.[19] The alleys of suburbia are the setting for chance encounters with various former and new acquaintances of the narrator, who display a markedly neurotic and grotesque behavior: a fellow pupil from primary school stutters

---

[18] "The nation fills the void left by the uprooting of communities and kin, and turns that loss into the language of metaphor. Metaphor, as the etymology of the word suggests, transfers the meaning of home and belonging across the 'middle passage,' or the central European steppes, across these distances, and cultural differences, that span the imagined community of the nation-people" (*Location* 139-40).

[19] This ethnography of the middle classes constitutes a harsh contrast to earlier documentary narrations of the nation from the standpoint of the Chilean diaspora, such as Littin's *Acta General de Chile*, which seeks the expression of nation-people in the working-class *poblaciones* of Santiago and Valparaiso.

and suddenly breaks out in tears, supposedly because of a puppy pet lost before the coup d'État; a former comrade from the Socialist youth organization tells stories about the times of the "ex-Unidad Popular" in "el ex-Santiago del ex-Chile;" his wife is afraid of a complot of stutterers in Santiago de Chile and has to be calmed by him. The contingency of these encounters and the idiosyncrasies of these grotesque personae add up to a national allegory, showing how deterritorialization has disembedded social relationships. On the one hand, the acquaintances try to cope with memories of the times before the military coup, which the narrator's presence seems to bring forth from the subconscious. On the other, the effects of telecommunication are omnipresent:[20] the camera follows two of the characters—the ex-comrade of the Socialist youth organization and the woman who turns out to be his neurotic wife—with extensive traveling shots at short distance, taken with a handheld camera from aside or swirling around the characters while they are walking down the alley and communicating with each other by cell phone. The whole setting breaks with the logics of spatial mimesis because the subjective camera suggests the narrator to be present at two places and to register both interlocutors simultaneously.

The background against which these images are shot shows the static social morphology of suburbia, with the bourgeoisie's private sphere defended against intruders with fences, gates or windows protected by iron bars. At a certain stage, the former socialist *compañero* invites the narrator to pass into the garden of his home. Once the frontier which excludes intruders from the intimacy of the bourgeois home has been trespassed, the rich green foliage of bushes and trees evokes a baroque idyll contrasting with the public space of the alley. The garden is visualized, however, in a manner deeply informed by the all-pervasive deterritorialized structure of feeling. The housewife shows the narrator around her collection of over thirty "animitas," little shrines for the souls of accident victims who, because of their innocent passing into afterlife, are believed to work miracles. In Chile, these shrines are originally set at road crosses where accidents took away the lives of the innocent. Moved to a bourgeois garden, and thus decontextualized, the animitas shrines break the intimacy of the bourgeois interior apart by introducing a strangely transient and transcendental dimension. In a grotesque manner, the film shows the animitas at work: performing miracles for the camera and receiving gifts in exchange. Lerencio, a supposed specialist in sore backs and inflammations, who is also believed to protect against plane crashes, starts

---

[20] The motif of telecommunication is related to a Baudrillardian effect of the hyperreal (cf. 166-84). Thus, the prop which is used by the narrator's former compañero as a cell phone turns out to be a TV remote control and it serves as a kind of *mise en abyme* to switch from this sequence to the next. The following sequence contains loosely threaded takes which blend together the ethnographic discourse of documentary film, for example, with the televisual rhetoric of financial news. The arrow icon of stock exchange values pointing down, for example, is inserted in images and used as a meta-narrative commentary on images of children ritually performing what is suggested to be the national anthem. These images question on the grounds of media reflexivity any claim to the documentary representation of profilmic reality.

to plead to a plane silhouette passing in the sky: "Aviones, aviones, ¡no se caigan todavía! ... ¡Sigan dando vueltas! ¡Vamos, sigan para otros paises!" ["Please, airplanes, do not fall out of the sky yet! ... Keep circulating! Come on, keep going on to other countries!"] Then, in the manner of a Brechtian effect of defamiliarization [*Verfremdungseffekt*], a model train is shown to traverse the garden, passing right through the animitas shrines and linking—as a montage effect—the garden scene to the next scenario, a social convention at one of Santiago's regional clubs.

This model train is part of a complex audio-visual leitmotif linked to deterritorialization. A product of the narrator's mind, it symbolizes the diasporic perception of space. In this first appearance of the motif in the film, the model train, the recontextualized animitas' shrines and the airplane linking distant spaces show how the core areas of the bourgeoisie's private sphere are constituted by the crossing of a whole array of different routes. By these means, this intimate place is turned into a kind of third, interstitial space—a space of "all-inclusive simultaneity," according to Soja:

> Everything comes together in Thirdspace: subjectivity and objectivity, the abstract and the concrete, the real and the imagined, the knowable and the unimaginable, the repetitive and the differential, structure and agency, mind and body, consciousness and the unconscious, the disciplined and the transdisciplinary, everyday life and unending history. (56-57)

These principles of Thirdspace inform the construction of space in *Cofralandes* in general; the film plays with the tension resulting from applying them to spaces which are conventionally related to stasis, primordiality, and continuity. This becomes particularly evident in the representation of the Andean landscape, which is re-signified in terms of spatial perception. In the conventional narration of nation, the landscapes of the countryside can be considered a very potent semantic of nationhood. The poetic impact of scenery elicits a highly affective response from the spectator, linking national identity with a naturalized and stable relation to place. These ideas have been exploited since early 19th century Romanticism—an era of aesthetic innovation which corresponds historically to the formational period of modern nationalism and devises with its sublime spaces and picturesque contrasts the complex aesthetic codes of landscaping (cf. Barlow Rogers). Naficy posits that these aesthetic conventions also play a crucial role in the style of accented filmmaking: contrasted to the historicity and fleeting character of urbanism associated by the deterritorialized filmmaker with the experience of everyday life in diaspora, the fetishized rural landscapes express a utopian longing for wholeness, primordiality, and rootedness. According to Naficy, shots of mountain sites in particular are related to the Bakhtinian idyllic chronotope on which landscape art is founded, as they appeal to the

> unity of an ancient complex and a folkloric time, which is expressed in the special relationship that space and time have within the idyll. This relationship is "an organic fastening-down, a grafting of life and its events to a place, to familiar territory with all its nooks and crannies, its familiar mountains, valleys, fields, rivers and forests, and one's own home." (155)

Cofralandes addresses the construction of landscape as a signifier of nationhood in two ways. On the one hand, Rainer Kraus, one of the three protagonists who accompany the narrator on his journey through Chile, is a German landscape artist who is shown to ceaselessly sketch the Chilean landscape and to philosophize on the importance of landscape for understanding the nation and its people. On the other hand, there is a series of sequences in which the documentary draws self-reflexive attention to the filmic montage of landscape images and thus effectuates a deconstruction of the documentary aesthetic.

With regard to the German landscape artist, it can be said that he does not only represent one of the film's principle approaches to the construction of ethnographic knowledge but is also one of the specular doubles of the filmmaker. Thus, he gives origin to one of the many facets of the meta-narrative *mise en abyme* in the film, mirroring in his art the landscape photography in film. His art form with its slow process of sculpting space by means of simple two-dimensional lines and traces seems oddly out of place and time when contrasted with the acceleration and rootlessness of urban life in Santiago. It is one of the many strategies with which the film slows down the pace in order to allow for moments of suspended time and ennui, which open the spectator's mind for contemplation in the midst of accelerated perception of a deterritorialized world.[21] Kraus explains at the end of the film in his "accented" Spanish why he is attracted to Chilean landscapes:

> Yo creo que, en Chile, uno hay que preocuparse por el paisaje. Ahí pasan las cosas intensas. Ya se nota que Chile es un país con hartas contradicciones que se expresan en el paisaje, un paisaje grande, denso, lindo. Las Cordilleras siempre a la vista, tremendas, la costa ... y en medio el ser humano que no sabe muy bien que hacer con estas cosas.[22]

The correspondence the landscape artist finds between the morphology of the natural surroundings and the state of mind which allows him to access the affective constitution of the nation people, is reminiscent of Romantic thought and its tradition of landscape painting. The association with Romanticism is highlighted by the film's use of Franz Schubert's "Die Nachtigall" as Kraus's signature tune. Although Kraus's access to the construction of ethnographic knowledge is relativized by his anachronistic ways, his accent, and "el aura gringo," as it is called in the film, his drawings and his stance on aesthetics are not discarded by the narrative instance. Instead, the film emulates at times a form of constructing landscape similar to Kraus's sketches. It mirrors the ways in which film and drawing register the same scenery through different, but analogous media, manifest similar forms of fictionalization of landscape

---

[21] Ruiz explores the importance of *ennui* in film aesthetics in the first chapter of his *Poética del cine*.

[22] I think that in Chile you have to preoccupy yourself with landscape. This is where the intense stuff happens. You will notice that Chile is a country with a lot of contradictions which find themselves expressed in landscape, a landscape which is huge, dense, lovely. The tremendous Cordilleras, the coast—they are always in sight ... and in their midst the human being who does not know what to make of these things.

and similarly aspire to poetic truths. By these means, the film foregrounds the mediality of filmic landscape representation and the particular perspectivism of landscape art: Kraus's drawings are always shown to be subject to re-elaboration and re-assessment from the artist's particular perspective on the surrounding space. This aspect is highly significant to the film's reflection on the perspectivism of ethnographic methodology, as will be explored in more detail in the following section of this essay.

The second, self-reflexive approach to landscape art in *Cofralandes* is linked to strategies of deconstructing landscape images by means of Avant-garde montage. Its most prominent feature with regard to this aspect is the counterpointing of the visual rhetoric of landscape with dissonant soundscapes, evocative of a distinct, deterritorialized perception of space. The scene which is most representative of this particular aporetic discourse on landscape is introduced midway through the film, after a sequence which evokes archetypal scenarios of homecoming and parting, set in the streets of Santiago and the train station at Limache. The exploration of the rural landscape is explicitly framed as a response to deterritorialized structures of feeling and constitutes a parenthesis in space and time, a mental journey with connotations of escapism.

The sequence starts with a travelling shot from a fast moving car, displaying a road trip through the lush green countryside, accompanied by lyrics and sounds of a folk song evoking the idea of a journey. Then it turns to a clearly topical representation of mountain sites with imposing, touristic visual impressions of the Andine landscape, picturing crosses and shadows in counter light, shot against the backdrop of a deep blue mountain lake, while elegiac chants evoke the unison of sublime space and spectator, suggesting a longing for calm and rootedness. The landscape changes abruptly to a highland plain. A female voice recites Gabriela Mistral's poetic evocation of a childhood in the Valle of Elqui and the longing for spaces afar: "Ibamos a ser reinas y todas íbamos llegar al mar." ["We were going to be queens and all of us were to reach the sea."] The poetry appeals to the topos of nature's femininity, the rhythmic and repetitive movement of the verses is in harmony with the paused and seemingly endless pan across the highland plain with its homogeneous visual impression of green bushes and mountain silhouettes. The pronouncedly slow circular pan to the left emulates a sovereign perspective on the unpopulated rural landscape.

When the recitation ends, sounds of a steam train blend into the birds' chant and produce a sudden rupture in the representational logic since they do not correspond to any visual motif of the diegetic world. Instead, they are revealed to be a product of the narrator's synaesthetic apperception of space, a reminiscence of his diasporic subjectivity. The panning of the camera comes to a halt, focusing on a group of cacti which break with the visual texture of the landscape dominated by green foliage. At this point, the sequence introduces a series of defamiliarizing effects, which run counter to the contemplative identification of observer and landscape. A small dirt road comes into sight, which is followed by the camera until it reaches the first vestiges of civilization to the sound of Kurt Schwitters's Dadaist evocation of train sounds in his

"Sonate in Urlauten." This seems like an irreverent reference to the regression to infancy. The "Urlaute," primordial sounds prior to language and meaning, contrast sharply with the naturalizing function of Mistral's poetry. As the camera continues to pan to the left, the rural landscape dissolves slowly into an urban scenario. For a fleeting moment the montage has the images of traffic passing by the camera at relatively close distance coincide with the imposing presence of the Andes.

The counterpointed use of sound effects, which marks the whole sequence, shifts the focus from the spectacle of landscape to the mobility of the spectator; the stasis and calm seem to trigger a cognitive effect which produces a self-reflexive distancing from the object and throws the narrator as spectator back onto himself and his solitude. The landscape images produce a (post)modern "deflection" or "reversal of the gaze," as is described by Augé:

> we should still remember that there are spaces in which the individual feels himself to be a spectator without paying much attention to the spectacle. As if the position of the spectator were his own spectacle. ... The spelling out of a position, or 'posture,' an attitude in the most physical and commonplace sense of the term, comes at the end of a movement that empties the landscape, and the gaze of which it is the object, of all content and all meaning, precisely because the gaze dissolves into the landscape and becomes the object of a secondary, unattributable gaze—the same one, or another. (86, 93)

Augé's description comes very close to the ways in which the film uses landscape as a disembedded signifier of nationhood: reminiscent of the modern nation's reach into the a-historic past (cf. Bhabha, *Nation* 1), but marked at the same time by a clearly postmodern self-reflexive and ironic distance from its object. There is a postmodern mixture of nostalgia and irony (cf. Hutcheon) present in the representation of the sublime mountain site, which is caused by the distance or mobility inscribed in the spectator's gaze, and the consciousness of the naturalized filiation of landscape art as being anachronistic.

The slow dissolve at the end of the sequence with its superimposition of urban and rural landscape can be conceived of as a metaphor for the deterritorialization of the nation: it enmeshes the two different spatial semantics in a way which translates between both spatial orders and produces a semantic shift in both of them. The mountain site as an expression of rootedness and national essence is deconstructed and deterritorialized in the eye of the beholder by the imminence of the historicity and change brought about by the accelerated urban scenario; the perception of city life and its fleeting temporality is predetermined by the recollection of the sublime space of the mountain site.

The following long-sequence shot of the traffic at the Plaza Baquedano in Santiago de Chile uses a similar filmic strategy. The two sequences complement each other as the second sequence basically constitutes a continuation of the camera movement in the previous scene, completing a slow 360 degrees circular pan to the left displaying the heterogeneous cityscape at Santiago de Chile's most prominent plaza. The Plaza Baquedano is an oval dominated by an equestrian statue of General Baquedano, one of the heroes of the Chilean independence, and it is an expression of city planning of the turn of the 19th century which structures the urban space, following contemporary European models, as the metropolitan center of the nation. The statue overlooks a monumental traffic circle which gives way to a series of boulevards and is passed by endless tides of urban traffic. This traffic circle is lined by a highly heterogeneous cityscape composed of buildings representing Santiago's urban development until the inception of high modernism.

The monument of Baquedano marks the beginning and the end of the 360 degree pan and evokes the spatial representation of the national "historia de bronze"—the myths of foundational history—, frozen to a halt and moved out of the everyday onto a pedestal. By means of the circular pan, the film diverts the attention from the monumentality of this representational space and moves the focus to the ceaseless flow of traffic. The documentary, thus, captures a different temporality than the ritual time of monumentality: it discovers the historicity and transitory nature of the everyday, of which the flow of urban traffic becomes a metaphor. This is done, as in the preceding sequence, by counterpointing the use of an extradiegetic soundscape to the image track. Fragments of oral memory, speculations and rumors uttered by a host of anonymous voices are localized in this urban scenery by white arrows pointing to specific localities—a balcony of an apartment block, a street corner, etc. At times cacophonic, these voices blend together individual memories ("Ahí hicimos un asado ...") ["We had a barbecue there once ..."], personal tragedies ("Yo estoy segura que en este departamento se cometió un asesinato") ["I am sure that in this apartment someone committed a murder"] and urban history ("Ahí nació el último veterano de ...") ["The last veteran of ... was born there"]. Sounds of a marching band allude to the times of the Unidad Popular, then a demonstration answers "ausente, ausente" ["absent, absent"] to voices shouting the names of the dead or disappeared, inverting, with a trace of irony, the political rituals of the Unidad Popular. The feeling of absence and past is what unites all sound fragments, spread over the urban space like an invisible social texture, made visible only by extradiegetic trick effects and symbolizing the deterritorializing power of the historic process. At the end of this sequence, in a self-ironic turn, the arrow introduced as a graphic icon to localize the invisible past is semantically linked to diaspora as it covers a life of its own, performing the landing of an airplane on a bus passing the Plaza Baquedano——a bus that carries the diasporic protagonists of the film on a tour through the city, as is suggested later on.

The spatial orders we have addressed so far——the *lieu de mémoire* of childhood memories, the suburban spaces, the sublime landscape, and the representational spaces of the city—are all imbued by the film's nomadic narration of the nation with a particular, deterritorialized sense of place. This sense of place is attributed both to the the diasporic observer and, in an indirect and much more ambivalent manner, to his "object" of representation, the Chilean nation-people the film sets out to depict ethnographically. An additional, but distinct spatial order of the nationscape the film plays with conceptually is what we can conceive of in Augé's terms as "non-places":

Clearly the word 'non-place' designates two complementary but distinct realities: spaces formed in relation to certain ends (transport, transit, commerce, leisure), and the relations that individuals have with these spaces. ... [N]on-places create solitary contractuality. (Augé 94)

According to Augé, non-places are defined by mobility and inhibit a sense of belonging. They suggest an experience of space in which social interaction is reduced to the consumption of services and commodities. The importance of these non-places for the contemporary constitution of the imagined community of the nation is addressed in various scenes of the film (for example, the hilarious scenes at the immigration office), but it is not until the end of the film that non-places become the predominant experience of space: an intertitle with a verse by the poet Jorge Carrera Andrade ("Te reconozco, viento del exilio, saqueador de jardines") ["I recognize you, wind of exile, expulser from gardens"] is shown against a black screen and triggers a flow of visual motifs clearly related to non-places. This particular sequence discovers spatial niches of passage and transition which expand national territoriality by a notion of mobility, exile and diaspora characteristic of the nomadic cultural position of the filmmaker.

The film enmeshes a series of visual impressions related to these imageries of non-places by means of a particular visual narration of space combining shots of street scenes, interior shots and props. It depicts them from a decentralized perspective. A street scene peopled by passengers dragging their luggage and shot through a metal grid is followed by low-angle shots of airport architecture and hotel lobbies, a close-up of a telephone in a hotel room, shots of a luxurious restaurant and close-ups of wine and beer glasses. In the first takes, there is a notion of frenzy mobility, a certain restive, contemplative and leisurely atmosphere, achieved by drawing on a haptic optic created by means of soft textures, dimmed lighting and the display of mouth-watering food. However, there is, simultaneously, a disturbing and transcendent presence of death in these images which profoundly changes the meaning of the category of the non-place and associates it with exilic loss and transitoriness. The subjective commentary, which is characteristic for most of the film's *auteur*-ish style, gives way in this sequence to silence: subtitles uttered by disembodied and deterritorialized voices take its place, suggesting anonymous people addressing other absent and distant people in a form of truncated communication. There is a remarkable tension between the glossy visual aesthetics of these non-places and the diasporic communication of loss and longing which, ultimately, stays beyond the reach of visualization. The strategic use of the written word is related to the trope of exilic and diasporic filmmaking, which Naficy has called "epistolarity" (cf. 101-51). Drawing on Kauffman, Naficy posits that letters and writing suggest a "'metonymic and metaphoric displacement of desire'—a desire to be with another and reimagine an elsewhere and other times" (101). In the "wind of exile" sequence of *Cofralandes*, epistolarity is characteristic for a nomadic narration which constructs an imagined community on the grounds of truncated dialogue and fragmented memory, which both have to do with the opaque mediality of telecommunication; meaning stays ambivalent, rumor-like, and inaccessible to an ultimate, textual authority on truth:

—Te escribo desde el aeropuerto de ...
—Llegue a Tokio, hay sol ...
—Un saludo desde ...
—Hoy cumplimos 12 años en Londres ...
—Llegamos sin novedad ...
—Me resfrié en Hong Kong ... Berlin ... Estocolmo[23]

While visual impressions of non-places pass fleetingly, the symphonic sound-track suddenly livens up as if it was evoking the wind of exile. Strings mark the rhythm for an oscillating visual background of neon signs while a subtitle saying "Ayer falleció Humberto ..." ["Yesterday Humberto passed away ..."] appears and slowly fades away. In an almost painful suspended rhythm, the names of eight fellow exiles are shown to appear as subtitles and fade away into oblivion. A nomadic narration, stripped down to the rudiments of communication, shows how the imagined community of exiles is slowly disintegrating against the backdrop of a leisurely cosmopolitanism which is both the stage for deterritorialization and, simultaneously, remains strange and impenetrable to the affective dimension of displacement.

The transient spatial order of the non-place does not erase the sense of community of the diasporic subject; instead, it evokes the separation and loss which time effectuates in the fluctuating networks of diasporic communities. This loss and separation problematizes language as a signifying system in a way which differs from Augé's assertions on the substitution of things by signs in the non-place of super-modernity: "Vocabulary has a central role here because it is what weaves the tissue of habits, educates the gaze, informs the landscape" (108). While Augé's interpretation of the role of language for non-places borders on the concept of the simulacrum, in Ruiz's film this simulacrum does not elude the disturbing presence of death and displacement. Instead, there is something in the transitory cultural location of exile and diaspora which disarticulates the simulacrum and the signifying system it is grounded on, producing a different epistemology or diasporic optic present in ways which transcend the a-history on the non-place.[24]

---

[23] —I write to you from the airport of ...
—I arrived at Tokio, it is sunny.
—Greetings from ...
—Today it is 12 years we live in London.
—We arrived without any news.
—I caught a cold in Hong Kong ... Berlin ... Stockholm.

[24] According to Augé, non-place is necessarily a-historic: "Everything proceeds as if space had been trapped by time, as if there were no history other than the last forty-eight hours of news, as if each individual history were drawing its motives, its words and images, from the inexhaustible stock of the unending moment of the present" (104). Cofralandes, to the contrary, posits loss and separation (as two diachronic effects of narration) to inflect on the simulacrum of non-space.

4. Epistemological Nomadism

This essay has shown so far that Ruiz's self-reflexive documentary *Cofralandes* undermines the conventional topology of the nationscape by approaching space from the
perspective of a deterritorialized sense of place. While conventional ethnographic discourse in documentary film presupposes a perception of space either from the neutral,
detached and godlike perspective of science, or the engaged and privileged perspective
of the participating observer, *Cofralandes* proposes a radical perspectivism which
unveils the necessarily limited narrative authority on space that either of these perspectives has. The cultural location from which the diasporic subject perceives and represents space is always transitory, and thus pinpoints to the common sense understanding
that the perception of space changes with the perspective, or trajectory, of its spectator.
In this sense, nomadic narration of space is based on the self-reflexive presupposition
that there can never be a conclusive authority in spatial representation. Ruiz opts, thus,
for a radical epistemological shift in ethnographic documentary filmmaking, which
can be associated with the concept of epistemological nomadism that Deleuze and
Guattari have proposed in their groundbreaking work *Thousand Plateaus*.

In their "Treatise on Nomadology," the two French poststructuralists use the spatial metaphor of deterritorialization to construct a subject position radically opposed to
the spatial order of the nation-state and private property that striate space by means of
fixed boundaries. In Deleuze and Guattari's approach, deterritorialization becomes
thus a metaphor for a certain form of radical nomadic criticism overcoming the spatial
order imposed by hierarchy and hegemony. Deterritorialization suggests a different,
nomadic conception of space: smooth and limitless space that constitutes a malleable,
"liquid" category. The "Treatise of Nomadology" translates this nomadic conception
of space to epistemology, postulating that in nomadic thought the reified subject-object
relation of Western logocentrism is overcome by an epistemology which resists clear-
cut distinctions between fact and fiction and questions ultimate authority or truth.

Deleuze and Guattari's position claims for itself to represent the cultural location
of a marginalized other—i.e. that of the nomad—, which has been one of the reasons
for questioning Deleuzian theory by postcolonial critics such as Gayatri Chakravorty
Spivak or Caren Kaplan, who posits: "The nomad serves as the site of this roman-
ticized imaginary entry into the 'becoming minor' of deterritorialization" (89). Kaplan
criticizes nomadology as being founded on an essentialization and lacking an awareness of the suffering and loss deterritorialization entails for exiled, diasporic or trans-
migrant populations.

Within the context of Ruizian filmmaking, however, the thought figure of the
nomadic is being used from the subject position of exile or diaspora within a clearly
postcolonial, albeit idiosyncratic framework of thought. The conceptual link established
by nomadology between a deterritorialized conception of space and epistemology is
highly relevant to this reflection on the methodology of ethnographic filmmaking.
Cofralandes' principle strategy is to establish a narrative instance for the construction of

ethnographic knowledge which is, in principle, dialogical. The narrative authority does not rest solely on the first person narrator, but is delegated, at least partially, to a series of protagonists accompanying him on his (auto)ethnographic quest and assuming the role of the filmmaker's doubles: the French journalist Bernard Pautrat, the German landscape painter Rainer Kraus, and the British sociologist Malcolm Coad. Each of these characters, introduced at the beginning of the film in the counts of the "vieja Paulina" as "tres príncipes hermanos que se fueron por mares y países lejanos" ["three princes and brothers who left home to travel seas and distant countries"] is acquainted with Chile and the idiosyncracies of its nation-people. The three are representatives of European diaspora and thus share, to a certain degree, the nomadic subjectivity of the narrator. Because of their foreignness, however, which is playfully constructed via their "aura de gringo" and the linguistic stigma of accent (cf. Naficy 21-25), they voice points of views which differ considerably from the role the filmmaker performs as a screen persona. By being the frequent target of irony and postcolonial critique, they legitimize the filmmaker's narrative authority and privileged access to his Chilean home culture, despite the long years of his absence and exile. The splitting of the narrative instance can thus be conceived as a strategy of displaying a sense of belonging on behalf of the filmmaker vis-à-vis the imagined community of the nation-people, while he is simultaneously using the presence of the foreign other, his travel companions, to keep the distance necessary for his (auto)ethnographic inquiries. Ethnographic meaning is thus negotiated in the film within a group of characters who do not only explore the Chilean nation from the perspective of their particular cultural locations, but also self-reflexively debate the nature of ethnographic construction of knowledge.

By means of each of the three doubles of the narrator, the film addresses a crucial problem of the nomadological construction of ethnographic knowledge. Malcolm Coad's fruitless sociological research on the phenomenon of a heightened suicide rate in various Chilean localities receives particular attention as it is mentioned twice in the film in almost the same words, once by himself and once by the first-person narrator. It is the meta-narrative allegory of an exotopic observer who has to acknowledge that each time he approaches a locality in which, by means of sociological research, a certain social problem is bound to be found, the problem vanishes when he arrives. This phenomenon repeats itself each time he approaches a new locality. The nomadic constitution of his object of study triggers a crisis within the epistemological framework of his understanding of science. The spatial order on which social science is grounded and which categorizes social phenomena according to the presupposition of spatial homogeneity and scientific neutrality becomes aporetic. These presuppositions are of no help at all when the phenomenon seems not only to disband when being approached on a local level, but, instead, moves from one place to another, leaving the sociologist on an unending and ultimately frustrating nomadic quest for knowledge.

Equally driven by a ceaseless search for knowledge, the landscapist Rainer Kraus is shown to adapt his methodology to the circumstances of his itinerant cultural location. In contrast to Malcolm Coad's ethnography, Kraus's landscape art does not aim at establishing verifiable truth on social phenomena from a supposedly neutral perspective. On the contrary, it is much more self-reflexive and aware of its perspectivism and performativity. While driving on a bus through Santiago, Kraus draws the interior of the bus with a fleeting reflection of the outside world. He explains to Bernard:

> Estoy dibujando aquí un poco, anotando impresiones que tengo del paisaje en este momento. ... Es parte del micro, interior, un poco de paisaje exterior, típico. ... No se nota muy bien porque la calidad del dibujo depende mucho de la calidad del pavimiento de la calle y un poco del ánimo del chofer también.[25]

His nomadic methodology does not only explore the country and the mentality of the people on a representational level. By continuously moving his point of view he feels to be subject to the outward influences which orient his drawings. He is, thus, conscious of the fact that at a pragmatic level he is as much the subject as the object of the social circumstances he interacts with while sketching the landscape.

The character of Bernard Pautrat, who, in this sequence, is filmed in a distorting extreme close-up on his glasses, trying to pry over Kraus's shoulders and to involve him in a conversation, introduces an element in the film which can most explicitly be related to a postcolonial deconstruction of Eurocentrism (cf. Shohat/Stam). Pautrat is actually the one who originally persuaded the filmmaker to undertake his (auto)ethnographic journey by extending an invitation to accompany him to Chile. Financed by a French magazine, he is to write a series of articles in the style of "un voyage au bout du monde, ou une connerie comme ça" ["a journey to the end of the world, or some stupid thing like that"]. The scene in which he presents the matter to the first-person filmmaker as well as the following dialogue are set in a Chinese restaurant in Paris. This dialogue is significant in staging the conflict over the postcolonial regime of gaze which is established in the film.

> Pautrat: Je te propose de venir avec moi au Chili.
> Filmmaker: Merci, mais tu n'as pas besoin de moi. Tu connais le Chili beaucoup mieux que moi.
> P.: Oui, mais ce n'est pas la question. Toi, tu n'as pas d'accent et tu es extrêmement bavard. Donc, tu parleras et je t'observerai.[26]

Pautrat proposes to use the auto-diegetic narrator as a guide and mediator, merely observing the interactions of the latter with the Chilean people. *Cofralandes*, however, inverts the hierarchy implicit in this regime of gaze by showing how the camera, which is related to the auto-diegetic point of view, assumes the role of a second-degree

---

[25] I am drawing a bit, taking note of the impressions of the landscape at this moment. ... This is a part of the interior of the bus with a bit of what is typical in the landscape outside. ... It's difficult to perceive because the quality of the drawing depends on the quality of the pavement of the street and also a bit on the mood of the driver.

[26] Bernard: I suggest that you accompany me to Chile.
Filmmaker: Thank you, but you do not need me. You know Chile much better than I do.
Bernard: Yes, but that's not the point. You don't have an accent and you're extremely communicative. Thus, you'll talk and I'll observe you.

"observer," registering how Bernard as a spectator forms part of the ethnographic spectacle in a conceptual move similar to that of the postmodern construction of landscape described on page 286 above. This postcolonial *mise en abyme* in the film, which has the observed observing his observer, breaks with the Eurocentrism of ethnographic filmmaking and allows for critical comments on the epistemological grounds on which Pautrat bases his journalistic explorations of the Chilean context: "Pero Bernard escribía sobre todo lo que veía. Veía y escribía, entendiendo sin entender este famoso Chile, el país del fin del mundo."[27] These lines contain an explicit postcolonial critique against the authority of the European ethnographer who makes use of an exotopic epistemology interpreting the postcolonial other as strange and exotic without reaching a more thorough understanding of what he describes.

The aporetic statement of Pautrat's "understanding without understanding" artfully undermines the authority of his descriptions without, however, delegitimizing his road of access to the construction of ethnographic knowledge altogether. Pautrat's views on Chile are informed by exotopism and stereotyping, but a series of his generalizations about the social psychology of the Chileans (and, in passing, about Europeans as well) are exemplified—and thus partially corroborated—by performative enactments of Chilean everyday life. His screen persona is, as the film shows, also characterized by his close acquaintance and affiliation with the Chilean context, which is even posited by the narrator (see dialog above). In this sense, his partial understanding of his object of study shows the generalizations and limitations of any ethnographic knowledge—a fact which is also true with regard to Ruiz's own (auto)ethnographic quest from the exotic perspective of diaspora. Pautrat is permitted some crucial, self-reflexive insights with regard to the lack of truthfulness and histrionic role-playing of his ethnographic "object," the Chileans; a fact which questions his ability to register their "real" life in a truthful manner. In one of his truly comical dialogues with Kraus, Pautrat affirms:

> Bernard: ... No hay que creer la gente que vive en Chile. Porque lo que pasa en Chile es que hay hartos, hartos mentirosos ... ¿Tu sabes eso, no?
> Rainer: No, no sé. Mentirosos hay en todas partes, ¿eh?
> B: Hartos, ¡sí!, pero más, más ... pero mentirosos con chispa, ¿no?
> R: ¿Con chispa? ¿Y por qué estás en Chile entonces?
> B: Porque a mi me gusta la mentira con chispa ... Hahaha, muy difícil, ¿no?[28]

---

[27] But Bernard was writing about everything he saw. He was seeing and writing, understanding without understanding this famous Chile, the land at the end of the Earth.

[28] Bernard: ... you should not believe the people who live in Chile. Because, what happens in Chile is that there are many, many liars. You know that, don't you?
Rainer: No, I don't! There are liars in all parts of the world, aren't there?
B: Very much so, but there are more, more ..., but there are more liars with an [ingenious] spark, don't you think?
R: With a spark? And why are you in Chile, then?
B: Because I like lies with this spark. Hahaha, that's very difficult to understand, isn't it?

His affirmation can be conceived of as a veiled meta-narrative commentary on the Ruizian auto-ethnographic travelogue in *Cofralandes*. The whole documentary is informed by this "mentira con chispa," the character of the auto-diegetic narrator being the foremost trickster and dreamer among all the Chilean "mentirosos con chispa" who appear in the film.

5. Conclusions

Cofralandes contains a mixture of documentary, fiction, performativity, and postcolonial mimicry, which does not answer to conventional truth claims of the documentary, but approximates the representation of reality by exploring both the deep structure of the Chilean society's fragmentation and histrionic role-playing as a consequence of a deterritorialized and uprooted structure of feeling. The Chilean "mentira con chispa" is thus an ingenious challenge *Cofralandes* poses to ethnographic filmmaking by reconfiguring the role of documentary discourse in the postmodern crisis of referentiality on the grounds of an epistemological nomadism. It does so by transcending the facile truth claims of documentary mimesis through a dialogical structure.

This crisis of referentiality is posited at the end of the film just before the final "wind of exile" sequence. It shows an acute interest in the ways in which deterritorialization and the non-places of cosmopolitan itineraries can be associated with a crisis of the signifying system of language, very much in accord with French poststructuralist thought. In his wake dream, the narrator starts to enmesh the spatial orders of here and there, his home in Santiago and his home in Paris. "Se me enrodó todo: la casa de allá y la casa de acá. ¡Qué cosa ...!" ["Everything became mixed up: the house there, the house here. How strange ...!"]. The different spatial orders of there and here, diaspora and homeland, start to dissolve in a way which deconstruct any clear limits and structures of the striated space. Space becomes smooth and liquid to the nomadic eye; it becomes impossible to root categories and fixed meaning in place. This process originates in the painful experience of feeling displaced as the narrator suffers the ultimate consequence of deterritorialization: the loss of language. To the sounds of Kurt Schwitters's primeval sounds from the gramophone, the film shows the world of objects to have received tags with words naming things—"lámpara," "gramofono," "cortina," "madera" ["lamp," "gramophone," "curtain," "wood"]—, i.e. signifiers naming the signified. This technique, a faint reminder of the insomnia plague and semantic dementia in Gabriel García Márquez' *Cien años de soledad*, expresses a desperate will to bridge the ongoing disassociation of things and names in diaspora. In this deterritorialized state of mind, it can no longer be guaranteed that language serves as a transparent vehicle of the ethnographic logos, and the increasingly abstract poetic quality of the image transcends the realistic mimesis of ethnographic documentaries. This sequence shows in the most radical way the challenge of deterritorialization to the construction of social knowledge. It illustrates, simultaneously, how a different, nomadic epistemology answers to this impossibility of establishing an ultimate, epistemic truth or of imposing a logic of closure on space and time in contemporary ethnographic documentary filmmaking.

Works Cited

Appadurai, Arjun. *Modernity at Large: Cultural Dimensions of Globalization.* Minneapolis: U of Minnesota P, 2000.

Augé, Marc. *Non-Places: Introduction to an Anthropology of Supermodernity.* London: Verso, 1995.

Aumont, Jacques, and Richard Neupert. *Aesthetics of Film.* Austin: U of Texas P, 1994.

Bahn, Eugene, and Margeret Bahn. *A History of Oral Interpretation.* Minneapolis: Burgess, 1970.

Barlow Rogers, Elizabeth. "What Is Romantic Landscape?" *Pückler and America.* Ed. Sonja Duempelmann. Special issue of *Supplement of the Bulletin of the German Historical Institute* 4 (2004): 11-24.

Baudrillard, Jean. "Simulacra and Simulations." *Selected Writings.* Ed. Mark Poster. Stanford: Stanford UP, 2001.

Bhabha, Homi K., ed. *Nation and Narration.* London: Routledge, 1990.

———. *The Location of Culture.* London: Routledge, 1994.

Bruzzi, Stella. *New Documentary: A Critical Introduction.* London: Routledge, 2010.

Buckland, Warren. *The Cognitive Semiotics of Film.* Cambridge: Cambridge UP, 2000.

Certeau, Michel de. *The Practice of Everyday Life.* Berkeley: U of California P, 2008.

Chanan, Michael. *The Politics of Documentary.* London: British Film Institute, 2007.

Deleuze, Gilles, and Félix Guattari. *A Thousand Plateaus: Capitalism and Schizophrenia.* Minneapolis: U of Minnesota P, 2003.

Frahm, Laura. *Jenseits des Raums: Zur filmischen Topologie des Urbanen.* Bielefeld: Transcript, 2010.

García Márquez, Gabriel: *Cien años de soledad.* Madrid: Cátedra, 1984.

Giddens, Anthony. *Consequences of Modernity.* Stanford: Stanford UP, 1990.

Hutcheon, Linda. "Irony, Nostalgia, and the Postmodern." *Methods for the Study of Literature as Cultural Memory.* Special issue of *Studies in Comparative Literature* 30 (2000): 189-207.

Jameson, Fredric. *The Political Unconscious: Narrative as a Socially Symbolic Act.* London: Routledge, 2002.

Kaplan, Caren. *Questions of Travel: Postmodern Discourses of Displacement.* Durham: Duke UP, 1996.

Kauffman, Linda. *Discourse of Desire: Gender, Genre and Epistolary Fictions.* Ithaca: Cornell UP, 1986.

Lefebvre, Henri. *The Production of Space.* Oxford: Blackwell, 1992.

Massey, Doreen B. *Space, Place, and Gender.* Minneapolis: U of Minnesota P, 1994.

Medel, Ingrid. "El documental político en Chile: La historia por desvelar." *El periodista* 3.60 (2004). http://www.elperiodista.cl/newtenberg/1627/article-60934.html.

Mouesca, Jacqueline. *El documental chileno.* Santiago de Chile: LOM Ed., 2005.

Naficy, Hamid. *An Accented Cinema: Exilic and Diasporic Filmmaking.* Princeton: Princeton UP, 2001.

Nichols, Bill. *Blurred Boundaries: Questions of Meaning in Contemporary Culture.* Bloomington: Indiana UP, 1999.

Nora, Pierre. *Lieux de mémoire.* Paris: Gallimard, 1984-1992.

Ruiz, Raúl. *Poética del cine.* Santiago de Chile: Sudamericana, 2000.

Said, Edward W. *The World, the Text, and the Critic.* Cambridge: Harvard UP, 1983.

Shohat, Ella, and Robert Stam. *Unthinking Eurocentrism: Multiculturalism and the Media.* London: Routledge, 1994.

Spivak, Gayatri C. "Can the Subaltern Speak?" *Marxism and the Interpretation of Culture.* Ed. Cary Nelson and Lawrence Grossberg. Urbana: U of Illinois P, 1988. 271-316.

Thies, Sebastian. "Dezentrierte Bildwelten Europas im Accented Cinema: *Trois vies et une seule mort* (1995) von Raúl Ruiz." *Europäischer Film im Kontext der Romania: Geschichte und Innovation.* Ed. Gisela Febel and Natascha Über. Zürich: LIT, 2007. 293-307.

———. "ImagiNaciones perdidas: La narración de la nación en el cine de la diáspora chilena." *Más allá de la nación.* Ed. Sabine Hofmann. Berlin: Frey, 2008. 195-216.

———. "Crystal Frontiers: Ethnicity, Filmic Space and Diasporic Optic in *Traffic, Crash, and Babel.*" *E Pluribus Unum? National and Transnational Identities in the Americas / Identidades nacionales y transnacionales en las Américas.* Ed. Sebastian Thies and Josef Raab. Berlin: LIT and Tempe: Bilingual Press/Editorial Bilingüe, 2009. 205-28.

Vázquez Rocca, Adolfo. "Raúl Ruiz: 'La recta provincia' o la invención de Chile." *Escáner Cultural* 97 (September 2007). http://revista.escaner.cl/node/377.

Filmography

Acta General de Chile. Dir. Miguel Littín. Chile and Cuba, 1985.

Calle Santa Fé. Dir. Carmen Castillo. Chile, France, and Belgium, 2007.

Chile: Memoria obstinada. Dir. Patricio Guzmán. Canada and France, 1997.

Cofralandes Part I: Rapsodia chilena. Dir. Raúl Ruiz. Chile and France, 2002.

Cofralandes Part II: Evocaciones y valses. Dir. Raúl Ruiz. Chile, 2002.

Cofralandes Part III: Rostros y rincones. Dir. Raúl Ruiz. Chile, 2002.

Cofralandes Part IV: Museos y clubes en la región antártica. Dir. Raúl Ruiz. Chile, 2002.

La cueca sola. Dir. Marilou Mallet. Canada, 2003.

La recta provincia. Dir. Raúl Ruiz. Chile, 2007.

Les maîtres fous. Dir. Jean Rouch. France, 1954.

IV.

DOCUMENTARY FILM

AS A MEDIUM OF CULTURAL MEMORY

Image History: Compilation Film and the Nation at War

CHRISTOF DECKER

Resumen

Este ensayo investiga las formas y funciones de los documentales de compilación preocupándose, en especial, de su papel en los procesos de cómo se inventa o se imagina la nación. Postulamos que las películas de compilación sobre la experiencia de la guerra pueden considerarse un medio importante de la memoria cultural para investigar el pasado histórico de los EE.UU., contribuyendo a la vez al surgimiento de una identidad nacional. Partiendo de las discusiones actuales sobre las películas de compilación y la intertextualidad, el artículo ofrece una conceptualización de las funciones del metraje e ilustra, sobre la base de una serie de análisis ejemplares, tres maneras distintas de reconstruir el pasado (o recordar la guerra), cada una de las cuales contribuye a crear la imaginación de una nación ya sea unida, dividida o en procesos de desintegración.

1. Introduction

The assumption that the images and sounds of documentary films are understood by the audience to refer to the historical world may be regarded as a relatively undisputed axiom in the recent theoretical discourse on the genre. Whether this reference is called a presumptive assertion, an indexical relation or a reference to the profilmic, the rhetorical claims of the form are seen to be predominantly based on the idea that what we see and hear establishes a privileged link with an event that belongs to the realm of the historical world (cf. Carroll; Nichols, *Representing*; Beattie). As Bill Nichols puts it, "we bring an assumption that the text's sounds and images have their origin in the historical world we share" (*Introduction* 35). This notion is a feature of the so-called contract between filmmaker and audience and it is reinforced not only by stylistic and formal elements but also by reading strategies on the part of the audience, and by cultural assumptions about technology and mass-mediated forms of communication.

Oddly enough, however, one form of filmmaking which negotiates the desire for historical referentiality in a particularly interesting way has received relatively little scholarly attention: the compilation film. In this case, especially, the notion of a photographic trace which might allow an unfettered or direct access to the historical world seems to be an indispensable premise. Furthermore, compilation films are particularly relevant for the creation of national self-images since they represent a primary way of relating to the past, and of assessing its significance for the present. Thus, the audience is presented with an 'image history,' which also entails a history of the image(s), making it necessary to consider both, the promise to show historical events based on archival footage and the specific (institutional and aesthetic) histories of the footage itself.

My aim in this essay is two-fold: on the one hand, I will address some recent attempts at defining the formal and stylistic features of compilation films in order to conceptualize them as media of cultural memory. On the other hand, I will examine a number of historical examples to assess how the compilation aesthetic is related to the idea of the U.S. American nation. I will focus on the depiction of war as a collective experience central to the compilation aesthetic as well as to the question of national identity. A time of crisis and challenge, war can be seen as a major if not *the* decisive historical moment for the self-definition of a nation. Consequently, its significance in many compilation films lies not just in testing the quality and intensity of patriotic feelings culminating in the willingness to die for one's country, but in making the good and evil qualities of the American national character manifest. Considering *Strange Victory* (Leo Hurwitz, 1948), *The Civil War* (Ken Burns, 1990) and *The Atomic Café* (Jayne Loader, Kevin Rafferty, Pierce Rafferty, 1982), I want to suggest that the design of compilation films remembering the experience of war has favored three forms of mediating cultural memory, in turn stressing the unity, division, or disintegration and "madness" of the nation.

2. Film, War and the Concept of the U.S. American Nation

In order to contextualize the compilation aesthetic and its relation to national self-images it is helpful to draw on Benedict Anderson's influential notion that nations are imagined political communities. According to this approach, nations are imagined as limited and sovereign. Furthermore, and most importantly for my purposes, they are "conceived as a deep, horizontal comradeship" (7). This becomes most relevant in times of war, as Anderson points out: "Ultimately it is this fraternity that makes it possible, over the past two centuries, for so many millions of people, not so much to kill, as willingly to die for such limited imaginings" (7).

Richard Slotkin has elaborated on Anderson's approach, arguing that myths play an important role for the invention of crucial components of national identity, including, for example, the notion of ethnicity. From this perspective, the concept of the (modern) nation only evolves *after* territorial borders have become established and fixed. And even then the nation is "a generalized or abstract place, which we inhabit through acts of patriotic imagination" (470). Anderson's idea of a nation as imagined is relevant to all modern states, yet Slotkin argues that the formation of the American republic, in particular,

> preceded the definition and popular acceptance of a distinctly "American" nationality. It was only after the Civil War and Reconstruction that the unitary American nation became a primary focus of ideology and power, superseding loyalties to and personal identification with particular provinces of the federal republic. (472)

The development of a unitary sense of the nation was strongly shaped by the myth of the frontier and the westward movement, yet Slotkin emphasizes that in certain historical periods new self-images emerge which create a new mythology and demonstrate that the nation as an imagined entity may change in rather substantial ways. The experience of war, in particular, seems to be a major catalyst for a changing representation of national images and identities. Focusing on combat films made during the Second World War, Slotkin argues that a major development took place which reconfigured the sense of the American nation. Against the background of nativism and cultural assimilationism prevalent in the first half of the 20th century, combat films indicated the "shift from the myth of America as essentially a white man's country, to that of a multiethnic, multiracial democracy" (470).[1]

For the history of documentary film, too, the idea that nations are imagined or invented communities puts a special emphasis on media of remembrance and cultural memory, which help to shape collective self-images. Remembering warfare is a crucial constructive act, a core site of patriotic imagination, which allows us to call compilation films representing the war experience a *mnemonic practice*.[2] Following Slotkin's approach we may ask: How has the U.S. American nation imagined itself with regard to the experience and waging of war? And, more specifically, how has the compilation aesthetic been employed to remember, represent and reinterpret the nation at war?

3. Defining the Compilation Film

Surprisingly little work has been done on compilation films, even though their significance, at least on German television, has been increasing steadily in recent years. Jay Leyda, who wrote an early book-length study on the genre, stated that historians seemed to be wary of archival footage, yet today what might be called image histo-

---

[1] The concept of the 'American nation' has become a hotly contested, if not the key, issue in the revisionary context of the New American Studies; for an introduction to this debate, cf. Kaplan/Pease and Pease/Wiegman.

[2] The significance of film as a medium of cultural memory can be distinguished at different levels, which are developed in more detail in Decker, "Interrogations." The first level concerns the materiality of the cinematic signifier; secondly, remembering can be seen as a process pertaining to and recollecting the past; thirdly, structural patterns are laid out to generate representations or models of memory. On the relation between fiction films and cultural memory, cf. Fluck, Erll/Wodianka; on the historiographic discourse about film, cf. Smith.

ries—i.e. historical narratives relying primarily on audiovisual material and eye-witness accounts—are a ubiquitous phenomenon that requires a more comprehensive scholarly treatment.

One difficulty of the discourse on compilations has been the question of which films should actually be classified as such. In her film dictionary Ira Konigsberg writes that a compilation film is

> made by combining footage from other films and assembling them in such a way that they achieve new significance from their present context. The term was first used by Jay Leyda in *Films Beget Films* (1964). Such films often deal with past political, social, and historical events. Drawn from old newsreels, propaganda films, and official archival footage, they are often compiled from a specific perspective. (60)

Useful as this definition seems to be at first, it also raises questions: How old does an 'old newsreel' have to be? If we draw footage from different sources, how can we *not* compile it from a specific perspective? Nevertheless, agreeing with Leyda, Konigsberg makes clear that compilation films are constructed synthetically out of prior material, and that this material is regarded as belonging to the past. In his 1964 study, Leyda added to these points that a compilation film should also give expression to an idea, thus separating it from being a 'mere document.' This formulation clearly echoes the Griersonian definition of documentary as a 'creative treatment of actuality,' which Grierson had introduced to separate it in a similar way from the less ambitious aesthetic of newsreels (cf. Grierson). In effect, then, Leyda was thinking of artistic reworkings of prior footage, which he went on to describe with considerable historical detail, even though his conceptual framework remains rather sketchy and insufficient for my purposes.

A key factor for the definition of compilation films seems to be the amount of archival footage used. There is a sense that a film based exclusively on this kind of material is the most 'pure' type of compilation (cf. Beattie). This could be seen as a call for a narrow definition of the term. However, I want to argue for a wider sense of compilations, first, because pure compilations are relatively rare, and second, because if we consider the use of archival footage as an important mnemonic practice, then we should also examine hybrid forms that combine archival footage with footage that is coded as contemporary or recent in order to engage in a dialogue between past and present. Obviously there is a gray area between genuine compilation films and other modes of documentary representation. A heuristic proposal might be to say that when the majority of footage used is archival and it is employed to present a historical argument that relies on its thoughtful, telling or provocative juxtaposition, we should call the production a compilation film.

The source material of compilation films has sometimes been called "found footage." However, as Keith Beattie rightly points out, the term "found footage" is misleading and glosses over the complicated strategies and ways of acquiring and selecting material included in a compilation film. It evokes the connotation of accidental discovery, easy, unhindered access, and creative artistic treatment that seems to disavow the economic and ethical imperatives underlying the modern business of trading with images. To be sure, the term "found footage" is closely linked to specific art movements such as collage art practiced in the Bay Area in the 1950s. In that context it does indeed refer to avant-garde artists like Bruce Conner, who did not have the financial means for more elaborate projects (cf. Peterson).

But as Jay Leyda has shown, the compilation praxis and aesthetic is much older. On the one hand, it goes back to the early, commercially motivated method of reusing material in order to save money on the production. On the other hand, it is related to the propaganda efforts following the First World War. In this second case we might more aptly speak of "captured footage" to stress the point that the recontextualization of anterior material constitutes a deliberate act of deconstructing existing newsreels or films to create a new rhetorical design. However, in order to address not just these cases of propaganda when discussing the compilation aesthetic, I want to propose that, at its most basic level, we should use the descriptive term "archival footage," which may refer to any kind of source material, i.e. not just newsreels or propaganda films but fiction films, home movies, advertising, industrial films and much more.

4. Compilation Film and Questions of Intertextuality

The process of reassembling material from prior texts shares many characteristics that in literary studies have been discussed as instances of intertextuality. Oddly enough, the rich theoretical discourse that has developed around this concept in the past thirty years has made little impact on film theory.[3] On the one hand, there are obvious similarities between literature and film. The reference to prior textual material may be implicit or explicit, it may have the status of an allusion, or it may be given as a direct quote (cf. Pfister). On the other hand, there is a major difference between the literary and filmic forms of intertextuality resulting from the respective semiotic systems. Put simply, the materiality of the sign appears to be less important for the medium of language than it is for the visual and auditory quality of film. This may be the central reason why a direct quote from prior material—i.e. an insertion of footage—is less frequent in fiction films than in literary texts because this insertion may potentially be much more disruptive and destabilizing with regard to narrative coherence. Even the highly reflexive films of the New Hollywood Cinema took great pains to motivate these direct quotes from old Hollywood films by inserting them only when the characters visited a cinema or watched television at home.[4]

---

[3] For a recent summary of concepts of intertextuality, cf. Allen.

[4] However, in contrast to direct insertions, allusions to prior material are much easier: body language, phrases or scenes are frequently, indeed increasingly, quoted; furthermore, parodies, which are seen to represent the highest degree of intertextuality, are a common filmic practice. On different forms of intertextuality, cf. Pfister.

The intertextual historical discourse of compilation films is, therefore, crucially dependent not only on formal and stylistic features like the literary intertext, but also on the aesthetic and technological codification of its source material. A highly intertextual modernist classic like John Dos Passos's *Manhattan Transfer* (1925), though fragmented and collage-like, seems to be relatively coherent in terms of its medium. This is different with filmic intertextuality based on direct quotes or insertions. Editing patterns, mise-en-scène, cinematography, and generic classifications represent highly specific formal and stylistic codes that are complemented by the materiality of the signifiers: film stock, color or black and white footage, the density of images, the speed of shooting, the sound quality—its frequency range, clarity, number of channels—and so on (cf. Arthur; James).

This semiotic specificity encoded in the material is primarily responsible for two basic notions that Paul Arthur has identified in the early praxis of compilations. First, it has informed the idea that archival footage is a historical sign: the "presumptive trace" that allows us to treat it as a transparent referent to historical events, thus stressing its evidential quality. Second, it has encouraged the contrary impulse to treat it primarily as an aesthetic phenomenon endowed with a certain materiality that can be reconfigured for new forms and meanings. In both cases, *something* has been encoded in the material that makes its physicality more important (and disruptive) than is the case with literary intertextuality. In the first instance, it is the indexical relation to the historical event; in the second, archival footage takes on an aspect that David E. James has termed *allegorical*. As an indication and trace of technological and financial means that went into the production of sounds and images, the footage signals a relative position within the context of the film industry indicative of economic and discursive power (cf. James 3-28).

The status of archival footage is thus shaped by both its presumed historicity and its materiality, and only by relating it to the social and cultural context in which it is produced and received can we fully grasp the complexity of the compilation aesthetic. As indicated, archival footage is usually not *found* as the term "found footage" would suggest, but traded. Just like other forms of documentary representation, therefore, compilation films are implicated in a network of power relations. First, access to and availability of footage is regulated by public or private institutions. Second, footage represents an economic source of income that is traded according to a value placed on images and sounds (cf. Beattie).

Finally, if we accept the premise that referential claims and socio-economic relations are encoded in the material, then archival footage also raises ethical issues. As many authors have argued, documentary filmmaking is not just based on a contract between audience and filmmaker but also between filmmaker and film subject (cf. Winston; Nichols, *Representing*). The interaction with 'real people' is a contested terrain shaping a social and ethical constellation that is inscribed in the sounds and images. Indeed, the relation between filmmaker and subject is usually not regulated by normative moral or legal guidelines and carries with it the constant negotiation of access and disclosure, of participation and professional distance. How should one deal with footage that was shot as a result of hierarchical power relations? Or, to put it more bluntly, how could or should a compilation film integrate footage shot in a concentration camp by German cameramen working for the Nazi regime? Who should trade these images? Who should profit from selling Gestapo footage shot in a ghetto? Should a compilation film indicate under which circumstances archival footage was created? In short, how can the specificity of a historical situation encoded as a complicated social, evidential, aesthetic and ethical 'trace' be adequately acknowledged?

As Jay Leyda recounts in his study, the creation of compilation films was professionalized during the Second World War as part of the propaganda efforts on both sides. Leni Riefenstahl's *Triumph des Willens* alone was recut by British editors three times between 1940 and 1943 (cf. Leyda 70). In times of war the ethical imperatives seemed to be simple enough. Film was understood as a weapon and the battle over footage became a military objective. As with literary intertextuality, the reassembling of prior film material indeed has this aspect of cannibalization and reappropriation, of deconstruction and counter-propaganda. Yet the ethical implications of dealing not only with historical events but also with power relations inscribed in the footage has not been adequately recognized. One reason for this strategic blindness may be the compelling promise of a transparent indexical reference corresponding with the desire to know—an "epistephilia," in Bill Nichols's sense—helping to disregard where the footage comes from (cf. *Representing*).

Yet, as Paul Arthur has argued, the authenticity and indexicality of scenes in compilation films and their role in the context of a rhetorical argument is complicated. Referring to a synthetic scene in *The Atomic Café* which joins American planes approaching Hiroshima and a Japanese man seemingly responding to the planes in the sky (looking up), who, Arthur claims, must have been taken from a fiction film, he writes:

> Documentarists who would never dream of restaging an event with actors do not hesitate in creating collages which amount to metaphoric fabrications of reality. The result is that guarantees of authenticity ostensibly secured by archival footage are largely a myth. In consequence, the binary opposition of unalloyed illustration—as the imperative of conventional documentary—and figurative reshaping is scarcely as absolute as some commentators suggest. (66)

Although I believe that Arthur misses the significance of this particular scene in *The Atomic Café*, the mythopoetic dimension of compilation films seemingly based on authentic historical 'traces' is an important factor highlighting the constructedness of many historical narratives.[5] Brian Henderson, in his discussion of *The Civil War* se-

---

[5] Arthur points out that the shot has been edited into *The Atomic Café* in a way that follows the temporal and spatial rules of continuity editing. However, the editing of *The Atomic Café* reverts to this pastiche of fictional editing at several points, especially at the end, where similar shots are combined to form the finale of an attack on the United States. In this case, the obvious diversity of the material (mixing, for instance, animated and real

ries, makes the similar point that Ken Burns's use of photographs deemphasizes the historical specificity of photography in favor of metaphorical renderings. Yet before contending that the authenticity of compilation films is a myth, we have to be more specific about the claims that are actually connected with the uses of archival footage.

5. The Uses and Rhetorical Functions of Archival Footage

Paul Arthur, Stella Bruzzi and Keith Beattie have recently made suggestions about the status of archival footage. At the most basic formal level, the key question seems to be which function the archival footage has for the design of the new textual whole.[6] How has it been employed? Beattie, following Arthur and Bruzzi, proposes to distinguish between a denotative use on the one hand and an expressive use on the other, which, in Arthur's article, corresponds to the schools of realism and constructivism, or documentary and avant-garde. These suggestions are helpful but I believe they do not really offer a comprehensive overview that does justice to the complexity of the compilation aesthetic. In semiotic terms, I find it problematic to designate the use of footage "denotative," since visual images are, compared with linguistic signs, far less bound by cultural conventions as to what constitutes denotative and connotative meanings. More importantly, I believe that, as a first step, we must distinguish between the use of archival footage for the new design on the one hand and the relation of the archival footage to the rhetorical argument on the other. In other words, the way archival footage is used in a compilation film and the function it has for the rhetorical argument do not have to be identical, and this should be acknowledged in our analytical framework.

In order to distinguish between different uses I propose three categories. First, the use may be *illustrative*: the footage gives an example or instance of something. Second, the use may be *evaluative*: the footage is questioned with respect to its worth or significance (as historical evidence or visual clue). Finally, the use may be *reconstructive*: the footage is reassembled in a way that stresses its (material or semiotic) specificity. The degree of reflexivity about the ways of dealing with archival footage increases as we move from illustrative to evaluative and reconstructive uses. However, these categories only refer to the use in the new textual organization. For a thorough assessment of the degree of intertextuality, one would have to look at both textual designs, since, obviously, the use of archival footage in the new text may correspond to, or differ from, the use in the prior text. For instance, a shot of Hitler greeting his troops in *Triumph des Willens* may first have signified powerful strength; this is employed in

---

action shots, and repeating scenes from the earlier 'duck and cover' sequence) highlights the artificiality of this strategy so that, retrospectively, the film makes clear that it has created false continuities and causal relationships all along (cf. Arthur).

[6]   On questions of textual functionality, cf. Bordwell.

a similar way by Leo Hurwitz, who retains the sense of a powerful menace but is most probably undermined by Len Lye to highlight a ridiculous case of self-stylization.[7]

The interrelation between textual designs and the functions that footage may have is not just a formalist concern that we should clarify in order to better analyze compilation films. Jay Leyda makes the interesting observation that in his opinion it is very difficult, if not impossible, to turn war propaganda against itself. He feels that Nazi material was not used with great success for anti-Nazi aims (cf. Leyda 63). In more general terms, this raises the question of whether we can discern recurring patterns of using archival footage. Which material has been used for compilations in specific ways? Which prior material appears to have a higher 'internal resistance' against being deconstructed and re-used in ways that would go against its original design? Put differently, how can the working with or against a prior generic, stylistic and rhetorical design be systematized and explained?[8]

One way of coming to terms with these questions is, as mentioned above, to distinguish between the uses of archival footage on the one hand and the relation between the footage and the argument the film is developing on the other—if, indeed, it is designed to be argumentative, a question which I will address below. Again, I propose to consider three categories. First, the use of footage may be in support of the argument: the footage is used as (putative) historical evidence confirming the verbal logic. Second, it may be used in contrast or opposition to the argument: the footage creates a tension between images or sounds and the verbal logic of the film. Finally, the use may be disassembling or destabilizing the argument: the footage, either deliberately or inadvertently, seems to go in a fundamental sense against the creation of a coherent argument.

It is important to stress that this proposal of categories is a very broad attempt at finding descriptive classifications for signifying practices that are actually very complex. For instance, the first category, using the footage in support of an argument, has to be qualified further concerning the (putative) status of footage as historical evidence. The referential claims it adds to the verbal logic may be specific or general, it may relate to identifiable events or persons, or to a general category evoking what may be called a setting, a time and place. Likewise, the second category of footage in contrast or opposition to an argument needs to be elaborated on. A major mode of this category is ironical inversion, in which official footage (like army information films or

---

[7] In my estimation of Len Lye's film *Swinging the Lambeth Walk* (1940) I am relying on Jay Leyda's description which makes this recontextualization highly probable. In any case, this example is only meant to be an illustration of an issue—different textual functions of the same sequences—that does not seem to be controversial (cf. Leyda 61-94).

[8] This is how Leyda puts the issue (in the German edition): "Steigert sich die Heftigkeit eines Materials vielleicht, wenn man es im Gegensatz zu seinem Inhalt bearbeitet?" (118). In her chapter on archival footage, Stella Bruzzi similarly mentions the "innate value and meaning" (39) of non-fictional records without, however, elaborating on its ontological status.

public announcements) is treated ironically. A complex (and not primarily ironic) case in point occurs in *In the Year of the Pig* (Emile de Antonio, 1968). The film begins with a shot of a press conference; sound and image are synchronous. An official spokesperson explains that Vietnamese prisoners have not been mistreated. While the sound continues, the image track changes. We see a Vietnamese man lying on the ground, being viciously kicked in the groin by an (American?) soldier who can only be seen from his waist down. Both image and sound track are used in an illustrative sense: the images show an instance of abuse, the sound track documents an instance of official announcements during the war. Yet they do not form a coherent argument—on the contrary, their asynchronous combination creates a particular tension. In this case, the images are meant to counter and question the verbal logic by uncovering that officials are lying.

Needless to say, the third category, too, has to be investigated further. What I have in mind here is the way the avant-garde has used archival footage, for example by breaking it up into different parts and reconstructing it according to a completely different logic that may be, as with Bruce Conner, more associational or poetic than rhetorical (cf. Arthur; on the modes, cf. Bordwell/Thompson). In this case it is appropriate, as Paul Arthur suggests, to discuss the mode of recontextualizing archival footage as metaphorical. Yet for the first two categories it seems wholly insufficient to link documentary realism only with an illustrative mode. In many if not most cases the relationship between images, sounds and rhetorical arguments goes beyond mere illustration by drawing on metonymic and synecdochical forms of historical referentiality.

In the last section of this essay I want to examine how these attempts at theorizing the compilation aesthetic can be connected with concrete historical examples. As indicated, I want to suggest that remembering different wars has revolved around three concepts of the U.S. American nation as divided, united, or disintegrating.

6.   The Nation at War: *Strange Victory*, *The Civil War* and *The Atomic Café*

Strange Victory (1948) by Leo Hurwitz is a little known film that deserves wider recognition. Though it is not mentioned in Jay Leyda's filmography of important compilation films, it seems to be exceptional for reappropriating the visual 'traces' of the war in Europe at a time of collective cultural amnesia, and in a way that relates them to the situation in the United States at the time of the film's release. In accordance with the practice of documentaries in the 1940s, the film combines reedited archival footage with scenes of contemporary America (e.g. street scenes, a newsstand) and acted sequences (e.g. a black war pilot applying in vain for a civilian job). Throughout the film the emotional appeal of the material is strongly coded by the musical score, while the rhetorical appeal relies almost exclusively on a male voice-over addressing the viewers directly and expressing a sense of urgency and anger. At one point in the film, when a pregnant woman is shown, the voice-over switches from a male to a female voice describing the promises connected with new-born babies. After this passage the male voice again takes over to counter and confront these visions of hope with the experience of racism, anti-Semitism and inequality in the United States.

The victory over Nazi Germany and its racist ideology is thus contrasted with the feeling that life in America seems not to have changed. Worse, fascist ideologies are seen to have slipped into the social fabric of the United States when the commentary mentions invisible yellow stars or the discrimination of babies according to color of skin, slant of eyes or religious denomination. It seems to be a strange victory, the narrator concludes, with "the ideas of the loser still active in the land of the winner." Though Hollywood films of the late 1940s like *Crossfire* (Edward Dmytryk, 1947) were made from a similarly 'progressive' political point of view, *Strange Victory*, with its much more explicit and aggressive critique, must clearly be seen in the tradition of the radical political left of the 1930s.[9] The compilation aesthetic that Hurwitz employs is polemical and drastic, joining the shot of a self-possessed Hitler with a ghastly composition of broken-out teeth, or an African-American baby with children being led out of a liberated concentration camp.

The selection of archival war footage centers around scenes of fighting, liberation or surrender and, most importantly, the rise of the Nazi movement in Germany. These scenes are mostly used illustratively, as historical evidence, yet there are several stylistic techniques that can also be seen as an evaluation or interrogation of the footage. The film begins with the fighting in 1942 and even though these events are not long in the past when *Strange Victory* is released in 1948, there seems to be a feeling among the filmmakers that a considerable resistance to this act of looking back has to be overcome. Repeatedly, the commentary remarks, "remember how it was?," as if having to counter the wish to forget. Thus, on the one hand, the film uses the footage as a verification of the war experience but, on the other, it also verbally creates a mood of distanced reflection that seems to anticipate the reservations against looking back.

A second way of interrogating the archival footage is connected with a more obvious treatment of the images as such. In one scene a close shot of Hitler, filmed in the typical heroicizing style from below, is superimposed with footage shot from a plane flying over a city in ruins, possibly Berlin (see Illustration 1). Creating a palimpsest-like composition, the posture of determination and power is inextricably linked with destruction and death. This might be called a dialectical composition joining together shots with synecdochical implications to create an interpretation of history: fascism means war. It represents one of the most effective ways of interrogating encoded meanings. But it also goes most clearly against the conventions of documentary realism and therefore seems to be much less frequent than other forms of critical evaluation.

A further instance of manipulating archival footage with technical means happens after the commentary has first praised the promise of babies only to counter this hopeful view with a 'face the facts' sequence that highlights the legacy of slavery, rac-

---

[9]   On the Hollywood films of the late 1940s, cf. Decker, *Blick* 434-91.

ism, anti-Semitism and religious intolerance. Suddenly, war footage is introduced that has been inserted running *backwards*. Thus the Nazi leaders who have been shown earlier as dead seem to be reanimated and the specter of Nazism rises again. This instance of trick photography ensures that although the footage is mostly used to support what the commentary has established as a historical assessment, there are also sequences that question its merely illustrative use, making the film at the same time rhetorical and reflexive.

Illustration 1: *Strange Victory* (Leo Hurwitz, 1948)

The function of the reversed motion scenes is, once again, to connect the past with the present in order to develop the film's argument that a particular form of fascist ideology is living on in the United States. At the core of this ideology is the idea of inequality based on the concept that one part of the population is seen or said to be superior. For Hurwitz this is epitomized in American society by the category WXP (white, Christian, Protestant), which is stamped on one of the baby cards. The conclusion drawn at the end is that the victory over German fascism has not had the desired effect at home. Juxtaposing archival footage with scenes from contemporary America is thus meant to commemorate the common fight and victory of the war but also to argue that the unified ideological front has given way to the disillusioned assessment that the conflict is not over. The battle for a more equal and democratic society has not been won, or as the commentary states at the end: "If we want victory, we'll still have to get it."

The lesson that *Strange Victory* propagates through its particular way of remembering the war is, then, that war against enemies like fascism is necessary and rewarding. Yet the struggle against external forces has to continue internally because the U.S. American nation is divided and dominated by racist and anti-Semitic sentiments. In a striking contrast to Frank Capra's *Why We Fight* series (1943-45) the war footage is not used to construct the vision of a unified nation but rather to emphasize its internal violence and disunity. Thus *Strange Victory* deflates the importance of the Second World War as a unifying force in favor of the domestic political struggles of the pre-war years. Instead of overcoming internal divisions, the war experience has intensified the feeling of injustice and anger.[10]

In the case of *Strange Victory* the mnemonic practice of compilation films drew on archival footage to stress the disunity of the American nation in the present. In contrast to this practice, the remembrance of wars via archival footage may also serve to emphasize the nation's unity. My case in point for this contention is *The Civil War*-series by Ken Burns whose compilation aesthetic relies on a unique mixture of elements that not only creates a high degree of intertextuality but also, by bringing together the temporal quality of film and the spatial quality of photography, a particular form of intermediality. On the whole, the series is characterized by the dominant expository logic established by a voice-over commentary. The historical narrative that evolves is complemented by interviews with historians, excerpts from diaries, newspaper articles or other source material, and, most importantly in terms of the series' visuality, by thousands of photographs.

By drawing on diaries, letters and other personal notes, the series achieves the personalization of cultural memory. Choosing eye-witnesses as privileged sources of information—individuals from both sides of the conflict and from different social classes—indicates the attempt at re-individualizing an experience that has become, as a precursor of modern wars, collective and all-encompassing.[11] As part of a mnemonic practice, the series adopts a celebratory and reconciliatory tone meant to stress the unity of the nation as the primary result of the war. As Gary Edgerton writes, *The Civil War* is "less a story of socio-political conflict than a poignant and mythopoetic lesson in national commitment, self-sacrifice, valor, and fulfillment" (58).

In order to create a sense of unity and unification through struggle, the compilation aesthetic goes to great lengths to establish connections between its elements, and to reinforce a sense of balance and closure. Indeed, the notion of coherence, both at a textual and at an idealized national level, seems to be a predominant aspiration behind

---

[10] The example set by Hurwitz was taken up twenty years later, albeit with different formal means, by Emile de Antonio's *In the Year of the Pig* (1968). Although de Antonio addresses a different military and political conflict the film basically adheres to the patterns established in *Strange Victory*: it employs archival footage for an argument about the past in order to point up a state of national disunity and internal rift in the present.

[11] The personalization of war histories has also affected other conflicts like the Vietnam War. In Errol Morris's *The Fog of War* (2003) remembering the war shifts fundamentally from the collective to the individual level, from the analytical assessment (of films like *In the Year of the Pig*) to the personal anecdotes and (largely unchallenged) interpretations of Robert McNamara.

the textual design. For instance, contemporary scenes showing former battlegrounds and the silhouettes of canons are shot at sunset or sunrise, thus stressing the circularity of natural processes, of endings and beginnings—the war ends, the new nation emerges.[12] Though the war represents a state of crisis and a challenge, in its mythological dimension it is also seen as a time for great leaders or great failures, bringing out patriotic virtues like honor, loyalty, dedication, and the willingness to die for one's country.

In the spirit of *The Civil War*-series, then, war is horrible but it is also a time for courageous and self-sacrificial behavior (cf. Edgerton). Furthermore, even though the series repeatedly shows the horrors of the war, it ultimately assesses the fight for freedom and the abolition of slavery as a unifying experience for the American nation. The promises of freedom have not been completely realized yet the 'honorable' way of remembering the war experience is meant to demonstrate the high degree of unity that has developed in the meantime. The Civil War as a time of interior division and struggle is thus reinterpreted as a first sign of overcoming the state of divisiveness. According to one of the series' experts, the U.S. American nation, formally a nation since gaining independence, was 'reborn' truly unified as a result of the war. Needless to say, this historical perspective, which has been characterized as liberal and pluralist, is a major departure from Leo Hurwitz's depiction of racism and violence against blacks as the major legacy of slavery.[13]

The final example in my analysis—*The Atomic Café*—employs yet a third way of relating to wars of the past. Here, archival footage is not used to stress the unity or disunity of the American nation (in the present) but rather to express its self-delusions and anxieties vis-à-vis a highly efficient yet at the same time highly irrational war machinery. In contrast to *Strange Victory* and *The Civil War*, *The Atomic Café* is an example of 'pure' compilations, made up exclusively of archival footage. No interviews or retrospective voice-overs contextualize the material (only some of the music seems to have been added). Structurally, the film begins with the atomic explosions at the end of the Second World War, and first reactions to the enormity of these events. The film then moves on to the Cold War, the spy hysteria, and the parallel development of legitimizing the potential use of atomic weapons against the Soviet Union, and of persecuting the political left at home. Finally, the compilation assembles material from popular culture and from official information films (with the famous 'duck-and-cover-sequence'), creating the impression of a hilarious but also horrifying disjunction between the enormity of the danger and the ridiculousness of coping with it in the public sphere.

---

[12] The underlying desire is suggested by Ken Burns himself: "we Americans who are not united by religion, or patriarchy, or even common language, or even a geography that's relatively similar, we have agreed because we hold a few pieces of paper and a few sacred words together, we have agreed to cohere, and for more than 200 years it's worked and that special alchemy is something I'm interested in" (qtd. in Edgerton 54).

[13] On Burns's politics, cf. Edgerton.

The central claim of *The Atomic Café* is that the political elite is characterized by an 'arrogance of power' in dealing with common people.[14] This is not suggested through explicit statements but revealed rather indirectly by showing, for instance, how the "natives" from Bikini are treated by the military superpower. Just like the pigs in the bomb blast area, they are considered to be test cases for the analysis of the weapon's effectiveness. While the voice-over from the official film (or newsreel) states that they are well and happy, we see images demonstrating that their hair can be pulled out in handfuls. In the tradition of de Antonio, the lies of the power elite are uncovered by deconstructing its official propaganda.

A related aspect of this kind of 'propaganda' is seen to rest in the images of the American family represented in advertising and other footage from the 1950s. In this case, too, the prevailing feeling is one of anxiety. As television sets enter the home, the idealized and indeed virtually sanitized white American family, watching in awe how the world changes in the atomic age, is connected with a sick reality that slowly seems to contaminate it. The film thus highlights a fundamental distrust of collective self-images and of the political authorities who are seen to have misinformed the American public in inflammatory ways about the destructive power of atomic weapons (cf. Bruzzi).

In this sense, *The Atomic Café* does not remember the war to stress the unity or the disunity of the nation, and the lessons to be drawn are neither conciliatory or divisive nor celebratory or critical. Rather, the film seems to be overwhelmed by the excessive logic of the atomic age—the paradoxical simultaneity of powerlessness and power, the unusual and normalcy, reasonable behavior and irrationality, chaos and order. The compilation aesthetic may uncover the 'schizophrenic' state of mind of the U.S. American nation but it cannot provide it with a deeper significance in the context of established historical master narratives. In this case, then, the investigation of archival footage unveils an amusing but also exhausted and ultimately horrifying archaeology of the pre-apocalyptic mind—a collage of a disintegrating nation.

7. Conclusion

I have argued that the compilation aesthetic has played a major role for the invention and imagining of the U.S. American nation. Here, in particular, remembering the experience of war has been a crucial way of relating to the past, and of shaping influential versions of cultural memory. How influential and pervasive these audiovisual forms actually are, has not been sufficiently realized, and much work on the compilation aesthetic remains to be done. Drawing on a number of historical examples, I have suggested categorical distinctions for the analysis of the compilation film genre and have argued that the representation of war has been characterized by an increasing tendency to personalize history. A second important change appears to have happened with re-

---

[14] On the pervasive influence of this theme in the 1960s, cf. Kraas.

gard to the issue of ethnicity and race. The very different assessment of the legacy of slavery by Leo Hurwitz in the 1940s and Ken Burns in the late 1980s is indicative of the new myth of the United States as a multiethnic and multiracial nation described by Richard Slotkin. Finally, as an afterthought, war compilations exhibit a remarkable predilection for the spectacle of destruction: the mushroom cloud of the atom bomb, carpet bombing in Japan, missiles launched at night from war ships—the visual spectacle of explosions and forms of mass destruction and death is slowed down for an intensified form of contemplation. Turning images of war into aesthetic objects may be a defense mechanism of survivors, yet it is striking to realize that archival footage has served so extensively as the material for what might be called, in analogy to the city films of the 1920s, war symphonies of matter, movement, and destruction. These sequences shockingly illustrate and often implicitly criticize the war machinery, yet at the same time they appear to be more ambiguous: not just signs of madness but disturbing projections of (national) power.

Works Cited

Allen, Graham. *Intertextuality*. London, New York: Routledge, 2000.

Anderson, Benedict. *Imagined Communities: Reflections on the Origin and Spread of Nationalism*. Revised Edition. London and New York: Verso, 1991.

Arthur, Paul. "The Status of Found Footage." *Spectator* 20.1 (1999/2000): 57-69.

Beattie, Keith. *Documentary Screens: Non-Fiction Film and Television*. Houndsmills and New York: Palgrave Macmillan, 2004.

Bordwell, David. "Neo-Structuralist Narratology and the Functions of Filmic Storytelling." *Narrative Across Media: The Languages of Storytelling*. Ed. Marie-Laure Ryan. Lincoln, London: U of Nebraska P, 2004. 203-19.

Bordwell, David, and Kristin Thompson. *Film Art: An Introduction*. 9th ed. New York: McGraw-Hill, 2009.

Bruzzi, Stella. *New Documentary: A Critical Introduction*. London and New York: Routledge, 2000.

Carroll, Noël. "Fiction, Non-fiction, and the Film of Presumptive Assertion: A Conceptual Analysis." *Film Theory and Philosophy*. Ed. Richard Allen, Murray Smith. Oxford: Clarendon P, 1997. 173-202.

Decker, Christof. *Hollywoods kritischer Blick: Das soziale Melodrama in der amerikanischen Kultur 1840-1950*. Frankfurt: Campus, 2003.

———. "Interrogations of Cinematic Norms: Avant-Garde Film, History, and Mnemonic Practices." *Amerikastudien/American Studies* 43.1 (1998): 109-30.

Edgerton, Gary. "Ken Burns's America: Style, Authorship, and Cultural Memory." *The Journal of Popular Film and Television* 21.2 (1993): 51-62.

Erll, Astrid, and Stephanie Wodianka, eds. *Film und kulturelle Erinnerung: Plurimediale Konstellationen*. Berlin: de Gruyter, 2008.

Fluck, Winfried. "Film and Memory." *Sites of Memory in American Literatures and Cultures*. Ed. Udo J. Hebel. Heidelberg: Winter, 2003. 213-29.

Grierson, John. "First Principles of Documentary." *Grierson on Documentary*. Ed. Forsyth Hardy. London, Boston: Faber and Faber, 1979. 35-46.

Henderson, Brian. "*The Civil War*: 'Did It Not Seem Real?'" *Film Quarterly* 44.3 (1991): 3-14.

James, David E. *Allegories of Cinema: American Film in the Sixties*. Princeton, NJ: Princeton UP, 1989.

Kaplan, Amy, and Donald E. Pease, eds. *Cultures of United States Imperialism*. Durham: Duke UP, 1993.

Konigsberg, Ira. *The Complete Film Dictionary*. New York: Meridian, 1987.

Kraas, Norbert. "'The Arrogance of Power' als zentrales Thema von Emile de Antonios *In the Year of the Pig*." *Der amerikanische Dokumentarfilm der 60er Jahre: Direct Cinema und Radical Cinema*. Ed. Mo Beyerle, Christine N. Brinckmann. Frankfurt: Campus Verlag, 1991. 354-73.

Leyda, Jay. *Filme aus Filmen: Eine Studie über den Kompilationsfilm*. Berlin: Henschel-verlag, 1967.

Nichols, Bill. *Introduction to Documentary*. Bloomington, Indianapolis: Indiana UP, 2001.

———. *Representing Reality: Issues and Concepts in Documentary*. Bloomington, Indiana-polis: Indiana UP, 1991.

Pease, Donald E., and Robyn Wiegman, eds. *The Futures of American Studies*. Durham: Duke UP, 2002.

Peterson, James. "Bruce Conner and the Compilation Narrative." *Wide Angle* 8.3-4 (1986): 53-62.

Pfister, Manfred. "Konzepte der Intertextualität." *Intertextualität: Formen, Funktionen, ang-listische Fallstudien*. Ed. Ulrich Broich and Manfred Pfister. Tübingen: Niemeyer, 1985. 1-30.

Slotkin, Richard: "Unit Pride: Ethnic Platoons and the Myths of American Nationality." *American Literary History* 13.3 (Fall 2001): 469-98.

Smith, Paul, ed. *The Historian and Film*. Cambridge and New York: Cambridge UP, 2008.

Winston, Brian. "The Documentary Film as Scientific Inscription." *Theorizing Documentary*. Ed. Michael Renov. New York, London: Routledge, 1993. 37-57.

Filmography

The Atomic Café. Dir. Jayne Loader, Kevin Rafferty, and Pierce Rafferty. U.S.A., 1982.

The Civil War. Dir. Ken Burns. U.S.A., 1990.

The Fog of War. Dir. Errol Morris. U.S.A., 2003.

In the Year of the Pig. Dir. Emilio de Antonio. U.S.A., 1968.

Strange Victory. Dir. Leo Hurwitz. U.S.A., 1948.

Swinging the Lambeth Walk. Dir. Len Lye. United Kingdom, 1940.
Triumph des Willens. Dir. Leni Riefenstahl. Germany, 1935.
Why We Fight. Dir. Frank Capra. U.S.A., 1943-45.

Compilación y patrimonio 'extraviado.' Reciclaje de material de archivo en el documental mexicano contemporáneo. *La línea paterna* (1995) y *Los rollos perdidos de Pancho Villa* (2003)

ITZIA FERNÁNDEZ ESCAREÑO

Abstract

The practice of recycling is ongoing in film history. The most striking change in the contemporary film production based on archival material is the conscious trace left. Recycling does not only give access to unknown materials, it also assigns new, open functions to the film document. Mexican cinema has a large and changing history of found footage films. This essay offers an analysis of two important compilation documentaries, *The Paternal Line* (1995), directed by José Buil and Maryse Sistach, and *The Lost Reels of Pancho Villa* (2003), directed by Gregorio Rocha. The film analysis is conducted on three levels: valorization of film collections, mise en scène (credits, sound, reediting, support manipulation), and interpretation of film h(H)istory. Both compilations perform the important function of preserving and reprogramming these images, but they also use oral history and other materials. The makers of these documentaries compiled traces of Mexican national culture from among the plurality of regional identities. While Rocha made a "greaser" manifesto from the north with transnational film fragments, Buil and Sistach compiled a family biography from home movies and amateur film collections originating in the south-center of Mexico. Recycling offers an option for saving film history—but with crucial consequences, since compilation documentary is film history in its own right.

La producción audiovisual contemporánea, basada en material de archivo, se encuentra extraordinariamente diversificada en la televisión, las series audiovisuales de la historia moderna, los programas didácticos, el cine de ficción, el documental, el cine experimental y los nuevos sectores multimedia. Sin embargo, la posibilidad técnica de remontar el pietaje fílmico ha sido una práctica inherente y permanente en la historia del cine. En nuestra época, la manipulación del material de origen se diferencia del pasado, porque la marca de ésta es consciente, reflexiva, realizada a través del propio soporte fílmico. La reapropiación es diametralmente distinta si el autor, al reciclar las imágenes, deja o no su marca en el montaje y la puesta en escena.

En consecuencia, se aprecia una innovación en la forma de dar acceso a los materiales reempleados. El documental de compilación explota el potencial de la copia fílmica y trasciende el valor atribuido inicialmente a este producto de la industria cultural. Es así, entonces, que el material fílmico adquiere otras funciones, tales como convertirse en un documento patrimonial, histórico, estético, económico, o, en un documento que forma parte de una colección de cine familiar o museográfica, o en un banco de imágenes, etc.

En México, el reciclaje tiene una larga tradición. La reutilización del pietaje de archivos es particularmente manifiesta en el material, tanto documental como de ficción, relativo a la Revolución Mexicana. Al respecto podemos citar algunos ejemplos clásicos. El pionero Enrique Rosas recicló parte de su propio documental en la película de ficción *El automóvil gris* (1919). También podríamos considerar compilaciones de este material "extraviado" a las dos versiones reducidas y sonorizadas, de los años treinta (1933 y 1937), reeditadas después de la muerte del realizador.[1] Documentalistas emblemáticas del reciclaje son Carmen Toscano y Nancy Cárdenas, con sus respectivas compilaciones de la Revolución Mexicana, *Memorias de un mexicano* (1950) y de la historia del cine mexicano, *México de mis amores* (1976).

En el documental mexicano actual, la práctica del reciclaje se ha diversificado debido a la posibilidad de acceder a archivos públicos y privados de cine, televisión y fotografías. Existe cierta continuidad en la producción de series colectivas que reexplotan materiales de archivo que muestran la forma como coexisten distintas tendencias. Por un lado, domina una producción homogénea con material de archivo para mercados definidos, como los canales especializados de la televisión cerrada y abierta. Por el otro, existe una producción independiente y diversa, que responde a otras necesidades sociopolíticas y estéticas, como son los documentales de compilación.[2]

---

[1]   Se trata del documental *Documentación nacional histórica 1915-1916* (Enrique Rosas, 1916) que incluía la escena del fusilamiento, el 6 de agosto de 1916, de los acusados de ser integrantes de la banda del automóvil gris (cf. la más completa filmografía del cine mexicano en línea: http://www.unam.mx/cgi-bin/filmoteca/busqueda.pl cuyo sitio está en reconstrucción; Ciuk et al., entrada "Rosas Aragón, Enrique." Otra ficción es producida por la concurrencia con tema similar: *La banda del automóvil* (Ernesto Vollrath, 1919; cf. Serrano et al.).

[2]   Respecto a esta cohabitación, nos referimos por ejemplo a ciertas series documentales transmitidas inicialmente en la televisión y/o editadas en VHS y luego en DVD, y basadas principalmente en archivos fílmicos como: colecciones producidas para Televisa por Editorial Clío libros y videos (desde 1998), por México Nuevo Siglo (desde 2001) y recientemente la serie *Clío en el bicentenario* (varios directores, 2010ss.); *18 Lustros de la vida en México en este siglo* (UNAM, 1990-1993) y *La vida en México en el siglo veinte* (varios directores, 2000); *Los que hicieron nuestro cine* (Alejandro Pelayo, 1984); el documental para el centenario del cine latinoamericano *Memoria/Enredando sombras* (varios directores, 1998); y la producción del Canal 6 de Julio.

Proponemos analizar dos documentales de compilación independientes que reutilizan imágenes de archivo. La elección de estos dos títulos responde a que los consideramos polos sintomáticos de las representaciones contemporáneas de lo "mexicano." Nos referimos a *La línea paterna* (1995) de José Buil y Maryse Sistach y *Los rollos perdidos de Pancho Villa* (2003) de Gregorio Rocha. En el tratamiento atípico que realizan del material de archivo, están en juego también dos nociones distintas de lo "mexicano" y del cine nacional. Ambos documentales se ocupan de la identidad nacional tanto en el plano público como en el privado, presentando un predominio de las representaciones de figuras masculinas.[3]

Abordamos el análisis de estos filmes refiriéndonos a la forma como cada documentalista recicla las imágenes de archivo con estrategias propias del cine de compilación. En especial, exploramos la valorización patrimonial de las colecciones de cine "extraviado," la puesta en escena de los gestos de la compilación: créditos, sonorización, remontaje y manipulación física del soporte y la reinterpretación de la h(H)istoria del cine nacional.

1. Rollos resucitados y nostalgia

La línea paterna es un documental codirigido por la pareja de cineastas José Buil y Maryse Sistach con guión y montaje del primero.[4] La película relata como José y su familia recuperan fotos y películas de la colección paterna de cine familiar y amateur. Estas películas fueron filmadas en 9.5 mm –con una cámara Pathé-Baby–, principalmente por su abuelo paterno, José Buil Belenguer, en el periodo entre 1925 y 1940, en Papantla, Veracruz. La historia abarca desde la migración de su abuelo, en 1909, desde Valencia (México) al norte de Veracruz. Allí, este médico, de origen español, fundó una familia numerosa con su segunda esposa, Remedios, y sus siete hijos. La película relata, además, la migración de otros miembros de la familia, en los años cuarenta, a la Ciudad de México, hasta el momento mismo del rodaje entre 1992-1994 (cf. anexo 1).

El documental de carácter autobiográfico, antropológico e histórico, tiene un elaborado trabajo de compilación y remontaje de películas familiares con intertítulos con-

---

[3] Un documentalista que ha explorado esta cuestión es Juan Carlos Rulfo. Cf., en particular, en *El abuelo Cheno y otras historias* (1995) y *Del olvido al no me acuerdo/Los caminos de Don Juan* (1999).

[4] José Buil Ríos (19.03.1953, Celaya, Guanajuato, México). Cineasta, guionista, director, editor, productor de numerosas películas desde finales de los setenta con Maryse Sistach: *Manos libres/Free Hands* (2005); *Perfume de violetas, nadie te oye* (2000, productor, guionista y editor); *El cometa* (1998, codirector y guionista); *La línea paterna* (1995, codirector, guionista y editor (documental)); *Anoche soñé contigo* (1992, guionista); *La leyenda de una máscara* (1989, director y guionista); *Los pasos de Ana* (1988, guionista y editor); *Conozco a las tres* (1983, guionista y editor); *Adiós, adiós ídolo mío* (1981, director, guionista y editor); *Apuntes para otras cosas* (1979, director, guionista y editor); *Mis amigos desempleados* (1978, director, guionista y editor); *Endre en la ciudad* (1977, director, guionista y editor).

temporáneos: foto fija familiar, documentación *non film* (folletería Pathé, correspondencias, diarios íntimos), sonorización accidental, musicalización y voz en *off* del poeta Ricardo Yáñez, quien representa la voz interna del cineasta José Buil.

2. La Patria Chica

El hilo conductor de la compilación es la colección fílmica de José Buil Belanguer desde 1925 hasta 1940. Se trata de registros de ritos y costumbres familiares: Día de Reyes, bailes –el predilecto es el jarabe tapatío–, fiestas, paseos, excursiones. Buil y Sistach logran identificar con eficacia años, personajes y espacios físicos de la colección familiar. Por medio de la voz en *off* y los créditos asignados, informan al espectador sobre cada uno de los planos y fragmentos reciclados. Este proceso aparece hasta en el interior mismo de la película, así por ejemplo, se cita en una imagen que la principal fuente de historia oral de la película fue el tío Julio (1.9).

La voz en *off* del poeta Yáñez se combina con la sonorización de otras voces que representan los pasajes citados de la correspondencia familiar, del diario del abuelo, de la folletería Pathé y de los testimonios orales. Hay una sonorización accidental suplementaria que acentúa la atmósfera evocada por las imágenes, entre otros, las campanas en la película de la boda de Cristina y los ruidos de la selva en las excursiones (1.7 y 1.8).

No sólo por el uso de la voz en *off*, sino también, por medio de los intertítulos y la descomposición de la imagen, se crea una cierta distancia con el material fílmico. No obstante, los intertítulos, las refilmaciones de los fotogramas, los ralentos, los congelamientos, etc. son sobrios; como en el caso del ralento de Pablo –el padre del cineasta–, cuando tenía doce años, durante una excursión al Tajín (1.7).

La línea paterna es un documental cronológico que expone simultáneamente el tiempo tanto linear como circular (el tiempo "interior"). Así, un simple pasatiempo como el jarabe tapatío se convierte en ritual a través de la compilación de los distintos fragmentos sobre el tema. Si bien el remontaje deja intacto el sentido original de algunos fragmentos, es decir tal cual fueron encontrados. De este modo, por ejemplo, se da testimonio de la primera película que vieron de la colección familiar (1.4).

Los "retratos animados" de la familia protagonista, son reciclados, en su temporalidad, también de forma dual. El paso del tiempo se muestra compilando las "poses," procedimiento que se asocia estrechamente al reempleo del cine familiar.[5] El documental trabaja el material para cada hermano de forma diferente, como un ejercicio único del paso del tiempo en cada miembro de la familia. Vemos así que, en la parte dedicada a Juan Manuel, uno de los hermanos, el ejercicio de montaje invierte el paso del tiempo y nos lo muestra de adulto a bebé. En cambio, el remontaje de las poses de los abuelos es cronológico y presenciamos el marcado proceso de su envejecimiento

---

[5] Un cortometraje experimental que logra este efecto con precisión singular es *Happy-End* (1996) de Peter Tscherkassky.

(1.8). Algunos autores señalan que, en general, el cine familiar no filma directamente la muerte o el deseo, sino es el "efecto" del paso del tiempo, a través del remontaje, lo que posibilita reinterpretar el cine de familia (cf. Simoni). En *La línea paterna*, la muerte no sólo ronda estas imágenes del pasado, también se encuentra en el rodaje del "presente" con las muertes de Pablo, el padre del cineasta, y del tío Juan Manuel (1.4 y 1.8). Al final, el cementerio es parte integral del espacio familiar y fílmico (1.9).

De todas maneras, la colección se caracteriza por ser no sólo un diario familiar, sino, también, la bitácora de un cineasta aficionado. El abuelo filmaba al mismo tiempo la manera como él y su familia socializaban en esa región étnica y cultural mixta del norte de Veracruz, la sierra del Totonacapan. Hay testimonios visuales invaluables de Papantla, que es denominada como "la ciudad que perfumó al mundo," "su país," el "ombligo del mundo." Otras escenas, como la "vuelta en el kiosko," las fiestas patrias y las excursiones, por ejemplo, expresan formas de socialización e identificación de esta familia mexicana (1.5-1.7). En esta dualidad Buil y Sistach asocian también otras películas familiares filmadas con la misma cámara, registros contemporáneos en vídeo, así como otros documentos *non film*. En la película se manifiesta una mirada antropológica e histórica al dar testimonio del paso del tiempo en la arquitectura de Veracruz y de la Ciudad de México. Además, los cineastas prolongaron esta tarea recreando los retratos, las "poses" de los totonacos durante la fertilización de las flores de vainilla y el vuelo en plena acción de los voladores de Papantla (1.5 y 1.7). Los secretos familiares revelados, muestran la existencia de otros lazos que los unen a la región. El mestizaje étnico se representa, de esta manera, en parte, por los medios hermanos paternos: Cristina y el hijo desconocido de Pablo (1.6 y 1.8).

La cuestión de género se expone de forma delicada y puntual. Hay diferencias en los roles que se les asigna a los niños y las niñas en los ritos: bailes, fiestas y expediciones. Ellos migran, ellas se arraigan. Casarse o no define invariablemente el estatus del personaje. El género determina cómo se vive la viudez o la soltería, cómo son las relaciones con los hijos fuera del matrimonio. Estas cuestiones propias a la microhistoria no pasan desapercibidas y por el contrario nos sensibilizan al respecto. En el cine familiar hay un metadiscurso que revela lo escondido y lo profundo tanto a nivel sociohistórico, como a nivel de la "verdad íntima." El potencial de estas imágenes aumenta por la exposición de la intimidad familiar, de sus secretos. La dimensión figural del filme familiar puede provocar en el espectador una reacción asociada a lo nostálgico y lo fusional (cf. Odin). Los cineastas reciclaron los fragmentos fílmicos tanto en sentido poético y analítico, como reflexivo y afectivo. La puesta en escena no esconde la muerte, ni el deseo, ni el secreto, ni el referente histórico de la memoria cinematográfica de la familia Buil. Por el contrario los "revela." *La línea paterna* es un caso ejemplar de la manera como el cine familiar está envuelto en un "aura" nostálgica. Ésta es una de las características clave en la tendencia mundial al reciclaje del cine familiar.[6] La obra de Buil y Sistach demuestra que determinada economía en los efectos

---

[6]   Uno de los cineastas más especializados en el reciclaje del cine familiar es el investigador social y archivista de origen húngaro Péter Forgács.

de la manipulación visual y sonora puede ser extraordinariamente eficaz para la puesta
en escena. Y por lo tanto lograr el difícil y sutil equilibrio de una lectura "nostálgica"
es decir afectiva como histórica.

3. Rollos extraviados y resistencia

Los rollos perdidos de Pancho Villa (2003) de Gregorio Rocha[7] es un documental ensayo en el que el autor relata su búsqueda de la película "perdida" *The Life of General
Villa* (1914), de William Christy Cabanné. Asimismo, Rocha da testimonio, con su
propia voz en *off*, de sus viajes, de su investigación y reflexión. Con música original,
compone mosaicos de imágenes en los que recicla materiales *non film* –prensa, contratos, fotomontajes, pósters, fotos– y fragmentos de los filmes localizados en archivos
fílmicos y documentales de Canadá, Inglaterra, EE.UU., los Países Bajos, Francia y
México. Entrevista a Kevin Brownlow, Rubén Osorio, Fernando del Moral, Stephen
Bottomore, el nieto de Charles Rosher y Paolo Cherchi Usai. El documental da créditos, por la asesoría, también a Aurelio de los Reyes, Frederick Katz, Herbert Reynolds,
Ivo Blom y Dario Díaz (cf. anexo 2).

4. Territorio transnacional

Rocha localizó materiales inéditos de ficción, pre-documentales (*non-fiction*) y documentales de la Revolución Mexicana en instituciones extranjeras y nacionales.[8] El titánico trabajo realizado por Rocha tiene el mérito de haber hecho múltiples hallazgos y,
de este modo, logra dar un panorama único en su tipo, hasta esta fecha, que incluye
fragmentos de archivos públicos y privados que redescubren imágenes de la Revolu-

---

[7]   Gregorio Rocha, documentalista y videoasta desde la segunda mitad de los años ochenta,
     se mueve entre EE.UU. y México. Se formó en el CUEC-UNAM. Docente del área docu-
     mental en el CCC, profesor invitado en la NY University. Encabeza el proyecto de archivo
     fílmico independiente Archivia y colabora con la filmoteca de la UNAM y el American
     Film Institute en proyectos de restauración. Su filmografía de documentales está basada en
     una preocupación social sobre la identidad fronteriza entre EE.UU. y México. Su obra se
     caracteriza por películas de carácter experimental y de ensayo personal, entre las que desta-
     can: *Guerras e imágenes* (1996-1999), *La flecha* (1996), *De placazos, vírgenes y tatuajes*
     (1996), *Ferrocarril a Utopía* (1995), *Historia de la fotografía en México* (correalizada con
     Sarah Minter, 1989), *Sábado de mierda* (1987), *Tijuana entre dos mundos* (1987), *Video
     Road* (correalizada con Sarah Minter, 1982).

[8]   Los archivos consignados en los créditos son: American Film Institute, Archivo Histórico
     Condumex, Bobst Library NY University, BFI, Cineteca Nacional, Columbus Historical
     Society, El Paso Public Library, Filmoteca UNAM, Imperial War Museum, Instituto de Es-
     tudios Históricos de la Revolución Mexicana, Library of Congress, Celeste Bartos Inter-
     national Film Study Center Museum of Modern Art, National Film Board of Canada,
     Netherlands Filmmuseum, New York Public Library, University of South Carolina,
     Department of Special Collections University of Texas.

ción Mexicana, que hasta ese momento eran consideradas "perdidas" por las filmografías del cine mudo. La voz en *off* de Rocha identifica la mayor parte de los materiales compilados.[9] Además es importante anotar que el autor consiguió localizar, en la colección Padilla[10], fragmentos del título que dio origen a su búsqueda.

Rocha se coloca a sí mismo en escena para mostrar las dificultades encontradas en el proceso de rescate. Por ejemplo, muestra cómo la película se desmorona entre sobreimpresiones de imágenes "fantasmas" de Villa. El cineasta evoca el fuerte olor del síndrome de vinagre, la condición del explosivo nitrato, la revisión del soporte fílmico en VHS, y cómo estos materiales se localizaron dispersos, fragmentados, relativamente sin identificar ni catalogar (2.3 y 2.4).

Los rollos perdidos de Pancho Villa es un documental caracterizado por una insistente manipulación de la imagen y por un arduo trabajo de sonorización y musicalización. El mito de Villa es revisitado por medio de los gestos de un montaje *collage*. Es decir que a través de "mosaicos," Rocha confronta el *non film* con fragmentos fílmicos para asumirse como *greaser*[11] (2.2 y 2.3). Las entrevistas a especialistas y su búsqueda del "Santo Grial," como lo llama, le sirven para autofilmarse entre sus viajes y sus interpelaciones a "Villa: A ti te pregunto … Te prestaste Villa … ¿Qué es lo que busco en ti, Villa, que no encuentro en mí? … ¿Quién te hizo esto?" (2.1 y 2.2). Sin embargo, Rocha no deja de hacer una historia crítica de cine cuando cita a algunos de los expertos consultados, tanto extranjeros y nacionales vivos, como Kevin Brownlow, Fernando del Moral (2.2), e incluso muertos, como Jay Leyda (2.3).

El documental expone con eficacia las formas de reapropiación de las imágenes de Villa que realizaron las productoras, los camarógrafos estadounidenses y europeos de la época (2.2). No obstante, también el director se "reapropia" de la representación cinematográfica de Villa. En su reflexión –que conocemos por su propia voz en *off*–,

---

[9] Sin embargo algunos de los materiales que se utilizan en el documental no se identifican durante el uso de la imagen, ni tampoco en los créditos. En los agradecimientos y créditos figuran las instituciones involucradas, pero no se consignan los títulos de las copias a los que corresponden las imágenes recicladas, por ejemplo, *Mexican Filibusterers* producida por Kalem en 1911.

[10] La descripción-análisis y los artículos publicados por Rocha (cf. "La colección," "*La venganza*") nos permiten establecer el origen para la mayor parte del pietaje reutilizado: Colección Stephens; *The Life of General Villa* (William Christy Cabanne, 1914, con Raoul Walsh); *Historia de la Revolución Mexicana* (Julio Lamadrid, 1928); pietaje propiedad de Lord Cardy, acerca del ferrocarril entre el Atlántico y el Pacífico inaugurado por Porfirio Díaz; *The Mexican Joan of Arc* (Kenean Buel, 1911); *The Colonel's Escape* o *El escape del Coronel* (Kenean Buel, 1912, con Rhys Pryce); *Een telegram uit Mexico* (Louis H. Chrispijn, 1914); pietaje a pedido de Victoriano Huerta del camarógrafo austríaco Fritz Arno Wagner; pietaje de Jesús Salas Barraza. Otra de las fuentes, *La venganza de Pancho Villa* (Félix y Edmundo Padilla, ca. 1930), a su vez contiene episodios del serial *Liberty, a Daughter of the USA* (episodios respectivamente de Jacques Jaccard del 1-15, y Henry MacRae del 16-20, 1916, USA, Universal Film Manufacturing Co.) y diversos noticieros.

[11] Expresión despectiva referida a las personas de origen mexicano, originada en el Suroeste de los EE.UU..

Villa es un síntoma de "lo que los cineastas quieren que veamos" (2.2). Rocha hace su propia historia del imaginario villista, "recrea" el mito. Y así asegura que la historia del cine es la historia del imaginario.

A partir de su condición de *greaser*, Rocha compila para conformar un manifiesto de resistencia cultural, como para reconstruir una historia del cine. El autor se inscribe abiertamente en un discurso de identidad nacional, que él mismo adjudica a la frontera norte de México (2.4). Su trabajo se singulariza de esta manera como la prolongación de su propio hallazgo fílmico, la compilación de las compilaciones: *La venganza de Pancho Villa* (Félix y Edmundo Padilla, ca. 1930) parte de la colección Padilla. El fragmento que Rocha finalmente localiza de *The Life of General Villa* (William Christy Cabanné, 1914) no adquiere la misma transcendencia que tiene la compilación de los Padilla citada. Ya que ésta última constituye un extraordinario ejemplo de resistencia cultural –distintivo del nacionalismo fronterizo–, y es, a la vez, una forma de combate en contra de la política antimexicana. La colección Padilla es, además, un testimonio de la historia de la exhibición y la recepción del cine en el norte de México, pues da a conocer la forma como se programaba en la frontera.[12]

Rocha trastoca los materiales de origen y les reasigna connotaciones que se ubican tanto a nivel ideológico, como histórico.[13] A través del discurso documental, el cineasta representa lo "mexicano" como una forma de resistencia cultural frente a la presencia del "otro," el gringo, el europeo. Una forma de contrarrestar las representaciones peyorativas de lo "mexicano" que se reciclan hasta la fecha en el "territorio" del imaginario colonialista (cf. De los Reyes).

5. Denominadores comunes y opuestos

Ambos documentales analizados presentan una serie de similitudes. Los dos compilan imágenes de archivo, en un caso "perdidas," en el otro, fuera de acceso. En ambos, estas imágenes pasivas son transformadas en colecciones fílmicas con valor patrimonial para el cine mexicano. En el marco del discurso documental exponen el mismo proceso de la búsqueda, el hallazgo y el rescate de imágenes "extraviadas." Las puestas en escena relatan el estado físico en que encontraron los materiales y, parcialmente, cómo abordaron su preservación. En este último aspecto hay instituciones vinculadas a la producción que tuvieron un rol particular. A modo de ejemplo, la colección del Dr. Buil Belanguer, fue preservada y restaurada por la filmoteca de la UNAM. En el procesamiento del material, el fotógrafo cinematográfico, Arturo de la Rosa, diseñó un aparato especial para procesar el material de 9.5 mm que entró en desuso. Por su parte,

---

[12] Rocha da testimonio, por ejemplo, de cómo, en las funciones del exhibidor Padilla, se incluía el sonido con un fonógrafo. También nos da a conocer que las copias sobrevivientes de los años veinte, son, en su mayoría, a color (cf. "La colección").

[13] Para un análisis fílmico de uno de los fragmentos privilegiados en el reciclaje de Rocha, *Een telegram uit Mexico* (1914), vinculado a la problemática de la identidad nacional y la migración, cf. Fernández, Donaldson 123.

Rocha emprendió un trabajo de colaboración interinstitucional para restaurar los materiales. Fundó la asociación Archivia, la cual administra la colección Padilla. Luego contando con la autorización de la familia, puso a disposición parte de ésta en el American Film Institute (EE.UU.) y ha preservado parte de ésta con el laboratorio Immagine Ritrovata (Boloña, Italia).[14]

Los dos documentales experimentan con la recreación de cómo estos materiales eran presentados en su forma original. Así, por ejemplo, musicalizan, sonorizan, comentan los materiales tal como, probablemente, se hizo en su época. Buil y Sistach hacen réplicas de "vistas" por lo tanto contemporáneas y retratos de los fertilizadores y los voladores de Papantla (1.5 y 1.7). Mientras Rocha atestigua el intento frustrado de filmar una versión en Durango (2.3) de la película extraviada de 1914, convertida así en un "Santo Grial." Este reciclaje nos habla de una forma posible de rescate del patrimonio y hasta qué punto, preservar y restaurar tienen implicaciones éticas.

En ambos documentales hay material de archivos familiares, pero de características diametralmente distintas. Uno era de uso comercial, que es el caso de los Padilla, mientras en el caso de los Buil, era estrictamente de uso privado. Por lo tanto, las dos colecciones están discontinuadas de sus usos originales. Buil y Sistach ponen nuevamente en escena su propia colección familiar. Mientras Rocha recicla la ficción extranjera sobre la Revolución Mexicana localizada en la colección Padilla, una familia de exhibidores.

Los dos documentales filman desde el "presente" del rodaje estableciendo, de este modo, relaciones entre estas colecciones y sus nuevos espectadores. Recontextualizan también los fragmentos fílmicos mediante los gestos del reciclaje. Asocian al pietaje visual, fragmentos musicales originales y no originales en la sonorización. Los créditos y la voz en *off*, por su parte, consignan los orígenes de los fragmentos reciclados. Los intertítulos, la manipulación del soporte y el remontaje son comunes, no obstante se aprecian métodos de remontaje que no son sólo diferentes, sino hasta opuestos. Buil y Sistach son sobrios y clásicos, mientras Rocha es experimental y posmoderno. Aún así, en las dos películas prevalece un titánico trabajo de identificación y de asociación de las imágenes. Ambos recurren y hacen un uso inédito de la documentación *non film* y de la historia oral, con personajes de ambas familias y expertos en la materia.

Los documentales contienen huellas de la conformación identitaria de México en dos sentidos. Por una parte, dentro de un marco nacional, ambos privilegian espacios regionales diferentes. Rocha trata de la zona fronteriza norte entre México y los EE.UU. En cambio Buil trata de las zonas centro-sur, particularmente la sierra totona-

---

[14] Los cineastas consignaron sus experiencias y hallazgos principalmente a partir de fuentes hemerográficas (cf. para Buil, el número consagrado al documental de *Nitrato de Plata* y para Rocha, sus artículos "La colección" y *"La venganza"*).

ca, en el estado de Veracruz.[15] Representan lo "mexicano" a partir de una pluralidad de "identidades." En Rocha, el móvil es un manifiesto cultural fronterizo *greaser*. Para Buil y Sistach se trata de retrazar una biografía familiar, tomando en consideración sus orígenes paternos y mestizos.

Por otra parte, los dos documentales son ensayos ambivalentes sobre la construcción de la identidad tanto en el ámbito público como en el privado. El universo que Rocha abarca es transnacional, cine de ficción, *non fiction* y documental. El corpus de Buil y Sistach es único ya que se trata de una colección personal y por lo tanto de cine familiar y de aficionados propia a la región totonaca, que incluye copias de ficción del catálogo Pathé (un corto del género *féerique*, un breve sketch de Chaplin, etc.; cf. Kessler).

6. Conclusiones

La compilación causa polémica o no en función de la legitimidad, generada por la reapropiación de las imágenes. Es decir que posibilita interpretar estas fuentes fílmicas, comprender la historia de los filmes y de su historia, en el marco de las posiciones e intenciones del compilador como de las lecturas potenciales del espectador.

Por ejemplo, por un lado *La línea paterna* tiene una relación indirecta, pero puntual con el imaginario revolucionario y villista (1.5). Pero más allá de esta curiosa coincidencia, hay una serie de personajes masculinos que operan como parámetros de identificación en ambos documentales: el abuelo paterno y Villa. Buil y Sistach definen su propia identidad mestiza a partir de cómo lo "íntimo" es representado por su abuelo migrante. Por otro lado, Rocha reinterpreta el modo como Villa ha sido representado negativamente por el "otro," el extranjero. Por lo tanto las dos formas de reutilización de estos "clichés" proponen una postura diferente frente al "extranjero," el otro.

La línea paterna es un documental histórico que se construye por medio del reciclaje del cine de familia y de aficionado. Desde la vida cotidiana Buil y Sistach reconstruyen no sólo una biografía familiar paterna, sino también una "Historia" de la región, adoptando un punto de vista socio-antropológico. En contraste, *Los rollos perdidos de Pancho Villa* es un documental que enfoca la historia de cine y del imaginario villista, principalmente a través de cine de ficción extranjero y exhibido en la frontera norte mexicana. Este material de reempleo se complementa con un ambivalente diario íntimo, entre ensayo personal y manifiesto militante del propio cineasta Rocha.

Ambos documentales proponen una historia de cine en soporte fílmico. Estos cineastas se han convertido en espectadores-intérpretes que utilizan las películas como un dispositivo, una especie de "máquina del tiempo." Estos documentalistas se han

---

[15] La filmografía que sobrevive de Gabriel García Moreno es la "punta del iceberg" de una fascinante producción de cine regional (Orizaba) veracruzano, durante el periodo del cine mudo (cf. Dávalos Orozco/Vázquez Bernal).

convertido en intermediarios que conectan a las huellas fílmicas del pasado con nuevos espectadores.

Anexos

Proponemos la descripción-análisis de ambos documentales a continuación.

Anexo 1

La línea paterna (1995)

1.1 Créditos de las productoras y responsables de la realización y la producción.

1.2 *Película 9.5 mm del abuelo Dr. José y su caballo el Huasteco.* Llegada a Papantla, al norte de Veracruz, en el Golfo de México. Presentan a la familia en fotos fijas. Pablo –padre de José, el cineasta– a los 34 años, con sus siete hermanos y la abuela Remedios. *Película 9.5 mm de 1925 con el rito de Los Santos Reyes* en que se regalan juguetes a los niños. El juguete de ese año es responsable de lo que vemos a lo largo del documental.

1.3 Parte dedicada a la llegada del juguete en 1924: un proyector de 9.5 mm Pathé Baby, modelo 1923. Mediante la correspondencia con el agente, presentan una proyección con dos niños: Pía, hija de los realizadores, y su primo Emiliano. Desfilan fragmentos fílmicos proyectados de películas de catálogo: *Películas 9.5 mm de Chaplin, una animación en versión francesa, un ballet "féerique."* Chaplin es el preferido para el tiempo de ocio. Así lo atestigua una *película 9.5 mm, de 1936, Charlotada por Irma y Pablo,* cuando éste tiene veintiún años, bailando un jarabe tapatío. La correspondencia del agente recomienda adquirir la motocámara para registrar a los seres queridos.

1.4 Intertítulo: "Poner en orden los recuerdos del cine," setenta años después. Registros en vídeo de agosto de 1992, con José, Pía y el abuelo Pablo, de 74 años, quienes viajan juntos a Papantla en busca de películas familiares. A través de foto fija cuentan parte de la carrera de Pablo como agente textil, sus viajes por todo el país y cómo conoció a su madre, Amparo, de Celaya, Guanajuato. En vídeo, registran calles y casas de Papantla. El abuelo, murió ahí, en 1959, a los 84 años. Y también muestran a Pablo la noche de su llegada, quien fue a morir a su tierra. En vídeo, la carretera es retomada para hacer una meditación acerca de la muerte de Pablo, padre del cineasta. En vídeo, la casa paterna se encuentra en ruinas, tal como la había dejado el abuelo. El interior de una casa, una "caja china" donde localizan un cofre con más de trescientas películas, de 1925 a 1940, con quince años de la vida familiar en Papantla. La primera película familiar que vieron fue una titulada *Vista 9.5 mm del cumpleaños 56 del abuelo con sus siete hijos.*

1.5   *Película 9.5 mm muestra cómo bailan el jarabe tapatío Juan Manuel y Ana.* Par-
      te dedicada a Ana, amamantada por su nodriza totonaca. Siguen fotos fijas y una
      Película 9.5 mm de la vuelta en el kiosko, en el "ombligo del mundo": Papantla,
      que "era su país." La voz en *off* cita pasajes del diario del abuelo y de la folletería
      Pathé. Parte dedicada a Meme la hermana menor. *Película 9.5 mm de 1930 de
      Meme* en la que aparece con sus hermanos con sólo un mes de vida. El abuelo,
      dado que era médico, ayudó a nacer a sus once hijos, de los cuales sólo siete
      lograron sobrevivir. Historia a través de las fotos fijas del primer matrimonio del
      Dr. Buil en Valencia hacia 1909, sus dos hijos –Juan Antonio y María de los De-
      samparados– y su esposa Dolores, todos fallecidos durante una epidemia. Gracias
      a su amistad con el Dr. Garí, el abuelo Buil se propone viajar a Ciudad de Méxi-
      co. En vídeo, Buil, con voz en *off* medita sobre la migración de su abuelo, en una
      secuencia en la playa. Al principio, el abuelo llega a Huejutla, Hidalgo, una ciu-
      dad muy necesitada de médicos durante la Revolución Mexicana. Por medio de
      fotos fijas cuentan cómo, en el corazón de la Huasteca, el abuelo conoce a Reme-
      dios (1912) con quien se casa. En 1913, viven en Valencia donde nace su primer
      hijo, Vicente. En 1915, de regreso a la Ciudad de México, en medio de un ataque
      villista, se ven obligados a refugiarse en Papantla. Se exponen las primeras razo-
      nes de haberse quedado en Papantla: por el movimiento armado durante la Revo-
      lución y la sociedad criolla en la que se insertaron. *Película 9.5 mm de un baile
      de la sociedad criolla.* También se quedaron por el olor de las flores blancas que
      al descomponerse producen la vainilla. Luego porque el primogénito, Vicente,
      muere y lo entierran en Papantla. La lápida se vuelve un lazo para permanecer
      allí. Silencio durante la secuencia en vídeo de la fecundación de la vainilla con
      "retratos" en blanco y negro de dos totonacos, Anastasio y Lucía.

1.6   *Película 9.5 mm en que se muestra cómo rompen piñata los niños.* El rumor de
      que la familia dispone de una cámara se dispersa en Papantla y la familia Buil so-
      cializa a partir de su uso. *Película 9.5 mm de la Reina Chabela de 1935* con Ani-
      ta y Meme de pajes. *Película 9.5 mm de excursión en la selva a caballo.* Se cuen-
      ta que Papantla quiere decir "lugar de papales" (pájaros). *Película 9.5 mm de los
      tendales de vainilla en las calles de Papantla.* Seguida de *Película 9.5 mm de
      1933 de fiestas patrias.* Comentarios sobre la integración y mestizaje del abuelo
      en la región totonaca. Parte dedicada a Cristina la hija mayor. Montaje de *Frag-
      mentos de películas 9.5 mm* con sus poses y retratos que sonorizan hasta la *Pelí-
      cula 9.5 mm de boda filmada por Pablo en junio 1938.* Parte dedicada a Amparo
      y Carmen a través de un montaje de *Fragmentos de películas 9.5 mm* de las her-
      manas inseparables. *Película 9.5 mm de la Rapsodia Húngara, en que ejecutan
      un jarabe tapatío. Película 9.5 mm con baile del "butaguit,"* luego en 1937, *Pelí-
      cula 9.5 mm con Amparo en baile de castañuelas.*

1.7   Excursión al Tajín. Retratos de totonacos sesenta años después. *Película 9.5 mm
      de 1933 del pasaje por la pirámide.* Cita el diario del abuelo. Pose de *Pablo doce
      años en ralento.* Parte dedicada a Pablo. Toma en vídeo de un juguete guardado y

que aparece luego en *Película 9.5 mm del 6 de enero de 1925*. Luego sigue *Pablo en película 9.5 mm del Día de Reyes* donde tiene veintidós años. Una *Película 9.5 mm de su visita acompañando a su padre a la Ciudad de México* en la Alameda y el centro histórico, junto a la familia del Dr. Garí. Pablo obtuvo entonces lo que más deseaba en el mundo: en vídeo registros de una credencial de volador de Papantla. *Película 9.5 mm sobre voladores* y luego en vídeo registro del volador en acción auto filmándose en tiempo real.

1.8   Parte dedicada a los abuelos Remedios y a José Buil. Montaje de *Fragmentos de películas 9.5 mm* con poses de los abuelos envejeciendo. El cineasta tenía cinco años cuando murió su abuelo. Pero, en la memoria, recuerda a su abuela como una viuda de pelo blanco, con más de veinte nietos, en su casa intacta. Parte dedicada a Juan Manuel quien enfermó durante el rodaje. Montaje de *Fragmentos de películas 9.5 mm*, partiendo de una foto fija de Juan Manuel adulto hasta cuando era bebé. "Máquina del tiempo, el cine familiar, de quien pidió que sus cenizas fueran esparcidas en el Tajín. Su muerte sucedió durante el rodaje." Parte dedicada al tío Julio Víctor, quien migró a la Ciudad de México en 1942: "Un enamorado que nunca se casó." En vídeo, el tío Julio, jubilado en 1994, quien fue la fuente oral de la identificación y catalogación de las películas. Calle en el norte de la Ciudad de México donde aparece el cineasta José con su hermano, mamá y nietos. *Película 9.5 mm en 1938 de Julio en un día de fiesta con chicas*. Pablo y Julio migraron juntos. El tío Julio le compraba la colección de Cine Mundial al cineasta, cuando éste era niño. *Película 9.5 mm de 1957, filmada con la misma Pathé Baby: sus padres, dos de sus hermanas y Pepe*. Eran un total de cinco hermanos. A cuadro una postal; corre el rumor de la existencia de un hijo de Pablo con una mujer totonaca. Rumor confirmado por el testimonio anónimo de una tía. Retratos de mujeres totonacas. Retratos registrados en vídeo durante el movimiento de voladores, con la edad probable de su medio hermano. *Película 9.5 mm de voladores*.

1.9   En vídeo, el cementerio, durante marzo de 1994, donde el cineasta ronda los cuarenta años y, acompañado por el equipo de rodaje, visita las tumbas de la familia, cuyas imágenes reviven sus recuerdos. Nace un nuevo miembro de la familia: Marcos. La vida sigue y Pía baila con Emiliano un jarabe tapatío moderno.

Anexo 2

La descripción se basa en los intertítulos con los que Rocha divide su documental *Los rollos perdidos de Pancho Villa* (2003).

2.1   El realizador Rocha da testimonio, con su propia voz en *off*, de su objetivo: localizar *The Life of General Villa* (William Christy Cabanné, 1914).

2.2   *Había una vez una película*. Rocha explora la colección Stephens en Canadá. En Londres entrevista al historiador Kevin Brownlow para confirmar que Pancho Villa y Frank N. Thayer, representante de la compañía de cine Mutual Film Corporation, se reunieron el 5 de enero de 1914, en una oficina de El Paso, Texas, para firmar un contrato de exclusividad. El propósito era realizar una película que permitiera filmar sus batallas, o su reconstrucción, y en las que Villa se interpretaría a sí mismo. La película se realizó y fue exhibida en Nueva York y Londres, pero desde entonces, ha desaparecido. Brownlow la consideraba un mito y con el contrato en la mano la califica de un evento histórico, por tratarse de un personaje histórico "real" que se interpreta a sí mismo. Tal como si Napoleón lo hubiese hecho hipotéticamente.

Entrevista a Rubén Osorio en Ojinaga, historiador regional. Se reconstruye parte del rodaje de la batalla de Ojinaga con fragmentos fílmicos.

Asimismo indaga, guiado por Kevin Brownlow, sobre el rol de los camarógrafos Charles Rosher y Charles Prior en estos rodajes.

Entrevista a Fernando del Moral quien identifica imágenes documentales de la Revolución en la película de ficción *Revolución o La Sombra de Pancho Villa* (1932) del ex militar carrancista Miguel Contrera Torres.

Entrevista a Kevin Brownlow quien expone el rol de D. W. Griffith en la película *Tragedy of Life of Pancho Villa*, interpretada por Raoul Walsh.

Entrevista a Stephen Bottomore en Londres acerca de cómo las películas de guerra, en general, fueron recreadas en lugares reales y/o en estudios.

En Nueva York y Londres, Rocha prosigue su búsqueda de la documentación *non film* del título perdido.

Luego en París –la "ciudad de los manifiestos"–, pronuncia su manifiesto *greaser* con el primer mosaico-compilación de fragmentos fílmicos.

2.3   *Búsqueda.* El autor realiza un panorama de algunos de los intentos, como el de Julio Lamadrid en 1928, de hacer una historia de la Revolución Mexicana a través de la compilación de imágenes de archivos.

Rocha retoma el proyecto que Jay Leyda no pudo realizar y lo cita por medio de su voz *off*, la que relata sus intenciones de compilar, a través de los archivos del mundo, las imágenes de la Revolución Mexicana. Rocha encuentra, en Londres y en Amsterdam, una serie de películas consideradas perdidas. Realiza el segundo mosaico-compilación con fragmentos de éstas.

En Rochester, entrevista a Paolo Cherchi Usai, quien define lo que es una película huérfana.

Asiste al congreso de filmes huérfanos (Orphans of the Storm), en Columbia, Carolina del Sur. Allí le muestran el hallazgo de un pietaje con Jesús Salas Barraza, el asesino de Villa. A la imagen de este pietaje asocia un fragmento del entonces presidente Plutarco Elías Calles, a quien considera el autor intelectual del asesinato.

Se hace un paralelo entre las invasiones de Villa a territorio estadounidense en Colombus, Texas (1911) y el atentado a las torres gemelas del 11 de septiembre en Nueva York (2001).

Al no encontrar la película central (Cabanné, 1914), Rocha decide recrear sus imágenes, proyecto que no logra realizar por falta de financiamiento. Da testimonio de los ensayos con actores en Durango, paisajes claves para la época de oro del *western*.

En San Diego, California, el nieto de Charles Rosher, Langdon Morell le da acceso a su colección, pero sin éxito alguno. Sigue sin localizar el material.

2.4 *Descubrimiento*. Rocha, gracias a una llamada telefónica anónima, da con un hallazgo inesperado. De paso, en Colombus, Texas, asiste al acto que recuerda el aniversario de la invasión villista.

Con un tercer mosaico-compilación retrata las incertidumbres históricas de la mítica invasión villista del 9 de marzo de 1916.

Luego en la biblioteca de El Paso, Texas, localiza documentos *non film* de *La venganza de Pancho Villa*, que forman parte de la colección Padilla de cine fronterizo (1920-1936). Gracias al testimonio de Edmundo Padilla –registrado en 1976 por su hija, Magdalena Padilla– Rocha tiene la posibilidad de examinar en dicha colección inédita, imágenes de Villa, recicladas por dichos exhibidores itinerantes.

Ya que *La venganza de Pancho Villa* resulta ser una compilación a base de películas pre existentes, que resulta ser una reconstrucción fícticia del asesinato de Villa, realizada por los Padilla en 1930, en ésta se localiza un fragmento de la película buscada por Rocha (Cabanné, 1914).

Rocha valora cómo esta película es una muestra de la resistencia cultural frente a la evolución peyorativa de la imagen de Villa. Se termina con el intertítulo *Paz a sus restos*. En lo que concierne a la historia de la colección Padilla, Rocha anuncia que ésa es otra historia.[16]

Bibliografía

Ayala Blanco, Jorge. "Los vestigios del futuro." *Nitrato de Plata* 21 (verano de 1995): 9-11.

Buil José. "Carta patria." *Nitrato de Plata* 21 (verano de 1995): 12.

———. "Texto para una película documental: *La línea paterna*." *Nitrato de Plata* 21 (verano de 1995): 16-23.

Cherchi Usai, Paolo. *The Death of Cinema Cultural Memory and the Digital Dark Age*. London: BFI, 2001.

Ciuk, Perla, et al. *Diccionario de directores. Cineteca Nacional*. CD-Rom. México, D.F.: Consejo Nacional para la Cultura y las Artes, 2000.

Dávalos Orozco, Federico y Esperanza Vázquez Bernal. *Carlos Villatoro. Pasajes en la vida de un hombre de cine*. México, D.F.: UNAM, 1999.

---

[16] Véase el documental *Acme & Co* (Gregorio Rocha, 2006).

De los Reyes, Aurelio. "Francisco Villa. The Use and Abuse of Colonialist Cinema." *Journal of Film Preservation* 63 (2001): 36-42.

Donaldson, Geoffrey. *Of Joy and Sorrow. A Filmography of Dutch Silent Fiction.* Amsterdam: Stichting Nederlands Filmmuseum, 1997.

Fernández Escareño, Itzia. "El batallón invisible. Territorio mexicano imaginario. Análisis de la película *Een Telegram Uit Mexico* (1914)." *Secuencia* 64 (enero-abril 2006): 233-56.

Katz, Friedrich. *The Secret War in Mexico. Europe, the United States and the Mexican Revolution.* U of Chicago P, 1981.

Kessler, Frank. "Féeries or Fairy Plays." *Encyclopedia of Early Cinema.* Ed. Richard Abel. New York: Routledge, 2005. 330-34.

Millán, Margara. *Derivas de un cine en femenino.* México, D.F.: Miguel Ángel Porrúa, 1999.

Nitrato de Plata 21 (verano de 1995).

Odin, Roger. "La famille Bartos de Péter Forgács, ou comment rendre l'histoire sensible." *Cinéma hongrois. Le temps et l'histoire.* Ed. Kristian Feigelson. Paris: IRCAV Presse Sorbonne Nouvelle, 2003. 193-207.

Orellana, Margarita. *La mirada circular. El cine norteamericano de la Revolución Mexicana 1911-1917.* México, D.F.: Cuadernos de Joaquín Mortiz, 1991.

Rocha, Gregorio. "La colección Edmundo Padilla. Un caso de arqueología cinematográfica." *Imágenes e investigación social.* Eds. Fernando Aguayo y Lourdes Roca. México, D.F.: Historia social y cultural, Instituto Mora, 2005. 155-61.

———. "*La venganza de Pancho Villa* (*The Vengeance of Pancho Villa*). A lost and found border film." *Journal of Film Preservation* 65 (2002): 24-29.

Serrano, Federico, et al., eds. *El automóvil gris. Guiones clásicos del cine mexicano.* Cuadernos de la Cineteca Nacional 10. México D.F.: Cineteca Nacional, 1981.

Simoni, Paolo. "Death at Work. And on Vacation Family Films Between Rediscovery and Oblivion." *Cinegraphie* 16 (2003): 371-80.

Filmografía

18 Lustros de la vida en México en este siglo. UNAM. México, 1990-1993.

Acme & Co. Dir.Gregorio Rocha. México, 2006.

Adiós, adiós ídolo mío. Dir. José Buil. México, 1981.

Anoche soñé contigo. Dir. Maryse Sistach. México, 1992.

Apuntes para otras cosas. Dir. José Buil. México, 1979.

Clío en el bicentenario. Varios directores/Editorial Clío/Grupo Televisa. México, 2010ss.

Conozco a las tres. Dir. Maryse Sistach. México, 1983.

De placazos, vírgenes y tatuajes. Dir. Gregorio Rocha. México, 1996.

Del olvido al no me acuerdo/Los caminos de San Juan. Dir. Juan Carlos Rulfo. México, 1999.

Documentación nacional histórica 1915-1916. Dir. Enrique Rosas. México, 1916.

Een telegram uit Mexico. Dir. Louis H. Chrispijn. Países Bajos, 1914.

El abuelo Cheno y otras historias. Dir. Juan Carlos Rulfo. México, Cuba, 1995.

El automóvil gris. Dir. Enrique Rosas. México, 1919.

El cometa. Dir. José Buil y Maryse Sistach. México, España, Francia, 1998.

Endre en la ciudad. Dir. José Buil. México, 1977.

Ferrocarril a Utopía. Dir. Gregorio Rocha. México, 1995.

Guerras e imágenes. Dir. Gregorio Rocha. México, 1996-1999.

Happy-End. Dir. Peter Tscherkassky. Austria, 1996.

Historia de la fotografía en México. Dir. Gregorio Rocha y Sarah Minter. México, 1989.

Historia de la Revolución Mexicana. Dir. Julio Lamadrid. México, 1928.

La banda del automóvil. Dir. Ernesto Vollrath. México, 1919.

La flecha. Dir. Gregorio Rocha. México, 1996.

La leyenda de una máscara. Dir. José Buil. México, 1989.

La línea paterna. Dir. José Buil y Maryse Sistach. México, 1995.

La venganza de Pancho Villa. Dir. Félix y Edmundo Padilla. México, EE.UU., ca. 1930.

La vida en México en el siglo veinte. Varios directores, UNAM. México, 2000.

Liberty, a Daughter of the USA. Dir. Jacques Jaccard y Henry MacRae. EE.UU., 1916.

Los pasos de Ana. Dir. Maryse Sistach. México, 1988.

Los que hicieron nuestro cine. Dir. Alejandro Pelayo. México, 1984.

Los rollos perdidos de Pancho Villa. Dir. Gregorio Rocha. México, Canadá, EE.UU., 2003.

Manos libres/Free Hands. Dir. José Buil. México, 2005.

Memoria/Enredando sombras. Varios directores. México, 1998.

Memorias de un mexicano. Dir. Carmen Toscano de Moreno y Salvador Toscano. México, 1950.

Mexican Filibusters. Kalem Production Company. EE.UU., 1911.

México de mis amores. Dir. Nancy Cárdenas. México, 1976.

Mis amigos desempleados. Dir. José Buil. México, 1978.

Perfume de violetas, nadie te oye. Dir. Maryse Sistach. México, Países Bajos, 2000.

Revolución/La sombra de Pancho Villa. Dir. Miguel Contrera Torres. México, 1932.

Sábado de mierda. Dir. Gregorio Rocha. México, 1987.

The Colonel's Escape/El escape del Coronel. Dir. Kenean Buel. EE.UU., 1912.

The Life of General Villa. Dir. William Christy Cabanné. EE.UU., 1914.

The Mexican Joan of Arc. Dir. Kenean Buel. EE.UU., 1911.

Tijuana entre dos mundos. Dir. Gregorio Rocha. México, 1987.

Video Road. Dir. Gregorio Rocha y Sarah Minter. México, 1982.

Los rubios (2003) de Albertina Carri – una poetología de la (pos)memoria[1]

DANIELA NOLL-OPITZ

Abstract

This essay focuses on the Argentinian documentary *Los rubios* (2003), directed by Albertina Carri, whose parents are among the 30,000 persons who "disappeared" during the last military dictatorship in Argentina (1976-1983). The film is first situated in the context of the politics of memory in contemporary Argentina; then it is analyzed with a focus on its particular aesthetics of *postmemory* (cf. Hirsch, "Surviving") and, more precisely, on its aspects of performativity and mediality. Carri questions not only the possibilities of remembering the traumatic past but also explores the limits of the documentary genre as "film of fact" (Renov 13). She liberates herself in *Los rubios* from being a victim of Argentinean history: by drawing on a particular performative aesthetic, she turns herself into the subject of her history and leaves behind the revolutionary discourse employed by the generation of her parents.

1. Introducción

Este ensayo enfoca la película documental argentina *Los rubios* (2003) dirigida por Albertina Carri cuyos padres forman parte de las 30.000 personas que fueron "desaparecidas" durante la última dictadura militar en Argentina (1976-1983). Después de contextualizar el filme en las políticas de la memoria en la Argentina contemporánea, analizaremos –siguiendo a Marianne Hirsch (cf. "Surviving")–, su peculiar estética de la posmemoria, haciendo hincapié en aspectos de la performatividad y de la reflexividad como dos facetas innovadoras en el discurso documental de Carri. La directora no sólo logra cuestionar las posibilidades de recordar el pasado traumático, sino también explora los límites del documental como "film of fact," como lo llama Renov (13). En un primer paso, considerando la performatividad como elemento constitutivo de la identi-

---

[1] Este ensayo forma parte del proyecto de investigación de mi tesis de doctorado que enfoca la memoria de la militancia de mujeres argentinas en los años sesenta y setenta tal y como se presenta en películas documentales. Agradezco a Sebastian Thies, Marietta Saavedra Arellano y a Ana Opitz por sus valiosos comentarios.

dad de la narradora en primera persona, demostraremos que Carri, en *Los rubios* se atribuye a sí misma el papel de una actriz predeterminada y trasciende así cualquier forma de victimización. Veremos que el discurso identitario basado en la performatividad le permite distanciarse del discurso político de la generación de sus padres y proponer –en vez de una afiliación a una identidad basada en lo familiar–, una afiliación a su equipo de filmación con el que comparte una identidad generacional. En un segundo paso enfocaremos la opacidad del documental como medio de la memoria que es otro aspecto clave en el que se basa la estética de la posmemoria en *Los rubios*. En este contexto, veremos en qué sentido Carri se distancia de un discurso de la memoria que confía plenamente en la posibilidad de que los medios brinden un acceso directo al pasado, que es la base conceptual del discurso sobre el documental, propagada, por ejemplo, por David Blaustein, coetáneo a sus padres, en *Cazadores de utopías* (1996).

2. El discurso oficial de la memoria en Argentina después de la última dictadura militar (1976-1983)

"Vengo a pedir perdón de parte del Estado nacional por la vergüenza de haber callado durante veinte años de democracia tantas atrocidades," esta frase pronunciada por el entonces presidente de Argentina, Néstor Kirchner, el 24 de marzo 2004, en el vigésimo octavo aniversario del golpe de estado de 1976 (Curia 3), evidenciaba que se había producido un cambio fundamental en el discurso oficial de la memoria de la última dictadura militar en Argentina.

Hubo una fase temprana en las políticas oficiales de la memoria en la que la publicación de *Nunca más* –el informe oficial de la Comisión Nacional sobre la Desaparición de Personas (CONADEP)–, en septiembre de 1984 y, un año después, la iniciación del proceso judicial, realizado por la justicia civil en contra de las tres juntas de la dictadura militar –conocido como el Juicio a las Juntas–, parecían prometer una reparación ética y jurídica de los crímenes cometidos durante los siete años de dictadura militar (1976-1983). Sin embargo, en los años siguientes se tomaron una serie de resoluciones políticas que acallaron estos crímenes y limitaron la persecución jurídica en contra de los responsables de las graves y masivas violaciones de los derechos humanos. Tales resoluciones se manifestaron, especialmente, en la Ley de Punto Final (1986) y la Ley de Obediencia Debida (1987).[2] En 1989, siguiendo la misma línea, Carlos Menem indultó tanto a los ex-miembros de las juntas militares que habían sido condenados a severas penas, como a los civiles enjuiciados por sus actividades guerrilleras. Según Hugo Vezzetti, ese indulto iba en contra de "las promesas de la repara-

---

[2] María Sonderéguer especifica que la Ley de Punto Final "fija una fecha tope para el llamado a prestar declaración indagatoria de los presuntos implicados en violaciones en los derechos humanos." La Ley de Obediencia Debida de 1987, a su vez, "discrimina grados de responsabilidad: quienes cumplían órdenes no pueden ser inculpados" (Sonderéguer 5 n. 6).

ción ética y jurídica que estuvieron en el nuevo origen de la democracia" (143). Incluso, a principios del nuevo milenio, el presidente Fernando De la Rúa continuó aplican-
do la misma política de la memoria a través de un decreto –diciembre de 2001– que
impedía la extradición de los ex-militares que habían sido acusados, en otros países,
por crímenes de lesa humanidad cometidos durante la dictadura militar.

Tomando en consideración estos hechos, se puede apreciar el profundo cambio
que se produce en la política oficial de la memoria con la llegada al poder de Néstor
Kirchner (2003-2007). En junio de 2003, Kirchner derogó el decreto de la no-extradi-
ción y, en agosto del mismo año, las leyes de Punto Final y de Obediencia Debida. En
septiembre de 2003, el Congreso argentino dio rango constitucional a la Convención
sobre la Imprescriptibilidad de los Crímenes de Guerra y de los Crímenes de Lesa Humanidad de la ONU. Finalmente, en marzo de 2004, se declararon inconstitucionales
los indultos del menemismo que habían permitido poner en libertad a seis integrantes
del Primer Cuerpo del Ejército. Hubo, también, actos simbólicos que marcaron este
cambio. Los ex detenidos-desaparecidos recorrieron junto con Kirchner las instalaciones de la Escuela de Mecánica de la Armada (ESMA), el centro clandestino de detención más tenebroso de la dictadura militar, que hasta el 24 de marzo de 2004 seguía
todavía en manos de las Fuerzas Armadas. También, el presidente Kirchner presidió la
ceremonia en la que se descolgaron los retratos de los ex-dictadores Jorge Rafael Videla y Reynaldo Bignone del Patio de Honor del Colegio Militar de la Nación. Al mismo tiempo, firmó un convenio con el Jefe de Gobierno de la Ciudad de Buenos Aires
que dispuso que la ESMA fuera convertida en un Espacio para la Memoria y la Promoción y Defensa de los Derechos Humanos.[3] En enero de 2006, Hebe de Bonafini,
presidenta de la Asociación de Madres de Plaza de Mayo, anunció que su asociación
realizaría por última vez la Marcha Anual de la Resistencia –que duraba 24 horas y no
coincidía con las marchas semanales de los jueves– aduciendo que "el enemigo ya no
está en la Casa Rosada como en la dictadura, como con los anteriores presidentes."
Concluyó asegurando que "a este gobierno [de Kirchner] ya no hay que resistirle, sino
acompañarlo" (Meyer s.p.; cf. también Dandan).

No obstante, otras organizaciones de derechos humanos condenaron la decisión
de las Madres (cf. Zibechi). El Encuentro Memoria Verdad y Justicia, organismo que
agrupa a más de trescientas cincuenta organizaciones de derechos humanos, ha critica-
do duramente tanto al gobierno de Néstor Kirchner como al de Cristina Fernández de
Kirchner, quien asumió la presidencia en diciembre de 2007. No sólo reprocha al gobierno argentino la dilatación de las investigaciones en el caso de la desaparición de
Julio López[4] o eludir su responsabilidad en la muerte del docente Carlos Fuentealba[5]

---

[3] El retiro de los retratos tanto como el acto en el que se firmó el convenio arriba mencionado tuvieron lugar el 24 de marzo de 2004 en el marco de la conmemoración del vigésimo
octavo aniversario del golpe de estado (cf. Verbitsky 6; Braslavsky 9).

[4] Jorge Julio López fue un testigo clave en el juicio contra el militar Miguel Etchecolatz, uno
de los integrantes más buscados del aparato de represión de la última dictadura militar argentina. El juicio contra Etchecolatz fue el primero, cuando, en 2003, se recomenzaron los

de Neuquén. También este organismo denuncia la represión de las protestas sociales tanto como la criminalización de éstas (cf. Encuentro). Gregoria Marín de la organización piquetera Frente Popular Darío Santillán se refiere al tema del respeto a los derechos humanos bajo el gobierno de Néstor Kirchner:

> La imagen de [Néstor] Kirchner es contradictoria. El tema de los derechos humanos lo relaciona en primer lugar con la dictadura militar. Nosotros, que, en parte, sufrimos la represión bajo la dictadura, estamos de acuerdo con la anulación de la amnistía y con los nuevos procesos contra los miembros de la junta militar. Sin embargo, bajo Kirchner, las violaciones constantes de los derechos humanos no han cesado. Argentina tiene un balance negro: en los últimos diez años, han sido asesinados centenares de activistas y la mayoría de estos asesinatos han quedado impunes. Por otra parte, también la extrema pobreza restringe los derechos humanos. En las noticias, los éxitos alcanzados en descubrir y castigar los crímenes de la dictadura ocultan, a menudo, la realidad social de este país.[6] (Berger s.p.)

Podemos concluir que no se puede negar que, con los Kirchner en la cúpula del gobierno, el discurso oficial de la memoria ha cambiado considerablemente. Sin embargo –como lo muestran las palabras de Gregoria Marín o Rodolfo Yanzón, abogado de la Liga Argentina de Derechos Humanos (LADH) (cf. Vogt)–, el compromiso de Néstor y Cristina Fernández de Kirchner con los derechos humanos se restringe, básicamente, al campo de la memoria de la última dictadura militar. Además, implica el riesgo de que las organizaciones de derechos humanos que se han comprometido con el gobierno sean instrumentalizadas por éste.

3. Una nueva generación y su modo de recordar

Nacido en 1950, Kirchner pertenece a la generación de argentinos que vivieron la época de la dictadura militar como adultos jóvenes, muchos de ellos militando[7] en organi-

---

juicios por crímenes de lesa humanidad, después de que el Congreso había anulado las leyes de Punto Final y Obediencia Debida. López desapareció el 17 de septiembre de 2006, un día después de la condena a cadena perpetua de Etchecolatz (cf. también Vogt).

[5] Carlos Fuentealba era maestro y activista sindical. Durante una protesta de los maestros para obtener mejoras salariales, recibió en la cabeza una bomba de gas lacrimógeno, lanzada por las fuerzas policiales que querían impedir un corte de ruta. Fuentealba murió el 5 de abril de 2007, un día después de haber sido herido.

[6] La entrevista a Gregoria Marín fue publicada únicamente en alemán. Esta cita en español es una traducción, hecha por la autora.

[7] Con María Rosa Valle y Graciela Destuet consideramos en este contexto "el concepto de militancia en sentido amplio, incluyendo más allá de la político-partidaria, la sindical, la feminista, la de corte religioso, la universitaria o la de las organizaciones guerrilleras, entre otras" (407). Es difícil dar cifras exactas de los jóvenes que militaban en los años sesenta y setenta en Argentina, partiendo, además, de una definición amplia de la militancia. No obstante, el hecho de que los Montoneros, una de las organizaciones armadas más importantes entre los sesenta y los setenta, hayan podido movilizar entre 50.000 y 150.000 personas en

zaciones políticas, sociales o eclesiásticas. Ya durante la dictadura militar, pero, sobre todo, en el tiempo inmediatamente posterior, dos generaciones de argentinos, víctimas de la dictadura militar –la de Kirchner y la de las Madres–, se organizaron en diversas asociaciones para defender los derechos humanos. Se puede nombrar, por ejemplo, la Asociación de Ex-Detenidos Desaparecidos y las Asociaciones de las Madres[8] o de las Abuelas de Plaza de Mayo. Especialmente las Asociaciones de Madres se hicieron famosas, no sólo en la misma Argentina, sino también en el extranjero. En innumerables manifestaciones, los integrantes de estas dos generaciones exigían castigo y justicia y se declaraban en contra del silencio y la impunidad. Por medio de manifestaciones culturales diversas[9], estas dos generaciones trabajaron especialmente en la década de los ochenta en contra del memoricidio (cf. Goytisolo) del discurso oficial de la memoria.

A contar de mediados de los años noventa, otra generación tomó la palabra: eran los hijos de los desaparecidos, asesinados, exiliados y presos políticos durante la época del terrorismo de Estado, éstos conformaron la agrupación Hijos por la Identidad y la Justicia contra el Olvido y el Silencio, conocido bajo la sigla H.I.J.O.S. La mayoría de sus integrantes vivió los primeros años de su infancia durante la dictadura y perdió a uno o a ambos padres a causa del terrorismo de estado. Lejos de dejarse reducir al papel de víctimas, H.I.J.O.S. exige que los culpables de los asesinatos y desapariciones sean llevados a juicio, al mismo tiempo, que se proponen continuar o recordar la lucha de sus padres. Sus miembros se consideran "una continuidad de la lucha de las Madres, las Abuelas, los Familiares y los Ex-Detenidos" (Ginzberg s.p.). Esta asociación introdujo un nuevo método de lucha en la guerra contra la impunidad: el "escrache." Éste no considera (solamente) los lugares simbólicos del poder, como la Plaza de

---

más de seis ocasiones (cf. Gillespie 134-35) da una impresión de la gran cantidad de jóvenes que militaban de una u otra forma.

[8]   En 1986 se produjo una escisión en las Madres, motivada por criterios diferentes en cuanto a la metodología de lucha bajo un gobierno constitucional y, también, en relación con actitudes autoritarias en la conducción del movimiento. Surge la Asociación Madres de Plaza de Mayo Línea Fundadora, llamada así porque la mayoría de las fundadoras se integran en esta línea. Sin embargo, ambos grupos, es decir tanto la Asociación Madres de Plaza de Mayo como la Asociación Madres de Plaza de Mayo Línea Fundadora, siguen concurriendo a la Plaza todos los jueves para reclamar verdad y justicia.

[9]   En este contexto, destacan algunos libros testimoniales (cf. Actis et al.; Leonidas Chaves/ Lewinger; Mattini; Pollastri; Ramus) o acciones como el "Siluetazo" que se tuvo lugar, en septiembre de 1983, por iniciativa de los realizadores plásticos Guillermo Kexel, Julio Flores y Rodolfo Aguerreberry. Eran todavía los tiempos de la dictadura. Miles de manifestantes produjeron siluetas de tamaño natural que representaban la "presencia de una ausencia" (Jelin, "Siluetas" 67) y daban cierta visibilidad a los desaparecidos. Con su documental *Cazadores de utopías*, David Blaustein, antiguo miembro de los Montoneros, trabajó contra el olvido en la década de los noventa. Eduardo Medici, nacido en 1949, y Daniel García, en 1958, son otros artistas cuyas obras enfocan la última dictadura militar. De especial interés, en este contexto, son las obras "Quiénes somos, adónde vamos, de dónde venimos" o "Tanto tiempo de tanta muerte" de Medici; "Camilla 1990," "Gran Requiem," "Lapidado" o "Estudio para un pañuelo" de García.

Mayo o la Plaza de los dos Congresos, sino que irrumpe en los espacios de la cotidianidad. Los escraches pueden ser definidos como "una denuncia popular en contra de
personas acusadas de violaciones a los derechos humanos o de corrupción, que se realiza mediante actos tales como sentadas, cánticos o pintadas" (Academia 298) en los
mismos barrios en los que viven los ex-represores, muy a menudo, sin que los vecinos
conozcan su pasado. H.I.J.O.S. pone en evidencia ese pasado silenciado y desenmasca-
ra a los culpables repartiendo fotos con sus rostros o pegando planos en las paredes
que indican el domicilio exacto del acusado. Esta asociación ha elegido así formas no-
vedosas para luchar contra la impunidad y, al mismo tiempo, recordar la represión (cf.
también Jelin, *Los trabajos* 118 n. 2), transformando los códigos de lucha heredados
de las Madres (cf. Taylor 169-70).

Mas, las formas de expresión de las que se sirve esta nueva generación para acu-
sar las violaciones de los derechos humanos durante la última dictadura militar, no se
limitan a estas acciones políticas, sino su búsqueda se extiende al campo artístico. El
documental, en este contexto, ocupa una posición preponderante en cuanto a que, según Oberti y Pittaluga "la dimensión veritativa a la que según Ricœur aspira la memoria, está presente desde el inicio en el género *documental*, que pone ante los ojos la documentación, la prueba; sea bajo la forma del testimonio, sea bajo la forma de la imagen de archivo" (126). Como detalla Ana Amado, los hijos de los desaparecidos "forman parte de una generación que en la cultura actual privilegia expresarse desde lenguajes artísticos diversos: vídeo, música, pintura, diseño gráfico, animación, fotografía, teatro" ("Las nuevas" 224). En este lenguaje artístico también caben las producciones audiovisuales como, por ejemplo, *En memoria de los pájaros* (2000) de Gabriela
Golder, *Historias cotidianas* (2001) de Andrés Habegger, el cortometraje *In absentia*
(2002) de Lucía Cedrón, *Papá Iván* de María Inés Roqué (2004), *Encontrando a
Víctor* (2005) de Natalia Bruschtein, *La matanza* (2005) de María Giuffra y también
Los rubios (2003) de Albertina Carri, película a la que a continuación nos dedicaremos
más a fondo. Concordamos con Amado en su consideración de que estas obras –producidas por jóvenes directores de cine cuyo padre o madre desaparecieron en la última
dictadura militar– están

> concebidas como homenaje y, a la vez, puesta al día del vínculo genealógico, [y que] no
> disimulan su raíz afectiva pero dejan entrever, de modo directo o figurado, menos una
> adhesión incondicional con la ideología de sus padres, que una voluntad de distancia y
> afirmación de sus propias opciones en el presente. ("Las nuevas" 224)

Esto es especialmente cierto para el documental *Los rubios* de Albertina Carri en
el que su directora plantea una voluntad de distancia y de afirmación de sus propias
opciones y –como ya lo ha dicho Amado– no sólo con respecto a la figura de sus padres militantes. Carri desafía tanto la manera en la que, hasta ese momento, se había
recordado el conflictivo pasado argentino, como las posibilidades del género documental como instrumento de la memoria. Esta posición hizo que este film provocara
una profusa reacción crítica (cf., por ejemplo, Aguilar, "*Los rubios*"; Amado, "Los ru-

bios"; Alonso, "Las nuevas", "Órdenes"; Garibotto/Gómez; Kohan, "La apariencia", "Una crítica").

El presente ensayo retoma el uso del concepto posmemoria como categoría de interpretación –introducida por Hirsch y aplicada por Nouzeilles a *Los rubios*–, pero lo hace concretizando lo que podría denominarse como una estética de posmemoria vinculada a los aspectos de performatividad y reflexividad.

El concepto de la posmemoria remonta a Marianne Hirsch quien lo usa para enfrentarse a la problemática de la memoria de los hijos de los sobrevivientes del Holocausto, o sea, a la memoria de la segunda generación. Pero, la misma Hirsch afirma que el concepto de la posmemoria "may usefully describe other second-generation memories of cultural or collective traumatic events and experiences" (*Family* 22). Según Hirsch, la posmemoria caracteriza la experiencia "of those who ... have grown up dominated by narratives that preceded their birth, whose own belated stories are displaced by the powerful stories of the previous generations, shaped by monumental traumatic events that resist understanding and integration" ("Surviving" 221). Define la diferencia entre memoria y posmemoria por medio de lo que llama la distancia generacional (cf. *Family* 22). Es así, entonces, que el eje central del concepto de la posmemoria es la distancia entre aquel que recuerda y el recuerdo. Los medios –fotos, películas, cartas, libros y, también, testigos– son los elementos que contrarrestan esta gran distancia temporal; pasan a ocupar el centro de la atención, se convierten en los portadores de la memoria y, en consecuencia, pueden ser considerados los elementos constituyentes de la posmemoria. En este contexto, Hirsch habla de la "textual nature" de la posmemoria y señala su "reliance on images, stories, and documents passed down from one generation to the next" ("Surviving" 222). Dicho de otro modo, la cuestión de la medialidad juega un papel decisivo para el concepto de la posmemoria.

Hirsch señala, además, que, como consecuencia de esta distancia temporal, el recuerdo no puede ser mediatizado a través de la recolección, sino a través de la representación, la proyección y la creación, muy a menudo, basadas,en el silencio y no en la palabra, en lo invisible y no en lo visible (cf. "Surviving" 221). En este mismo sentido, Hirsch aclara que, para la posmemoria, la mediación del recuerdo sólo funciona a través de un "imaginative investment and creation" (*Family* 22).

4. La estética fílmica de la posmemoria en *Los rubios* de Albertina Carri

4.1. La performatividad

Una característica importante de la estética de la posmemoria que aparece en *Los rubios* y que constituye en gran parte este "imaginative investment and creation" (Hirsch, *Family* 22), es la performatividad. En *Blurred Boundaries*, Bill Nichols introduce, como modelo de análisis, una modalidad de representación performativa en las películas documentales, que se distingue por dar relevancia a aspectos subjetivos y afectivos en un discurso tradicionalmente objetivista (cf. *Blurred* 95). Stella Bruzzi, en su obra *New Documentary. A Critical Introduction* también se ocupa de la modalidad performativa, pero la define de manera algo distinta a la de Nichols. En concordancia con Judith Butler y John Langshaw Austin, Bruzzi considera que un documental es performativo siempre y cuando, simultáneamente, lleve a cabo la misma acción que está describiendo (cf. 154). Considera la modalidad performativa como estrechamente relacionada con la modalidad reflexiva al señalar que "the ethos behind the modern performative documentaries is to present subjects in such a way as to accentuate the fact that the camera and crew are an inevitable intrusion that alter any situation they enter" (157). Esto significa que un documental performativo es reflexivo en tanto se exhiben los mecanismos de representación. Esta combinación entre aspectos performativos y reflexivos es especialmente característica en *Los rubios*, un documental que representa fílmicamente el proceso de producción. Una secuencia clave del principio de la película nos sirve para ejemplificar esta combinación; en ella presenciamos la filmación de una escena en la que la actriz Analía Couceyro performa el papel de la directora Carri y, al mismo tiempo, aparece la figura de Carri comentando su actuación "performance."[10] Primero, con la presentación de diferentes imágenes fijas, se nos muestran los preparativos para la filmación de la escena. En la primera imagen vemos a un miembro del equipo de filmación que tiene en su mano una cámara; en otra vemos una mesa de trabajo llena de papeles, lápices y otras cosas; en una tercera, distinguimos a tres miembros del equipo, uno de ellos con un aparato de medición de luz en la mano. Paralelamente a estas imágenes una voz femenina en *off* dice: "Dat n° siete de ficción, vamos a rodar ficción. Hoy es ... ¿Qué día es hoy? ¿Siete? Siete de julio de 2002, domingo, y vamos a ..." En ese momento se interrumpe el sonido y escuchamos otra voz –esta vez masculina– diciendo: "Entrevista 'Vaquita de San Antonio' toma uno." Este comentario acerca de la ficcionalidad de la secuencia, nos hace reflexionar sobre la autenticidad de lo que vamos a ver[11], teniendo presente –como señala, por ejemplo, Nichols en *Blurred Boundaries*– que el género documental no es opuesto a la ficción sino, por el contrario, se sirve de estrategias narrativas propias de las películas de ficción.[12] Por lo tanto, no puede haber una delimitación nítida entre las películas documentales y las de ficción y la presentación de esta escena como "ficción" nos revela el carácter híbrido del documental.[13]

---

[10] Para un análisis detallado de la presencia de la actriz Analía Couceyro haciendo el papel de Albertina Carri véase más abajo en este apartado.

[11] Cuando Couceyro lee una parte del libro de Roberto Carri y, en el fondo, distinguimos la palabra "Teatro," se trata de un comentario metanarrativo que tiene la misma función como el que acabamos de mencionar.

[12] En cuanto a estrategias narrativas en películas documentales y etnográficas, cf., por ejemplo, a Kiener.

[13] Así, Carri se distancia de los documentales sobre el conflictivo pasado argentino como *Montoneros, una historia* o *Cazadores de utopías* que consideran el documental como "film of fact" (Renov 13), el que transmite si no la verdad, por lo menos, una verdad. Carri, al contrario, señala el caracter construido de cualquier verdad histórica en el discurso docu-

En la siguiente escena –muy breve– se muestra, en blanco y negro, en primer plano, cómo se cierra la claqueta mientras que, en plano medio, distinguimos un micrófono y, al fondo, Couceyro sentada en una silla. En la escena siguiente, todavía en blanco y negro, en un primer plano distinguimos a Carri, que da la espalda a la cámara, filmando a Couceyro. Esta última aparece en un segundo plano pronunciando un monólogo. Carri interrumpe la toma para dar indicaciones a la actriz que la personifica. Mientras explica a Couceyro cómo se imagina el monólogo, se enfocan sus manos junto a la cámara con la que acaba de filmar y que ahora está en un trípode. La toma se repite en blanco y negro, pero esta vez, en un primer plano del perfil de Carri y parte de la cámara que enfoca a Couceyro mientras ésta última pronuncia el monólogo. Carri sonríe durante la toma y la termina con las palabras "Buenísima, corte." Después de otra repetición, en la última escena de esta secuencia –a diferencia de las escenas anteriores filmada en color sugiriendo que se trata de la versión definitiva– el espectador ve a Couceyro de frente en una toma de primer plano pronunciando el monólogo antes ensayado.

Presenciamos, de esta manera, los diferentes pasos necesarios para llegar a la escena en su versión final. Es, en este sentido, que podemos llamar a *Los rubios* una película performativa en el sentido de Bruzzi (cf. 157): Carri exhibe lo representacional y, a la vez, lo pone en escena, dejando en claro que se trata de una construcción fílmica. Al principio de la secuencia descrita, a través del comentario en *off*, nos ubica en el momento de la filmación, el siete de julio de 2002, y nos da a conocer, mediante las diferentes imágenes fijas, algunos de los preparativos.

La secuencia descrita es sólo un ejemplo, entre muchos otros, que presentan y subrayan el alto grado de construcción de lo que vemos en la pantalla. Simultáneamente la película hace hincapié en las posibilidades y límites de la cámara con respecto a la documentación de la realidad. Comparando *Los rubios* con otras películas documentales que se caracterizan por resaltar elementos performativos, podemos afirmar con Bruzzi:

> The fundamental issue here is honesty. The performative element could be seen to undermine the conventional documentary pursuit of representing the real because the elements of performance, dramatisation and acting for the camera are intrusive and alienating factors. Alternatively, the use of performance tactics could be viewed as a means of suggesting that perhaps documentaries should admit the defeat of their utopian aim and elect instead to present an alternative 'honesty' that does not seek to mask their inherent instability but rather to acknowledge that performance—the enactment of the documentary specifically for the cameras—will always be the heart of the non-fiction film. (155)

---

mental. La estética de la posmemoria que Carri elige para representar el pasado es altamente reflexiva y crítica; en vez de propagar verdades, las cuestiona. De esta forma Carri, de cierta manera, ataca a la generación de sus padres que basa su identidad de ex-militantes en verdades epistémicas derivadas de un materialismo histórico o un nacionalismo peronista.

No obstante todo lo que se ha dicho hasta aquí, existe otro aspecto que nos parece central en el contexto de la performatividad que ni Nichols ni tampoco Bruzzi toman en consideración. La performatividad también se puede encarar desde el punto de vista de un discurso identitario. El hecho de que la figura de la directora se desdoble de manera performativa y dé indicaciones a la actriz que la representa le permite salir del papel de víctima. En consecuencia, no se reduce al papel de una persona cuyos padres fueron secuestrados y asesinados expresando, por esta causa, su gran sufrimiento. La impresión que prevalece es la de Carri como directora cinematográfica que da indicaciones y decide la manera como hay que hacer las cosas. De este modo, se crea a sí misma una identidad que le permite convertirse en el sujeto de su propia historia.

La identidad que Carri construye para sí misma en *Los rubios*, recurriendo a la performatividad, no es monológica. Se trata más bien de una identidad desdoblada, abierta, que se manifiesta por la actuación de Analía Couceyro en el papel de Albertina Carri. La primera, después de haber introducido a Albertina Carri, se presenta a sí misma mirando hacia la cámara y diciendo: "Mi nombre es Analía Couceyro, soy actriz y en esta película represento a Albertina Carri." Es decir, los mecanismos de la representación se exhiben en vez de esconderlos. Como lo formula Kohan, este procedimiento pone a *Los rubios* "en la esfera evidente de las técnicas del distanciamiento brechtiano" dado que se suprime todo efecto de identificación en los espectadores y, por lo tanto, la aliviadora descarga catártica ("La apariencia" 26). Tal vez sea en este contexto en el que tenemos que ubicar la breve escena en la que vemos una mano escribiendo en un cartón "identificación meca" sin que se termine de escribir, lo que suponemos que debería ser la palabra "mecánica." El hecho de que la palabra quede inconclusa puede interpretarse como una alusión a esa falta de identificación del espectador con la protagonista Carri representada por una actriz.

La película da todavía un paso más en esta dirección. Como ya vimos en la secuencia de la entrevista sobre las vaquitas de San Antonio, la directora misma aparece en la película como figura autodiegética. Nouzeilles distingue incluso, por lo menos, a tres Albertina Carri en *Los rubios*:

> Albertina, the author behind the frame; Albertina the *auteur* inside the film, who appears holding the camera, giving instructions and discussing the movie with the crew; and Albertina, the daughter in a state of memory, who stands before the camera delivering a rehearsed testimony. The latter is played by the actress Analía Couceyro. (269)

En la pantalla presenciamos la manera en que se efectúa la negociación entre las diferentes subjetividades relacionadas con Carri. Estamos de acuerdo con Kohan cuando señala que Carri dice las palabras que después va a decir Couceyro "bajo la forma mecánica y expeditiva de las indicaciones de filmación" y que el texto "se neutraliza" y hasta se vuelve inquietantemente impersonal ("La apariencia" 26). Indudablemente, se percibe cierta distancia entre Carri y el texto; pero, decir que esa distancia sea "absoluta," como concluye Kohan, y que "no hay nada más remoto de estas palabras que Albertina Carri" ("La apariencia" 27) no convence. Lo que consideramos como decisivo en este contexto no es tanto la distancia entre el texto enunciado por

Couceyro y Carri, la (supuesta) autora de las palabras, sino el hecho de que la presencia de la actriz permite a Carri salir del papel de víctima. El desdoblamiento le permite percibirse y dirigirse a sí misma. Esta identidad desdoblada y desplazada le permite, al mismo tiempo, hablar desde el lugar de la persona cuyos padres fueron secuestrados y asesinados, un lugar asociado con una alta carga afectiva, y dar indicaciones sobre cómo deben ser enunciadas las palabras, o sea, convertirse en una autoridad que maneja el discurso.

El concepto de una identidad no estable, alterable, lo encontramos también en otros momentos de la película. Con ayuda de una figurita de *playmobil* a la que se le cambia el sombrero, Carri escenifica su concepto no esencialista, no estático de la identidad. Cada vez que le cambia el sombrero a la figura, cambia la identidad de ésta. La misma directora señala que la figurita "pasa de ser sheriff a astronauta o a ama de casa, así que va variando su rol en el mundo" (Zapata/Rozas/Gasparini s.p.). Consiguientemente, la identidad no se concibe como un concepto fijo, inalterable sino, por el contrario, como algo que se construye y que, por lo tanto, puede variar.[14]

Esta misma concepción de identidad la vemos reflejada al final de la película, cuando los miembros del equipo de filmación caminan en grupo hacia el horizonte campestre, todos llevando pelucas rubias. Estas pelucas aluden al testimonio de una vecina del barrio en el que vivía Albertina Carri de niña con sus padres, antes de que éstos fueran secuestrados. La vecina recuerda que toda la familia era rubia: "Son tres nenas rubias, el señor es rubio, la señora rubia, todos rubios." La voz en *off* de Analía Couceyro, aclara inmediatamente después: "Cuando le mostré a mi tía el testimonio de la señora se puso a gritar: 'Mi hermana nunca fue flaca y nunca fue rubia.'" Compartimos la interpretación de la mayoría de los críticos que relaciona el supuesto cabello rubio de la familia Carri –que incluso da el título a la película– con el hecho de que eran miembros de la clase media que vivían en un barrio obrero. Entonces, cuando la vecina –teñida de un negro azabache, como muy perspicazmente, observa Aguilar (cf. "*Los rubios*" 179)– dice acordarse de que los Carri eran todos rubios, no quiere referirse tanto al color del cabello, sino más bien a que los Carri llamaban la atención en el barrio, porque eran distintos (cf., por ejemplo, Nouzeilles 268; Sarlo 151; Aguilar, "*Los rubios*" 179). Al ponerse pelucas rubias, el equipo de filmación toma al pie de la letra el testimonio de la vecina y, de cierta manera, se adapta a este testimonio asumiendo la identidad que la vecina creó con sus palabras.

El concepto de identidad que propone *Los rubios* y que se concretiza en la última escena, no sólo resalta por su renuncia a cualquier esencialismo, sino, además, transmite la importancia de la comunidad. Son todos los miembros del equipo de filmación –y no, como vemos en una escena anterior, únicamente Couceyro– los que caminan, uno al lado del otro, unidos por las pelucas rubias que llevan puestas. Se trata de una comunidad que va más allá de los lazos de sangre que unen a la familia y la experiencia del trauma. Amado señala que la familia más cercana, las hermanas de Albertina

---

[14] Al mismo tiempo, a través del playmobil y la performatividad del juego infantil, Carri deconstruye el discurso documental y su postulado de veracidad.

Carri, no aparecen en *Los rubios*. Con ellas "no hay comunidad ni concordancia posible en el ejercicio de la memoria" ("Órdenes" 77). En un momento de la película Couceyro dice: "Mi hermana Paula no quiere hablar frente a cámara, Andrea [la otra hermana] dice que sí quiere hacer la entrevista, pero todo lo interesante lo dice cuando apago la cámara" (34.05). La comunidad que reemplaza a la familia en *Los rubios* es el equipo de filmación, los "nuevos rubios" por decirlo así, todos jóvenes de la misma generación que Albertina Carri, jóvenes que comparten el proyecto de (pos)memoria que Carri se propuso realizar con *Los rubios* (cf. Amado, "Órdenes" 77-78; Nouzeilles 266, 271).

4.2. La medialidad opaca de la memoria

Cuando en lo que sigue hablamos de los medios de la memoria en *Los rubios*, nos referimos no sólo a fotos, libros o cartas, sino también a los testimonios de familiares y antiguos compañeros de militancia de los padres de la directora que aparecen en la película. Los consideramos como medios portadores de la memoria en la medida en que estos testimonios acerca del pasado –como veremos– son mediatizados. Estos testimonios aparecen en diferentes momentos de la película. Pero, salta a la vista que en ningún caso se nombra al testigo o se especifica su identidad. Por consiguiente, el espectador sólo puede deducir, del contexto fílmico en que se encuentra, la índole del testimonio. Contrariamente a Sarlo que interpreta el hecho de que los testigos permanezcan en el anonimato como "un signo de separación, e, incluso, de hostilidad" (149-50), consideramos que estos testimonios anónimos crean, más bien, esa "bruma de la memoria" de la que se habla en *Los rubios* en otro momento (29.28). Al dejar a los testigos en el anonimato, la documentalista nos enfrenta con una memoria en la que las diferentes voces no se dejan ubicar con exactitud en el pasado.

Los testimonios de los familiares o de los antiguos compañeros de militancia de sus padres Roberto Carri y Ana María Caruso son presentados, en la gran mayoría de los casos, por medio de un televisor en cuya pantalla vemos hablar al testigo y en la que se introducen comentarios metanarrativos, como por ejemplo, "reproducir," es decir, una inscripción que originariamente proviene de la videograbadora. De esta suerte, en vez de crearse un efecto de inmediatez, que por lo general se asocia con el testimonio oral, se insiste, por el contrario, en la mediación (doble) y en la distancia que conlleva esta última.

En este contexto, vale la pena detenerse también en la instancia narrativa intradiegética de la directora –representada por la actriz Analía Couceyro– frente a los testimonios. La mayoría de las veces, Couceyro en su papel de Albertina Carri, da la espalda al televisor en el que se ve a los testigos y parece prestarles poca atención. En vez de escuchar atentamente lo que dicen, se pone a hacer otra cosa. Según Kohan esta actuación de Couceyro es "el despliegue de un vasto muestrario de modos de desconsideración" ("La apariencia" 28). No obstante, no vemos en esta actitud, un gesto de alejamiento, como luego lo plantea Kohan (cf. "La apariencia" 28). Partimos de la hipótesis de que el gesto de la directora no se refiere tanto a los testigos como personas, sino a los testigos en su calidad mediatizada. A nuestro entender, muestra una cierta desconfianza frente a la capacidad de los testimonios para dar cuenta de la historia. Aún más, empleando los testimonios de la manera señalada, se distancia de las películas documentales sobre la militancia argentina de los años sesenta y setenta, como *Cazadores de utopías* en las que la autoridad narrativa se basa en los testigos que presentan un discurso "todo armadito" –como lo formula Aguilar ("Maravillosa" 29)– dando a conocer una imagen supuestamente nítida del pasado sin incongruencias. En este aspecto, seguimos a Alonso quien opina que en *Los rubios*, por el contrario, "las entrevistas se presentan como un método siempre conflictivo y pocas veces estable" pero que "antes que un descrédito o una nulidad, la mediatización que Carri les dedica a [los] testimonios produce una mengua en sus efectos de transferencia" (165).[15]

Este conflicto entre una memoria que se basa en la autoridad de los testigos y que presenta una imagen nítida del pasado frente a otra memoria que, precisamente, cuestiona la autoridad narrativa de los testigos como exclusiva e, igualmente, toda posibilidad de llegar a un conocimiento unívoco del pasado, se aprecia con mucha claridad en el conflicto entre Carri y su equipo con el Instituto Nacional de Cine y Artes Audiovisuales (INCAA). La película nos revela que Carri solicitó un subsidio al INCAA; éste –en un telefax, cuyo contenido se lee en la misma película—, exige a Carri un "mayor rigor documental" y reclama "una búsqueda más exigente de testimonios propios" que podrían concretarse con "la participación de los compañeros de sus padres." De esta forma, se representa un conflicto entre dos generaciones que disputan la manera como recordar el pasado argentino de los años sesenta y setenta: por un lado, está la generación de los testigos de la época –simbolizada por el INCAA– y, por el otro, está la generación de los hijos representada por Albertina Carri. Obviamente, la generación que vivió la época en cuestión no está de acuerdo con el nuevo proyecto, puesto que, al fin y al cabo, pone en duda la autoridad de los testigos y, en la película, se manifiesta un claro escepticismo frente a los testigos como medios para recuperar la memoria (cf. también Nouzeilles 274).

Este escepticismo lo encontramos también en la utilización de otros medios, como por ejemplo, en las fotografías. Éstas abundan en la película: decoran las paredes del estudio organizadas en un collage o las vemos en aparente desorden cubriendo el escritorio. En la mayor parte de las fotos vemos a bebés o a niños y, en algunos casos, podemos concluir, con ayuda de inscripciones en la ropa o a partir de una fecha escrita al lado, que se trata de la propia directora cuando era niña o que, probablemente, estamos frente a una foto de bebé de uno de sus padres.

---

[15] Compartimos la opinión de Aguilar quien detalla en este contexto que "la aparición de *Los rubios* ... hace que nuestra visión de los primeros documentales realizados sobre la militancia de los setenta aparezca bajo una nueva luz y revela que aquello que pretendía ser una evocación natural y espontánea debe ser observado como otra construcción artificial para dominar la memoria presentándola, toscamente, como pasado" ("Maravillosa" 19).

Sin embargo, la película le niega al espectador la imagen del rostro de los padres de Albertina Carri. La manera en que son empleadas las fotos se opone muy claramente a su utilización en la retórica en torno a los desaparecidos de las organizaciones de derechos humanos. Para éstas, las fotos de los desaparecidos funcionan "como el pivote sobre el que se organiza el recuerdo y se proclama la continuidad de la búsqueda" (Garibotto/Gómez 118): a cada rostro se le asigna el nombre, se le atribuye una identidad sin que quede lugar a dudas su veracidad.[16] En *Los rubios* tal atribución no se realiza. Las personas de las fotografías quedan en el anonimato y, en vez de hacer revivir la apariencia física de Roberto Carri y de Ana María Caruso y esbozar una imagen nítida y concreta de ellos, causan aún más las preguntas acerca de su identidad. Además, ellas nunca muestran a la familia Carri Caruso completa, o sea, a los padres y las tres hijas. Casi siempre vemos a uno o dos niños, solos o de la mano de un adulto del que únicamente se distinguen las piernas. En vez de mostrar un todo, enseñan fragmentos y, en vez de dar cuenta de una continuidad temporal, hacen hincapié en lagunas temporales, por ejemplo, cuando vemos una foto de Roberto Carri de niño junto a una foto de sus hijas cuando eran muy pequeñas (cf. también Nouzeilles 270).

De este modo, la fotografía no se presenta como un medio portador transparente de la memoria, sino que, por el contrario, subraya la opacidad, una cierta resistencia a entregar el pasado y a eliminar, al mismo tiempo, todas las dudas. Esta opacidad, la directora la transfiere a una imagen concreta: cuando el equipo de rodaje emprende su labor documental –están sentados en un auto, mirando las fotos de un antiguo álbum–, alguien decide cubrir las fotos con una funda de pergamina; la escena termina así: el papel semi-transparente cubriendo las fotos –que, además, se muestran invertidas– de modo que es imposible distinguir nítidamente a las personas. Se simboliza, de esta forma, de manera metafórica, la resistencia de la fotografía a entregarnos la memoria y, al mismo tiempo, se pone de relieve su calidad de ser "a bizarre medium" como es denominada por Roland Barthes en su obra *Camera Lucida*. Éste concluye:

> La Photographie devient alors pour moi, un *medium* bizarre, une nouvelle forme d'hallucination: fausse au niveau de la perception, vraie au niveau du temps: une hallucination tempérée, en quelque sorte, modeste, *partagée* (d'un côté «ce n'est pas là», de l'autre «mais cela a bien été»): image folle, *frottée* de réel. (177)

Además de las fotos, Carri se sirve de un libro escrito por su padre y de algunas cartas como medios transmisores de la memoria. Es un ensayo titulado *Isidro Velázquez. Formas prerrevolucionarias de la violencia*, del cual, en el documental, aparecen dos ediciones. Una antigua con los bordes desgastados –probablemente de 1968, año de la primera edición– la cual aparece sobre una mesa de trabajo entre otros papeles, periódicos y fotos. La otra edición de 2001, está en la misma mesa de trabajo y es de ella que Couceyro –representando a Carri– lee una parte al principio de la película. En nuestra opinión, la elección de la nueva edición no significa que Carri rechace el

---

[16] Para un estudio detallado del uso de las fotos por las Madres de Plaza de Mayo, cf. Taylor 176-89.

pasado, como lo plantea Kohan (cf. "La apariencia" 28), sino, por el contrario, subraya la importancia del presente para nuestra manera de percibir el pasado. Como detalla Reinhart Koselleck en su obra *Vergangene Zukunft*: "La experiencia es pasado *actualizado* [la cursiva es nuestra], cuyos sucesos pueden ser incorporados y recordados."[17] Esta actualización del pasado en el presente –tan importante para la memoria– es la posición que encontramos reflejada cuando la actriz lee un fragmento del libro de Roberto Carri eligiendo la nueva edición.[18]

No obstante, el fragmento leído en voz alta no corresponde a la creación del padre. Lo que lee Couceyro es una cita de la *Historia de las agitaciones campesinas andaluzas* (1929) de Juan Díaz del Moral que el padre incluyó como epígrafe en su libro. Es decir, las palabras que –automáticamente y sin ponerlas en duda– atribuimos a Roberto Carri pertenecen, al fin y al cabo, a otra persona. Nouzeilles no da importancia a este hecho y señala que lo que escuchamos da cuenta de la posición política del padre de Carri y es necesario considerarlo como una especie de testamento político que el padre transmite a sus hijas, de la misma manera que la carta que el Ché Guevara escribió a sus hijos (cf. Gambini 276) o la carta del asesinado ex-líder montonero Juan Julio Roqué, que su hija María Inés lee al principio de su documental *Papá Iván* (cf. Nouzeilles 271-72). Sin embargo, queremos poner de relieve que así como las fotos no nos facilitan una idea exacta de la apariencia física de Roberto Carri y de Ana María Caruso, el libro, que prometía un acceso directo a las palabras de Roberto Carri, nos niega finalmente esta posibilidad y nos ofrece algo completamente inesperado. De nuevo se manifiesta la resistencia del medio –en este caso del libro– a brindar un acceso fácil, directo a la memoria.

Se puede constatar algo semejante con respecto a las cartas que los padres escribían en la cárcel y enviaban a sus hijas. Como señalan Garibotto y Gómez, la narradora se refiere en más de una ocasión a estas cartas, pero, sin embargo, "solamente una vez puede leerse claramente la letra de la madre que felicita a Albertina con ocasión de su cumpleaños" (118-19). Mientras que en algunas películas, como por ejemplo *Raymundo* (2003), los manuscritos mostrados se atribuyen a su autor a través de la voz en *off*, de manera que no quedan dudas respecto a la autoría de los manuscritos, en *Los rubios*, en cambio, parecen favorecerse tales dudas: en diferentes momentos la cámara barre una serie de manuscritos sin que se aclare a quién pertenecen. En este aspecto estamos de acuerdo con Garibotto y Gómez cuando afirman

> El film genera una expectativa, anticipa una construcción y, una vez creado ese espacio de recepción, lo deja alevosamente vacío: el espectador comienza a delinear el rostro del desaparecido, pero más tarde se le confunde con otros; vislumbra su letra, pero es inca-

---

[17] En el original alemán Koselleck dice: "Erfahrung ist gegenwärtige Vergangenheit, deren Ereignisse einverleibt und erinnert werden können" (354). Agradezco la traducción a Marietta Saavedra Arellano.

[18] Para la importancia del presente para nuestra percepción del pasado, cf. también Jelin, *Los trabajos* 12-13.

paz de leer lo que dice; empieza a oír su voz y después descubre que no le pertenece.
(119)

De esta manera, ninguno de los medios que aparecen en la película –los testigos,
las fotos, el libro y las cartas– transmiten de manera transparente la memoria y, por
tanto, son incapaces de corporizar al desaparecido, de devolverle cierta materialidad o,
incluso, de darle una identidad. Por el contrario, en *Los rubios*, se subraya la resistencia –y tal vez incluso la impotencia– de los medios para ofrecer la memoria del desaparecido. Así, *Los rubios* propone un contradiscurso a los discursos de la memoria dominantes en Argentina cuyo principal soporte son los medios enfocados en este trabajo.

5. Conclusión

En *Los rubios* se propone una estética fílmica que exhibe la puesta en escena del documental y subraya su performatividad. Por esta vía Carri reflexiona y cuestiona la manera en que se recuerda el pasado traumático. Desde el punto de vista de un discurso
identitario, la estética de la posmemoria le brinda la posibilidad de plantear una identidad no esencialista, que se construye en un proceso de desdoblamiento y negociación
entre Carri y Couceyro. Este procedimiento no sólo le permite poner de manifiesto la
puesta en escena –que es característica principal de la película documental– e introdu-
cir un momento brechtiano en *Los rubios*. Posibilita además –lo que consideramos mucho más importante– que la directora construya una identidad propia y generacional.
Esta identidad desdoblada que se negocia entre Couceyro y Carri, pone a Carri en el
lugar de la directora de cine que dirige y decide. Es decir, se niega –como lo constata
también Aguilar– a "presentarse exclusivamente en la pose de duelo y a entregarnos
un personaje trágico" ("*Los rubios*" 189). Lejos de eso, Carri se emancipa del papel de
la víctima paralizada a la que la dictadura militar le quitó padre y madre y se convierte
en el sujeto de su historia.

Además, el discurso identitario basado en la performatividad permite a Carri
emanciparse del discurso revolucionario de sus padres. La herencia revolucionaria del
padre sí está presente en el fragmento en el que Couceyro lee del libro del padre al
principio de la película. No obstante, es el equipo de filmación el que se convierte en
el grupo de referencia clave para Albertina Carri como lo demuestra la escena final en
la que todos –incluida la misma directora–, llevando pelucas rubias como indicadores
de esta nueva identidad construida sobre una memoria volátil, caminan hacia el horizonte campestre. Es decir, el grupo en el que se integra no es el de la familia ni el de
un grupo político militante, como podría ser el de H.I.J.O.S., lo que la convertiría básicamente en hija de desaparecidos (cf. también Nouzeilles 273). El grupo en el que se
integra –al que dirige–, por el contrario, es el del equipo de filmación; a éste no la
unen lazos de sangre ni tampoco un proyecto político, como en el caso de los Montoneros a los que pertenecían sus padres. Al contrario, su vínculo es el trabajo amistoso,

colectivo y dialógico en un proyecto fílmico que propone una nueva estética de la pos-memoria.

Esta comunidad en la que Carri se inserta comparte, en cierto modo, con los pa-dres de Carri la característica de "ser rubios." Los padres eran "rubios," o sea, diferen-tes, por una cuestión de clase social: pertenecer a la clase media y vivir en un barrio obrero. Carri y su equipo de filmación se convierten en "rubios" cuando vuelven a este mismo barrio como gente de cine, con sus cámaras, micrófonos y grabadoras de soni-dos (cf. también Sarlo 151). Carri y su equipo se convierten también en "rubios" y dis-tintos porque rechazan las formas preestablecidas de otras películas documentales so-bre la memoria al recurrir a la estética de la posmemoria y al cuestionar, así, las posibi-lidades de la memoria (cf. también Aguilar, *"Los rubios"* 180).

Esta estética de la posmemoria se manifiesta también en la opacidad de los me-dios que plantea el documental. Libros, fotos y cartas se resisten a entregar una imagen unívoca del pasado. Pasa lo mismo con los testimonios de los que fueron los compañe-ros de los padres de Carri. Están presentes, pero no se les concede la autoridad narrati-va que tienen en otros documentales. Por el contrario, Carri deja entrever un claro es-cepticismo frente a los testimonios y a la posibilidad de llegar, por su intermedio, a una imagen unívoca del pasado. Al hacer esto, la directora, inevitablemente, se enfren-ta a la generación de los que vivieron la época de los setenta como adultos jóvenes, re-presentados en *Los rubios*, por ejemplo, a través del comité de preclasificación del In-stituto Nacional de Cine Argentino. Por lo tanto, *Los rubios* puede considerarse como la emancipación de Albertina Carri de un discurso de la memoria que confía plena-mente en la posibilidad de los medios y, en primer lugar, en los testimonios para posi-bilitar un acceso directo al pasado. Como representante de la generación de la posme-moria, Carri implementa un concepto diferente de la memoria conduciendo, de esta forma, los debates acerca de la memoria, en Argentina, a un nivel reflexivo. De esta manera también enfrenta las limitaciones del género documental y cumple con el pos-tulado de veracidad en un grado mayor que eludiendo estas limitaciones.

Bibliografía

Academia Argentina de Letras. *Diccionario del habla de los argentinos*. Buenos Aires: Es-pasa, 2003.

Actis, Munú et al. *Ese infierno. Conversaciones de cinco mujeres sobrevivientes de la ESMA*. Buenos Aires: Sudamericana, 2001.

Aguilar, Gonzalo. *"Los rubios*. Duelo, frivolidad y melancolía." *Otros mundos. Un ensayo so-bre el nuevo cine argentino*. Gonzalo Aguilar. Buenos Aires: Santiago Arcos Editor, 2006. 175-91.

———. "Maravillosa melancolía. *Cazadores de utopías*: una lectura desde el presente." *Cines al margen. Nuevos modos de representación en el cine argentino contemporáneo*. Ed. María José Moore y Paula Wolkowicz. Buenos Aires: Libraria, 2007. 17-32.

Alonso, Mauricio. "*Los rubios.* Otra forma, otra mirada." *Imágenes de lo real. La representación de lo político en el documental argentino.* Ed. Josefina Sartora y Silvina Rival. Buenos Aires: Libraria, 2007. 157-69.

Amado, Ana. "Las nuevas generaciones y el documental como herramienta de historia." *Historia, género y política en los '70.* Ed. Andrea Andújar et al. Buenos Aires: Feminaria, 2005. 221-40.

———. "Órdenes de la memoria y desórdenes de la ficción." *Lazos de familia. Herencias, cuerpos, ficciones.* Ed. Ana Amado y Nora Domínguez. Buenos Aires: Paidós, 2004. 43-82.

Barthes, Roland. *La chambre claire. Note sur la photographie.* Paris: Gallimard, 1980.

Berger, Timo. "'Man wollte uns dämonisieren.' Ein Gespräch mit Mitgliedern der Piquetero-Organisation Frente Popular Darío Santillán." *Lateinamerika Nachrichten* 397/398 (Jul/Aug 2007). http://www.lateinamerikanachrichten.de/?/artikel/1172.html.

Braslavsky, Guido. "Una orden cargada de símbolos." *Clarín* 25 de marzo de 2004: 9.

Bruzzi, Stella. *New Documentary. A Critical Introduction.* London: Routledge, 2005.

Calveiro, Pilar. *Poder y desaparición. Los campos de concentración en Argentina.* Buenos Aires: Colihue, 1998.

Carri, Roberto. *Isidro Velázquez. Formas prerrevolucionarias de la violenc*ia. Buenos Aires: Colihue, 2001.

Curia, Walter. "Kirchner en la ESMA. En nombre del Estado, vengo a pedir perdón." *Clarín* 24 de marzo de 2004: 3.

Dandan, Alejandra. "Acto final para una marcha de 25 años." *Página 12* 27 de enero de 2006. http://www.pagina12.com.ar/imprimir/diario/elpais/1-62192-2006-01-27.html.

Diaz del Mora, Juan. *Historia de las agitaciones campesinas andaluzas – Córdoba: antecedentes para una reforma agraria.* Madrid: Revista de Derecho Privado, 1929.

Encuentro Memoria Verdad y Justicia. "Documento del 24 de marzo de 2008." http://www.30anios.org.ar/frameset.htm.

Gambini, Hugo. *El Ché Guevara.* Buenos Aires: Stockcero, 2002.

Garibotto, Verónica y Antonio Gómez. "Más allá del 'formato memoria.' La repostulación del imaginario postdictatorial en *Los rubios* de Albertina Carri." *Contra Corriente. Una Revista de Historia Social y Literatura de América Latina/ Contra Corriente. A Journal on Social History and Literature in Latin America* 3:2 (2006): 107-26.

Gillespie, Richard. *Soldiers of Perón. Argentina's Montoneros.* Oxford: Clarendon P, 1982.

Ginzberg, Victoria. "Diez años de H.I.J.O.S." *Página 12* 17 de abril de 2005. http://www.pagina12.com.ar/imprimir/diario/elpais/1-49866-2005-04-17.html.

Goytisolo, Juan. "Lo que no se dice de Sefarad." *El País* 21 de diciembre de 1999. http://sirio.deusto.es/abaitua/kanpetzu/primate/sefarad.htm.

Hirsch, Marianne. *Family Frames. Photography, Narrative, and Postmemory.* Cambridge: Harvard UP, 1997.

———. "Surviving Images. Holocaust Photographs and the Work of Postmemory." *Visual Culture and the Holocaust.* Ed. Barbie Zelizer. London: Athlone P, 2001. 215-46.

Jelin, Elizabeth. *Los trabajos de la memoria.* Madrid: Siglo XXI de España Editores, 2002.

———. "Siluetas." *Escrituras, imágenes y escenarios ante la represión.* Ed. Elizabeth Jelin y Ana Longoni. Buenos Aires: Siglo XXI, 2005. 69-77.

Kiener, Wilma. *Die Kunst des Erzählens. Narrativität in dokumentarischen und ethnographischen Filmen.* Konstanz: UVK Medien, 1999.

Kohán, Martín. "La apariencia celebrada." *Punto de Vista* 78 (2004): 24-30.

———. "Una crítica en general y una película en particular." *Punto de Vista* 80 (2004): 47-48.

Koselleck, Reinhart. *Vergangene Zukunft. Zur Semantik geschichtlicher Zeiten.* Frankfurt a.M.: Suhrkamp, 1989.

Leonidas Chaves, Gonzalo y Jorge Omar Lewinger. *Los del 73. Memoria Montonera.* La Plata: De la campana, 1998.

Mattini, Luis. *Hombres y mujeres del PRT-ERP (La pasión militante).* Buenos Aires: Ediciones Contrapunto, 1990.

Meyer, Adriana. "Una polémica sobra la continuidad de la Marcha de la Resistencia." *Página 12* 17 de enero de 2006. http://www.pagina12.com/diario/elpais/1-61782-2006-01-17.html.

Nichols, Bill. *Blurred Boundaries. Questions of Meaning in Contemporary Culture.* Bloomington: Indiana UP, 1994.

———. *Representing Reality. Issues and Concepts in Documentary.* Bloomington: Indiana UP, 1991.

Nouzeilles, Gabriela. "Postmemory Cinema and the Future of the Past." *Journal of Latin American Cultural Studies* 14.3 (2005): 263-78.

Oberti, Alejandra y Roberto Pittaluga. *Memorias en montaje. Escrituras de la militancia y pensamientos sobre la historia.* Buenos Aires: El Cielo por Asalto, 2006.

Pollastri, Sergio. *Las violetas del paraíso. Una historia montonera.* Buenos Aires: Ediciones El Cielo por Asalto, 2003.

Ramus, Susana Jorgelina. *Sueños sobrevivientes de una montonera. A pesar de la ESMA.* Buenos Aires: Colihue, 2000.

Renov, Michael. "Toward a Poetics of Documentary." *Theorizing Documentary.* Ed. Michael Renov. New York: Routledge, 1993. 12-36.

Sarlo, Beatriz. *Tiempo pasado. Cultura de la memoria y giro subjetivo, una discusión.* Buenos Aires: Siglo XXI Editores Argentina, 2005.

Shapiro, Ann-Louise. "How Real is the Reality in Documentary Film? Jill Godmilow in Conversation with Ann-Louise Shaprio." *History and Theory* 36.4 (1997): 80-101.

Sonderéguer, María. "El debate sobre el pasado reciente en Argentina. Entre la voluntad de recordar y la voluntad de olvidar." *Hispanoamérica* 87.29 (2000): 3-15.

Taylor, Diana. *The Archive and the Repertoire. Performing Cultural Memory in the Americas.* Durham/London: Duke UP, 2003.

354   Daniela Noll-Opitz

Valle, María Rosa y Graciela Destuet. "La visibilidad de la mujer en la creación de la política en los '70." *Historia, género y política en los '70*. Ed. Andrea Andújar et al. Buenos Aires: Feminaria, 2005. 407-32.

Verbitsky, Horacio. "Cuadros de situación." *Página 12* 21 de marzo de 2004: 6-7.

Vezzetti, Hugo. *Pasado y presente. Guerra, dictadura y sociedad en la Argentina*. Buenos Aires: Siglo XXI Editores Argentina, 2002.

Vogt, Jürgen. "Keine Spur von Julio López." *Lateinamerika Nachrichten* 390 (Dez 2006). http://www.lateinamerikanachrichten.de/?/artikel/1001.html.

Welzer, Harald. "Im Gedächtniswohnzimmer." *Die Zeit* 25 de marzo de 2004. http://zeus.zeit.de/text/2004/14/st-welzer.

Zapata, Hugo, Julieta Rozas y Diego Gasparini. "Entrevista a Albertina Carri, directora de *Los Rubios*." *Toma Uno. Magazine periodístico de cine*. http://www.toma-uno.ar/entrevistas/losrubios.htm.

Zibechi, Raúl. "Madres de la Plaza." *La Jornada* 11 de febrero de 2006. http://www.jornada.unam.mx/2006/02/11/index.php?section=politica&article=026a2pol.

Filmografía

Cazadores de utopías. Dir. David Blaustein. Argentina, 1996.

El tiempo y la sangre. Dir. Alejandra Almirón. Argentina, 2004.

En memoria de los pájaros. Dir. Gabriela Golder. Argentina, Francia, 2000.

Encontrando a Víctor. Dir. Natalia Bruschtein. Argentina, 2005.

Historias cotidianas. Dir. Andrés Habegger. Argentina, 2001.

In absentia. Dir. Lucía Cedrón. Argentina, 2002.

La matanza Dir. María Giuffra. Argentina, 2005.

Los rubios. Dir. Albertina Carri. Argentina, 2003.

M. Dir. Nicolás Prividera. Argentina, 2007.

Montoneros, una historia. Dir. Andrés Di Tella. Argentina, 1995.

Papa Iván. Dir. María Inés Roqué. Argentina, 2004.

Raymundo. Dir. Ernesto Ardito y Virna Molina. Argentina, 2002.

V.

BEYOND THE CANON:
REDISCOVERING DOCUMENTARY FILMS
AND FILMMAKERS

Las mujeres y el reportaje-documental en México (1920-1936)

PATRICIA TORRES SAN MARTÍN

Abstract

This essay seeks to raise awareness of the film work carried out by Adriana and Dolores Elhers as well as Elena Sanchez Valenzuela. These Mexican women were pioneers in the nation's documentary cinema at a time when this type of film, which had impacted Mexican society since the beginning of the twentieth century, had moved past its experimental stages. Their efforts and visionary work brought about innovations in documentary filmmaking and newsreels, in the use of technology, and in the creation of film archives.

Despite their important work these women have been all but forgotten. They do not occupy their just positions in the history of cinema because their films cannot be accessed. However, a variety of sources have made it possible to gain insight into their work. This project in film archeology thus aims to draw a more complete and complex picture of Mexican film history.

1. Introducción

En el presente texto me interesa rescatar el trabajo de las primeras mujeres mexicanas que incursionaron en la práctica cinematográfica del documental, cuando este oficio era apenas un terreno de experimentación, aunque ya se advertían sus influencias en la sociedad mexicana de principios del siglo XX.[1] Me importa destacar los aspectos que tienen que ver con dos contextos históricos que marcaron un antecedente importante para la historia de nuestro país: el México revolucionario que encontró en el cine el mejor de sus aliados para internacionalizar uno de los capítulos históricos más álgidos en nuestro país, la Revolución Mexicana (1910-1920)[2], y el México cardenista (1934-1940)[3] gobierno que significó para nuestro país una puerta de entrada al "socialismo."

---

[1] En esta época del cine silente, hubo otras realizadoras mexicanas en el terreno de la ficción que tuvieron una destacada participación: María Herminia Pérez de León, mejor conocida como "Mimi Derba" y Cándida Beltrán Rendón (cf. Miquel; Torres, "Mujeres").

[2] Se conoce con el nombre de Revolución Mexicana la etapa histórica de México de 1910 a 1920, período muy complejo debido a la intervención de diferentes jefes militares y políti-

Las hermanas Elhers filmando (fuente: Sánchez-García)

En este contexto se desarrolló el trabajo de las hermanas veracruzanas Adriana (1894-1972) y Dolores Elhers (1896-1983)[4] como pioneras en todos los territorios de la incipiente cinematografía: se formaron en el oficio; filmaron documentales; procesaron películas; vendieron aparatos de proyección; trabajaron para la primera oficina de censura que hubo en nuestro país, y participaron de forma activa en la política cinematográfica de la Revolución Mexicana.

En este mismo ámbito se encuentra Elena Sánchez Valenzuela (1900-1950), distinguido personaje que, como las hermanas Elhers, intervino en la política cultural mexicana bajo la presidencia de Lázaro Cárdenas. Se destacó como protagonista de la película muda *Santa* (1918), primera versión de la novela homónima de Federico Gamboa, dirigida por el periodista Luis G. Peredo[5], asimismo fue cronista cinemato-

---

cos. Dicho movimiento se desató a causa de las repetidas reelecciones del general Porfirio Díaz y del malestar económico derivado de las condiciones del campesino, así como también de los conflictos obreros surgidos en los últimos años de su gobierno.

[3] Este período político de México lleva el nombre de "cardenismo" por el apellido del Presidente General de la República, Lázaro Cárdenas (1896-1970), quien se caracterizó desde muy joven por su compromiso con la causa constitucionalista y con la lucha de los rebeldes, lo cual le significó el cargo de Gobernador interino de su estado natal, Michoacán, a los 25 años. Desde su cargo como Gobernador desarrolló una impresionante labor en pro de la educación; democratizó la universidad, fundó escuelas rurales y repartió tierras entre los campesinos. En 1929, fue nombrado presidente del entonces Partido Revolucionario Nacional, hoy PRI.

[4] El *Diccionario de directores del cine mexicano* da 1903 como fecha de nacimiento de Dolores Elhers. Sin embargo, aquí seguimos a Sánchez-García quien indica que Dolores Elhers nació en 1896.

[5] *Santa* ha sido llevada a la pantalla en cuatro ocasiones. La primera versión muda (Luis Peredo, 1918) donde actúa Elena Sánchez Valenzuela. La segunda versión de Antonio Moreno (1931), actor de origen español, quien dirigió a Lupita Tovar. La tercera es de Norman Foster (1943), teniendo como protagonista a Esther Fernández. Finalmente Emilio

gráfica y, en 1942, fundó la primera filmoteca de Latinoamérica. En 1936, el presiden-te Cárdenas le encargó la dirección del proyecto "Brigadas Cinematográficas," con-virtiéndose ella así en una de las pioneras del documental sonoro en México.

Estas voluntades creativas femeninas han quedado sumergidas en el olvido y en la invisibilidad. La historia no ha podido hacerles justicia, debido a la pérdida, destruc-ción o la conservación parcial tanto de sus obras cinematográficas como de fuentes documentales e impresas, aunque ya existen avances que nos plantean esta tarea his-toriográfica como una empresa de arqueología fílmica.[6]

2. El documental, un encuentro con la historia

En México, desde los albores del cine mudo, el registro de la realidad a través de la cámara fue una práctica desarrollada con entusiasmo y mucho fervor propagandístico; gracias a ello, la Revolución Mexicana quedó registrada y documentada en los trabaja-dos de Salvador Toscano (1872-1947) y Jesús H. Abitia (1881-1960), por mencionar a los más importantes. De lo que tuvo que haber sido un extraordinario testimonio fílmico lo único que se conserva en la actualidad son materiales incluidos en otras películas, tales como: *Memorias de un mexicano* (Carmen Toscano de Moreno, 1950) y *Epopeyas de la revolución* (Gustavo Carrero, 1961).

Vale destacar que, desde las primeras imágenes fílmicas que captaron la realidad mexicana, estuvieron presentes los hermanos Carlos, Eduardo, Salvador y Guillermo Alva quienes documentaron esa época a través de un nutrido registro fílmico (1905-1915) que logró captar el ambiente político urbano, que para la primera década del sig-lo pasado, ya era un detonante sociocultural importante.[7]

Las imágenes de ese momento histórico, vertidas en "vistas fílmicas," llevaron a determinar la función social del cine, en un tiempo en el que apenas se estaba transi-tando de la invención científico-artística al espectáculo masivo de entretenimiento.

Gómez Muriel (1968) dirige a Julissa en la última película basada en esta novela. En una versión libre de la novela de Gamboa, María Novaro dirigió un breve homenaje a *Santa* en un episodio de *Enredando sombras* (1997), serie coordinada por el documentalista cubano Julio García Espinoza.

[6] Tanto los materiales filmados por las hermanas Elhers, como los documentales del proyec-to "Brigadas Cinematográficas," coordinado por Elena Sánchez, pasaron de la Secretaría de Gobernación al Archivo General de la Nación y de ahí a la Cineteca Nacional en donde muchos de sus trabajos fueron destruidos por un incendio en 1982.

[7] Los hermanos Alva son reconocidos como los documentalistas más importantes de la pri-mera época del cine mudo mexicano: en 1905 se inician como exhibidores, en 1906 se ha-cen empresarios de la Sala Academia Metropolitana, y entre 1906 y 1914 registran una larga serie de filmes entre los que destacan: *Fiestas del centenario de la Independencia* (1910), *Insurrección en México* (1911), *Viaje del señor Madero de ciudad Juárez a la ciudad de México* (1911), *Entrevista Díaz-Traft* (1909), *Revolución orozquista* (1912) (cf. Ciuk).

En este marco, las hermanas Adriana y Dolores Elhers, huérfanas de padre, tuvieron la difícil tarea de enfrentar una sociedad donde las mujeres profesionales eran pocas; sin embargo, su ambiente familiar de mujeres solas, y su trabajo compartido para lograr mantenerse sembraron en ellas una mentalidad liberal y antiporfiriana que las llevó a apoyar, primero, a Francisco Ignacio Madero y, luego, a Venustiano Carranza.

El encuentro con este último, el primer Jefe Constitucionalista[8] –cuando fue a Veracruz y ellas fueron llamadas a fotografiarlo–, les abrió las puertas de un mundo casi vedado para las mujeres, ya que el político les agradeció su trabajo otorgándoles una beca para estudiar fotografía en Boston, Massachussets. De este modo, en 1916, se integraron en los estudios Champlain para aprender la técnica fotográfica, a la vez que, por las noches, asistían a una escuela de arte para maestros. Al terminar el año, Carranza les concedió una prórroga para estudiar cinematografía y se incorporaron al Army Medical Museum en Washington D.C., en donde el gobierno estadounidense había concentrado recursos para hacer películas que orientaran, en asuntos de salud, a los soldados que luchaban en la Primera Guerra Mundial. Las hermanas aprendieron entonces, bajo estricta disciplina militar, a filmar, revelar, procesar, copiar y titular películas. Posteriormente se fueron a vivir a Nueva York, completando allí su formación con las técnicas para hacer filmes artísticos en la Universal Pictures Company, en Jacksville, New Jersey.

A su regreso a México, en 1919, instalaron en los bajos de su casa un negocio en el que vendían aparatos de proyección e, igualmente, enseñaban su utilización. Al mismo tiempo, el gobierno de Carranza les asignó funciones en la Secretaría de Gobernación: Adriana, como Jefa del Departamento de Censura, y, Dolores, como Jefa del Departamento Cinematográfico. Allí tenían a disposición un laboratorio en el que revelaban las películas de carácter documental que filmaban. Tal medida provocó una ola de recriminaciones en su contra; se les acusó "de ejercer su cargo sin ninguna preparación artística" y sus cintas fueron descalificadas por no tener "un ápice del sentimiento artístico de la vida" (cf. Sánchez-García).

El Departamento de Censura había sido creado con la intención de filtrar los mensajes denigrantes que eran lugar común en las películas estadounidenses y que V. Carranza consideraba negativos para México, además se cortaban las escenas supuestamente ofensivas para la moral pública. La Secretaría de Gobernación, a través de este Departamento, ejercía una doble censura, primero sobre el libreto y luego sobre la película. La Iglesia, por su parte, atendía los mensajes morales calificando las películas de "lícitas" o "ilícitas."

En el laboratorio las hermanas Elhers procesaban las películas que ellas mismas realizaban y con las que se pretendía contrarrestar la imagen de México como un país

---

[8] Venustiano Carranza (1859-1920) fue el Primer Jefe del Ejército Constitucionalista (1917), defensor de la Constitución de 1857. Su carrera política se inició cuando el presidente Francisco I. Madero lo designó miembro de su gabinete como Ministro de Guerra y Marina. A la muerte de Madero formuló en 1913 el "Plan de Guadalupe" en el que desconocía a Victoriano Huerta y a los poderes legislativo y judicial.

atrasado. Rodaron desfiles, manifestaciones y lugares de interés cultural, tales como las grutas de Cacahuamilpa, las ruinas de Teotihuacán y el Museo Nacional de Arqueología, Historia y Etnografía, además de un largo documental acerca del tratamiento de agua potable, filmación que les llevó meses y que las colocó en situaciones peligrosas. Igualmente exhibían sus materiales fílmicos en escuelas, fábricas, dependencias del gobierno e instituciones de beneficencia.

El hecho de ser mujeres fue un argumento constante en contra de ellas, se movían en un ambiente exclusivo de varones, por esta razón llevaban pantalones para poder realizar las tareas asignadas. En 1920, al morir V. Carranza, su gran protector, y con el ascenso de Álvaro Obregón a la presidencia de la República, Adriana y Dolores fueron alejadas de sus cargos. Durante un tiempo, Adriana pudo filmar y procesar películas en un pequeño laboratorio casero que habían instalado, como la que hizo sobre el petróleo para la International Petroleum Company, que se exhibió en 1922 en los Estados Unidos de América. Entre 1922 y 1931 realizaron unos noticieros semanales que llamaron *Revistas Elhers*, donde mostraban los acontecimientos del momento –catástrofes, desfiles, manifestaciones etc.– y que vendían directamente a los exhibidores. Por algunos años más continuaron con la "Casa Elhers" ofreciendo aparatos de proyección y sus repuestos. Dolores abandonó el trabajo de filmación debido a una grave enfermedad, mientras que Adriana seguiría activa hasta su muerte en 1972 (cf. Martínez de Velasco).

Adriana y Dolores Elhers murieron sin pena ni gloria, y a la fecha no ha sido posible rescatar ninguno de sus materiales fílmicos, ni tampoco se ha realizado una acuciosa investigación documental que nos dé fe de la exhibición y recepción que sus documentales tuvieron en nuestro país.

El caso de Elena Sánchez Valenzuela debe entenderse como uno de los más destacados del cine nacional durante la época de transición del cine mudo al sonoro. Durante la incipiente época del cine mudo mexicano trabajó como actriz en dos películas que sentaron precedentes: *Santa* –que ya he mencionado– y *En la hacienda* (1921) de Ernesto Vollrath.[9] La historiografía del cine mexicano también nos informa que Elena estaba encargada de la crónica de cine en *El Día* durante los años treinta. A la fecha he podido constatar que su iniciación en el periodismo cinematográfico fue a partir de 1920 en el diario *El Demócrata*; en 1921, fue corresponsal de este mismo diario en Los Angeles, a su regreso a México, en 1922, colaboró para *El Universal Gráfico* en la columna "El cine y sus artistas;" un año después estableció la reseña de cine diaria y, en 1929, fue nombrada corresponsal en París donde permaneció por cuatro años.

Instaurada la industria cinematográfica mexicana, Elena tuvo una participación afortunada; en 1942 fundó la primera Filmoteca Nacional, entonces ubicada en la Secretaría de Educación Pública. Esta última labor la llevó a convertirse, no solamente

---

[9]   Ambas películas marcaron el nacimiento de dos géneros cinematográficos que proliferaron por varias décadas en el cine nacional: el melodrama prostibulario y el melodrama ranchero.

en la precursora de la conservación del material fílmico mexicano, sino también la hizo responsable de la promoción de este proyecto en toda Latinoamérica. La presencia de Elena Sánchez en varios países de América Latina –Argentina, Uruguay, Ecuador, Guatemala y Perú–, dejó un vivo testimonio de su capacidad de convocatoria. Dio charlas y conferencias sobre la importancia de establecer una red de filmotecas en América Latina en el marco de dos importantes eventos: el primer Congreso Interamericano de Mujeres en Guatemala (1947) y el Primer Festival de Cine Argentino (1948).

De hecho, esta participación fue una difícil incursión en un terreno hasta entonces descuidado, y que, por cierto, tampoco ha merecido reconocimiento alguno de parte de las autoridades encargadas de la cinematografía; de ese modo su trayectoria apenas se conoce y, en particular, otros capítulos importantes de su paso por el cine eran desconocidos hasta 1992, cuando encontré en referencias hemerográficas –proporcionadas por su hermano David Valenzuela– que Elena, en 1936, había empezado a incursionar en el género documental.

Sánchez Valenzuela trabajó como documentalista en un proyecto denominado "Brigadas Cinematográficas" propulsado por el propio presidente Cárdenas y auspiciado también por el Ala Izquierda del Bloque Nacional Revolucionario de la Cámara de Diputados, dirigida entonces por Luis Mora Tovar[10], quien, además de político, era poeta y ensayista.

Las referencias localizadas nos hablan de una película titulada *Michoacán*, que ella misma dirigió y fotografió a decir de la nota siguiente:

> He aquí una serie de bellísimas viñetas entresacadas del Cine-reportazgo que acaba de hacer Elena Sánchez Valenzuela en el Estado de Michoacán. Se trata de una película documental de interés indiscutible y de gran valor artístico e histórico. Elena, la primera mujer en la América Latina que concibe, planea y ejecuta una película, logró captar con una formidable intuición artística y un absoluto sentido periodístico centenares de escenas a cual más bellas y sugerentes –escenas que están hablando– que exponen a maravilla detalles desconocidos de la vida de los campesinos de Michoacán; gente humilde, limpia, sana y laboriosa, que rebosa optimismo, como si se sintiera contagiada por la exuberancia de su tierra natal, llena de prodigios de belleza.
>
> "Michoacán" se llama este primer Cine-reportazgo de Elena Sánchez Valenzuela, del cual publicamos aquí algunas escenas.[11]

---

[10] Mora Tovar, importante escritor y político –diputado y senador de la república–, que se distinguió entre otras cosas por haber sido el fundador de la Procuraduría de Pueblos en la República. Fue un político combativo lo que en tiempos del Movimiento Armado revolucionario lo condujo siete veces al encarcelamiento. Autor de varios libros: *La caída del símbolo y otros poemas* (1931), *Prosas para la bien amada* (1929), *La revolución y el magisterio* (1932), *Los motivos de Judas* (s.f.).

[11] A la fecha no se ha podido corroborar fuente y fecha de esta nota periodística proporcionada por el señor David Valenzuela, ni tampoco esta película.

Viñetas de *Michoacán* (1936) de Elena Sánchez Valenzuela

Las fotografías que ilustran la nota anterior guardan en su composición una similitud con los encuadres logrados por el fotógrafo neoyorkino Paul Strand en la cinta *Redes* (1934) de Fred Zinnemann y Emilio Gómez Muriel[12]: escenarios del Lago de Pátzcuaro y sus pescadores, rostros populares de los pescadores y campesinos, símbolos bellos y vigorosos.

Estaba previsto hacer estos documentales en toda la República y difundirlos a nivel nacional e internacional. Su propósito no era solamente la propaganda turística, sino, de la misma manera, dar a conocer los logros del régimen cardenista. En la parte musical participaron el maestro Miguel Lerdo de Tejada y un técnico alemán de apellido Blum, cuyo cargo específico ha sido imposible localizar.

En un contrato firmado por la propia Elena Sánchez Valenzuela y el señor Manuel Espinoza Tagle queda sentado que el documental *Michoacán* tenía un metraje de 4.000 a 5.000 pies, lo cual significa que este trabajo filmado en 35 mm o en 16 mm era un largometraje, también se especificaba que las copias de este documental no podrían ser explotadas comercialmente.

Investigaciones actuales me llevaron a encontrar en una serie de películas no identificadas en la Filmoteca de la Universidad Nacional Autónoma de México (UNAM), las copias en vídeo de varios documentales que, por sus títulos y las imágenes de la época, coincidirían con el de *Michoacán*. Esto permitiría suponer que eran parte de ese paquete de documentales de las "Brigadas Cinematográficas."

Los documentales localizados se titulan Veracruz, el paraíso del trópico; Puebla, el relicario colonial de América; Así es Oaxaca, semilla de una raza; Acapulco, paraíso de América; Así es Morelos, ciudad de virreyes y Así es Campeche. Estos filmes fueron producidos por Antonio Fuentes, fotografiados por Max Lizt, Moisés Cervantes y Ezequiel Carrasco[13] y narrados por Carlos V. Salazar. Sin embargo, no aparece ningún otro crédito, como sería el de director, o directora para el caso que nos ocupa, o bien, coordinador. De todos modos, podemos asegurar que corresponden a la década de finales de los años treinta por las imágenes y el estilo que guardan todos en su conjunto.

Ciertamente son trabajos documentales de carácter promocional y turístico, ya que lo que muestran son recorridos por los principales sitios de las ciudades seleccionadas, y sin lugar a dudas, llevaban el propósito de destacar la política socialista del General Lázaro Cárdenas. En todos ellos se resaltan los sitios arquitectónicos y arqueológicos más importantes, como el Convento de Santo Domingo, las ruinas de Mitla y Monte Albán para el de Oaxaca, o bien, el Palacio de Cortés y el templo de Nuestra Señora del Carmen, para el del Estado de Morelos, y así para los demás. Hay dos aspectos que llaman la atención y que atestiguan la presencia de una consigna

---

[12] Primer largometraje mexicano que recibió el apoyo estatal de la Secretaría de Educación Pública. Es una película de gran contenido social sobre la lucha de un grupo de pescadores en contra de sus explotadores.

[13] En el caso de Ezequiel Carrasco, se sabe que tuvo una importante participación como fotógrafo durante la época del cine silente, lo mismo que Max Lizt. Sobre el trabajo de Moisés Cervantes no se tienen referencias.

nacionalista; por un lado, vemos imágenes de mujeres nativas, mixtecas y chapanecas engalanadas con sus mejores trajes típicos y, por el otro, se aprecia la utilización, en términos de narrativa, de un recurso muy novedoso para ese tiempo: las inserciones escénicas que complementan el tema. Por ejemplo, en el documental referido al puerto más turístico de México, Acapulco, vemos este recurso referido a un capítulo histórico acaecido en 1683 –mejor conocido como la "Nao de la China"– y que remite a la llegada de naves mercantiles españolas que además de mercancías, transportaban migrantes, y entre éstos venía una china.[14]

Igualmente se filmaron imágenes frecuentes de obreros en sus faenas, o bien, hay alusiones muy significativas al trabajo político de los gobernantes de turno. El tono del narrador cumple las funciones de recurso informativo y la música era el perfecto elemento de acompañamiento que reforzaba los noticieros de la época.

Sin embargo, no hay fuentes que corroboren el año de producción, ni tampoco he ubicado ningún dato hemerográfico que testimonie dónde se exhibían estos documentales. Estas informaciones ausentes no me permiten asegurar la posible existencia de un vínculo directo con el documental *Michoacán*, pero existe la certeza de que pretendía ser un material de comercialización. Solamente puedo asegurar que, por las viñetas que se publicaron sobre este documental en la nota periodística antes mencionada, hay una coincidencia en el tipo de imágenes sociales que quería ser difundido. El problema más serio de esta investigación es que todo este material se mantenía en la Filmoteca que la propia Sánchez Valenzuela había fundado y que se encontraba en la Secretaría de Educación Pública. Más tarde todos los materiales fílmicos pasaron a formar parte de la Cineteca Nacional, la que después del terrible incendio de 1982, dejó a México sin memoria visual.[15] Iniciativas oficiales, colectivas e incluso de productores independientes han permitido que a lo largo de estas dos décadas se hayan ido localizando materiales nacionales en otros lotes fílmicos, sin embargo, para el caso de los documentales de este proyecto coordinado por Sánchez Valenzuela todavía no se ha podido rescatar el total de los trabajos de esta empresa cardenista.

3. A manera de conclusión

El cine mexicano de esa época se caracterizaba por los arrebatos históricos, revolucionarios y posrevolucionarios de los años veinte y treinta, los temas de seducción y abandono, castidad y pecado y los ambientes rurales y campiranos, como fantasías nacionalistas. En este contexto, el surgimiento de una corriente documentalista repre-

---

[14] De este capítulo histórico derivó la leyenda sobre la tan nombrada "China poblana."

[15] Durante el período presidencial de José López Portillo (1976-1982), su hermana Margarita estaba a cargo de la dirección de la Cineteca Nacional, que en ese momento dependía directamente de la Secretaría de Gobernación. El incendio se originó en las bóvedas donde se encontraban los materiales. Fue resultado de un absoluto acto de negligencia de la funcionaria, quien contando con el presupuesto designado para las instalaciones de un equipo de protección y conservación idóneas, no cumplió con su deber.

sentó, sin duda, un acontecimiento curioso, pero digno de ser considerado como el principio de una identidad cinematográfica que, a lo largo de muchos años, ha estado luchando por imponerse en el ámbito fílmico nacional. Actualmente el género documental ha conseguido un lugar en la cinematografía mexicana y ya no es necesario debatir sobre si es un género cinematográfico establecido, o, solamente, es un territorio de exploración. De la misma manera, tampoco es preciso considerar el trabajo de las documentalistas como una práctica marginal dentro de la marginalidad en la que por tanto tiempo se ubicó al documental mismo.

El caso de estas mujeres documentalistas y adelantadas a su momento histórico, puede parecernos aislado, no obstante encuentro más de una coincidencia que nos habla de la urgente necesidad de seguir investigando la otra historia del cine nacional que está por escribirse y reconstruirse. Lo que hicieron las hermanas Elhers fue mostrar otra imagen del México posrevolucionario y devastado, o bien el México rural costumbrista, que, por supuesto, no era el entorno real ni social ni cultural de esos años. En otro sentido, estas iniciativas inauguraron un género por lo demás popular hasta los años ochenta: el "noticiero fílmico" que ya en la década de los cuarenta gozaba de gran éxito.

Por su parte, Elena Sánchez Valenzuela, como documentalista y fundadora de la primera Filmoteca de Latinoamérica, impulsó una labor que hasta la actualidad todavía no es reconocida en su justa dimensión histórico-social.

Ahora bien, también llama la atención que ambas empresas femeninas fueran promovidas por jefes políticos importantes, y que ello, sin lugar a dudas, significó un parteaguas para los posteriores trabajos que fueron apoyados por las instituciones oficiales; a la vez, se puede entender mejor el impulso nacionalista que prevaleció en este campo de la cinematografía. Empero, quedan muchas vetas de análisis sobre el trabajo de estas figuras precursoras, sobre todo, a causa de la ausencia de los materiales fílmicos, lo cual no permite hacer ningún tipo de análisis estético, o incluso comparativo con el resto de los documentales de esas décadas.

Esta situación apremiante nos habla también que todavía hay mucho que investigar en este terreno, y muestra de ello es que todavía seguimos encontrando trabajos inéditos o atesorados en stocks fílmicos, gracias a los cuales podremos seguir reconstruyendo la historia del documental mexicano.[16] No obstante, el camino que estas mujeres abrieron a las generaciones futuras, es digno de escribirse con mayúsculas.

Respecto de las brechas generacionales que se dan entre el trabajo de estas pioneras, y las cineastas, que en los años setenta se decidieron por el documental, no ya como un terreno de exploración personal y social, sino de denuncia política, pienso que hay coyunturas de orden cultural y político que marcaron un momento histórico importante. Así, podemos nombrar la incorporación formal de la mujer mexicana a la República al conseguir el derecho a voto en 1953, los movimientos feministas de los

---

[16] Un ejemplo muy reciente son los materiales fílmicos de la Revolución que el documentalista Gregorio Rocha encontró en el acervo privado de la familia Padilla, y que ahora se encuentran restaurados y editados en el filme *Los rollos perdidos de Pancho Villa* (2003).

sesenta y la celebración del Año Internacional de la Mujer en México, en 1975, de donde se derivaron reacciones e iniciativas que impulsaron y recuperaron propuestas feministas, más con un fervor personal y subjetivo, pero que a la fecha suscriben un trabajo insólito en la historia del documental en México.

Bibliografía

Ayala Blanco, Jorge. *La Aventura del Cine Mexicano (1931-1967)*. México, D.F.: Ed. Posada, 1984.

Ciuk, Perla, ed. *Diccionario de directores del cine mexicano*. México, D.F.: Ed. Consejo Nacional para la Cultura y las Artes (CNCA), 2000.

Dávalos Orozco, Federico. *Albores del cine mexicano*. México, D.F.: Clío, 1996.

———— y Esperanza Vázquez Bernal. *Filmografía general del cine mexicano (1906-1931)*. Puebla: Benemérita Universidad Autónoma de Puebla (BUAP), 1985.

García Riera, Emilio. *Historia documental del cine mexicano*. Tomo 1. Guadalajara: Universidad de Guadalajara, 1992.

————. *México visto por el cine extranjero (1894–1940)*. Tomo 1. Guadalajara: Eds. Era, Universidad de Guadalajara, Centro de Investigaciones y Enseñanza Cinematográficas, 1987.

González Casanova, Manuel, ed. *El cine y la Revolución Mexicana*. México, D.F.: Ed. Filmoteca de la UNAM, 1979.

Martínez de Velasco, Patricia. *Directoras de cine: Proyección de un mundo oscuro*. México, D.F.: Ed. IMCINE y CONEICC, 1991.

Meyer, Eugenia. "Dolores Ehlers." *Cuadernos de la Cineteca Nacional* 9 (1979).

Miquel, Angel. *Mimi Derba*. Colección Cine de Mujeres en México. Guadalajara: Archivos Agrasánchez y Universidad de Guadalajara, 2002.

Mora Tovar, Luis. *La caída del símbolo y otros poemas*. Morelia: Ed. Mora Tovar, 1931.

————. *La revolución y el magisterio*. Morelia: Ed. Mora Tovar, 1932.

————. *Los motivos de Judas*. s.l., s.f.

————. *Prosas para la bienamada*. Morelia: Eds. Nezahualcóyotl, 1929.

Rashkin J., Elissa. *Women Filmmakers in Mexico. The Country of Which We Dream*. Austin: U of Texas P, 2001.

Reyes, Aurelio de los. *Filmografía del cine mudo mexicano: 1924-1931*. México, D.F.: Universidad Nacional Autónoma de México (UNAM), Dirección General de Actividades Cinematográficas, 2000.

Sánchez-García, José Manuel. Sin título. *Novedades* [Ciudad de México] 25 de febrero de 1945: n-c.

Torres, Patricia. *Adela Sequeyro*. Colección Cine de Mujeres en México I. Guadalajara: Ed. Archivos Agrasánchez/Universidad de Guadalajara, 1997.

————. "Elena Sánchez Valenzuela." *DICINE* 47 (1992): 14-16.

————. "Las mujeres del celuloide en México." *Acordeón* 17 (1996): 68-76.

————. "Mujeres detrás de cámara. Una historia de conquistas y victorias en el cine latinoamericano." *Revista Nueva Sociedad* 218 (2008): 25-38.

————. "Scènes et spaces feminins: quelques cinéastes latinoamericaines." *ALEPH* (2001): 87-101.

Tuñón, Julia. "Cuerpo y amor en el cine mexicano de la Edad de Oro. Los besos subversivos de la Diosa Arrodillada." *Cuidado con en el corazón. Los usos amorosos en el México moderno.* Ed. José Joaquín Blanco. México: Instituto Nacional de Antropología e Historia, 1999. 103-142.

Filmografía

Acapulco, paraíso de América. Dir. desconocido. México, s.a.

Así es Campeche. Dir. desconocido. México, s.a.

Así es Morelos, ciudad de virreyes. Dir. desconocido. México, s.a.

Así es Oaxaca, semilla de una raza. Dir. desconocido. México, s.a.

En la hacienda. Dir. Ernesto Vollrath. México, 1921.

Enredando sombras (Serie de documentales). Coord. Julio García. Cuba, México, 1998.

Entrevista Díaz-Traft. Dir. Salvador, Guillermo, Eduardo y Carlos Alva. México, 1909.

Epopeyas de la revolución. Dir. Gustavo Carrero. México, 1961.

Fiestas del centenario de la Independencia. Dir. Salvador, Guillermo, Eduardo y Carlos Alva. México, 1910.

Insurrección en México. Dir. Salvador, Guillermo, Eduardo y Carlos Alva. México, 1911.

Los rollos perdidos de Pancho Villa. Dir. Gregorio Rocha. México, Canadá, Estados Unidos, 2003.

Memorias de un mexicano. Dir. Carmen Toscano de Moreno y Salvador Toscano. México, 1950.

Michoacán. Dir. Elena Sánchez Valenzuela. México, 1936.

Puebla, el relicario colonial de América. Dir. desconocido. México, s.a.

Redes. Dir. Emilio Gómez Muriel y Fred Zinnemann. México, 1934.

Revista Elhers. Dir. Adriana Elhers y Dolores Elhers. México, 1922.

Revolución orozquista. Dir. Salvador, Guillermo, Eduardo y Carlos Alva. México, 1912.

Santa. Dir. Luis Peredo. México, 1918.

Santa. Dir. Antonio Moreno. México, 1931.

Santa. Dir. Norman Foster. México, 1943.

Santa. Dir. Emilio Gómez Muriel. México, 1968.

Veracruz, el paraíso del trópico. Dir. desconocido. México, s.a.

Viaje del señor Madero de ciudad Juárez a la ciudad de México. Dir. Salvador, Guillermo, Eduardo y Carlos Alva. México, 1911.

Mining and the Dignity and Indignities of Work: From *Salt of the Earth* to Hector Galán's *Los Mineros*

GARY FRANCISCO KELLER

Resumen

Un análisis histórico del tema de la explotación minera de su principio con la llegada de los conquistadores en América y de su representación en películas americanas, mexicanas, y chicanas a partir de 1954 a 1991. El énfasis está en *Salt of the Earth* (Herbert J. Biberman, 1954), *Cananea* (Marcela Fernández Violante, 1978) y *Los mineros* (Hector Galán, 1991). Estas películas se analizan en el contexto de un grupo de películas internacionales conocidas que se desarrollan en ambientes de la explotación minera o que se dedican a la dignidad y los derechos de los trabajadores, incluyendo: adaptaciones de la novela *Germinal* de Émile Zola (de 1913 hasta 1993), *Strike* (1925) y *Battleship Potemkin* (1925) de Sergei Eisenstein, *Kameradschaft* (1931) de G.W. Pabst, *Black Fury* (1935) de Michael Curtiz, *The Stars Look Down* (1940) de Carol Reed, *How Green Was My Valley* (1941) y *The Grapes of Wrath* (1940) de John Ford, *Sól Ziemi Czarnej* (1970) de Kazimierz Kutz [vesión inglesa, *Salt of the Black Earth*], *The Molly Maguires* (1970) de Martin Ritt, *Harlan County, USA* (1976) de Barbara Kopple, y *Matewan* (1987) de John Sayles.

Affiliated Web Site

This paper uses numerous full-color or black and white images—together with relevant information about this visual material—that are available for the long term at the affiliated Web site, http://www.asu.edu/clas/hrc/Keller. In addition, on this same Web site appears a suggestive list of films, worldwide, that develop the theme of dignity and exploitation in the mines or fields, going from Sergei Eisenstein's *Strike* (1925) through Sergio Arau's *A Day Without a Mexican* [*Dia sin Mexicanos*] (2004).

*   *   *

The setting of the mine has been deeply significant in both Mexican and Mexican American/Chicano history, culture, and political activism, and as such it has always received a great deal of attention in literature, and ultimately, film. It also is a primary setting for literature and films of social justice around the world. This paper examines three such films of the Latina/o world and it also provides brief descriptions of the canon among films world wide through an attached inventory (at http://www.asu.edu/clas/hrc/Keller).

Silver and gold, much of it mined in Mexico, were the main source of Spain's wealth and power during its empire days of the late 16th through late 18th century. Precious metals represented 84% of all exports from New Spain (now Mexico) to the *madre patria*. Most of the colonial-era cities of New Spain were known for their rich silver mines. But mining activities spurred profoundly oppressive practices during the conquest and colonial periods of Mexico, although not as oppressive as slavery in the colonies of America and in other places around the world. It is therefore no surprise that the mining district was the cradle of Mexican independence.

The issue of the exploitation of labor in the mines and fields in Hispanic America begins with the Spanish conquest of the great Amerindian civilizations—Aztec, Mayan, Incan, and others—and the subsequent coercing of native peoples into labor forces through such legal instruments as the *encomienda* system and its successor, the *repartimiento de labor*. Neither system was slavery in that the worker was not owned outright—being free in various respects other than in the dispensation of his or her labor—and the work was intermittent. However, these systems often created slavery-like conditions in the mines. The *encomienda* has been interpreted by historians variously as a subterfuge for slavery at one extreme, and, at the other, as the equivalent of a draft, such as for a military obligation.

As we know, the Spanish conquistadors came to the Americas partly in search of material wealth, especially gold and silver. This became almost immediately apparent to the Amerindians, who, when they captured a European, sometimes gave him what he desired in the form of a molten ingestion. Theodor de Bry, in around 1590, produced some bracing engravings on the subject of Conquistador atrocities and Amerindian retaliation. (See Section A of http://www.asu.edu/clas/hrc/Keller for several images about conquistador atrocities and Amerindian retaliation related to mining.)

Feeding conquistadors molten gold became something of a trope during the conquest and colonial period. For example, subtribes of the Jíbaro (also written Xébaro and Zíbaro) people of Ecuador, who successfully withstood the efforts of the Peruvian Incas to subjugate them, were placed under enforced labor in the mines beginning in 1541. They rebelled under the leadership of Anirula in 1599 and with a force estimated at 20,000 warriors stormed Logroño, killing every inhabitant of the 12,000, excepting the young women who were carried off. According to contemporary accounts, the governor was done in by pouring molten gold down his throat "in order that he might have his fill of gold."

The most famous instance of molten retaliation refers to Pedro de Valdivia, the conquistador of what is now Chile. During the uprising of 1553, Valdivia was captured and put to death by indigenous peoples. Among the many legends surrounding his death the most prominent was that Valdivia was tied to a stake with his mouth forced open while a high priest poured molten gold down his throat in order to "finally quench the Conquistador's endless hunger for gold."

One of the supplementary objectives of this paper is to provide some orientation to films world wide on the topic at hand. While we do not have the space to review the films related to Amerindian-European encounters which sometimes resulted in the exploitation of labor,[1] I do need to observe that non-Hollywood Chicano films as well as Mexican, Chilean, Bolivian, and other Latin American films, no matter what time period they treat, are clearly informed about and typically sub-contextualize issues of exploitation of Amerindian labor by their European masters in the mines and the fields of Latin America over centuries.

The mining regions of central Mexico are often referred to as the nation's "cradle of independence." Nowhere was the independence conflict between colonial New Spain and mother Spain more heightened than in this geographic area. The father of the 1810 War of Mexican Independence, Padre Miguel Hidalgo y Costilla, launched the "Grito de Dolores," the battle cry of independence, on September 16, 1810 from the small town of Dolores, near one of Mexico's most prominent mining cities, Guanajuato. This event has assumed a mythopoetic status. Since the late 19th century, Hidalgo y Costilla's "battle cry" has become emblematic of Mexican independence. Each year on the night of September 15, the President of Mexico re-enacts the event by ringing the bells of the National Palace in Mexico City. He repeats a cry of patriotism based upon the "Grito de Dolores" from the balcony of the palace, to the assembled crowd of up to half a million spectators in the *Plaza de la Constitución* (also known as the *Zócalo*). (See Section B of http://www.asu.edu/clas/hrc/Keller for José Clemente Orozco's famous mural depicting Padre Hidalgo.)

The historical and conceptual triad: mining, oppression of workers, and worker struggles for freedom from oppression does not stop with the 1810 War of Independence. Far from it, for a time in 1863 during the French invasion of Mexico, the mining city of San Luis Potosí served as the capital of the republican government under President Benito Juárez. Thus, it was appropriate that when Mexico's revolution against dictator Porfirio Díaz began on November 20, 1910, Francisco Indalecio Madero named his revolutionary manifesto, the *Plan of San Luis Potosí*.

The problems of exploitation and worker grievances have gone into the 20th and the 21st century, despite the moderate triumph of the Revolution of 1910 and its insti-

---

[1]   Some of the best of these films include Werner Herzog's *Aguirre, the Wrath of God* (1972), and *Fitzcarraldo* (1982), both starring Klaus Kinski; Roland Joffé's *The Mission* (1986), starring Robert De Niro and Jeremy Irons, screenplay by Robert Bolt; Carlos Saura's *El Dorado* (1988), starring Abel Viton; and Bruce Beresford's *Black Robe* (1991), starring Lothaire Bluteau.

tutionalization by the Partido Revolucionario Institucional (PRI). In one gripping manifestation, strikers rallied naked except for their miner hats and boots, calling riveting attention to their dearth of means. (See Section C of http://www.asu.edu/clas/hrc/Keller.)

This triad—mines, oppression, struggle for freedom—is a historical and conceptual inheritance from Mexico to the Mexican American/Chicano communities that were intimately involved in the mining of the Southwest of the United States such as the copper, gold, or silver mines of Arizona, California, Colorado, New Mexico, Nevada, Texas, and Utah and just across the U.S.-Mexico border, such as in Cananea, run by an American company, the Cananea Consolidated Copper Company.

A review of the mining-focused literature of Chicano culture is beyond the scope of this essay, but we do concentrate on film beginning with *Salt of the Earth* (1954), the progenitor of Chicano film. Also, I have provided (on the accompanying Web site) a sampling of additional salient Chicano and some related non-Chicano docudramas and documentaries that treat the subject of the dignity of work and workers' rights. Most of these films are set in the environment of the mines and a few, in a supplemental fashion, in the fields. Special attention is placed on the setting of the mines, inasmuch as this setting has received very scant attention, except for *Salt of the Earth*, in Chicano/Latino film scholarship.

On the Web site, http://www.asu.edu/clas/hrc/Keller, I have included a descriptive inventory of a universe of notable international films set in mining environments or intensely dedicated to the dignity of and rights of workers that inform and contextualize the films examined in depth by this paper. These films include adaptations of Émile Zola's seminal novel, *Germinal* (the earliest in 1913, the most recent to my knowledge in 1993), Sergei Eisenstein's *Strike* and *Battleship Potemkin*, G.W. Pabst's *Kameradschaft*, Michael Curtiz's *Black Fury*, Carol Reed's *The Stars Look Down*, John Ford's *How Green Was My Valley* and *The Grapes of Wrath*, Kazimierz Kutz's *Sól Ziemi Czarnej* [English language release as *Salt of the Black Earth*], Martin Ritt's *The Molly Maguires*, Barbara Kopple's *Harlan County, USA*, and John Sayles's *Matewan*. These are films that have had considerable influence over world cinema.

Chicano, in this paper, is used in two important ways. It refers to the depiction of Chicanos (or Mexicans) in films, irrespective of the level of control of or creative input into the films by Hispanics. The second usage includes the first one, surely, but *additionally*, it encompasses the level of control or creative input by Hispanics. Thus, the 1930 *The Arizona Kid* is Chicano in only one sense, in its depiction of the Kid as "Mexican," but it is not Chicano at all in the second sense, since Hispanics had no financial or creative control over that film, and participated only secondarily in its acting. The main characters are Warner Baxter, an Anglo who plays a "Mexican" miner, and Carol Lombard, the blonde temptress. Argentine actress Mona Maris has a supporting role as Lorita, one of a number of señoritas who interrelate with the Kid. In marked contrast, Hector Galán's *Los Mineros* (1991) is Chicano in both senses. It depicts Chicano characters and it is financially and artistically controlled by Chicano filmmakers. Separately and analogically for an understanding of Mexican film, Marcela Fernández Violante's film, *Cananea*, is a Mexican film in every sense of the word, both thematically and with respect to production, creative control, director and cast.

Salt of the Earth (1954)

> You are the salt of the earth; but if the salt has lost its taste, how shall its saltiness be restored? ... You are the light of the world.
> —Matthew 5:13-16

The Sermon on the Mount begins with the Beatitudes. It tells us that those who are poor, those who are hungry, those who weep, those whose hearts are pure, those who work to establish peace, those who suffer for the cause of justice, they are all blessed in the kingdom of God. Then the Sermon on the Mount speaks of the response of those who are blessed. It tells us: "You are the salt of the earth, you are the light of the world." All who are blessed are called to a responsibility.

The responsibility that in 1950–1952 real New Mexican miners and their families undertook was to bear the burden of social injustice in order to become a model of social justice. That model was vivified by the artistry of, respectively, blacklisted director Herbert J. Biberman, producer Paul Jarrico, and writer Michael Wilson.

In 1954, writer/director Herbert J. Biberman, undaunted by the months he had spent in a federal prison for refusing to squeal to the red-baiting House Un-American Activities Committee (HUAC), directed *Salt of the Earth* in collaboration with writer Michael Wilson and producer Paul Jarrico. All had been blacklisted by the Hollywood establishment, which itself was coerced by the forces of McCarthyism with the justification that these film professionals had been involved in socialist politics. While *Salt of the Earth* is not a Chicano film per se, it has assumed a key role as a foundational work in the analysis of the development of Chicana/o cinema. (See Section D of http://www.asu.edu/clas/hrc/Keller for relevant visual material from *Salt of the Earth*.)

Salt of the Earth is based on a true story. Jarrico found the subject matter while on a family vacation in New Mexico, where he heard about a mining strike in Grant County. The strikers were predominantly Mexican Americans, members of the Union of Mine, Mill, and Smelter Workers, a union the Congress of Industrialized Organizations (CIO) ejected in 1949 for alleged Communist influences. The strikers demanded that the Empire Zinc Corporation give them the same benefits and wages it gave the region's Anglo miners. The strike nearly collapsed after eight months when Empire Zinc opened the mine to scab labor and obtained a court injunction prohibiting union pickets on company property. Then the wives and mothers of the union's Ladies' Auxiliary circumvented the injunction by marching in place of the men. This living, factual reality is the basis of *Salt of the Earth*.

The same year that *Salt of the Earth* was released, another movie about belea-
guered workers opened to quite a different reception. *On the Waterfront* (1954, director: Elia Kazan, writer: Budd Schulberg, starring Marlon Brando), like *Salt of the
Earth*, was based on an actual situation. Both movies were shot on location with the
participation of those who had lived the real stories. And both movies shared a history
in the Hollywood blacklist. There the similarities ended. Kazan and his writer, Budd
Schulberg, had both named names—identified movie people they said were Communists—when questioned by the House Un-American Activities Committee (HUAC).
Some saw their movie, in which Brando's character testifies against the racketeers
who run the docks, as an allegory in support of informing. The people behind *Salt*, in
contrast, were unrepentant blacklistees whose leftist political affiliations derailed their
careers during the Red scares of the 1950s. *On the Waterfront* was a hit and is
remembered as a classic film. The makers of *Salt of the Earth* struggled to find theater
owners willing to show their incendiary movie, yet it has become a classic cult film, at
least on college campuses. To paraphrase William Faulkner's Nobel Prize speech, *Salt*
"not only endures, but prevails."

It required a great deal of optimism to make a left-leaning movie like *Salt of the
Earth* in the early 1950s, but director Herbert Biberman was, by many accounts, a
great optimist. The director of now-forgotten films such as *Meet Nero Wolfe* and *The
Master Race*, Biberman had helped found the Screen Directors Guild, which later
became the Directors Guild of America. He was also a Communist and one of many
movie professionals who found inspiration in the Soviet Union—that is, in what
dictator Joseph Stalin allowed the world to see of the Soviet Union. Throughout the
1930s, the Communist Party USA remained active in Hollywood, establishing guilds
to give writers and actors bargaining clout against the studios, and fighting against
fascism abroad by championing the Spanish Republic and rallying against the Third
Reich. Stalin's pact with Adolf Hitler in 1939 disillusioned many a Beverly Hills
Bolshevik, though some, like Biberman, remained unswayed.

When the United States entered World War II in 1941, the Soviet Union became
an ally, and Hollywood began to make movies that celebrated our newfound comrades.
Those films returned to haunt the movie industry when World War II ended and the
Cold War pitted the United States against the Soviet Union. Suddenly the U.S. government began casting a critical eye on the movie industry, and HUAC began investi-
gating Communist influences on the silver screen.

HUAC's most visible targets were the so-called Hollywood Ten, filmmakers the
committee charged with contempt of Congress in 1947 after they refused to answer
questions about Communist affiliations. In 1950, the Supreme Court declined to consider the filmmakers' appeals, and the Hollywood Ten began serving their sentences.
Herbert Biberman, 50, served six months at a federal institution at Texarkana, Texas.
Incarcerated with him was another of the Ten, writer Alvah Bessie. Compared to the
ebullient Biberman, Bessie was a dour cynic. He cringed at Biberman's incessant good
manners and his penchant for preaching politics to guards and prisoners, but he did

have to admire Biberman's dedication to his beliefs, especially when he learned that the director had offered to serve six extra months to get Bessie released earlier.

In 1951, HUAC increased the pressure on the movie industry with a new batch of subpoenas for Communist Party USA members, past members, and even non-affiliated liberals. The studios fell in line and expanded their unofficial blacklist. Actors, producers, directors, and other industry professionals whom the studios deemed tainted by leftist beliefs suddenly found themselves unemployable. Biberman, fellow Ten member and producer Adrian Scott, theater owner Simon Lazarus, and blacklisted screenwriter Paul Jarrico saw possibilities for that discarded talent. They teamed up to form Independent Productions Corporation and set out to find a story to tell.

In New Mexico's mining strike that succeeded in 1952, the filmmakers had found their story. In extraordinary fashion, the filmmakers made changes in the script that came directly from their interaction with the people. They wanted to tell the story from the participants' point of view and use their feedback to fine-tune the screenplay. So when he finished his script treatment, screenwriter Michael Wilson took it to Grant County. People there objected to one scene where the main character had an extramarital fling and another in which he purchased whiskey with his last paycheck. Wilson cut those scenes. They were perfectly acceptable as drama, he explained to his partners: "But we're dealing with something else. Not just people. A people." As Wilson labored to complete a final script over the next year, he had union members and their wives look over all his drafts.

At the end of January, the miners and their wives flocked to Silver City's theater to watch the first rushes, and they laughed and applauded at their images on the big screen. Yet even as the movie progressed, storm clouds were forming. A Silver City schoolteacher wrote to Walter Pidgeon, president of the Screen Actors Guild, and expressed concern that a Communist film company was manipulating the local Mexican Americans. Soon the media and the government began scrutinizing the maverick movie troupe. Columnist Victor Riesel pointed out the production's proximity to the Los Alamos atomic research facility. Congressman Donald Jackson said the film was "deliberately designed to inflame racial hatreds and to depict the United States of America as the enemy of all colored peoples." It was, he said, "a new weapon for Russia."

The negative publicity created problems. Pathé Laboratories suddenly refused to process the daily rushes, so Biberman could no longer review each day's work and had to print scenes blind. Immigration officials came for Revueltas—they had sudden concerns about her passport—and deported her back to Mexico. Biberman had to use a stand-in for some sequences, but he still needed the actress for voice-overs and frontal shots. Eventually, Revueltas recorded narration under clandestine circumstances in a dismantled Mexican sound studio, and the crew shot final footage of her in Mexico and then smuggled it like contraband over the border.

By the beginning of 1954, the moviemakers had turned their raw footage into a movie. The next hurdle was to find theaters to show it. Roy Brewer, the anti-Com-

munist head of the IATSE, represented projectionists, and he was hardly likely to steer
Salt on to movie screens. As he wrote to Congressman Jackson, "The Hollywood AFL
Council assures you that everything which it can do to prevent the showing of *Salt of
the Earth* will be done." In New York City the production found a theater owner
whose projectionists belonged to a different union. After much persuasion he agreed to
host the film's opening. *Salt of the Earth* premiered at the Grande Theater on March
14, 1954, to mostly positive reviews. *The New York Times'* Bosley Crowther wrote
that "an unusual company made up largely of actual miners and their families plays the
drama exceedingly well." While several found it unfairly pro-labor, few saw it pro-
Red, save a young writer named Pauline Kael, who wrote that it was "as clear a piece
of Communist propaganda as we have had in many years."

Communist or not, lines such as "This installment plan, it's the curse of the
working man," indicate the shortcomings of writing for "a people" instead of people.
In his account of the blacklist era, *A Journal of the Plague Years*, Stefan Kanfer referred to Wilson's "clanking, agitprop prose." Nevertheless, *Salt* ran at the Grande for
nine weeks, taking in a more-than-respectable $50,000, and opened in another dozen
or so American theaters. The film was warmly received overseas, especially in France,
and it won the grand prize from the Paris Academy of Film. *Salt* also triumphed at its
premiere in Mexico City, where audiences considered Rosaura Revueltas a star. In
1956 the film company filed an anti-trust suit charging more than 100 industry figures
with conspiracy. That done, Biberman and Jarrico resigned from the company to move
on to other work. After eight years of litigation, they lost their suit.

Many of the people blacklisted never found work in movies again. Some writers
found employment by working under pseudonyms or having others front for them.
Michael Wilson won Oscar attention for his scripts, even though his name did not
appear on the final films. In later, friendlier years he would get credit for writing
Friendly Persuasion and for his contributions to *The Bridge on the River Kwai* and
Lawrence of Arabia.

Biberman developed land in Los Angeles and wrote a book, *Salt of the Earth:
The Story of a Film*, published in 1965. He directed one more movie, *Slaves*, a poorly
received variation on *Uncle Tom's Cabin*. He died of bone cancer in 1971.

Jarrico wrote scripts in Europe and returned to the United States in the late
1960s, his Communist years long behind him. "I'm probably the only writer who has
been blacklisted on both sides of the Iron Curtain," he said. He found television work
and wrote films such as *The Day That Shook the World*. He also fought to get blacklisted writers the screen credits denied them. Jarrico died in 1997 in an automobile
accident near Ojai, California, at the age of 82. The day before he had received honors
at a star-studded Beverly Hills soirée entitled *Hollywood Remembers the Blacklist.*

Salt became a historical phenomenon and has assumed a cult following especially on college campuses not in spite of but because of its treatment by the United States
establishment (politicians, journalists, studio executives, and other trade unions). It is
one of the first pictures to advance the feminist social and political point-of-view. It is

also notable for its union funding from the International Union of Mine, Mill, and Smelter Workers. Here the triad that *Salt* developed was the first nationally significant feminist, union-financed, worker-focused film about Chicanos.

Closely following factual reality, the docudrama tells the story of an extended and challenging strike during 1950–1952, in the fictional village of Zinc Town, New Mexico, a strike led by Mexican American and Anglo miners against the Empire Zinc Company. The film shows how the miners (the union men and their wives), the company, and the police, react during the strike. In neorealist style the producers and director used actual miners and their families as actors in the film.

While the film is not free from stereotypes (evil Anglo lawmen and mine-company officials), what makes it both memorable and revolutionary is the strength and grace of the women led by veteran Mexican actress Rosaura Revueltas who defer to their macho husbands until a Taft-Hartley injunction makes it necessary for the womenfolk to replace the miners on the picket line. As the women find their voice, the film's affirmation of perseverance, justice, as well as gender and racial equality appears almost as radical and rousing today as it did in the dark days of McCarthyism.

Salt of the Earth has been so enduring that it generated a docudrama of its own about the story of its making. The recent *One of the Hollywood Ten* (2001, director: Karl Francis, starring Jeff Goldblum, Greta Scacchi, Ángela Molina) treats the story of Herbert Biberman, several of his Hollywood blacklisted associates, and his wife, Gale Sondergaard, and their struggles to make *Salt*. It is a gripping movie and it makes viewing the 1954 film even more rewarding. (See Section E of http://www.asu.edu/clas/hrc/Keller for relevant visual material from *One of the Hollywood Ten*.)

Cananea (1978)

Marcela Fernández Violante, known as one of Mexico's best filmmakers, is also among the most enduring, inasmuch as she has had to deal with the tumultuous political climate of an industry dominated by men and highly influenced by the Mexican federal government. She began her career in 1971 and her first film was a documentary about artist Frida Kahlo. The film won an Ariel—the Mexican Academy Award—for "Best Documentary." Her first feature film was *De todos modos Juan te llamas* (1975), which tells the story of the peasant-run and Catholic Church-supported Cristero insurrection against the government of 1926–29.

Cananea (1978, starring Carlos Bracho, Yolanda Ciani, Steve Wilensky) is not the only significant film about the town of Cananea, Sonora, close to the U.S.-Mexico border and the town of Douglas, Arizona. In 1961 appeared *La carcel de Cananea* (director: Gilberto Gazcón, starring Pedro Armendáriz and Agustín de Anda).[2] The

---

[2] *La carcel* is not a musical but its title and plot are tied to one of the most famous Mexican *corridos* of all times, "La carcel de Cananea," which has been sung by numerous Mexicans as well as by the Mexican American singer from Arizona, Linda Ronstadt. This *corrido* was written in 1917, in the midst of the Revolution. It describes the experiences of a man

popular Pedro Armendáriz is a federal lawman who captures a youthful criminal played by Agustín de Anda. After the capture by the federal deputy, the two men begin to have a greater appreciation for each other. This friendship of sorts does not ameliorate the conclusion that the enforcer and the fugitive foresee: the prison that waits at the end of their journey. (See Section F of http://www.asu.edu/clas/hrc/Keller for relevant visual material from *La carcel de Cananea*.)

The two Cananea films, 1961 and 1978, are loosely connected by the Mexican Revolution. *Cananea* is a film that treats an important revolt by miners that was a precursor to the Mexican Revolution of 1910. The revolt took place in 1906 and was seminal to the post-revolutionary nationalization of Mexican mines. At the time of the strike, the population of 23,000 included 7,000 Americans and 5,000 Chinese. The large number of Chinese in the town is consistent with the murder topic of the song, "La carcel de Cananea."

Cananea is also a consummate border film that treats the differences between Anglo-American and Mexican values, attitudes, and culture. The film has psychological depth, partly because the point of view alternates between the Mexican miner and the idiosyncratic American mine owner, Colonel Green. Green is no stereotype, but rather a full-fledged character. The film displays the sure instincts and expert directorial control of Fernández Violante. Nevertheless, while his character is portrayed with veracity and depth, the film exposes the undeniable fact that his profitable American-owned Cananea copper mine in the Sonora desert was notable for its relentless exploitation of the Mexican people who worked in the mines. (See Section G of http://www.asu.edu/clas/hrc/Keller for relevant visual material related to *Cananea*.)

The most moving and politically incendiary film sequences deal with the ruthless suppression of the striking Mexican miners by Arizona Rangers who crossed the border at will into the Mexican town. The actual Cananea Strike of 1906 resulted in the death of 23 people in the fight between the strikers and the posse led by Arizona Rangers. This multiple outrage that included violating the sovereignty of Mexico and the killing of numerous Mexican miners and other citizens was important to the subsequent trajectory of the Mexican Revolution of 1910, which nationalized mines, petroleum, and other subsoil assets.

Despite the achievements of the Revolution of 1910, all is not well in the mines around Cananea. The Cananea copper mine, one of the largest in the world, is less than an hour from the U.S. border and it has not escaped the ongoing problems that affect border towns, including the exploitation of workers and violence related to drug running and smuggling. As recently as 2007, workers were involved in violent confrontations with the new Mexican owners of the Cananea copper mine as a result of the privatization conducted by the Mexican government and plans to greatly reduce the unionized workforce and bring in poorly paid workers from southern Mexico. Ad-

---

accused of murdering Chinese immigrants who was incarcerated in the town jail. The song is semi-anonymous, allegedly written by a man called Francisco, nicknamed "El Cucharón de Batuc" ("The Big Spoon of Batuc," a town in the geographic area), in 1917.

ditionally, there was a recent violent episode attributable to the activities of drug cartels.

Los Mineros (1991)

Los Mineros (1991, producer/director: Hector Galán,[3] telescript: Paul Espinosa and Hector Galán, narrator: Luis Valdez) is a documentary produced by the Public Broadcasting System (PBS) American Experience series. It combines archival footage, letters and personal testimony to recount the 50-year struggle of Mexican American miners to form a union. (See Section H of http://www.asu.edu/clas/hrc/Keller for relevant visual material from *Los Mineros* as well as Chicana/o works of art depicting the crossing of the border.)

One aspect of history that *Los Mineros* drives home is the long story of Mexicans working in the United States. The historical differences over the decades and centuries are sadly bound together by the commonality of Anglo-American nativism, xenophobia, and racism. This is the case of undocumented workers who today come of their own accord and are welcomed in certain exploitive corners as landscapers, construction workers, or hotel and restaurant employees. But the same reality faced the Mexicans who were actively recruited into the United States in prior decades.

The push to electrify American cities and towns created a huge demand for copper at the turn of the 20th century. By 1910, thousands of Mexican miners—*los mineros*—had come to Arizona, including the sister towns of Clifton-Morenci, to mine ore for American copper companies, supplying the raw material for electric power lines.

Over the decades *los mineros* became U.S. citizens but they were not fully accepted as American. The Anglo foremen delegated the most dangerous tasks to the Mexican Americans. Working 10-to-12 hour shifts in tunnels 4,000 feet underground, *los mineros* made only half as much as "Anglos" through the imposition of the contemptible "dual-wage system." In addition, they were forced to live in shacks on the "Mexican" side of town and were cheated in company stores. The film is played out against the backdrop of the stark landscape of desert and mountain Arizona broken by clusters of miners' shacks facing the giant Phelps-Dodge mining operation.

---

[3] Hector Galán has been creating documentary films for over thirty years. He has produced and directed eleven films for the PBS series *Frontline*, two films for *The American Experience*, and numerous critically acclaimed and award-winning independent films such as feature documentaries, music documentaries, and documentary series. Galán founded his company, the Austin, Texas based Galán Inc. Television/Film in 1984. Galán Inc. productions include the series *Chicano! History of the Mexican American Civil Rights Movement*, *New Harvest, Old Shame*, *Shakedown in Santa Fe*, *Cuba: A Personal Journey*, *The Hunt for Pancho Villa*, *Songs of the Homeland*, *Forgotten Americans*, *Vaquero: The Forgotten Cowboy*, *Accordion Dreams*, and many more.

As early as 1903, the Mexican American miners organized strikes against unfair wages and substandard living conditions, but these were brutally contained by the Arizona Rangers and federal troops, including rounding up strikers into boxcars and droving the boxcars into the remote desert with no food or water.

Things got worse when the bottom dropped out of the copper market in 1931. Mexicans were deported to Mexico as part of a government "repatriation" plan. With the recovery of the mines in the mid-1930s, the Mexican American miners were permitted to return but found the dual-wage system still firmly entrenched. A union was finally formed during World War II which brought Mexican American men a new sense of identity and energized them to demand their rights in a country they valiantly helped defend. Galán's camera captures the passionate memories of living *minero* veterans, such as Ed Montoya, whose Okinawa tale lends *Los Mineros* extraordinary moral power.

The exploiters still did not cave in. The union was not recognized until 1956, when a 104-day strike led by Mexican American World War II veterans ended in victory and the miners won the concessions they had been demanding for so long.

*   *   *

In this paper we have reviewed three Chicano or proto-Chicano films about workers in the mines and their struggle for dignity and economic redress. In doing so, we have had occasion to highlight the history of mining oppression at certain historical times, namely the conquest and colonial periods of Mexico, the period immediately before and leading to the Mexican Revolution of 1910, and the period of aftermath of World War II in New Mexico and Arizona. Additionally, we have referenced the three films under primary consideration, *Salt of the Earth*, *Cananea*, and *Los Mineros*, against the backdrop of numerous films of worldwide importance that treat the dignity of work and the indignities of oppression in the mines and in the fields.

Certain conclusions can be derived from this effort. One is that the three films in question, and virtually all of the films in this domain of struggle against worker oppression, come out of real-life events. It would be difficult to invent the grist for filmic conflict that the actual events offered the filmmakers. The second is that the three Latina/o films conclude with worker victory although only after tribulations of biblical proportions. This is not always the case of some analogous international films, where ultimately the only justice that is achieved is poetic justice, the documentation through artistry of the human tragedy of events and circumstances. It may be that a *movimiento social*, recent and still in its enthusiastic stage, has something to do with this thematic triumphalism when compared with certain films set in Europe. Finally, there is a notable interface and interaction with the topics and themes of the film and the personal lives of the filmmakers. It is clearly not coincidental that the most important female filmmaker of her times, Marcela Fernández Violante, would direct a mining film about events that led to a signal advance in the social conditions of Mexico. Nor is it coincidental that a group of black-listed Hollywood professionals would be drawn to and develop a film about the triumph in New Mexican mines of an ethnically oppressed group, a union declared as Communist and therefore subversive, and a gender constrained by masculinism but, in the end, triumphant over that traditional oppression in an atmosphere of camaraderie, reconciliation, and utter innovation. Nor is it mere happenstance that Chicano documentary filmmaking's most veteran director, writer, and producer, Hector Galán, would be drawn to a plot and setting characterized by extraordinary stamina on the part of *mejicanos*/Chicanos.

Further Reading

Berg, Charles Ramírez. *Latino Images in Film: Stereotypes, Subversion and Resistance.* Austin: U of Texas P, 2002.

———. "Stereotyping and Resistance: A Crash Course on Hollywood's Latino Imagery." *The Future of Latino Independent Media: A NALIP Sourcebook.* Ed. Chon A. Noriega. Los Angeles: UCLA Chicano Studies Research Center, 2000. 3-13.

Berumen, Frank Javier Garcia. *Brown Celluloid: Latino/a Film Icons and Images in the Hollywood Film Industry.* New York: Vantage P, 2003.

Biberman, Herbert. *Salt of the Earth: The Story of a Film.* Boston: Beacon P, 1965.

———. *The Chicano/Hispanic Image in American Film.* New York: Vantage P, 1995.

The Bronze Screen: 100 Years of the Latino Image in Hollywood. DVD. Narrated by Wanda De Jesús. Chicago, IL; Questar, Inc., 2002.

Bruce-Novoa, Juan. "There's Many a Slip between Good Intentions and Script: *The Milagro Beanfield War.*" *Post Script* 16.1 (1996): 53-63.

CineWorks: A Latino Media Resource Guide. San Francisco: Cine Acción, 1993.

Cosandaey, Mikelle. "Combining Entertainment and Education: An Interview with Robert Redford." *Cineaste* 16.1-2 (1987-1988): 8-12.

de Góngora Marmolejo, Alonso. *Historia de Todas las Cosas que han Acaecido en el Reino de Chile y de los que lo han gobernado (1536–1575).* Universidad de Chile. Colecciones Documentales en Texto Completo. http://www.historia.uchile.cl/CDA/fh_complex/0,1393, SCID%253D10200%2526ISID%253D404%2526JNID%253D12,00.html.

de Vivar, Jeronimo. *Crónica y relación copiosa y verdadera de los reinos de Chile.* Artehistoria Revista Digital. Crónicas de América. http://www.artehistoria.jcyl.es/cronicas/contextos/11498.htm.

Ferriss, Susan, and Ricardo Sandoval. *The Fight in the Fields: Cesar Chavez and the Farmworkers Movement.* New York: Harcourt Brace, 1997.

Fregoso, Rosa Linda. *The Bronze Screen: Chicana and Chicano Film Culture.* Minneapolis: U of Minnesota P, 1993.

Friedman, Lester D., ed. *Unspeakable Images: Ethnicity and the American Cinema.* Urbana: U of Illinois P, 1991.

Gallegos, Aaron. Review of *The Fight in the Fields: Cesar Chavez and the Farm Workers' Struggle. Sojourners* 26.3 (May-June 1997): 59-62.

Goodman, Walter. Review of *Chicano! History of the Mexican-American Civil Rights Movement*. *New York Times* April 12, 1996: B8(N), D18(L).

———. Review of *The Fight in the Fields: Cesar Chavez and the Farm Workers' Struggle*. *New York Times* April 16, 1997: B6(N), C18(L).

Habell-Pallán, Michelle, and Mary Romero, eds. *Latino/a Popular Culture*. New York: New York UP, 2002.

Hadley-Garcia, George. *Hispanic Hollywood: The Latins in Motion Pictures*. New York, NY: Carol Pub. Group, 1990.

Harvey, Dennis. Review of *The Fight in the Fields: Cesar Chavez and the Farmworkers' Struggle*. *Variety* Jan 26, 1997. http://www.variety.com/review/VE1117911720?refcatid =31.

Herrera-Sobek, María, and Helena María Viramontes, eds. *Chicana (W)Rites: On Word and Film*. Series in Chicana/Latina Studies. Berkeley, CA: Third Woman P, 1995.

Hinojosa, Rolando. "*I Am Joaquín*: Relationships Between the Text and the Film." *Chicano Cinema: Research, Reviews, and Resources*. Ed. Gary D. Keller. Binghamton, NY: Bilingual P, 1985. 142-45.

Kanfer, Stefan. *A Journal of the Plague Years*. New York: Atheneum, 1973.

Keller, Gary D. *A Biographical Handbook of Hispanics and United States Film*. Tempe, AZ: Bilingual P, 1997.

———. *Hispanics and United States Film: An Overview and Handbook*. Tempe, AZ: Bilingual P, 1994.

———, ed. *Cine Chicano*. Mexico: Cineteca Nacional, 1988.

———, ed. *Chicano Cinema: Research, Reviews, and Resources*. Binghamton, NY: Bilingual P, 1985.

King, John, Ana M. López, and Manuel Alvarado. *Mediating Two Worlds: Cinematic Encounters in the Americas*. London: BFI, 1993.

Limón, José E. "Stereotyping and Chicano Resistance: An Historical Dimension." *Aztlán* 4.2 (1973): 257-70.

List, Christine. *Chicano Images: Refiguring Ethnicity in Mainstream Film*. Garland Studies in American Popular History and Culture. New York: Garland Pub., 1996.

López, Ana M. "Are All Latins from Manhattan?—Hollywood, Ethnography, and Cultural Colonialism." *Unspeakable Images: Ethnicity and the American Cinema*. Ed. Lester D. Friedman. Urbana: U of Illinois P, 1991. 404-24.

———. "Celluloid Tears: Melodrama in the 'Old' Mexican Cinema." *Iris* 13 (Summer 1991): 29-52.

López, Oliva M. "Proyección chicana en *Raíces de Sangre*." *Cine Cubano* 100 (1981): 75-80.

Maciel, David R. "'Yo Soy Chicano': The Turbulent and Heroic Life of Chicanas/os in Cinema and Television." *Chicano Renaissance: Contemporary Cultural Trends*. Ed. David R. Maciel, Isidro D. Ortiz, and Maria Herrera-Sobek. Tucson: U of Arizona P, 2000.

———, and María Herrera-Sobek, eds. *Culture Across Borders: Mexican Immigration and Popular Culture*. Tucson: U of Arizona P, 1998. 227-58.

————, Isidro D. Ortiz, and María Herrera-Sobek, eds. *Chicano Renaissance: Contemporary Cultural Trends.* Tucson: U of Arizona P, 2000. 131-68.

Mariño de Lobera, Pedro. *Crónica del Reino de Chile, escrita por el capitán Pedro Mariño de Lobera....reducido a nuevo método y estilo por el Padre Bartolomé de Escobar.* Edición digital a partir de Crónicas del Reino de Chile. Madrid: Atlas, 1960. 227-562 (Biblioteca de Autores Españoles; 569-575). Biblioteca Virtual Miguel de Cervantes. http://www.cervantesvirtual.com/obra/cronica-del-reino-de-chile--0/.

Martinez, Eliud. *"I Am Joaquin* as Poem and Film: Two Modes of Chicano Expression." *Journal of Popular Culture* 13 (1980): 505-15.

Mora, Carl J. "Mexican Cinema in the 1970s." *Mexican Art of the 1970s.* Ed. Leonard Folgarait. Nashville, TN: Vanderbilt University, Center for Latin American and Iberian Studies, 1984.

————. *Mexican Cinema: Reflections of a Society, 1896-1980.* Rev. ed. Berkeley, CA: U of California P, 1989.

Mora, Sergio de la. "Chicanos and Film: A Re/View of the Field." *Studies in Latin American Popular Culture* 14 (1995): 287-95.

Morales, Alejandro. "Expanding the Meaning of Chicano Cinema: *Yo soy Chicano, Raices de sangre, Seguin." Chicano Cinema: Research, Reviews, and Resources.* Ed. Gary D. Keller. Binghamton, NY: Bilingual P, 1985. 121-37.

Nericcio, William Anthony. "Autopsy of a Rat: Odd, Sundry Parables of Freddy Lopez, Speedy Gonzales, and Other Chicano/Latino Marionettes Prancing about Our First World Visual Emporium." *Camera Obscura* 37 (Jan. 1996): 189-237.

Noriega, Chon A. "The Aesthetic Discourse: Reading Chicano Cinema since *La Bamba." Centro de Estudios Puertorriqueños Bulletin* 3.1 (Winter 1990–91): 55-71.

————. "Chicano Cinema and the Horizon of Expectations: A Discursive Analysis of Film Reviews in the Mainstream, Alternative, and Hispanic Press, 1987–1988." *Aztlán* 19.2 (1988–90): 1-32.

————. "Citizen Chicano: The Trials and Titillations of Ethnicity in the American Cinema, 1935–1962." *Social Research* 58.2 (Summer 1991): 413-38.

————. "In Aztlán: The Films of the Chicano Movement, 1969–79." *New American Film and Video Series* 56. Pamphlet no. 56 (January 1991): 9-27.

————. "U.S. Latinos and the Media: Theory and Practice." *Jump Cut* 39 (June 1994): 57-112.

————, ed. *Chicanos and Film: Essays on Chicano Representation and Resistance.* Garland Reference Library of Social Science, vol. 710. New York: Garland Pub., 1992.

————, ed. *Chicanos and Film: Representation and Resistance.* Minneapolis: U of Minnesota P, 1992.

————, ed. *The Future of Latino Independent Media: A NALIP Sourcebook.* Los Angeles: UCLA Chicano Studies Research Center, 2000.

————, ed. *Shot in America: Television, the State, and the Rise of Chicano Cinema.* Minneapolis: U of Minnesota P, 2000.

————, and Lillian Jiménez. "La indirecta directa: Two Decades of Chicano and Puerto Rican Film and Video." *New American Film and Video Series 61*. New York: Whitney Museum of American Art, 1992.

————, and Ana M. López, eds. *The Ethnic Eye: Latino Media Arts*. Minneapolis: U of Minnesota P, 1996.

Pettit, Arthur G. *Images of the Mexican American in Fiction and Film*. College Station: Texas A&M UP, 1980.

Reyes, Luis, and Peter Rubie. *Hispanics in Hollywood: An Encyclopedia of Film and Television*. Garland Reference Library of the Humanities, vol. 1761. New York: Garland Pub., 1994.

Richard, Alfred Charles, Jr. *Contemporary Hollywood's Negative Hispanic Image: An Interpretive Filmography, 1936–1955*. Bibliographies and Indexes in the Performing Arts, no. 14. Westport, CT: Greenwood P, 1993.

————. *Contemporary Hollywood's Negative Hispanic Image: An Interpretive Filmography, 1956–1993*. Bibliographies and Indexes in the Performing Arts, no. 16. Westport, CT: Greenwood P, 1994.

————. *The Hispanic Image on the Silver Screen: An Interpretive Filmography From Silents Into Sound, 1898–1935*. New York: Greenwood P, 1992.

Rodríguez, Clara E. *Heroes, Lovers, and Others: The Story of Latinos in Hollywood*. Washington, D.C.: Smithsonian Books, 2004.

————, ed. *Latin Looks: Images of Latinas and Latinos in the U.S. Media*. Boulder, Colo.: Westview P, 1997.

Sandoval-Sanchez, Alberto. *José, Can You See?: Latinos on and off Broadway*. Madison: U of Wisconsin P, 1999.

Saragoza, Alex M. "The Border in American and Mexican Cinema." *Aztlán* 21.1-2 (1992–96): 155-90.

————. "Mexican Cinema in the United States 1940-1952." *History, Culture, and Society: Chicano Studies in the 1980s*. National Association for Chicano Studies. Ypsilanti, MI: Bilingual P, 1983. 107-24.

Tatum, Charles M. *Chicano Popular Culture: que hable el pueblo*. Tucson: U of Arizona P, 2001.

Weintraub, Irwin. Review of *The Fight in the Fields: Cesar Chavez and the Farmworkers' Struggle*. *Library Journal* 122.13 (August 1997): 152-53.

Woll, Allen. "Bandits and Lovers: Hispanic Images in American Film." *The Kaleidoscopic Lens: How Hollywood Views Ethnic Groups*. Ed. Randall M. Miller. Englewood, N.J.: Ozer, 1980.

————. "Hollywood Views the Mexican-American: From the *Greaser's Revenge* to *The Milagro Beanfield War*." *Hollywood as Mirror: Changing Views of "Outsiders" and "Enemies" in American Movies*. Ed. Robert Brent Toplin. Westport, CT: Greenwood P, 1993. 41-51.

Filmography

Accordion Dreams. Dir. Hector Galán. PBS. U.S.A., 2001.

Aguirre, the Wrath of God. Dir. Werner Herzog. Germany, 1972.

The Arizona Kid. Dir. Alfred Santell. U.S.A., 1930.

Battleship Potemkin. Dir. Sergei Eisenstein. Soviet Union, 1925.

Black Fury. Dir. Michael Curtiz. U.S.A., 1935

Black Robe. Dir. Bruce Beresford. Canada, Australia, 1991.

The Bridge on the River Kwai. Dir. David Lean. United Kingdom, U.S.A., 1957.

Cananea. Dir. Marcela Fernández Violante. Mexico, 1978.

Chicano! History of the Mexican American Civil Rights Movement. Dir. Hector Galán. PBS. U.S.A., 1996.

Cuba: A Personal Journey. Dir. Hector Galán. PBS. U.S.A., 1984.

The Day That Shook the World. Dir. Veljko Bulajic. Yugoslavia, Czechoslovakia, Hungary, Germany, 1975.

A Day Without a Mexican [Dia sin Mexicanos]. Dir. Sergio Arau. U.S.A., Mexico, Spain, 2004.

De todos modos Juan te llamas. Dir. Marcela Fernández Violante. Mexico, 1976.

El Dorado. Dir. Carlos Saura. Spain, France, Italy, 1988.

Fitzcarraldo. Dir. Werner Herzog. Germany, 1982.

Forgotten Americans. Dir. Hector Galán. PBS. U.S.A., 2000.

Friendly Persuasion. Dir. William Wyler. U.S.A., 1956.

Germinal. Dir. Albert Capellani. France, 1913.

Germinal. Dir. Claude Berri. France, Belgium, Italy, 1993.

The Grapes of Wrath. Dir. John Ford. U.S.A., 1940.

Harlan County, USA. Dir. Barbara Kopple. U.S.A., 1976.

How Green Was My Valley. Dir. John Ford. U.S.A., 1941.

The Hunt for Pancho Villa. Dir. Hector Galán. PBS. U.S.A., 1993.

Kameradschaft. Dir. Georg Wilhelm Pabst. Germany, France, 1931.

La carcel de Cananea. Dir. Gilberto Gazcón. Mexico, 1960.

Lawrence of Arabia. Dir. David Lean. United Kingdom, 1962.

Los mineros. Dir. Hector Galán. PBS. U.S.A., 1991.

The Master Race. Dir. Herbert J. Biberman. U.S.A., 1940.

Matewan. Dir. John Sayles. U.S.A., 1987.

Meet Nero Wolfe. Dir. Herbert J. Biberman. U.S.A., 1936.

The Mission. Dir. Roland Joffé. United Kingdom, 1986.

The Molly Maguires. Dir. Martin Ritt. U.S.A., 1970

New Harvest, Old Shame. Dir. Hector Galán. PBS. U.S.A., 1990.

On the Waterfront. Dir. Elia Kazan. U.S.A., 1954.

One of the Hollywood Ten. Dir. Karl Francis. Spain, United Kingdom, 2001.

Salt of the Earth. Dir. Herbert Biberman. U.S.A., 1954.

Shakedown in Santa Fe. Dir. Hector Galán. U.S.A., 1988.

Slaves. Dir. Herbert Biberman. U.S.A., 1969.

Sól Ziemi Czarnej. Dir. Kazimierz Kutz [English version: *Salt of the Black Earth*]. Poland, 1970.

Songs of the Homeland. Dir. Hector Galán. PBS. U.S.A., 1995.

The Stars Look Down. Dir. Carol Reed. United Kingdom, 1940.

Strike [English language release of *Stachka*]. Dir. Sergei Eisenstein. Soviet Union, 1925. U.S.A., 1961.

Vaquero: The Forgotten Cowboy. Dir. Hector Galán. PBS. U.S.A., 1988.

Una nación desconocida: Chile en las películas de Pedro Chaskel (1960-1970)[1]

MANFRED ENGELBERT

Für Heiner Ross, in Dankbarkeit

Abstract

This essay explores the early documentaries by the Chilean director Pedro Chaskel, focusing on films like *Aquí vivieron* (1964), *Testimonio—hospital psiquiátrico de Iquique* (1968/69) and *Venceremos* (1970). It argues that the Latin American documentary film production of the 1960s is wrongly considered to be primarily a militant and therefore aesthetically impoverished kind of filmmaking. Political commitment and aesthetic proficiency do not exclude one another but can be fruitfully combined in what is called here the synthesis of the "politartistic."

In addition to analyzing the three above-mentioned films in detail the essay contextualizes them by discussing the conditions of filmmaking in the *Centro de Cine Experimental*, where Chaskel worked with Sergio Bravo, a director who influenced the whole generation of prominent Chilean filmmakers of the *Unidad Popular*. By focusing on structural concerns and the interrelation of visual and auditory discourse, the film analysis demonstrates that Chaskel's work not only successfully denounces an unjust social order but that it also manifests a distinct documentary aesthetic.

Según la opinión generalizada de los estudiosos del documental latinoamericano, este género, en general, y el de los años sesenta, en particular, tendría como meta desarrollar una conciencia nacional y hemisférica a través del cambio sistemático de la función del cine. En palabras de Ana M. López:

> The goal has been to develop through the cinema (and other cultural practices) a different kind of national and hemispheric consciousness by systematically attempting to transform the function of the national cinema in society and the place of the spectator in the national cinema. (142)

Esta empresa habría sido desde sus inicios "revolucionaria" y "antiimperialista," según otra autoridad en el campo, Zuzana M. Pick: "The New Latin American Cinema

---

[1] Una primera versión de este artículo fue publicada en la *Revista de cine* 10 (2008): 11-35.

launched a project of cinematographic renewal that was defined from the outset as revolutionary and antiimperialist" (190). Frente a las imágenes controladas por la oligarquía, los cineastas latinoamericanos habrían buscado expresar la "realidad nacional" escondida. Julianne Burton afirma:

> scores of young Latin American filmmakers assembled the minimum equipment necessary and undertook to produce films about and for and eventually with the disenfranchised Latin American masses. They sought to express "national reality," which they believed to be hidden, distorted, or negated by the dominant sectors and the media they controlled. (xi)

Asimismo, algunos de los propios chilenos –tanto los estudiosos del cine como los cineastas de los cuales me voy a ocupar en esta ponencia– compartían la misma visión del fenómeno. De esa manera, María Angélica Illanes Oliva habla del Chile de los sesenta como "el tiempo del *desocultamiento*" (23), dando como ejemplo *El chacal de Nahueltoro* (1969), que, por cierto, no es un documental, pero cuyo equipo realizador, dirigido por Miguel Littin en el cual destacan Héctor Ríos, responsable de la cámara, y Pedro Chaskel en el montaje, viene directamente de la experiencia y de la pericia cinematográfica aprendida con el documental.[2] En un coloquio-retrospectiva que organicé en la Georg-August-Universität de Göttingen, Alemania, el mismo Chaskel recordó una frase que, en los cincuenta, habrían utilizado mucho sus amigos cinéfilos y él: "Chile no tenía imagen en la pantalla" (22 de octubre 2003, archivo casette).

Mi título tiene, pues, su justificación. Pero una mirada más atenta va a revelar las imprecisiones y la falta de valor explicativo de una historiografía que identifica construcción nacional revolucionaria y quehacer cinematográfico. No es mi intención menoscabar los méritos de lo que Paulo Antonio Paranaguá ha llamado "la historiografía anglosajona especializada" (16) sobre el documental, a la cual hay que sumar, en el caso chileno, las obras de Jacqueline Mouesca, en particular su libro *El documental chileno*, de reciente publicación (2005). Lo que sí quiero –aprovechando las líneas generales ya elaboradas por la crítica– es trabajar en contra del peligro de "un prejuicio o un estereotipo," como ha sido señalado por Paranaguá, según el cual el documental latinoamericano sería –y no sería más que eso– "una película militante, pobre e improvisada, maniquea y burda, sin estructura ni originalidad" (16). Una vez más reivindicaré aquello que ya traté de hacer con la música de los Quilapayún y con la obra inmensa de Violeta Parra (cf. Parra, Violeta; Engelbert, "Poesía," "Notas") y que he llamado lo "politartístico" para demostrar que, lejos de excluirse, lo político y lo artístico pueden unirse en feliz síntesis cuando una creadora o un creador lo intentan seriamente.

---

[2] Chaskel ha sido montajista de Littin y Patricio Guzmán. En esa calidad aparece en el libro de Jorge Ruffinelli, que en su monografía sobre Guzmán incluye una visión panorámica de la historia del cine chileno (cf. 187-91). Ruffinelli también se refiere a algunas de las películas que Chaskel realizó en Cuba: *Los ojos como mi papá* (1979), la trilogía sobre el Che Guevara *Una foto recorre el mundo* (1981), *Constructor cada día, compañero* (1982) y *Che, hoy y siempre* (1983) (cf. 201-02).

Al esbozar un análisis de tres de las películas documentales realizadas por Pedro
Chaskel (*1932, en Alemania), en muy estrecha colaboración con Héctor Ríos,
(*1927) quiero destacar, por un lado, la lenta gestación de esa expresión politartística
que prueba su vigor hasta en condiciones precarias de realización y momentos de ur-
gencia política. Por otro lado, me parece necesario subrayar que, si bien Chile es el
marco geográfico-regional en el cual se desarrolla la actividad cinematográfica de
Chaskel, sus creaciones de los años sesenta no se pliegan a términos de una concepción política basada en el concepto de la "nación," ni en el sentido conservador de la
palabra como baluarte de los intereses creados del capital, ni en el sentido progresista
de una alternativa liberadora frente a las estructuras de dependencia global. Tampoco
conviene del todo un marco de interpretación personal como categoría de explicación
estética, lo que he querido indicar hablando de la cooperación privilegiada con Héctor
Ríos. Para Chaskel vale, como vamos a ver, lo que Marx dice en sus "Tesis sobre
Feuerbach" acerca del ser humano en general: que éste es el conjunto de sus relaciones
sociales[3]. Pero Chaskel también es un creador de cine por derecho propio.

Quiero añadir una nota personal en cuanto a la elección de las películas de
Chaskel (y de Ríos). Tal vez habría sido más justo destacar aquí la obra todavía demasiado poco conocida de Sergio Bravo (*1927) cuyo esplendor descubrí solamente hace
poco. Desgraciadamente no es de fácil acceso esta obra genial que no necesitó de la
visita a Chile de John Grierson en 1958, ni de la de Joris Ivens en 1963, ni de la co-di-
rección de *A Valparaíso* para ponerse a la altura del mejor cine documental en el mundo. Subyace una cierta ironía en el hecho de que el rigor y la independencia absoluta
de Bravo con la intención de salvar intacta su obra sea, tal vez, una de las causas de su
relativo desconocimiento.[4] Las películas de Chaskel, Ríos, Sapiaín y, en general, las
del Cine Experimental de la Universidad de Chile tuvieron la suerte de encontrar en
Alemania, ya a comienzos de los años setenta, una distribuidora y un archivo en la
asociación *Freunde der Deutschen Kinemathek* de Berlín. Críticos y cinéfilos como
Peter B. Schumann y Heiner Ross supieron reconocer tempranamente el valor de este
cine.[5] Gracias a que compraron copias y firmaron contratos de distribución ventajosos
para estos cineastas sin medios, estas películas fueron exhibidas y se conservaron a
salvo de la furia de los golpistas del 11 de septiembre de 1973.[6]

---

[3] "In seiner Wirklichkeit ist es [das menschliche Wesen] das Ensemble der gesellschaft-
lichen Verhältnisse" (Marx 140).

[4] Sergio Bravo puso a disposición de Verónica Cortínez de la Universidad de California, Los
Angeles, copias de sus obras. Cortínez y yo estamos preparando un estudio detallado sobre
las primeras películas de Bravo.

[5] Los libros de Schumann –*Film und Revolution in Lateinamerika* (1981) y, en particular,
Historia del cine latinoamericano (1987)– siguen siendo imprescindibles para una primera
orientación en el campo. *Film und Revolution* ofrece un currículo de Chaskel hasta 1970 y
una descripción básica de *Venceremos* (cf. 109).

[6] Personalmente debo mi conocimiento de este patrimonio de la cultura mundial a Heiner
Ross quien también estableció los contactos con Pedro Chaskel. Les agradezco a ambos
que pudimos armar el coloquio-retrospectiva de Göttingen.

Vale recordar que el Nuevo Cine en Chile, que siempre se asocia con la calidad sorprendente de los primeros largometrajes de Miguel Littin, Raúl Ruiz, Helvio Soto y Aldo Francia, no irrumpe en el Segundo Festival del Nuevo Cine Latinoamericano de Viña del Mar en 1969. Los logros de esa explosión estética sólo se explican sobre la base del largo desarrollo de una cultura cinematográfica dentro del campo cultural. Jacqueline Mouesca alude con toda razón al impulso inicial dado por la política del Frente Popular bajo la presidencia de Pedro Aguirre Cerda a inicios de los años cuarenta y a la importancia de las actividades culturales múltiples fomentadas por las instituciones universitarias (cf. *Plano secuencia* 13-15; *El documental* 53). Estas actividades están lejos de provenir únicamente de la Universidad de Chile, según pretende Mouesca –con su posición habitual en favor de lo que ella considera de izquierda–; opinión, por lo demás, compartida por John King (cf. 169). Son el resultado, más bien, de la iniciativa de estudiantes, graduados en profesiones liberales y profesores universitarios tanto de la Universidad Católica como de la Universidad de Chile. El Teatro de Ensayo de la Universidad Católica (TEUC) se funda a comienzos de los cuarenta, poco después del Teatro Experimental de la Universidad de Chile (TEUCH) y no fue un hecho excepcional que ambos cooperaran entre sí. La voluntad de innovación y de cambio, unía a jóvenes de ambientes socioculturales muy distintos caracterizados tanto por el movimiento obrero como por la Acción Católica. Crear una cultura propia y apropiarse, con este fin, de las manifestaciones más modernas del ámbito internacional del teatro, la música, la pintura, la arquitectura y el cine eran las dos caras de una misma moneda. Sergio Bravo afirma, en un mensaje electrónico a Verónica Cortínez, que su ingreso a la Facultad de Arquitectura de la Universidad de Chile estuvo marcado por la efervescencia nacida de la reforma universitaria de 1947, la "aplicación de la poética de la BAUHAUS de Weimar" por "Tibor Weiner, ex-miembro de la Bauhaus, llegado desde España a bordo del Winnipeg."[7] Y Bravo sigue: "fue ese clima efervescente de vida universitaria, con un programa de estudios recientemente reformado, el crisol desde donde surgió la poética que me indujo a la realización de cine documental" (mensaje electrónico del 1ero de noviembre 2005).[8] Más allá de las diferencias políticas, que empiezan a perfilarse sólo a partir de la segunda mitad de los cincuenta y que se agudizarán en la década siguiente, el impulso dominante es el de crear arte frente a la ramplonería y el anquilosamiento de los anticuarios de la cultura oficialista, oligárquica. Cabe pensar que la mejor expresión directa –es decir contemporánea– de es-

---

[7] El gobierno del Frente Popular encargó a Pablo Neruda la "expedición del Winnipeg," barco en el cual dos mil republicanos refugiados e internados en Francia lograron escapar de Europa y exiliarse en Chile. Remito al artículo de Francisco Caudet quien ensalza –con datos– "esa magnífica obra humanitaria" (439).

[8] En este contexto vale mencionar también la obra de Germán Becker, hombre de espectáculos y, finalmente, cineasta, demasiado vilipendiado por su adhesión al pinochetismo tras una larga militancia en la Democracia Cristiana. En su libro –aún no publicado– sobre el cine chileno bajo Frei, Verónica Cortínez dedica un largo capítulo al aporte estético de Becker.

ta efervescencia cultural es el proyecto poético de Neruda, tal como éste lo concretiza en *Canto general*.

Las actividades en el campo del cine empiezan a desarrollarse a comienzos de los cincuenta. Como señala Mouesca, el Departamento de Foto y Microfilm[9] de la Universidad de Chile produjo, en 1952, una película histórico-documental en la cual, característicamente, colaboraron actores del TEUCH de la categoría de Roberto Parada y María Maluenda (cf. *El documental* 61). La Academia de Cine y Fotografía de la Universidad Católica se fundó en 1953. Duró poco, pero en 1954 la misma Universidad Católica "pondrá en marcha un ambicioso plan de trabajo apoyado en cuatro departamentos" (*El documental* 64). El Cine Club Universitario de la Federación de Estudiantes de Chile fue fundado en 1954[10] por iniciativa de Pedro Chaskel. En ambas universidades nacieron, a mediados de los cincuenta, instituciones diferentes que –según parece– se enfrentaban a un cierto inmovilismo dentro de las estructuras creadas anteriormente. El Instituto Fílmico de la Universidad Católica se creó en 1955, dirigido por el sacerdote jesuita Rafael Sánchez[11] que, en los sesenta, fue un documentalista de calidad (cf. Vega et al., *Re-visión* 269-70, 381-82; Mouesca, *El documental* 64). Sergio Bravo fue alumno de este instituto (cf. Vega et al., *Re-visión* 265; Mouesca, *El documental* 69) y recibió el título de ayudante en dirección en diciembre de 1956 (cf. mensaje electrónico a Verónica Cortínez, 31 de octubre 2005). En 1957, Bravo fundó el Centro de Cine Experimental. Se trataba de algo así como de una "secesión" de las estructuras académicas y es curioso notar que, otra vez, el mismo fenómeno se dio en el caso del teatro, más claramente con la creación del Ictus[12] en 1955. El impulso mayor de la iniciativa de Bravo partía de su deseo de pasar a la práctica después de una fase de apropiación – necesariamente pasiva– del lenguaje cinematográfico de autores destacados como Grierson y Birri, sin olvidar a Rouch y Resnais. Tanto Bravo como Chaskel, quien rápidamente se unió al grupo formado alrededor de Bravo, insisten en este aspecto al describir los motivos de su búsqueda de estructuras alternativas para la creación.[13] Bravo, en mensaje electrónico a Verónica Cortínez del 28 de octubre de 2005, cuenta que

---

[9] La aclaración sobre el nombre del departamento viene de Pedro Chaskel (cf. mensaje electrónico del 14 de marzo 2006). Mouesca habla del "Departamento de Cine." La película mencionada es *Chile y su pueblo*.

[10] Me atengo a la fecha que entregó Chaskel en el coloquio-retrospectiva de Göttingen (22 al 25 de octubre de 2003). Se comprueba en el "Editorial" firmado por Pedro Chaskel y Daniel Urria, publicado en el primer número de la revista *Séptimo Arte* en agosto de 1955 como órgano del mismo club.

[11] A Sánchez se debe un importante manual sobre el montaje cinematográfico.

[12] Este grupo, imprescindible para comprender la historia del teatro en Chile, desarrollará, bajo la dictadura de Pinochet y a partir de una iniciativa de Claudio di Girolamo –uno de los fundadores del Ictus–, una labor innovadora con documentales en video (cf. Mouesca, *El documental* 87-89).

[13] Chaskel matiza que "el Centro de Cine Experimental, éramos él y yo. Bravo la locomotora y yo una especie de vagón de cola, aunque trabajando a la par con él" (mensaje electrónico del 14 de marzo 2006).

su expulsión del Cine Club por haber comenzado a filmar sin respetar los estatutos, lo llevó a fundar el Centro de Cine Experimental:

> La experimentación en base a vivencias directas y el análisis cinético que yo postulaba era inaceptable. Se llamó a reunión para tratar de mi caso, proponiendo [Manuel Gallardo] mi expulsión del Cine-Club, la que fue aprobada, significándome a la vez un buen impulso para decidir la fundación del Centro de Cine Experimental (8 de julio de 1957).

En 1985, Bravo declaró a Mouesca: "Nosotros queríamos aportar un nuevo lenguaje, independizarnos totalmente de lo que veíamos como cine oficial chileno," destacando, al mismo tiempo, la importancia de la escuela de documentalistas de Fernando Birri en Santa Fe, Argentina, que se había convertido en un polo de atracción para muchos estudiantes de cine (*Plano secuencia* 18).

De este fervor fundado en profundos conocimientos nacieron películas como *Mimbre* (1957) y *Trilla* (1958) en las cuales se produjo el encuentro entre la genialidad cinematográfica de Bravo y la musicalidad de Violeta Parra. Más que un mero "rescatar para el cine de valores nacionales" (Vega et al. 381), esta labor, en su conjunto, está caracterizada por el anhelo de salvaguardar y de perpetuar en y por la obra de arte el valor del ser humano amenazado por el desarrollo del mundo moderno. Como afirman Vega et al., los cineastas "liberados de las presiones impuestas por las necesidades de éxito comercial, trabajan con equipos artesanales y manifiestan en un nivel de escritura su interés por la geografía y habitantes del país" (381). Son conscientes de la precariedad de sus medios que los hace comprender, y hasta compartir, las circunstancias de pobreza en la cual sobreviven los artesanos. Al mismo tiempo, saben combinar la exaltación de actividades potencialmente no alienadas con la acusación de las circunstancias alienantes que condicionan esta misma pobreza. Las primeras películas de Bravo, por ejemplo, son, a la vez, testimonios de actividades populares y obras de arte cinematográficas.[14] Por consiguiente, el compromiso político nace del compromiso con un arte profundamente humanista y no al revés. *Ahora le toca al pueblo* (1962), *La marcha del carbón* (1963) y *Banderas del pueblo* (1964) son la expresión politartística, independiente de las consignas del día y de la militancia comunista de Bravo.

Pedro Chaskel pasa por etapas muy parecidas.[15] La fundación del Cine Club de la FECH en 1954 y su trabajo de animación particularizaron la primera etapa de su formación. La revista de cine que codirige en aquellos momentos lleva el título de *Séptimo Arte*. La adopción del francés *Septième Art* expresa la influencia del cine francés en Chaskel quien habla con admiración de Marcel Carné, Jean Cocteau y Alain

---

[14] Sería interesante analizar Mimbre, a partir de sus imágenes del producto artesanal, como un discurso sobre el cine.

[15] En el coloquio-retrospectiva de Göttingen, Chaskel recalcó la importancia de Bravo, especialmente para el montaje de imágenes y música, lamentando lo poco que se tomó en cuenta su obra durante el gobierno de Allende (al comentar su trabajo con Carlos Flores en 1973 sobre *Descomedidos y chascones*, 23 de octubre 2003). Además subrayó lo mucho que aprendió al trabajar con Bravo a finales de los cincuenta (al hablar sobre *Organilleros*, el 25 de octubre 2003).

Resnais sin olvidar a Claude Autant-Lara o Christian-Jacque (coloquio-retrospectiva de Göttingen, octubre de 2003).[16] En 1957, en el momento de su acercamiento al Centro de Cine Experimental pasó –como Bravo– por el Instituto Fílmico de la Universidad Católica. En ese mismo tiempo empezó su carrera profesional en el cine al trabajar como asistente de producción, dirección y montaje en el largometraje de ficción *Tres miradas a la calle* (1957) de Naum Kramarenco. Con este cineasta más bien convencional trabajó otra vez, en 1961, como asistente de dirección y montaje en *Deja que los perros ladren*. Fuerte debe de haber sido el contraste entre las miradas al cine tradicional –en el cual confiesa haber aprendido mucho de su oficio– y las miradas al cine innovador de Bravo con quien colaboró en *Día de organillos* (1959). Esta película –una balada de Santiago– sirvió de inspiración a cineastas como Patricio Guzmán (*La batalla de Chile*, 1975–79, y *Chile, la memoria obstinada*, 1997), Sergio Castilla (*Gringuito*, 1998) y al propio Chaskel (*Venceremos*, 1970, y *Organilleros*, 1996).[17] En 1963 sucedió a Bravo en la dirección del departamento Cine Experimental[18] de la Universidad de Chile, cargo en el que permaneció hasta ser expulsado de la universidad por los golpistas en 1973.

Aquí vivieron, el primero de sus "delicados cortometrajes"[19] (Paranaguá 77), es de 1964 y en lo que sigue me ocuparé brevemente de él, del mismo modo que de *Testi-*

---

[16] El programa del Cine Club Universitario de la FECH, publicado en el número de agosto ya citado, menciona, sin embargo, cuatro títulos entre los cuales no se encuentra ninguna francesa: *Milagro en Milán* (*Miracolo a Milano*, Vittorio De Sica, 1951), *Odio que fue amor* (*The Browning Version*, Anthony Asquith, 1951), *Los asesinos están entre nosotros* (*Die Mörder sind unter uns*, Wolfgang Staudte, 1946), *El fugitivo* (*The Fugitive*, John Ford, 1947). Es sorprendente la presencia de Staudte en Chile en un momento en el cual era muy mal visto en la República Federal por haber filmado en la República Democrática. *Die Mörder sind unter uns* es la primera y una de las pocas películas alemanas que hablan y condenan la impunidad de muchos de los criminales nazis que logran iniciar una nueva vida después de la liberación de Alemania (la derrota, según ellos y muchos más).

[17] Me refiero, por supuesto, a la imagen del carretonero al comienzo de *Día de organilleros* (filmado en picada vertical) que parece dar inicio a su carrera por el cine chileno. Chaskel, en la entrevista que le hace Ruffinelli, subraya, a propósito de las imágenes del carretonero de *La batalla de Chile III. El poder popular*, que "ese personaje es alguien que todos los chilenos han filmado alguna vez" (190-91). En cuanto a la colaboración de Chaskel, los créditos de *Día de organilleros* ponen "Iluminación: Pedro Chaskel."

[18] El Cine Experimental fue creado como organismo sucesor del Centro Experimental a instancias del propio Bravo quien fue su director entre mayo de 1961 y junio de 1963, fecha en la cual debió abandonar ese puesto por problemas de política universitaria. Chaskel había sido director de la recién creada Cineteca de la Universidad de Chile que, junto con el Centro Experimental y la TV universitaria formaban el Departamento Audiovisual (cf. mensaje electrónico de Sergio Bravo, "Precisiones en torno al origen del Centro de Cine Experimental," 24 de noviembre 2005).

[19] Paranaguá, como Ruffinelli, se refiere a las películas *Los ojos como mi papá* (1979) y *¿Qué es...?* (1980) que tratan del exilio cubano. Pero me parece lícito aplicar este término a la obra entera de Chaskel.

monio (1968–69) y *Venceremos* (1970), es decir, consideraré la mitad de las seis películas que Chaskel realizó en la década de 1960 a 1970. Las tres obras escogidas muestran de qué manera la obra de Chaskel se inscribe a lo largo de los sesenta en el contexto de la creciente concientización y polarización política, aunque siempre sobre la sólida base de la práctica estética de su oficio de cineasta. Como en Bravo, su compromiso político es una consecuencia de su compromiso artístico.

Aquí vivieron –que alguna vez se mencionó como *Arqueología en el norte* (cf. Mouesca, *Plano secuencia* 21)– se filmó bajo condiciones técnicas pobres y sin planificación previa, "durante los trabajos de investigación efectuadas por el arqueólogo Profesor Jean Christian Spahni en el litoral norte de Chile junto a la desembocadura del río Loa," según la información del intertítulo inicial de la película. Los créditos especifican la estrecha cooperación entre Chaskel y Ríos quienes se conocieron en su trabajo con Kramarenco en *Deja que los perros ladren* (1961).[20] La realización se adscribe a ambos, la fotografía y el montaje a Chaskel, y la producción, a Ríos. En realidad, los dos aprovechan la posibilidad de unirse a la expedición de Spahni para hacer cine, con una cámara 16mm a cuerda (lo que permitía una toma máxima de 20 segundos) y 10 rollos de 2 minutos y medio de duración. Chaskel tenía predilección por el paisaje, en tanto que Ríos se enfrentaba al reto de la luz.[21] El resultado final de 16 minutos y 100 tomas muestra que este escaso material se utilizó con eficacia, mas no para hacer una película educativa sobre los antepasados del norte de Chile, sino para realizar un ensayo poético sobre el incesante pasar del ser humano por la tierra, marcado por los elementos, el trabajo y la muerte que desemboca en otras vidas. En vano se buscarán en ella informaciones, más allá de las imágenes, sobre los habitantes de la costa nortina en un momento remoto de la historia que nunca se concretiza.[22] Apenas se entregan algunos comentarios sobre la tarea de los arqueólogos que son comparados con los campesinos, pues descubren con la pala y la mano los misterios –que guarda la tierra– de los que vivieron aquí: seres humanos de todos los tiempos. La dureza de este lugar desértico –inaccesible por tierra en 1964–, cuyos habitantes dependieron del único río del norte que de la cordillera baja al mar, se utiliza magistralmente para estilizar el trabajo arqueológico como trabajo campesino y, en verdad, tan precario como el de los antepasados. El marco marítimo repetido en un plano recurrente del vuelo de los alcatraces hace pensar en "la mer toujours recommencée" –"la mar siempre recomenzada" del "Cimetière marin" de Paul Valéry (223)– como origen y símbolo de la vida. Los planos que presentan los hallazgos de los arqueólogos insisten, a partir de la muerte, en la vida (una calavera en primer plano se une por un *travelling lateral* a los restos de su vestimenta y su herramienta; segmento 3) y el comentario –voluntaria-

---

[20] Ríos fue asistente de cámara.

[21] Todas las indicaciones técnicas que siguen se refieren a los respectivos esquemas del montaje que se encuentran al final del artículo.

[22] Quien quiera informarse rápidamente sobre la prehistoria del Norte Grande de Chile puede hacerlo, por ejemplo, a partir de las páginas de Osvaldo Silva Galdames en la *Historia de Chile* de Villalobos et al. (cf. 12-21).

mente poético (de Ernesto Fontecilla) en emulación del ejemplo de Resnais y pronunciado por uno de los grandes actores del teatro y del cine de la época, Héctor Duvauchelle– subraya "la elocuencia de la muerte" (plano 42) que se da a conocer en "aquello que en vida fueron sus posesiones:" "los hombres se prolongan en sus cosas, humildes" (plano 63).

Si el filme se empezó sin planificación, su montaje final revela una estructura minuciosamente concebida. Valga como ejemplo el segmento central de la película, el cuarto de 7, de una duración de 102 segundos en 13 planos. El segmento funciona como resumen y, a la vez, como una pausa que invita a la reflexión. El ritmo cuidadoso del montaje combina un plano de conjunto que muestra a los arqueólogos perdidos en la extensión desértica entre la cordillera y el mar con otro de un buitre y un tercer plano, medio, que muestra a uno de los campesinos-arqueólogos casi en actitud amorosa con un esqueleto dentro de un hoyo-tumba. Esta primera parte del segmento (planos 45 a 50) se cierra con una de las variantes del plano ya mencionado de los alcatraces (aparecen por primera vez en el plano 18) y sigue la descripción de un recreo que termina con otro plano de aves marinas (plano 57). La ausencia de comentario (es el único segmento sin palabras) forma parte de la lograda construcción del segmento, además de la parca utilización de la música compuesta por Gustavo Becerra, uno de los grandes compositores chilenos de la segunda mitad del siglo junto a Luis Advis y Sergio Ortega.

El respeto absoluto a la vida del ser humano fundamentado en la conciencia misma de su fragilidad ante la muerte va a ser la constante del cine de Chaskel y de Ríos.[23] *Testimonio* empieza a filmarse a finales de 1968 y se termina en 1969. Otra vez el comienzo del rodaje se debe a una casualidad. En un viaje de comisión al Altiplano, el director de la clínica psiquiátrica de Iquique pide a Chaskel y Ríos que documenten la miseria de la cual tiene que hacerse responsable. El espanto que sienten frente al abandono casi completo de los enfermos mentales se transmite a los siete minutos de película –y, todavía hoy, a los espectadores. Ese espanto –Chaskel relata cómo Ríos y él sintieron la cámara como un parapeto contra la agresividad de los hechos y, a la vez, como un medio de mantener una distancia respetuosa dada la intrusión de la cámara– se combina con una petición intrínseca de respeto que se desprende precisamente del trabajo con la cámara. Ésta se fija en la descripción del lugar como patio trasero y basural de una clínica moderna (segmento 1, sin seres humanos). Traspasando una reja (plano 12), la cámara documenta los hechos básicos del interior (segmento 3) y de la vida de los internos (segmento 4) que insiste en la reclusión (planos 16 y 26). Culmina con una serie de retratos de los internos y otra de las internas (segmento 5, dos minutos), retratos que –tanto por el movimiento y los gestos de los seres humanos, como por el movimiento de la cámara– captan de manera sobrecogedora la curiosidad, el

---

[23] Con la experiencia de la dictadura de Pinochet en la cabeza, es inevitable que algunos momentos de *Aquí vivieron* hagan pensar en *Fernando ha vuelto* (Silvio Caiozzi, 1998), por ejemplo, el segmento 5 con el siguiente comentario al plano 60: "Nada hace más sobrecogedor el recuerdo de los desaparecidos que aquello que en vida fueron sus posesiones."

miedo y la consideración de este encuentro-desencuentro entre mundos que se desconocen. También este segmento repite las rejas de la reclusión (planos 27 y 32). El balance final es una constatación de alienación y de cosificación impuesta (segmento 6, de dos planos sin ser humano). Cuando en las imágenes se muestran las paredes y las rejas (el último plano, el 47) que con letreros como "policlínico" contienen promesas de ayuda que no se cumplen la voz del comentario habla de los seres humanos que no se ven en la pantalla:

> Estos hombres no votan,
> no son de ningún partido político,
> no pagan impuestos,
> no hacen el servicio militar,
> no escriben cartas a los diarios,
> no defienden a la patria,
> no rezan,
> no sirven a ningún patrón,
> y además no tienen dinero.

De repente se impone la impresión de que los locos somos nosotros que permitimos tales abusos.

Venceremos se considera como "un modelo del género" del "documental político" (Mouesca, *El documental* 71). No cabe duda de que el motivo de la realización de la película es político. Se hace –según Chaskel– para apoyar al gobierno de la Unidad Popular contra las acciones agresivas de la derecha, en el contexto del secuestro y asesinato del general René Schneider, después de que el Congreso había confirmado a Salvador Allende como Presidente de la República en octubre de 1970. Pero si la película se mira con atención se descubre que ésta no es la expresión de un programa político. No hay retratos de Allende –su nombre aparece fugazmente en el titular de un diario que se agita como una bandera más (plano 188, al comienzo del segmento 14), y el símbolo de la Unidad Popular (la X que combina la V de "victoria" y la A de "Allende") se puede ver algunos instantes más tarde (plano 203).[24] La película es antes que nada la expresión de la enorme esperanza colectiva de poder terminar con una sociedad injusta y alienante. Es esta sociedad la que *Venceremos* acusa en claro y duro blanco y negro, sin una palabra de comentario explícito. La primera parte (segmentos 2-9, min. 00.28-09.57, que corresponde a las dos terceras partes del tiempo) opera con una serie de sintagmas conopiales en montaje paralelo.[25] Los segmentos pares de 2 a 8 representan la pobreza (son cuatro sintagmas conopiales), los segmentos impares de 3

---

[24] En Göttingen, Chaskel subrayó la intencionalidad de esta puesta en escena. Se quería evitar cualquier atisbo de "culto a la personalidad" (en el contexto de la discusión sobre la trilogía guevarista, 25 de octubre 2003).

[25] Está demás indicar que me sirvo de la "grande syntagmatique" de Christian Metz. En cuanto a la formación de unidades más largas que los sintagmas de Metz me atengo a la propuesta de Fledelius (cf. 48-49). Es notable que la organización del tiempo de las dos partes de *Venceremos* corresponda a las proporciones (en principio espaciales, es cierto) de la "sección áurea" (5:8) (cf. Sánchez 72-79).

a 9 ilustran la riqueza (otra vez cuatro sintagmas conopiales) y estos ocho sintagmas forman, a su vez, cuatro super-sintagmas paralelos. Esta organización puede parecer esquemática, pero su eficacia se revela al considerar el montaje de las imágenes con la banda sonora. La película insiste primero en la miseria de la alienación (segmento 2). La letra nada política (en un sentido restringido) de la canción "Santiago" de Ángel Parra da su pleno sentido a las tomas de los hombres que, por la mañana, van camino al trabajo, a pie o en "micro" (autobús):

El tiempo cambia de espacio
el hombre no encuentra su alma
el tiempo le da dinero
y oscurece la mañana.

Pero los "ricos" tampoco parecen felices. La canción italiana "Vivere" –vivir sin melancolía y reírse ("ridere") de las locuras del mundo– acompaña el segmento 3 que muestra fachadas de mansiones más o menos fastuosas. No se escucha cuando se ven hombres (y el plano de una mujer) que van aislados y aburridos cada uno en su automóvil. El eco de esta canción amargamente frívola cobra matices doblemente irónicos por el efecto de su ausencia y su reemplazo por el ruido de los motores. Se sugiere el cinismo de "los ricos" frente al mundo y se contrasta con la mirada distanciada de la cámara sobre la falta de calidad humana de su vida: son fachadas de seres humanos.[26] La bisagra del plano 42 –un carretonero en medio de autos– muestra la pobreza en medio de la riqueza, formando ambos el cuadro de una sociedad alienada. Con este plano pasamos a la parte central (segmentos 4 a 9) que después de la exposición del tema en el primer sintagma paralelo (segmentos 2 y 3), lo desarrolla ampliamente. Después de insistir en el esfuerzo de los pobres para sobrevivir mediante dos planos de otro carretonero (43 y 44), cuya cara ocupa la pantalla a medida que se va aproximando a la cámara, sigue una serie de fotos que acompaña a la canción –comprometida con los pobres sin ser directamente política– "Quisiera volverme noche" de Ángel Parra[27]:

---

[26] La canción de Cesare Bixio fue compuesta en los años treinta. En vez de quejarse de la infidelidad de su amor, el "yo lírico" de la canción se felicita de su "libertad recobrada." El refrán bipartito dice: "Vivere senza malinconia / Vivere senza più gelosia / Senza rimpianti / Senza mai più conoscere cos' è l'amore / Cogliere il più bel fiore / Goder la vita e far tacere il cuore. // Ridere sempre così giocondo / Ridere delle follie del mondo / Vivere finché c'è gioventù / Perché la vita è bella / La voglio vivere sempre più."
Le agradezco esta información a la Dra. Ilva Fabiani, lectora de italiano en el Seminario de Románicas de la Universidad de Göttingen.

[27] Ángel e Isabel Parra, los hijos de Violeta Parra y Luis Cereceda, forman un núcleo de la cultura alternativa que surge durante los años sesenta. En 1965 fundaron la ya mítica "Peña de los Parra" (en el número 340 de la santiaguina Calle del Carmen), una "verdadera academia de la canción y de la artesanía" según Osvaldo Rodríguez, "el Gitano" (31). De la "Peña" salieron al mundo Víctor Jara y Patricio Manns; por la "Peña" pasan Atahualpa Yupanqui y Paco Ibáñez, entre muchos otros. Las canciones de Ángel Parra y Alejandro Reyes que aparecen en *Venceremos* provienen de la labor en la "Peña" (cf. Parra, Ángel).

Quisiera volverme noche
para ver llegar el día
que mi pueblo se levante
buscando su amanecida.

En el segmento siguiente (5), los jóvenes propagandistas de "Fiducia," un grupo universitario "gremialista" de extrema derecha, distribuyen su revista en las calles de los barrios altos. Su pensamiento, que parece justificar la miseria, se da a conocer en la página de una revista que se muestra en primer plano (un inserto, plano 60) que reproduce un artículo titulado "Verdades olvidadas," en el que se comenta que "la igualdad de clases corrompe las costumbres." De esta defensa del *status quo*, subrayada por una música disonante (tomada de *La historia del soldado*, de Igor Stravinsky), volvemos a las imágenes de la pobreza (segmento 6, otra serie de fotos) y a la voz de Ángel Parra que continúa:

Quisiera ser leña seca
Pa' calentar el invierno
de los pobres de mi tierra,
de los que nacen muriendo.

El segmento 7 –sorprendentemente actual– presenta un retrato del consumismo como expresión de la riqueza existente y como sueño paliativo contra la miseria real. En sus imágenes se combinan un materialismo crudo (artículos de consumo lujosos: el auto rápido, la ropa exquisita, los perfumes, comidas y bebidas en profusión), con el machismo (la mujer rebajada a artículo de consumo: maniquíes en los escaparates, imágenes de mujeres desnudas en revistas como *Viejo verde*) y con la agresividad (camuflada de justiciera en cómics de origen norteamericano: *Batman*, "el hombre murciélago campeón de la justicia," *Superman*, *Hopalong Cassidy*, *Gene Autry*, dirigida contra mujeres "problema" –imagen de *Susy, secretos del corazón*). Las imágenes van acompañadas por la canción pop "El triunfador" del grupo uruguayo Los Iracundos:

Yo quiero ser un triunfador
de la vida y del amor.
Y seguiré buscando
felicidad,
porque en alguna esquina
la encontraré.
Con el saco sobre el hombro,
voy cruzando la ciudad,
uno más de los que anhelan
el amor que es de verdad.
Calles, parques, muchos bares
son testigos de mis ansias,
y el amor que estoy buscando
es mi única esperanza.[28]

---

[28] Se trata de la segunda parte de la canción. Las dos primeras estrofas son: "Con el saco sobre el hombro / voy buscando mi destino, / no me importa a mí la gente / mas yo sigo mi

La interacción de ambos medios es perfecta en el sentido de que las imágenes ilustran con elocuencia el espíritu arribista de la canción y ésta complementa, sin doblarlas, las imágenes del sueño consumista a través de la mención explícita de los sueños supuestamente individuales e idealistas en oposición a los objetos de consumo y al ser humano reducido a tal objeto. También queda de manifiesto que no se trata de una riqueza de verdad sino de una imagen, de una (mala) utopía para los que tienen poco o nada.[29]

El consumismo del individuo "triunfador" se contrapone con el escándalo de la desnutrición en el segmento 8.[30] La contradicción entre la extrema miseria de los niños en el basural y en la clínica, su pertenencia a "los que nacen muriendo," y los juegos amenos, solidarios, evocados por la ronda "Dame la mano" de Gabriela Mistral es punzante:

> Dame la mano y danzaremos;
> dame la mano y me amarás.
> Como una sola flor seremos,
> como una flor y nada más.
> El mismo verso cantaremos,
> al mismo paso bailarás.
> Como una espiga ondularemos,
> como una espiga, y nada más.
> Te llamas Rosa y yo Esperanza;
> pero tu nombre olvidarás,
> porque seremos una danza
> en la colina, y nada más. (217)

Finalmente, otra vez con la melodía de "Vivere" (segmento 9), la alienación y el cinismo irónico llegan a su paroxismo en el contraste de los pasatiempos supuestamente elegantes de la clase alta aburrida y esnob. La única conclusión que admiten las imágenes filmadas de una competencia de animales mimados al máximo es que los perros, en este "mondo cane," parecen obtener más atención que los niños.[31] El plano bisagra

---

camino. // Con el saco sobre el hombro / y mil sueños en la mente / de la vida no me asombro, / si luchar es lo corriente."

[29] Chaskel recuerda con una pequeña nota de desencanto que este segmento fue el que más asombro y aplausos causó cuando se mostró en las poblaciones santiaguinas en 1970 y los años siguientes (coloquio-retrospectiva de Göttingen, 25 de octubre 2003). El conjunto uruguayo Los Iracundos fue muy popular en el Chile de finales de los sesenta y comienzos de los setenta y sus melodías todavía se recuerdan hoy en día.

[30] Se aprovechan imágenes de la película *Desnutrición infantil*, de 1969, dirigida por Ramiro Álvarez, con la fotografía de Ríos.

[31] El largometraje documental *Mondo cane* (Gualtiero Jacopetti et al., 1962) que da cuenta – de un modo algo sensacionalista, por fines de comercio– de algunas atrocidades toleradas forma parte de una lista que entregó Patricio Guzmán al hablar de las películas que le habían impresionado profundamente (cf. Ruffinelli 364). Esta lista empieza con *The Living Desert* (Walt Disney, 1953) y termina con *Mourir à Madrid* (Frédéric Rossif, 1963) y contiene también *Mein Kampf* (Erwin Leiser, 1960). Para Román Gubern, *Mondo cane* forma

(137) resume este escándalo con la imagen de la niñita desnutrida de los planos 114 y 115.

La consecuencia de este estado del Estado –como diría Matta– es la confrontación violenta de las "masas populares" con las "fuerzas del orden" que muestra el siguiente sintagma conopial (segmento 10).[32] Es el resumen del super-sintagma antecedente (2-9) y, al mismo tiempo, la primera parte del segundo super-sintagma que forma junto con el segmento 11 (otro sintagma conopial).[33] La parte final del segmento 10 (planos 160-74), el paroxismo de la violencia, se combina con la "Elegía" de Eduardo Carrasco, entonada por el emblemático grupo Quilapayún. Se construye de esa manera un homenaje a todos los que contribuyeron, sufriendo, al triunfo de la Unidad Popular.[34]

Las tomas que documentan las manifestaciones masivas y alegres para celebrar la victoria de Allende funcionan como alternativa contra la alienación y la violencia de las estructuras sociales vigentes. La índole alternativa se marca por la bisagra del plano 184 –la pantalla negra– y el "BASTA" en el muro del primer plano (185). Es en este momento en que aparece –en tres planos no seguidos (189, 193, 195)– la bandera chilena. Pero no se vuelve emblema de una "nación." Forma parte de la alegría común que necesita del viejo símbolo para expresar el intento de renovación y, por qué no, de revolución. La canción "Gallo de amanecida," cantada por el conjunto Lonquimay, se une a las imágenes y subraya el ambiente de comienzo esperanzado, de redención sin redentor:

> Un gallo de amanecida
> abre las alas y canta,
> entre tinieblas y rocío
> la esperanza se levanta.
> Este gallo que canta no tiene dueño,
> no es tuyo, ni mío, ni del vecino
> es el gallo que canta nuestro destino.[35]

---

parte "de una retahíla de paraísos artificiales, con desnudos de celuloide y horrores al gusto del 'divino marqués'" (367).

[32] Chaskel destacó, como una de las ideas centrales de *Venceremos*, la preocupación de Ríos por la violencia cotidiana, estructural, como problema inevitable de la sociedad capitalista (coloquio-retrospectiva de Göttingen, 22 de octubre 2003).

[33] Los dos super-sintagmas (paralelos) forman un mega-sintagma (paralelo) que en su duración de 16 minutos corresponde casi exactamente a la estructura típica que se deduce de las pesquisas de Fledelius para documentales de esta duración (49).

[34] La película épica *La tierra prometida* (1973) de Miguel Littin está dedicada enteramente a conmemorar a los que cayeron en los decenios de lucha del movimiento obrero.

[35] La canción sigue con marcadas notas cristianas, incluyendo de este modo también a los simpatizantes de la Democracia Cristiana sin los cuales no habría sido posible la elección de Allende: "Le escuchan todos los que están vivos, / los bondadosos, los oprimidos, / rezando al Cristo de la igualdad, / de la belleza, de la verdad, / el desafío y la dignidad, / los hambrientos y sin camisa, / los con el alma nunca sumisa, / los de la cólera y la sonrisa.

Se excluye cualquier culto al individuo para insistir en la necesidad de un cambio profundo de la sociedad en el cual todos tienen que participar. Este cambio se ve como un largo camino, (una revolución lenta, si se me permite este casi oxímoron). El plano 215 muestra otro muro con la inscripción "Pueblo: Abierto está el camino" y solamente en el plano siguiente (216) se completa la frase con "hacia el nacimiento del hombre nuevo" para formar el "mane, thecel, phares" positivo que se propone como programa político.[36] La cámara nos presenta esta parte del "nacimiento" mediante un *zoom* invertido, el *fade in* de la nada triunfalista "Elegía" se hace más fuerte y acompaña, casi en contrapunto, la imagen final (plano 217) del "VENCEREMOS" que aparece en una muralla llenando la pantalla. Todas estas murallas deberían abrirse para que se volviera realidad la esperanza de crear entre todas y todos las condiciones para una vida humana con dignidad.[37]

Nada más apreciable ni nada más difícil de realizar. A la postre sorprende no tanto la ingenuidad o el romanticismo que el propio Chaskel nota en su película (cf. Mouesca, *El documental* 71), sino más bien la clarividencia del cuadro social que se plasma en ella. Clarividencia en cuanto a quienes son los opositores del gobierno de Allende, como el grupo "Fiducia," escogido como representante de la derecha política y de cuyas filas salió el propagandista más hábil de la dictadura de Pinochet, Jaime Guzmán Errazurriz[38]. Y clarividencia en cuanto a la violencia contenida en una estructura social marcada por la injusticia. La globalización de la pobreza y de la exclusión no se pueden negar –cayó el muro de Berlín, hay muro entre Europa y África en Ceuta y Melilla, hay muro entre los israelíes y los palestinos, hay muro entre América del Norte y América del Sur, hay ghettos en nuestras grandes ciudades. Y en todos estos lugares crece la violencia. Es tiempo de que tomemos en serio el "mane, thecel, phares" y la propuesta humana que se encuentran en las películas documentales de Sergio Bravo, Héctor Ríos, Claudio Sapiaín, Álvaro Ramírez, Carlos Flores, Sergio

---

// Cristo que nunca vendió su nombre, / no tuvo miedo de ser un hombre. // Este gallo nos canta de contrapunto,/ todos los hombres vamos bailando juntos, / el que no quiera oírlo no se disculpe, / es un canto de vida y no de muerte, / el que quiera bailarlo que se despierte. // Los campesinos y los mineros, / enfierradores y carpinteros, / los tejedores, los estudiantes, / organilleros y caminantes, / excavadores y electricistas, / los escribientes y las modistas, / los anhelantes, los solitarios, / los cesantes y funcionarios, / los pescadores entumecidos, / mil corazones en un latido, / mil corazones en un latido."

[36] Mientras la inscripción en los muros de la sala de fiestas del rey Baltasar predice la destrucción de Babilonia, las inscripciones murales de *Venceremos* formulan una visión utópica optimista.

[37] Es de notar que la conocida marcha "Venceremos" de Sergio Ortega y Claudio Iturra, cantada por los Inti-Illimani y los Quilapayún no se escucha en la película de Chaskel/Ríos.

[38] Como se sabe, Guzmán fue asesinado en 1991. Para una exposición de su doctrina –que se apoya en las teorías de Carl Schmitt, que a su vez trató de legitimar la toma del poder por Hitler– se puede consultar el libro de Renato Cristi.

Castilla, y –con todos los que no nombro– de Pedro Chaskel, quien actualmente está
trabajando en una película sobre la "Operación Cóndor."[39]

Anexo: protocolos de secuencia de las películas analizadas

Aquí vivieron
Cine Experimental de la Universidad de Chile, 1964
16 mm, b/n, 16 minutos

Producción: Héctor Ríos
Realización: Pedro Chaskel, Héctor Ríos
Fotos y montaje: Pedro Chaskel
Texto: Ernesto Fontecilla
Voz: Héctor Duvauchelle
Sonido: Francisco Cares
Música: Gustavo Becerra
Esquema del montaje:

Segmento	Duración	Contenido	No. de planos
0	00.00-00.58	Créditos	
1	00.58-03.13	El lugar desierto	1-19
2	03.14-04.14	La tarea de los arqueólogos	20-25
3	04.15-08.10	Labor de manos para descubrir	26-44
4	08.11-09.53	Hombre de hoy como el de ayer	45-57
5	09.54-12.02	Trabajo de detalles fundamentales	58-73
6	12.03-13.14	Viviendas: sabiduría de los que aquí vivieron	74-83
7	13.15-16.00	El regreso	84-100

Testimonio –hospital psiquiátrico de Iquique
Cine Experimental de la Universidad de Chile, 1968–69
16mm, b/n, 7 minutos

Dirección y montaje: Pedro Chaskel
Asistente: Claudio Sapiaín
Fotografía: Héctor Ríos

---

[39] Organizada por Manuel Contreras –quien gestó el asesinato de Orlando Letelier–, esta operación supranacional –participaron activamente Argentina, Bolivia, Paraguay y Uruguay–
se proponía dar caza coordinada a todo lo que las dictaduras de los setenta consideraban de
izquierda (cf. Cuya).

Música: Kodaly Schidlowsky
Voz: Héctor Noguera

Esquema del montaje:

Segmento	Duración	Contenido	No. de planos	Sonido/Música
1	00.00-00.48	Un basural: patio de una clínica	1-7	
2	00.49-01.05	Créditos	8-11	
3	01.06-02.19	Información sobre hechos básicos	12-15	Voz: "Servicio de psiquiatría del hospital regional de Iquique –Diciembre de 1968. Servicio de hombres: 29 enfermos para cuya atención existen una clínica sin lavatorio, sin agua, sin ventilación, sin iluminación ..."
4	02.20-04.22	Condiciones de vida de los enfermos (celdas, comidas)	16-26	
5	04.23-06.24	Seres humanos excluidos de la sociedad	27-45	
6	06.25-07.00	Balance final: alienación y cosificación	46-47	Voz: "Estos hombres no votan ..." (cf. p. 396)

Venceremos
Cine Experimental Universidad de Chile, 1970
16mm, b/n, 15.40 minutos

Realización: Pedro Chaskel, Héctor Ríos
Cámara: Samuel Carvajal
Sonido: Leonardo Céspedes

Canciones: "Santiago," "Quisiera volverme noche," Ángel Parra
                    "Dame la mano," Gabriela Mistral
                    "Un gallo de amanecida," Alejandro Reyes
                    "Elegía," Eduardo Carrasco

Intertítulo (plano 5):

"Los materiales de esta película provienen de filmaciones de Cine Experimental,
Noticiario de Canal 9, fotografías del archivo del diario *El Siglo* y de Patricio
Guzmán."

Esquema del montaje:

Segmento	Duración	Contenido	No. de planos	Sonido/Música
1	00.00-00.28	Créditos (sin título)	1-5	Guitarra sola
2	00.29-01.58	Barrios pobres transporte en micro	6-22	Ángel Parra: "Santiago"
3	01.59-03.04	Barrios ricos, autos privados	23-41	Cesara Bixio: "Vivere" (planos 25-34)
	03.05-03.16	(bisagra) Carretonero entre autos	42	Ruido de autos
4	03.17-04.07	Imágenes de la extrema pobreza I	43-56	Ángel Parra: "Quisiera volverme noche"
5	04.08-04.48	Barrios ricos: "Fiducia"	57-63	Cobres que suenan falsos (de Igor Stravinsky, *La historia del soldado*)
6	04.49-05.15	Imágenes de la extrema pobreza II	64-71	Ángel Parra continúa, "Quisiera ser leña seca"
7	05.16-06.49	Sueños de consumidor macho, y de consumidora domesticada	72-104	Los Iracundos: "El triunfador"
8	06.50-08.26	Imágenes de la extrema pobreza III: niños sin comida	105-116	Canción, letra de Gabriela Mistral: "Dame la mano"

Chile en las películas de Pedro Chaskel (1960-1970) 405

Segmento	Duración	Contenido	No. de planos	Sonido/Música
9	08.27-09.49	Ocios y aburrimiento de ricos	117-136	"Vivere," retomada
	09.50-09.57	(bisagra) Bebé desnutrido (retoma plano 114)	137	Mudo
10	09.58-12.39	La miseria produce violencia	138-183	Tambores; planos160-174: Eduardo Carrasco/ Quilapayún: "Elegía"
	12.40-12.42	(bisagra) Pantalla negra	184	*fade in* sonido masas
11	12.43-15.37	La alternativa	185-217	Planos 187-214 Alejandro Reyes/ conjunto Lonquimay: "Un gallo de amanecida;" planos 216-217: "Elegía," retomada
	15.38-15.40	FIN	218	

Bibliografía

Burton, Julianne. "Introduction." *Cinema and Social Change in Latin America. Conversations with Filmmakers*. Austin: U of Texas P, 1986. ix-xvi.

Caudet, Francisco. "Chile, Pablo Neruda y los dos mil del *Winnipeg*." *Texto social. Estudios pragmáticos sobre literatura y cine. Homenaje a Manfred Engelbert*. Ed. Burkhard Pohl y Annette Paatz. Berlin: Tranvía, 2002. 425-40.

Chaskel, Pedro y Daniel Urria. "Editorial." *Séptimo Arte* 1 (agosto 1955): 1.

Cristi, Renato. *El pensamiento político de Jaime Guzmán. Autoridad y libertad*. Santiago de Chile: LOM, 2000.

Cuya, Esteban. "La 'Operación Cóndor.' El terrorismo de Estado de alcance transnacional." *Ko'âga Roñe'êtâ* VII (1996). http://www.derechos.org/koaga/vii/2/cuya.html.

Engelbert, Manfred. "Notas a la poesía chilena. La lírica de Quilapayún." *Revista Chilena de Literatura* 55 (noviembre 1999): 137-48.

———. "Poesía y pintura en la vida de Violeta Parra." Actas del primer simposio internacional en Berlín occidental sobre literatura y crítica literaria de mujeres de Latinoamerica. Ed. Esther Andradi et al. Berlin: LAI, 1989. 91-110.

Fledelius, Karsten. "Syntagmatic Film Analysis—With Special Reference to Historical Research." *Untersuchungen zur Syntax des Films*. Papiere des Münsteraner Arbeitskreises für Semiotik/PAPMAKS 8. Münster, 1979. 31-68.

Godoy Quezada, Mario. *Historia del cine chileno*. Santiago de Chile: sin editorial, 1966.

Gubern, Román. *Historia del cine*. Barcelona: Editorial Lumen, 1989.

Illanes Oliva, María Angélica. "Apocalipsis en el sur. Chile a partir de la década de los 60." *Chile: 1968-1988*. Ed. José Luis Gómez-Martínez y Francisco Javier Pinedo. Athens: Georgia Series on Hispanic Thought, 1988. 11-29.

King, John. *Magical Reels. A History of Cinema in Latin America*. London, New York: Verso, 2000.

López, Ana M. "An 'Other' History. The New Latin American Cinema." *New Latin American Cinema*. Ed. Michael T. Martin. Volume One: Theory, Practices and Transcontinental Articulations. Detroit: Wayne State UP, 1997. 135-56.

Marx, Karl. "Thesen über Feuerbach." *Karl Marx – Friedrich Engels. Philosophie* Ed. Iring Fetscher. Vol. 1. Frankfurt a.M.: Fischer Taschenbuch, 1966. 4 vols. 139-41.

Mistral, Gabriela. "Dame la mano." *Poesías completas*. Ed. Margaret Bates. Madrid: Aguilar, 1966. 217.

Mouesca, Jacqueline. *El documental chileno*. Santiago de Chile: LOM, 2005.

———. *Plano secuencia de la memoria chilena. Veinticinco años de cine chileno (1960–1985)*. Madrid: Ediciones del Litoral, 1988.

Neruda, Pablo. *Canto general*. Madrid: Ediciones Cátedra, 1990.

Ossa Coo, Carlos. *Historia del cine chileno*. Santiago de Chile: Editora Nacional Quimantú, 1971.

Paranaguá, Paulo Antonio. "Orígenes, evolución y problemas." *Cine documental en América Latina*. Ed. Paulo Antonio Paranaguá. Madrid: Ediciones Cátedra, 2003. 13-78.

Parra, Ángel. *Canciones de amor y muerte. Peña de los Parra*. VBP-297. LP. 1969.

Parra, Violeta. *Lieder aus Chile*. Ed. Manfred Engelbert. Frankfurt a.M.: Vervuert, 1978.

Pick, Zuzana M. *The New Latin American Cinema. A Continental Project*. Austin: U of Texas P, 1996.

Rodríguez, Osvaldo. *Cantores que reflexionan. Notas para una historia personal de la Nueva Canción Chilena*. San Fernando de Henares: LAR, 1984.

Ruffinelli, Jorge. *Patricio Guzmán*. Madrid: Ediciones Cátedra, 2001.

Sánchez, Rafael C. *El montaje cinematográfico. Arte de movimiento*. Santiago de Chile: Ediciones Nueva Universidad, 1971.

Schumann, Peter B., ed. *Film und Revolution in Lateinamerika*. Oberhausen: Verlag Karl Maria Laufen, 1981.

———. *Historia del cine latinoamericano*. Buenos Aires: Editorial Legasa, 1987.

Silva Galdames, Osvaldo. "Prehistoria." *Historia de Chile*. Ed. Sergio Villalobos et al. Santiago de Chile: Editorial Universitaria, 1990. 12-34.

Valéry, Paul. "Le cimetière marin." *Charmes*. Paris: Gallimard, 1955. 221-40.

Vega, Alicia et al. *Re-visión del cine chileno*. Santiago de Chile: Editorial Aconcagua, 1979.

Filmografía

A Valparaíso. Dir. Joris Ivens, co-director Sergio Bravo. Francia, Chile, 1963.

Ahora le toca al pueblo. Dir. Sergio Bravo. Chile, 1962.

Aquí vivieron. Dir. Pedro Chaskel. Chile, 1962.

Banderas del pueblo. Dir. Sergio Bravo. Chile, 1964.

Che, hoy y siempre. Dir. Pedro Chaskel. Cuba, Chile, 1983.

Chile y su pueblo. Dir. Edmundo Urrutia y Raúl Barrientos. Chile, 1952.

Chile, la memoria obstinada. Dir. Patricio Guzmán. Francia, Canadá, Chile, 1997.

Constructor cada día, compañero. Dir. Pedro Chaskel. Cuba, Chile, 1982.

Deja que los perros ladren. Dir. Naum Kramarenco. Chile, 1961.

Descomedidos y chascones. Dir. Carlos Flores. Chile, 1972.

Desnutrición infantil. Dir. Ramiro Álvarez. Chile, 1969.

Día de organillos. Dir. Sergio Bravo. Chile, 1959.

Die Mörder sind unter uns. Dir. Wolfgang Staudte. Alemania, 1946.

El chacal de Nahueltoro. Dir. Miguel Littin. Chile, 1969.

Fernando ha vuelto. Dir. Silvio Caiozzi. Chile, 1998.

Gringuito. Dir. Sergio Castilla. Chile, 1998.

La batalla de Chile. Dir. Patricio Guzmán. Venezuela, Francia, Cuba, Chile, 1975-79.

La marcha del carbón. Dir. Sergio Bravo. Chile, 1963.

La tierra prometida. Dir. Miguel Littin. Chile, Cuba, 1973.

Los ojos como mi papá. Dir. Pedro Chaskel. Cuba, 1979.

Mein Kampf. Dir. Erwin Leiser. Suecia, Alemania, 1960.

Mimbre. Dir. Sergio Bravo. Chile, 1957.

Miracolo a Milano. Dir. Vittorio De Sica. Italia, 1951.

Mondo cane. Dir. Gualtiero Jacopetti, Paolo Cavara y Franco Prosperi. Italia, 1962.

Mourir à Madrid. Dir. Frédéric Rossif. Francia, 1963.

Organilleros. Dir. Pedro Chaskel. Chile, 1996.

¿Qué es...?. Dir. Pedro Chaskel. Cuba, 1980.

Testimonio. Dir. Pedro Chaskel. Chile, 1968-69.

The Browning Version. Dir. Anthony Asquith. Gran Bretaña, 1951.

The Fugitive. Dir. John Ford. Estados Unidos, México, 1947.

The Living Desert. Dir. Walt Disney. Estados Unidos, 1953.

Tres miradas a la calle. Dir. Naum Kramarenco. Chile, 1957.

Trilla. Dir. Sergio Bravo. Chile, 1958.

Una foto recorre el mundo. Dir. Pedro Chaskel. Cuba, 1981.

Venceremos. Dir. Pedro Chaskel y Héctor Ríos. Chile, 1970.

VI.

PERSPECTIVES ON THE PRACTICE OF
DOCUMENTARY FILMMAKING

La idea de nación y el problema de identidad en el Ecuador: un acercamiento desde el cine documental

JUAN MARTÍN CUEVA

Abstract

In this essay, the Ecuadorian filmmaker Juan Martín Cueva, who lived in the Latin American diaspora in Europe in the 1990s and 2000s, situates his documentary *El lugar donde se juntan los polos* (2002) in the context of the narration of nation in Ecuador. First, Cueva points out in which ways the process of creating a documentary is highly influenced by the filmmaker's social context, commenting also on the role which reception plays in the constitution of meaning in documentary film. Secondly, Cueva turns to the concept of nation and highlights the heterogeneity of Ecuador's population—which implies diverging possibilities of access to education and political power. Cueva considers Ecuador a nation whose inhabitants lack a shared national identity and who are consequently unable to perceive themselves as part of a whole but rather think of themselves as fragments not related to one another. In his view the most recent Ecuadorian documentaries—which, in one way or another, all express a quest for the identity of the Ecuadorian nation—are related to this missing sense of belonging. As Cueva points out, *El lugar donde se juntan los polos* also focuses on this problem and has to be understood as a proposition to narrate the Ecuadorian nation from the decentred perspective of diaspora. In this filmic narration the indigenous movements are portrayed as a rising force that Cueva considers capable of creating a new sense of national belonging.

Quiero empezar diciendo que no estoy seguro de poder contribuir de modo muy importante a lo que aquí se discute, pienso que será más interesante para ustedes ver mi documental que escucharme hablar y creo, además, que tendrá mayor interés lo que ustedes puedan opinar sobre mi documental, o sobre otros temas que mi documental les traiga a la mente, que lo que yo pueda decir de este tema tan complejo: ImagiNaciones, el cine documental y la narración de la nación en las Américas.

El juego de palabras ImagiNaciones –si lo entiendo bien– se refiere a las formas de representación de lo que somos, de los individuos y de las colectividades que existen en América, y de las naciones o sociedades que hemos construido, en las cuales hemos nacido y que seguimos reproduciendo. Se refiere también –supongo– a esa palabra que se ha puesto tan de moda en los últimos tiempos: el imaginario. O cómo nos perciben y cómo nos percibimos nosotros mismos. El imaginario europeo o alemán, de inicios del siglo XXI, sobre la identidad americana, confrontado al imaginario de los propios americanos sobre su realidad, expresado a través del cine documental.

Me gustaría afirmar dos cosas sobre el trabajo del documentalista: primero, que el cineasta expresa muchas veces conceptos e ideas muy complejos en su trabajo, pero una buena parte de esas ideas no han sido desarrolladas por él de manera totalmente consciente y racional, sino intuitivamente. Y segundo, que la reflexión y la confrontación con otros puntos de vista que uno provoca cuando realiza una película documental es sólo el comienzo de un proceso más largo, alimentado por cada una de las proyecciones del documental y por cada uno de los comentarios que cada espectador –al ver la película y reaccionar frente a ella– transmite al director. Mi documental *El lugar donde se juntan los polos* (2002), que hoy veremos, tiene casi cuatro años, y sin embargo no es una obra cerrada. Desde hace tres días los escucho hablar, reaccionar ante el trabajo de otros documentalistas, yo mismo observo el trabajo de ellos. De esta manera se produce un proceso de reflexión colectiva que me entrega otra mirada sobre mi propio trabajo y sobre los temas que desarrollo en él, al punto que si hoy me pusiera a filmar nuevamente este mismo documental, ya no sería el mismo: mil cosas las diría de manera distinta y mil cosas cambiarían. Es en ese sentido que –me parece– debe interpretarse esa afirmación, que se hace un poco fácilmente, de que la obra no pertenece más al director en el momento en que éste la pone a consideración del espectador.

Ahora bien, no sé si el simple hecho de venir de América Latina sea suficiente para poder hablar de lo que es América Latina, de las sociedades que se han construido en esta región del mundo, de las características de la nación a la que uno pertenece. Ustedes apreciarán que en esta película documental se intenta hacer una reflexión sobre el tema de la nación, de la identidad, de la pertenencia a una sociedad y a una cultura, aunque nunca me lo haya planteado en esos términos exactos. No sé si esa reflexión se desarrolla de manera pertinente o torpe, oportuna o caprichosa, pero, en todo caso, trata de acercarse –desde el cine documental– a lo que es el Ecuador, al momento que se está viviendo, a lo que ha sido la historia de la segunda mitad del siglo XX en América Latina, a lo que nos han dejado generaciones de luchadores sociales y políticos a los seres humanos –escépticos e individualistas– de principios de este siglo. Desde esta perspectiva, me parece que es coherente integrar este documental en la reflexión que se está produciendo en esta conferencia sobre la narración de la nación. En el caso de mi documental, se trata de una narración subjetiva, como lo son todas, puesto que se trata justamente de narraciones: quien dice narración, dice narrador, es decir, una subjetividad. La realidad de la que me ocupo puede ser expresada como el problema de la nación o de la identidad nacional de los ecuatorianos, pero no es sólo el Ecuador, o no es sólo el Ecuador aislado: es el proceso que vive el Ecuador puesto en la perspectiva del proceso político que vive América Latina desde hace medio siglo, desde la Revolución Cubana. Además, todo esto visto desde mi perspectiva, desde París, desde una familia determinada, en unas circunstancias determinadas, utilizando los elementos que yo tenía a mano o de los que podía disponer, que en realidad es mi memoria, la de mi familia, las anécdotas y testimonios de quienes estaban a mi alrededor y los archivos que pusieron a mi disposición determinadas personas a las que por alguna razón, y por fortuna, tuve acceso. Yo sé que, finalmente, esto es cuestión de fabricación del documental y el espectador no necesita saberlo para poder verlo. Pero, sí tengo ganas de contarles, en esta conferencia, que, por ejemplo, quise usar "Sandinista" –una canción de The Clash– y fue imposible, lo cual cambió el resultado final del documental; o que me pasé meses buscando unas tomas hechas en los años setenta –cuando yo era un niño– por un grupo de estudiantes de cine latinoamericanos que filmó un cortometraje en 16 mm y en el cual actuábamos, mi hermano y yo, en un parque parisino. Nunca encontré esas tomas que habrían cambiado la película.

Creo que todos los documentales son el producto de una serie de limitaciones y de casualidades, y eso hay que tomarlo en cuenta cuando miramos estos trabajos como narraciones: imagínense si Raymundo Gleyzer no se hubiera filmado con su hijo, la película sería otra; si no hubiera grabado sus conversaciones con el niño, todo habría sido diferente. Él no estaría tan presente en la película como lo está, gracias a una increíble serie de circunstancias: que él se haya grabado, que se hayan guardado las cintas, que las hayan puesto a disposición de los realizadores, que ellos las hayan usado de ese modo y no de otro. La narración está asentada en casualidades, en memorias humanas –y la memoria humana es muy frágil y muy caprichosa–, en las voluntades, en los estados de ánimo de los realizadores en el momento en que estaban filmando y, luego, cuando estaban editando, en las circunstancias que rodeaban a los personajes cuando los estaban filmando; en fin, es una construcción muy frágil.

El cine documental siempre narra, consciente o inconscientemente, el lugar donde fue producido. Queriéndolo o sin querer, a través de historias que pueden o no referirse explícitamente al tema, el documentalista cuenta quién es, de dónde viene, cómo es el país en el que imaginó y realizó su obra. Por eso, el documental siempre es la narración de la nación, siempre es la narración autobiográfica o autodescriptiva de quien lo hace y del medio y la época en las que vive o vivió. El cine documental está a medio camino entre estética y narración, entre pensamiento e intuición, entre sentimiento y razón, a veces un poco más allá, a veces un poco más acá.

Al ser invitado a esta conferencia donde reina la razón, el pensamiento, lo intelectual, me pareció que lo mínimo que podía hacer era preparar un poco seriamente lo que me pedían que expusiera, y la solución más fácil que encontré fue abrir el diccionario y buscar la definición de "nación." Resulta que nación es una "sociedad natural de hombres a los que la unidad de territorio, de origen, de historia, de lengua y de cultura inclina a la comunidad de vida y crea la conciencia de un destino común," según el *Pequeño Larousse*. La verdad es que la definición del diccionario no coincide por ningún lado, en casi ningún punto, con lo que yo conozco de mi país, con lo que yo percibo de esa nación a la que pertenezco.

Si en lugar de abrir el diccionario, abren un prospecto turístico, verán que el Ecuador son unos indios pequeñitos, con ojos rasgados y pómulos salientes, vestidos con ponchos y ropas de lana muy coloridas que viven en unos paisajes andinos impresionantes de montañas nevadas y valles verdes. Si tienen suerte, detrás de ellos habrá unas cuantas llamas y, a lo lejos, un pueblito con una iglesia blanca muy bonita. ¿Esto es el Ecuador? Tampoco esta imagen coincide con lo que conozco de él. Por último, si en lugar del diccionario y del plegable de una agencia de viajes, prenden el televisor, verán otro país: si tenemos la "suerte" de que el Ecuador sea mencionado en los noticiarios de CNN, lo que se ve es en general otra cosa: gobiernos derrocados por manifestaciones callejeras, una crisis muy seria de la estructura institucional, asambleas populares, intentos de una Asamblea Constituyente para formular una nueva Constitución, ausencia de la Corte Suprema de Justicia, mal funcionamiento del Parlamento, etc.

Desde hace una década, el Ecuador vive un proceso de descomposición del sistema democrático, de crisis permanente de la institucionalidad, de reinado de la corrupción y el oportunismo, de improvisación y generación repetida de ilusiones colectivas en las que la gente cree unos meses y, al poco tiempo, deja de creer. La imagen que proyecta el Ecuador de sí mismo son muchas imágenes, y todas tienen una parte de verdad, y ninguna es la verdad en sí. Son reflejos deformados, no somos ni la definición literal de una nación civilizada, ni el paraíso terrenal andino habitado por un Adán y una Eva indios que, en lugar de la manzana, tienen una papa y, en lugar de la serpiente, una llama, ni tampoco somos un infierno que recuerde a Somalia o a Liberia con una falta absoluta de gobernabilidad y de orden democrático. Somos todo eso y, como toda sociedad, somos un tejido muy complejo de miles de problemas y aspectos distintos. Entender el Ecuador no es cosa de sentarse a tomar un café y describir el funcionamiento de una sociedad en la que tienen que convivir desde hace ya 500 años indios y blancos.

De frustración en frustración, de intento en intento, de tumbo en tumbo: así la nación ecuatoriana va construyéndose o destruyéndose. Algo parecido, en algunos aspectos, le sucedió a la Argentina hace unos años, pero la nación argentina tuvo más de dónde agarrarse y la situación se fue normalizando, se fue resolviendo la crisis y, así, se mantuvo intacto aquello que hace que Argentina sea Argentina. En cambio, en el Ecuador se está dando, ya por muchos años, aquello que en francés llaman una "fuite en avant," un avanzar vertiginoso y descontrolado hacia no se sabe dónde.

Da la impresión de que eso de la nación se parece un poco al arco iris; cada vez que uno se acerca, el asunto se aleja, siempre está más allá, o más bien, nunca está en ningún lugar: es una imaginación, una creación de nuestra mente, una percepción de nuestros ojos, un juego de luz.

¿Cómo es el ecuatoriano típico? Permítanme el ejemplo más cercano: yo. Soy ecuatoriano, quizás soy el primer ecuatoriano que ustedes conocen. ¿Así son los ecuatorianos? No lo sé. Lo que sé es que cuando viajo por Europa, la mayoría de la gente, si se fija en mí, jamás adivinaría de dónde vengo. Muchos de ustedes pueden pensar "cuestión suya," a mí qué me importa que este tipo tenga apariencia de africano, de danés o de boliviano, pero por ahí podemos acercarnos a un problema más colectivo, un problema nacional, un problema de los ecuatorianos. En el propio país, es difícil que cualquier habitante, cualquier ciudadano, reciba un trato igualitario por el solo hecho de ser ciudadano de ese país.

Hay una anécdota muy significativa sobre lo que le ocurrió a una mujer indígena que con el tiempo se convirtió en dirigente del movimiento de los indígenas en el Ecuador. Ella había migrado del campo, de la provincia de Cotopaxi, a Quito. Allí trabajó como empleada doméstica, y para hacerlo tuvo que cambiar su manera de vestir y su apariencia, disimular su pertenencia a la comunidad indígena de la que venía. Después de unos años, estudió y quiso obtener una beca que ofrecía una agencia de cooperación extranjera, y se presentó a los exámenes. Le dijeron que lamentablemente esa beca estaba exclusivamente destinada a los indígenas, y que ella no era indígena. Tuvo que volver a su apariencia indígena y "probar," mediante testimonios y documentos, que era indígena. Una vez, yo estaba haciendo un documental sobre los migrantes ecuatorianos en España, y éstos no me querían dejar entrar en la iglesia que se habían tomado en Madrid, porque decían que yo no era ecuatoriano. Les tuve que mostrar mi cédula de identidad para poder entrar. Yo me considero ecuatoriano exactamente de la misma manera que lo es Lourdes Tibán, la mujer indígena de quien conté la anécdota: somos ciudadanos del mismo país, de la misma época, tenemos más o menos la misma edad, tenemos posiciones políticas bastante cercanas, pero ni ella me considera a mí su semejante, ni yo a ella la considero igual que a mí, aunque me esfuerce. Y lo peor no es eso, sino que toda la sociedad, el sistema, las instituciones, las miradas culturalmente determinadas que los demás posan sobre nosotros, no nos consideran iguales y, por eso, no somos iguales. Porque una cosa es lo que dice la Constitución –que nadie o casi nadie conoce– y otra es lo que nos dicen diariamente de mil maneras, mil veces repetida la evidencia de que no somos iguales.

Sobre la base de una imposición sobre otra imposición, de una aculturación sobre otra aculturación, se ha producido una sociedad que no se puede pensar a sí misma como un todo, que se piensa por pedacitos. Ni siquiera es cuestión de percepciones o de subjetividades: es un hecho que en el país conviven varias sociedades, varias historias, varias realidades, diferentes las unas de las otras. Yo pertenezco a una realidad bastante parecida a la de Miami. Salgo a la calle y veo avenidas grandes, grandes centros comerciales, llenos de lujo y de productos para el consumo, familias blancas, con niños rubios, dentro de unos cuatro por cuatro impresionantes y, sólo a dos cuadras de mi casa hay un barrio que era una comunidad indígena –Amagasí del Inca– que ha sido tragada por la ciudad; la realidad que se vive ahí no tiene nada que ver con lo que acabo de describir: calles mal asfaltadas, algunas de tierra, gente descalza, escuelas muy mal equipadas, una iglesia de cemento armado sin pintar, comercios ambulantes, familias indígenas caminando por las calles. Al llegar a la esquina yo sigo derecho para llevar a mis hijos a la escuela. Bastaría con que doblara a la izquierda y bajara la calle de las Farsalias para entrar en otra dimensión.

En estas condiciones es difícil construir una nación que corresponda a la definición que leímos hace un momento. Siendo sincero, yo encuentro en mí mucho más cosas en común con un blanco mestizo colombiano, con un argentino o hasta con un español, que con un indígena de idioma quichua o con un secoya, shuar o tsáchila de mi propio país. Los veo a ellos como extranjeros, y ellos me ven a mí como extranjero. Esa manera de vernos, esa concepción que tenemos los ecuatorianos de nosotros mismos y de nuestra pertenencia, esa idea de que no somos parte de una nación sino de un grupo de gente similar dentro de una sociedad desmembrada, se refleja, lógicamente, en la producción artística, cinematográfica y, en particular, en el documental. ¿Quiénes somos? ¿Qué es el Ecuador? Muchos de los documentales ecuatorianos de los últimos años están construidos a partir de esas dos preguntas, son variaciones sobre el mismo tema, casi todas podrían tener por subtítulo: "La narración de la nación en el Ecuador."

En la sicología de los ecuatorianos, esta situación se expresa como un vértigo permanente, una gran angustia, una incertidumbre que conduce a muchos a la desesperación. Concretamente, esto ha llevado a más de uno de cada diez ecuatorianos al exilio, a la emigración, a buscar mayor seguridad en otro lugar. Con esta idea un poco esotérica de lo que es la "nación" trato de explicarme lo que ha pasado con mi país. Es una sensación como de orfandad, como de no tener referentes, de no tener una nación a la que uno pueda sentir que pertenece y a la que uno puede volver si no encuentra otra cosa en la cual sostenerse.

He descrito lo que sucede en el Ecuador desde hace una década, pero hay estudios que plantean que el problema, aunque se haya evidenciado en estos últimos diez años, viene de mucho más lejos. El historiador Pablo Ospina sostiene que el problema es que, desde que se desarmó la estructura de poder que se expresaba en el Estado oligárquico –antes de la Segunda Guerra Mundial–, la clase dominante nunca pudo construir otra alternativa real de poder político que se expresara en una nueva forma de Estado. Alguien dijo que en el Ecuador hay una clase dominante, pero no una clase dirigente. Pienso que lo que se está jugando en mi país, particularmente con el fortalecimiento del movimiento indígena, es la constitución de una nueva clase dirigente –que no es precisamente la clase dominante, sino un sector dominado–, que son los indígenas. Quizás ellos tengan un poco más claro, más profundamente integrado en su ser, en su mentalidad, en su ideología, en su cultura, la noción de identidad y de pertenencia, y por eso les sea más fácil formular posibilidades reales de nación, de un nuevo país, de una realidad distinta que supere esta indefinición y esta convivencia caótica de muchas identidades en un mismo país, que es la situación que tenemos hoy.

Hace poco tiempo se rodó en el Ecuador un documental sobre el proceso electoral en una zona muy aislada de la Amazonía sur, en Tiwintza, zona habitada por indígenas shuar y por colonos: *Tu sangre*, dirigido por Julián Larrea (2005). Esta película parece decirnos que es una reflexión sobre nuestra identidad, cuando nos muestra esa población durante las elecciones municipales: eso somos también. Otro largometraje documental reciente –*Ecuador vs. resto del mundo* de Pablo Mogrovejo, 2004– habla de las muchas maneras que tuvimos los ecuatorianos de vivir y festejar la clasificación, por primera vez en la historia, de la selección nacional de fútbol a un Mundial, y nos dice de otra manera: eso también somos. El documental *Problemas personales* (2002), de Manolo Sarmiento y Lisandra Rivera, establece un retrato de la sociedad ecuatoriana desde la migración en España. Una vez más: eso también somos o, si se quiere, así también nos podemos representar, así también podemos vernos a nosotros mismos, pensarnos, entendernos.

El conjunto de la producción documental reciente busca dar respuesta a esta misma pregunta sobre la identidad ecuatoriana, y lo hace desde una perspectiva nueva, contrapuesta, quizás, con la de los documentalistas de los ochenta, cuyas producciones Gabriela Alemán –especialista en cine latinoamericano– describió como trabajos que sepultan una parte de la realidad ecuatoriana, la encierran en el pasado al querer establecer una unidad artificial y falsa y al negar la diversidad que realmente nos constituye. Ahora esa diversidad, los componentes marginales de la sociedad ecuatoriana, vuelven en los documentales, y me pregunto si esto va a contracorriente de la búsqueda de identidad que, de algún modo, debería ser el paraguas que nos cubra a todos, o si busca entender más bien la complejidad de lo que somos desde la diversidad que es el Ecuador.

En mi documental *El lugar donde se juntan los polos*, después de un recorrido por casi medio siglo de intentos de cambiar la situación en América Latina, pasando por la Cuba revolucionaria, el Chile de Allende, la Nicaragua Sandinista, termino mencionando a los indígenas ecuatorianos como los portadores de una nueva esperanza para el país y el continente. Varios espectadores, sobre todo en el Ecuador, me criticaron ese optimismo, incluso alguien me dijo que casi había un racismo al revés, porque en un momento dado hablo de la ilusión que provocaba en mí la posibilidad de que el Ecuador fuera gobernado por un indio. Evidentemente no se trata del color de la piel de la persona que pueda ocupar la presidencia de la República: no es por ahí que se va a resolver el problema, pero sí hay una especie de impaciencia irracional para que accedan al poder los sectores que nunca han podido poner en práctica su propuesta de nación y, sobre todo, un escepticismo muy grande hacia toda propuesta que venga de los mismos sectores que ya han hecho muchos intentos y no han podido construir una nación en la cual todos los ecuatorianos sintamos que pertenecemos en igualdad de condiciones.

Pienso que las naciones no sólo se construyen con elementos reales, con una determinada organización institucional, reglas de juego legales, una moneda, una bandera, un escudo, sino con sensaciones subjetivas que son producto de determinadas situaciones y manifestaciones de distintas construcciones culturales muy complejas. En la actualidad, el Ecuador no tiene moneda propia, las instituciones no funcionan, una gran parte de la sociedad se siente excluida de todo el sistema estatal, el servicio de salud, la seguridad social y la educación pública son un desastre, la décima parte de la población ha salido del país y, por último, la principal fuente de ingreso del país es el dinero que envían a sus familias los que se han ido: ese dinero hace vivir la economía ecuatoriana; a veces, cuando el precio del petróleo sube, nos da ligeramente algo más que los emigrantes, ésas son las fuentes de ingresos de la economía ecuatoriana.

Creo que todo documental, en la medida en que sea realizado por gente mínima-mente sensible, habla necesariamente de los problemas con los que nos enfrentamos los ecuatorianos y a los que habrá que dar una solución creativa, audaz, que nos permi-ta sobrevivir como nación. Si revisamos los temas que han tratado los documentales y el cine ecuatoriano en general, encontraremos muchas derivaciones de este gran tema que es la no existencia de una nación constituida, la sensación de no tener una identi-dad muy clara, la incertidumbre de lo que somos y de lo que podríamos construir.

Esta situación tan difícil para el país, para sus habitantes, es, contradictoriamente una fuente muy rica de historias, de personajes, de reflexiones que inspiran a los cine-astas, y yo pienso que, por esta razón, es en el cine, y más particularmente en el género documental, en el que se expresa con más riqueza la creación ecuatoriana contemporá-nea.

Postdata

Releo mi ponencia, y en esta relectura puedo constatar que, ya en ese momento, había varias ideas algo incorpóreas, escondidas en algún rincón de mi mente, esperando que, tiempo después, les diera cuerpo y vida al escribir el guión de otro documental mío, *Este maldito país* (2008).

Uno de los personajes principales de este documental es justamente Lourdes Ti-bán, la mujer indígena de identidades, aparentemente, cambiantes, y sus reflexiones dan a conocer, desarrollan y confirman la conclusión a la que yo quería llegar en la ponencia: la cuestión de la identidad no es asunto de "buscar, explorar y encontrar" la verdadera esencia de uno, aquello que hace que seamos como somos. La identidad es, más bien, el definirse uno mismo en referencia a los universos a los que pertenece o va perteneciendo como un proceso complejo y nunca terminado. En este mismo docu-mental, el escritor Jorge Enrique Adoum, uno de los pensadores más lúcidos que he-mos tenido en Ecuador, resume –creo yo–, de modo más acertado mi posición frente a la cuestión de la identidad: "La identidad no es un retrato pintado o una escultura hecha y definitiva, sino que tú le vas añadiendo cosas. Teníamos una tradición corta, pequeña ... vinieron los españoles y hubo que pegarle a ese retrato algunas cosas más. Después se fueron los españoles dejándonos cosas aquí, buenas y malas. ¿Identidad? No es algo que uno hereda y se queda ahí, sino algo que uno va transformando tam-bién." Y eso es lo que demuestran Lourdes y los otros personajes del documental.

Por otra parte, también en esta relectura, compruebo que aquello que expresaba yo acerca el movimiento indígena e incluso sobre el contexto político ecuatoriano ha cambiado radicalmente: en el año 2000 los indígenas participaron decisivamente, a tra-vés de la CONAIE (Confederación de Nacionalidades Indígenas del Ecuador), en una movilización popular que terminó con el derrocamiento del gobierno de Jamil Mahuad (hasta este hecho era donde llegaban mis reflexiones en *El lugar donde se juntan los polos).* Meses después, la CONAIE y su brazo político, el partido Movimiento de Unidad Plurinacional Pachakutik-Nuevo País, acordaron apoyar la candidatura del coronel Lucio Gutiérrez, quien ganó las elecciones y fue presidente de Ecuador desde 2002 hasta 2005. Pero, a los seis meses de su gobierno, Gutiérrez excluyó del gobierno a las mismas organizaciones indígenas que lo habían llevado al poder y, éstas, en la oposición, participaron en las jornadas ciudadanas de movilización que terminaron anticipadamente con el gobierno de Gutiérrez. Luego, en el año 2007, –por razones que sería muy largo de exponer aquí–, no apoyaron en las elecciones a Rafael Correa, el actual presidente. Hoy en día existe una relación muy tensa entre las organizaciones indígenas con el gobierno ecuatoriano, que, supuestamente, quiere llevar a cabo un cambio revolucionario en el país. Aunque los indígenas han logrado imponer ciertos temas en la nueva constitución y en los debates para definir nuevos rumbos en lo económico, en la política ecológica, etc., no forman parte orgánica del conglomerado de fuerzas que rodean y sostienen al gobierno. La propia Lourdes Tibán –mencionada en mi ponencia de Bielefeld y, luego, personaje central de mi documental *Este maldito país*–, fue elegida como asambleísta del partido Pachakutik y, en la actualidad, se manifiesta públicamente como oponente a la política de Rafael Correa.

Filmografía

Ecuador vs. resto del mundo. Dir. Pablo Mogrovejo. Ecuador, 2004.

El lugar donde se juntan los polos. Dir. Juan Martín Cueva. Ecuador, Francia, Bélgica, 2002.

Este maldito país. Dir. Juan Martín Cueva. Ecuador, Brasil, 2008.

Problemas personales. Dir. Manolo Sarmiento y Lisandra Rivera. Ecuador, 2002.

Tu sangre. Dir. Julián Larrea. Ecuador, 2005.

Reconstruyendo la historia oculta de una nación a partir de la mirada de un hombre y su cámara

ERNESTO ARDITO

Abstract

In this essay the Argentinean filmmaker Ernesto Ardito situates his documentary *Raymundo* (2002), which he directed in collaboration with Virna Molina, in the context of Argentina's politics of memory, and thus of the narration of nation. Telling the story of the Argentinean Marxist filmmaker Raymundo Gleyzer, who was murdered during the last dictatorship in Argentina (1976–1983), *Raymundo* bridges the gap between the 1960s/70s and the present.

The decades prior to the dictatorship were marked by a highly mobilized youth, who demanded social justice in socialist and Marxist revolutionary movements. Gleyzer and his group of filmmakers, *Cine de la Base*, supported this struggle; consequently, they were among the 30,000 Argentineans who disappeared and were murdered during Argentina's dictatorship. As Ardito points out, in the first decade after the return to democracy in 1983 there were few signs left of the militancy that had characterized a major part of the population in the 1960s and 1970s. In film schools the work of groups such as *Cine de la Base* was not even mentioned. With their film *Raymundo*, Ardito and Molina combat this silencing and pursue two main goals: first, they aim to re-establish the memory of Raymundo Gleyzer, and second, they show the continuity of the militancy of Argentinean cinema of the 1960s and 1970s within the context of the current social mobilization in Argentina.

A fines de la década de los cincuenta surge en la Argentina, en la provincia de Santa Fe, la Escuela de Cine del Litoral. Una escuela preponderantemente documentalista, dirigida por Fernando Birri, basada en conceptos que éste incorporó del neorrealismo italiano. Así, por primera vez existía en nuestro país una escuela de formación crítica e ideológica que, a partir del análisis de la realidad, tomaba como sujeto al oprimido, al marginado, al explotado. El cine se convertía de este modo en una herramienta de denuncia social.

En 1957, Birri y todos sus alumnos rodaron en forma colectiva *Tire dié*, película estrenada en 1958, que señala el inicio del cine revolucionario argentino. El grupo de jóvenes cineastas documentalistas que lo llevaron adelante se diferenciaban absolutamente de otros grupos de realizadores, como Rodolfo Kuhn, Manuel Antín, David José Kohon, Leopoldo Torre Nilsson, entre otros, enmarcados en la ficción, que con su cine miraban a Europa, inspirados en los conflictos y en la estética propuesta por la Nouvelle Vague francesa. Estos otros grupos describían también una realidad argentina, pero los conflictos no eran sociales, sino psicológicos, el sujeto no era el oprimido, sino el opresor, es decir, el burgués, los niños ricos con corazón triste.

De este modo, estos grupos narraban dos naciones completamente diferentes, dos realidades opuestas, a pesar de que el territorio en donde se desarrollaban las historias era el mismo. Todo esto sucedía en tanto que la masa de espectadores consumía un cine industrial que sostenía el orden moral, político, religioso y social del sistema.

Así como en la Argentina, también a partir de los años sesenta, comenzaron a aparecer en los diferentes países de Latinoamérica focos del nuevo cine revolucionario que, sin embargo, se desconocían entre sí. No existía aún una unidad de acción. Los primeros contactos entre estos cineastas se produjeron sólo a partir de los festivales latinoamericanos de cine de Viña del Mar (Chile) de 1967 y 1969. Allí pudieron intercambiar experiencias, conocer las diferentes producciones y debatir sobre la función del cine como herramienta de lucha para la liberación de América Latina del imperialismo de los Estados Unidos. Es allí también donde cobró vida la concepción de que Latinoamérica era como una sola nación, pues los procesos económicos y políticos de cada país eran similares o idénticos, ya que todos formaban parte del mismo modelo de dominación.

Los cuestionamientos de cada uno de los filmes, provenientes de las diferentes regiones latinoamericanas se retroalimentaban entre sí, en función de una lucha única. Es decir, se desarrollaba el concepto internacionalista del marxismo, según el cual el capitalismo no tiene fronteras y la clase obrera y campesina es explotada del mismo modo y por los mismos intereses sin consideración de los límites territoriales.

El cineasta argentino Raymundo Gleyzer fue uno de los principales referentes de esta generación y, en su trabajo, predominó desde un principio este fundamento ideológico. Su internacionalismo se aprecia ya en su primera película *La tierra quema*, del año 1963, cuyo argumento se desarrolla en el Brasil. Filmada en el nordeste brasileño, narra la vida de una familia de campesinos que emigra en busca de agua sufriendo a causa del hambre y por la muerte de varios hijos. "Toda Latinoamérica debe mirarse en el nordeste de Brasil" –decía Gleyzer. Esta película nos muestra que su mirada crítica no se reducía a las fronteras de su país, vale decir, su cine no veía a Argentina como su única nación, sino que ésta era parte de la gran nación que era Latinoamérica.

Otro ejemplo emblemático de la filmografía de Gleyzer es *México, la revolución congelada* (1971), película filmada casi clandestinamente en México y cuyo tema es la traición del PRI (Partido Revolucionario Institucional) a los ideales originales de la

Revolución Mexicana. En él analiza el papel de este partido gobernante como reflejo directo del papel burocrático, populista y demagógico del peronismo en la Argentina. Hacia 1970, este cine revolucionario se hizo eco de la evolución de las corrientes políticas revolucionarias entendiendo que la realidad latinoamericana no sólo había que denunciarla, sino transformarla y, en este sentido, el cine debía ser una herramienta al servicio de esta lucha. Surgió, de esta manera, un cine militante, en el que sus realizadores comenzaron a formar parte de las diferentes agrupaciones políticas transformándose en los brazos cinematográficos de las mismas.

El cine militante de los setenta no era un movimiento aislado, sino parte de un amplio movimiento revolucionario integrado por jóvenes militantes, estudiantes, trabajadores, artistas, intelectuales, científicos que luchaban por la liberación del país y por la implantación del socialismo. Esta generación de militantes revolucionarios consideraba que tomar el poder era posible, ya fuera en forma democrática como el modelo chileno de Allende, o en forma insurreccional como la Revolución Cubana. Y esto lo sabía bien el poder económico y político argentino, del mismo modo que los Estados Unidos, potencia que veía como amenaza la expansión del socialismo por toda Latinoamérica. El temor más grande era que el pueblo comenzara a identificarse de forma masiva con los ideales de esta vanguardia ideológica. Y lo que estaba en juego era el modelo de país: socialismo versus capitalismo.

En la Argentina, la represión comenzó a operar activamente hacia finales de 1974 con comandos clandestinos de ultraderecha que perseguían y asesinaban a los militantes de izquierda, amparados por el gobierno democrático de Isabel Perón. En el ambiente cinematográfico, esta situación llevó a que muchos cineastas y artistas tuvieran que exiliarse o pasaran a la clandestinidad. Es en ese mismo período en que la guerrilla, el ala más radicalizada del movimiento revolucionario, fue prácticamente aniquilada por el ejército y otras fuerzas de orden público. El gobierno de Isabel Perón perdió el consenso popular y en marzo de 1976, la presidenta fue depuesta por un golpe militar.

En mayo de ese mismo año, Raymundo Gleyzer fue secuestrado por un comando paramilitar y desde entonces está desaparecido.

La dictadura militar, encabezada por el general Jorge Rafael Videla (1976–1983), institucionalizó un plan de exterminio, aniquilando por completo la insurrección popular y a su vanguardia ideológica. Sembró el terror en la población y, de esta manera, tuvo el campo libre para empezar a poner en marcha, en forma veloz y sin resistencia, el modelo económico neoliberal que hoy tenemos. Este plan condujo al país a la ruina, benefició solamente al 2% de la población y condenó al 53% de ella a descender a la línea de pobreza. En 1983, la dictadura que ya había cumplido su función, empezó también a perder apoyo tras la guerra de las Malvinas: el poder económico reaccionó dando nuevas bases a su dominio y, así, reemplazó el poder político dictatorial por una nueva democracia.

Con el comienzo de la presidencia de Raúl Alfonsín (1983–1989), el gobierno empezó una política de transición basada en lo que la izquierda argentina denominó la "teoría de los dos demonios," la que ganó mucha fuerza en la opinión pública. Esta teoría sostenía que en la década del setenta había habido dos bandos minoritarios y armados que se habían enfrentado oscureciendo la historia del país: los militares y los guerrilleros de izquierda. En el medio estaban las instituciones democráticas y el pueblo, víctimas inocentes de esta lucha violenta.

Los formadores de opinión pública proclamaban que la violencia de la izquierda había traído como consecuencia la dictadura militar y que ambos bandos habían cometido crímenes de lesa humanidad. Pero lo cierto es que la guerrilla argentina ya había sido destruida en su mayor parte antes de marzo de 1976 y, por tanto, no constituía ningún peligro para la democracia. Los guerrilleros no sumaban más de 1.500 y los desaparecidos del período de la dictadura fueron 30.000. El verdadero peligro estaba en la conciencia de esta generación y no en las armas.

El origen de esta mentira histórica está cimentada en dos aspectos, el económico y el político. En cuanto al primero, los líderes democráticos fueron cómplices activos de sus antecesores militares al continuar con su plan económico. La clase dominante que se benefició con el exterminio o el exilio de los militantes de izquierda, seguía siendo la misma y el Estado seguía estando a su servicio. En cuanto a lo político, era necesario borrar de la memoria colectiva a la intelectualidad de los sesenta y los setenta y los ideales que representaba, a partir de los cuales todo un pueblo había empezado a transitar hacia el socialismo y no hacia una democracia neoliberal.

En síntesis, para ocultar la verdad, también había que ocultar la historia.

Desde 1976 en adelante se empezó a hablar de los desaparecidos, de los crímenes de la dictadura, de las torturas, de los centros clandestinos de detención, siempre de un modo paralizante y aterrorizador para los nuevos jóvenes. Y nunca se hablaba del pasado anterior a 1976, sobre quiénes habían sido esos desaparecidos, por qué habían luchado, qué modelo habían querido cambiar.

¿Cómo iba a permitir la cultura dominante de esta nueva democracia que las nuevas generaciones se vieran identificadas con los sueños e ideologías de la generación del setenta, que quisieran continuar con esta lucha y acabar con el orden establecido y el neoliberalismo?

En el caso de Gleyzer, lo lógico que tendría que haber hecho el gobierno democrático desde un comienzo, habría sido recuperar su obra y difundirla por sus canales públicos. Pero no lo hizo, porque los cuestionamientos de los filmes de Gleyzer continuaban siendo vigentes. En otras palabras, también en la democracia se censuró implícitamente a Raymundo Gleyzer y lo mismo sucedió con la obra de otros intelectuales y artistas militantes.

Asimismo, la dictadura había producido una generación de padres que habían quedado aterrorizados ante la posibilidad de cualquier participación política de sus hijos por temor a que les pasara lo mismo que a los desaparecidos. La palabra "política" era una palabra vinculada con la muerte. En este caso, también esta generación tenía algo que ocultar, tanto por sus hijos como por ellos mismos: se avergonzaban de su propio miedo, de haber amparado la desaparición de personas con su propio silencio y sumisión. (Bien se sabe que, a veces, los regímenes violentos sacan del ser humano lo peor de sí). De esta manera, la memoria colectiva ocultó este trauma y colaboró con la desaparición de su propio pasado.

Por otra parte, muchos personajes ligados al poder político, económico, eclesiástico y mediático habían participado activamente en el gobierno militar y al restablecerse la democracia, se reorganizaron, se lavaron la cara y continuaron actuando, por esto, también había que ocultar ese pasado oscuro.

¿Y qué sucedió con los sobrevivientes que habían militado en alguna agrupación revolucionaria? Eran mal vistos y muchos se reinsertaron en la sociedad callando su pasado. La sociedad los hacía sentirse culpables. Todo, por donde se mirara, encuadraba a favor del silencio. Y lo cierto es que la vanguardia cultural y el avanzado debate ideológico de los años setenta nunca más volvieron a repetirse.

El film documental emblemático de este período fue *La república perdida* (1983–1986) dirigido por Miguel Pérez, que recorre la historia de nuestro país desde comienzos del siglo XX. En esta revisión histórica, la Nación eran los partidos políticos en una lucha maniquea y constante en contra del poder militar para poder controlar el poder estatal, eliminando de la historia las luchas populares. En su representación de la historia de los setenta, esta película reproduce sistemáticamente el discurso oficial de "los dos demonios" y omite la voz, el pensamiento y la humanidad de los militantes revolucionarios. El período previo a 1976 era mostrado como una etapa oscura, violenta, potenciando en las nuevas generaciones el tabú histórico y la ignorancia. Para los que no vivimos ese período, por ser muy niños o no haber nacido, la palabra de la historia oficial era la palabra verdadera, cierta. Se habían encargado de dinamitar el puente entre las dos generaciones.

El primer gobierno democrático dirigido por Raúl Alfonsín, lejos de impartir justicia en contra de los delitos de lesa humanidad cometidos por la dictadura militar, dictó la *Ley de punto final* (1986) –conocida también como la ley de impunidad– que impidió continuar con los juicios contra los torturadores y asesinos.

En el segundo gobierno democrático asumió el poder Carlos Menem (1989–1995) quien indultó a los pocos militares que habían sido condenados, bajo la premisa de que, para lograr la pacificación del país, era preciso mirar hacia el futuro y no hacia el pasado. Menem profundizó el plan económico iniciado por la dictadura, privatizó las empresas estatales e impuso la ley de flexibilización laboral; acciones que hicieron retroceder en el tiempo la legislación laboral y despojaron a los trabajadores de todas las conquistas logradas en casi un siglo de lucha. El desempleo aumentó de manera abrumadora, las riquezas del país se evaporaron hacia el extranjero y se instaló, ya sin pudor, la cultura de la corrupción en la sociedad. Era la ley de "sálvese quien pueda, a costa de cualquiera y por cualquier medio."

El mismo temor a perder la vida que había imperado en la dictadura, ahora se había transformado en el temor a perder el empleo y el estatus. La extorsión del sistema llevó a la gente a no comprometerse, a no mirar qué le pasaba al compañero despedido, incluso en algunos casos, la obligó a traicionar para salvarse, y, sobre todo, a agachar la cabeza.

La "teoría de los dos demonios" de los ochenta desembocó posteriormente en la teoría de que "las ideologías están muertas," bajo el abrigo cultural del posmodernismo y la idea de que el sistema era un monstruo inabarcable, imposible de derrotar. Por su lado, los partidos de izquierda colaboraron a esta situación con sus propios fraccionamientos y con sus errores de comunicación. No existía una alternativa real, al menos en la conciencia de la gran masa de la población.

Éste es el marco sociohistórico en el que fuimos formados en la Escuela de Cine. Nunca nos pasaron una película de cine político militante. A diferencia de la Escuela de Birri, ésta era una formación sin identidad, muy lejana de un contexto social desbastador. Analizábamos el modelo de Hollywood o el europeo. Es decir, el concepto de nación en este sentido no existía. Se trataba de reproducir modelos de narración de otras naciones, con otras realidades completamente diferentes de las nuestras. Y esto generaba filmes con contenidos híbridos. Además nos enseñaron a que no se podía filmar fuera de los cánones de la industria, y que el cine era sólo para unos elegidos que se acoplaban a las reglas del sistema.

Virna Molina y yo, siendo integrantes de esta generación, discrepábamos de esta situación, hecho que nos condujo a construir nuestro propio modelo de producción para poder realizar una película en forma independiente o artesanal, fuera de los cánones impuestos por la industria. De hecho, muchos cineastas independientes de nuestra generación nacieron de esta misma manera. En el marco de este modelo cultural sus filmes comenzaron a innovar en las formas, en los modelos de producción o en los personajes a desarrollar, pero sus contenidos no cuestionaban de forma frontal el sistema, sino lo oxigenaban y, en definitiva, lo legitimaban. Desde esta posición generacional de que "nada se puede cambiar" –que implica el temor a afrontar la lucha–, algunos buscaron una superación con respecto a la realidad. Representaban la crisis de su país desde un punto de vista irónico, como más allá del bien y del mal, ante un contexto para ellos, inamovible. Otros describían el folclorismo o las crisis psicológicas de los marginados, u otros, simplemente, omitían todo, con contenidos aislados de un país que se estaba cayendo a pedazos. El derrotismo era, en definitiva, lo que predominaba y se transformó en una cualidad comercial, porque las películas premiadas en Europa o en Estados Unidos, mostraban lo mal que estábamos de un modo original, innovador y audaz, pero no proponían ninguna salida.

Las propuestas del cine militante de los sesenta y los setenta no habían tenido continuadores, morían encapsuladas en el tiempo.

Hacia el año 1996 se realizó una retrospectiva fílmica de Gleyzer dirigida a un público intelectual, pero que no llevó a un debate sobre los contenidos de sus películas y, de hecho, éstas fueron consideradas una rareza cinematográfica. De esta misma manera, también en algunos documentales y en la literatura, se empezó a hablar nuevamente de la generación revolucionaria, pero la tesis que planteaban estas producciones y este paradigma cultural era que los sujetos protagonistas de ese momento histórico vivían una realidad, una cotidianidad, completamente diferente de la nuestra. Por lo tanto, sus objetivos de lucha quedaban anulados, dado que nosotros no teníamos los mismos conflictos que ellos. Es en este marco en que se filmó la película documental *Cazadores de utopías* (1995), dirigida por David Blaustein, cuyo mismo título define ya la perspectiva adoptada. El sistema estatal difunde este film masivamente, tal como lo había hecho en los años ochenta con *La república perdida*.

Cazadores de utopías basa su argumento en los testimonios de militantes revolucionarios –los montoneros– dando un panorama visual y testimonial de diferentes sucesos, pero tiene una particularidad especial: el punto de vista es peronista. Tras la "teoría de los dos demonios," hacia finales de los noventa, el cine pasó a otro modo de acercamiento al pasado caracterizado por la subjetividad peronista. De hecho en las imágenes de archivo que allí aparecen, se quitó toda referencia visual a los grupos marxistas. Ahora el modelo negado era el marxista. El peronismo, que tenía el control del Estado, intentaba reconstruir la memoria histórica desde su visión monopolizadora y excluyente.

En el año 1997, el peronismo como única fuerza gobernante conducía al país a una crisis social y económica terrible, por esto debía reivindicar su pasado heroico de lucha y resistencia para legitimar su poder. Pero esta ventana que se abría hacia el pasado, fue el origen del encuentro entre las dos generaciones. Así muchos jóvenes comenzamos a descubrir que habían existido artistas, intelectuales, políticos, dirigentes sindicales de base que habían luchado por otro país, con herramientas concretas para lograrlo. Necesitábamos tomarlos como referentes para darle sentido a nuestras vidas en el desierto de corrupción y deterioro moral en que vivíamos.

Virna Molina y yo comenzamos a indagar sobre la historia del cine argentino y nos encontramos con que había existido toda una generación de cineastas revolucionarios que había sido perseguida, exiliada y que uno de sus más grandes referentes, Raymundo Gleyzer, estaba desaparecido.

Logramos tener acceso a sus películas *Los traidores* (1973) y *México, la revolución congelada* (1971). Luego hallamos un libro sobre él editado en Uruguay. Mas allá de esto no había nada en la Argentina, sólo un par de artículos en revistas especializadas. Su trabajo, su existencia, había sido borrada del mapa. La cultura oficial había cumplido muy bien su labor negadora. En el libro de la Cinemateca Uruguaya, gran parte de sus amigos, compañeros y familiares habían escrito algunas líneas recordándolo, todo en un marco de mucha angustia, eran casi como cartas de despedida. Éste fue nuestro primer acercamiento a su persona.

Sin embargo, para nosotros, lo revelador de este libro es que también contenía entrevistas y documentos en los que el grupo Cine de la Base, que Raymundo había creado, explicaba su teoría y su modo de producción, cómo realizaban y difundían sus filmes de forma clandestina sorteando la censura y la persecución. Nuestra identificación con esos contenidos fue enorme. La censura política que rodeaba al grupo Cine de la Base y contra la cual desarrollaba sus estrategias, era igual a la censura económica que nos rodeaba a nosotros, la cual devenía a su vez de una censura política implícita.

Éste fue el comienzo de nuestra nueva escuela, la del cine político-militante y la ruptura con el paradigma que nos rodeaba. Entendimos, a su vez, que era necesario realizar una película sobre esta experiencia para las nuevas generaciones, que era preciso romper con la brecha cultural e ideológica que había generado la dictadura y la "teoría de los dos demonios." Comenzamos a rearmar ese puente destruido, piedra por piedra.

La tarea del armado de *Raymundo* llevó cinco años, siendo ésta, una película de descubrimiento y de desenmascaramiento de un tabú histórico. El primer gran obstáculo fue que la obra completa de Gleyzer no estaba en el país, sino desperdigada por el mundo. Había sido llevada al exilio para salvaguardarla de la hoguera de la dictadura. Así comenzamos con una doble tarea, la de armar el film y la de hallar, clasificar y restaurar la obra de Gleyzer. Su esposa Juana Sapire tenía en Nueva York gran parte de ella. Otros filmes aparecieron en los lugares menos pensados o diversos.

Había tan poca información en nuestra generación sobre este período que sentimos la necesidad de reconstruir la historia oculta de nuestra nación a partir de la mirada de Raymundo Gleyzer. Es decir, su biografía fue el medio para descubrir y reflexionar sobre este pasado censurado, perdido, desaparecido.

Los archivos oficiales no tenían imágenes de las luchas populares de las décadas de los sesenta y los setenta. Buscamos entonces en la obra de otros cineastas revolucionarios, en los archivos familiares, en bibliotecas independientes, arañando toma por toma, foto por foto, texto por texto, para encontrarnos con Raymundo y su tiempo. Luego, en el exterior, se hallaron imágenes inéditas de cómo Raymundo filmaba, de su vida personal, del cine revolucionario y de la historia política argentina.

Cuando iniciamos el proyecto no existía en Argentina una foto donde se viera claramente el rostro de Raymundo. Con el correr del tiempo y la constancia en el trabajo, diferentes familiares y amigos de Raymundo nos fueron brindando su confianza y, con ella, sus archivos personales –fotografías, cartas y películas– donde íbamos encontrando las piezas de ese rompecabezas tan complejo que era nuestro pasado reciente. En unas carpetas que guardaba Juana en Nueva York, encontramos documentos –diarios de viaje, entrevistas, reflexiones y guiones de Gleyzer– que nos dieron la posibilidad de poder reconstruir su historia y la de nuestro país desde su propia mirada.

Realizar las entrevistas para el film fue complicado. Muchos no querían hablar para no recordar ese pasado que les causaba tanto dolor. Otros omitían los puntos de conflicto. Así también entre las diferentes voces sobre un mismo hecho histórico, existían versiones contrapuestas sobre una misma "verdad histórica." En términos generales, el sentimiento de derrota, acentuado por la marginación que la cultura oficial ejercía sobre los militantes, era muy fuerte. Había desconfianza de lo que nosotros, como parte de otra generación, pudiéramos llegar a hacer con la revisión de sus vidas.

Esta situación nos motivó para realizar un análisis minucioso de cada hecho histórico-político que se narra en el film. Vivimos la historia desde adentro, paso a paso, no sólo nos exigíamos la búsqueda más completa posible de información y documentación, sino el debate constante sobre los mismos y sobre las diferentes posiciones. La tarea fue muy prolongada, pero sentíamos la responsabilidad de estructurar esta revisión para que lo narrado no quedara encapsulado en los sucesos del pasado. El film debía ser una herramienta para que el espectador tuviera las bases para comprender la actualidad.

La imagen construida por el Estado sobre la Argentina de los setenta, eran fragmentos oscuros, en blanco y negro, como de un pasado lejano, prehistórico, como de algo que hubiera sucedido hace siglos, ajenos –desde todo punto de vista– a nuestro presente y a nuestra realidad cotidiana. Había una imposibilidad de identificación.

Por esto nuestra tarea no fue sólo de indagar en el archivo de sucesos históricos, en los filmes, sino en la cotidianidad, buscando imágenes de los protagonistas o del pueblo en donde el espectador actual pudiera reconocerse. Desde lo humano se unen las dos realidades para que el pasado funcione activamente en el presente, cuestionándolo.

La verdadera construcción histórica de una nación está en el análisis de la subjetividad de sus protagonistas, es decir, el pueblo, de acuerdo al momento histórico en que transitan. Esto es lo que construye la identidad de una nación, su ser. Por esta misma razón había la necesidad de comprender a Raymundo y a los militantes de los setenta en su totalidad, no sólo en su aspecto ideológico.

Esto también define la estructura del film como un túnel del tiempo donde el espectador se sumerge y recorre la historia de la mano de los protagonistas para comprender desde su mismo universo cada motivación, sentimiento o reflexión de los mismos. Por eso, el lugar del entrevistado en cámara o las imágenes del presente que buscan hacia el pasado, ceden su lugar para dar cabida a las imágenes familiares, de trabajo, de los hechos históricos, de sus filmes, de la televisión etc., de modo que la mirada del espectador sea la mirada del protagonista en ese momento.

Raymundo era militante marxista y esto nos permitió dar un vuelco al revisionismo de los setenta desde el cine. Al narrar la historia desde este punto de vista, nos permitimos una reflexión crítica sobre el peronismo, pero sin omitir su posición.

El film lo iniciamos en el año 1997 y lo finalizamos en noviembre de 2002. En diciembre de 2001, el modelo neoliberal llegó a su punto más álgido y colapsó. La sociedad reaccionó unitariamente, tanto la clase media como los sectores marginados, estallaron. La confiscación de ahorros, el altísimo desempleo, las condiciones de trabajo infrahumanas, motivaron un estado de protesta y reacción constante: cayó el gobierno de De la Rúa. El pueblo gritaba: "Que se vayan todos" y comenzó a cuestionar el papel del Estado y de sus instituciones. Frente a la falta de respuestas de éstos, surgieron una serie de organizaciones generadas por la misma gente: *asambleas populares* para resolver los problemas que tenía cada barrio; *fábricas ocupadas* por sus trabajadores y puestas a producir sin los patrones que las habían cerrado y desaparecido; *casas tomadas* para solucionar los problemas de la falta de viviendas; *movimientos de desocupados* que brindaban una forma de lucha contra el hambre y la exclusión. Así, muchos llegaron a la conclusión de que todo tenía su origen en el plan económico instaurado por la dictadura y continuado por los gobiernos democráticos siguientes. Comenzaron a preguntarse, por ejemplo, quiénes habían sido los desaparecidos o por qué modelo de país habían luchado. El mismo pueblo había provocado una apertura histórica. De hecho, esta misma explosión popular construye el final del film, terminando de colocar la última piedra en ese puente destruido de la memoria.

Cuando *Raymundo* estuvo listo, empezamos a preocuparnos de su proyección. La gente nos llamaba e íbamos con la película a los barrios. Luego, después de la exhibición, se generaban siempre largos debates. Fue precisamente en estos nuevos espacios sociales de discusión, fuera del sistema, donde circuló el film durante todo el año 2003 y también el 2004.

No sólo nosotros utilizábamos esta dinámica de difusión. En ese momento, surgió un movimiento muy amplio conformado por colectivos y cineastas que comenzaron a registrar este período, a realizar informes y a difundirlos de esta misma manera. El cine documental ahora no sólo reflejaba la realidad, sino que la cuestionaba e interactuaba con ésta. El cine volvía a ser una herramienta de concientización y de lucha.

Se cerraba así, un ciclo interrumpido por la dictadura y las democracias cómplices del silencio. De esta manera se retomaba el modo de hacer cine del Cine de la Base y de otros grupos revolucionarios. Raymundo Gleyzer se convirtió en el referente de estos nuevos documentalistas y, finalmente, sus documentales volvieron a proyectarse para el pueblo. La vigencia del contenido de sus películas permitía un debate constante sobre situaciones puntuales de la actualidad. Su memoria estaba viva, estaba activa.

La idea de Nación narrada por estos nuevos grupos de cine militante, se construye desde la subjetividad del mismo sujeto en conflicto, el pueblo. Y el cineasta opera como parte de esta lucha con su herramienta que es el cine. Una mirada que inmersa en el devenir de la coyuntura, es quizás incompleta, al no permitirse un análisis a distancia de lo que está sucediendo, pero es clara, en el sentir de los protagonistas y de la denuncia o reclamo llevada por los mismos.

En conclusión, bajo el modelo cultural en que nos criamos, en ese estado de las cosas, comenzamos esta búsqueda desesperada por rearmar el rompecabezas de nuestra historia a partir de la vida de un hombre y, así, poder también encontrarnos a nosotros mismos, saber de donde veníamos y el por qué de nuestra realidad, ya que aprender a analizarla desde sus raíces era definir nuestra nación.

Filmografía

Cazadores de utopías. Dir. David Blaustein. Argentina, 1995.

La república perdida. Dir. Miguel Pérez. Argentina, 1983–1986.

La tierra quema. Dir. Raymundo Gleyzer. Argentina, 1963.

Los traidores. Dir. Raymundo Gleyzer. Argentina, 1973.

México, la revolución congelada. Dir. Raymundo Gleyzer. Argentina, 1971.

Raymundo. Dir. Ernesto Ardito y Virna Molina. Argentina, 2002.

Tire dié. Dir. Fernando Birri. Argentina, 1958.

México, tan lejos de Dios...

CARLOS MENDOZA

Abstract

This essay discusses the narration of nation in contemporary Mexican documentary film in the context of processes of economic integration and the loss of national sovereignty. It shows how the erosion of nationalism in hegemonic discourse makes national sentiment the domain of popular resistance to neoliberal globalization. In this context, the social documentary in Mexico offers alternative perspectives on the nation and its constituents, although the critical representation of social reality is smothered by government censorship and by commercial television's lacking interest in independent documentaries. Contrasting *Editorial Clio*, a commercial production company and part of *Televisa*'s media empire, with the independent production collective *Canal 6 de julio*, which expresses counter-hegemonic perspectives and relies on alternative and precarious broadcasting and distribution channels, the essay outlines both potentials and limitations for the impact of independent filmmaking on discourses of national identity.

En México la cultura nacional está siendo agredida por la globalización. En contra de los pronósticos optimistas que hacían la mayor parte de los intelectuales mexicanos en 1993 ante la inminencia de la entrada en vigor del Tratado de Libre Comercio con América del Norte, hoy ese conjunto de nociones, mitos, obras, instituciones, tradiciones y creadores imprescindibles que podemos definir como cultura nacional está siendo erosionada por el efecto de la llamada integración económica.

El discurso dominante que caracteriza a los más altos funcionarios gubernamentales, –que repiten los medios de comunicación y la inmensa mayoría de las instituciones educativas privadas–, corresponde al pensamiento de un grupo pequeño y poderoso de magnates que se impone a la mayoría. Este discurso ha dejado de lado los valores tradicionales del nacionalismo mexicano para ponderar las cualidades que tendríamos que cultivar con miras a la supuesta inserción de nuestro país en un mundo que nos presentan como competitivo, aunque quienes elaboran dicho discurso hayan forjado su éxito en las relaciones públicas, o sea, esquivando precisamente la competencia.

La llamada modernización económica de México, impulsada en 1988 por el gobierno de Carlos Salinas (1988–1994) –gobierno que provenía de una elección fraudulenta–, engendró un pequeño grupo de multimillonarios que se beneficiaron con las privatizaciones y cuyos nombres figuran en la lista de la revista Forbes entre los más ricos del mundo, trajo consigo un alarmante deterioro de los servicios públicos de educación y salubridad, amparó la sobrevivencia de un sistema de justicia obsoleto y corrupto, y generó una nación cuyos habitantes están divididos por un abismo profundo entre los muchos pobres y los pocos ricos que coexisten en ella. De este contexto proviene precisamente ese discurso que pretende presentar los efectos del actual modelo económico como si se tratara de fenómenos naturales y que contrapone el concepto de soberanía al de competitividad, siempre utilizando el *espanglish* como idioma oficial.

Los gobernantes mexicanos y sus aliados son especialistas en la prestidigitación semántica y recurren al eufemismo como su recurso retórico predilecto. Según ellos, la soberanía empieza a ser un valor obsoleto, de ahí que no tengan inconvenientes –por ejemplo– en aceptar que nuestros aereopuertos se llenen de agentes norteamericanos que salvaguardan desde nuestro territorio la soberanía estadounidense. Con el vocablo "proteccionismo" sucede algo parecido. Esta palabra es mal vista por el gobierno mexicano, porque los tecnócratas consideran que los subsidios son premodernos, no les importa que nuestros socios comerciales lo vean de otro modo y ellos sí subsidien a sus agricultores. Lo mismo ocurre cuando se habla del precio del barril de petróleo, de migración o de cine. En estos tres temas, como en muchos otros, la preferencia del gobierno mexicano por lo estadounidense está por encima de cualquier compromiso con lo nacional. De este modo el petróleo mexicano es vendido a los Estados Unidos a un precio inferior del que se exige al resto de los compradores, mientras la Secretaría de Relaciones Exteriores da su beneplácito para que la policía fronteriza estadounidense dispare balas de goma rellenas de gases tóxicos a los migrantes ilegales. Entre tanto los encargados de la burocracia cultural ofrecen las salas cinematográficas nacionales a Hollywood, al extremo de que por cada película nacional que se exhibe, son alrededor de quince filmes norteamericanos los que ocupan nuestras pantallas.

El nacionalismo mexicano que, a principios del siglo XX era factor de cohesión pluriclasista, se fue a refugiar años más tarde en las clases populares que lo volvieron bravucón y clasista. Actualmente, éste se refugia en lo más oculto del imaginario colectivo y se manifiesta, sin pronunciar su propio nombre, en la vida política nacional. De hecho, lo que se conoce generalmente como izquierda mexicana, es decir, los partidos políticos que representan a la izquierda electoral institucional, son en realidad grupos de orientación nacionalista. Su modelo es el llamado nacionalismo revolucionario, la doctrina inspiradora de los sectores progresistas del Partido Revolucionario Institucional (PRI), partido que gobernó durante setenta y un años el país y mereció la denominación de la "dictadura perfecta" del escritor Mario Vargas Llosa.[1] Estos sectores

[1] El comentario de Mario Vargas Llosa se dió en el marco de una discusión televisada en el marco del coloquio *El siglo XX: la experiencia de la libertad* (1990) y produjo por el con-

desarrollaron lo mejor de la obra social de un régimen definido por Octavio Paz como "el ogro filantrópico." La inspiración de esta "izquierda" es el gobierno del general Lázaro Cárdenas (1934–1940) que llevó a cabo una importante reforma agraria, expropió la industria petrolera a las compañías extranjeras, impulsó un modelo educativo denominado "educación socialista" y recibió a decenas de miles de exiliados republicanos españoles; aunque, por otra parte, avaló la fundación de un sindicalismo corporativo, corrupto y criminal, que ha sojuzgado de por vida a la clase obrera mexicana, no permitió elecciones libres e impuso como su sucesor en la presidencia a un político católico y conservador, Manuel Avila Camacho, en 1940.

No obstante, según el escritor Carlos Monsiváis, el nacionalismo se desvanece en este país, vecino de Estados Unidos en plena época de Bush, "por lo que se requiere de resistencias políticas, sicológicas y culturales, y esto ha sido el sentimiento nacional y no el nacionalismo" (Corral Arrazola).

¿Sentimiento nacional o nacionalismo? Quién sabe, la frontera entre uno y otro es demasiado sutil.

No obstante, es necesario vislumbrar en el nacionalismo mexicano –incluso con sus contradicciones– la alternativa mexicana opuesta al modelo económico que devasta al país. También es válido hablar de algo parecido a una batalla sorda que se libra en el campo de la cultura entre el *American way of life* y la cultura mexicana. La realidad mexicana ofrece ejemplos que incluso sobrepasan los hechos de la siguiente noticia: en el año 2004, un pequeño grupo de personas, agrupadas en el Frente Cívico de Defensa del Valle de Teotihuacán, intentó impedir con ardor y, como era previsible, sin éxito, la instalación de un almacén Walmart en la inmediaciones de Teotihuacán, una de las joyas más representativas de la cultura prehispánica mexicana, literalmente sembrada de vestigios arqueológicos (cf. Salinas/Camacho). Después de una disputa de algunos meses en los que el Instituto Nacional de Antropología e Historia y el Consejo Nacional para la Cultura y las Artes guardaron silencio, la construcción del almacén prosiguió. Hoy, por supuesto, el Walmart de Teotihuacán atiende a su clientela muy cerca de la Pirámide del Sol y el asunto apenas tuvo resonancia en la mayor parte de la prensa mexicana. Sin embargo, más allá de episodios como éste, que se repiten con demasiada frecuencia, existen preocupantes síntomas de la profunda erosión que la moda globalizadora provoca en los valores y en la identidad nacionales. Carlos Monsiváis señala que "por primera vez es ostensible el cambio en el habla, antes atenida a las características del campo y modificaciones urbanas, y hoy sojuzgada por la caída de la sintaxis conocida y por los vocablos provenientes del inglés." Y continúa: "Se quiera o no, y seguramente se quiere, el habla es el español, a diario modificado por el inglés y defendido por el ADN de la costumbre; el *espanglish* es el idioma del porvenir cotidiano y el español, la lengua irrenunciable que también incorpora el *espanglish*" (Corral Arrazola). Otra voz autorizada, la del historiador Enrique Florescano, lamentaba hace apenas unos días que los antiguos símbolos de la identidad nacional no provoquen ya

flicto posterior entre Vargas Llosa y Octavio Paz un escándalo en el campo académico en México.

ninguna reacción en las nuevas generaciones de mexicanos aunque, según Florescano, "la culpa no es sólo del gobierno, sino del conjunto social, de la desinformación en la que vivimos: no sabemos cómo están educando las familias a sus niños, no sabemos siquiera quiénes son los nuevos mexicanos que están naciendo en el campo, en las ciudades, los cuales tienen unas necesidades totalmente distintas de las de quienes se formaron con otros ideales, con otro proyecto cultural y nacional" (Mateos-Vega).

Para Monsiváis el nacionalismo mexicano hoy es apenas "un ritual de la memoria que convierte en ideología sentimental gran parte de lo vivido y lo imaginado históricamente." Afirma que quienes integran la minoría dominante "sólo vuelven al gentilicio mexicano en las ocasiones afectivas, ante un gol, una canción, una fiesta, un desastre amoroso, una indignación moral y política" (Corral Arrazola). Estos trazos retratan con fidelidad a los propietarios de las dos principales cadenas de televisión comercial mexicana, Televisa y TV Azteca, que, obsesionadas por los beneficios económicos y por el poder supraestatal que constituyen, influyen sin contrapesos en una población que, en su mayoría, pasa con grandes dificultades por el deficiente sistema educativo mexicano, cuya obra se desvanece por los efectos del "amable" e incesante entretenimiento banal que le ofrece la pantalla chica. Entretenimiento "globalizado" que desdeña la cultura nacional y que hasta 1972 había conseguido, entre otras cosas, que a la mayor parte de los niños que recibían educación primaria les fuera más familiar Supermán que el general Emiliano Zapata.[2] Abundando sobre este tema es preciso volver a Florescano quien señala que "el sistema educativo nacional es un desastre: los niños no aprenden nada en la primaria o abandonan la escuela. Y cuando el sistema educativo fracasa alguien tiene que tomar el lugar. Hoy ese lugar lo ocupa Televisa; proximamente serán las cadenas internacionales de televisión las que se ocuparán de hacer los programas educativos; vendrán de Inglaterra, Francia, Japón o China. Nosotros nos quedaremos rezagados porque la tecnología que han desarrollado los medios de comunicación no está en las aulas de la escuela mexicana."

Ante semejante panorama es natural que el sentimiento nacional sea preservado en distintas expresiones tradicionales, artísticas y sociales alejadas de la influencia de los grandes medios de comunicación y del *status quo*. También es lógico que el arte y el periodismo críticos se conviertan en reductos de resistencia cultural en los que nadie, ni siquiera ellos mismos, se identifican bajo esa denominación. Uno de esos espacios es el cine documental mexicano que sobrevive con dificultades lejos de la televisión y de las audiencias masivas.

En México, el documental ha sido un género constantemente marginado por la burocracia cultural, por los productores, distribuidores y exhibidores; por las empresas televisoras e incluso por las instituciones encargadas de la enseñanza del cine. Su condición de género relegado obedece a tres factores: las preferencias estéticas de quienes han encabezado las instituciones culturales y de enseñanza, el predominio de los intereses comerciales e ideológicos de Hollywood y, por último, la censura.

---

[2] A este resultado llegó un estudio realizado por el Instituto Nacional del Consumidor, aplicado a 1.800 niños, realizado en 1981 (cf. Riding 373-451).

A pesar de la diversidad temática que presenta hoy el documental mexicano, la inclinación natural de la mayor parte de los cineastas dedicados a esta especialidad ha desembocado en un trabajo principalmente interesado en las temáticas sociales y políticas que, sin duda, son muy abundantes en nuestro país. Tras la aparición del documental *¡Torero!* (1956) de Carlos Velo –prácticamente el primero exhibido comercialmente en México– y tras una larga noche en la que los únicos filmes de este género contenían únicamente propaganda gubernamental, obligatoria antes de cada exhibición comercial, la película *El grito* (Leobardo López Aretche, 1968), una crónica del cruento movimiento estudiantil de 1968 producida por la Universidad Nacional Autónoma de México, marcó el inicio de una serie de trabajos realizados durante la década de los setenta y ochenta. Trabajos que, con espíritu crítico, miraban la realidad circundante y al gobierno autoritario, que entonces cumplía ya medio siglo en el poder bajo el precepto inspirador de "A balazos llegamos y a balazos nos tienen que sacar," aludiendo a sus orígenes en la Revolución Mexicana y a su carácter autoritario. No es extraño, pues, que, de modo instintivo, el grupo gobernante y sus aliados miraran con desconfianza el género documental. Tampoco causa asombro que el cine mexicano de ficción, desde tiempos inmemorables, se haya ocupado muy poco o nada de la convulsa realidad nacional y que, en tiempos del neoliberalismo, se le haya despertado una súbita pasión por las comedias basadas en el tema de la pareja que impiden ver –ni siquiera como trasfondo– la lucha de los mexicanos por el voto efectivo, el alzamiento indígena en Chiapas, el fenómeno de la migración, el gravísimo crecimiento de los poderes fácticos o la corrupción que carcome la vida pública del país. No se pretende atribuir al documental mexicano la vocación unívoca por lo político y por lo social, entre otras razones porque sería falso, tampoco presentarlo como un refugio del sentimiento nacional de mayor envergadura de la que en realidad tiene. No obstante, es cierto que en las narraciones documentales mexicanas, sí están presentes una abundante diversidad de temas nutrientes de la identidad que como Nación, o como conjunto de naciones, caracterizan a México.

¿Por qué las miradas a la realidad de los documentalistas mexicanos se convierten en narraciones audiovisuales nacionales? La primer respuesta es obvia: la generosa variedad cultural mexicana es casi inagotable, al igual que la que deriva de la historia más o menos remota y de la conmocionada realidad social actual. Afirmar que hoy en México la realidad supera a la fantasía no es un tópico. Es muy probable que un poco de sensibilidad y de conocimiento de la realidad circundante basten para explicar el porqué de la inclinación mayoritaria de los documentalistas jóvenes y no tan jóvenes por abordar temas "nacionales," toda vez que no existen corrientes ni grupos ni grandes debates acerca de este tema que pudieran incidir en las tendencias del documental mexicano. No obstante, los documentales producidos en los últimos años demuestran una gran variedad de temas relacionados con lo nacional: así, por ejemplo, se produjeron documentales sobre la bebida nacional, el pulque (*La canción del pulque*, Everardo González, 2003), la Virgen de Guadalupe (*El pueblo mexicano que camina*, Juan Francisco Urrusti, 1996), la vida de Guty Cárdenas –cantante popular asesinado en 1932–

(*Sencillamente Guty*, Marco Rubio, 2005) o la historia de un asaltante de bancos que además era cantante de rancheras (*El charro misterioso*, José Manuel Cravioto, 2005). También se encuentran documentales sociales dedicados al asesinato de una defensora de los derechos humanos (*Digna, hasta el último aliento*, Felipe Cazals, 2003), a las peripecias de decenas de hombres y mujeres que encontraron protección en México huyendo de la guerra civil española (*Los niños de Morelia*, Juan Pablo Villaseñor, 2004), a la migración centroamericana en la frontera sur (*De nadie*, Tin Dirdamal, 2005), a la vida del guerrillero Lucio Cabañas (*La guerrilla y la esperanza: Lucio Cabañas*, Gerardo Tort, 2005) o a los asesinatos de mujeres en Ciudad Juárez (*Señorita extraviada*, Lourdes Portillo, 2001).

Temáticas nacionales que corresponden al trabajo ya sea de cineastas experimentados que incursionan por vez primera en el documental, o de estudiantes de cine, o de hombres y mujeres que, de manera empírica, realizan su primer film no ficcional. Independientemente de su origen, del formato en el que fueron realizados y de su resultado final, todos ellos delimitan con claridad la vocación del documental mexicano por la narración de lo nacional y contraponen sus trabajos al discurso que desde los medios de comunicación audiovisuales se repite hasta el infinito.

Por la diversidad de sus orígenes es pertinente aclarar que estos documentales son de muy variada calidad, que la mayoría de ellos fueron realizados en vídeo digital y muy pocos, en material fotosensible, pero todos enfrentan un mismo problema: su casi nula difusión.

Con las puertas de la exhibición comercial prácticamente cerradas –apenas se han exhibido cuatro o cinco documentales mexicanos en las salas comerciales durante los últimos quince años–, bloqueado absolutamente su acceso a los canales de la televisión comercial mexicana –incluso buena parte de la supuestamente cultural–, el documental sólo se encuentra con su público en las escasas proyecciones organizadas por los propios realizadores y por aquellos interesados en difundirlo, o en el marco de los escasos festivales nacionales que se ocupan de este género, o en eventos culturales aislados.

Con la relativa excepción del Canal 6 de julio, del que nos ocuparemos más adelante, el documental mexicano es apenas conocido y suele tener una pobre recepción fuera de sus fronteras. La ya mencionada mezcla de desdén y rechazo oficial a los trabajos de este género lo mantienen en una marginalidad casi subterránea. No obstante, la exhibición en México de la película *Fahrenheit 9/11* (2004) de Michael Moore, impulsó favorablemente este género y consiguió reavivar ligeramente el interés por él, despertando una suerte de auge que se muestra principalmente en la creciente producción de documentales, sobre todo en el ámbito estudiantil. Sin embargo, no se trata hasta el momento de una tendencia clara que pueda rescatarlo de su marginalidad.

La excepción que confirma esta regla la aporta el consorcio Televisa cuya filial, Editorial Clío, produce documentales y los presenta en un canal de televisión abierta una vez por semana. A través de las series tituladas *México siglo XX* y *México nuevo siglo*, el consorcio abrió, en 1998, una ventana con buenos augurios al género de la no ficción. El primer trabajo exhibido sobre la represión estudiantil de 1968, parecía anunciar, al fin, una tardía preocupación de Televisa por el lado oscuro de la realidad nacional, siempre ausente en su programación. El proyecto, además, auspiciaba la participación de varios de los más destacados documentalistas mexicanos. Sin embargo, lamentablemente, el instinto comercial del consorcio fue convirtiendo el proyecto en una fábrica de monografías instantáneas, cada vez con menor audiencia debido a la exhibición de documentales que dejaban ver su origen en una banda de producción que uniformaba fondo y forma, eliminaba el estilo personal de los realizadores, quienes naturalmente se fueron alejando de la aventura, al menos los más serios y prestigiados. La decadencia del proyecto se empezó a manifestar con claridad a lo largo de 2005 cuando *México nuevo siglo* empezó a producir "documentales" que contaban la historia color de rosa de las empresas que eran propiedad de las familias más poderosas del país, familias que gustosas patrocinaban los halagos fílmicos. Estos trabajos, mezcla de autopromoción empresarial y apología de clase, ocultan los pecados públicos de una clase patronal poco escrupulosa, exhiben el profundo desprecio que en Televisa existe por el documental, representan una pésima escuela y una forma de vacunación masiva contra este género.

Así, la única expresión documentalista presente en la televisión comercial mexicana que nació con una incipiente vocación crítica y un tímido interés por abordar temas relativos a la identidad nacional, ya siete años más tarde se ocupa de adular por encargo a los ricachones mexicanos conduciendo al intimidado género documental a una forma de prostitución similar a la que padeció en las década de los sesenta cuando se le asignó –como ya se ha señalado– el papel de propagandista gubernamental. El discurso de *México siglo XX* está construido, debido a su vocación eminentemente comercial, en forma de epopeya. Según él, la construcción del México civilizado se debe fundamentalmente a los barones de la iniciativa privada quienes solían volver su mirada generosa hacia los prescindibles obreros. La premura con que se investiga y luego se elaboran los guiones para estos documentales conduce a frecuentes inexactitudes históricas, omisiones y juicios de valor carentes de base. Si bien es una derivación del discurso dominante, en este caso específico se trata de una expresión culta y adecentada de éste a causa de las pretensiones intelectuales de quienes encabezan el proyecto. En 2004 el súper consorcio incursionó nuevamente en el terreno del documental y produjo una serie titulada *México: la historia de su democracia*, en la que relata, no sin sesgos, la lucha del pueblo mexicano por llegar a esa forma de convivencia política; no obstante el resultado de dicho trabajo es un discurso legitimador del sistema político imperante que aún no supera del todo las prácticas electorales fraudulentas y que padece el virtual secuestro de las instituciones republicanas por parte de ese pequeño grupo de multimillonarios del que aquí ya se ha hablado. Al final de cuentas, es la historia oficial en la que Televisa suprime toda información acerca del papel que tuvieron los medios de comunicación –específicamente ellos mismos– para impedir durante décadas toda forma de avance democrático en el país.

Del lado exactamente opuesto a estas experiencias documentalistas se ubica la producción de un pequeño grupo llamado *Canal 6 de julio* que en veinte años ha producido más de cincuenta documentales de temas políticos y sociales. Se trata tal vez de la productora que mantiene la difusión más consecuente del documental mexicano, si bien su audiencia es claramente minoritaria. El discurso de estos trabajos suele estar basado en la crítica directa al modelo económico vigente y a una clase política, en su mayoría, desacreditada ante la sociedad. Los contenidos de estos trabajos –en muchos casos con enfoques marcados por el humor, una cualidad distintiva de muchas expresiones de la cultura mexicana–, han convertido a Canal 6 de julio en uno de los medios más censurados de la historia reciente de México. Tras las prohibiciones ocultas bajo argumentos administrativos de que fue objeto el documental *Crónica de un fraude*, en 1988, el Canal 6 de julio, vivió otros relevantes capítulos de censura, como los cuatro allanamientos a su estudio, en enero de 1994, durante la insurrección zapatista; así como innumerables episodios de obstaculización a su labor tanto de exhibición, como de registro de imágenes. El camino que esta productora debe seguir para la difusión de su trabajo habla por sí mismo, ya que alcanza a su público a través de la venta de copias de los documentales en las librerías. Así, en México se pueden producir narraciones audiovisuales con tecnología digital del siglo XXI, pero se deben difundir de mano en mano, igual que en el siglo XI, cuando se inventó la imprenta. Una serie de documentales del Canal 6 de julio, como el ya citado *Crónica de un fraude* (1988), *Chiapas, la otra guerra* (1994), *Las píldoras del doctor Barnés* (sobre la huelga de la UNAM en 1999) y *Tlatelolco, las claves de la masacre* (2002), alcanzaron una amplia difusión, mediante su distribución de mano en mano, que se puede contabilizar en decenas de miles de copias distribuidas en tan sólo algunas semanas.

Esta paradoja es, a fin de cuentas, la alegoría de un país cuyo grupo gobernante intenta figurar en los foros internacionales al lado de los jefes de estado de los países desarrollados, y cuya clase empresarial está claramente representada en la lista de los hombres más ricos del mundo, mientras su sistema educativo es peor que el de países como Nigeria, Zimbabue o Jamaica, y cuyas regiones más pobres son comparables con las zonas más miserables del continente africano. Un país dividido en el que la mayoría de la gente intenta reencontrarse con un proyecto de nación, mientras la minoría privilegiada sueña con la integración de México en su vecino del norte, dando la espalda al patético episodio que, en 1847, le costó al país la pérdida de más de la mitad de su territorio. Pero, la historia real es para los tecnócratas que dominan la Nación, una materia desagradable porque produce agruras y comezón en la memoria. Esto explica también el hecho de que en febrero de 2005 fuese clausurada la carrera de Historia junto con la de Filosofía en la Universidad Autónoma de Nuevo León, el estado de la República del que proviene el núcleo duro de la clase empresarial mexicana (cf. Carrizales). Se adujo que era debido al escaso mercado de trabajo que encuentran sus egresados, como si en México hubiera egresados de alguna otra carrera que sí encuentran trabajo. Esta decisión en nombre de la eficiencia académica globalizada tuvo lugar unos meses después de que un programa difundido por Televisa y auspiciado veladamente por el Departamento de Estado del gobierno estadounidense titulado *Oppenheimer presenta*, aleccionara a la audiencia para exigir a nuestras universidades formar más ingenieros y menos filósofos y otros humanistas, como en el muy globalizado Singapur, la potencia exportadora a la que deberíamos imitar.

Pobre México, dice la conseja popular, tan lejos de Dios y tan cerca de los Estados Unidos.

Bibliografía

Carrizales, David. "Desaparecen carreras de historia y filosofía en la UANL; el mercado, la causa." *La Jornada*, 9 de febrero de 2005. http://www.jornada.unam.mx/2005/02/09/049n2soc.php.

Corral Arrazola, Victor. "El nacionalismo de hoy es un ritual de la memoria, dijo Carlos Monsiváis." *La Jornada*, 29 de octubre de 2005. http://www.jornada.unam.mx/2005/09/24/a05n1cul.php.

Mateos-Vega, Mónica. "Deplora Florescano la apatía de los nuevos mexicanos por los símbolos nacionales." *La Jornada*, 29 de octubre de 2005. http://www.jornada.unam. mx/2005/10/29/a08n1cul.php.

Paz, Octavio. *El ogro filantrópico: Historia y política 1971–1978*. México, D.F.: Joaquín Mortíz, 1979.

Riding, Alan. *Vecinos distantes. Un retrato de los mexicanos*. México, D.F.: Joaquín Mortíz, 1985.

Salinas, Javier y Fernanado Camacho. "Teotihuacán, testimonio de un gobierno que no defiende la cultura: Sánchez Vázquez." *La Jornada*, 5 de noviembre de 2004. http://www.jornada.unam.mx/2004/11/05/03an3cul.php?origen=index.html&fly=1.

Filmografía

Chiapas, la otra guerra. Dir. Carlos Mendoza. México, 1994.

Crónica de un fraude. Dir. Carlos Mendoza. México, 1988.

De nadie. Dir. Tin Dirdamal. México, 2005.

Digna, hasta el último aliento. Dir. Felipe Cazals. México, 2003.

El charro misterioso. Dir. José Manuel Cravioto. México, 2005.

El grito. Dir. Leobardo López Aretche. México, 1968.

El pueblo mexicano que camina. Dir. Juan Francisco Urrusti. México, 1996.

Fahrenheit 9/11. Dir. Michael Moore. Estados Unidos, 2004.

La canción del pulque. Dir. Everardo González. México, 2003.

La guerrilla y la esperanza: Lucio Cabañas. Dir. Gerardo Tort. México, 2005.

Las píldoras del doctor Barnés. Dir. Canal Seis de Julio. México, 1999.

Los niños de Morelia. Dir. Juan Pablo Villaseñor. México, 2004.

México: la historia de su democracia. Varios Directores. México, 2004.

México nuevo siglo. Varios Directores/Editorial Clío. México, 2001.

México siglo XX. Varios Directores/Editorial Clío. México, 1998.

Oppenheimer presenta. Dir. Gustavo Marrazo. Estados Unidos, 2003ss.

Sencillamente Guty. Dir. Marco Rubio. México, 2005.

Señorita extraviada. Dir. Lourdes Portillo. México, Estados Unidos, 2001.

Tlatelolco, las claves de la masacre. Dir. Carlos Mendoza. México, 2003.

¡Torero!. Dir. Carlos Velo. México, 1957.

The Ruins of Modernity[1]

JESSE LERNER

Resumen

Este trabajo centra su atención en el significado que los antiguos mayas del sur de México adquieren en el imaginario modernista poniendo de relieve que su cultura se ha convertido en una fuente inagotable de inspiración de las ideas e iconografía de artistas, arquitectos, cineastas, fotógrafos y otros productores de cultura visual no sólo en México, sino también en los EE.UU., Europa y, en general, en el mundo entero. Es un tema al cual he dedicado un documental con el título de *Ruins* (1999), que compila –de manera cuasi arqueológica– las huellas audiovisuales de esta tradición mayista moderna y reflexiona acerca de la construcción de la verdad tanto en la arqueología como en el documental. Mary Louise Pratt afirma que "la metrópoli imperial es imaginada como la determinación de la periferia, pero habitualmente no se considera la forma en que la periferia determina la metrópoli." Considerando esta afirmación es que postulamos que el modernismo maya se desarrolla como un fenómeno de ida y de vuelta: entre Chichén Itzá y la región sureste de México (es decir, la periferia de la periferia), la Ciudad de México (el centro de la periferia) y los centros metropolitanos de los EE.UU. y Europa. Esta visión del modernismo es un poco más complicada que un simple conjunto de ideas, que supondría que, en primer lugar, se desarrolló en la metrópoli y luego se extendió hacia otros lugares, en tanto que otro conjunto de objetos de los mayas, las imágenes, su base material o materias primas, se habrían expandido en la dirección contraria. En vez de esto, apreciamos un sistema complejo de ida y vuelta que conlleva en sí los objetos ambulantes y los artistas, los migrantes y los peregrinos, los intercambios e influencias. Este acercamiento existe en la mayor parte de la narrativa del primitivismo moderno, pero difiere de manera significativa de los relatos más conocidos de cómo se trajo desde Oceanía o África Occidental un botín colonial que más tarde despertó la imaginación de los vanguardistas modernos de principios del siglo XX. Es decir, aquellas vanguardias que existían sin conocer aquello que les había servido de inspiración. En oposición a esta visión, entendemos por modernismo maya, un fenómeno que es mucho más el producto de todo un continente, en ocasiones, de todo el mundo y que se logra a través del diálogo, del con-

---

[1] A different version of this text appears in my book *The Maya of Modernism*.

tacto. Una modernidad en el ámbito panamericano, caracterizada por una serie conti-
nuada de reinterpretaciones, colaboraciones e intercambios. Tal modernidad está representada en este trabajo por autores tan diversos como Robert Smithson, Sergei
Eisenstein, Albert Lewin, Waldemaro Concha Vargas y Robert Stacy Judd.

This essay focuses on the significance which the ancient Maya in the South of Mexico
acquire in the modernist imagination, stressing that their culture has become an inexhaustible source of inspiration, ideas, and iconography for artists, architects, filmmakers, photographers, and other producers of visual culture not only in Mexico, but
also in the United States, Europe, and throughout the world. This topic is at the heart
of my fake documentary *Ruins* (1999), an experimental film essay on the history of
collections and exhibitions of Mesoamerican antiquities in the West. My film com-
piles—in an almost archeological manner—audiovisual references to Mayan modernism, while reflecting on the construction of truth in both archeology and documentary
filmmaking. I take Mayan modernism to be a phenomenon of to and fro between
various spaces: between Chichén Itzá (Yucatán) and the surrounding southeast of
Mexico (as the periphery of the periphery), Mexico City (as periphery) and the metropolitan centers of the United States and Europe. Thus I envisage a complex system of
mutual exchange that extends to moveable artifacts, artists, migrants, and pilgrims.
This approach is part of the larger narrative of modernist primitivism, but it contradicts
traditional views of a one-way influence with indigenous artifacts being taken to
Europe, exhibited in museums there, and later inspiring expressionists, cubists, and
other modernist trends of the early twentieth century. I view Mayan modernism much
more as the product of an entire continent and, in some instances, of the whole world,
the result of an ongoing pan-American conversation and exchange. This kind of
modernity is presented in this essay through figures as diverse as Robert Smithson,
Sergei Eisenstein, Albert Lewin, Waldemaro Concha Vargas, and Robert Stacy Judd.

A 1961 television documentary film called *Expedition: Treasure of the Sacred
Well* records the construction and operation of an extraordinary artificial archeological
geyser within the "Sacred Cenote" at Chichén Itzá. The site is a focal one for Mesoamerican archeology. Chichén Itzá, the ancient Maya city, is represented by and has
been replaced with the modern tourist destination and research site built upon (and
from) its ruins. There, as elsewhere throughout the Yucatán peninsula, the erosion of
the soft limestone just below the thin layer of impoverished topsoil has over the centuries produced innumerable caves and underground passages. When the roof of these
subterranean cavities can no longer hold, the collapse yields a sinkhole, or, in local
parlance, a *cenote*. The ancient Maya used these as a source of fresh water as well as a
place for religious offerings and, most notoriously, for ritual human sacrifices. The
prospect of recovering the remnants of whatever was heaved into this water during
pre-Cortesian rituals—and, of course, the eternally tantalizing visions of dark-skinned,
beauteous young virgins, generously bedecked in gold and jade, tumbling downward
to the water's surface and death—have made the "Sacred Cenote" a site of a series of

archeological follies, from Edward H. Thompson's destructive dredging to the atomic-age attempts to clear the water by chlorination.[2]

Expedition: Treasure of the Sacred Well and the complementary articles in "National Geographic," generously illustrated with photographs, chronicle the process whereby scientists from the Smithsonian, the National Geographic Society and Mexico's *Instituto Nacional de Antropologia e Historia* (National Institute of Anthropology and History, or INAH), supported by divers from a Mexican scuba club (CEDAM), insert a long metal tube perpendicularly into the well, and then, by pumping air to the bottom of the pipe, suck mud, water, and hundreds of archeological fragments up through the pipe and release them into the air in a veritable pre-Columbian gusher.[3] The effect of this practice upon the artifacts uncovered is predictably destructive: the narrator notes that all the pottery recovered is in the form of broken fragments (and disingenuously concludes that "perhaps the Maya broke these pots in order to symbolically kill them"). Still, the archeological geyser does function perfectly as a metaphor for the subject of my research; Chichén Itzá and the other celebrated Maya sites of Mexico as a veritable cornucopia of artifacts and inspirations which, once dislodged from their resting places, are scattered in all directions to new destinations, where they take on remarkable lives unimaginable to the artisans who originally crafted them.

In addition to the daring bi-national team of divers and archeologists who, risking life or mortal injury for the sake of science and knowledge, the television documentary features two local Mayas who were employed by the team as assistants. Avelino Canul, introduced as "an ordinary local farmer," earns repeated praise from the narrator for his "keen eyesight" and other "virtues" that make him "a wonderful helper." "Little José, our youngest helper," as he is introduced in the film, also merits commen-

---

2   For more on Thompson's dredging and diving in Chichén Itzá's *cenote*, cf. my "Thompson y el cenote sagrado," 23-26. The attempt to clear the water of the *cenote* by chlorination in order to make it possible for divers to see well enough to recover the material below is described in Ediger, *The Well of Sacrifice*. For my purposes the image of the archeological booty spurting upward through the water's surface and into the air is a more suggestive image. More on human sacrifices will follow below, but for the moment it should suffice to reference what is perhaps the most imaginative account of the ritual at Chichén's sacred *cenote*: T.A. Willard's remarkable pseudo-historical fantasy novels *Bride of the Rain God: Princess of Chichen-Itza,*), *The Wizard of Zacna: Lost City of the Mayas* and his celebration of Edward H. Thompson's life and work, *The City of the Sacred Well*.

3   The project is also recorded in Eusebio Dávalos Hurtado, "Into the Well of Sacrifice: Return to the Sacred Cenote" as well as in Bates Littlehales, "Into the Well of Sacrifice: Treasure Hunt in the Deep Past." The objects collected during Thompson's dredging and diving, the archeological vacuum cleaner described above, and the de-chlorination project are reproduced and analyzed in Lothrop, *Metals from the Cenote of Sacrifice, Chichen Itza, Yucatán*; Proskouriakoff, *Jades from the Cenote of Sacrifice, Chichen Itza, Yucatán*; Clemency Chase Coggins and Orrin C. Shane, III, eds., *Cenote of Sacrifice: Maya Treasures from the Sacred Well at Chichen Itza* and *Artifacts from the Cenote of Sacrifice, Chichen Itza, Yucatán*.

dations in the documentary's voice-over. In the *National Geographic* article he is additionally highlighted and even given the benefit of a last name, being presented as "[t]wentieth-century Maya, young José Burgos." Much is made of the fact that these modern Maya were able to "learn to use an Aqua-Lung" (Littlehales 552) and that one proves "to be a superb diver"(553). The interest in Maya using Aqua-Lungs, and more broadly, in the Mexican Indians' embrace of modern technology and of modernity more generally, is noteworthy and recurrent. Elsewhere in this same issue of *National Geographic*'s thematic section on Mexico, for example, the reader is presented with a scene from Veracruz of "overalled Indians bid[ding] their bare-breasted wives *maj nioj*—goodbye in their ancient Aztec tongue—and set[ting] off to build one of the world's most modern chemical plants" ("New Atlas Map" 539).

As this trope suggests, the rejection, indifference, miscomprehension or, as in this case, ready adoption of new technologies by an ancient people, and by extension, the potential for those people to fully enter the modern world, is a site of curiosity and anxiety, and one of the explicit or implicit themes of the many Western representations of the Maya, both popular, like this television program and magazine article, and scholarly. The question at the heart of this text is: what place, if any, do the Maya have in the modern world? What do the astonishing ruins scattered across southeastern Mexico, Belize, Guatemala and Honduras tell us about the living Maya and their potential to enter into modernity? How should they be cast in that most treasured Western narrative, that of "progress" toward modernity? Might their past aesthetic and architectural accomplishments form the basis for a modern, uniquely American (Pan-American, Mexican, Latin American or just plain "American," with all of that adjective's ambiguities) modernism? How is it possible—or indeed, is it possible—to be both Maya and modern?

Nearly four decades after the misguided archeological exploits documented in *Expedition*, I was in Mérida, Yucatán as a guest of a film festival, the *Festival Regional Cine-Video-Sociedad*. I had come to show my fake documentary *Ruins* (1999), an experimental film essay on the history of collections and exhibitions of Mesoamerican antiquities in the West. The film festival took place in a variety of venues around the city—a restored movie palace from Mexican cinema's golden age, the municipal cultural center on the city's central plaza, and a commercial multiplex that had allowed the festival use of one of its theaters. My film was shown at this latter location; next door, the Dreamworks© animated feature *The Road to El Dorado* was showing: a revisionist (at best) treatment of the Spanish conquest of the Maya, whose English-language version features the voices of Kevin Klein, Kenneth Branagh and Rosie Perez. The steps out of my screening and into the theater next door meant a return, once again, to the sacred *cenote*. The candy-colored caricatures of Mesoamerican artifacts that the animated Maya on the screen tossed into the well of sacrifice formed a psychedelic rainbow of pre-Columbian loot. All the while the animated participants in the imaginary ritual danced in abandon like the pre-Columbian rock-and-roll version of a demented Radio City chorus line, mouthing the original score composed by Elton

John and Tim Rice. The children in the audience—and there were many—were enraptured.

The "twenty-first century Maya," to update *National Geographic*'s designation, were eating it up. It occurred to me that my film and the Dreamworks© *Road to El Dorado*, as different as they might be in their modes of production, intentions, styles, and so on, were both trapped in the same hall of mirrors—U.S. representations of Mexico, re-imported to Mexico for consumption and reinterpretation—that had been going on for at least the past century and a half. As with a hall of mirrors, where each reflection implies further distortions, these film screenings imply a back and forth of mutual (mis-)interpretations and creative re-readings.

My work digs beneath this hall of mirrors to find fragments of the meanings which the ancient Maya of southern Mexico had in the modernist imagination, scattered around and below the hall's foundations like so many dislodged, reflective shards.[4] It reveals that, like the ancient fragments suctioned off the bottom of the "Sacred Cenote," propelled up into the air and scattered in all directions, the Maya past has proven to be a boundless source of inspiration, ideas and iconography for artists, architects, filmmakers, photographers and other producers of visual culture in Mexico, the United States, Europe and beyond. More specifically, it looks at the ways in which these ancient fragments have been used within the contexts of divergent strands of modernism and of visual culture. "While the imperial metropolis imagines itself as determining the periphery," Mary Louise Pratt writes, "it habitually blinds itself to the ways in which the periphery determines the metropolis" (6).

The phenomenon I am calling Maya modernism takes place within the framework Pratt describes, a back and forth between the periphery of the periphery (Chichén Itzá, the Yucatán and more generally the Maya region in Southeastern Mexico), the center of the periphery (Mexico City), and the metropolitan centers of the United States and Europe. The dynamics of these reflections and reinterpretations are as delirious as the hailstorm of antiquities depicted in *The Road to El Dorado*, though typically not colored with the same saturated garish pop tones as those of the cornucopia of *ersatz* artifacts that appear in the animated feature. The specifics of this history complicate the simple notion that a set of modernist ideas is first developed within the metropolis and then exported elsewhere, while a set of objects, images and artifacts of the Maya and the material basis for explanations of what they might mean travel in the other direction. Instead, we see a complex back and forth involving itinerant objects and artists, migrants and pilgrims, dialogues, collaborations and exchanges. This history exists within the larger narrative of modernist primitivism, but differs in significant and intriguing ways from the more familiar narratives of how Oceanic or West African objects, brought back to Europe as colonial loot and warehoused in mu-

---

[4]   The Maya region extends beyond Mexico over the entire territory today occupied by the nations of Guatemala and Belize as well as into Northern Honduras and along El Salvador's Pacific slope. These are countries with histories very different from Mexico's, which I have left out of this study for precisely that reason.

seums, later sparked the imagination of the German expressionists, Parisian cubists and other modernist vanguards of the early twentieth century.

While the modernist primitivism of the cubists of Montmartre, for example, existed without the knowledge of the West Africans whose radical geometries provided such provocative inspiration, what I am calling Maya modernism is significantly the product of a hemispheric—or at times even global—dialogue, an ongoing pan-American conversation. Whether it was the North American visits of the Mexican muralists and their impact, most famously the W.P.A. muralists emulating Diego Rivera and his expansive vision, or the influence of Eisenstein's never-completed film *Que Viva Mexico!* on Mexican cinema's "Golden Age," the modernism that finds inspiration in the ancient Maya is not, as a rule, the product of individuals working in isolation. As will become clear shortly, the motivations and the ideological charge of this modernist spirit may have been very different for artists from the north and those from the south. But what distinguishes this regional (or hemispheric) history of primitivism from the more familiar Parisian case, or that of the Fauves, Gauguin in Tahiti, and so on, is that it is the product of an exchange in which Yucatecans, Mexicans and foreigners, mestizos, Mayas and others, all participate, in which each is free to respond to, endorse, misunderstand, reinterpret or reject each other's ideas.

There are exceptions; Charles Olson's *Mayan Letters* show that while living in Yerma, Campeche, he had more significant long distance intellectual engagements with Robert Creeley and Cid Corman than with any of his Mexican hosts or neighbors.[5] Robert Smithson, with his wife Nancy Holt and gallerist Virginia Dwan, driving southward from Mérida towards Chiapas and staging the photographs later published as *Incidents of Mirror Travel in Yucatán*, are likewise minimally engaged with locals. But for the most part this regional history of modernist primitivism is characterized by a continuing series of dialogues, reinterpretations, collaborations, imitations, rebuttals, reuses and exchanges. By tracing these interactions and mutual influences, this study aims to further deepen and complicate the analysis of that facet of modernism problematically labeled "primitivism."

Many of the scholarly conversations on these topics use the much-criticized 1984 exhibition *"Primitivism" in Twentieth Century Art: Affinities of the Tribal and the Modern* at the Museum of Modern Art in New York as a point of reference. That exhibition, its problematic use of "affinities" as a device to link modernist and non-Western objects, and its erasure of the colonial projects that brought the material culture of Africa and Oceania to the European studios of the artists represented: all these factors merit close scrutiny and criticism.[6] With the exception of a section in the exhibition catalog's final chapter, as if added as an afterthought, the role of Mesoamerican objects in this dynamic was not mentioned. Even a preliminary review of

---

[5] Cf. Charles Olson, *Mayan Letters*; Charles Olson and Robert Creeley, *The Complete Correspondence*; and Charles Olson, *Letters for Origin, 1950-1956*.

[6] Cf., for example, James Clifford, "Histories of the Tribal and the Modern" and Thomas McEvilley, "Doctor Lawyer Indian Chief."

that role reveals a history strikingly different from the narrative, repeated and pre-served by art historians, of cubists purchasing Dagon masks at the *marché-au-puce* and returning to their studios newly inspired, ready to challenge Renaissance perspec-tive.

Scholars have of late begun to piece together the narratives that constitute a dis-tinctive New World primitivism. W. Jackson Rushing's *Native American Art and the New York Avant-Garde* looks at the role of Indian objects from the area that today is the U.S. in the development of a North American modernism, from Marsden Hartsley to Jackson Pollock, from John Sloan to Adolph Gottlieb. Cesar Paternostro's *The Thread and the Stone* examines the impact of Andean, especially Inca, visual cultures upon abstract artists in the twentieth century. Barbara Braun's *Pre-Columbian Art and the Post-Columbian World* looks closely at the work of five important individual artists and architects—Paul Gauguin, Frank Lloyd Wright, Diego Rivera, Henry Moore and Joaquin Torres-García—each influenced in some significant ways by an-cient art of ancient South or Middle America. Other scholars have explicitly addressed the political context for this New World primitivism and explored the impact of this context. Holly Barnet-Sánchez's doctoral dissertation, *The Necessity of Pre-Columbi-an Art*, offers an astute analysis of the political context for the movement of pre-Co-lumbian objects from the museum of natural history to the museum of art, in relation-ship to the "Good Neighbor" policy during the Second World War and the need to forge a common hemispheric heritage.[7] Other recent monographs have explored these connections in relationship to the work and careers of individual artists.[8] My research builds on their contributions as it takes on questions yet to be thoroughly studied by cultural critics.

Equally important is other recent revisionist scholarship on Mexican regional histories and archeology in the Maya region. In contrast to the paucity of academic studies once available, Gilbert M. Joseph announced twenty years ago that the Yucatán had become "one of the three Mexican regions," along with the Northwest and Oaxa-ca, "of greatest interest to the new generation of local historians" (*Rediscovering* 8) whose work had significantly complicated the dominant national historical narrative. Joseph himself is in no small measure one of the sources for this energetic inquiry into local history, and his *Revolution from Without* provides a critical political context for the cultural history that follows. Joseph's collaboration with Allen Wells, *Summer of Discontent, Seasons of Upheaval*, and Ben Fallaw's analysis of the region's turbulent transformations during the 1930s, *Cárdenas Compromised*, both make significant con-tributions to our understanding of the local political context for much of what follows here. Paul Sullivan's brilliant analysis of one aspect of the history of archeological endeavors in the region, *Unfinished Conversations*, and his nineteenth-century inter-nationalist whodunit, *Xuxub Must Die*, are testaments to the rewards of meticulous

---

[7]   Unfortunately, this latter effort has yet to be published.

[8]   For example, Cuauhtémoc Medina on Gunther Gerzso in *Risking the Abstract: Mexican Modernism and the Art of Gunther Gerzso*.

archival research. So are *Romancing the Maya*, R. Tripp Evans' work on nineteenth-century archeologists and explorers, as well as the conjectures of armchair romantics—from Désiré Charnay to Joseph Smith—whose engagements with Mesoamerican antiquities function at some level as a prelude to this study. Quetzil Casteñeda's study of tourism at Chichén Itzá, *In the Museum of Maya Culture*, emerges from an ethnographic tradition but effectively critiques the way anthropology has used the site towards a variety of problematic ends. All of these studies contribute to making Mexico's southeast an exciting place for historical research, a site of an ongoing engaged dialogue on the region's complex and exceptional past.

Finally, there is an exciting body of literature on Mexican national identity that contributes a theoretical foundation critical to this analysis. Roger Bartra's landmark study of *lo Mexicano*, *La jaula de la melancolía*, is first and foremost in importance. His boldly conceived survey and critique of the ways Mexican intellectuals, from Octavio Paz to Manuel Gamio, have invented and studied a national character and the role of "the Indian" in those formulations, invites further explorations and is particularly relevant to the discussion of visual culture. Some scholars, especially Tarek Elhaik and Gabriela Zamorano Villarreal, have answered this challenge, and my work is intended to complement their efforts.

This history is constituted by the traditional objects of the art historian's scrutiny—paintings, sculpture, prints, fine art photography and so on—but also by architecture, television, films, television documentaries and other expressions of popular culture beyond the scope of "high art" (cf. Mirzoeff). Antecedents for this approach include not only the recent studies of visual culture but also the writings of Jean Charlot, whose *Art from the Mayans to Disney* contains essays on popular culture and "high" art, ancient and modern—*pulqueria* paintings, the ancient murals at Chichén Itzá and Carlos Mérida's drawings—each scrutinized and analyzed with the same intelligence and respect. Charlot understood that images hold a special power in Mexico's history, making this extraordinarily rich terrain for such an approach.

A gift, quite literally "from the Maya to Disney," is documented in the 1942 travelogue of a hemispheric goodwill tour by a team of that studio's animators, *South of the Border with Disney*. While providing accommodations to the group visiting from Hollywood, "the young employees of the Mayan Hotel" present Walter Disney with a cake adorned with a likeness of Mickey Mouse, rendered in icing. The film's narrator tells of another technology that the Maya have readily embraced. "Every one of" the Maya employees, we are told, "was an enthusiastic picture fan." Serge Gruzinski has analyzed how, centuries before there were any Maya "picture fans," images had been deployed in the New World as part of complex struggles of power and faith among participants with vastly different belief systems:

> For spiritual reasons (the imperatives of evangelization), linguistic reasons (the obstacles of many indigenous languages), and technical reasons (the spread of the printing press and the rise of engraving), the image exerted a remarkable influence on the discovery, conquest and colonization of the New World in the sixteenth century. Because the image—along with written language—constitutes one of the major tools of Euro-

pean culture, the gigantic enterprise of Westernization that swooped down upon the American continent became in part a war of images that perpetuated itself for centuries and—according to all indications—may not even be over today. (2)

Gruzinski's daring projections of *Blade Runner*'s dystopian, corporate-dominated Los Angeles (or is it Mexico City?) of the future, with its flat-topped pyramids housing malevolent corporations and a plethora of large-screen outdoor projections, suggest that this dynamic does not end with modernity but rather accelerates with the exponential increase of images spewing from new technologies designed for their ever more rapid dissemination. Gruzinski looks to the Conquest of the Americas, in its political, artistic, spiritual and linguistic dimensions, as the point of origin for the forces of globalization that are transforming our world today. This study focuses on visual culture, primarily from the twentieth century, and contemplates its trajectory through the hemisphere and beyond.

The Mayas' encounter with the European world can be said to begin with Columbus' landfall on the Yucatecan coast, with the first Spanish sailors shipwrecked on their shores, or with the Spanish Conquest of the peninsula early in the sixteenth century. In the nineteenth century, lithographs and early photographs form the first mechanically reproduced and mass distributed images of the Maya ruins, and in the twentieth century these representations multiply exponentially. I believe that there are four cardinal points, or paradigms, around which these representations and the ideas that inform them are clustered. These four cardinal points structure and expose commonalities shared by artists of different eras and nationalities, working in distinct media by foregrounding the conceptual foundations and assumptions of these otherwise quite divergent representations.

Time, many scholars have proposed, was an obsession for the ancient Maya. The prediction of eclipses, the cyclical and "long count" calendars, and numerous complex astronomical calculations all figured large in their world. But the element of time operating here is something altogether different. Modernity's narratives unfold in linear time. For the Maya—living or ancient—to make sense, they had to be positioned in relationship to the region's, the nation's and the Americas' past, present and future. Are the contemporary Maya living fossils, melancholic lingerers haunting the scene of their past glories like phantoms lost in time? Will they ever regain some of their past splendor, or will they quietly fade away, leaving only their monumental crumbling ruins as a reminder of what they once were? And if they are to enter modernity, what would that look like? This is the fundamental question for self-styled intellectual architects of Mexican modernity: what about the Indians?

At the center of my work is an understanding, sometimes explicit and more often implied, of the relationship of the living Maya to the ruins in their midst and the modern world impinging upon them. In the first paradigm, we have a series of diverse images that all operate on the assumption and seek to convince us that the Maya are themselves remnants, living artifacts of an exhausted culture. This conviction reoccurs through history and permeates Mexican visual culture in pernicious and troubling ways. The first images of Maya ruins and their contemporary descendants to receive wide distribution are those of Frederick Catherwood, a pioneering photographer and adventurer who traveled extensively in the Maya region in the mid-nineteenth century. Catherwood's images and the text of John Lloyd Stephens that they illustrate (*Incidents of Travel in Central America, Chiapas, and Yucatán*, 2 vols., 1841) are both reinterpreted by Yucatecan commentators, initiating a cavalcade of reflections in the pan-American hall of mirrors; contemporary artists have also revisited Catherwood's formative depictions. Stephens and his Yucatecan translator disagree on the possibility or probability that the disparaged, modern-day Indian may be the descendent of the builders of monumental ruins. Stephens brings home the origins of the Maya culture, the source which Ignatius Donnelly located in Greece, Hugo Grotius identified as coming from Nordic lands, Lord Kingsborough as Israelite, T.A. Willard as Hebraic, and which Harold Gladwin had attributed to Alexander the Great.[9] By situating the Maya as heirs to the ruins, Stephens, his translators and commentators all weigh in on the relationships between the Maya, their past and the modern world. The orthodoxies of an official Mexican construction of the ancient and modern Maya propagated by the *Partido Revolucionario Institucional* (PRI) after the consolidation of their monopoly on political power in the years following World War II are exemplified by the feature film *Raíces* (1954).

The second paradigm is premised on a disappearing act. Susan Stewart writes that "in the New World, for example, antiquarianism centered on the discovery of a radical cultural other, the Native American, whose narrative could not easily be made continuous with either the remote past or the present as constructed by non-native historians" (141). One way to establish that continuity is to remove the Maya from the picture. The radical otherness is no longer an issue if the ruins are depopulated; there is then a heritage unclaimed that is free for the taking. This strategy allows for a continuity to be established by virtue of geographical proximity, pushing aside issues of racial and cultural difference. Two disparate examples, one contemporary and one from the first half of the twentieth century, might illustrate this paradigm: *Photogravity*, Gabriel Orozco's series of sculptures commissioned by and exhibited at the Philadelphia Museum of Art, and the English architect Robert Stacy-Judd. Here we have a Maya modernism without the Maya; the ancient objects are a blueprint and a vindication for the modern, but the indigenous Mexican is nowhere to be seen. Orozco's project specifically addresses the collecting practices of one pair of important collectors of modern art and pre-Cortesian objects, Walter and Louise Arensberg. It asks some of the more general questions that arise when modernism recontextualizes non-Western objects—likely objects coming from societies without a concept equivalent to what we call "art"—and relocates them to a museum or gallery space. A

---

[9] A levelheaded survey of a great range of these kinds of speculative schemes and delirious conjectures, from Kon Tiki to Mu, with detours through Belshazzar's Chaldean banquet hall and Lemuria, is offered by Robert Wauchope in his *Lost Tribes and Sunken Continents*.

similar impulse exists in architecture, contrasting the history of Mesoamerican references within modern visual arts with that of Maya Revival architecture.

For the post-Revolutionary Mexican state, the ancient Maya and their accomplishments were a usable past, one that could effectively be deployed to address a burning political and social imperative. Gathered around the third cardinal point we find many visions of Maya modernism that celebrate the possibility or reality of the Maya themselves "catching up," entering the modern world and becoming active subjects in a new world of their own making. A little-known newsreel from the 1930s, several paintings and photographs, and key works of Mexican Maya revival architecture illustrate this dynamic. A distinct Latin American strain of Maya revival architecture, and the theoretical discourses that motivated it, contrasts with the North American variant.

Finally there is another scenario, that of the aoristic Maya, a culture and people that transcends and conflates the ancient and the modern. Here the role of the Maya is neither to catch up with the progress defined elsewhere, nor to offer up validation for modern aesthetic projects from their distant past, but rather to engage fully with the modern world as actors in charge of their own destinies. Sergei Eisenstein's *Que Viva Mexico!*, which, in spite of its profound influence and monumental accomplishments, is one which (arguably) does not exist, and which certainly does not exist in the form its director envisioned. Eisenstein's materials for the film are instructive in that they reveal his thought process evolving, flirting with two of the dominant paradigms in his sketches for the film's introduction and conclusions before settling on a highly individual understanding of Maya culture as an aoristic continuity transcending the ages. The long-standing fascination of the surrealist movement with the Native American cultures generally and with the Maya specifically produced artifacts as strange as Alfred Lewin's potboiler *The Living Idol* (1957), which brings the paradigm of the aoristic Maya into the realm of the Hollywood feature film. The earthworks artist Robert Smithson's significant engagement with the ancient Maya produced a parody of an art historian's slide lecture entitled "Hotel Palenque." In this artist talk disguised as a lightweight whimsical bit of Aquarian Age humor, Smithson reveals the continuity between a lowly form of contemporary Mexican vernacular architecture and the most exalted structures of the past, revising both the category of Maya revival architecture and of Maya modernism itself.

Throughout this history, the Maya represent a complex puzzle for the Western mind. To call the Maya, their architecture or the collapse of their civilization "a mystery" is the most clichéd of truisms. Since the arrival of the first European, the native people of the Americas have been frequently seen as savages. Yet the sophisticated architectural ruins, paintings and sculptures left behind by the ancient Maya do not fit comfortably into this pervasive misconception. Alice Le Plongeon accurately characterized this discrepancy when she wrote in the late nineteenth century:

> The nations that peopled the American continent prior to the coming of the Spanish conquerors are all spoken of as Indians. The word *Indian* immediately calls up a

vision—at least in the mind's eye of many people—of a dark-skinned savage; not overly burdened by clothing, but elaborately tattooed and smeared with paint, a towering ornament of gaudy feathers on his head, a tomahawk in his hand ... It is in Southern Mexico, Guatemala and Honduras, down to Darien, that the traveler pauses in amazement before splendid monumental remains that are scattered over vast territories. Who were the builders? The people found there at the time of the Conquest said they did not know; if any traditions existed among them they remained untold. (106-7)

The Maya are thus perceived as an anomaly within the category of "Indian;" their writing system, monumental architecture, mathematical endeavors and vivid intellectual life seem to set them apart. Within the long and troubled history of "Whites" trying to make sense of who the "Indians" are or were, what would become of them, and how to comprehend, or at least explain, their worldview, so radically different from that of the Old World, the Maya often seemed to be a particularly puzzling exception. Today we may more readily recognize the many traits the ancient Maya shared with other Mesoamerican peoples, and this sense of anomalousness is lost. Before, the impression of the ancient Maya's uniqueness and even superiority gave their image a special charge for observers. On the one hand, the accomplishments of the ancient Maya may make them seem less distant or less alien to some Western observers. For many, they seemed to constitute a *usable* past; when cast as the Greeks of the New World, their heritage was a powerful repertoire from which numerous artists and architects could draw. Yet much else was more difficult to assimilate. First and foremost, there is the practice of human sacrifice, profoundly difficult for the Western mindset to assimilate and accept. Some, intent on remaking the ancient Maya in their own image, have denied this practice. Others, searching for an ancient Maya culture that is radically other, have chosen to celebrate it. These complexities inform the assimilation of ancient Maya culture into the project of modernism.

Works Cited

Barnet-Sánchez, Holly. *The Necessity of Pre-Columbian Art: U.S. Museums and the Role of Foreign Policy in the Appropriation and Transformation of Mexican Heritage.* Diss. UCLA, 1993.

Barta, Roger. *La jaula de la melancolía: Identidad y metamorfosis del mexicano.* Barcelona: Debolsillo, 2005.

Braun, Barbara. *Pre-Columbian Art and the Post-Columbian World: Ancient American Sources of Modern Art.* New York: Harry N. Abrams, 2000.

Casteñeda, Quetzil E. *In the Museum of Maya Culture: Touring Chichén Itzá.* Minneapolis: U of Minnesota P, 1996.

Charlot, Jean. *Art from the Mayans to Disney.* New York: Sheed and Ward, 1939.

Clifford, James. "Histories of the Tribal and the Modern." *The Predicament of Culture.* Cambridge: Harvard UP, 1988. 189-214.

Coggins, Clemency Chase, ed. *Artifacts from the Cenote of Sacrifice, Chichen Itza, Yucatán.* Cambridge, MA: Peabody Museum of Archaeology and Ethnography, 1992.

———, and Orrin C. Shane III, eds. *Cenote of Sacrifice: Maya Treasures from the Sacred Well at Chichen Itza.* Austin: U of Texas P, 1984.

Dávalos Hurtado, Eusebio. "Into the Well of Sacrifice: Return to the Sacred Cenote." *National Geographic* 120.4 (October 1961): 540-49.

Ediger, Donald. *The Well of Sacrifice.* Garden City, NY: Doubleday, 1971.

Evans, R. Tripp. *Romancing the Maya.* Austin: U of Texas P, 2004.

Fallaw, Ben. *Cárdenas Compromised: The Failure of Reform in Postrevolutionary Yucatán.* Durham, Duke UP, 2001.

Gruzinski, Serge. *Images at War: Mexico from Columbus to* Blade Runner *(1492-2019).* Trans. Heather MacLean. Durham, NC: Duke UP, 2001.

Joseph, Gilbert M. *Rediscovering the Past at Mexico's Periphery: Essays on the History of Modern Yucatán.* Tuscaloosa, AL: U of Alabama P, 1986.

———. *The Revolution from Without: Yucatán, Mexico and the Unites States, 1880-1924.* Durham: Duke UP, 1988.

———, and Allen Wells. *Summer of Discontent, Seasons of Upheaval: Elite Politics and Rural Insurgency in Yucatán, 1876-1915.* Stanford: Stanford UP, 1996.

Le Plongeon, Alice. *Here and There in Yucatán: Miscellanies.* New York: J. W. Bouton, 1887.

Lerner, Jesse. "Thompson y el cenote sagrado." *Alquimia* 5.13 (Sept-Dec 2001): 23-26.

———. *The Maya of Modernism.* Albuquerque: U of New Mexico P, 2011.

Littlehales, Bates. "Into the Well of Sacrifice: Treasure Hunt in the Deep Past." *National Geographic* Vol. 120 No. 4 (October 1961): 550-61.

Lothrop, Samuel Kirkland. *Metals from the Cenote of Sacrifice, Chichen Itza, Yucatán.* Cambridge, MA: Peabody Museum of Archaeology and Ethnography, 1952.

McEvilley, Thomas. "Doctor Lawyer Indian Chief." *Artforum* 23 (November 1984): 55-60.

Medina, Cuauhtémoc. *Risking the Abstract: Mexican Modernism and the Art of Gunther Gerzso.* Madrid: Turner, 2003. http://tortugamarina. tripod.com/articulos/medina/gerzso. htm.

Mirzoeff, Nicholas. "What Is Visual Culture?" *The Visual Culture Reader.* Ed. Nicholas Mirzoeff. London: Routledge, 1998. 3-14.

"New Atlas Map Focuses on Fast-growing Mexico and Central America." *National Geographic* 120.4 (October 1961): 539.

Olson, Charles. *Mayan Letters.* Ed. and with Preface by Robert Creeley. London: Cape Editions, 1968.

———. *Letters for Origin, 1950-1956.* Ed. Albert Glover. London: Cape Goliard P, 1970.

Olson, Charles, and Robert Creeley. *The Complete Correspondence.* George F. Butterick, ed. Santa Barbara, CA: Black Sparrow, 1983.

Paternostro, César. *The Stone and the Thread: Andean Roots of Abstract Art.* Trans. Esther Allen. Austin: U of Texas P, 1996.

Pratt, Mary Louise. *Imperial Eyes: Travel Writing and Transculturation.* New York: Routledge, 1992.

Proskouriakoff, Tatiana. *Jades from the Cenote of Sacrifice, Chichen Itza, Yucatán.* Cambridge, MA: Peabody Museum of Archaeology and Ethnography, 1974.

Rushing, W. Jackson. *Native American Art and the New York Avant-Garde.* Austin: U of Texas P, 1995.

Smithson, Robert. "Hotel Palenque." *Parkett* 43 (1995): 117-32.

Stewart, Susan. *On Longing: Narratives of the Miniature, the Gigantic, the Souvenir, the Collection.* Durham, NC: Duke UP, 1993.

Sullivan, Paul. *Unfinished Conversations: Mayas and Foreigners Between Two Wars.* Berkeley: U of California P, 1989.

———. *Xuxub Must Die: The Lost Histories of a Murder on the Yucatán.* Pittsburgh: U of Pittsburgh P, 2004.

Wauchope, Robert. *Lost Tribes and Sunken Continents: Myth and Method in the Study of American Indians.* Chicago: U of Chicago P, 1962.

Filmography

Blade Runner. Dir. Ridley Scott. U.S.A., Hong Kong, 1982.

Expedition: Treasure of the Sacred Well. ABC-TV. U.S.A., Mexico, 1961.

The Living Idol. Dir. Alfred Lewin and René Cardona. U.S.A., Mexico, 1957.

Que Viva Mexico! Dir. Sergei Eisenstein. Soviet Union, U.S.A., Mexico, 1979.

Raíces. Dir. Benito Alazraki. Mexico, 1954.

The Road to El Dorado. Dir. Bibo Bergeron et. al. U.S.A., 2000.

Ruins. Dir. Jesse Lerner. U.S.A., Mexico, 1999.

South of the Border with Disney. Dir. Norman Ferguson. U.S.A., 1942.

Contributors

Gabriela Alemán is lecturer at the Universidad Andina Simón Bolívar in Quito, Ecuador. She holds a PhD from Tulane University, where she worked with Ana Lopez. Her main research interests are Ecuadorian and Latin American film history, documentaries, and film theory. Her recent publications include: "Epilogue: At the Margin of the Margins: Contemporary Ecuadorian Exploitation, Cinema and the Local Pirate Market" (in *Latsploitation, Exploitation Cinemas, and Latin America*, ed. by Victoria Ruétalo and Dolores Tierney, Routledge, 2009) and "An International Conspiracy" (in *Journal of Latin American Cultural Studies*, Travesia, Volume 13, Issue 1, 2004). Since 2005 she has been a regular contributor to the *International Film Guide* edited by Wallpaper Press.

Ernesto Ardito is an independent Argentinean documentary filmmaker. He studied Social Communication at the Universidad de Buenos Aires and Film Studies at the Instituto Avellaneda de Artes Cinematográficas in Buenos Aires, Argentina. Ernesto Ardito taught at the International Summer School "Cine documental latinoamericano: teoría, historia, práctica" (2008) organized by the University of Bielefeld, and he was part of the selection committees for documentary film of the National Council of Culture and Arts in Chile and the National Institute of Film and Audiovisual Arts in Argentina. His feature film *Raymundo* (2002), codirected by Ardito and Virna Molina, received a number of important awards at international festivals. *Corazón de fábrica*, his second feature film, also directed with Virna Molina, came out in 2008 and portrays a factory in the Argentinean south managed by its workers.

Juan Martín Cueva is an Ecuadorian filmmaker. He directed the film festival *Cero Latitud* in Quito, Ecuador from 2003 to 2009 as well as the second international documentary film festival *Encuentros del Otro Cine* (2003). Cueva studied cinema in Belgium and sociology in Quito. He has taught at the Universidad San Francisco, at INCINE, at the School of Cinema, Acting, and Visual Anthropology of FLACSO, and at the University of the Americas in Ecuador. His filmic oeuvre focuses on documentaries. Among his recent films are *586K, Frontera (sin) norte* (2010), *Las siete cumbres* (2009), *Los ecuatorianos* (short version of *Este maldito país* for TV, 2008), *Este maldito país* (2008) and *El lugar donde se juntan los polos* (2002).

Christof Decker is Associate Professor of American Studies at the University of Munich (LMU). He received his PhD in 1994 from the Free University Berlin and was an Honorary Fellow at the University of Wisconsin-Madison. His research interests are media and visual culture studies, American literature and culture, critical theory, race and gender studies, and cultural studies. His most recent publication is *Visuelle*

456 Contributors

Kulturen der USA: Zur Geschichte von Malerei, Fotografie, Film, Fernsehen und Neuen Medien in Amerika (2010).

Wiebke Engel teaches American literature and culture at the University of Duisburg-Essen. Her scholarly interests include reflections of American society through popular music and film, U.S. American political and cultural identity and modern American drama. At present, she is working on her dissertation, which examines the effects of September 11, 2001 on catastrophe films set in New York City (working title: *The Big Applecalypse—Depictions of New York City in Pre- and Post-Nine-Eleven Disaster Films*).

Manfred Engelbert, professor emeritus of Romance Philology at the Georg-August-Universität Göttingen, Germany is currently a research fellow in the Department of Spanish and Portuguese at the University of California, Los Angeles. For his promotion of French cinema in Germany and for his studies on the history of French film he received the "Ordre des Palmes Académiques" (France, 1992). For his promotion of Chilean culture and his publications in this field he was appointed "Comendador de la Orden Gabriela Mistral" (2007). His major publications include books on Pedro Calderón de la Barca, Violeta Parra, and Jean Renoir.

Álvaro Fernández Bravo is director of New York University in Buenos Aires and researcher at CONICET, Argentina. He received his PhD from the Department of Romance Languages at Princeton University and holds the title of *Licenciado en Letras* by the University of Buenos Aires. Fernández Bravo has taught at Temple University, Philadelphia, University of Buenos Aires, and National University of Mar del Plata (both in Argentina), among others. He has published and edited numerous books and articles, including *Episodios en la formación de redes culturales en América Latina* (with C. Maíz, 2009), *El valor de la cultura* (with L.E. Cárcamo-Huechante and A. Laera, 2007), and *Sujetos en tránsito* (2003).

Itzia Fernández Escareño, a sociologist from Universidad Autónoma Metropolitana-Azcapotzalco, is researcher in film studies, specializing in gender studies, silent movies, film archives, film history, found footage, documentaries about Mexico as well as European cinemas. She obtained her PhD in Film Studies from Université Paris III Sorbonne-Nouvelle, with a dissertation on the compilation work of the Dutch filmmaker Peter Delpeut with the Nederlands Filmmuseum, during the '90s. She has catalogued film collections for Cineteca Nacional and Filmoteca UNAM in Mexico City. Itzia Fernández Escareño has curated several film programs and has been teaching and giving lectures in different institutions in Mexico, France and the United States. She has published for Cineteca Nacional and the journals *Luna Córnea* and *Secuencia*, among others. At present, she is working with Laboratorio Audiovisual de Investigación Social (LAIS)-Instituto Mora (CONACYT).

Jens Martin Gurr has been Chair of British and Anglophone Literature and Culture at the University of Duisburg-Essen since April 2007. His research interests include contemporary Anglophone fiction, urban cultural studies, the politics of identity in the Americas, film and film theory, 17th- and 18th-century British literature, and British Romanticism. He is director of the University of Duisburg-Essen's joint research agenda "Urban Systems."

Birte Horn is a PhD candidate in American Studies at the University of Duisburg-Essen, Germany. Her research interests are film and television studies, gender studies, African American literature, and American history. In her dissertation she examines the use of mythology and archetypes in selected American television series with a focus on the female superhero.

Gary Francisco Keller is director of the Hispanic Research Center of Arizona State University. Recent publications include *Triumph of Our Communities: Four Decades of Mexican American Art* (2005); *Journal of Hispanic Higher Education* vol. 5, no. 3 (July 2006): *Latino Achievement in the Sciences, Technology, Engineering, and Mathematics*; and *The Cisco Kid: American Hero, Hispanic Roots* (2008). A recent Internet project is "Saint Francis and the Americas": http://sanfrancisco.asu.edu.

Anne Lakeberg holds a B.A. in Spanish and Latin American Studies as well as Social Sciences and an M.A. in Sociology from the University of Bielefeld, Germany. During her studies she spent a year in Argentina at the University of Buenos Aires.

Jesse Lerner is a documentary filmmaker based in Los Angeles. His short films *Natives* (with Scott Sterling, 1991), *T.S.H.* (2004) and *Magnavoz* (2006) and feature-length films *Frontierland* (with Rubén Ortiz-Torres, 1995), *Ruins* (1999), *The American Egypt* (2001) and *Atomic Sublime* (2010) have screened at New York's MoMA, the Rotterdam and Sundance Film Festivals, and the Guggenheim Museums in New York and Bilbao. His books include *F is for Phony: Fake Documentary and Truth's Undoing* (with Alexandra Juhasz) and *The Shock of Modernity*.

Chris Lippard holds a PhD in Film, Literature, and Culture from the University of Southern California. He is currently Associate Professor of Film Studies and Director of Graduate Studies in Film at the University of Utah. He has published work on Abbas Kiarostami, Derek Jarman, Dennis Potter, F.W. Murnau, Jorge Sanjinés, and the Sundance Film Festival and has an essay forthcoming on issues of identity formation among immigrant groups in the United States. He was co-chair of the Society for Cinema and Media Studies Middle Eastern Caucus from 2004 to 2007, and is co-editor of *The Historical Dictionary of Middle Eastern Cinema* (Scarecrow Press, 2011). Chris Lippard is past chair of the Utah Film and Video Center, and in 2009 he was a fellow of the Inter-American Research group, "E Pluribus Unum?—Ethnic

Identities in Transnational Integration Processes in the Americas," based at the Center for Interdisciplinary Research (ZiF) in Bielefeld.

Carlos Mendoza is founder and director of the independent Mexican production company Canal 6 de Julio and has directed more than sixty documentary films. He has received numerous awards for his oeuvre, both in Mexico and internationally. Carlos Mendoza graduated from Centro Universitario de Estudios Cinematográficos at the Universidad Nacional Autónoma de México, where he is professor for documentary film. His work focuses primarily on political and social documentaries. He is the author of *El Ojo con memoria* (1999) and *La invención de la verdad* (2008), which received the National University Prize (UNAM). In 2002 Carlos Mendoza was awarded the special "Volcán" prize at the festival Pantalla de Cristal (Mexico City) for his lifework.

Daniela Noll-Opitz is a PhD candidate in Spanish and Latin American Studies at the University of Bielefeld, Germany. Her doctoral thesis explores representations of Argentinean women involved in the armed struggle during the 1960s and '70s in contemporary documentary films. She studied in Bielefeld, Lyon, Madrid, and Buenos Aires and obtained her Master's in Spanish, Latin American, and Romance Studies at the University of Bielefeld in 2004. She was one of the organizers of the International Symposium "Ethnicity under (Visual) Construction in the Americas" (2009). From 2007 to 2010 she was a research assistant of "E pluribus unum?—Ethnic Identities in Transnational Integration Processes in the Americas," an inter-American research group, at the Center of Interdisciplinary Research (ZiF), Bielefeld.

Lorena Ortiz is a videographer and script writer. She holds the title of *Licenciada* in Communication (B.A.) from ITESO, Guadalajara, Mexico and has an M.A. in Film Studies from the University of Guadalajara. She twice received a grant from the Program for the Encouragement of Creation and Artistic Development by the National Council for Culture and Arts in Mexico. Her videos have been featured at festivals in Argentina, Mexico, Canada and Germany, and she has taught at Bielefeld University. In 2010 she co-organized and taught in the International Summer School "Documentary Cinema of the Americas," offered by the Universities of Bielefeld and Guadalajara. Lorena Ortiz is a collaborator for the movie section of the *O2 Cultura* supplement of *La Gaceta*, published by the University of Guadalajara, and she also writes for the electronic journal *El ojo que piensa*.

Hannah F. Osenberg is an M.A. student of European Media Studies at the University of Potsdam. After spending a year at the Universidad Complutense de Madrid, Spain she graduated in Spanish and Latin American Studies from the University of Bielefeld, obtaining a Bachelor of Arts in 2007. She was one of the organizers of the International Summer School "Cine documental latinoamericano: teoría, historia, práctica" (Bielefeld, 2008) and she participated in an interactive film project for the exhibition

"German Unity at Lake Balaton—a European History" at the Collegium Hungaricum in Berlin. She is director of the EMERGEANDSEE Media Arts Festival in Berlin.

Gabriele Pisarz-Ramírez is Professor of American Studies and Minority Studies at Leipzig University. Her key research interests are in the fields of Inter-American Studies, Ethnic and Intercultural Studies, and Early American Studies. Her publications include a book on Mexican American cultural productions (*MexAmerica*, 2005) and a study on inter-American cultural relations (*The Americas in the 19th Century*, 2008).

Burkhard Pohl obtained his PhD in Romance Philology with a dissertation on the Spanish publishing sector and its impact on Latin American novels during the 1960 and '70s (*Bücher ohne Grenzen*, 2003). He has worked as an assistant professor in the Department of Romance Philology at the Georg-August-Universität Göttingen, Germany and is currently teaching at a high school and various universities. His main research interests include Spanish cinema of the democracy, transnationalism, road movies, the Spanish-speaking literary market, Argentinean narrative, and Cervantes. His recent publications include: *Miradas glocales* (ed. with J. Türschmann, 2007) and *Texto Social. Estudios pragmáticos sobre literatura y cine* (ed. with A. Paatz, 2003).

Josef Raab is Professor of North American Studies at the University of Duisburg-Essen and Founding President of the International Association of Inter-American Studies. His research focuses on Inter-American Studies, North American literature and culture, television, film, ethnicity, and borders. From 2007 to 2010 he was co-chair (together with Sebastian Thies and Olaf Kaltmeier) of the international Research Group "E Pluribus Unum?—Ethnic Identities in Processes of Transnationalization in the Americas." He is co-editor of the book series "Inter-American Studies | Estudios Interamericanos" and of several collections of essays, including *E Pluribus Unum?— National and Transnational Identities in the Americas / Identidades nacionales y transnacionales en las Américas* and *Hybrid Americas: Contacts, Contrasts, and Confluences in New World Literatures and Cultures*.

Madalina Stefan is a PhD student of Spanish and Latin American Studies at the University of Bielefeld, Germany. She studied in Madrid, Bielefeld, and Guadalajara and holds a B.A. in Spanish and Latin American Studies and German as a Foreign Language as well as an M.A. in Inter-American Studies from the University of Bielefeld. Madalina Stefan was a junior fellow of the Inter-American Research Group "E Pluribus Unum?—Ethnic Identities in Transnational Integration Processes in the Americas." Her research interests are Film and Space Theory, Postcolonial and Cultural Studies as well as Migration Studies. Her audiovisual work focuses on Migration and Space. Most recently she completed the short films *Retrovisor* (2008) and *In between* (2010) as well as the medium-length film *Alicias* (2010).

Sebastian Thies is Associate Professor of Hispanic Literatures and Media Studies at the University of Bielefeld, Germany. His research interests include media studies, Latin American documentary film, postcolonial studies, and Latin American literature. He has published a monograph on the contemporary historical novel in Mexico, *"La verdadera historia es el olvido": Alterität und Poetologie der Memoria in der mexikanischen historischen Erzählliteratur der Gegenwart* (2004) and co-edited a series of volumes on contemporary Mexican literature, Latin American exiles in Europe and the U.S.A as well as national and transnational identities in the Americas. Since 2004 he has co-organized the series of International Conferences of Bielefeld Inter-American Studies and he headed, together with Josef Raab and Olaf Kaltmeier, the ZIF Research Group "E Pluribus Unum?—Ethnic Identities in Processes of Transnationalization in the Americas" (2007-2010).

Patricia Torres San Martín, is professor for Mexican and Latin American cinema at the University of Guadalajara, Mexico where she has been teaching in the History Department and the Master's of Cinema Studies and History since 1990. For her PhD in Social Anthropology she wrote a dissertation entitled *From the Subject to the Film: Reception and Audience of Contemporary Mexican Cinema*. Patricia Torres's books include *Crónicas tapatías del cine mexicano (1917-1940)* (1993), *Cine y género. La representación social de lo femenino y masculino en el cine mexicano y venezolano* (2001), and *Mujer y cine en América Latina* (2004). Her articles have been published in national and international journals such as *DICINE, Acordeón, La Ventana, Pantalla, The Journal of Film and Video* (Georgia State University), *Texto Crítico* (Stanford University), and *CINEMAIS* (Brazil).

Wanja von der Goltz is lecturer of Business English, academic advisor, and coordinator in the School of Business Administration at the University of Duisburg-Essen, Germany. He studied American Studies, British Literature, and Business Administration in Germany and Great Britain. Apart from film and media studies he also works on 20th-century American literature. For his PhD he wrote a dissertation on *Functions of Intertextuality and Intermediality in "The Simpsons."*

Inter-American Studies | Estudios Interamericanos
Ed. by Josef Raab and Sebastian Thies

This interdisciplinary series examines national and transnational issues in the cultures, societies, and histories of the Americas. It creates a forum for a critical academic dialogue between North and South, promoting an inter-American paradigm that shifts the scholarly focus from methodological nationalism to the wider context of the Western Hemisphere.

2   Wilfried Raussert, Michelle Habell-Pallán (Eds.):

Cornbread and Cuchifritos. Ethnic Identity Politics, Transnationalization, and Transculturation in American Urban Popular Music

Selected Articles: *Wilfried Raussert:* Introduction: Ethnic Identity Politics, Transnationalization, and Transculturation in American Urban Popular Music: Inter-American Perspectives · *John Carlos Rowe:* The Death of Francis Scott Key and Other Dirges: Music and the New American Studies · *Martin Butler:* Towards a Topography of Hybridization in U.S. Urban Popular Music · *María Elena Cepeda:* When Latina Hips Make/Mark History: Music Video in the "New" American Studies
ISBN 978-3-86821-265-5, 292 pp., paperb., € 29,50 (2011)

3   Martin Butler, Jens Martin Gurr, Olaf Kaltmeier (Eds.):

EthniCities. Metropolitan Cultures and Ethnic Identities in the Americas

Selected Articles: *Christoph Marx:* Globalizing Cities: Ethnicity and Racism in Vancouver and Johannesburg in the First Wave of Globalization · *Olaf Kaltmeier:* Historic City Centers in Globalization Processes: Cultural Heritage, Urban Renewal, and Postcolonial Memories in the Americas · *Eva Marsch:* The Construction of Ethnic Identities in Street Art · *Marc Simon Rodriguez:* Latino Mural Cityscapes: A Reflection on Public Art, History, and Community in Chicago after World War II · *Alexandra Ganser:* Navigating Little Italy: Carceral Mobility in Martin Scorsese's *Mean Streets* · *Karin Höpker:* The Cab and the City: Chance Encounters and Certalian Perspectives in Jim Jarmusch's *Night on Earth*   **ISBN 978-3-86821-310-2, 268 pp., paperb., € 29,50 (2011)**

4   Jens Martin Gurr, Wilfried Raussert (Eds.):

Cityscapes in the Americas and Beyond
Representations of Urban Complexity in Literature and Film

Selected Articles: *Jens Martin Gurr:* The Representation of Urban Complexity and the Problem of Simultaneity: A Sketchy Inventory of Strategies · *Hatice Bay:* Paul Auster's *In the Country of Last Things*: A Journey into a Thousand Heterotopias and Flows of Becoming · *Marcus Hartner:* Psycho-geography and (In)Sanity: Walking London, New York, and Dubai with Will Self · *Christoph Schaub:* Conflicting Imaginaries of Urban Socio-Cultural Complexity: Diversity and Division in Contemporary U.S.-American Cultural Production · *Betsy van Schlun:* Berlin – A Mazing Metropolis: Representations in Films of the Weimar Republic **ISBN 978-3-86821-324-9, 300 pp., paperb., € 29,50 (2011)**

Wissenschaftlicher Verlag Trier · Bergstr. 27 · 54295 Trier
Tel.: 0651/41503 · Fax: 0651/41504 · www.wvttrier.de · E-Mail: wvt@wvttrier.de